ALTERNATIVE SENTENCING,

INTERMEDIATE SANCTIONS

AND PROBATION

SECOND EDITION

Andrew R. Klein

anderson publishing co.
p.o. box 1576
cincinnati, oh 45201-1576
513-421-4142

To My Parents and Family,
Stephanie, Jessica and Alexander

Alternative Sentencing, Intermediate Sanctions and Probation, Second Edition

ISBN 0-87084-486-5
Library of Congress Catalog Number 96-85360

The text of this book is printed on recycled paper.

Elisabeth Roszmann Ebben *Editor*

Elizabeth A. Shipp *Assistant Editor*

Editor in Chief Kelly Grondin

Foreword

. . . what we call necessary institutions are often no more than institutions to which we have grown accustomed. . . .

Alexis de Tocqueville

There is a reason why restitution, community work service, monitored home confinement and all the other alternative sanctions discussed in this book are rapidly gaining acceptance in courts throughout the country. It is because there is now a clear consensus that our traditional sentencing approaches are failing. Whether it is the victim who goes uncompensated, the public that pays more and more for an ever-expanding prison system and *still* feels unprotected or the offender who is dehumanized by his incarceration, all are critical of the criminal justice system, and with justification.

The problem has been that we have followed a course locking us into two extremes in attempting to deal with crime—an extraordinary reliance on imprisonment on one hand, and a shortsighted policy of doing little or nothing with unconfined offenders on the other.

We have paid dearly for following this course of action and for not having implemented the array of intermediate sanctions that are now being advanced in this publication. The more deliberate and selective process at the sentencing stage for each individual has now been replaced by mandatory minimum jail sentences and presumptive sentencing guidelines that paint all defendants with the same confining brush. Our answer to the drug problem is to merely jail more and more offenders for longer and longer periods. Our answer to drunk driving is the same. Name the crime and the answer is simply more time.

What has been the result? We have not made a dent in preventing the drug trade and its related crime. We have not in any way reduced the rates of recidivism among convicted drunk drivers. Violence in our society continues to grow. What we have achieved, however, is a serious crisis of prison and jail overcrowding and an insatiable call for more and more facilities to warehouse offenders at costs that are now prohibitive.

Alternative sentencing has gained considerable currency within the criminal justice system due to the limitation of cells resulting from prison and jail overcrowding. However, it will not be utilized to its fullest potential until we dispel the myth that incarceration is the only safe option for most offenders. As soon as we dismiss this notion, we will discover a world of sentencing options available to us.

When I was first appointed to the bench in 1974, I presided over the Quincy District Court, a typical busy, urban court, abutting Boston, Massachusetts. Due to the baby boom and the rise of drug use, our criminal caseload had already exploded to the second largest in the state. However, our county jails were under a federal court order to depopulate due to overcrowded conditions. We were therefore restricted in both the number and the length of time we could sentence even violent and repeat offenders.

Fortunately we learned a great deal from the alternative sentencing programs both Mr. Klein and I developed in the late 1970s. In 1975 we established the Earn-It Program, the first and largest court restitution program in the nation. It taught us that we could build accountability into an offender probation plan. Over the first two years, offenders paid their victims almost $100,000 in restitution. By the time I left the bench in 1993, that amount exceeded one million dollars for the same period.

We also learned that we could put hundreds of offenders to work in the community under proper supervision doing free community service to make up for their offenses. Offenders who had vandalized a municipal skating rink were made to work an entire summer fixing it. Other offenders were regularly put to work in community projects like Habitat for Humanity, building houses for the poor, or working with the food pantry to provide meals to homeless shelters, not to mention thousands of others placed in a vast community network of private nonprofit and public agencies.

We learned that most violent and repeat offenders were addicted to alcohol, drugs or both and that our efforts to get them sober required on-site alcohol and drug testing and, in many cases, monitored home confinement until they established a track record of being clean and sober. These offenders also required *saturation surveillance,* an intensive probation of strict monitoring of their activities, sometimes over the entire 24-hour period of each day.

The application of these alternative, intermediate sanctions I termed the *community cell.* It served as a means of incapacitating or tightly monitoring and controlling the behavior of serious offenders while they were being treated in the community. Just like a jail cell, we discovered that the community cell could lock offenders up in the community, not behind bars, but at their monitored community service jobs during the day, at their monitored AA meetings in the evening, and at their electronically monitored homes at night. Testing would also warn us if the offender was trying to escape from his alcohol and drug abuse treatment regimen, in which case he would be immediately brought back to court for a probation violation and sentenced to the precious few jail cells at our disposal.

Can there be a better example of the value of the array of alternative and intermediate sanctions than those now being advanced in Mr. Klein's publication? By use of these sanctions, a lawyer can draft an alternative sentence to jail for a client who is a serious offender. The lawyer can recommend to the court that his client, and not the state, pay for the defendant's (home) confinement, for his own treatment, for restitution to the victim, perform community work service, and have a better opportunity to rehabilitate himself, without any significant threat to public safety.

That is why this book is so important. It details in many contexts the ways in which we can fashion substantial sanctions and controls for serious, even violent offenders without incarceration, and, as important, without unduly subjecting the community to increased risk of harm.

What impresses me about *Alternative Sentencing* is that the author, Mr. Klein, has succeeded in producing a guide for practitioners that is exhaustive in both range and detail. The numerous examples of alternatives span the entire spectrum of crimes and types of offenders that we see in court. Most importantly, the book will equip lawyers, judges, probation officers and other practitioners with state-of-the-art techniques and, at the same time, provide them with cases that they can cite as legal precedents and as examples of alternatives that have been successfully implemented in the past.

For students who need to know how the system really operates as opposed to how we say it operates, I can think of no better text. A student reading this book will have the same exposure and hands-on level of understanding of the criminal justice system, prosecution, defense, sentencing and probation as if they had just completed a year-long internship working in a busy public defender's office, probation department, judge's chamber or correctional agency.

I believe the book will make a significant contribution toward reforming our sentencing practices. I have been a strong advocate of restitution, community service and other forms of alternative sentencing since the days they were pioneered in the mid-1970s. As a founder of the National Institute for Sentencing Alternatives at Brandeis University, and as a national lecturer in the field, I have had the opportunity to make presentations on alternatives to a substantial portion of the judiciary and criminal justice professionals in almost every state. I know of their commitment to a more effective and humane system of justice. It is for this reason that I cannot imagine a capable defense lawyer, a conscientious prosecutor, a competent probation officer or a caring judge who would want to discharge his or her responsibilities without thoroughly exploring the sentencing examples, techniques, philosophies, procedures and strategies outlined in this guide.

Albert L. Kramer
Former First Justice, Quincy District Court
Trial Court of Massachusetts

Preface

This book is written by a practitioner for both students and practitioners. For students, it provides a comprehensive look and insight into the real world of criminal justice, criminals, courts and probation as only a practitioner in the front lines of the criminal justice system for more than 20 years could know and reveal. For practitioners, including defense attorneys, prosecutors, judges and probation officers, it provides real solutions to criminal sentencing. Although much has been written about criminal law and procedure, once an offender admits guilt or is found guilty by a judge or jury of his peers, there is little information available that is of practical use about criminal sentencing. There is even less that deals exclusively with criminal sentencing, particularly alternative, intermediate and other forms of sentencing that do not rely on incarceration on the one hand or traditional probation on the other.

Alternative Sentencing, Intermediate Sanctions and Probation details sentences that effectively punish offenders for their crimes and addresses common sentencing concerns including rehabilitation, deterrence, retribution and justice. In addition, it provides basic analysis and information necessary to match the sentence with the offender, whether that offender is a sexual predator, perpetrator of domestic abuse, drunk driver or drug addict, to name but a few.

The book is divided into four sections. The first section describes the state of sentencing in America today, the dilemma of prison overcrowding as well as the collapse of traditional probation and how we got there. It examines the crucial criminal sentencing process as it actually functions, as well as the role of practitioners involved in it. As it explains, if practitioners seeking alternative sentences wait to act until the defendant is before the judge at disposition, the defendant probably will leave the courtroom in handcuffs. Special attention is focused on four factors that influence the ultimate court-ordered disposition: plea bargaining, presentence investigation reports, the participation of crime victims and the sentencing hearing.

Because probation is the original alternative sentence and remains basic to constructing and enforcing alternative and intermediate sentences, this section also discusses the institution of probation, what it entails, how it operates and the standard and special conditions of a probationary sentence. While probation operations vary dramatically across the country, general insights, issues and case law common to all of them are analyzed and presented.

The second section presents examples of alternative and intermediate sentences for specific types of crimes, ranging from nonviolent property crimes to homicides and most in between, including manslaughter, motor vehicle homicide, sexual assaults, arson, an assortment of armed and unarmed assaults and batteries, burglaries, robberies, thefts, larcenies, drug offenses and miscellaneous white collar crimes. Examples are drawn from a variety of courts and jurisdictions from around the country, both state and federal. They include specific examples of alternative sentences imposed upon high-risk, chronic offenders whose records qualify them for life imprisonment in many jurisdictions with "habitual offender" or "three strikes and you're out" statutes. All of the examples presented are both described and analyzed.

The third section examines each of the major components of alternative and intermediate sentences. This section includes an exhaustive compilation of federal and state case and statutory law pertaining to restitution, community work service, monetary sanctions other than restitution, mandatory treatment, intermediate sanctions, incapacitation without incarceration and alternative uses of incarceration. The discussion of restitution focuses in particular on victim involvement, usually as either recipients of court-ordered restitution or active participants in court-ordered victim/offender confrontations. The discussion of monetary sanctions, among other things, looks at the new innovative imposition of "day fines" in this country. Treatment describes the new generation of behavioral and cognitive change programs specifically geared for resistant offenders who only enter treatment because they are forced to do so. New treatment technologies and behavior-altering drugs are examined, ranging from penile plethysmographs for sex offenders to naltrexone for alcoholics. Incapacitation without incarceration details various intensive supervision programs, electronic monitoring, day reporting centers, boot camps and more, whether administered by traditional probation or new intermediate sanction agencies. Alternative uses of incarceration examines various split, shock and intermittent sentences.

Each alternative and intermediate sanction component is analyzed in some detail. First the history and rationale for each component's use are presented. Its use is reviewed, followed by legal analysis of the statutory and case law defining it. Its practical use as a sentencing option is discussed. This includes how each can be fashioned and monitored even where sentencing jurisdictions do not have a formal program or available probation resources for its imposition. In addition, analysis of pertinent research of each component's effectiveness is summarized.

Finally, the fourth section looks at how these sentences can be enforced by the court, probation officials and others, as well as how they can be evaluated. The discussion of enforcement provides a comprehensive look at the role of probation supervision and revocation. This section, combined with those in the first section detailing what probation is, should provide both students and practitioners with an in-depth understanding of probation in America, how it actually works, and often does not work, as well as its future role in the criminal sentencing and corrections.

The book concludes with detailed checklists for practitioners and those interested in analyzing sentencing, which cover the factors that should be considered in fashioning, determining, enforcing and evaluating criminal sentences. Because the laws of each state differ, as do the opinions of the various circuits of the United States Courts of Appeals, one book cannot definitively describe the exact content of sentencing law in each jurisdiction. The checklists, however, raise the pertinent questions that determine the fundamental parameters defining what is permissible in each jurisdiction.

Effective and responsible sentencing of criminals is everyone's legitimate concern, criminal justice practitioners and nonpractitioners alike. It is my hope that *Alternative Sentencing, Intermediate Sanctions and Probation* will help expand sentencing options by acquainting its readers with existing alternatives and by demonstrating to both that criminals can be effectively punished without reliance upon long-term jail sentences to the exclusion of other alternatives that, in the final analysis, may not only be significantly cheaper than long-term incarceration, but significantly more effective and just for victims of crime, offenders and the community at large.

Andrew R. Klein
February, 1996

Acknowledgments

I wish to acknowledge the assistance of Sarah Raymond, an attorney who double checked the legal cites for me. This book would not have been possible except for the experience I have gained over the past 20 years as a probation officer at the Quincy Court. To all members of that community, especially my own probation staff, I offer my heartfelt thanks and appreciation. Finally, my family has given me the support and encouragement necessary to get this book finished, almost on deadline.

Contents

Chapter 1

Sentencing and Justice in America

§1.01   Sentencing Criminals in America

Targeting Minorities

When it comes to sentencing offenders, we sentence and lock up minorities disproportionately. Which particular minority is affected varies state by state depending upon local demographics. In almost all states where African Americans reside in substantial numbers, they are most affected. Across the country, as of 1990, the incarceration rate of African Americans was five times that of whites.[1] But in other states, other minorities are also overrepresented, including Eskimos in Alaska, Native Americans in the Southwest and elsewhere, Samoans in Hawaii and Hispanics in many other states, to name a few.

Nearly one-third (32.2%) of African American males between the ages of 20 and 29 (827,440) were under correctional supervision in this country on any given day as of October, 1995. African American women experienced the greatest increase in the rate of incarceration, increasing almost 80 percent from 1989 to 1994. By June 30, 1995, 6.8 percent of all black male adults were in prison or jail compared to less than one percent of white adult males.[2]

The impact on minorities is enormous. In 1990, for example, 609,690 young African Americans ages 20 to 29 were involved in the criminal justice system. In that same year, only 436,000 African Americans of any age were involved in higher education. This contrasts sharply with white youth. While 1,054,508 white youths between the ages of 20 and 29 were involved in the criminal justice system that year, more than 4.5 million were involved in higher education.[3]

Between 1980 and 1993, the percentage of African American inmates rose in the nation's prisons from 46.5 percent to 50.8 percent. By the end of 1993, African Americans were seven times more likely than whites to have been incarcerated in a state or federal prison. As of December 31, 1993 the rate of incarceration for African Americans in these institutions was 1,471 per 100,000, compared to 207 per 100,000 for whites. In this same period, the length of sentences of more than one year rose 195 percent. The number of white males so sentenced rose 163 percent, but the number of African American males rose 217 percent. The increase in African American male prisoners (304,800) accounted for nearly half of the total increase during the 13-year period.

Hispanics are the fastest growing minority group in prison, increasing from 7.7 percent of all state and federal inmates in 1980 to 14.3 percent in 1993. Their rate of incarceration tripled from 163 per 100,000 to 529 per 100,000. At the end of 1993, 139,000 Hispanics were in state or federal prisons. The number may actually be higher because of poor record keeping in many jurisdictions. On December 31, 1993, nearly two-thirds of all sentenced prison inmates were black, Asian, Native American or Hispanic.

Some have argued that racism accounts for the overrepresentation of minorities in correctional caseloads. Certainly it is indisputable that racists exist within the ranks of police officers, prosecutors and judges who come down harder on minorities than others. Major police scandals in Los Angeles and Philadelphia, centered on corruption based largely on racist practices in both departments, give graphic public testimony to this. Less public racism exists throughout the system. A three-year study by a special commission in New York, for example, found that New York courts are "infested with racism." In fact, the commission found there are two justice systems at work in the courts of New York State, one for whites, and a very different one for minorities and the poor.

> Many minorities in our courts receive 'basement justice' in every sense of the phrase—from where their courts are located . . . to the 'assembly line' way in which their cases are decided. . . . [I]nequality, disparate treatment and injustice remain hallmarks of our state justice system.[4]

A similar 1991 study in California yielded similar results regarding plea bargaining. An analysis of 700,000 criminal cases conducted by the *San Jose Mercury News* found that "[a]t virtually every stage of pretrial negotiations, whites are more successful than nonwhites. Of 71,000 adults with no prior records who were arrested on felony charges, a third of the whites but only a quarter of the blacks or Hispanics had their charges reduced to misdemeanors or infractions."[5]

On the other hand, African Americans are most heavily populated in jurisdictions with the toughest sentencing patterns (i.e. the south). While both African Americans and whites are incarcerated at above normal rates in these areas, there are a disproportionate number of nonwhites living there.

Although racism has traditionally played a substantial role in the American criminal justice system,[6] other antecedent and intervening variables also contribute to this overrepresentation of minorities. Specifically, the "war on drugs," pursued by successive national administrations since the 1970s, has fueled this disproportionate impact. Drug offenders represent the largest proportional growth of inmates nationally in recent years, increasing by 510 percent from an estimated 58,000 in 1983 to 353,564 in 1993. During this same period, the percentage of offenders sentenced for other crimes decreased, violent crime decreased from 57 to 45 percent and property crime from 30 to 22 percent. The rise among drug offenders was greater among federal inmates, constituting 60 percent of all inmates in the federal prisons, up from 25 percent in 1980. But within state prisons, ten times as many offenders were serving time for drugs in 1993 as in 1980.[7]

Further, the drugs targeted by the criminal justice system and punished most severely are those most available to and used by minorities. In 1995, for example, despite recommendations of the United States Sentencing Commission, Congress refused to make the punishment of crack cocaine, predominately used by poorer, urban minorities, the same as that of powered cocaine, used by more affluent, white suburbanites.

Several years earlier, faced with the same disparities, the Minnesota Supreme Court declared unconstitutional state statutes that called for a sentence of four years in prison for a first-time conviction for possession of crack but probation for possession of powered cocaine. The Court found that 96.6 percent of all persons charged with the former were African-Americans and 79.6 percent of those charged with the latter were white. The Court found that the "*correlation between race and the use of cocaine base or powder and the gross disparity in resulting punishment cries out for closer scrutiny of the challenged laws* (emphasis added)."[8]

As a result of the war on drugs, for example, the number of black women incarcerated just for drug offenses in state prisons increased more than 800 percent from 1986 to 1991. One study suggests that while African Americans account for only 13 percent of monthly drug users, they are involved in 35 percent of the arrests for drug possession, 55 percent of the convictions and 74 percent of the prison sentences.[9] Blacks and Hispanics totaled 91 percent of all drug possession offenders sentenced to prison in New York and 71 percent in California according to a 1993 study. In New York, African Americans and Hispanics convicted of drug possession are three times more likely to be sentenced to prison than whites. In California, they are twice as likely to receive a prison sentence.[10]

To deal with the vast increase in the number of drug arrests, many jurisdictions have formed special drug courts such as those in New York City, opened in 1987. Due to the explosion of crack cocaine cases, felony drug arrests increased 159 percent between July 1985 and July 1987 in that city. The drug courts were designed to reduce the number of continuances and time required to resolve most drug cases from eight continuances taking six months to resolve the case to one taking six days to resolve the case.[11] For quick admissions, many offenders, even those with prior records, are offered more lenient sentences. From April 1987 to February 1988, the Manhattan drug court accepted 2,000 pleas. Similar results were obtained in the Bronx with 1,300 pleas and Brooklyn with 400.

Critics charge that overworked public defenders are pressured to accept pleas immediately without exploring the prosecutor's case for weaknesses for fear the plea agreement will be withdrawn. Quick acceptance also precludes an independent grand jury review of police conduct and evidence.

> The defendants are getting chewed up here. The pressure is enormous to push cases through. People are taking felony pleas and getting state prison time with the same consideration that someone would get if they came in for drunk driving.[12]

The increased penalties for crack over powdered cocaine is just one example of the disproportionate impact of the "war against drugs" on minorities. Lest it be ignored, arguably the most destructive drug of all is comparatively ignored by the criminal justice system. Although this drug accounts for the greatest number of arrests per year, its users remains largely unpunished. Its abusers are mostly white. The drug is alcohol, which is, of course, legal for most to possess in most situations. However drunk driving, which is not legal, accounts for 1.8 million arrests per year. All other drug offenses account for only 1.1 million arrests per year.

While both alcohol and other drugs can be harmful, drunk drivers alone kill more people than those who die as a result of drug-related deaths through overdoses, disease or the violence associated with the drug trade, 22,000 versus 21,000 annually.[13] Yet even repeat drunk drivers rarely are sentenced as felons, even when they are convicted of motor vehicle homicide. In New York State, for example, drug possession convictions are three times as likely to result in jail sentences and 24 times as likely to result in prison sentences as convictions for drunk driving.

While, for example, Georgia first offenders can and are sentenced to prison from 2-15 years for simple drug possession, a 1991 study by the *Atlanta Journal and Constitution* documented more than 16,000 Georgia drivers who had at least *five* drunk driving convictions. Typically, they were not sent to prison. One, for example, received a fine of $440 for his twentieth conviction. He had never been imprisoned nor placed on probation for his drunk driving convictions.[14]

> Drunk drivers are 70 percent white, 20 percent Hispanic and only 9 percent black.

In short, by selecting only certain drugs to target, minorities have been also targeted disproportionately as defendants. If society, for example, declared that drug users should be treated as leniently as drunk drivers or vice versa, the racial and demographic disparities in incarceration and sentencing would dramatically dissipate across the country.

The Continuing Love Affair with Prisons

Until recent political revolutions in the Soviet Union and the Union of South Africa, this country could always point to two other Western countries that relied more heavily on incarceration to punish its offenders. Now, with the demise of the Soviet Union and the end of apartheid in South Africa, the United States tops all developed countries in locking up its citizens.

By 1990, the United States surpassed South Africa with an incarceration rate of 455 per 100,000 compared to 311 per 100,000. The incarceration rate for black males in this country was 3,370 per 100,000 compared to 681 per 100,000 in South Africa as of 1992.[15] By December 31, 1994, the U.S. rate was 565 including inmates in local jails as well as state and federal prisons. Russia's rate was 558 per 100,000.[16]

As of December 31, 1994, more than one million Americans were behind state and federal prison bars, up almost nine percent from the year before. If jail populations were included, the figure would top 1.5 million. An additional 2.8 million were under probation supervision and 671,000 on parole. The incarceration rate has almost tripled since 1980. Texas has led the way with a rate of 636 per 100,000 and North Dakota has the lowest with 78 per 100,000.

Ever since the Quakers invented the modern prison, or penitentiary, America's love affair with incarceration as a preferred form of sanctioning offenders has remained steadfast. One consequence is the enormous impact on minorities. It is a sobering statistic indeed to realize that in this country a young black male has a better chance of going to prison than college. What this portends for the future of all Americans can only be catastrophic.

Another consequence is the enormous fiscal impact on all Americans who must bear the costs of our frantic effort to keep up with ever-expanding prison populations. Although experts have been warning us for the past several decades that we cannot build our way out of the prison overcrowding crisis, propelled by our politicians, we keep trying. As of 1991, this country was spending $16 billion alone to operate its overcrowded prisons.[17] As of 1994, prisons held 15.4 percent more inmates than their rated capacities. Their costs ranged from an average of $7,557 a year in Arkansas to $30,302 in Minnesota.

The newest federal maximum security prison, located in Florence, Colorado, opened in 1994 at a cost of $60 million or $123,751 per bed. Designed to hold 484 of America's worst federal criminals, it housed 243 as of August, 1995.[18]

Desperate for cheaper alternatives, in 1995 Alabama and Arizona reintroduced chain gangs assigned to do road maintenance. Correctional commissioner, Ron Jones of Alabama, told the press: "we are running a budget deficit, and if I use chains, I can put 40 inmates on Highway 72 near Limestone with but one shotgun guard. Without chains, I'd need two guards."[19]

Not only is the number of inmates increasing, but so is the age of inmates. With older inmates come increased costs. From 1987 to 1994, the percentage of inmates 55 years or older increased almost 45 percent. Increased medical costs mean the average older inmate with medical problems costs $60,000 a year.[20]

"Get tough" legislation, including "three strikes and you're out" laws, first passed in California in 1994, will increase costs even more. If all the pending "get tough" legislation passes, the National Council on Crime and Delinquency projects a prison population of 7.5 million within a generation. Prison construction will cost at least $376 billion and the annual operating costs will rise to $133 billion.[21]

By the end of the 1980s, correctional spending averaged five percent of state budgets. A decade later, that percentage doubled. Correctional programs have remained the second fastest growing part of state budgets, surpassed only by health care costs, according to the National Conference of State Legislatures.[22] As correctional spending continues to grow, spending for other human services must shrink. Education spending is often the victim.

Nowhere is this more apparent than in California. State prison spending has increased from two percent in 1980 to 9.9 percent in 1995 while spending on higher education has dropped during the same period from 12.6 to 9.5 percent. In the last 15 years, the state's inmate population has increased from 23,511 to 126,140 and the state has built 17 new prisons. With the "three strikes and you're out" law effective in 1995, costs for still more prisons are expected to increase dramatically. The state will need 15 more prisons by the year 2000 at a cost of $4.5 billion. And this expenditure will just allow the state to stay at its current overcrowded rate of 182 percent capacity. If "three strikes" is fully implemented, a Rand study predicts that California will have to spend 18 percent of its total state budget on corrections by the year 2002. The "three strikes" law mandates a prison sentence of 25 years to life for third-time offenders convicted of felonies.[23]

California's statistics reveal more. With an African American population of 13 percent, state prison population was 31 percent black as of 1995. That same year six percent of Berkeley's freshman class was African American.

According to the Governor of California, each prisoner in that state consumes the annual tax bill of seven Californians. While students cost $6,000 each per annum, inmates cost $20,000 each per annum. While the state used to pay 60 percent of the operating budget of the universities in that state, it now pays 25 percent. By one standard, however, prisons and the state university have achieved parity. The annual salary for an assistant professor at the University of California is the same as that of a prison guard at San Quentin, about $45,000 a year.[24]

The experience in California is not unique. In a survey of state spending conducted in the mid-1990s, six states were found to have shifted resources from schools to prisons. The states included Connecticut, Florida, Massachusetts, Michigan and Minnesota.[25] Correctional spending for 1995 and appropriations for 1996 continue as in most recent years to lead state spending increases, based on budget reports from 34 states and tax reports from 44. In 1995, corrections became by far the fastest growing area of state appropriations, as states funded staffing for newly constructed and planned facilities. The 13.3 percent corrections increase far exceeded Medicaid's 7.2 percent increase. That same year saw South Carolina actually complete a brand new prison that it had to leave vacant because it was unable to pay its operating costs.

Florida led the nation with increased appropriations of 50.2 percent for corrections in 1995.[26] Texas' prison population has tripled since 1991 at a cost of $36 million to build almost 100,000 beds. The system is expected to reach capacity by 1996. To fill the beds, Texas reduced parole from 70 percent of inmates to 15 percent, increasing average sentence length from 18 percent in 1991 to 28 percent in 1994. The prison operating budget is now six percent of the state budget, up 2,000 percent in the last 10 years. Although the crime rate in Texas has decreased from 1991 to 1994 by 25 percent, the re-imprisonment rate for Texas prisoners within three years is 43 percent, guaranteeing, in effect, future demands for the same beds.[27]

Economists worry that prisons are capital-intensive. Money spent on anything else would create more employment. Additionally, if inmates were carried in the annual unemployment figures, the national rate would jump from six percent to 7.5 percent as of 1995.[28]

The Rise of Determinate Sentencing

It is expected that the number of persons in prison will soon surpass the number of full-time college students in this country.

One of the reasons for the increase in imprisonment in the United States is the growth over the past two decades of determinate sentencing systems adopted by the federal and many state criminal justice systems. In determinate systems, the law defines the punishment, limiting judicial discretion to release convicted offenders. Begun in Maine in 1976, many systems have adopted determinate sentencing. By the end of the 1980s, a dozen states had adopted such systems in whole or in part, including California, Connecticut, Florida, Illinois, Indiana, Minnesota, New Mexico, North Carolina and Washington. Colorado had determinate sentencing but went back to indeterminate sentencing in 1985.

Other jurisdictions have guidelines written into statutes that prescribe ranges of sentences based on the offender and the offense. These include the United States federal courts, Florida, Louisiana, Maryland, Minnesota, New Jersey, Ohio, Pennsylvania and Tennessee. Utah has guidelines established by court rule rather than statute, as do Massachusetts, Michigan, Rhode Island and Vermont in part.

Almost all states also have some statutes imposing mandatory sentences for certain crimes. A dozen others have presumptive sentencing systems that prescribe a range of punishments for normal cases but allow the judge to depart for extraordinary reasons.[29] Punishment is based on statutorily prescribed aggravating and mitigating circumstances. Usually appellate courts have characterized aggravating factors as willful conduct by the defendant and mitigating as conduct that is beyond his control. For example low intelligence must be a mitigating, not aggravating factor.[30]

Generally, sentencing in determinate systems relies on incarceration more than systems with indeterminate systems. A national survey of 28 felony courts in 1985, for example, found that incarceration rates in determinate sentencing systems were almost three times as high as in indeterminate systems, 45 percent to 17 percent for serious felonies. Sentences in the former are from 40 to

50 percent longer as well. Probationary sentences are less frequent, given 44 percent of the time versus 52 percent in indeterminate sentencing systems.[31]

California was one of the first states to enact determinate sentencing in 1977 and illustrates the typical impact of these sentencing schemes. Judges must sentence offenders to a middle term set by law unless they establish specific mitigating or aggravating factors. Terms are fixed by law. The old Parole Board was abolished. The system came about because of general discontent with indeterminate sentencing, where judges were given a freer hand to sentence, and parole boards to release sentenced offenders early. Originally the legislated terms were based on what inmates, on average, were currently serving. As a result, the new scheme was seen as "truth-in-sentencing" and was supported by both liberals and conservatives. As the California Parole Administrator writes, "[t]he agreement lasted about as long as it took the Governor's signature to dry on the bill."

As soon as the system passed, legislators went to work. First they lengthened a wide range of sentences. Then they created tougher sentences for specific crimes, including sex crimes, burglary and so on. Then they added still others, from welfare fraud and drugs to vehicular manslaughter. More crimes were made felonies requiring prison time. In 1987, in fact, the legislature passed 104 bills revising the state penal code. The following year, they passed 119. In 1989, they passed 27. And so on until 1994 when they passed 170. While judges also evolve in their sentencing practices over time, they probably would not have changed as quickly and as radically as the legislators have changed the penal code year by year.

As a result, the prison population quadrupled in California. In 1977, there were 19,623 inmates incarcerated at a rate of 86 per 100,000. By 1993, the number rose to 119,995 at a rate of 375 per 100,000. Most recently, the state enacted "three strikes" legislation that threatens even greater incarceration.

Not only has the number and rate of incarceration increased dramatically, but sentencing discrepancies did not diminish as expected. Discretion simply passed from judges to prosecutors. For example, while the state prison rate of sentenced offenders averaged 13.5 percent in 1991 for felony arrests, it varied county by county from a low of 4.5 percent in Santa Cruz to a high of 30.3 percent in Madera County. Almost 73 percent of offenders are prosecuted as felons in Madera but only 24 percent are so prosecuted in Alameda County. Even adjacent counties with similar demographics vary widely. A felon arrested in San Bernardino is only half as likely to end up in Superior Court or go to prison as in Riverside.[32]

Since the federal sentencing guidelines were adopted, effective in 1987, replacing indeterminate sentencing, the number of federal offenders going to prison has increased. In 1984, slightly more than 50 percent of offenders went to prison. By 1990, that figure rose to almost 75 percent. Probationary sentences declined from 63 percent in 1986 to 44 percent in 1990. In addition to implementation of the guidelines, Congress also enacted several mandatory sentencing provisions affecting large numbers of offenders.

The Introduction of Community Corrections Acts

To counter the impact of determinate and mandatory sentencing programs, about one-half of the states have moved to provide for community-based alternative sentencing programs. Michigan provides a typical example. Overcrowding finally caught up to Michigan in the 1980s, a state with a traditionally high incarcerate rate of between seventh and fifth in the nation. The legislature had to enact emergency legislation giving the governor the power to release inmates out the back door once prison capacity was exceeded. Once the governor was forced to use this power more than six times, the state tried to build its way out of the problem, constructing half a dozen new prisons. The state quickly realized it did not have the money to staff the facilities that filled as soon as they were opened. As a result, in 1988, the state passed the Community Corrections Act. Approximately $20 million was appropriated to be returned to local communities that would come up with responsible plans to divert state prison inmates.

Eventually all but two or three counties within the state came aboard, noticeably reducing the number of felons going straight to prison. When longer sentences and mandatory sentencing laws continued to overcrowd prisons, the state once again responded with increased prison construction, but also increased community corrections funding by another $10 million when $58 million was appropriated for new prison beds. Michigan's overall prison commitment rate decreased from 29.9 percent in 1991 to 24 percent in 1994.[33]

Connecticut has attacked the problem with a state-sponsored community alternative sentencing scheme, called the Alternative to Incarceration Program (AIP) administered by a Judicial Office of Alternative Sanctions. Begun in 1987, by 1995 the state committed $27 million that year on alternative programs for 4,500 offenders. Only 15 percent of the money goes to administrative costs. The goals are to reduce overcrowding and offer meaningful alternative sanctions. The AIP contracts out a myriad of community-based sentencing programs ranging from residential programs and day reporting centers to community work service programs and drug testing programs. These programs are not administered by probation.

Among other achievements, AIP offenders did the maintenance and cleanup work for the Special Olympics held in that state in July, 1995. The year before, offenders in AIP performed over 200,000 hours of community work service. Many wore sweatshirts labeled: "We are giving something back."

While the average prison slot costs $25,000, the average AIP slot costs $5,000, saving the state $84 million. This does not include the costs of building a new prison which would have been necessary without the program.[34] As a result of these savings, the state was able to reserve room for other offenders to stay in prison longer. For those sentenced to more than two years, the length of stay increased to 55 percent of their sentence as opposed to 13 percent served in 1990.

Fiscal reality, if nothing else, is forcing many states to reduce their ardor for imprisonment. By the end of the 1980s, nearly every state began to experiment with alternative sentences for at least nonviolent offenders. While expert opinions are mixed as to whether these programs are more successful in turning offenders around, they all agree that they are from 25 to 50 percent cheaper. Although many of these programs have been in existence for five years, by 1991 only 41,500 of 802,000 offenders in federal, state and local correctional systems were in alternative programs, according to the Criminal Justice Institute in New York.[35]

§1.02   Making Probation an Alternative Sentence

Many expert criminologists agree with Gilbert and Sullivan's admonition in *The Mikado* that the punishment should fit the crime. The task, however, remains difficult to perform, particularly given the paucity of traditional sentencing options available to courts. Although probation has served as an all-purpose treatment alternative to incarceration, growing disenchantment with rehabilitation as a central aim of sentencing and, hence, a corresponding lack of faith in probation have diminished the role of probation as an alternative to jail. Instead, probation has increasingly been used as a token punishment in lieu of doing nothing in cases in which the court would not commit the offender anyway.

However, even if the traditional rehabilitation model of probation has not fulfilled the earliest vision of John Augustus, the father of probation, the probationary sentence remains the basic root of alternative sentencing. Almost all alternative sentences are specific conditions of probation—usually but not always, monitored and enforced by probation officers. Rather than "treaters" or "counselors," probation officers function as "enforcers" of these conditions. This is not to suggest that alternative sentences are unconcerned with behavior change or devoid of rehabilitation. Alternative sentences, however, address all of the aims of traditional sentencing, including retribution, reparations, deterrence and incapacitation, in addition to rehabilitation. The tools to accomplish these varying aims are usually probation conditions. The profusion of permissible probation conditions, departing from the standard condition of traditional probation—do not get rearrested—provide the rich soil from which alternative sentences grow. These conditions may be attached to straight probationary, suspended or split sentences.

The court has the ability to impose probation conditions that involve the victim, require the offender to make various payments, mandate him to participate in treatment programs, or otherwise modify his behavior. It can incapacitate the offender without the use of traditional incarceration or employ traditional incarceration in alternative ways. In such a manner, alternative sentences can retain the punitive, deterrent and incapacitative aspects of traditional sentences while avoiding the high costs of long-term incarceration. As a result, discerning judges, assisted by capable defense and prosecuting attorneys and probation officers, possess powerful tools in fashioning alternative sentences that fit not only the crime, but the criminal, the victim and the community. Further, these alternative sentences may be fashioned even in cases in which it would be unconscionable to allow the offender to pass through the system unpunished yet again or leave the public exposed to a defendant whose unconstrained liberty threatens its safety.

The criminal justice system has become so accustomed to all-or-nothing sentences for cases ranging from petty thievery to mass murders that it has come to accept the proposition that sentences can either address deterrence or rehabilitation, but never both. For example, when incarceration was first proposed as a condition of probation, many in the field reacted with shock, viewing it as an insidious plot to pollute probation, confusing incapacitation with rehabilitation and putting punishment into probation.

A single alternative sentence can be multifaceted. It need not be all or nothing. The alternative sentence can be partially punitive, rehabilitative, retributive and/or incapacitative. Deterrence can be achieved without long-term incarceration. All of this can be imposed without endangering the public or provoking its disapproval. Alternative sentencing need not mean lack of control or punishment.

Such sentences do mean lack of uniformity. They must be tailored to each offender, unlike traditional sentencing in which one cell fits all. Fortunately, there are as many alternative sentences as there are offenders and victims. Choosing or fashioning the appropriate alternative sentence is the challenge facing the criminal justice system. An excellent example of fashioning an alternative sentence was provided by Nebraska District Court federal judge Charles Urbom, who was faced with sentencing a series of defendants for massive bid rigging and fraud.

After exhaustively analyzing the nature of the offense, the offenders, the community in which the offenses were committed and the victims, as well as his sentencing goals and objectives, the judge imposed various probation conditions combined with an alternative use of traditional long-term incarceration to create a sentence hailed by a panel of United States Court of Appeals Eighth Circuit judges as "creative, innovative and imaginative." They noted with approval that "[t]he arsenal of the sentencing judge . . . contain[s] more than the traditional weapons of fine and imprisonment simpliciter." [36]

In fashioning the sentence, Judge Urbom began by reviewing the purposes of sentencing.

> Retribution, deterrence, incapacitation, and rehabilitation are the usually stated reasons for punishment. As applied to the cases before me, I accept the views (1) that society does have a right, perhaps a duty, to balance the universe, to speak in clear terms that it has been offended, (2) that punishment has some effect in deterring some persons from similar crimes, (3) that the likelihood of future repetition by these particular defendants is remote enough to rule out incapacitation—that is, the need for rendering them unable to do further

damage, and (4) that rehabilitation is to be sought in reforming whatever bents of mind rationalized the practice of bid rigging to be
acceptable behavior.[37]

The judge then examined the striking features of the crime, the criminals
and the community in order to insure that the sentence addressed each to
achieve its appropriate purposes.

First, (the crimes) involved collusion. . . . No one undertook any of
the criminal acts for beneficent purposes or with beneficent results.

Second, they involve people of splendid reputation, of strong talent,
of excellent education, with proven leadership qualities.

Third, they involve a defrauding, not of strangers, but of friends, cus-
tomers, the defendants' own state government.

Fourth, there is no sign of sudden passion, no fit of temper, no
grudge to square, no desperate need for drugs, no alcoholic lessening
of judgment, no psychopathic sign of illness, no pressure of poverty,
no rudderlessness of broken homes, but deliberate acts by people well
equipped to live by the accepted ways of society.

Fifth, there is repetition—each defendant admits doing the same or
similar illegal acts over and over again.

Sixth, there is a large amount of money involved in each case.

Seventh, there is difficulty of detection.

Eighth, there is no violence or threat of violence involved.

Ninth, every defendant has admitted guilt.

Tenth, the money lost by the state did not directly inure to the benefit
of the individual defendants, although all relied in one degree or
another on it and shared it indirectly.

Eleventh, none of the defendants has been convicted of any crime
before this.[38]

The judge, while rejecting long-term incarceration, also rejected no incarceration. The crime, he averred, called for a sentence that shocks, to gain the
attention of the defendants and other contractors who may be tempted. No sentence but prison or jail, he concluded, could provide the appropriate shock
effect. Yet incarceration alone was not enough. To come up with alternatives,
the judge reached out to the community, as well as to the defense attorney.

A sentence should be constructive, if possible. I have been pleased to
have the imaginative assistance of defense counsel and of Gregory
Lamm of Crime and Community, Inc. and Gary Mears of Nebraska
Center on Sentencing Alternatives in developing ideas for causing
the defendants to give back to the society they have offended more

than merely idleness in prison or jail, while at the same time causing the defendants to be disrupted in their usual routines and styles of life. The alternative sentences will be designed to be firm, specific, unpleasant for the defendants and constructive for them and others. They have the additional strength of being aimed in most instances at helping directly people who are in the criminal justice population or are prime candidates for it. If the community service features of the sentences are correctly devised they will not have decreased the amount of punishment, but will have increased the usefulness and decreased the expensiveness of it.[39]

The judge rejected direct monetary restitution to the public because no agreement existed as to the exact amount of loss by the state.

The resulting sentences against the defendants were in two parts, against the companies and against the company officers. In regard to one of the latter, the sentence is summarized as follows:

1. The defendant shall spend six months in a jail type facility, followed by probation for five years.

2. Upon release, the defendant must reside for 30 days and nights at Good Samaritan Village . . . and spend at least 72 hours each week in unpaid services to the Village during his residency there. Seven chores are listed for the defendant, including trimming trees, making an energy survey and painting.

3. The defendant must pay for his room and board at a rate of $12 per day at the Village.

4. Following his stay in the Village, the defendant must continue to perform community service of ten hours per week for twenty consecutive weeks for the . . . County Fair Association in analyzing and correcting drainage problems at the Association's facility under the supervision of the Association and the probation officer.

5. For the next 20 weeks, the defendant must perform community service for the YMCA at the rate of ten hours per week.

6. The defendant must pay a fine of $25,000 within 60 days or donate it to the Village and, if the latter, not take it as a charitable deduction from his taxes.

7. The defendant must inform probation of any approaches for illegal business transactions during the course of his business.

8. The defendant must pay $35 court cost.[40]

Although a United States Court of Appeals Eighth Circuit panel upheld this particular sentence, subsequently the Circuit, sitting *en banc,* ruled in a related case that federal probation law precludes the imposition of cash donations as a condition of probation.[41] In the meantime, however, Congress enacted legislation specifically authorizing cash donations in cases in which the victim so consents.[42]

Judge Urbom's sentence contained several common alternative sentencing components including incapacitation without incarceration (in this case, confinement in a non-correctional institution), orders of community work service, the imposition of supervision fees, court costs and a fine or cash donation, as well as additional probation conditions restricting the defendant's activities and associations. The above alternative sanctions were attached to a split sentence. Other common alternative sentencing components, not employed by the judge, include the imposition of other monetary sanctions such as restitution, mandatory support orders, treatment fees, the posting of performance bonds and forfeitures. They include, in addition to orders of community work service, direct victim service in which the offender works directly for the victim, often repairing the very damage he caused. They also include mandatory treatment orders, particularly where the defendant exhibits crime-related behavior dysfunctions such as alcoholism, drug addiction, compulsive gambling or sexual deviance. They include means to incapacitate offenders without the use of incarceration, ranging from house arrest to intensive probation supervision. Finally, alternative sentences may use incarceration, including various forms of split sentencing such as shock sentencing, incarceration being a condition of probation or intermittent sentencing.

The growth of alternative sentencing is attributable to the growth of permissible probationary conditions. This growth began with the development of formal probation at the turn of the last century. In addition to the establishment of probation, a dozen of these early statutes linked restitution to probation, mandating the former as a condition for the latter.

Restitution as a dispositional alternative played a crucial role in the development of alternative sentencing. It was among the first alternative sentencing components that forced the courts to look beyond the interests of either the state, on the one hand, or the offender on the other. Rather, it focused the court's attention on the specific crime victim and the community in which the crime occurred.

However, it was not until after large infusions of federal funds in the 1970s, accompanied by a burgeoning victim rights movement, that large-scale use of this alternative sentencing disposition began to surface around the country. Specific restitution programs, generally administered by courts through their probation departments, proliferated across the country. These programs spawned other alternative sentencing options including "symbolic" or "community" restitution orders, which have come to be known as community work service orders.

Community work service orders were also encouraged as the result of Supreme Court decisions and the uproar over drunk drivers. First, the Court ruled in the early 1970s that judges could no longer sentence offenders to a dollar or a day in prison, allowing wealthier defendants to escape incarceration by paying fines while incarcerating those unable to pay them. As a result, courts had to find alternatives to fines for sentencing indigent defendants. Many courts began to order community work service instead. Community work service programs spread across the country. Second, Mothers Against Drunk Driving and others influenced the majority of state legislatures to stiffen drunk driving sanctions. Rather than add to already overcrowded jails, a dozen states provided for community work service sanctions supplemented by mandatory treatment.

Other alternative sentencing options, introduced in the last several decades, originated from prison officials, judges, religious leaders and others. In order to relieve the worst prison overcrowding in the nation's history, officials developed community-based restitution centers. Pioneered in Minnesota in the early 1970s, correctional restitution centers spread to Georgia, Mississippi and Texas. Just as court orders of restitution require probationers to leave their homes to go to work to pay back their victims, these programs require inmates to leave their cells to go to work to pay back their victims.

In Ohio, judges developed a system of sentencing which came to be known as "shock sentencing," a split sentence where the offender's original long-term commitment is later revised to allow his release on probation. The idea quickly spread around the country. The Oklahoma Department of Corrections recently added another element to the sentence. Before inmates may be released, they must meet with their victims and arrange a restitution contract agreeable to the victim and the sentencing judge. A federal judge in New York developed weekend sentencing, an innovation that subsequently spread to many state courts.

A Mennonite church in Canada, in concert with a local probation department, established a victim/offender mediation program that not only included the victim in the sentencing process but as part of the disposition. The program, known as the Victim Offender Reconciliation Program (VORP), quickly spread across the United States. Expanding beyond its Mennonite roots, the VORP model has been incorporated into many restitution programs.

Elsewhere, the National Center for Institutions and Alternatives (NCIA) was established by Jerome Miller, former juvenile corrections commissioner in Massachusetts who de-institutionalized that state's juvenile corrections. NCIA may be hired by defense attorneys to develop saleable alternative dispositions to incarceration for otherwise jail-bound defendants. While not introducing new specific alternative sentencing options, NCIA developed what it labeled "Client Specific Planning," which repackaged the standard probation presentence investigation report to develop realistic alternative sentences. It also developed a routine of dispositional advocacy successful in winning the backing of prosecutors and judges for a wide variety of alternative sentences.

The nation's media, searching for an answer to ever-worsening prison overcrowding, as well as a good story, focused attention on alternative sentencing. *60 Minutes* profiled the Earn-It program, one of the oldest court restitution and community work service programs, located in Quincy, Massachusetts. Bell Associates syndicated nationally a program titled *Going Straight,* which focused on Earn-It, an American VORP program in Elkhart, Indiana, and on several individual examples of alternative sentences obtained by the NCIA.

As with any sentencing reforms, appellate courts were not unanimous in accepting these new alternative sentencing options. However, no sooner did appellate courts reject one, than the appropriate legislature acted to provide for the option in law. For example, a New York appellate court rejected community work service as a condition of probation.[43] The New York Legislature amended its state probation law allowing it.[44] An Oregon appellate court rejected an award of restitution to relatives of a homicide victim.[45] The state legislature quickly amended the law to allow for it.[46] A Colorado appellate court rejected incarceration as a condition of probation.[47] The state legislature enacted legislation providing for incarceration as a condition of both misdemeanor and felony probation.[48] Various United States Circuit Courts rejected cash donations as conditions of probation.[49] The United States Congress amended the federal criminal code to allow for such donations with the concurrence of the crime victim.[50]

Accompanying these changes in the laws and on the bench, probation departments also began to undergo transformations. Departments across the country began the slow transition from a traditional casework model to what have been called "justice" and "limited risk control" models of probation. Departments began to develop risk classifications, allowing them to concentrate on high-risk offenders. Intensive supervision programs were developed, incorporating many alternative sentencing sanctions including restitution and community work service.

Suddenly, judges around the country in state, municipal and federal courts discovered that, like Judge Urbom, they have at their disposal a powerful arsenal for alternative sentencing. And, as the following chapters reveal, they are increasingly imposing alternative sentences for all kinds of crimes and categories of criminals.

Before examples of alternative sentences are presented and analyzed, however, the context for such sentences will be examined. First, the criminal sentencing process will be briefly discussed. Then, probation will be explored both as the original alternative sentence and as it can be used today for alternative sentencing.

Notes

[1] Maurer, M. (1992). AMERICANS BEHIND BARS: ONE YEAR LATER. Washington DC: The Sentencing Project.

[2] Sniffem, M. (1995). *US Inmate Population Soars in '95*. ASSOCIATED PRESS.

[3] Maurer, M. (1990). YOUNG BLACK MEN AND THE CRIMINAL JUSTICE SYSTEM: A GROWING NATIONAL PROBLEM. Washington, DC: The Sentencing Project.

[4] *Panel Says New York Courts Are Infested with Racism.* CRIMINAL JUSTICE NEWSLETTER, 22:12 (June 17, 1991).

[5] Schmitt, C. (1991). *Plea Bargaining Favors Whites as Blacks, Hispanics Pay Price.* SAN JOSE MERCURY NEWS, Dec. 8.

[6] Friedman, L. (1993). CRIME AND PUNISHMENT IN AMERICAN HISTORY. New York, NY: Basic Books (gives a historical account of criminal justice in this country including the role of racism and its influence within the system).

[7] Beck, A. and D. Gilliard (1995). *Prisoners in 1994.* BUREAU OF JUSTICE STATISTICS BULLETIN (August). Washington, DC: U.S. Department of Justice.

[8] *State v. Russell,* 477 N.W.2d 886 (Minn. 1991).

[9] YOUNG BLACK AMERICANS AND THE CRIMINAL JUSTICE SYSTEM: FIVE YEARS LATER. Washington DC: The Sentencing Project, 1995.

[10] Shine, C. and M. Mauer (1993). DOES THE PUNISHMENT FIT THE CRIME? DRUG USERS AND DRUNK DRIVERS, QUESTIONS OF RACE AND CLASS. Washington, DC: The Sentencing Project.

[11] Kerr, P. (1988). *New Court Succeeds in Cutting Backlog of Drug Cases.* NEW YORK TIMES, Feb. 6.

[12] Quote from Martin Murphy, criminal defense division of legal aid society of Manhattan. In Kerr, P. *New Court in New York Succeeds in Cutting Backlog of Drug Cases.* NEW YORK TIMES, Feb. 6, 1988.

[13] Shine, C. and M. Mauer (1993). DOES THE PUNISHMENT FIT THE CRIME? DRUG USERS AND DRUNK DRIVERS, QUESTIONS OF RACE AND CLASS. Washington, DC: The Sentencing Project, March.

[14] Gelb, A. (1991). *Scales of Justice Tip Toward Drunks.* ATLANTA JOURNAL AND CONSTITUTION, Nov. 5.

[15] Maurer, M. (1992). AMERICANS BEHIND BARS: ONE YEAR LATER. Washington, DC: The Sentencing Project, February.

[16] Sniffen, M. (1995). *US Inmate Population Soars in '95.* ASSOCIATED PRESS.

[17] Anderson, D. (1991). *A World Leader, in Prisons.* NEW YORK TIMES, March 2.

[18] Gavzer, B. (1995). *Life Behind Bars.* PARADE MAGAZINE, August 13.

[19] *Ibid.*

[20] Study by American Correctional Association, reported in PARADE MAGAZINE.

[21] James Austin, Executive Vice President, quoted in PARADE MAGAZINE.

[22] Reported in Hinds, M. (1992). *Feeling Prisons' Costs, Governors Weigh Alternatives.* NEW YORK TIMES, August 7.

[23] Butterfield, F. (1995). *New Prisons Cast Shadow Over Higher Education.* NEW YORK TIMES, April 12.

[24] Nolan, M. (1995). *California Sees Prisons Filling as Colleges Decline.* BOSTON GLOBE, August 28.

[25] Survey conducted by Center for the Study of the States, State University of New York, cited in Butterfield, op. cit.

[26] Proband, S. (1995). *Corrections Leads State Appropriations Increases for '96.* National Conference of State Legislatures, Denver, CO, quoted in OVERCROWDED TIMES, October.

[27] Grunwald, M. (1995). *Texas May Find Surplus of Cells a Fugitive Fix.* BOSTON GLOBE, November 12.

[28] Richard Freeman, economist, quoted in G. Zachary (1995). *Economists Say Prison Boom Will Take Toll.* WALL STREET JOURNAL, September 29.

[29] Bureau of Justice Statistics (1988). *Report to the Nation on Crime and Justice, Second Edition.* Washington, DC: U.S. Department of Justice.

[30] *Commonwealth v. Ennis,* 394 Pa. Super. 1, 574 A.2d 1116 (1990).

[31] Cunniff, M. (1987). SENTENCING OUTCOMES IN 28 FELONY COURTS IN 1985. Washington, DC: Bureau of Justice Statistics.

[32] Holt, N. (1995). *California's Determinate Sentencing: What Went Wrong?* PERSPECTIVES, Summer.

[33] Deegan, P. (1995). *Community Corrections for the Year 2010: All Corrections is Local: Building Partnerships for Public Safety, II.* THE IARCA JOURNAL ON COMMUNITY CORRECTIONS, VII:1, September.

[34] Speech, Hon. Aaron Ment, Chief Court Administrator, Connecticut, to Massachusetts probation Conference, Randolph, MA, May 11, 1995.

[35] Hinds, M. (1992). *Feeling Prisons' Costs, Governors Weigh Alternatives.* NEW YORK TIMES, August 7.

[36] *United States v. William Anderson Co. Inc.,* 698 F.2d 911 (8th Cir. 1982).

[37] *United States v. William Anderson Co. Inc.,* 1982-2 Trade Cas. § 64,896 (D.C. Neb. 1982).

[38] *Id.*

[39] *Id.*

[40] *United States v. Werner Construction, Inc.,* 1982-2 Trade Cas. § 64,897 (D.C. Neb. 1982).

[41] *United States v. Missouri Valley Construction Co.,* 741 F.2d 1542 (8th Cir. 1984).

[42] Pub. L. No. 97-291, 96 Stat. 1248 (codified at 18 U.S.C. § 3579(b)(4) (1982) (redesignated § 3663 effective Nov. 1, 1986).

[43] *People v. Mandell,* 50 A.D.2d 907, 377 N.Y.S.2d 563 (1975).

[44] N.Y. PENAL LAW § 65.10(2)(h) (McKinney Supp. 1986) (as amended by P.L. 1978 c. 505 § 1 and P.L. 1980 c. 471§ 22).

[45] *State v. Stalheim,* 275 Or. 683, 552 P.2d 374 (1970).

[46] OR. REV. STAT. § 137-103(4) (1977).

[47] *People v. Ledford,* 173 Colo. 194, 477 P.2d 374 (1970).

[48] COLO. REV. STAT. § 16-11-202 (1978) (enacted by R. & R.E., L. 72, p. 240 § 1).

[49] See, *e.g.,* *United States v. Prescon Corp.,* 695 F.2d 1237 (10th Cir. 1982).

[50] 18 U.S.C. § 3579(b)(4) (1982).

Chapter 2

Sentencing Criminals

§2.01   The Process of Criminal Sentencing

Theoretically, the sentencing process follows a deliberate, consistent course, whether the ultimate disposition is long-term incarceration or an alternative sentence. After a full trial and a finding of guilt by the judge or the jury, the court recesses to give all parties time to prepare argument for disposition. A professionally trained probation officer, in the interim, conducts a full presentence investigation and drafts a comprehensive, unbiased social and criminal history report, concluding with pertinent sentencing recommendations.

Immediately prior to sentencing, both prosecution and defense are provided with copies of the presentence report. They each review it carefully and prepare their own presentations for court. They spend as much time and energy on their dispositional arguments as they spent preparing for the trial on the facts. Rejecting repetition of rote pleas for or against mercy and leniency, they prepare detailed, individualized sentencing alternatives that address not only the crime, but also the criminal and the circumstances of the crime victim.

The judge digests the presentence report prior to the dispositional hearing but enters the courtroom with an open mind, ready to hear from all parties. After insuring that defense and prosecution have had sufficient time to prepare for the hearing and review the presentence report, the judge invites the defense to speak on the client's behalf. After the defense attorney concludes, the judge inquires if the defendant would care to present information in his own behalf in mitigation of punishment. Having been alerted by his attorney before the hearing of his right of allocution, the defendant states his argument.

The prosecution follows, summarizing the pertinent facts of the trial and presenting information provided by the crime victim, amplifying the data contained in the "victim impact statement" already provided to all parties. Mindful of the American Bar Association's admonition that prosecutors should not make sentencing recommendations for fear that they may compromise judicial considerations,[1] the prosecutor carefully concludes his remarks, including any information that might accrue to the benefit of the defendant.

During the proceedings, first the defense attorney and later the prosecutor call pertinent witnesses to aid the court in sentencing.

Finally, the judge considers all the information and makes a decision, mindful of enthusiastic endorsements of a probationary presumption in sentencing by the American Bar Association, the President's Commission on Law Enforcement and Administration of Justice, the National Advisory Commission on Criminal Justice Standards and Goals and the American Law Institute.[2] The judge announces the disposition, carefully explaining and recording the reasons for it.

The defendant agrees to pay the fee. He then exits the courtroom under his own power or escorted by the court officers. The clerk calls the next case.

That is what is supposed to happen, based on the Federal Rules of Criminal Procedure. However, in this country's packed criminal courts, the sentencing process usually begins before the case is called for trial. Defense and prosecution counsel get together, often in the crowded courthouse corridors, and engage in some quick negotiations. The defense exchanges the right to force the State to prove his client's guilt by a jury for reduced charges or an agreed-upon disposition or both. The prosecutor exchanges his right to proceed on the original, more serious criminal charges for a chance to clear the case quickly, freeing himself and office and police resources for the next case.

In point of fact, more than 90 percent of all criminal cases are disposed of through such a process, called plea bargaining. A study of felony arrests in the 1980s revealed that guilty pleas ranged from 81 percent of all cases in Louisville to 97 percent in the Manhattan Borough of New York City.[3] In fact, other studies reveal that 61 percent of all criminal cases are disposed of with a guilty plea at arraignment in the latter jurisdiction.[4] More recently, in 1990 Manhattan criminal courts handled 17,010 felony cases. Eighty-four percent pled out, almost nine percent were dismissed and only 5.5 percent went to trial. Similarly, that same year, Brooklyn criminal courts handled 45,700 felony cases. Almost one-half (44%) were reduced to misdemeanors. Of those that remained felonies, only 811 received verdicts after trials. The conviction rate was 67.4 percent. As an experienced practitioner told the New York Times, "[i]n New York and around the country, the administration of justice is rough. There are compromises at every turn."[5]

As a result of a statewide ballot initiative, Proposition #8, passed in 1982, California voters eliminated plea bargaining in serious felony cases and drunk driving cases unless there is insufficient evidence to prove the people's case, or testimony or a material witness cannot be obtained or a reduction or dismissal would not result in a substantial change in sentence.[6] Defendants do not have a right to plea bargain.[7]

The ultimate outcome of any criminal case, plea bargained or not, has a lot to do with the type of sentencing system the jurisdiction has. Historically, sentencing was left to the courts. The legislatures and Congress allowed them broad discretion to sentence as they deemed fit. As previously described, that changed in the mid-1970s as more and more jurisdictions adopted determinate and other sentencing schemes that limited judicial discretion. Where indeterminate sentencing schemes were dropped, incarceration rates generally increased.

Sentencing studies reveal, not surprisingly, that probation rates are the lowest for homicide (14%) and robbery (26%) and highest for drug cases (66%) and larcenies (57%) among the serious felonies examined, which also included rape, aggravated assault and burglary. Interestingly, the percentage of cases plea bargained is equivalent in both determinate and indeterminate systems, averaging about 89 percent in the instant study.[8]

Similarly, in the federal system, although the imposition of the Sentencing Guidelines in 1987 has seen an increase in incarceration, plea bargaining has been unaffected. A study of the first 2,324 cases from November 1987 to March 31, 1989 revealed that 90.2 percent of all federal cases were still pled out. This figure mirrors the ratio of pleas before the Guidelines.[9]

Plea Bargaining

What is usually referred to as plea bargaining actually covers different kinds of bargains. In exchange for the defendant's plea of guilt and foregoing of a trial, the prosecutor can agree to a specific disposition or sentence. The prosecutor can also agree to reduce the charges from a felony to a misdemeanor or the number of counts charged against the defendant. The prosecutor can also agree not to make any sentencing recommendation at all.

Even if the prosecutor makes no promises, offenders are generally rewarded for admitting their guilt and saving the government the costs and uncertainty of trying them. Although offenders cannot be punished for demanding a trial, judges can legally reward them for admitting their guilt because it is deemed to demonstrate the offender's remorse and atonement.

Obviously, plea bargaining varies depending upon the underlying sentencing scheme in the relevant jurisdiction. Also, in jurisdictions that require formal presentence investigation reports by probation officers, the bargain may be conditional upon the findings of that report. For example, a federal sentencing court that accepts a plea agreement providing for a specific sentence is not bound by the agreement until after it has had an opportunity to examine the presentence report. If the report reveals facts that differ from those agreed upon, the plea can be rejected and the defendant given an opportunity to plead anew.

In an example of the above, a defendant charged in a drug case agreed to a plea that stipulated the amount of drugs involved to be 99 grams—just short of the amount needed to increase the offense level in the federal sentencing guidelines. The court accepted the plea, which limited sentence to the low end of the guidelines. The sentencing report, however, revealed the amount of drugs to be over 100 grams. The court then changed its mind and sentenced the offender to more time in prison. The rejection of the plea was upheld by the relevant Circuit Court on appeal.[10]

Similarly, plea bargains may be vacated if the restitution amount eventually ordered was not known at the time of the plea if the restitution amount is relevant and material to the making of the agreement.[11] On the other hand, appellate courts in Arizona have not allowed for pleas to be overturned where the defendant who plead was unaware that he would be placed on home detention because the latter did not constitute a "severe deprivation of liberty."[12] Similarly, an Indiana appellate court held that only conditions that impose a "substantial obligation of a punitive nature" must be specified in the plea agreement.[13] And a Michigan appellate court refused to allow a defendant to withdraw his plea even though the conditions imposed went beyond those agreed to in the plea arrangement. The Court reasoned that because the conditions of probation are, at all times, alterable and amendable without notice or an opportunity to be heard in that state, the sentencing judge could depart from the agreed-upon conditions at sentencing.[14]

Generally, plea bargains proceed as follows. The judge hears a recitation of the facts as captured by the arresting police officer in his report. Defense and prosecutors make a perfunctory argument on behalf of the bargain. If the bargain does not include an agreed-upon disposition, the defense and prosecution make brief arguments, asking for mercy on the one hand and consideration of the public safety on the other. Defense puts in a *pro forma* plea for probation.

If the jurisdiction is New York City or Los Angeles, the parties are cognizant of the fact that probation supervision may mean the probationers send in a postcard to the office once a month at most. If the probation department is represented, an officer hands the judge an often incomplete copy of the defendant's prior record if he has one. And, in some cases, the parties may also know that the local jails and correctional facilities are overcrowded, releasing inmates out the back door as quickly as they enter the front door.

The judge ratifies the plea bargain and the next case is called.

Although plea bargaining was not formally recognized by the United States Supreme Court until 1970,[15] the Court acknowledged in a 1977 case that "[f]or decades it was a *sub rosa* process shrouded in secrecy and deliberately concealed by participating defendants, defense lawyers, prosecutors, and even judges."[16]

Legal acceptance of plea bargaining has led to the formulation of specific rules. The Federal Rules of Criminal Procedure, for example, outline the following procedure for federal plea negotiations:

> The attorney for the government and the attorney for the defendant, or the defendant when acting pro se may engage in discussions with a view toward reaching an agreement that, upon the entering of a plea of guilty or nolo contendere to a charged offense or to a lesser or related offense, the attorney for the government will do any of the following:
>
> (A) move for a dismissal of charges; or

(B) make a recommendation, or agree not to oppose the defen-
    dant's request for a particular sentence, with the under-
    standing that such recommendation or request shall not be
    binding upon the court; or
(C) agree that a specific sentence is the appropriate disposition
    of the case.
The court shall not participate in any such discussion.[17]

The Federal Rule goes on to provide that, once reached, the plea agreement
must be presented in open court. If the agreement is in regard to either (A) or
(C), the judge must wait until after considering the presentence report before
endorsing or rejecting it. If (B), the court shall advise the defendant that if it
does not accept the agreement, the defendant may withdraw the plea.

Although plea bargains are not binding on judges and the judges reserve
the right to call for additional sentencing information, including but not limited
to full presentence investigation reports by probation officials as mandated in
the federal courts, studies reveal that judges overwhelmingly endorse what is
presented to them. A National Institute of Justice study, for example, found that
in plea-bargained cases, judges do not concern themselves with the strength of
the case against the defendant, but whether unfair coercion was used to induce
the plea. The study found further that judges reject the plea bargain in only two
percent of cases.[18]

As a result of plea bargaining, frequently the crime the defendant admits to
is not the crime for which he was arrested. Another Justice Department study
revealed that of 858 offenders convicted of violent crimes in Oregon in 1979,
only one-third were convicted of the same offense for which they had been
charged.[19] The larger number, two-thirds, were convicted of a lesser offense. This
reduction in charges is significant. Of the offenders convicted of the original
charges, 73.4 percent were incarcerated. Of those whose charges were reduced,
only 55.9 percent were incarcerated. The same pattern prevailed in regard to
property offenses, but less dramatically. A little less than half of the property
offenses were reduced. Those with reduced charges were incarcerated at a rate
of 35 percent as compared to 40.5 percent for those convicted of the same
charges for which they were arrested. In both types of crimes, charge reductions
were due to plea bargaining as well as independent prosecutorial decisions.

In addition to such mundane but important considerations from how
crowded the criminal docket is to such concerns as the various parties' notions
of what constitutes justice, there are some common considerations that affect
plea bargaining. For the defense, the primary concern is limiting the defendant's exposure to lengthy incarceration. Even if a full jury trial may see the
client exonerated, the risk of conviction of a serious crime may convince
defense to seek a plea bargain. The Supreme Court, in recognition of this, has
expressly allowed defendants who do not admit guilt to enter into plea
bargains.[20] At the same time, the prosecutor is often more concerned with
obtaining a conviction and clearing the case than in the particular sentence sub-

sequently imposed. While the prosecutor, rightly or wrongly, receives the credit or the blame for the case finding, the judge must bear the burden for imposing the sentence.

Both prosecution and defense are concerned with the costs of trying the case. If the prosecutor's office is backlogged, understaffed and dependent upon overextended police resources, it may be vulnerable to the threat of a long, drawn-out trial.

Both prosecution and defense are influenced by what some commentators have called the "going rates,"[21] the typical sentencing patterns established in various jurisdictions for common offenses. If it is clear that the defendant is likely to be sentenced a certain way no matter what either side recommends or what particular facts come out during the trial or dispositional hearing, it may be in neither's interest to try the matter.

Other matters external to the prosecutor and defense attorney may also influence plea bargaining. Local jail or prison overcrowding may play a role. If the local institution is under court order to maintain a cap on its population or is already letting offenders out the back door to reduce its population, there may be little incentive for the prosecutor to press for long-term incarceration. The Denver Bar Association found, after polling area judges, that judges were more reluctant to incarcerate nonviolent offenders as a result of jail overcrowding.[22]

Pretrial publicity affects plea bargaining. If the case has obtained notoriety, there may be no deal acceptable to the prosecutor, no cost too great for prosecution of the case to the fullest. On the other hand, pretrial publicity can accrue to the benefit of the defense. Widespread sympathy for the defendant may convince the prosecutor to forego a trial and the adversarial sentencing process.

The victim can also affect plea bargaining. Although specific legislation giving the victim veto power over the prosecution's plea arrangements is limited, victim influence in sentencing is increasing. Almost a half-dozen states, for example, suggest or mandate victim involvement in the plea bargaining process itself. In Florida, the state attorney is permitted to consult with the victim or the victim's family concerning any plea agreement.[23] In Nevada, the court may interview witnesses, including the victim, to see if the offense is more serious than the plea submitted.[24] In Indiana, a judge may not consider a prosecutor's recommendation of a felony plea bargain unless the prosecutor has notified the victim of the plea negotiations, the prosecutor's recommendation, and the victim's right to be present and address the court when the judge considers the plea.[25] Maine and Minnesota have similar provisions.[26] Considering that the vast majority of criminal cases never go beyond this stage, this is an important victim right.

However, at least one state supreme court has ruled that a state prosecutor may not, pursuant to Oregon state law, condition his acceptance of a plea upon the concurrence by the parents of the murder victim. The condition, the court wrote, constituted an impermissible delegation to the victim's parents of the prosecutor's statutory discretion. Further, it held that a prosecutor who engages in plea negotiations must be guided by public policy considerations relating to the effective administration of the criminal justice system and not delegate this duty to others.[27]

Whether or not the victim is involved in the plea bargaining process by statute, there is some case law developing that suggests that appellate courts are looking to see if the plea bargain served the victim's interests as well as the public interest. In a 1984 West Virginia case, for example, the state's highest court ruled that the sentencing court had not only the right but the duty to consider "the interests of the victim as well" in determining whether a plea bargain met the standard of being "consistent with the public interest in the fair administration of justice."[28] The court noted that "[w]e are reinforced in this view by the . . . legislative findings (the preamble to legislation establishing certain victim rights, such as having a victim impact statement introduced before sentencing) enacted by the 1984 legislature . . . entitled "Victim Protection Act of 1984."[29]

At least in regard to felonies, the federal courts and one-half of the state courts, like West Virginia's, require victim impact statements. Others allow victims to address the court at sentencing, matching the defendant's right of allocution. Still others provide for victim's statements of opinion at sentencing. As a result, both prosecutor and defense must be mindful that the victim's feelings may eventually be presented to the court. For the prosecutor, while it may prove fairly easy to negotiate dispassionately even a complicated case with the defense, explaining this to an aggrieved, angry and confused victim may prove difficult indeed. On the other hand, if the victim is in agreement, plea bargaining may be expedited.

Then, too, there are the details of the particular case that affect plea bargaining. The defendant may have information the prosecutor wants for another case, or the defendant may have valuable goods the prosecutor wants returned. The defense may have already compensated or promised to compensate the victim. Plea bargains, in fact, may be conditioned upon the defendant's agreement to cooperate with law enforcement or pay victims restitution.[30]

In addition to the above, other seemingly extraneous factors often come into play which may influence the plea bargain. In 1995, for example, the *Boston Globe* completed an exhaustive survey of how that state's property seizure law was working. The law enables prosecutors to forfeit and seize the house, car or drug profits of various drug offenders. The proceeds go directly to the local prosecutor's office or the office of the state attorney general. The drug money then becomes part of their operating budgets.

> It would be bad enough if the drug money were merely converted to a kind of (District Attorney's) slush fund. What's worse, as the (Globe) revealed, is that this system sets up incentives for prosecutions to trade long prison sentences for drug money. The guy who can provide the DA with hundreds of thousands of dollars in drug profits gets short time and fingers some street dealer who takes the fall for the long prison sentence. . . . On average, $50,000 in drug profits brought a 6.3 years sentence reduction. . . .

To be precise, an asset seizure law intended to punish major dealers has the effect of helping them get off easier. Drug asset seizures amount to about 12 percent of the prosecutors' budgets, and in some counties the figure goes over 20 percent.[31]

Lack of concern for crime victims, particularly women victims, may also play an enormous role in criminal proceedings. The same newspaper revealed in another exposé, completed the year before, that based on their assessment of the importance of domestic abuse cases, some district attorneys routinely dismissed up to 66 percent of these cases compared to others who dismissed only 18 percent. The sample examined criminal violations of over 40,000 restraining orders, large enough to control for individual case characteristics.[32]

Most importantly, plea bargains are influenced by the bottom line: what both sides are seeking. If the proposed alternative sentence sought by the defense is reasonable and meets the particular sentencing aims of the state, this may be the best guarantee of a successful plea negotiation between defense and prosecution.

In light of the prevalence of plea bargaining and its vast importance in the determination of the ultimate sentence, dispositional advocacy must begin long before the case reaches the judge. The place for the defense to begin advocating an alternative sentence is in the prosecutor's office. At the very least, if the prosecutor cannot be convinced to endorse an alternative sentence, the defense should try to win the prosecutor's agreement to remain silent before the court and let the judge decide.

§2.02   Probation Presentence Investigation Reports

If the defense and prosecution have reached a plea bargain, the sentence is almost guaranteed in most courts. However, in some jurisdictions, two steps remain. First, the probation department must conduct a presentence investigation report. Second, the court must receive the report and conduct a dispositional hearing before imposing sentence. Neither the presentence report nor a formal dispositional hearing is required, but both may be requested by the court in all jurisdictions. Both may be essential to convince the court to impose an alternative sentence.

As many judges will admit, when it comes time to sentence, they are left "wandering in deserts of uncharted discretion."[33] The judge knows little about the person before him, except what may have emerged from the trial, or more likely the admission. Apart from this, all the judge has is the defendant's prior record if there is one, and the defendant's posture or facial expressions observed during the proceedings. To supplement this, the judge must rely on the information presented by the defense and prosecution. The only neutral party the court can turn to for information is the probation officer. Although a public employee, the probation officer reports directly to the judge.

As the Colorado Supreme Court declared in a 1983 decision:

> The information and recommendations presented to a trial court by
> its probation department in connection with a sentencing hearing are
> of great importance to the trial judge's ultimate sentencing decision. .
> . . The report is not designed to further the sentencing interests of
> either the prosecution or the defendant: rather, it is in the nature of
> an evaluation and recommendation by an impartial expert in the
> field of effective sentencing alternatives.[34]

Any plea bargain, for this reason, is not binding on the probation officer. The probation officer has no duty to conform his sentencing recommendations to the plea agreement.

The presentence report alone may contain the data necessary for the judge to address both the offense and the offender in the sentence. More jurisdictions are also requiring information on the crime victim to be introduced before sentencing. The presentence report may provide a convenient vehicle, and probation officers may provide available manpower to accomplish this mandate. Even in the nine states that have comprehensive determinate sentencing schemes, judges often require presentence reports to learn of any mitigating or aggravating factors that will affect the ultimate sentence imposed.

Over the years, almost all of the major prescriptive studies of sentencing have endorsed increased use of presentence reports. The American Bar Association, for example, recommends that "all courts trying criminal cases should be supplied with the resources and supporting staff to permit a presentence investigation and a written report of its results in every case."[35] The Bar qualifies, however, that such reports be mandatory only if the defendant faces a year or more imprisonment or if the defendant is under 21 or a first-time offender. Similarly, the National Advisory Commission on Criminal Justice Standards and Goals recommends presentence reports where incarceration, felonies or minors are involved.[36] The entire scheme of judicial discretion in sentencing, it suggests, "is subverted if adequate investigation is not provided."[37]

Presentence investigations go back to the beginning of probation in the 1840s. In fact, the first probation statute, enacted in Boston in 1878, included the provision that "the probation officer will investigate persons convicted of crimes and misdemeanors and make recommendations to the courts regarding the advisability of probation."[38] The modern presentence report, however, can be traced back to William Healy, Director of the Juvenile Psychiatric Institute of Chicago, who championed individual diagnosis of each offender in order to pursue rational treatment.

By 1943, the federal courts published formal presentence report guidelines and formats. In 1965, the Administrative Office of the United States Courts published comprehensive standards, including 16 separate areas to be covered, ranging from prior record to marital history, home and neighborhood, finances and "interests and leisure."

The United States Supreme Court validated the use of presentences in a 1949 case, *Williams v. New York*.[39] In this case, although the jury recommended leniency, the court imposed the death penalty based on a presentence report containing unproven hearsay information obtained outside the court, which alleged that the defendant had committed 30 other burglaries for which he had not been convicted, had a "morbid sexuality" and represented a "menace to society." Ruling that the "punishment must fit the defendant and not merely the crime," the Supreme Court upheld the disposition. Williams died.

Despite the popularity of presentence reports, both by criminal justice commentators and study commissions, their actual use has become subject to debate. A study of presentence reports conducted in the early 1960s, for example, found that judges seldom looked beyond the current offense, prior record and indications of stability.[40] The 1967 Presidential Crime Commission questioned the efficacy of some of the material in presentence reports:

> [I]n many cases [they] have come to include a great deal of material of doubtful relevance to dispositions in most cases. The orientation of many probation officers is often reflected in, for example, attempts to provide in all presentence reports comprehensive analyses of offenders, including extensive descriptions of their childhood experiences.[41]

Nevertheless, by the mid-1970s, another Justice Department study found widespread use of presentences.[42] Of 3,303 agencies identified as performing probation services, 2,540 reported doing presentence reports. It also found that what passed for presentence reports varied tremendously. With the exception of the offender's name, no two reports included the same headings. Similar to earlier studies, however, the report found that judges were uninterested in complete social histories, concentrating instead on information concerning the offense, prior record, and the defendant's stability in the community. What they valued most was the added time that ordering the presentence reports allowed the courts before imposing sentence, as well as the special medical or psychiatric data the reports could provide.[43]

Reviewing the state of the art several years later, experts reported their bafflement over presentence reports:

> In summary, research into presentence investigation reports leaves us in somewhat of a quandary. First, we see that sentencing decisions tend to be made on relatively few pieces of information. Second, we see that in spite of this, there is a rather steady demand for more complete and accurate presentence investigation reports. On one hand, we see little evidence that conclusively indicates that presentence investigation reports are worth their massive costs; on the other, the traditional logic for them is persuasive and the demand of judges for them can hardly be denied.[44]

In a major study of presentence reports completed for Californian felons, the Rand Corporation found in general no statistical difference in the recidivism rates of those persons probation officers recommended for probation from those they recommended for prison.[45] The mere order of a presentence report does not mean that it will be complete, relevant or read by the judge.

§2.03   —Federal Presentence Reports

When the federal guidelines went into effect in the late 1980s, the role of federal probation officers completing presentence reports was dramatically altered. In place of providing general background information on the defendant, the probation officer must now concentrate on factors the court must consider in computing the sentence pursuant to the guidelines. The amended Federal Rules of Criminal Procedure call for:

> information about the history and characteristics of the defendant, his prior criminal record, if any, his financial condition, and any circumstances affecting his behavior that may be helpful in imposing sentence or in the correctional treatment of the defendant.[46]

In addition, the probation officer is instructed to provide "unless the court orders otherwise, information concerning the nature and extent of non-prison programs and resources available for the defendant" as well as "such other information as may be required by the court."[47] To accommodate the court in fitting the sentence within the guidelines, the probation officer's report is to contain:

> the classification of the offense and of the defendant under the categories established by the Sentencing Commission . . . that the probation officer believes to be applicable to the defendant's case; the kinds of sentence and the sentencing range suggested for such category of offense committed by such a category of defendant as set forth in the guidelines issued by the Sentencing Commission . . . and an explanation by the probation officer of any factors that may indicate that a sentence of a different kind or of a different length than one within the applicable guidelines would be more appropriate under all the circumstances.[48]

The post-Guidelines federal presentence report has six parts: (1) The Offense (charges and convictions; obstruction of justice, if any; acceptance of responsibility); (2) Defendant's Criminal History; (3) Sentencing Options (custody, supervised release and probation provisions); (4) Offender Characteristics (family ties, family responsibilities and community ties, mental and emotional data, physical condition, employment record); (5) Fines and Restitution; (6) Factors that May Warrant Departure from Guidelines. These sections are followed by the Sentencing Recommendation as well as the probation officers' recording of any objections raised by either the Government or the Defendant to the report.

Probation officers have a Worksheet to calculate: (1) Offense level; (2) Multiple Counts or Stipulations to Additional Offenses; (3) Criminal History; (4) Guideline Worksheet (final scoring). The probation officer must report what he or she believes to be true. He cannot merely summarize what the parties tell him or mediate between the defense and prosecution. He must come up with a single version to present to the judge. The probation officer must therefore carefully document where he obtains the information on which he relies. The information within the report must be proved by a preponderance of the evidence.[49] The judge resolves all disputes.

After the guidelines went into effect in 1987, the probation officer's role in helping the court determine the sentence was challenged as a violation of separation of powers. The Ninth Circuit upheld the probation officer's role, saying the court had the power to appoint an independent investigator to gather appropriate information even though the Guidelines no longer identify rehabilitation as the goal of sentencing. As the court recognized, presentence reports need not be tied to the rehabilitation model. A court needs as much detailed information if it seeks to impose a uniform sentence as it needs if it seeks to rehabilitate offenders.[50]

Because the presentence report is so crucial for sentencing, at least one federal Circuit has ruled that the defendant may not waive it.[51] The judge must personally insure that the defendant has read the report.[52] In a related area, even though it is not covered in the Federal Rules of Criminal Procedure governing presentence investigation reports, the First Circuit insists that if the court uses material in sentencing that is not contained in the presentence report, this too must be revealed to the defendant.[53]

Generally before the federal guidelines, the federal courts ruled that a defendant did not have the right to counsel when he meets with the probation officer working on the report. This did not represent a crucial stage of the criminal process. The information in the report, after all, was for the judge's use, not the prosecutor's use.[54] The defendant does not have *Miranda* rights at routine presentence meetings with his probation officer. After all, he has already admitted to or been found guilty prior to the presentence report being ordered.[55] On the other hand, while refusing to say that a defendant has a Constitutional right to a lawyer when meeting with the probation officer preparing the report, the Ninth Circuit ruled in 1990 that, given the importance of the report in determining sentencing since imposition of the Guidelines, pursuant to the court's supervisory power, defense lawyers must be allowed to attend presentence interviews.[56] Besides, the court added optimistically, the lawyer may well facilitate matters by stressing the importance of telling the truth to the probation officer.

The Fourth Circuit ruled, on the other hand, that because the probation officer is neutral in preparing the presentence report, his changing role with the implementation of federal guidelines still did not make the preparation of the presentence report a critical stage of the proceedings covered by the Sixth Amendment right to counsel. As a result, *ex parte* communication between the probation officer and judge, in the instant case, did not violate the offender's Sixth Amendment rights. The court would not presume that the probation officer acted improperly.[57] The Tenth Circuit has ruled that there is no Sixth Amendment right to counsel during presentence interviews, despite imposition of the federal guidelines.[58] Similarly, it has ruled that probation officers need not give offenders their *Miranda* rights in these interviews.[59]

A reason defendants may want their counsel at these meetings is because if they provide false information to the probation officer for inclusion in the presentence report, they may be prosecuted for obstruction of justice.[60]

Presentence reports may include conduct not charged in the indictment, as long as the defendant is aware of its inclusion.[61] For example, in one case, the defendant was sentenced for use of counterfeit money in excess of that charged in the indictment. The latter amount was $10,840, but the former was more than $1,000,000. The million dollars was found in the home of a codefendant. At the sentencing hearing, the government connected the defendant to the larger amount of money because he was the mastermind, he possessed the paper on which the currency was printed and he was with the codefendant at the time of the crime.

At least one federal circuit has allowed disclosure of presentence reports to third parties. The Ninth Circuit has ruled that third parties, including newspapers, may have access if they make some threshold showing that disclosure will serve the ends of justice.[62] In that case, the victim's family wanted to see the probation presentence report used to help free a felon who then went on to kill the victim. The victim was the offender's former prosecutor. The offender had earlier threatened to kill the prosecutor who had successfully prosecuted him for arson. Nonetheless, the offender was released after another conviction, even though it involved the defendant having an arsenal of weapons. The defendant then killed the victim and committed suicide when police closed in on him. Originally the District Court judge ruled no access to third parties. A three-judge panel of the Ninth Circuit overruled the judge, holding that the denial was a "clear error of judgment." The information in the presentence report was held to be the only source of relevant information available to the victim's relatives in their wrongful death action. Even so, subsequently the District Court released only information contained in the report, excluding internal working documents such as risk prediction scores, chronologicals and case reviews not available to the offender himself at sentencing.[63]

While the fact situation in the above case is unique, pursuant to this ruling, other courts have released presentence reports to the Immigration and Naturalization Service to facilitate deportation of a drug offender.[64]

The Seventh Circuit Court of Appeals has prohibited general disclosure under the Freedom of Information Act. Further, disagreeing with the Ninth Circuit, it restricted disclosure only for a particularized, compelling need.[65] In one case, the court allowed the release of a presentence report where the defendant had claimed to the press that he was being prosecuted for failing to file his tax return because he was black. While the defendants have a right to privacy because much of the information in the presentence reports are not related to the offense, the court noted that the sentencing hearing itself is public and therefore it is hard to say that the presentence report should never be public. In addressing the same issue, the Fifth Circuit amended a disclosure order it reviewed to exclude defendant characteristics.[66]

Federal probation officers have immunity in the preparation of presentence reports.[67]

§2.04   —State Presentence Reports

Presentence reports are not uniformly mandated in the states. The United States Supreme Court has, in effect, demanded that presentence reports be completed in all courts in cases in which the death penalty is possible.[68] State laws vary. A number of states mandate presentence reports for felony cases.[69] Some require them if the defendant faces incarceration for a certain amount of time. In Delaware, for example, the time is six months; in New York, 90 days.[70] Others require them if the defendant is to be placed on probation.[71] Appellate courts have held that, absent language requiring presentence reports, there is no inherent right to have one considered prior to sentencing.[72]

Standards and practices for state presentence reports vary tremendously among and within individual states. Standard formats, if they exist, are general, often confined to one county or one court's jurisdiction. Typical presentence report standards, for example, are contained in New York's Criminal Procedure Law and the Division of Probation Rules.[73] They provide that reports include the circumstances concerning the crime, the defendant's criminal history, employment history, family situation, economic status, education and personal habits, and the defendant's physical and mental condition. The court is also authorized to order a physical or mental examination if the defendant has been convicted of a felony or serious misdemeanor. As is common, the standard provides for the inclusion of any other information that the court directs to be included. An abbreviated investigation and "short form" report is specifically authorized for misdemeanants.

In 1981, the New York probation service completed 108,408 presentence investigation reports—44,506 for felonies and 63,902 for misdemeanants. Thirty-seven thousand were completed in New York City, averaging 25 per month per probation officer.[74] Such a workload, exacerbated by the layoff of 140 probation officers between 1974 and 1981, severely restricted probation officers' ability to meet the two-week deadline in completing their reports. Complained one such officer to a reporter:

> We no longer are allowed to get input from the victims, the arresting officer or out-of-state records. Much of the report is based on what the defendant says—and that's often bull.[75]

Texas' state probation commission has also adopted a statewide format for its presentences. The format consists of a single page standard fact sheet, supplemented as the probation officer or court deems proper. As the commission explained in introducing its standard one-page format, "(a) fully read and considered (presentence report) is more effective than a lengthy one not considered and used."[76]

Perhaps one of the most detailed formats exists in Orange County, California. Just the instructions for completing the report consist of a dozen single-spaced pages. The format begins with a face sheet that covers the defendant's identification, prior record, employment history, marital history, family data, education background, military record and personal information. Following the face sheet, the probation officer is instructed to address the circumstances of the offense, covering damages, injuries, codefendants, defendant attitude and so on. Next follows a victim statement. If the defendant has been incarcerated pending trial, a jail adjustment category follows. Then comes a summary of the defendant's statement and a comparison of it with the arresting or investigating police officer's report. The defendant is asked to give references who must then be contacted and interviewed by the probation officer and whose interview will be included in the next section of the report. Prior record follows, including police contacts that did not result in conviction. Then comes social history, followed by an evaluation of mitigating and aggravating factors discovered. Next to each aggravating or mitigating factor, the probation officer is advised to insert the applicable Judicial Council rules defining legally recognized aggravating and mitigating factors. The rules also serve as guidelines for whether the probation officer determines the defendant suitable for probation in unusual cases. Finally the probation officer inserts his sentence recommendation, a "meaningful" supervision plan, a recommendation of whether the defendant should be incarcerated as a condition of his probation and if so where, and any unique probation conditions the court should impose. These may include, for example, "have no blank checks in possession" for a larcenist. Twenty-six other conditions of probation are also attached for the probation officer to choose from if proposing a probationary sentence. In the last section, the probation officer must determine whether the defendant can afford the $32 per month probation supervision fee.

As can be seen by the range in content required in just the few jurisdictions described above, there are few limits as to what information may be included. As the United States Supreme Court held in a 1969 case, "[t]here are no formal limitations on [presentence reports'] contents, and they may rest on hearsay and contain information bearing no relation whatever to the crime with which the defendant is charged."[77]

In preparing presentence reports, probation officers may consult a wide assortment of sources, including, most importantly, the defendant himself. Except in Oregon as the result of a unique decision,[78] attorneys do not have the right to accompany their clients at these interviews. They may, of course, meet with them to assist them in preparing for the interviews. Any statements the defendant makes to the probation officer may be used against him. The United

States Supreme Court held, in fact, that probation officers are not required to give probationers their *Miranda* rights before questioning them.[79] In this case, the probationer admitted, in response to his probation officer's question, that he had murdered someone. The admission was admitted as evidence against him at a subsequent trial.

Probation officers may generally also include material specifically excluded from the trial. In a leading case, *United States v. Schipani*,[80] the Second Circuit Court of Appeals held that the exclusion of such evidence from the judge's consideration at sentencing would "not add in any significant way to the deterrent effect of the [exclusionary] rule" on law enforcement officers. In *Schipani,* the judge increased the defendant's sentence based on the evidence obtained from illegal wiretaps because it revealed the defendant to be a "professional criminal." A number of appellate courts have followed suit, although some have not.[81]

The information in presentence reports must be accurate and reasonably complete. The New Jersey Superior Court has laid out perhaps one of the most specific criteria in reviewing the qualitative aspects of presentence reports. In this case, the presentence was declared to be inadequate as well as biased. The details of the offense consisted of a summary copied from the prosecutor's file: past criminal history, limited to an abbreviated summary of the record; education, restricted to the fact that the defendant had dropped out of school after eighth grade; family, which contained only names, ages and religion of family members and the defendant's statement that he had never been married; employment, which listed his job and military record; and finally, the report concluded under "leisure time activities" the fact that the defendant admitted to drinking too much. The court concluded that "[t]here is little in the report that would give a judge an accurate idea of defendant's personal background—his mentality, personality, habits and the like—or of the family background which would give the case a meaningful setting."[82] The court also found "strong indications in the record suggesting that if defendant had been fairly interviewed by a probation department representative in whom [he] had some confidence, and the entire background of the occurrence disclosed, the degree of his offense might well have been tempered and his punishment proportionately lightened."[83]

Most jurisdictions provide for limited disclosure of presentence reports, assuring that defense attorneys will challenge biased, incomplete, inaccurate or misleading information.[84] The Wyoming Supreme Court has specifically ruled that the defendant has no right to see the background material summarized in the formal presentence report.[85] Similarly, a California appellate court ruled that the defendant has no right to cross-examine the probation officer who prepared the presentence report.[86] It is incumbent upon both the defense and prosecuting attorney to examine the presentence report carefully to insure accuracy, completeness and competence. They must challenge any data found to be lacking and be prepared to provide supplemental material where necessary. The United States Supreme Court has held that states need not require that information in presentence reports surpass the standard of preponderance of the evidence.[87] If the presentence report provides more descriptive than prescriptive material, the task confronting both prosecution and defense is to come up with a realistic disposition based on the information revealed in the report. This task is particularly vital if either seeks the court to impose an alternative sentence.

Finally, defendants do not have the right to have presentence reports completed unless mandated by statute. The Massachusetts Supreme Judicial Court, for example, specifically ruled that such reports are not required as long as the defendant is given the opportunity to present evidence in mitigation of a sentence.[88]

§2.05   —Private Presentence Reports

Before leaving the presentence report, it is important to note a new phenomenon in the field, namely private presentence reports available for a fee. Given the high correlation between presentence recommendations by probation officers and court acceptance, in some instances estimated to be as high as 90 percent,[89] it was perhaps inevitable that probation's monopoly in the field would not last forever.

The impetus for private presentence reports has come from several directions. First, cutbacks in probation services have forced some courts to look for cheaper methods of obtaining presentences. Private entrepreneurs, often former probation officers, have taken up the challenge.[90] Because local departments find themselves ill-equipped to perform investigations of foreign nationals, a former probation officer founded an agency that specializes in "international sentencing reports."[91] These reports are particularly useful in drug importation cases in which defendants may not be American citizens. Finally, defense attorneys have demanded tailor-made reports for their clients that provide the background information necessary to convince the prosecutor or the court to grant their client an alternative sentence. The organization that pioneered this activity is called the National Center for Institutions and Alternatives and it calls its presentence reports Client Specific Plans. Founded by Jerome Miller, former Massachusetts Youth Services Commissioner, who deinstitutionalized that state's juvenile corrections in the early 1970s, the Center will only accept work where defendants are believed to be jail-bound. It is funded largely by the Edna McConnell Clark Foundation of New York.

The Client Specific Plan is designed to help judges and prosecutors justify alternative sentences by including in each plan specific controls on the defendant, paybacks and treatment services, as well the names of community members who endorse it. Each plan presented to the court specifies the individuals who will work with and monitor the offender, the specific programs that the offender will participate in, and the frequency and duration of the plan's conditions. In order to individualize the plans to each defendant, the staff analyzes the offense and the offender, identifies the offender's emotional, financial, behavioral, medical or other problems, as well as his skills and abilities. After completing these tasks, the staff examines the community and the court, including local conditions, sentencing practices, jail conditions and laws. While no formula is used to equate therapy, community service, restitution payments or other alternative sentencing components with days in jail, the plan is designed to realistically provide sanctions and controls consistent with the seriousness of the offense.

Unlike many presentence reports, the plans are mainly prescriptive rather than descriptive, geared to the specific defendant, his problems and what he is going to do about them, and, equally important, what he is going to do to make up for the crime. If the defendant is found, for example, to have a drug problem, a placement in a local drug treatment center is secured. The plan also spells out where the defendant is going to live, how he will support himself and how leisure time will be spent, how he will pay for the treatment and restitution if offered. The court is presented with various options. The plan may call for the defendant to live with his parents or in a particular county or in a halfway house to be monitored by the local probation officer or a community sponsor such as a local church official. Community service options are also arranged for the court's selection and so on. Examples of plans adopted by various courts include cases in which defendants convicted of arson, causing $4.5 million worth of damage, and manslaughter, killing ten people in a car accident, were not sentenced to one day in jail but were given alternative sentences developed by the Center.

Private presentences can be particularly suited to promoting alternative sentences due to the difference between them and traditional presentence reports completed by probation. The essential difference is that private presentence reports go beyond focusing on who the defendant is and what he has done. They also specifically address what the defendant should do and what should be done to the defendant to make up for the offense. The prescriptions include detailed plans for alternative sentence implementation and enforcement.

By and large, the Center reports that judges welcome their recommendations. During its initial period of operation between 1979 and 1981, the Center took on 350 cases. The courts accepted 70 percent of the Center's recommended plans.[92] Client Specific Planning programs are being franchised around the country by the Center. Similar programs are developing independently. The Center itself maintains offices in Washington D.C., New York, Texas and Florida.

By 1995, there were 220 defense-based alternative sentencing programs across the country in 27 different states, a dramatic increase from just 17 a decade earlier. According to the National Directory of Felony Sentencing Services, distributed by the Washington, D.C. Sentencing Project, in 1989, 44 of the projects were affiliated with public defender offices and 71 were privately based. North Carolina had 13 locally funded programs. New Mexico public defenders had nine staff members in six offices for this purpose. These agencies provided services for 16,000 felons that year.

Where private presentence agencies are unavailable, a conscientious defense attorney, working with his client, can assemble a client specific plan. If a regular presentence report has been completed by probation, the defense attorney may supplement its content to include the essential prescriptive component.

§2.06   Common Information Used in Sentencing

Law and presentence report practices vary. However, studies reveal that what judges are looking for and actually use in sentencing offenders is information they believe indicates offender risk of recidivism and dangerousness. As a result of recent legislation and pressures brought on the court, judges also seek information regarding the victim of crime. The above information is not necessarily obtained through formal presentence investigation reports.

§2.07   —Predicting Offender Risk and Danger

In addition to presentence reports, judges typically seek information regarding offender risk and dangerousness by scrutiny of the offender's prior record and psychiatric and other related expert evaluations. Courts are more apt to incarcerate offenders they believe to represent a high risk of recidivism or future violence. Many jurisdictions prohibit judges from imposing probationary sentences for offenders who commit certain crimes of violence or who possess a weapon during the crime. The revised 1984 federal criminal code, for example, calls for sentences "at or near maximum" for crimes of violence, or if the defendant's record contains two or more previous felonies involving violence. The model criminal codes, developed over the past several decades, all advise that violent offenders be punished more severely than nonviolent ones.[93] If the court is not to incarcerate such offenders, it must be persuaded that the alternative sentence contains suitable measures to mitigate offender risk and dangerousness.

Unfortunately, much of the information courts commonly rely upon to determine offender risk and dangerousness has been proven to have little if any statistical significance as a crime predictor. Leading the list are psychiatric and other related expert evaluations, despite the fact that criminal codes readily provide for them in sentencing. The United States Criminal Code provides, for example, that if the court cannot obtain the requisite material it needs from the probation presentence report, it may order another study of the defendant "conducted in the local community by qualified consultants" or if the court "desires more information than is otherwise available to it as a basis for determining the mental condition of the defendant, it may order that the defendant undergo a psychiatric or psychological examination and that the court be provided with a written report of the results of the examination."[94] Many states have similar provisions in their statutes.

Many jurisdictions also allow the court to commit defendants to in-patient diagnostic institutions to the same end. Again, the federal code provides for 60-day commitment if the court finds "compelling reason" to do so. The time may be doubled if necessary. Illinois allows for a 60-day commitment; New York—30 days; Massachusetts—up to 40 days. Available institutions vary. In California, the Department of Corrections operates several Reception Guidance Centers to evaluate both offenders and defendants awaiting sentence. In Massachusetts, judges may use private or state mental hospitals, including the state hospital for the criminally insane to evaluate particularly threatening defendants.

There is some case law suggesting that in certain circumstances where presentence reports are mandatory and resources available, mental examinations may be required before sentencing. The Circuit Court of Appeals for the District of Columbia, for example, overturned a sentence in which the trial judge refused to refer the defendant for a psychological evaluation although the presentence report labeled him a "psychopathic offender."[95] The court held that the presentence report should include whether the defendant suffers from physical, intellectual or emotional difficulties and how they affect his behavior, the likelihood of societal adjustment without special treatment, the effect of various sentences and the chances of rehabilitation. Lest the court's ruling be misinterpreted, in a later case, the same court ruled that no error attached by the trial court's failure to provide for an evaluation where the defendant had been previously examined and found competent to stand trial, witnesses had testified as to his mental health at the trial, and a presentence report had been provided to the court.[96]

Despite the widespread use of psychiatric and related evaluations aimed at predicting dangerousness used by judges in sentencing, the process is fraught with hazards. Few experts even agree on the definition of what constitutes a violent offender. Is a violent offender defined by the crime he commits, or by his character? According to noted criminologist Norval Morris, even if society set out to lock up all violent criminals and to let the nonviolent free, the results would be small. "The concept of dangerousness is so plastic and vague—its implementation so imprecise—that it would do little to reduce either the present excessive use of imprisonment or social injury from violent crime."[97]

Nonetheless, in 1983 in the case of *Barefoot v. Estelle*,[98] the United States Supreme Court upheld Texas law, which gives exclusive weight to psychiatric predictions of dangerousness in the jury's decision of whether certain murderers warrant the death penalty. In that case, two psychiatrists had testified before the jury that, based on the defendant's characteristics (they had not met the actual defendant), he met the test of being "a continuing threat to society." One labeled him a "criminal sociopath" and the other as having a "typical sociopathic personality disorder." On appeal, the American Psychiatric Association, participating as *amicus curiae,* informed the Court that "the unreliability of psychiatric predictions of long-term future dangerousness is by now an established fact within the profession."[99] The Association went on to state that two out of every three predictions of future dangerousness made by psychiatrists are simply wrong.

Based on this and other testimony, the dissenters on the Court concluded that such psychiatric predictions are too unreliable to be admissible as evidence. "In a capital case," they argued, "the specious testimony of a psychiatrist colored in the eyes of an impressionable jury by the inevitable untouchability of a medical specialist's word, equates with death itself."[100] However, the majority argued that the testimony of the psychiatrists goes to the weight of the evidence, not its admissibility. They went on to note that although many have questioned such predictions, one noted expert, Dr. John Monahan, who had originally been a doubter, concluded after an exhaustive study that "there may be circumstances in which prediction is both empirically possible and ethically appropriate."[101] The Court's dissenters also cited Monahan to support their arguments.

Monahan believes that only short-term prediction of violence is possible and that prediction must be based on actuarial, not solely clinical data.[102] Further, he argues that the offender's immediate environment may be as important in attempting to predict future violence as individual defendant characteristics. If, for example, the offender has a long history of brawling in taverns when drunk, future violence may be prevented if that offender is kept from drinking in bars or from drinking at all. Common environmental factors that must be considered in predicting future violence include the offender's family context: is the offender's mother Ma Kettle or Ma Barker? The peer group: does the offender run around with a gang or a glee club? Employment: is the offender likely to find employment? Victim access: will the offender be able to get at his potential victims? Weapons: does the offender have easy access to them? Drugs and alcohol: does the offender have easy access to them?

Numerous studies reveal that specific actuarial information has statistically valid predictive value. Nowhere, however, have researchers been able to establish a method of prediction that is more than 60 to 70 percent accurate for more than a small population of offenders. Not surprisingly, prior record information is among the best predictors of future criminal behavior.

As is the case with psychiatric and other related expert evaluations, consideration of prior record information in sentencing is expressly accommodated by case and statutory law. In 1959, the United States Supreme Court specifically ruled that sentencing judges could base a defendant's sentence, in part, on his past record of crimes.[103] As long as the prior record is accurate and the prior conviction was obtained when the defendant was represented by counsel, the court may consider it in sentencing.[104] In addition to convictions that meet constitutional standards, other record information is generally allowed, including arrests, indictments, acquittals and so forth as long as the sentencing judge makes it abundantly clear on the record that these items are being considered for what they are worth and not equated with convictions. Appellate courts have generally assumed that judges possess the discernment to interpret such information correctly.

All of the following information derived from prior records has been found to have a correlation with future criminal behavior: age at first offense—the younger a defendant's age at first offense, the greater is the risk of recidivism; the number of previous offenses—the larger the number of past offenses, the greater is the risk; the seriousness of the offenses—the more serious the past offenses, the greater the risk; past periods of incarceration and/or probation revocations—the more times an offender has been incarcerated or had his probation revoked, the greater the risk.

Prior record information may also reveal alcohol and other drug abuse. Substance abuse correlates with risk of recidivism. Prior convictions for drug offenses are usually indicative of drug addiction or dependency. Prior convictions for drunk driving are indicative of alcohol abuse. Notwithstanding how defense counsel may portray their clients to the court, numerous studies agree that even first offender drunk drivers are more often than not either alcoholics or problem drinkers.[105] Substance abuse, however, may not be immediately apparent from the defendant's prior record.

The current offense also correlates with risk. An offender who commits a property crime is more likely to reoffend than one who commits a crime against persons. Other aspects of the current crime, including the number of victims, the amount of damage or injury caused, whether an offender cooperated with law enforcement or testified against codefendants, have no correlation with risk.

In addition to prior and current record information, other actuarial data that reveal the defendant's stability in the community correlate with risk: the number of address changes—the more times an offender moves, the greater is the risk; the length of employment or school attendance—the shorter period an offender remained in school or on the job in the year immediately prior to the crime, the greater is the risk; the family structure—the less secure and stable the defendant's family structure, the greater is the risk.

Finally, some researchers have found that a defendant's attitude correlates with risk. If the offender rationalizes his behavior, the risk is greater.

As can be seen, the above information may be obtained without the need for a long, drawn-out presentence investigation. It can be obtained through an examination of the criminal record and a brief interview with the offender. The defendant's attitude may be revealed by his demeanor in court.

A number of probation and parole agencies in disparate jurisdictions across the country have developed recidivism risk scales in order to quantify risk assessments. To develop these scales, researchers made multiple regression analyses comparing common characteristics of criminals with recidivism rates.

The Massachusetts risk scale is utilized throughout that state's probation service to determine appropriate level of probation supervision and has been validated over a number of years with thousands of juvenile, misdemeanor and felony probationers. Reviewing the profile of its recidivists, Massachusetts probation officials concluded:

> The average probation failure (recidivist) was male, under 19 years of
> age, had committed a crime against property, had been employed for
> six months or less during the last year, had a substance abuse prob-
> lem, as well as a general attitude problem.[106]

The highest risk offenders, the 15 percent of Massachusetts probationers who scored 10 or below on the scale which ranges from four to 30, recidivate at a rate of 70 percent. The lowest risk offenders, the 30 percent who scored above 25 on the scale, recidivate at a rate of only 10 percent. The average probationer in the state recidivates at a rate of 30 percent. Interestingly, the Massachusetts study found that nearly 90 percent of those probationers who recidivate do so within six months of being placed on probation.

The United States Parole Commission has developed a similar risk scale that it uses to determine whether inmates are good parole risks. If an inmate is determined to represent a bad risk, the sentence length is not decreased. The federal parole scales, as well as those developed in Massachusetts, Wisconsin and Ohio follow. All are composed of slightly different individual risk factors. All also predict recidivism in general and not violence per se.

Massachusetts Probation Service Assessment of Offender Risk[107]
(Scoring: 2-10, highest risk; 11-15, high risk; 16-24, moderate risk;
25 and over, minimum risk.)

MASSACHUSETTS PROBATION SERVICE
ASSESSMENT OF OFFENDER RISK

NAME _____
           (First)   (Middle)   (Last)

D.O.B. ___/___/___ S.S. ___/___/___ Sex _____ CT # _____

Date Assessed ___/___/___ Assessed by _____ _____ _____
                                       (First)   (Middle)   (Last)

Supervising Probation Officer _____

Offense(s) #1 _____ #2 _____

#3 _____ Probation From ___/___/___ to ___/___/___

		SCORE AT:		
		INITIAL	FOUR MOS.	TEN MOS.	TERM
---	---	---	---	---	---
1.	PRIOR RECORD (ADULT OR JUVENILE) DURING PAST 5 YEARS 0=3 or more 1=two 2=one 4=none				
2.	NUMBER OF PRIOR PERIODS OF PROBATION SUPERVISION DURING PAST 5 YEARS 0=2 or more 1=one 4=none				
3.	AGE AT FIRST OFFENSE 0=16 or younger 1=17-19 2=20-23 3=24 or older				
4.	NUMBER OF RESIDENCE CHANGES DURING PAST 12 MONTHS 1=2 or more 2=one 3=none				
5.	EMPLOYED/SCHOOL ABSENCE DURING PAST 12 MONTHS EMPLOYED / SCHOOL ABSENCE 0=2 months or less / 0=26 or more days 1=3-4 months / 1=21-25 days 2=5-6 months / 2=16-20 days 3=7-8 months / 3=11-15 days 4=9 months / 4=10 days or less				
6.	FAMILY STRUCTURE 0=currently resides away from family, few or no family ties 1=resides in one-parent home 2=parent not supporting children 3=single, emancipated from parental home, strong family ties, or married no children 4=resides in two-parent home 5=parent supporting children				
7.	ALCOHOL OR DRUG USAGE PROBLEMS 0=frequent abuse, needs treatment 1=presently in treatment 2=occasional abuse, some disruption of functioning 3=prior problem 4=no apparent problem				
8.	ATTITUDE 1=rationalizes negative behavior; not motivated to change 2=dependent or unwilling to accept responsibility 3=motivated to change; receptive to assistance 4=motivated; well-adjusted; accepts responsibility for actions				
	TOTAL RISK SCORE				

(OCPR-1/82)

U.S. Parole Commission, Salient Factors[108]
(Scoring: 9-11, very good parole prognosis; 6-8, good prognosis;
4-5, fair prognosis; 0-3, poor prognosis.)

U.S. Department of Justice
United States Parole Commission

U.S. Probation Officer's Parole Guideline Worksheet

Name: _____ Docket No.: _____ Date: _____

[Note: The following is only an estimate of the parole guideline range as the U.S. Parole Commission will compute the actual parole guideline range at the time of the parole hearing.]

Offense Severity Rating is assessed as Category _____ because _____

_____

_____

_____

_____

SALIENT FACTORS

A. PRIOR CONVICTIONS/ADJUDICATIONS *(ADULT OR JUVENILE)* .... ☐
    None = 3; One = 2; Two or three = 1; Four or more = 0

B. PRIOR COMMITMENT(S) OF MORE THAN THIRTY DAYS *(ADULT OR JUVENILE)* .... ☐
    None = 2; One or two = 1; Three or more = 0

C. AGE AT CURRENT OFFENSE/PRIOR COMMITMENTS .... ☐
    Age at commencement of the current offense:
    26 years of age or more = 2***; 20-25 years of age = 1***;
    19 years of age or less = 0
    ***EXCEPTION: If five or more prior commitments of more than
        thirty days (adult or juvenile), place an "x" here _____
        and score this item = 0

D. RECENT COMMITMENT FREE PERIOD *(THREE YEARS)* .... ☐
    No prior commitment of more than thirty days (adult or juvenile) or
    released to the community from last such commitment at least three years
    prior to the commencement of the current offense = 1; Otherwise = 0

E. PROBATION/PAROLE/CONFINEMENT/ESCAPE STATUS VIOLATOR THIS TIME .... ☐
    Neither on probation, parole, confinement, or escape status at the time
    of the current offense; nor committed as a probation, parole, confinement,
    or escape status violator this time = 1; Otherwise = 2

F. HEROIN/OPIATE DEPENDENCE .... ☐
    No history of heroin/opiate dependence = 1; Otherwise = 0

TOTAL SCORE .... ☐

The applicable Guidelines are: (Adult) (Youth/NARA)

Estimated Guideline Range _____ months.

Particularly Aggravating/Mitigating Factors (Optional): _____

_____

_____

_____

_____

PAROLE FORM F-5
FEB 84

Wisconsin Assessment of Client Risk[109]
(Scoring: 0 to 8, low risk; 9-15, moderate risk; 16 and more, high risk.)

Department of Health and Social Services
Division of Corrections
DOC-502 (Rev. 9/80)

ADMISSION TO ADULT FIELD CASELOAD
ASSESSMENT OF CLIENT RISK

State of Wisconsin

Client Name Last	First	MI	Case Number
Probation Control Date or Institution Release Date (Month, Day, Year)	Agent Last Name		Area Number

Select the appropriate answer and enter the associated weight in the score column. Total all scores to arrive at the risk assessment score.

SCORE

Number of Address Changes in Last 12 Months: ....
(Prior to incarceration for parolees)
- 0 None
- 2 One
- 3 Two or more

_____

Percentage of Time Employed in Last 12 Months: ....
(Prior to incarceration for parolees)
- 0 60% or more
- 1 40% - 59%
- 2 Under 40%
- 0 Not applicable

_____

Alcohol Usage Problems: ....
(Prior to incarceration for parolees)
- 0 No interference with functioning
- 2 Occasional abuse; some disruption of functioning
- 4 Frequent abuse; serious disruption; needs treatment

_____

Other Drug Usage Problems: ....
(Prior to incarceration for parolees)
- 0 No interference with functioning
- 1 Occasional abuse; some disruption of functioning
- 2 Frequent abuse; serious disruption; needs treatment

_____

Attitude: ....
- 0 Motivated to change; receptive to assistance
- 3 Dependent or unwiling to accept responsibility
- 5 Rationalizes behavior; negative; not motivated to change

_____

Age at First Conviction: ....
(or Juvenile Adjudication)
- 0 24 or older
- 2 20 - 23
- 4 19 or younger

_____

Number of Prior Periods of
Probation/Parole Supervision: ....
(Adult or Juvenile)
- 0 None
- 4 One or more

_____

Number of Prior Probation/Parole Revocations: ....
(Adult or Juvenile)
- 0 None
- 4 One or more

_____

Number of Prior Felony Convictions: ....
(or Juvenile Adjudications)
- 0 None
- 2 One
- 4 Two or more

_____

Convictions or Juvenile Adjudications for: ....
(Select applicable and add for score. Do not
exceed a total of 5. Include current offense.)
- 2 Burglary, theft, auto theft, or robbery
- 3 Worthless checks or forgery

_____

Conviction or Juvenile Adjudications for
Assaultive Offense within Last Five Years: ....
(An offense which involves the use of a
weapon, physical force or the threat of force)
- 15 Yes
- 0 No

_____

TOTAL _____

Ohio's Risk-Screening Instrument[110]
(Scoring: the higher the score, the greater the risk.)

Number of prior felony convictions (or juvenile adjudications)	0 2 4	None One Two or more _____
Arrested within 5 years prior to arrest for current offense (excludes traffic)	0 4	No Yes _____
Age at arrest leading to first felony conviction (or juvenile adjudications)	0 2 4	24 and over 20-23 19 and under _____
Amount of time employed in last 12 months (prior to incarceration for parolees)	0 1 2 0	More than 7 months 5 to 7 months Less than 5 months Not applicable _____
Alcohol usage problems (prior to incarceration of parolees)	0 2 4	No interference with functioning Occasional abuse: some disruption of functioning Frequent abuse; serious disruption; needs treatment _____
Other drug usage problems (prior to incarceration of parolees)	0 2 4	No interference with functioning Occasional abuse; some disruption of functioning Frequent abuse; serious disruption; needs treatment _____
Number of prior adult incarcerations in a State or Federal institution	0 3 6	0 1-2 3 and above _____
Age at admission to institution or probation for current offense	0 3 6	30 and over 18-29 17 and under _____
Number of prior adult probation/ parole supervisions	0 4	None One or more _____
Number of prior probation/ parole revocations resulting in imprisonment (adult or juvenile)	0 4	None One or more _____
		Total _____

Michigan Department of Corrections Assaultive Risk Screening Sheet[III]

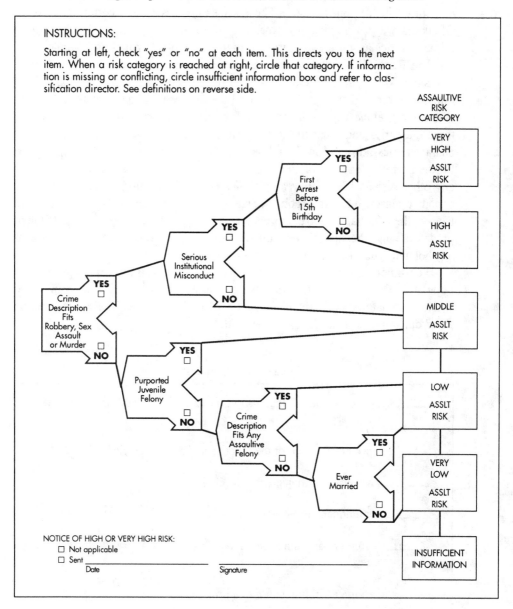

INSTRUCTIONS:

Starting at left, check "yes" or "no" at each item. This directs you to the next item. When a risk category is reached at right, circle that category. If information is missing or conflicting, circle insufficient information box and refer to classification director. See definitions on reverse side.

ASSAULTIVE RISK CATEGORY

VERY HIGH ASSLT RISK

HIGH ASSLT RISK

MIDDLE ASSLT RISK

LOW ASSLT RISK

VERY LOW ASSLT RISK

INSUFFICIENT INFORMATION

First Arrest Before 15th Birthday — YES / NO

Serious Institutional Misconduct — YES / NO

Crime Description Fits Robbery, Sex Assault or Murder — YES / NO

Purported Juvenile Felony — YES / NO

Crime Description Fits Any Assaultive Felony — YES / NO

Ever Married — YES / NO

NOTICE OF HIGH OR VERY HIGH RISK:
☐ Not applicable
☐ Sent _____
Date _____   Signature _____

A growing body of empirical evidence suggests that there exists a very small group of habitually violent offenders who can be identified. Similar to general recidivism risk scales, various dangerousness or violence scales have been developed. Most were developed in the context of confined inmate populations peculiar to specific prisons around the country. They are used primarily by paroling authorities to determine which inmates are safe to release early from prison. The Michigan Department of Corrections, for example, found that less than five percent of its released inmates accounted for 40 percent of all the repeat violent acts. Those rated low for future assault committed less than three percent of them upon release.[112] These scales are based on a common formula. Offenders with prior violent crimes are more likely to commit future violent crimes, particularly if they committed their first violent crimes as juveniles.

The Rand Corporation also interviewed prison populations in California, Texas and Michigan to develop its scale.[113] It found that a small proportion of the inmates committed the lion's share of all the crimes to which inmates admitted. While the average California inmate, for instance, admitted to two robberies, three burglaries and eight thefts per year, a specific subpopulation with similar characteristics admitted to 34 robberies, 68 burglaries and 22 thefts per year. Further, while members of this subpopulation might specialize in burglary, or any other serious felony, they also confessed to committing a number of other serious offenses, including robbery, assault and drug offenses. As a result, Rand labeled these inmates "violent predators." The difference between the "violent predators" and the rest of the inmates, Rand found, was primarily the use of alcohol and drugs among the "violent predators."

The other common risk characteristics were also found to apply to this population. While other inmates also committed sporadic violent crimes, the "violent predators" committed them at a much higher rate. The Michigan and Rand dangerousness prediction scales follow.

Violent Predators Scale[114]

_____ incarcerated more than half of the two-year period prior to the most recent arrest.

_____ a prior conviction for the crime that is being predicted.

_____ juvenile conviction prior to 16.

_____ commitment to a state or federal juvenile facility.

_____ heroin or barbiturate use in the two-year period prior to the current arrest.

_____ heroin or barbiturate use as a juvenile.

_____ employed less than half of the two-year period preceding the current arrest.

Prediction scales, whether for general risk or dangerousness, share some fundamental problems. First, none of these prediction models is perfect. All predict some offenders will fail who do not, and vice versa. A Massachusetts study, for example, reveals that 30 percent of offenders judged to represent maximum risk (scoring 10 or less) did not recidivate, and 10 percent of those judged to be of lowest risk (scoring 25 or more) did recidivate, just like their highest risk peers.[115] The Rand Corporation, in another study, completed an analysis of California felons released on probation, principally from Los Angeles County.[116] The researchers found that information on prior record, income at arrest, living arrangements, education, race, drug and alcohol abuse and type of crime committed improved the accuracy of prediction by only 15 percent over chance. The base rate for recidivism was 54 percent. With the above information, researchers could predict recidivism with 69 percent accuracy. Rand researchers concluded that "[u]ntil statistically based predictions can be made more accurate, basing sentencing decisions on them would raise obvious moral and legal questions."[117]

Another Rand study admitted that its prediction scale, based on prison interviews and self-reported crimes, was of little use. At the time of sentencing, authorities may only consider crimes for which offenders have been arrested. Rand found no correlation between actual records and self-reported records of inmates.[118] Other Rand researchers found, ironically, that many so-called low-rate offenders, as determined by their official criminal records, actually have more extensive criminal records than their so-called high-rate peers as determined by their official criminal records. It turns out that the latter are simply caught more often. They are not as good criminals as those who are caught less often. They commit proportionately fewer crimes but are arrested more often than their more proficient, officially labeled low-rate peers.[119]

There exist specific criminal subgroups that may not be identified by typical risk prediction scales. Perpetrators of domestic violence and certain sex offenders may not be predicted accurately by existing risk scales. White collar pedophiles with clean criminal records but lifelong cravings for children will typically be discounted for future criminality wrongly. Batterers who feel entitled to ownership of their wives or children, who seek death before divorce, for example, may also register low on risk scales. Yet they may be more likely than the average high-risk offender to be tomorrow's headline for murder or murder/suicide.

Second, a particular problem in sorting out high- and low-risk offenders is that many factors relating to risk correlate with race and socioeconomic class. Without due care, risk instruments, instead of sorting out risk, may simply be discriminating on the basis of wealth and ethnicity. It is for this reason that Congress admonished the United States Sentencing Commission, created by its 1984 federal criminal code revision, to be wary:

> The Commission shall assure that the guidelines and policy statements, in recommending a term of imprisonment or length of a term of imprisonment, reflect the general inappropriateness of considering the education, vocational skills, employment record, family ties and responsibilities, and community ties of the defendant.[120]

Third, many question the fairness of sentencing an offender based on what he might do, as opposed to what he did do. However, it is a widely accepted practice in this country to consider public safety in sentencing. As the United States Supreme Court held in a 1976 case:

> It is, of course, not easy to predict future behavior. The fact that such determination is difficult, however, does not mean that it cannot be made. Indeed, prediction of future criminal conduct is an essential element in many of the decisions rendered throughout our criminal justice system. . . . [A]ny sentencing authority must predict a convicted person's probable future conduct when it engages in the process of determining what punishment to impose.[121]

While specific prediction scales may be statistically valid, *i.e.* probabilistic, they have obvious difficulties in predicting individual outcomes. Further, the sentence imposed, particularly an alternative sentence requiring substantial behavior modification, may alter the defendant's behavior, mitigating future violence or recidivism. For this reason, even the federal sentencing guidelines, which focus primarily on the offense, not the offender, allow sentencing courts to assess the offender's potential for things like successful drug treatment. The Fifth Circuit ruled, for example, that sentencing courts in the federal system should be free to consider all relevant information concerning the offender's background, character and conduct. Thus a defendant's potential for rehabilitation is the sort of factor that a court may take into account in sentencing within the guidelines. The court distinguished this offender potential from other offender characteristics rejected as legitimate sentencing considerations, including the defendant being "gifted, talented," or having in him "something good."[122]

State appellate courts also have directed sentencing courts to pay attention to intervening factors that may mitigate risk, such as drug treatment. For example, a New York appellate court, agreeing with probation presentence recommendations, overturned an order of incarceration where the offender had completed, among other things, a drug treatment program pre-trial.[123]

Notwithstanding the validity of certain risk prediction scales or the morality of using them in sentencing, dispositional recommendations that fail to address issues of risk or dangerousness are destined to be ignored.

§2.08   —Assessing the Victim

As a result of the victim rights movement and recent case and statutory law, judges are required to consider information about the crime victims—often whether or not the jurisdiction requires presentence reports. A Presidential Victim Task Force, commissioned by President Reagan shortly into his first term, went so far as to recommend a constitutional amendment to the Sixth Amendment: "Likewise, the victim, in every criminal prosecution shall have the right to be present and to be heard at all critical stages of judicial proceedings."[124] Congress did enact comprehensive victim rights legislation in 1982.[125] This legislation, called the Victim and Witness Protection Act, requires federal courts to impose restitution in certain cases and requires a victim impact statement to be considered at disposition. The latter provision, amended in 1984, calls for the probation officer to include in the presentence report "verified information stated in a nonargumentative style containing an assessment of the financial, social, psychological, and medical impact upon, and cost to, any individual against whom the offense has been committed."[126]

While Congress was still debating this Act, the voters of California amended by ballot initiative their state's constitution, creating a Bill of Rights for Victims.[127] Called Proposition # 8, the initiative created, among other things, a victim right to restitution as well as a right for the victims to be notified of, attend and participate in sentencing and parole hearings.

Prompted by what commentators call the most successful civil rights movement in the country's history, almost half of the states have added some victim rights laws to their books in the last few years. The following states all joined California in passing comprehensive victim bills of rights: Delaware, Florida, Illinois, Maine, Massachusetts, Minnesota, Nebraska, Nevada, Rhode Island, South Carolina, Washington and Wisconsin.[128] As of 1984, some nineteen states had enacted laws mandating the involvement of victims in sentencing, usually through the device called "victim impact statements."[129] These statements are similar to the statement demanded by the federal code. The Maryland statute, for example, mandates victim impact statements for felonies or misdemeanors that resulted in serious physical injury or death to the victim. It instructs probation officers to "itemize any economic loss suffered by the victim as a result of the offense; identify any physical injury . . . along with its seriousness and permanence; describe any change in the victim's personal welfare or familial relationships as a result of the offense; and contain any other information related to the impact of the offense upon the victim that the court requires."[130] If a presentence report is not ordered, the victim impact statement must be completed by the prosecutor's office. A model victim impact statement form employed in Maryland follows.

Victim Impact Statement[131]

STATE VS _____

CASE # _____

SENTENCING DATE _____

_____

TO ASSIST THE COURT IN ITS EFFORT TO WEIGH ALL FACTORS PRIOR TO IMPOSING SENTENCE, WE REQUEST YOUR *VOLUNTARY* COOPERATION IN COMPLETING THIS FORM. THIS STATEMENT IS INTENDED TO BE SUBMITTED TO THE JUDGE IMPOSING SENTENCE HEREIN.

_____

NAME OF VICTIM: _____

ADDRESS: _____

DATE OF BIRTH: _____

1. Please describe the nature of the incident in which you were involved.

    _____

    _____

2. As a result of this incident, were you physically injured? _____
    If yes, please describe the extent of your injuries.

    _____

    _____

3. Did you require medical treatment for the injuries sustained? _____
    If yes, please describe the treatment received and the length of time treatment
    was or is required.

    _____

    _____

4. Amount of expenses incurred to date as a result of medical
    treatment received: $ _____
    Anticipated expenses: $ _____

5. Were you psychologically injured as a result of this incident? _____
    If yes, please describe the psychological impact which the incident has had
    on you.

    _____

    _____

6. Have you received any counseling or therapy as a result of
    this incident? _____
    If yes, please describe the length of time you have been or will be undergo-
    ing counseling or therapy, and the type of treatment you have received.

    _____

    _____

7. Amount of expenses incurred to date as a result of counseling or
    therapy received: $ _____

8. Has this incident affected your ability to earn a living? _____
    If yes, please describe your employment, and specify how and to what extent
    your ability to earn a living has been affected, days lost from work, etc.

    _____

    _____

9. Have you incurred any other expenses or losses as a result of
    this incident? _____
    If yes, please describe.

    _____

    _____

10. Did insurance cover any of the expenses you have incurred as a result of
    this incident? _____
    If yes, please specify the amount and nature of any reimbursement.

    _____

    _____

11. Has this incident in any way affected your lifestyle or your family's lifestyle? If yes, please explain.

_____

_____

12. Are there any other residual effects of this incident which are now being experienced by you or by members of your family?

_____

_____

13. Please describe what being the victim of crime has meant to you and to your family.

_____

_____

14. What are your feelings about the criminal justice system? Have your feelings changed as a result of this incident? Please explain.

_____

_____

15. Do you have any thoughts or suggestions on the sentence which the court should impose herein? Please explain, indicating whether you favor imprisonment.

_____

_____

THIS FORM IS SUBSCRIBED AND AFFIRMED BY THE VICTIM AS TRUE UNDER THE PENALTIES OF PERJURY. THE INFORMATION AND THOUGHTS YOU HAVE PROVIDED ARE VERY MUCH APPRECIATED.

DATE: _____

SIGNATURE _____

Where victim impact statements are not available, courts may obtain the same information directly from the victim by inviting him or her to testify at the time of sentencing.

Even where required by law, appellate courts have been very forgiving where courts allow cases to proceed without victim impact statements. Originally, for example, an Indiana appellate court held that the failure of the presentence report either to include a written statement by the victim or a certification that the probation officer attempted to contact the victim to obtain it required case remand for inclusion of the statement. Later, the decision was overruled.[132] In a related situation, a California probation officer failed to notify the victim of his right to attend the sentencing hearing. On appeal, the appellate court said that the law mandating the same was "directory," not mandatory in its effect. Further, the law provided no remedies for the failure of probation officers to carry it out, leaving the court no authority to afford any relief.[133]

Whether legally mandated or not, presentence reports that ignore victims may simply be inadequate, depriving the court of the ability to address legitimate victim concerns in the sentence, precluding many alternative sentencing components such as victim work service and restitution orders.

Despite the lack of enthusiasm and rigor displayed in enforcing victim rights, the most dramatic setback to the victim's rights movement occurred in 1987 when the U.S. Supreme Court struck down victim impact statements in capital cases, ruling that such victim (actually, relative of the victim) statements "create a constitutionally unacceptable risk that the jury may impose the death penalty in an arbitrary and capricious manner."[134] Further, two years later, the highest court expanded its ruling to include statements of the victim's character made by the prosecutor in his summation before the jury. That, too, was deemed to pose an unacceptable risk to the defendant facing life or death.[135]

In line with these decisions, some state courts moved to reign in victim impact statements, at least to insure that defendants had the opportunity to counter them in court. For example, the Nevada Supreme Court in 1990 held that certain procedural safeguards were required when the victim's oral impact statement refers to prior bad acts of the defendant. In such cases, when the victim goes beyond describing the impact of the crime or the losses suffered, the sentencing court must afford the defendant certain due process rights. These include prior notice of the testimony and an opportunity to cross-examine the victim. In addition, the court ruled that the victim must testify under oath.[136] In the Nevada case, the defendant had accidentally shot his wife. His mother-in-law, at sentencing, testified regarding prior acts of abuse committed by the defendant against the victim and his child. While declining to rule out the hearsay testimony of the mother-in-law, the court ruled that due process required the above procedural safeguards.

With such safeguards, courts have accepted victim statements and statements from friends of the victim. Convicted of gross vehicular manslaughter while drunk, a defendant complained in California that he was denied due process when the sentencing court reviewed letters from the victim's family and unrelated friends. The appellate court held that because the defendant had been given the opportunity to review the letters and rebut them, his due process was not violated. The appellate court pointed out that the sentencing court also considered "responsible" unsworn out-of-court letters on behalf of the defendant, too.[137]

In 1991, the United States Supreme Court, with a more complete conservative membership, overruled the previous decisions that limited victim impact statement use in capital cases. In *Payne v. Tennessee,* the defendant was convicted of murdering a woman and her daughter. At the trial, the defendant presented evidence regarding mitigating aspects of his background and character. The state countered with the mother of the victim who testified, among other things, that the surviving son cried for his mother and his sister. The prosecutor also commented about the effects of the crime on the son and other family members before the jury in closing argument. The jury sentenced the defendant to death.

A majority of the Supreme Court, in an opinion by Justice Rehnquist, held that the Eighth Amendment does not prohibit a jury from considering "victim impact" evidence either from the victim or the prosecutor at capital trials. The overturned cases incorrectly limited sentencing hearings in capital cases solely to "blameworthiness." In fact, the new majority held, assessment of harm caused by the criminal and the crime is relevant in determining both the elements of the crime and the appropriate punishment. Victim impact evidence is simply another way of informing the court or jury of the specific harm in question. Beside, it noted, the original decisions were held by a slim majority and were inconsistently applied by the lower courts.[138]

By 1991, eight states enacted constitutional amendments to include victim rights, including California, Rhode Island, Florida, Michigan, Texas, Washington, Arizona and New Jersey. In the last state, the amendment was passed four to one by the voters in a November 1, 1991 election. In addition, victim impact statements were permitted in 48 states. A handful of states mandate victim involvement in plea bargaining itself, including New York, Kentucky, Michigan, Missouri, South Carolina, South Dakota and West Virginia. Six others merely state that victims have the right to be consulted. Three others say the victims must be informed, but not consulted. Alabama actually gives the victim the right to sit next to the prosecutor at trial.[139]

As a result of such victims' rights laws, in New York, for example, the only reason the state was allowed to accept a plea mid-trial in the notorious "preppie" murder trial of Robert Chambers Jr. was because the victim's parents agreed to the five- to 15-year sentence for first degree manslaughter. On the other hand, pursuant to California's Victims' Bill of Rights, the state's offered plea agreement was rejected by the victim's father. He bluntly addressed the court:

> When you consider the lack of punishment already mentioned and the apparent lack of professionalism on the part of the prosecution, I hope you'll agree that justice has not been served in this case . . . The [defendant] is a murderer and should be charged accordingly.[140]

As a result, the plea was withdrawn.

In a related situation, on the other hand, a probation officer's failure to obtain a required victim impact statement for a presentence report or certify that the victim was offered the opportunity to make a statement did not make the sentence invalid according to the Indiana Supreme Court.[141] The victim impact statement is designed, it ruled, to give the victim an opportunity to have some input. It is not intended as an additional benefit to the defendant.[142]

Impact of Victim Rights Laws in Sentencing

An early study of the implementation of California's Victim Bill of Rights revealed that these rights have had little actual effect on the criminal justice system and sentencing in general in that state. Mostly, victims choose not to participate. Victims only came to court three percent of the time. A study poll indicates why. It found that 37 percent trust the District Attorney to do the right thing. Another 30 percent think their appearance will not make any difference anyway. Twenty-eight percent are afraid or too upset to come. Another five percent said it was too costly to come.

Victims preferred to give statements to the probation officer for inclusion in the presentence report rather than coming to court themselves. Nearly one-half of those who did submit statements reported having help from family members, advocates like MADD or the district attorney in completing them. Interestingly, as many prosecutors (two-thirds) like victim allocution in court as judges found it unnecessary.

The study concluded that victim appearances have little effect because they are so rare. Not understanding plea bargaining, even though 56 percent know of their right to speak in court, most victims do not understand the appropriate time to speak up. Victims are more interested in knowing about their cases than directing them. Some who did appear in court did so not to speak, but to see what was going on. The vast majority of victims believe they should have the right to speak up even though they do not choose to exercise the right very often. The form letter sent by probation to victims was deemed inadequate. Of those who spoke out at sentencing, 56 percent wanted long sentences, 15 percent sought emotional relief, 12 percent wanted restitution and 17 percent wanted light sentences.

The results convinced the researchers that merely grafting victim rights onto an existing system will simply be cosmetic and not transform the system.[143]

§2.09 The Sentencing Hearing

Before imposing sentence, many jurisdictions require that the court convene a dispositional hearing. The federal rules spell out a complete scenario for the hearing, illustrated at the beginning of this chapter. Many other jurisdictions follow suit.[144] Others specify at least partial hearing content, including the victim's statement of crime impact or opinion regarding sentence or testimony in aggravation or mitigation of sentence.[145] However, absent specific legislation, courts need not provide dispositional hearings.[146]

Common elements of sentencing hearings include: (1) defendant allocution; (2) victim allocution; (3) other dispositional witnesses; and (4) defense and prosecution dispositional arguments.

1. Defendant Allocution

Beginning with King Henry II of England, a common law right for the defendant to speak in mitigation of punishment has come to be recognized in many jurisdictions. Others provide for it by law. The United States Supreme Court has recognized the power of such statements. In ruling that a presentation by the defendant's counsel does not satisfy this right of allocution, the Court held that "[t]he most persuasive counsel may not be able to speak for a defendant as the defendant might, with halting eloquence, speak for himself."[147]

It is the responsibility of the defense attorney to prepare the defendant to exercise this right or to choose to waive it when appropriate.

2. *Victim Allocution*

Many jurisdictions have given the victim an equal right of allocution. These jurisdictions allow the victim to speak in court at sentencing or submit through a probation officer, the prosecutor or a victim advocate a written statement of either the crime's impact on the victim or the victim's opinion as to sentence or both. The Massachusetts law, for example, provides:

> Before disposition (in felony and motor vehicle homicide cases) . . . the district attorney shall give the victim actual notice of the time and place of sentencing and of the victim's right to make a statement to the court, orally or in writing at the victim's option, as to the impact of the crime and as to a recommended sentence. Before disposition, the court shall allow any victim who elects to make such an oral statement the opportunity to do so in the presence of the defendant. Before disposition, the district attorney shall file any such written statement with the court and shall make it available to the defendant. If the victim is unable to make an oral or written statement because of his mental, emotional or physical incapacity or his age, his attorney or a designated family member shall be provided the notice and the opportunity to make a statement prescribed in this paragraph.[148]

The statute goes on to provide that the court "shall allow the defendant to have the opportunity to rebut the victim's oral or written statement and the district attorney's written statement if the court decides to rely upon such statements or parts thereof in imposing sentence."[149]

The right of allocution is considered so crucial that the Sixth Circuit Court of Appeals admonished judges to personally and unambiguously invite defendants to speak on their own behalf.[150] The Fourth Circuit ruled that it is not enough for the defendant to have testified at trial, he must also be invited to speak at disposition.[151]

In addition to Massachusetts, a number of states require similar victim participation at sentencing, including: Arizona, California, Connecticut, Maine, New Hampshire, Rhode Island and West Virginia.[152] Other jurisdictions that do not provide for victim allocution provide that statements of impact or opinion must be provided to the court at sentencing.[153]

3. *Other Dispositional Witnesses*

In addition to the defendant and the victim, the court may allow a variety of witnesses to speak at the sentencing hearing. Generally these witnesses testify in mitigation or aggravation of sentence, but they may also testify on any other matter relating to the sentence and its imposition. The National Center for Institutions and Alternatives, for example, enlists witnesses who will endorse the sentencing alternatives' development as well as state their commitment to its implementation. If the defendant has a drug problem, the witness might be called to verify that diagnosis and recommend suitable treatment. Another may be called to inform the court that he administers such a treatment program and will admit the defendant and report to the court on his progress.

The probation officer who prepared the presentence report may also be called to provide additional information. However, appellate courts have ruled that the defense has no constitutional right to cross-examine the probation officer or other experts called to testify in regard to sentencing.[154] But if the content of the report is challenged as incorrect and is important in the court's consideration of the sentence, fundamental fairness may require the court to either ignore the report or permit the defense to confront and cross-examine the probation officer.[155]

4. *Defense and Prosecution Arguments in Sentencing*

When all of the other witnesses have been called and the presentence report, if ordered, is reviewed, the defense and prosecution may be allowed to make their final arguments in regard to sentencing. If the sentencing recommendation is the result of a plea bargain, the prosecution has an obligation to present and explain it on the record. The defense may want to add his support of the recommendation on its merits.

Where there is no agreement, defense still has an affirmative obligation to advocate for his client at disposition. In *Wood v. Georgia,*[156] the United States Supreme Court held that it is the defense's duty "to seek to convince the court to be lenient" and failure to do so may violate due process. Similarly, the American Bar Association has promulgated a number of standards positing various defense obligations at sentencing, holding that dispositional advocacy may, in many cases, be "the most important service" defense attorneys can offer their clients. The Bar advised defense attorneys to familiarize themselves with all sentencing alternatives as well as the normal patterns of sentences:

> In appropriate cases, the attorney should make special effort to investigate the desirability of a disposition which would particularly meet the needs of the defendant, such as probation accompanied by employment at community facilities or commitment to an institution for special treatment. If such a disposition is available and seems appropriate, the attorney, with the consent of the defendant, should make a recommendation at the sentencing proceeding that it be utilized.[157]

Federal District Court Judge Joseph L. Tauro has dispensed some particularly appropriate advice on the subject:

> Some lawyers think, mistakenly, that they are doing a favor for their bank robber client, with a three-page rap sheet, by asking for straight probation, without offering any rational basis for such a request other than shopworn cliches such as "one more chance" or " my bank robber's wife, mother and child will be heartbroken if he goes away." If that is all they have to say, then more than likely their bank robber's wife, mother and child are going to be heartbroken.[158]

The Judge advises, instead, that the defense attorney present real alternatives to the judge. If the defendant's imprisonment is inevitable, the defense can still mitigate the sentence by offering some alternatives.

> It is very refreshing and very effective, for a lawyer to begin his sentencing presentation by stating flatly to the judge that the defendant should be jailed. That type of overture causes the judge to listen with particular care. This is the lawyer's opportunity to argue convincingly, and with credibility, for a short sharp dose of jail, as opposed to a longer term.[159]

As Judge Tauro goes on to advise, this is the time for the defense to plead for an alternative sentence.

For his part, the prosecutor has a special obligation in each case to see that justice is done. According to the American Bar Association, he should recognize that the severity of the sentence is not necessarily an indication of the effectiveness or the efficacy of his office.

> [R]egular, specific sentencing recommendations, particularly if attended by heavy publicity and if the judge is elected, can put the court under unwarranted and unfair pressures. The related point is that systematic recommendations from the office of the prosecution might induce too much reliance by the court as a substitute for independent formulation at the sentence.[160]

There is no more difficult task than sentencing. The task is made all the more difficult by the lack of credible sentencing alternatives. American corrections are, to put it succinctly, in a shambles. On the one hand, a majority of states have acted to impose stiffer terms of incarceration for certain classes of offenders or offenses. On the other hand, a majority are also presently being sued, often successfully, to reduce jail overcrowding. As a result, many of the same jurisdictions that are putting more offenders into prisons are releasing others under court order. Meanwhile, local probation departments cling to an outmoded casework model, which the sheer number of sentenced offenders makes obsolete. In many jurisdictions, the cutback in probation resources reduces the ability of the departments to monitor, much less enforce non-institutional sanctions.

The situation, in the words of District Judge Tauro, demands "new and imaginative sentencing initiatives that will buttress the weakness of the existing system, and yet preserve its great strength—the individualized judgment based on a comprehensive assessment of the defendant, dimples as well as warts."[161] The challenge facing all the parties to criminal sentencing is to come up with those "new and imaginative sentencing initiatives" as well as develop probation departments' capacities to help carry them out. The first challenge can be met in the traditional sentencing process if addressed in plea bargaining, presentence reports and dispositional advocacy. The second challenge requires reform of traditional probation practices or the development of alternative methods of supervising offenders.

Notes

[1] STANDARDS RELATING TO SENTENCING ALTERNATIVES AND PROCEDURES, § 5.3(c) (Approved Draft, 1968).

[2] STANDARDS RELATING TO PROBATION § 1.3(a) (Approved Draft 1970) (endorses a probationary sentence unless imprisonment is necessary to protect the public, to provide correctional treatment, or to avoid diminishing the gravity of the offense); PRESIDENT'S COMMISSION ON LAW ENFORCEMENT AND ADMINISTRATION OF JUSTICE TASK FORCE, CORRECTIONS 28 (1967); NATIONAL ADVISORY COMMISSION ON CRIMINAL JUSTICE STANDARDS AND GOALS, CORRECTIONS, Standard 5.2 (1973); MODEL PENAL CODE § 7.01(1) (Proposed Official Draft, 1962) (endorses a probationary sentence unless imprisonment is necessary for public protection).

[3] Bureau of Justice Statistics (1983). *Prosecution of Felony Arrests.* Washington, DC: U.S. Department of Justice.

[4] Fried (1983-1984). *Responses.* 12 N.Y.U. REV. L. & SOC. CHANGE 199 (relying on an unpublished analysis of 1981 data by the New York City Criminal Justice Agency).

[5] Baquet, D., M. Gottlieb and E. Shipp (1991). *Slaying Casts a New Glare on Law's Uncertain Path.* NEW YORK TIMES, June 25.

[6] CAL. PENAL CODE § 1192.7 (West Supp. 1996), upheld in *Brosnahan v. Brown,* 32 Cal. 3d 236, 651 P.2d 274, 186 Cal. Rptr. 30 (1982).

[7] See, *e.g., United States v. Osif,* 789 F.2d 1404 (9th Cir. 1986).

[8] Cunniff, M. (1987). *Sentencing Outcomes in 28 Felony Courts in 1985.* Bureau of Justice Statistics. Washington DC: U.S. Department of Justice.

[9] *Judges Complying: First Statistical Analysis by U.S. Sentencing Commission Finds Guidelines Working Well.* CORRECTIONS DIGEST, 20:40 (1989).

[10] See, *e.g., United States v. Kemper,* 908 F.2d 33 (6th Cir. 1990).

[11] See, *e.g., State v. Crowder,* 155 Ariz. 477, 747 P.2d 1176 (1987); *cf. Roullette v. Quincy Division of the District Court Department,* 395 Mass. 1008, 480 N.E.2d 1033 (1985).

[12] *State v. Perkins,* 159 Ariz. 381, 767 P.2d 729 (Ariz. Ct. App. 1988).

[13] *Buck v. State,* 580 N.E.2d 730 (Ind. Ct. App. 1991); *cf. State v. Wilka,* 464 N.W.2d 630 (S.D. 1991) (need not tell defendant of collateral consequences of plea, to wit, condition of counseling, because latter is nonpunitive).

[14] *People v. Johnson,* 534 N.W.2d 255 (Mich. Ct. App. 1995).

[15] *Brady v. United States,* 397 U.S. 742, 90 S. Ct. 1463, 25 L. Ed. 2d 747 (1970).

[16] *Blackledge v. Allison,* 431 U.S. 63, 76, 97 S. Ct. 1621, 1630, 52 L. Ed. 2d 136, 148 (1977).

[17] FED. R CRIM. P. 11(e).

[18] McDonald, W. (1983). *Plea Bargaining: The Issues and the Practice.* summarized in BUREAU OF JUSTICE STATISTICS, REPORT TO THE NATION ON CRIME AND JUSTICE: THE DATA 65.

[19] Bureau of Justice Statistics (1984). SENTENCING PRACTICES IN 13 STATES. Washington, DC: U.S. Department of Justice.

[20] *North Carolina v. Alford,* 400 U.S. 25, 91 S. Ct. 160, 27 L. Ed. 2d 162 (1970).

[21] See Harris (1983-1984). *Strategies, Values and The Emerging Generation of Alternatives to Incarceration.* 12 N.Y.U. REV. L. & SOC. CHANGE, 148, n.21; C. Silberman (1983). CRIMINAL VIOLENCE, CRIMINAL JUSTICE, 291-93 (cites research showing all but 7-10 percent of sentences imposed can be explained by court norms revolving around the offense and the prior record).

[22] Udevitz (1985). *More Would Go To Jail If Prisons Weren't So Full Judges Say In Poll.* DENVER POST, March 16.

[23] FLA. STAT. ANN. RULES OF CRIM. PROC. 3.171(b)(1)(ii) (West Supp. 1986).

[24] NEV. REV. STAT. § 174.055 (1985).

[25] IND. CODE ANN. § 35-35-3-2 (Burns Supp. 1985).

[26] ME. REV. STAT. tit. 15 § 812 (Supp. 1985); MINN. STAT. ANN. § 611A.03 (West Supp. 1986).

[27] *State v. McDonnell,* 310 Or. 98, 794 P.2d 780 (1990), *app. aft. rev.,* 313 Or. 478, 837 P.2d 941 (1990).

[28] *Myers v. Frazier,* 319 S.E.2d 782, 790 (W. Va. 1984).

[29] *Id.* at 790, n.11.

[30] See, *e.g., State v. Jarvis,* 310 S.E.2d 467 (W. Va. 1983) (in which the defendant's incarceration was upheld after the prosecutor alleged that the defendant failed to cooperate with authorities as agreed upon in the plea bargain and the probation presentence was changed to recommend incarceration in endorsement of this position, although, in the instant case, the sentencing judge stated that he would have denied probation in any event); see also *Patton v. State,* 458 N.E.2d 657 (Ind. App. 1984) (in which the court upheld the defendant's incarceration after the defendant failed to make the promised restitution.)

[31] Kuttner, R. (1995). *State Should "Get Real" On Perverse Asset-Seizure Law.* BOSTON GLOBE, Dec. 11.

[32] Bass, A., P. Nealon and D. Armstrong (1994). *The War on Domestic Abuse.* BOSTON GLOBE, Sept. 25.

[33] Frankel, M. (1972). CRIMINAL SENTENCES 7-8.

[34] *People v. Wright,* 672 P.2d 518, 521 (Colo. 1983).

[35] STANDARDS RELATING TO SENTENCING ALTERNATIVES § 4.1 (Approved Draft, 1968).

[36] STANDARDS AND GOALS, CORRECTIONS, Standard 5.14. National Advisory Commission on Criminal Justice Standards and Goals (1973).

[37] *Id.* at 576.

[38] MASS. GEN. LAWS, ch. 198 (1878).

[39] *Williams v. New York,* 337 U.S. 241, 69 S. Ct. 1079, 93 L. Ed. 1337 (1949).

[40] Carter, R. (1978). PRESENTENCE REPORT HANDBOOK 4.

[41] *Id.* at 18-19.

[42] THE PRESENTENCE INVESTIGATION REPORT 1 (1978). Washington, DC: U.S. Department of Justice.

[43] *Id.* at 10-14.

[44] Banks, J., E. Carlson, J. Dahl, J. Debro, K. Kirkpatrick and L. Varnon (1978). IMPROVED PROBATION STRATEGIES. Washington, DC: U.S. Department of Justice.

[45] Petersilia, J., S. Turner, J. Kahan and J. Peterson (1985). GRANTING FELONS PROBATION. Santa Monica, CA: The Rand Corporation, R-3186-NIJ.

[46] FED. R. CRIM. P. 32(2)(A) (effective Oct. 1, 1987).

[47] *Id.* at 32(2)(E), (F).

[48] *Id.* at 32(2)(B).

[49] *United States v. Lee,* 818 F.2d 1052 (2d Cir. 1987), *cert denied,* 484 U.S. 956, 108 S. Ct. 356 (1987).

[50] *United States v. Belgard,* 894 F.2d 1092 (9th Cir. 1990), *cert. denied,* 489 U.S. 860, 111 S. Ct. 164, 112 L. Ed. 2d 129 (1990).

[51] *United States v. Turner,* 905 F.2d 300 (9th Cir. 1990).

[52] *United States v. Lewis,* 880 F.2d 243 (9th Cir. 1989).

[53] *United States v. Curran,* 926 F.2d 59 (1st Cir. 1991).

[54] See, *e.g., United States v. Jackson,* 886 F.2d 838 (7th Cir 1989); *Brown v. Butler,* 811 F.2d 938 (5th Cir. 1987); *Bauman v. United States,* 692 F.2d 938 (9th Cir. 1982).

[55] See, *e.g., United States v. Cortes,* 922 F.2d 123 (2d Cir. 1990); *United States v. Miller,* 910 F.2d 1321 (6th Cir. 1990), *cert. denied,* 498 U.S. 1094, 111 S. Ct. 980, 112 L. Ed. 2d 1065 (1990); *United States v. Rogers,* 899 F.2d 917 (10th Cir. 1990), *cert. denied,* 112 L. Ed. 2d 83, *vacated,* 921 F.2d 975 (1990).

[56] *United States v. Herrera-Figueroa,* 918 F.2d 1430 (9th Cir. 1990).

[57] *United States v. Smith,* 935 F.2d 47 (4th Cir. 1991).

[58] *United States v. Gordon,* 4 F.3d 1567 (10th Cir. 1993), *cert. denied,* 114 S. Ct. 1236, 127 L. Ed. 2d 79 (1993).

[59] *United States v. Washington,* 11 F.3d 1510 (10th Cir. 1993), *cert. denied,* 114 S. Ct. 1404, 128 L. Ed. 2d 76 (1993).

[60] *United States v. Hicks,* 948 F.2d 877 (4th Cir. 1991), *cert. denied,* 112 S. Ct. 1762, 118 L. Ed. 2d 424 (1991).

[61] *United States v. Ignacio Munio,* 909 F.2d 436 (11th Cir. 1990), *cert. denied,* 449 U.S. 938, 111 S. Ct. 1393, 113 L. Ed. 2d 449 (1990); *accord, United States v. Allen,* 886 F.2d 143 (8th Cir. 1989); *United States v. Sarasti,* 869 F.2d 805 (5th Cir. 1989).

[62] *United States v. Schlette,* 842 F.2d 1574 (9th Cir. 1988), *modified,* 854 F.2d 359 (9th Cir. 1988).

[63] *United States v. Schlette,* 699 F. Supp. 222 (N.D. Cal. 1988), *aff'd,* 842 F.2d 1574 (1980).

[64] *United States v. Villa,* 701 F. Supp. 760 (D. Nev. 1988).

[65] *United States v. Corbitt,* 879 F.2d 224 (7th Cir. 1989); *United States v. Charmer Industries, Inc.,* 711 F.2d 1164 (2d Cir. 1985).

[66] *United States v. Huckaby,* 43 F.3d 135(5th Cir. 1995).

[67] *Dorman v. Higgins,* 821 F.2d 133 (2d Cir. 1987).

[68] *Woodson v. North Carolina,* 428 U.S. 280, 96 S. Ct. 2978, 49 L. Ed. 2d 944 (1976) (in which the Court ruled that the sentencing court must consider the defendant individually).

[69] See, *e.g.,* P.A. 77-2097, as amended, ILL. ANN. STAT. ch. 38, § 1005-3-1 (Smith-Hurd 1982) (unless sentence is agreed).

[70] N.Y. CRIM. PROC. LAW § 390.20(2)(b)(c) (McKinney 1983).

[71] See, *e.g.,* CAL. PENAL CODE § 1203(b) (West Supp. 1986) (for felony probationary sentences); OHIO REV. CODE ANN. § 2951.03 (Anderson 1982) (probation for convicted felons); N.Y. CRIM. PROC. LAW § 390.20(2)(a) (McKinney 1983); TENN. CODE ANN. § 40-21-104 (1982).

[72] See, *e.g., United States v. Hazelrigg,* 430 F.2d 580 (8th Cir. 1970); *United States v. Williams,* 254 F.2d 253 (3d Cir. 1958); *Pulliam v. State,* 264 Ind. 381, 45 N.E.2d 229 (1976); *Commonwealth v. Rancourt,* 399 Mass. 269, 277-278, 503 N.E.2d 960, 966 (1987).

[73] N.Y. CRIM. PROC. LAW § 390.30 (McKinney 1983 & Supp. 1986); N.Y. ADMIN. CODE tit. 9, § 350.4 (1982).

[74] New York Division of Probation (1981). ANNUAL REPORT.

[75] Raab (1981). *New York Probation Aides Assert Office Fails to Watch Thousands.* NEW YORK TIMES, August 3.

[76] Texas Adult Probation Commission (undated). EXPLANATION OF THE PRESENTENCE REPORT FORMAT.

[77] *Gregg v. United States,* 394 U.S. 489, 492, 89 S. Ct. 1134, 1136, 22 L. Ed. 2d 442, 446 (1969), *reh'g denied,* 395 U.S. 917, 89 S. Ct. 1738, 23 L. Ed. 2d 232 (1969); *accord, People v. Forman,* 108 Ill. App. 2d 482, 247 N.E.2d 917 (1969); see also *Williams v. Oklahoma,* 358 U.S. 576, 79 S. Ct. 421, 3 L. Ed. 2d 516 (1959) (sentencing data should be completely unfettered.)

[78] *State ex rel. Russell v. Jones,* 293 Or. 312, 317, 647 P.2d 904, 906 (1982) (majority held that defendant is entitled to the assistance of counsel "to the same degree when the judge seeks sentencing information from him in open court and when the judge does so indirectly through the out-of-court agency of a probation officer." The court went on to add that a "conscientious defense attorney would not necessarily feel obliged to attend to protect his client's interests." Id. at 317-318, 647 P.2d at 907; *cf. State v. Cox,* 147 Vt. 421, 519 A.2d 1144 (Vt. 1986), *cert. granted,* 107 S. Ct. 1283 (1987) (jailed defendant who pled *nolo contendere* had residual Fifth Amendment right to refuse to answer probation officer who was completing a court-ordered presentence report in which information supplied led the judge to increase the severity of the sentence beyond plea agreement); *People v. Baker,* 158 Ill. App. 3d 756, 511 N.E.2d 219 (Ill. Ct. App. 1987) (judge cannot force defendant to complete an alcohol evaluation prior to disposition without affording him the right to counsel or right to refuse to answer questions that may violate his Fifth Amendment rights without being subject to contempt of court).

[79] *Minnesota v. Murphy,* 465 U.S. 420, 104 S. Ct. 1136, 79 L. Ed. 2d 409 (1984), *reh'g denied,* 466 U.S. 945, 104 S. Ct. 1932, 80 L. Ed. 2d 477 (1984).

[80] *United States v. Schipani,* 435 F.2d 26, 28 (2d Cir. 1970), *cert. denied,* 401 U.S. 983, 91 S. Ct. 1198, 28 L. Ed. 2d 334 (1971); see also *United States v. Graves,* 785 F.2d 870 (10th Cir. 1986); *United States v. Vandermark,* 522 F.2d 1019 (9th Cir. 1987); *United States v. Larios,* 640 F.2d 938 (9th Cir. 1981).

[81] See *State v. Jones,* 110 Ariz. 546, 521 P.2d 978 (1974) (en banc), *cert. denied,* 419 U.S. 1004, 95 S. Ct. 324, 42 L. Ed. 2d 280 (1974), overruled by 669 P.2d 584 (1983); *State v. Banks,* 157 N.J. Super. 442, 384 A.2d 1164 (1978). *Contra, Verdugo v. United States,* 402 F.2d 599 (9th Cir. 1968), *cert. denied,* 402 U.S. 961, 91 S. Ct. 1623, 29 L. Ed. 2d 124 (1971) (in which the court ruled that use of illegally seized evidence would provide a substantial incentive for unconstitutional searches and seizures); *People v. Belleci,* 24 Cal. 3d 879, 598 P.2d 473, 157 Cal. Rptr. 503 (1979) (in which the court also prohibited the use of excluded evidence in presentence reports based on state statute).

[82] *State v. Leckis,* 79 N.J. Super. 479, 487, 192 A.2d 161, 165 (1963).

[83] *Id.* at 486, 192 A.2d 165.

[84] See, *e.g.,* FED. R. CRIM. P. 32(c)(3)(A) ("The court shall upon request permit the defendant, or his counsel if he is so represented, to read the report of the presentence investigation exclusive of any recommendation as to sentence . . .) (effective Oct. 1, 1987, defense will also have access to victim impact information and the like. FED. R. CRIM. P. 32(e)(A), as amended by Acts of Oct. 12, 1984, P.L. 98-473, § 215(g), 99 Stat. 2017); N.Y. CRIM. PROC. LAW. § 390.50 (McKinney 1983 & Supp. 1986); CAL. PENAL CODE § 1203(b)(West Supp. 1986); P.A. 77-2097, as amended, ILL. ANN. STAT. ch. 38, § 1005-3-4 (Smith-Hurd 1982); TEXAS CODE CRIM. PROC. ANN. art. 42.12 § 6(4) (Vernon Supp. 1986). *Contra,* OHIO R. CRIM. P. 32.2(c)(1) (Except in cases of aggravated murder, the report of the presentence investigation shall be confidential and need not be furnished to the defendant or his counsel or the prosecuting attorney unless the court, in its discretion, so orders.)

[85] *Alexander v. State,* 823 P.2d 1198 (Wyo. 1992).

[86] *People v. Leftel,* 242 Cal. Rptr. 456, 196 Cal. App. 3d 1310 (1987).

[87] *McMillan v. Pennsylvania,* ___ U.S. ___, 106 S. Ct. 2411, 91 L. Ed. 2d 67 (1986) (preponderance standard satisfied due process clause of Fourteenth Amendment in context of state presentence reports); see also *State v. Walker,* Mich. No. 79649 (9/22/87) (adopts ABA Standard for Criminal Justice, 18-6.4 (c) preponderance required for presentence content).

[88] *Commonwealth v. Rancourt,* 399 Mass. 269, 503 N.E.2d 960 (1987).

[89] Kulis (1983). *Profit in the Private Presentence Report.* 7 PERSPECTIVES 5.

[90] For example, Criminological Diagnostic Consultants, founded in 1981 by two brothers, William and Robert Bosic, one a former prison counselor and the other a probation officer, is located in Riverside, California. It is described in Granelli (1983). *Presentence Reports Go Private.* NATIONAL LAW JOURNAL, May 2.

[91] National Legal Services was founded by Marcia G. Shein, a former United States Probation officer, and maintains offices in Georgia, Florida and Texas. See n. 84.

[92] Hoeffer (1982). *Make the Sentence Fit the Felon,* 21 JUDGES JOURNAL 48-62; *see also* Berman (1983). *Meeting the Goals of Sentencing: The Client Specific Plan.* 9 NEW ENG. J. CRIM. & CIV. CONFINEMENT 331-342.

[93] See, *e.g.,* MODEL SENTENCING AND CORRECTIONS ACT § 3-109 (1979).

[94] 18 U.S.C. § 3552(b), (c) (1984) (effective Nov. 1, 1987).

[95] *Leach v. United States,* 353 F.2d 451 (D.C. Cir. 1965), *cert. denied,* 383 U.S. 917, 86 S. Ct. 911, 15 L. Ed. 2d 672 (1966).

[96] *United States v. Carter,* 436 F.2d 200 (D.C. Cir. 1970).

[97] Morris, N. (1974). THE FUTURE OF IMPRISONMENT 62.

[98] *Barefoot v. Estelle,* 463 U.S. 880, 103 S. Ct. 3383, 77 L. Ed. 2d 1090 (1983) (Blackmun, J., dissenting), *reh'g denied,* 464 U.S. 874, 104 S. Ct. 209, 78 L. Ed. 2d 185 (1983).

[99] *Id.* at 920, 103 S. Ct. at 3408, 77 L. Ed. 2d at 1121.

[100] *Id.* at 916, 103 S. Ct. at 3406, 77 L. Ed. 2d at 1119.

[101] *Id.* at 899-901 n. 7, 103 S. Ct. at 3397-3398 n.7, 77 L. Ed. 2d at 1108-1109 n. 7 (maj. op.) (quoting from J. Monahan (1981). THE CLINICAL PREDICTION OF VIOLENT BEHAVIOR).

[102] Monahan, *supra* note 98, at 82.

[103] *Williams v. Oklahoma,* 358 U.S. 576, 79 S. Ct. 421, 3 L. Ed. 2d 516 (1959), *reh'g denied,* 359 U.S. 956, 79 S. Ct. 737, 3 L. Ed. 2d 763 (1959).

[104] See *State v. Tucker,* 404 U.S. 443, 92 S. Ct. 589, 30 L. Ed. 2d 592 (1972) (in which the court held that the defendant's prior record, which included an incarceration for 5½ years on a chain gang following a trial for which the defendant had no counsel, could not be used in sentencing except for historical fact that the defendant's rights had previously been violated.)

[105] National Highway Traffic Safety Administration (1985). ALCOHOL AND HIGHWAY SAFETY STUDY 1984: A REVIEW OF THE STATE OF THE KNOWLEDGE.

[106] Cochran, D., M. Brown and R. Kazarian (1981). EXECUTIVE SUMMARY OF RESEARCH FINDINGS FROM THE PILOT COURT RISK/NEED CLASSIFICATION SYSTEM, REPORT #4. Massachusetts Office of the Commissioner of Probation; see also Beck (1987). *Recidivism of Young Parolees.* BUREAU OF JUSTICE STATISTICS SPECIAL REPORT (May) (recidivism highest among male dropouts who committed property crimes, had more prior arrests and had begun criminal career before age 17).

[107] *Id.* at 92.

[108] U.S. Parole Commission, *Salient Factors* (1981). In A. Partridge, A. Chaset and W. Eldridge, THE SENTENCING OPTIONS OF FEDERAL DISTRICT JUDGES 19 (1983).

[109] Wisconsin Department of Health and Social Service (1980). *Admission to Adult Field Caseload, Assessment of Client Risk.* In S. Baird, S. Christopher, R. Heinz and B. Bemus, PROJECT REPORT # 14, A TWO YEAR FOLLOW UP REPORT, THE WISCONSIN CASE CLASSIFICATION/STAFF DEVELOPMENT PROJECT (1979)).

[110] *Ohio's Risk-Screening Instrument.* In V. Oleary and T. Clear (1994). DIRECTIONS FOR COMMUNITY CORRECTIONS IN THE 1990's 10. Washington, DC: National Institute of Corrections, U.S. Department of Justice.

[111] Michigan Department of Corrections (1977). ASSAULTIVE RISK SCREENING SHEET. (found in Monahan, supra note 101, at 102).

[112] J. Monahan, *supra* note 101, at 103.

[113] Chaiken, J. and M. Chaiken (1982). VARIETIES OF CRIMINAL BEHAVIOR. Santa Monica, CA: The Rand Corporation, R-2814-NIJ, August.

[114] Greenwood, P. and A. Abrahamse (1982). SELECTIVE INCAPACITATION. Santa Monica, CA: The Rand Corporation, R-2815-NIJ, August.

[115] Brown, M. and D. Cochran (1984). EXECUTIVE SUMMARY OF RESEARCH FINDINGS FROM THE MASSACHUSETTS RISK/NEED CLASSIFICATION SYSTEM, REPORT #5. Massachusetts Office of the Commissioner of Probation.

[116] Petersilia, J., S. Turner, J. Kahan and J. Peterson (1985). GRANTING FELONS PROBATION. Santa Monica, CA: The Rand Corporation, R-3186-NIJ.

[117] *Id.* at 92.

[118] Rolph, J. and J. Chaiken (1987). IDENTIFYING HIGH RATE SERIOUS CRIMINALS FROM OFFICIAL RECORDS. Washington DC: National Institute of Justice, April.

[119] Greenwood, P. and S. Turner (1987). SELECTIVE INCAPACITATION REVISITED. (Washington, DC: The Rand Corporation, National Institute of Justice).

[120] COMPREHENSIVE CRIME CONTROL ACT OF 1984, Title II, Pub L. No. 98-473 (to be codified at 28 U.S.C. § 994 (e)).

[121] *Jurek v. Texas,* 428 U.S. 262, 274-275, 96 S. Ct. 2950, 2957-2958, 49 L. Ed. 2d 929, 940 (1976), *reh'g denied,* 429 U.S. 875, 97 S. Ct. 198, 50 L. Ed. 2d 158 (1976).

[122] *United States v. Lara-Velasquez,* 919 F.2d 946 (5th Cir. 1991).

[123] *People v. Aylesworth,* 532 N.Y.S.2d 322, 143 A.D.2d 353 (N.Y. Sup. App. 1988).

[124] President's Task Force on Victims of Crime (1982). FINAL REPORT vi.

[125] VICTIM AND WITNESS PROTECTION ACT, Pub. L. No. 97-291, 96 Stat. 1248 (codified at 18 U.S.C. §§ 1512-1515, 3146(a), 3579, 3580 (1982) and amending FED. R. CRIM. P. 32(c)(2)).

[126] COMPREHENSIVE CRIME CONTROL ACT OF 1984, Pub. L. No. 98-473, 1984 U.S. CODE CONG. & AD. NEWS (98 Stat.) 2015 (amending FED. R. CRIM. P. 32).

[127] CAL. CONST. art. I, § 28(B).

[128] See, *e.g.,* P.A. 83-1432 §§ 1-9, ILL. ANN. STAT. ch. 38, §§ 1401-8 (Smith-Hurd Supp. 1986); N.Y. EXEC. LAW §§ 640-645 (McKinney Supp. 1986); R.I. GEN LAWS § 12-28-1 through 9 (Supp. 1985); WASH. REV. CODE ANN. 7.69.010-030 (Supp. 1986).

[129] Victim impact statements are mandated in Illinois, Indiana, Kansas, Maryland, Minnesota, Nebraska, Nevada, New Jersey, New Mexico (by state judicial policy), New York, Ohio, Oregon, Virginia, West Virginia and Wisconsin; Victim Statements of Opinion are mandated in California, Rhode Island, Maine and West Virginia; and victim allocution is mandated in Arizona, Connecticut, New Hampshire and West Virginia as of 1984 according to National Organization for Victim Assistance, VICTIM RIGHTS AND SERVICES: A LEGISLATIVE DIRECTORY (1984).

[130] MD. ANN. CODE art. 41, § 124 (c)(2)-(4) (Supp. 1985).

[131] National Organization for Victim Assistance (1984). VICTIM RIGHTS AND SERVICES: A LEGISLATIVE DIRECTORY 58-60.

[132] *Isom v. State,* 479 N.E.2d 61 (Ind. Ct. App. 1985), *overruled,* 554 N.E.2d 1129 (1990).

[133] *People v. Superior Court,* 154 Cal. App. 3d 319, 202 Cal. Rptr. 585 (1984).

[134] *Booth v. Maryland,* 482 U.S. 496, 107 S. Ct. 2529, 96 L. Ed. 2d 440 (1987), *reh'g denied,* 108 S. Ct. 311 (1987).

[135] *South Carolina v. Gathers,* 490 U.S. 805, 109 S. Ct. 2207, 104 L. Ed. 2d 876, *reh'g denied,* 110 S. Ct. 24 (1989).

[136] *Buschauer v. State,* 106 Nev. 890, 804 P.2d 1046 (Nev. 1990).

[137] *People v. Mockel,* 276 Cal. Rptr. 559, 226 A.3d 581 (Cal. Ct. App. 1990).

[138] *Payne v. Tennessee,* 501 U.S. 808, 111 S. Ct. 2597, 115 L. Ed. 2d 720 (1991), *reh'g denied,* 115 L. Ed. 2d 1110 (1991).

[139] *Network Newsnotes* 7:1, MADD (Spring 1992).

[140] *People v. Stringham,* 206 Cal. App. 3d 184, 253 Cal. Rptr. 484 (Cal. Ct. App. 1988).

[141] Ind. Code § 35-38-1-9 (requires presentence report to include victim's statement or probation officer's certificate that the victim was offered the opportunity to make a statement).

[142] *Schwass v. State,* 554 N.E.2d 1127 (Ind. 1990).

[143] *Victim Appearances at Sentencing Under California's Victim Bill of Rights.* Research in Brief (1987). Washington, DC: National Institute of Justice, August.

[144] See, *e.g.,* P.A. 77-2097, as amended, Ill. Rev. Stat. ch. 38, § 1005-4-1 (Supp. 1986) (includes presentence report, defendant allocution, evidence in aggravation/mitigation, sentencing alternatives, victim statement etc.)

[145] See, *e.g.,* Ariz. R. Crim. P. 26.7 (a hearing may be ordered subject to a motion by either defense or prosecution to present mitigating or aggravating circumstances); Cal. Penal Code § 1203(b) (West Supp. 1986) (a hearing is required to determine the defendant's application for probation).

[146] See, *e.g., State v. Foy,* 224 Kan. 558, 582 P.2d 281 (1978) (in which the court held that the sentencing court could move directly to imposition of sentence after a finding of guilt notwithstanding the defense request for a special report.)

[147] *Green v. United States,* 365 U.S. 301, 304, 81 S. Ct. 653, 655, 5 L. Ed. 2d 670, 673 (1961).

[148] Mass. Gen. Laws Ann. ch. 279 § 4B (West Supp. 1986).

[149] *Id.*

[150] *United States v. Thomas,* 875 F.2d 559 (6th Cir. 1989).

[151] *United States v. Miller,* 849 F.2d 896 (4th Cir. 1988).

[152] See, *e.g.,* 1981 Conn. Gen. Stat. 54091C (1985).

[153] See, *e.g.,* Kan. Stat. Ann. § 21-4604 (Supp. 1985) (provides that the court *may* order a presentence report for misdemeanors, but *must* for felonies, and a victim impact statement is required in all such reports). See also Md. Ann. Code § 5124C (Supp. 1985).

[154] See, *e.g., People v. Arbuckle,* 22 Cal. 3d 749, 587 P.2d 220, 150 Cal. Rptr. 778 (1978) (in which the courts held that the defense had no right to cross-examine the report writer or to introduce expert witnesses to attack the method by which the report was prepared); *accord, State v. Harmon,* 147 Conn. 125, 157 A.2d 594 (1960).

[155] See, *e.g., United States v. Weston,* 448 F.2d 626 (9th Cir. 1971) (court ignored presentence report and vacated for resentencing), *cert. denied,* 404 U.S. 1061, 92 S. Ct. 748, 30 L. Ed. 2d 749 (1972): *United States ex rel. Brown v. Rundle,* 417 F.2d 282 (3d Cir. 1969) (court ruled defense should have been allowed to cross-examine report writer).

[156] *Wood v. Georgia,* 45 U.S. 261, 272, 101 S. Ct. 1097, 1103, 67 L. Ed. 2d 220, 230 (1981).

[157] Standards Relating to Sentencing Alternatives and Procedures, § 5.3(e),(f)(v) (1968).

[158] Tauro (1983). *Sentencing, A View from the Bench.* 9 N.E.J. Crim. & Civil Confinement 323, 329.

[159] *Id.* at 328-329 n. 98.

[160] Standards Relating to Sentencing Alternatives and Procedures, § 5.3(3),(f)(v) (1968).

[161] Tauro at 324-325 note 158, *supra.*

Chapter 3

Probation and Alternative Sentencing

§3.01   Probation, the Original Alternative Sentence

Probation is the original alternative sentence. From the first day Boston shoe cobbler John Augustus entered the Boston Police Court and persuaded it to release into his custody a wretched looking drunkard, probation stood as an alternative to incarceration. In fact, the work of John Augustus, the nation's first unofficial probation officer, was bitterly opposed by police, court clerks and turnkeys who received payments only when defendants were incarcerated.[1]

In 1917, the Massachusetts Commissioner of Probation testified at a meeting of the American Bar Association regarding probation's efficacy as an alternative to jail:

> Meanwhile (as a result of probation) the number of commitments to institutions has declined proportionately. Probation became universal in (Massachusetts) courts in 1898, and in the period that has elapsed, while the population of the state has increased by nearly a million, no additions have been built to its penal institutions, either state or county, and practically half their cells are vacant today. The great causative factor in such a result is conceded to be the use of probation.[2]

Over the last several decades, the various sentencing commissions have all endorsed the use of probationary sentences, focusing on their use as an alternative to jail. The American Bar Association, for example, holds that probation "avoids the negative and frequently stultifying effects of confinement which often severely and unnecessarily complicate the reintegration of the offender into the community."[3] Similarly, the National Advisory Commission held that "[t]he prison, the reformatory, and the jail have achieved only a shocking record of failure. There is overwhelming evidence that these institutions create crime rather than prevent it. . . . The blueprint for corrections must read: more alternatives, more programs, more professionals to conduct these programs, and more public involvement in the processes of corrections."[4] The Supreme Court has also joined the chorus, declaring in a 1928 decision that probation provides a means to insulate from the contaminating influence of prison certain offenders who are well-suited to rehabilitation.[5] In a later case, the Court repeated a description of probation from the Fifth Circuit, declaring it to be an "ambulatory punishment."[6]

After being invented by John Augustus, probation's use became widespread both in this country and around the world. Before his death in 1859, Augustus personally bailed out 1,946 defendants whose cases were then dismissed if they abided by Augustus' terms. The Massachusetts legislature enacted the world's first probation statute in 1878. Maryland followed in 1894. The practice, however, spread more quickly than specific enabling legislation. As it spread, legal challenges were heard and state appellate courts handed down contradictory decisions.[7] In 1916, as a result of a case brought by the United States Attorney General, the Supreme Court struck down probation in federal courts.[8] Notwithstanding the decision, probation expanded, partially because the ruling encouraged legislatures to enact specific laws. By 1910, 19 states had enacted such statutes. The development of juvenile courts further spurred on probation's use. Congress enacted federal probation in 1925, though it was still opposed by the Attorney General, whose office declared that probation was "part of a wave of maudlin rot of misplaced sympathy for criminals that is going over the country."[9] By the 1940s all but seven states had probation laws. By 1956, Mississippi became the last of the contiguous states to adopt probation. Alaska and Hawaii subsequently followed suit.

Probation agencies are varied. There exist today an estimated 885 agencies that administer adult probation services in over 2,400 local offices spread across the country. The average state employs 305 probation officers who actually supervise probationers, in addition to those who perform administrative functions. The federal courts employ 1,574 more. Probation is administered in widely varied manners. In some states, it is totally administered locally by either executive or judicial agencies. Still other states have abolished public probation departments and contract for probationary supervision with the Salvation Army or other public and private agencies. In other states, probation departments are administered either locally by the courts or by a statewide executive agency. Probation budgets range from less than one million dollars in North Dakota to more than $115 million in New York. The average state expends approximately $17.6 million per year on probation.[10]

While probation administration is quite varied, its use across the country is enormous and growing. While the crisis of jail and prison overcrowding is well known, probation too is overcrowded and has matched prisons in exponential growth.

Until 1965, the number of persons in prison outnumbered those released on probation. Since then, there has been no contest. By 1984, there were 1.7 million Americans on probation, one out of every 35 adult men in the United States. This compares to only 464,000 incarcerated in state or federal institutions. Nationwide, 63 percent of all offenders were placed on probation, compared to 26 percent incarcerated and another 11 percent on parole. The rates of defendants placed on probation vary among the individual states. As of 1984, the mean was 450 per 100,000 and the median was 380 per 100,000.[11] That compared to a national incarceration rate of 188 per 100,000.[12] By the end of 1994, the number of Americans on probation rose to 2.8 million with an additional 671,000 on parole. The number in prison or jail was 1.5 million.[13]

Probation caseloads increased by 154 percent between 1980 and 1993.[14]

Nationally, probationers are evenly divided between misdemeanants and felons. The proportion varies widely, however, as does the definition of what constitutes either. North Carolina, for example, dependent upon convict labor to complete its interstate highway system, at one point made almost all crimes state felonies so that offenders were sentenced to state, rather than county, chain gangs. In Massachusetts, on the other hand, almost 98 percent of all crimes are prosecuted as misdemeanors. Unlike the vast majority of other states, the maximum sentence for a misdemeanor in Massachusetts is two and one-half years in jail, not a year or less as is usual in most other states.

As of 1990, Georgia topped the states in use of probation with 2,838 per 100,000 on probation followed by Texas with 2,538, Delaware with 2,430, Washington with 2,353, Maryland with 2,291 and Florida with 2,093. The national average was 1,443 per 100,000.[15] Reflecting federal sentencing guidelines and mandatory incarceration provisions for certain career and drug offenders effective in the mid-1980s, federal probation dropped to 58,222, one thousand less than the year before.

By 1995, prison population experienced the second largest yearly increase, 83,000 more inmates, expanding state and national prison populations to over one million, 948,704 in state prisons and 95,034 in federal prisons. An additional 500,000 inmates were serving time in local jails. The probation population, meanwhile, surged to 2.9 million with an additional 690,000 on parole, up two percent from the year before. This represented a rate of 1,540 per 100,000 or 1.9 percent of all adults in the country. Texas and California led the nation with the highest numbers of persons on probation and parole, slightly over one-half million in the former and 370,000 in the latter, with rates of 3,017 and 1,253 respectively. In Texas more than 3.8 percent of all adults were on probation or parole. North Dakota had the lowest rate of offenders on probation or parole, followed by West Virginia, Mississippi and Kentucky (450, 517, 552 and 553 per 100,000 respectively).

Alabama had the largest increase in its probation population, increasing by 14.5 percent. Twelve states and the federal probation system reported a decrease, led by South Dakota (down 6.2%), California (5.8%) and federal probation (6.8%). Twenty-one percent of the probationers were women, 58 percent were white and 32 percent were African American.[16]

As of 1995, according to the President of the American Correctional Association, nearly 88 percent of offenders in the community were on general supervision. Six percent were on intensive supervision, two percent were on electronic monitoring and five percent were on specialized caseloads.[17] The average probation/parole officer's caseload was 118 as of January 1994.[18] In Los Angeles, which has the largest probation department in the country, caseloads were much higher. Three-quarters of all probationers are under the supervision of a team of two probation officers who monitor 2,000 offenders each.[19]

By 1996, another 119,000 were added to the probation and parole roles, increasing the total by 3.2 percent, slightly less than the 3.4 percent average yearly increases since 1990. There were more than 3,090,000 on federal, state or local probation and more than 700,000 on parole. Meanwhile, jail and prison populations increased by six percent.

As a result, since 1980, the total number of Americans under correctional supervision has almost tripled to include 2.8 percent of all adults. Texas still maintained the largest number on probation and parole, followed by California. In Texas, 3.9 percent of all adults were on probation or parole.[20]

Statutes defining probation eligibility vary. Some narrowly prescribe eligibility. Others leave it completely open to the court. Some spell out eligibility offense by offense. Others define broad categories of eligibility based on the offense or offender characteristics. Nine states have enacted comprehensive sentencing guidelines, specifying legitimate sentence ranges for all crimes. The 1984 federal criminal code recodification legislation imposed a similar scheme.

Despite the profusion of probation agencies and the number of offenders placed on probation, probation has not stemmed the tide of prison overcrowding. Some question whether judges generally impose probationary sentences for serious offenders or merely reserve it for less serious offenders who were not jail-bound in any event. At least one correctional historian questions whether probation was ever intended to serve as an alternative to prison. Rather, he posits, it offers a paper solution to the need to clear cases through courts. For prosecutors, defense and judges, probation offers them a way of doing "something."[21]

What judges would have done with an offender if probationary sentences had not been available is difficult to research. What is apparent from studying probation statistics throughout the United States is that there is no overall inverse correlation between use of probation, on the one hand, and use of imprisonment on the other. If probation were being used exclusively as an alternative to incarceration, one might expect to find that the states that imposed more probationary sentences would have a lower than average incarceration rate and vice versa. Such is not the case, however. Generally, states that have a relatively high per capita imprisonment also have a relatively high per capita use of probation. Texas, for example, has one of the highest state imprisonment rates in the country (sixth highest) and the highest rate of probation impositions. Similarly, Southern states generally place persons on probation at a rate of 520 per 100,000, higher than the national average. They also generally incarcerate more than the rest of the nation. The Northeastern states generally have low rates of incarceration. They also have relatively low rates of probation, 400 per 100,000, less than the national average.[22]

What these figures indicate is that, with some exceptions, certain states are more aggressive in sentencing than others. Those that are aggressive are more likely to incarcerate some offenders and place others on probation. Those that are less aggressive incarcerate less and place fewer on probation. Generally speaking, there is no correlation between rate of incarceration and rate of crime in the community. Some states that have an exceptionally high incarceration rate also have a higher-than-average crime rate. Other states with low incarceration rates also have lower-than-average crime rates. But such is not uniformly the case.

The apparent reluctance of many judges to sentence serious offenders to probation has its roots in the very development of probation. Probation evolved in the common law as a means to escape the harshness of existing sentences. In the middle ages, first ecclesiastics and then anyone who could both read and write could claim "benefit of clergy" to escape punishment for a crime. The practice followed the Pilgrims to the New World. In fact, the British soldiers convicted for the murder of the American colonials at the Boston Massacre escaped punishment by claiming this convention and consequently were simply branded on their hands and released. Benefit of clergy was eliminated after independence. However, a new custom quickly arose replacing it, allowing judges to release convicted defendants on their promise of "good abearance."[23]

John Augustus and the probation officers later created by subsequent statute merely added casework to probation. Probation was not considered a sentence and even today only three states have enacted legislation declaring probation as a sentence, although the term "probationary sentence" is used ubiquitously. Further, from the beginning, caseloads were restricted to minor offenders. John Augustus, who was a crusading temperance worker, dealt almost exclusively with drunkards, bailing them from jail only after they agreed to take a pledge of sobriety. The only offenders he bailed who were charged with more serious crimes were children, many as young as six or seven. Notwithstanding such restricted caseloads, the impact on corrections was enormous at that time. As Augustus' meticulous records reveal, a substantial number of offenders incarcerated in his day were drunkards. From 1842 to 1851, he recorded that, of 8,494 persons incarcerated in Massachusetts, 4,168, almost half, were sentenced as "common drunkards."[24] As a result, the original use of probation, though a "non-sentence," could and did serve as an alternative to incarceration.

Since then, not only has drunkenness been largely decriminalized, but faith in rehabilitation as a goal (or possibility) in sentencing has seriously declined. Widely publicized research completed in the 1970s, purportedly proving that community-based corrections does not work, has cast doubt on probation's efficacy in dealing with offenders.[25] The 1979 Model Sentencing and Corrections Act, devised by the National Conference of Commissioners on Uniform State Laws, disavows rehabilitation as a sentencing goal.[26] In 1985, the Rand Corporation released a widely publicized study of felony probation in several California counties, principally Los Angeles.[27] It found that while serious offenders were routinely placed on probation, 51 percent were subsequently reconvicted of a crime. The report concluded that felony probation represented a substantial risk to the public safety. Rand did note that often the offenders placed on probation received almost no supervision due to these counties' expanding caseloads and budgetary cutbacks in probation services. Probation, with its historic commitment to rehabilitation, has come to be seen as irrelevant, if not dangerous. Reflecting this sentiment, the *Wall Street Journal* characterized probation in its one and only news report on the subject in 1983 with the headline: *Risk to Society*.[28] Public sentiment has also hardened, demanding increased punishment for offenders.

Despite this changing sentiment in corrections, most state statutes authorizing probation continue to adopt the common law formulation of probation as an alternative to the restraints of sentencing.[29] As a result, despite the admonitions of the American Bar Association and others that there be few restrictions on probation eligibility, more and more jurisdictions have enacted legislation proscribing its use. In the past decade, for example, 37 states enacted legislation providing for mandatory incarceration for various gun law violations. The 1984 federal criminal code recodification directed the new United States Sentencing Commission to see that prison sentences are generally increased for entire classes of offenders and offenses. It specifically encouraged probationary sentences only for nonviolent, first offenders of nonserious crimes.[30]

The declining faith in rehabilitation, coupled with the increasing demand for punishment, saw prison budgets increase while probation budgets declined in many jurisdictions. Cutbacks were the rule of the day in the early 1980s. In New York City, for example, authoritative sources charged that the city's 40,000 probationers went virtually unwatched, largely because the probation staff itself was cut by 35 percent between 1974 and 1981.[31] In 1989, probationer Steven Smith murdered Dr. Kathryn Hinnant in her New York hospital. Mr. Smith had not seen his probation officer for eight months, even though he had been arrested twice in that interval and been in two hospitals for suicide attempts. The incident focused attention on the fact that 800 city probation officers were supervising 55,000 probationers as well as completing presentence reports on them. Caseloads averaged over 250. Judge Burton Roberts, Administrative Judge of the Bronx Supreme and Criminal Courts, explained that probation "has been the stepchild of the criminal justice system." He continued:

> Nothing is wrong with probation. It is the execution of probation that is wrong. If the City does not fund the agency properly, then tragedies like this are going to happen.[32]

Similarly, Los Angeles' probation department, once the largest correctional agency in the world, suffered a 2,000-person cut during the same period. As a result, most of the newer, younger probation officers lost their jobs, leaving the department with 75 percent of its members over 40. The local probation officer union president publicly charged that in Los Angeles, "probation is no longer viable."[33]

One expert reported in 1988 that for every dollar spent on corrections in this country, probation received only three cents![34]

The cutbacks made many judges and others even less likely to utilize probation for more serious offenders. Reflecting this, the United States Supreme Court commented in a 1983 case that probation supervision was likely to be so minimal in practice that its successful completion constituted "little, if any, assurance that [the defendant] is a person who can be trusted. . . ."[35]

Cutbacks continued into the 1990s. After interviewing probation officers throughout California in the 1990s, one researcher concluded that probation in that state had entered an era of "extreme austerity." Flooded with new clients without the resources to deal with them, many California probationers were "banked," placed on a list of clients who would not be supervised in any meaningful way.[36]

Across the country, New York City probation was again hit with cutbacks. In 1993, the probation union agreed to a 19 percent cut in personnel through attrition, reducing the number of probation officers from 383 to 310 in order to save the city $3.3 million. As a result of the cutbacks, the department announced it would no longer see nonviolent offenders in person, relying instead on electronic kiosks. Positive identification mechanisms such as biometric fingerprint reading devices would insure that the electronic interview was conducted with the intended probationer. Special counseling for violent offenders would be conducted in groups rather than individually.[37] By 1995, the department reported that it had shifted its resources to providing high-risk, violent offenders with "cognitively based group intervention."[38]

Despite their declining fortunes, probation officials were slow to change or reform in the 1970s and 1980s. A government-sponsored study of probation, completed in the mid-1970s, found that "the mainstream of probation and parole is not grossly different from what it was a decade ago. Too often new and innovative efforts are essentially 'side shows'—intriguing, existing, but devoid of major impact upon the overall operation."[39] A survey completed by the American Probation and Parole Association a half-dozen years later found the same conservatism at work. The field, it revealed, continued to cling to a "clinical casework ideology," stressing a "treatment-oriented approach" that relies to a large degree on "psychoanalytical foundations and social work techniques and principles." In practice, this treatment approach has often been reduced to perfunctory office encounters of probationer and probation officer.

The survey, however, did find the beginnings of several new schools of probation, including one based on the sentencing theory of "just deserts."

> Yet another view . . . still in its embryonic stages of development, is termed the "justice" approach and stresses the need . . . to monitor court orders for compliance, serve as the mediator between the offender and the court, the offender and the community and the offender and the victim.[40]

Probation reform finally began to accelerate toward the end of the 1980s and into the early 1990s. Most importantly, punishment is unashamedly finding its way into the probationary sentence. The "Justice Model" of probation calls for probation to be considered a sentence, in and of itself, that provides the courts with an intermediate punishment between release and incarceration.[41] To add to its punitive content, the Justice Model abandons rehabilitation as its central content and replaces it with such sanctions as restitution and community work service to be imposed in accordance with the crime's seriousness. Indicative of this trend toward punishment, in a dramatic break with the past, more and more jurisdictions since the 1970s have authorized the incarceration of probationers as a condition of probation. This has occurred despite the vehement arguments of probation purists that this introduction of punishment into probation has negated its legitimate purpose. In California, the majority of misdemeanant and felony probationers are now sentenced to jail as a condition of their probation. But old ideologies do not die easily. While upholding the incarceration of probationers up to one year as a condition of probation, the Florida Supreme Court came up with the following tortured reasoning to explain that their ruling did not make the probationary sentence punitive:

> A sentence and probation are discrete concepts which serve wholly
> different functions. Imposed as a sentence, imprisonment serves as a
> penalty, as a payment of defendant's "debt to society." Imposed as an
> incident of probation, imprisonment serves as a rehabilitative device
> to give the defendant a taste of prison.[42]

Other appellate courts have been more forthright, frankly admitting that punishment may be a proper rationale for a probation requirement. As the Nebraska Supreme Court declared in commenting on incarceration as a condition of probation as opposed to a sentence, "[J]ail time is jail time."[43] In another case challenging incarceration as a condition of probation, an Illinois appellate court held that the seriousness of the offense made the condition of incarceration appropriate. In regard to another challenged condition of probation, a New Mexico appellate court similarly held that probation "[i]s not meant to be painless. It has an inherent sting and the restrictions on the probationer's freedom are realistically punitive."[44] Reflecting the increasingly punitive content of probation, cases are even beginning to be reviewed where probationers are demanding incarceration in lieu of probation because the former is less onerous.[45]

The Rand Corporation, extremely critical of probation practices in its 1985 study, endorses probation as an "alternative intermediate form of punishment."

> We believe the criminal justice system needs an alternative, interme-
> diate form of punishment for those offenders who are too antisocial
> for the relative freedom that probation now offers, but not so serious-
> ly criminal as to require imprisonment. A sanction is needed that
> would impose intensive surveillance, coupled with substantial com-
> munity service and restitution. It should be structured to satisfy pub-
> lic demands that the punishment fit the crime, to show criminals that
> crime really does not pay, and to control potential recidivists.[46]

The Rand formula adds risk control to the "just deserts" model of probation, increasing the penalty based not only on the severity of the crime, but on the risk posed by the defendant for future crime. Both models depend upon common alternative sentencing components to add to the punitive content of the probationary sentence.

By embracing punishment, probation, the original alternative sentence, could finally reclaim its original correctional identity as an alternative to incarceration even for serious offenders. As a result, what used to be called "alternative sentencing," relabeled "intermediate sanctions" in the 1980s, is really nothing more than particular probation conditions, often punitive in content, attached to a probationary or a split sentence.

However, as discussed in the preceding chapter, probation no longer has a monopoly when it comes to administering these newer, intermediate sanctions. In an increasing number of jurisdictions, agencies other than probation administer these new sanctions. These agencies may be privatized correctional agencies such as outfits that provide electronic home monitoring, or other agencies within the criminal justice system such as county sheriffs. Sometimes, the sanction programs are specifically written into the criminal code. Some probation departments have aggressively claimed intermediate sanctions for themselves. If Connecticut's Alternative to Incarceration Program represents a statewide non-probation agency administering these intermediate sanctions, Georgia's probation department exemplifies a probation department's dramatic transformation into an intermediate sanctioning agency.

Georgia probation is an example of how a new, "tougher" probation can provide both a better safe alternative to jail as well as deal more effectively with the level of risk posed by increasingly violent probationers. It also allows probationary sentences to be utilized to provide a range of intermediate sanctions heretofore unavailable to judges.

Georgia probation has been the bellwether in this movement to make probation a tougher alternative. As an enthusiastic *New York Times* editorial described in 1991:

> In Georgia, probation doesn't necessarily mean a free pass. The state's system of graduated sanctions for convicts in the community has drawn national attention. About one fifth of the $500 million Georgia spends annually on corrections goes to keep people on probation, rather than in jail or prison. That's far more than most other states spend on probation, but officials say the investment pays off handsomely. Keeping offenders under supervision in the community, working and participating in substance abuse treatment, education and community service projects, has saved Georgia hundreds of millions on prison construction.[47]

Georgia probation's transformation began during the administration of then-Governor Jimmy Carter. At that time, in the mid-1970s, the state housed 4,000 inmates in one central overcrowded prison. A federal suit forced the state to decarcerate. A blue ribbon committee was formed to address this correctional crisis. It became apparent to the commission that relying on traditional probation and prisons alone was doomed to failure. At the time, Georgia led the nation in incarceration, with more than half of its inmates sentenced for nonviolent crimes. In some rural counties only 15 percent of all sentenced offenders were released on probation, while other counties probated 50 percent of all offenders.

The panel quickly realized that the key to reform was creating and marketing a tougher probation system. Some of the toughest sentencing judges in the state were interviewed and questioned about what alternative sentences they could support. They talked about curfews, drug-free caseloads, more than once-a-week reporting, mandatory employment and restitution to crime victims coupled with regular record checks.

In 1982, the probation department created its intensive probation program which it described in a department brochure as "turning up the heat on probation." The department created a new category of probation officers, named "surveillance officers" to emphasize the monitoring/enforcement role of probation as distinguished from a counseling/supportive role. In 1989, Georgia probation established shock detention centers within established prisons to hold offenders for the first 90 days of their probationary period. The probationer detainees were separated from the other inmates by an interior prison fence. The officer in charge was a former military man and he introduced military style marching and discipline in the centers.

The detention centers led to the establishment of freestanding boot camps. The boot camps became popular among judges and soon expanded to both probationers and regularly sentenced inmates. Recently the department has put treatment programs within the camps and established aftercare components for graduates. Campers still are required to arise at 5:00 A.M. and complete hard physical labor.

The department also began operating four diversion centers (formerly called restitution centers), including one for female offenders.

To provide a sanction for recalcitrant probationers other than prison, the department established a dozen probation detention centers exclusively for probationers in 1993. Probation violators or probationers who commit drunk driving infractions are sentenced to the centers from 60 to 120 days. They perform community work service, wear uniforms and participate in a variety of treatment programs including working on development of life skills and basic education. State law was also changed mandating that probation violators could not be sent to prison but must be sent to these centers.

As a result of "toughened" probation, a snapshot of corrections in the state looked much different in 1995 than it did in Governor Jimmy Carter's time, 20 years earlier. On a typical day in 1995, 131,000 would be on probation and 32,000 in prison. Of those on probation, 3,415 would be on intensive probation supervision, 1,000 would be in probation-run diversion centers, 2,330 would be in detention centers and 475 in boot camps. In short, 6,985 offenders would be in toughened probation programs each day. Over a full year, 19,437 probationers would go through these programs. As a result, Georgia's incarceration rate dropped from first in the nation to twelfth.[48] The hierarchy of tougher probation sanctions allows the state to select people for these programs at less cost and reduced threat to community safety. As the *Times* editorial concluded, "That's a bargain no state ought to overlook."

While the Georgia Probation Department has developed specific programs, by specifically fashioning individual probationary conditions, individual judges anywhere in the country are similarly constructing toughened probationary sanctions, one defendant at a time. As a result of this trend, for the first time, appellate courts are hearing more and more appeals of defendants who are demanding prison over probation, finding the latter more restrictive than the former. Appellate courts have split on the requests. Some rule that probation is not a quasi-contract that the defendant is free to accept or reject.[49] On the other hand, Minnesota's Supreme Court has ruled that if probationary terms are more onerous, the defendant may opt for jail.[50]

§3.02   Probationary Conditions

Once an offender is found guilty and released on probation, the sentence is either suspended or its execution stayed, pending the defendant's compliance with specific probationary conditions. Without these conditions, probation is essentially devoid of content. Conditions can make probation a significant sanction, serving a variety of correctional ends. These conditions are established either by the jurisdiction's authorizing probation statutes or by the court. They are usually imposed at the time of sentencing, although they may be changed during the probationary period. Only Alaska restricts the court's choice in enumerating conditions other than those mandated by statute.[51]

§3.03   —Statutory Conditions

Most jurisdictions share the same basic statutory conditions. First, probationers must obey all laws. Second, they must report periodically to their probation officer. Third, they must obey all court orders, including payment of court-ordered fines, costs, fees, restitution, support and other financial assessments. Fourth, they must remain within the jurisdiction of the court. Fifth, they must participate in and often pay for prescribed treatment.

In addition, more and more statutes specify that probationers may be ordered to perform community work service. More than a dozen states allow probationers to be sentenced to jail as a condition of probation, some up to two years. Some jurisdictions require that probationers submit to various kinds of searches to enforce probationary conditions and submit to random urine tests to enforce abstinence from drugs or alcohol. Others require probationers to refrain from possessing firearms, to avoid certain associations or types of employment. Some have broad conditions such as "avoid injurious and vicious habits" or "persons or places of disreputable or harmful character."

Many individual states have more unique statutory conditions. North Carolina, for example, provides that a probationer must "[a]t a time to be designated by his probation officer, visit with his probation officer at a facility maintained by the Division of Prisons."[52] California statute authorizes the condition that a probationer post a bond "for the faithful observance and performance of any or all of the conditions of probation."[53] In other examples, Nebraska bars probationers from serving as undercover agents or employees of any law enforcement agency of the state or political subdivision. To enforce this law, it bars any evidence derived in violation of this prohibition in any proceedings whatsoever.[54] Arizona's Supreme Court requires all adult and juvenile probationers to be tested for literacy. If found to be illiterate, the sentence can include mandated literacy training.[55] Louisiana mandates similar participation in an adult education or reading program until the probationer obtains a sixth grade reading level.[56]

Some statutes mandate specific conditions for specific crimes. A California statute requires, for example, AIDS testing and education for individuals convicted of soliciting an act of prostitution.[57] Similarly, a Louisiana law orders all sex offenders placed on probation to submit to a blood and saliva test.[58] An Illinois law mandates that perpetrators of domestic violence must pay restitution to any shelter their victims were forced to flee to.[59]

Until 1984, federal probation law enumerated only five conditions. The federal criminal code recodification changed that, listing 20 conditions. Only one of these, to obey federal, state and local laws, is required of all federal probationers.[60] Felons, however, must also abide by at least one of the following three conditions:

(1) Pay a fine imposed . . . (the law sets out prescribed ranges of fines based on offense seriousness from $250,000 maximum for a felony or misdemeanor that results in loss of life to $25,000 maximum for a misdemeanor and to $1,000 for an infraction, with higher limits if defendant is an organization).

(2) Make restitution to a victim of the offense.

(3) Work in community service as directed by the court.[61]

In addition, federal courts may impose the following 17 other conditions against a probationer:

Support his dependents and meet other family responsibilities.

Give the victim of the offense the notice ordered. (Defendants guilty of fraud or other intentionally deceptive practices must make offense conviction known through the media or other means, if necessary, at a cost not to exceed $20,000.)

Work conscientiously at suitable employment or pursue conscientiously a course of study or vocational training that will equip him for suitable employment.

Refrain, in the case of an individual, from engaging in a specified occupation, business, or profession bearing a reasonably direct relationship to the conduct constituting the offense, or engage in such a specified occupation, business, or profession only to a stated degree or under stated circumstances.

Refrain from frequenting specified kinds of places or from associating unnecessarily with specified persons.

Refrain from excessive use of alcohol, or any use of a narcotic drug or other controlled substance . . . without a prescription by a licensed medical practitioner.

Refrain from possessing a firearm, destructive device, or other dangerous weapon.

Undergo available medical, psychiatric, or psychological treatment, including treatment for drug or alcohol dependency, as specified by the court, and remain in a specified institution if required for that purpose.

Remain in the custody of the Bureau of Prisons during nights, weekends, or other intervals of time, totaling no more than the lesser of one year or the term of imprisonment authorized for the offense. . . during the first year of the term of probation.

Reside at, or participate in the program of, a community corrections facility for all or part of the term of probation.

Reside in a specified place or area, or refrain from residing in a specified place or area.

Remain within the jurisdiction of the court, unless granted permission to leave by the court or a probation officer.

Report to a probation officer as directed by the court or the probation officer.

Permit a probation officer to visit him at his home or elsewhere as specified by the court.

Answer inquiries by a probation officer and notify the probation officer promptly of any change of address or employment.

Notify the probation officer promptly if arrested or questioned by a law enforcement officer.

Finally, the federal statute specifies that the offender must "satisfy such other conditions as the court may impose."[62]

Almost all state probation statutes have a similar provision, allowing the court to add other conditions not spelled out in the statute. Some of the statutes add a qualifying phrase such as "as the court shall deem proper and reasonable." California's probation statute allows additional conditions "as it (the court) may determine are fitting and proper to the end that justice may be done, that amends may be made to society for the breach of the law, for any injury done to any person resulting from that breach, and generally and specifically for the reformation and rehabilitation of the probationer. . . ."[63] Even the absence of such language has not been held to preclude the imposition of additional nonstatutorily defined conditions.

§3.04   Discretionary Conditions

In determining conditions of probation, courts have been afforded the widest latitude by appellate courts. Appellate courts have been wary of second guessing sentencing judges. Typical of this, for example, is the language used by an Arizona appellate decision upholding a particular condition of probation:

> The fundamental principle established by Arizona decisions is that unless the terms of probation are such that they violate fundamental rights or bear no reasonable relationship whatever to the purpose of probation over incarceration, the appellate courts will not interfere with the trial court's exercise of discretion in the formulation of the terms and conditions of probation.[64]

The sentencing court's discretion is not total. There are five general rules to which conditions must conform to pass legal muster.

1. Conditions Must be Reasonably Related to the Crime

Adopting the same general framework, appellate courts typically allow conditions of probation that are *reasonably related* to the crime committed or to the prevention of future criminal behavior by the defendant or satisfy other legitimate probationary goals. Generally the legitimate goals of probation are defined quite broadly, as in the following Fifth Circuit decision:

> A condition of probation satisfies the statute so long as it is reasonably related to rehabilitation of the probationer, protection of the public against other offenses during its term, deterrence of future misconduct by the probationer or general deterrence of others, condign punishment, or some combination of these objectives.[65]

For this reason, the following orders have all been upheld as valid conditions: banishment from Irish pubs; mandatory wearing of metal taps on the probationer's shoes; staying 500 yards away from an abortion clinic; not collecting any money from speaking, writing or coverage concerning the crime; staying out of a specific bowling alley; not running for state public office; and not possessing credit cards or a personalized checking account. In the first case, the probationer had been convicted of gun-running for the IRA out of Irish pubs.[66] In the second, the probationer was convicted of sneaking up on his victims and snatching their pocketbooks.[67] In the third, the probationer was convicted of vandalizing an abortion clinic.[68] In the fourth, the probationer embezzled and converted public funds.[69] In the fifth, the probationer got in trouble drinking with his buddies in a bowling alley.[70] In the sixth, the probationer was convicted of forging names on political nomination papers.[71] In the seventh, the probationer was convicted of two counts of bank fraud.[72]

For the same reason, the following conditions have been vetoed: a condition ordering a probationer convicted of possession of marijuana to get a haircut;[73] a condition of abstinence from alcohol for a probationer convicted of assault and battery while sober;[74] a condition ordering a probationer convicted of burglary to refrain from playing professional basketball;[75] a condition barring pregnancy except by the husband for a woman convicted of grand theft and battery;[76] a bar on contacting his wife for a man convicted of forging political nomination papers;[77] an order not to contact the Department of Corrections on any prisoner's behalf except her own for a woman convicted of obstructing justice after she hindered the apprehension of her husband;[78] or a condition requiring the probationer to sell off his used car business for a man convicted of possession of marijuana.[79]

However, appellate courts have upheld some conditions less directly related than others, especially as they affect the offender's rehabilitation and public safety. For example, even though the probationer had been convicted of possession of cocaine, an appellate court upheld a condition of abstinence from alcohol because it found it reasonable to guard against the probationer simply switching from one drug to another, alcohol.[80] Also, the Alaska Court of Appeals upheld a condition requiring a sex offender to abstain from alcohol as the order "enhanced" chances for "successfully addressing his problems with immaturity, anger and impulsiveness."[81] Similarly, the Ninth Circuit upheld a ban on possession of handguns for probationers convicted of assaulting an elderly woman and attempting to burn her home. No guns were used but the Court held that the probationers' past conduct raised serious questions about their dangerousness. They had been getting drunk for years and their treatment of the elderly was outrageous. The condition satisfied deterrent, punishment and public protection goals, notwithstanding the legal challenge by the two Native American probationers that they should be exempt from the ban because they needed guns to participate in ceremonial tribal hunts and religious practices.[82]

Finally, although not related to the offense of burglary and theft for which the defendant was placed on probation, a Wisconsin appellate court upheld a ban on telephoning any female, except family, without the prior approval of his probation officer. The defendant had *prior* convictions in 1988 and 1990 for making harassing telephone calls of a sexual nature to women. The Court found the condition reasonably related to the defendant's rehabilitation.[83] Similarly, an Alaskan appellate court upheld sex offender treatment for a probationer convicted of burglary because the defendant had a prior record of sexual assault and criminal trespass. The court ruled that the condition need not relate to the offense for which the defendant was convicted if it is supported by the record that it is essential for the protection of the defendant and the public.[84] A California appellate court upheld AIDS education as a related condition when a defendant was convicted of selling crack cocaine, because cocaine in powder form could be injected and that could lead to AIDS. Therefore, the court reasoned that the condition was reasonably related to both the crime and the defendant's future criminal conduct.[85]

2. *Conditions Must be Doable*

In addition to being reasonably related to the offense, the offender's rehabilitation or community protection, probation conditions must be *doable*. The condition must be both achievable and intelligible. An unemployed, indigent probationer, for example, cannot be ordered to pay restitution of $250 and a fine of $500 by a specific date as a condition of probation.[86] Nor can a borderline retarded juvenile probationer be ordered to maintain satisfactory grades at school.[87] Nor can a probationer be barred from all places of business that sell alcohol, because, as one court found, alcohol is sold in so many stores as to make the ban unrealistic.[88] Nor can a probationer be ordered to report four times a week if employed and seven times a week if unemployed for his 30-year probationary sentence.[89] Nor can a 20-year-old probationer maintain a 9:00 P.M. curfew for the term of his probation. In the latter case, the Louisiana Supreme Court ruled the condition so harsh that the probationer was destined for failure.[90]

To be doable, courts have insisted that conditions be specific and intelligible, not vague and subject to varying interpretations. Typically, boilerplate conditions that used to be standard in probation such as "refrain from associating with persons of bad character" or refrain from "antisocial conduct" do not make it past appellate review.[91] The courts worry about situations such as the following. A sex offender was ordered to have no contact with children. Subsequently he went into an area not authorized by his work release facility and was seen to drive by a playground where his victim was playing, blow the car horn and smile. The sentencing court revoked his probation but the revocation was overturned on appeal as the appellate court found the no-contact term too ambiguous so as to deprive the defendant of due process.[92]

On the other hand, a "no association" with persons of "harmful or disreputable character" was upheld where the probationer was accused of associating with his co-defendant for whom he served as a lookout in the crime for which he was placed on probation. The probation officer had also specifically told the probationer not to associate with the co-defendant and the probationer had told the probation officer he would not do so. Given these facts, the court deemed that the probationer understood that he should not have associated with the co-defendant.[93] Similarly, the Ohio Supreme Court reversed a lower court to uphold a no-association order with anyone under the age of 18 for a probationer convicted of contributing to the delinquency of a minor. The Supreme Court declared that a "common sense" reading of the condition provided the defendant with fair notice. Although a literal reading would be unreasonable, the Court could not find that the condition imposed would be unreasonably enforced in the future.[94]

Regarding the problem of varying interpretations, the Maine Supreme Court, for example, found the condition "cooperate fully to the satisfaction of the probation department with law enforcement personnel in regard to trafficking cocaine" to be unconstitutionally vague.[95] For similar reasons, a Minnesota appellate court altered a condition that a motor vehicle homicide probationer read and understand his victim impact statement and write an appropriate letter of apology. The court sanctioned the reading of the statement and writing of the letter but not the subjective conditions that he understand what he read.[96]

While probation conditions must be doable, this is not to imply that conditions must be easy. Appellate courts approve of making probationers sweat from time to time, even in regard to monetary conditions. In upholding a large restitution order, the Pennsylvania Court, for example, ruled that it might well be necessary for the defendant to make "substantial sacrifices," requiring "additional or alternative employment," a "reduction in expenses," and "even a temporary change in lifestyle." The court went on to hold that sacrifice may be judged too much only when the payments ordered are "so unreasonable in view of the defendant's financial circumstances and ability to work that, despite good faith efforts, the defendant cannot hope to comply."[97] A New Mexico appellate court put it this way:

> Probation is not meant to be painless. It has an inherent sting and the restrictions on the probationer's freedoms are realistically punitive.[98]

3. Conditions Must Not Overly Restrict Constitutional Rights

While conditions may prescribe an offender's otherwise constitutionally protected rights, they must do so as conservatively and narrowly as possible while still achieving their desired goal of rehabilitation or crime prevention.

They may not, in short, be *overbroad*. In grappling with this issue, the California Court of Appeals made an analogy with standards used to judge the legality of a publicly conferred benefit conditioned on a waiver of constitutional rights.

> . . . [T]hat the value accruing to the public from imposition of these conditions manifestly outweighs any resulting impairment of constitutional rights; and that there are available no alternative means less subversive of constitutional rights, narrowly drawn so as to correlate more closely with the purposes contemplated by conferring the benefit.[99]

Another California case demonstrates the concern appellate courts have in approving conditions that overly restrict constitutional rights. In this case, a California appellate court struck down a ban on pregnancy for a heroin addict, declaring that even if related to the crime or future criminality on the part of the probationer, it was impermissibly overbroad.[100] The court found that other, less far-reaching conditions could protect unborn children from the heroin use of their mother. In fact, a number of other appellate decisions have excised conditions that bar pregnancy among probationers, noting that such conditions would force pregnant probationers to forego prenatal care to hide their pregnancy or have an abortion. One asked, what if the probationer used birth control and it failed to work?[101]

The following cases are instructive where appellate courts have drawn the line in specific cases. While one California appellate court struck down a condition that a probationer convicted of assault during a demonstration refrain from speaking at "any college, high school, or junior high school campus or at any organization advocating protest,"[102] another upheld a narrower ban against the probationer participating in any demonstration similar to the one in which he had originally been when he was arrested.[103] Another appellate court upheld a ban on a probationer coming within one and one-half miles of a drug house, as the constitutional infringement was deemed to be minimal while the condition met a legitimate need of law enforcement.[104]

An instructive case was decided by the Maine Supreme Court in 1994. The defendant was convicted of unlawful sexual contact with a dangerous weapon. The crime was committed against a 14-year-old girl and he had a history of similar crimes. The sentencing court ordered that he was to have no contact with any minor children, including his own. The state supreme court held:

> [T]he general prohibition of Coreau from contact with children under the age of sixteen is reasonably related to the crimes for which [he] has been convicted, furthers the rehabilitation process by reducing the risk of [his] committing further crimes against minors, and protects the public safety. Extending that restriction to *unsupervised* contact with his own children bears a sufficient relationship to the crimes for which he has been convicted, reduces the risk of further criminality, and is a protection for the children. See State v. Whitechurch, 155 Vt. 134, 577 A.2d 690 (1990). The court's prohi-

> bition of any type of contact between [him] and his children, includ-
> ing supervised or monitored contact, however, goes well beyond the
> language (of probation statute) and the purposes of probation. The
> condition is not sufficiently related to the crimes for which he was
> convicted and has little to do with public safety. There is no evidence
> that (he) has abused any of his own children, and there is nothing in
> the record to indicate that his presence would be psychologically
> damaging to his children.[105]

In short, while the condition could restrict the probationer's access to his own children, it went too far in restricting all access, even supervised access. Not only did it go too far, but as will be discussed in the next general rule, it contradicted public policy in Maine, namely the public policy to maintain families whenever possible.

In a landmark United States Supreme Court case upholding a Wisconsin statute requiring probationers to submit to warrantless searches by probation officers, the Court noted that probation supervision presented the state with a "special need," which justified departure from "the arrest warrant and probable cause requirements."[106] Most states have followed suit.[107] New Hampshire's Supreme Court upheld probation searches based on superior court rules.[108]

Following the United States Supreme Court decision, some appellate courts have also allowed such conditions absent a state statute or regulatory scheme spelling out when a probation officer can exercise such a warrantless search. In such cases, the individual search condition must be reasonable and narrowly drawn for the circumstances of each case by the sentencing court.[109] Montana's Supreme Court in 1988 reversed an earlier 1980 decision to uphold a search by a probation officer based on reasonable suspicion.[110] Still other appellate courts have upheld waivers of Fourth Amendment rights simply on the fact that probationers agreed to the condition in accepting probation, even though the alternative would have been jail.[111] On the other hand, some state appellate courts refuse to allow warrantless searches absent statutory authority, even if the probation department promulgated official departmental rules and procedures governing such warrantless searches.[112]

Appellate courts have also upheld mandatory drug testing of probationers, rejecting arguments that the testing constituted a warrantless search. Probation officers do not need probable cause to demand that a test be done if such tests are imposed by the court.[113]

Courts have upheld conditions that compromise probationers Fifth Amendment rights. For example, polygraph tests as conditions of probation have been okayed.[114] In one case, for example, the polygraph was declared to be necessary to enforce conditions imposed against a juvenile adjudicated of lewd and lascivious conduct who was ordered to have no unsupervised contact with girls. In another case, the Eleventh Circuit upheld the revocation of a defendant's probation when he invoked his Fifth Amendment rights when his probation officer asked him to account for $25,000 income reported on his tax returns. The court decided that while the probationer had a right to avoid self-incrimination, the state had the right to revoke his probation for a refusal to answer his probation officer "truthfully and completely" as required by his probation conditions. The court concluded that the issue was not the invocation of his privilege, but his failure to report to his probation officer.[115]

As the above cases all underscore, the appellate courts look favorably upon conditions that make the probationer's good behavior in the community easier for the probation officer to enforce.

Finally, appellate courts have allowed conditions that impinge upon probationers' First Amendment rights as well as more general right of privacy, usually claimed to be found in the First, Fourth and Fifth Amendments. The Ninth Circuit supported the condition that two police officers convicted of perjury after making false statements in a civil rights suit be required to make a public apology. The court noted that the condition was particularly appropriate because neither defendant admitted his guilt or took responsibility for his conduct.[116] Mandatory treatment has also withstood the challenge that it violated the defendant's right to privacy. In upholding the condition, the Third Circuit wrote:

> The district court carefully . . . determined that in view of [the defendant's] courtroom behavior and criminal record, psychological counseling could both promote his rehabilitation and decrease the likelihood that his aberrant behavior would recur to the potential harm of society. We therefore agree with the district court that the condition was reasonably related to the purposes of probation and that the impact on [the defendant's] rights was no greater than necessary to carry out these purposes.[117]

Similarly, the Wyoming Supreme Court upheld a condition that a defendant convicted of forging political nomination papers submit to a psychological stress test given his long history of aberrant behavior.[118]

Once ordered into treatment, the probationer has no right to patient-doctor confidentiality. For example, the Alabama appellate court held that such disclosure not only did not compromise the purpose of treatment, but "common sense" dictated that if treatment is a condition of probation, the court and probation officer must have some means of determining whether the defendant is in compliance with that treatment.[119]

Finally, probation conditions have withstood Ninth (prohibition of cruel and unusual punishment) and Thirteenth (bar on involuntary servitude) Amendment attacks. Because probation is not a sentence, the Ninth Amendment has been held not to apply.[120] Mandatory employment was held to relate to the defendant's rehabilitation, including his support or payment of fines and restitution owed.[121]

4. *Conditions Must be Consistent with Public Policy*

Over the years, there has been a class of conditions rejected by the courts for contravening public policy. Banishment from one state to another is an obvious and consistent example. Obviously, while solving one state's problem, banishment does harm to another.[122] While a ban on pregnancy fails to meet the "overly broad" test previously detailed, it also promotes abortion or prenatal neglect if the pregnant probationer seeks to hide her pregnancy, both of which are against public policy.[123]

The Michigan Supreme Court struck down the mandatory use of the drug Depo Provera as a sex suppressant for a pedophile, in part because the drug had not been approved by the FDA for that purpose.[124] Nor could a Florida court force a probationer to sell her house to pay her remaining restitution because Florida public policy prohibited the forced sale of a homestead.[125]

Finally, an Illinois appellate court struck down the requirement that a drunk driver publish a public apology that included his police booking picture in the newspaper. The court worried that the condition would add public ridicule as a condition.[126] The court also expressed its concern that the condition seemed to contradict the legislative intent of the state's drunk driving statute, which was to promote drunk drivers' rehabilitation through psychological or psychiatric treatment. Other appellate courts, however, have upheld conditions requiring drunk drivers to put bumper stickers on their cars notifying passing motorists of their probationary status.[127]

5. *Conditions Must Not Usurp Legislative Role*

Courts may not invent specific conditions that are preempted by or inconsistent with statutory laws. Although courts do have wide discretion in fashioning individual conditions of probation, if the state has laid down a series of related conditions, the court may not ignore them in favor of its own. For example, the Tennessee Supreme Court did not allow a judge to order a convicted drunk driver to forfeit his car for the duration of his license suspension. The state legislature, it ruled, had already provided a number of specific penalties for drunk driving and it, not the sentencing judge, "is both the appropriate branch of government to prescribe procedures in cases such as this and is capable of mandating the extent and nature of available punishments as well as the conditions of probation for the offense of driving under the influence."[128]

Various federal circuit courts of appeals have disallowed the imposition of charitable donations as a condition of probation, holding that Congress intended monies to be paid only to those enumerated in relevant statutes.[129]

Where statutes are silent, appellate courts look at what has been enacted in related areas to establish legislative intent. A Pennsylvania court, for example, in deciding against auto forfeiture in a drunk driving case, analyzed all 13 statutory conditions of probation in the state's probation statute. It found that all

13 constituted "behavioral restrictions, restricting actions or directing actions," aimed at rehabilitation, not punishment. With the exception of restitution, none authorized economic deprivation such as property forfeiture. The court also criticized the judge, who, while ordering forfeiture for drunk driving, had failed to order the probationer to abstain from drinking or driving. In this light the condition was found not to be rehabilitative and therefore not authorized by statute.[130]

The Wyoming Supreme Court refused to allow a condition of probation requiring a sex offender to submit to DNA testing. The condition, the court explained, went beyond *any* statutory authority. It did uphold another condition requiring the probationer to pay child support as an order of restitution because the defendant admitted to unlawful sexual intrusion that could have resulted in the minor victim's pregnancy.[131]

Nor can a judge usurp another agency's or court's functional responsibility and prerogatives. For example, a judge cannot order an alien to leave the country as a condition of probation, because the power to deport by law is entrusted to the United States Attorney General.[132] Nor can a child abuser be ordered not to seek custody of her child in juvenile court without the sentencing judge's permission as the condition interfered with the juvenile court's authority and put the mother in a position of having to choose between the juvenile court if it awarded her custody and jail for violating her probation.[133] In a similar case in Oregon, that state's supreme court ruled that the judge could not order the probationer not to contest custody provisions in the civil courts. It could, however, have legally ordered him to comply with other court orders and notify criminal court of any civil action so the sentencing court's concern could have been communicated to the civil court.[134]

A Maryland court was similarly barred from prohibiting a narcotics distributor from working in pharmacies without the court's permission even though he obtained a valid pharmaceutical license. The appellate court held that the defendant's suitability to be a pharmacist should be determined by the state pharmacy board, not the trial court. The latter could not usurp the authority of the former.[135]

On the other hand, a Maryland appellate court upheld an order of 1,000 hours of community service for a juvenile, even though the state's statute specifically limited the number of hours to 20 for a first offender and 40 for a second. The court, instead, unabashedly opted for other statutory authority, specifically the part of the statute authorizing "reasonable conditions that promote the goals of probation."[136]

§3.05   —Imposing Probationary Conditions

While conditions of probation may be broad, the authority to impose them is limited. With the exception of conditions mandated to all probationers, in most circumstances, only the judge can impose them. The judge may not delegate his or her imposition to third parties, including, in most instances, probation officers.

Especially in regard to monetary terms such as restitution, appellate courts have insisted that the judge alone actually spell out both the amount owed and the specific payments due. At least one appellate court is so concerned with protecting the judge's monopoly on sentencing that it even demands that not only must the judge alone order the performance of community work service as a condition of probation, but the judge must also establish the type of community service to be completed and the schedule for its performance.[137]

Most courts, however, are less extreme, allowing for reasonable delegation of terms necessary for the implementation of judicially ordered conditions. For example, an Illinois appellate court upheld judicial delegation of completion time of a community work service order to probation, deeming it "impossible for the sentencing judge to detail in its probation order every aspect which would lead to successful completion of the public service requirement."[138]

In general, appellate courts allow for limited delegation of what they label "derivative" conditions, terms that flow logically from the general court order. The Florida Supreme Court, for example, refused to find it an illegal delegation that the probationer was to undergo substance abuse screening and, if deemed necessary by probation, receive counseling. The court ruled that the delegation in question would not lead to a punitive result or amount to usurpation of an essentially judicial function.[139]

By its rules of criminal procedure, Arizona gives probation officers authority to impose regulations necessary to implement the conditions imposed by the court. Such regulations must be in writing.[140]

On the other hand, a California court found it illegal for a probation officer, in implementing the judge's condition that the defendant was not to associate with gang members, to mandate that the probationer abide by a curfew and stay out of a section of the city where gangs operated.[141] Similarly, it was ruled an illegal delegation for the judge to order that the probation officer determine whether some of the probationer's 10- to 40-day sentence would be waived, based on the probation officer's satisfaction with the defendant's program completion.[142]

Judges cannot delegate to non-probation officers either, including treatment experts. For example, the North Dakota Supreme Court barred a judge from delegating to an addiction evaluator the course of treatment a probationer was to follow. In the end, the court held, the final decision must be the judge's.[143] This is not to say, however, that the judge must determine all the specifics of an offender's treatment program. For example, another appellate court allowed a judge to delegate to a treatment program promulgation of its behavioral rules that the probationer must follow. The court ruled that in this case, at least, the court was doing nothing more than requiring the probationer to abide by the parameters of a program established to provide a structure within which his probation and rehabilitation could proceed to a successful conclusion.[144]

Probation officers have an independent right of action in only half a dozen states that specifically authorize it by statute. A few states, also by statute, authorize probation officers themselves to order treatment conditions. Even if the sentencing judge does not so order, the probation officer may still order the probationer into treatment. The Vermont Supreme Court, for example, pursuant to such a state statute, allowed a probation officer to mandate sex abuse counseling even though the sentencing judge had not checked the box in the sentencing form ordering mental health counseling.[145] The reason such delegation of treatment conditions is not seen as a usurpation of the judge's function in sentencing probably goes back to the common law evolution of probation as a non-punitive "non-sentence."

Once conditions of probation are legally imposed, it is incumbent upon the judge to insure that the probationer is aware of them and understands them. Consequently, many jurisdictions insist that conditions of probation be reduced to writing and given to the probationer. The federal criminal code, for example, specifies: "[t]he court shall direct the probation officer to provide the defendant with a written statement that sets forth all the conditions to which the sentence is subject, and that is sufficiently clear and specific to serve as a guide for the defendant's conduct and for such supervision as required."[146]

On the other hand, even where specifically mandated by statute, the failure of the court to provide defendants with written conditions of probation may not constitute a legal problem if it can be shown that the probationer was made aware of their content.[147] But if the record fails to demonstrate that the probationer knew what was expected of him in the way of specific probationary conditions, unwritten conditions have no effect. As one appellate court made clear, "a term not recorded at sentencing and not furnished in writing to the defendant has no effect."[148] The one universal exception is the most fundamental term of probation—not to commit any new offenses. Whether this was provided to the probationer or not, no appellate court yet has excused offenders from it.

Of course, even though written, some conditions may be problematic if their meaning is vague or unclear. A New York court admonished probation in that state for providing standard written conditions that contained phrases such as "refrain from consorting with disreputable persons" and "refrain from frequenting unlawful or disreputable places." The Court found the phrases to be unhelpful, "ornate and imprecise."[149]

Probation officers can help translate such conditions to probationers. While a Michigan appellate court, for example, found a condition barring "antisocial conduct" to be impermissibly vague, it upheld the parolee's revocation for antisocial conduct because the officer had explained to the probationer that the phrase meant "fighting."[150] In other words, boilerplate conditions such as "avoid persons of disreputable character" may be enforced if probation officers can demonstrate that they supplied probationers with a list of specific persons to be avoided, such as codefendants.

A 1985 New York appellate court ruling sets forth a fairly representative standard in deciding whether conditions meet this "clearness" test. In this case, the appellant claimed that the condition that he not "abuse alcohol" was unclear and his probation therefore could not be revoked for a violation of that term.

The court ruled, however, that "[t]he condition is sufficiently explicit to inform a reasonable person of the conduct to be avoided." Because the probationer had become intoxicated and disrupted a wedding, the court had little trouble upholding the revocation.[151]

§3.06   —Modifying Conditions of Probation

Once imposed, probation is not a binding contract, immutably set for the course of the probationary period. This is true even if the originally probated sentence was the product of a plea.[152] Probationary terms may be modified by the court. In some jurisdictions, this is spelled out by statute and in others it has been upheld by appellate courts.

The federal criminal code provides an example of the former:

> The court may, after hearing, modify, reduce, or enlarge conditions of
> a sentence of probation at any time prior to the expiration or termi-
> nation of the term of probation, pursuant to the provisions applicable
> to the initial setting of the conditions of probation.[153]

In Michigan, an appellate court upheld a state law that allowed for conditions to be "at all times alterable, and amendable, both in form and in substance, in the court's discretion" without notice.[154] Most jurisdictions require notice before conditions may be modified. Typically, the Massachusetts Supreme Judicial Court authorizes courts to modify conditions absent statutory authority as a matter of "well-established common law."[155]

The Vermont Supreme Court has similarly allowed for modification of conditions but only with either the probationer's consent or a finding that circumstances surrounding the probationer have changed.[156] Other jurisdictions, such as Illinois, demand only a hearing but do not require the state to provide any evidence that the modification is desirable.[157]

Jurisdictions have split on whether the probationer is entitled to counsel for such a hearing. A Wisconsin appellate court ruled that a hearing to extend probation, for example, was not a "grievous loss" like a revocation and the presentation of evidence is not complex.[158] A Florida appellate court, on the other hand, has nullified probation extensions even when the probationer consented because no hearing was held and counsel was supplied.[159]

A number of jurisdictions provide that probation may be automatically extended if the probationer fails to pay restitution orders even if the nonpayment is nonwillful.[160] An Oregon appellate court similarly held that probation can be extended without a probation violation, as is the normal course in that state, if the extension is directed toward the defendant's rehabilitation. In that case, the probationer had not completed psychiatric counseling and had used drugs while on probation.[161]

Of course, probation may also be modified or extended after the court has found the probationer in violation of his probationary conditions.

Some states and the federal system limit the length of probationary sentences by court rule or statute. Others provide no limits. Georgia, for example, provides for a maximum term of four years except upon written order of the court necessary to enforce restitution or fine payment, or for further protection of a victim or class of victims. Thus, a state court upheld the imposition of a 20-year probationary period for a child sex molester.[162]

Notes

[1] Augustus, J. (1939). A REPORT OF THE LABORS OF JOHN AUGUSTUS 11.

[2] H. Parsons, remarks before The American Institute of Criminal Law and Criminology, American Bar Association, New York, 1917. In Grinnell (1917). *Probation As An Orthodox Common Law Practice in Massachusetts Prior to the Statutory System.* 2 MASS. L. Q. at 613.

[3] STANDARDS RELATING TO PROBATION § 1.2(III) (Approved Draft 1970).

[4] National Advisory Commission on Criminal Justice Standards and Goals (1973). STANDARDS AND GOALS, CORRECTIONS, 311.

[5] *United States v. Murray,* 275 U.S. 347, 48 S. Ct. 146, 72 L. Ed. 309 (1928).

[6] *Korematsu v. United States,* 319 U.S. 432, 435, 63 S. Ct. 1124, 87 L. Ed. 1497 (1943) (quoting from *Cooper v. United States,* 91 F.2d 195, 199 (5th Cir. 1937).

[7] See, *e.g., People ex rel. Forsyth v. Court of Sessions,* 141 N.Y. 288, 36 N.E. 386 (1894) (in which the court upheld probationary sentences without explicit statutory authority); *contra, Neal v. State,* 104 Georgia 509, 30 S.E. 858 (1898).

[8] *Ex parte United States,* 242 U.S. 27, 37 S. Ct. 72, 61 L. Ed. 129 (1916).

[9] Goldfarb, R. and L. Singer (1973). AFTER CONVICTION 215.

[10] Camp, G. and C. Camp (1984). THE CORRECTIONS YEARBOOK.

[11] Bureau of Justice Statistics (1985). PROBATION AND PAROLE, 1984.

[12] Bureau of Justice Statistics (1984). PROBATION AND PAROLE, 1983; Bureau of Justice Statistics (1984). PRISONERS IN 1984.

[13] Stern, H. (1995). *State, Federal Prisons Reach Record 1 Million Inmate Level.* ASSOCIATED PRESS, August 10.

[14] Bureau of Justice Statistics (1994). *Probation and Parole Populations Reach New Highs.* Press Release, Washington DC, Sept. 11.

[15] *Probation and Parole 1990* (1991). NCJ-125833, November.

[16] Gilliard, D. and A. Beck (1995). *The Nation's Correctional Population Tops 5 Million.* Bureau of Justice Statistics, August 27.

[17] Huskey, B. (1995). *The Future of Community Corrections: A National Perspective.* THE IARCA JOURNAL ON COMMUNITY CORRECTIONS, VII: 1 (September).

[18] Criminal Justice Institute (1994). THE CORRECTIONS YEARBOOK: PROBATION AND PAROLE 1994.

[19] SEEKING JUSTICE (1995). New York, NY: Edna McConnell Clark Foundation.

[20] Bureau of Justice Statistics (1996). *Probation and Parole Population Reaches Almost $3.8 Million*. U.S. Department of Justice Press Release, June 30.

[21] Rothman, D. (1981). THE DISCOVERY OF THE ASYLUM.

[22] PRISONERS IN 1984, *supra* note 12.

[23] Grinnell, *supra* note 2.

[24] Augustus, *supra* note 1 at 45.

[25] See, *e.g.,* Martison (1974). *What Works? Questions and Answers About Prison Reform.* 35 PUBLIC INTEREST.

[26] MODEL SENTENCING AND CORRECTIONS ACT §§ 3-101, 3-102(5) (1979). National Conference of Commissioners on Uniform State Laws.

[27] Petersilia, J., S. Turner, J. Kahan, and J. Peterson (1985). GRANTING FELONS PROBATION. Washington, DC: National Institute of Justice, R-318186-NIJ.

[28] Penn (1983). *Risk to Society, Reliance on Probation is Increasing, and So is Opposition to Its Use.* WALL STREET JOURNAL, May 16.

[29] See, *e.g.,* CAL. PENAL CODE § 1203(b) (West Supp. 1986) (allows for the imposition of probation where the court finds "circumstances in mitigation of the punishment prescribed by law. . ."); N.Y. PENAL LAW § 65.00 (1)(i) (McKinney 1975 & Supp. 1986) (directs judges to consider whether "institutional confinement for the term authorized by law . . . may not be necessary for the protection of the public" before placing an offender on probation).

[30] 28 U.S.C. § 994(j) (Supp. II 1984) (effective Nov. 1, 1987); but see *Rodriguez v. United States,* ___ U.S. ___, 107 S. Ct. 1391, ___ L. Ed. 2d ___ (1987) (in which the court held that probation is authorized unless specifically excluded by statute).

[31] Shenon (1984). *City Probation is Assailed as Overwhelmed and Ineffective.* NEW YORK TIMES, April 28.

[32] Bohlen, C. (1989). *Probation Agency Faces a Double Burden.* NEW YORK TIMES, January 8.

[33] California Probation, Parole, and Correctional Association (1984). THE POWER OF PUBLIC SUPPORT 3543; Blackmore (1980). *Treatment? There's No Treatment Going on Here,* CORRECTIONS MAGAZINE 13 (December); Penn, *supra* note 28.

[34] Petersilia, J. (1988). *Probation Reform.* In Scott, J. and T. Hirschi (eds.), CONTROVERSIAL ISSUES IN CRIME AND JUSTICE. VOL 1. Newbury Park, CA: Sage Publications.

[35] *Dickerson v. New Banner Institute, Inc.,* 460 U.S. 103, 121, 103 S. Ct. 986, 996, 74 L. Ed. 2d 845, 859 (1984), *reh'g denied,* 461 U.S. 911, 103 S. Ct. 1887, 76 L. Ed. 2d 815 (1983) (according to the defendant, his supervision consisted of "occasionally report[ing] that [he] had not been arrested.").

[36] Lemert, E. (1993). *Visions of Social Control: Probation Considered.* 39 CRIME AND DELINQUENCY 447.

[37] Hicks, J. (1993). *Accord Made to Cut Staff for Probation.* NEW YORK TIMES, January 29.

[38] Domurand, F. (1995). *Supervising the Violent Offender in the Community: An Unmet Challenge.* Paper presented to National Institute of Corrections Workshop, Maryland, March, 17.

[39] Banks, J., E. Carlson, J. Dahl, J. Debro, K. Kirkpatrick and L. Varnon (1978). IMPROVED PROBATION STRATEGIES 1. Washington, DC: U.S. Department of Justice.

[40] R. Polisky (1981). *Introduction* to AMERICAN CORRECTIONAL ASSOCIATION DIRECTORY OF PROBATION AND PAROLE.

[41] See D. Fogel (1975). WE ARE LIVING PROOF: THE JUSTICE MODEL FOR CORRECTIONS; P. McAnany, D. Thomson and D. Fogel (eds.) (1984). PROBATION AND JUSTICE.

[42] *Villery v. Florida Parole and Probation Commission,* 396 So. 2d 1107 (Fla. 1981) (citations omitted).

[43] *State v. Stastny,* 223 Neb. 903, 395 N.W.2d 492 (Neb. 1986).

[44] *State v. Baca,* 90 N.M. 280, 282, 562 P.2d 841, 843 (1977) (citations omitted).

[45] See, *e.g., State v. Randolph,* 316 N.W.2d 508 (Minn. 1982); *State v. Sutherlin,* 341 N.W.2d 303 (Minn. App. 1984) (in which the court reaffirmed *Randolph,* allowing the probationer to serve his sentence of 15 months for unauthorized use of a motor vehicle rather than the probationary sentence that required him to be committed to the county workhouse for one year and seek alcohol treatment upon his release. Allowing for good time, the sentence amounted to a maximum of 10 months, two months shorter than the probationary commitment.)

[46] Petersilia, *supra,* note 26, at ix.

[47] Anderson, D. (1991). *Probation, Georgia Style.* NEW YORK TIMES, July 17.

[48] Fallon, V., paper to Office of the Commissioner of Probation, Boston, MA, April 24, 1995.

[49] See, *e.g., Yates v. State,* 792 P.2d 187 (Wyo. 1990); *United States v. Howard,* 577 F.2d 269 (5th Cir. 1978); *cf. People v. Dingert,* 139 Ill. 2d 248, 554 N.E.2d 1376 (Ill. 1990).

[50] *State v. Rasinksi,* 472 N.W.2d 645 (Minn. 1991); *State v. Carmickle,* 762 P.2d 290 (Or. 1988). (special conditions may infringe on constitutional rights, therefore legislature could not have meant that defendants had to accept probation without consent).

[51] *Sprague v. State,* 590 P.2d 410 (Alaska 1979) (construing ALASKA STAT. § 12.55.100 (1985)) (exclusion of absent remedies should be inferred from inclusion of specified remedies.) See generally, Cohen, N. and J. Gobert (1983). THE LAW OF PROBATION AND PAROLE (provides a comprehensive breakdown of probation conditions).

[52] N.C. GEN. STAT. §15-1343(b)(11) (1983).

[53] CAL. PENAL CODE § 1203.1 (West Supp. 1986) (effective until Jan. 1, 1989).

[54] NEB. REV. STAT. § 29-2262.01 (Supp. 1994).

[55] Gordon, F. (1993). *Literacy Programs for Those on Probation: Do They Make a Difference?* 32 JUDGES JOURNAL 2 (Winter).

[56] LA. CODE CRIM. PROC. ANN. art. 895(G) (West Supp. 1995).

[57] CAL. PENAL CODE §1202.6 (West Supp. 1995), upheld in *Love v. San Francisco County Superior Court,* 226 Cal. App. 3d 736, 276 Cal. Rptr. 660 (1990) (found not an unreasonable search).

[58] LA. CODE CRIM. PROC. ANN. art. 895(E) (West Supp. 1995).

[59] ILL. ANN. STAT. ch. 38, § 1005-5-6(b).

[60] 18 U.S.C. § 3563(a)(1) (Supp. II 1984) (effective Nov. 1, 1986).

[61] *Id.* at § 3563(b)(2), (b)(3), (b)(13).

[62] *Id.* at § 3563(b)(1), (b)(2-12), (b)(14-20).

[63] CAL. PENAL CODE § 1203.1 (West Supp. 1986).

[64] *State v. Turner,* 142 Ariz. 138, 144, 688 P.2d 1030, 1036 (Ariz. Ct. App. 1984) (citations omitted).

[65] *United States v. Tonry,* 605 F.2d at 148 (5th Cir. 1979).

[66] *Malone v. United States,* 502 F.2d 554 (9th Cir. 1974), *cert. denied,* 419 U.S. 1124, 95 S. Ct. 809, 42 L. Ed. 2d 824 (1975).

[67] *People v. McDowell,* 59 Cal. App. 3d 807, 130 Cal. Rptr. 839 (1976).

[68] *Markley v. State,* 507 So. 2d 1043 (Ala. Ct. App. 1987).

[69] *United States v. Terrigno,* 42 Crim. L. Rptr. 2374 (9th Cir. 1988).

[70] *State v. Salyers,* 239 Neb. 1002, 480 N.W.2d 173 (1992).

[71] *Hamburg v. State,* 820 P.2d 523 (Wyo. 1992).

[72] *United States v. Laughlin,* 933 F.2d 786 (9th Cir. 1991).

[73] *Inman v. State,* 124 Ga. App. 90, 183 S.E.2d 413 (1971).

[74] *People v Burton,* 117 Cal. App. 3d 382, 172 Cal. Rptr. 632 (1981).

[75] *People v. Higgins,* 22 Mich. App. 479, 177 N.W.2d 716 (1970).

[76] *People v. Dominguez,* 256 Cal. App. 2d 623, 64 Cal. Rptr. 290 (1967).

[77] *Hamburg v. State,* 820 P.2d 523 (Wyo. 1991).

[78] *State v. Maynard,* 47 Ohio App. 301, 547 N.E.2d 409 (1988).

[79] *State v. Matheny,* 884 S.W.2d 480 (Tenn. Crim. App. 1994).

[80] *Smith v. State,* 513 So. 2d 1367 (Fla. Dist. Ct. App. 1987).

[81] *Allain v. State,* 810 P.2d 1019 (Alaska Ct. App. 1991).

[82] *United States v. Juveniles # 1 & 2,* 38 F.3d 470 (9th Cir. 1994).

[83] *State v. Miller,* 175 Wis. 2d 204, 499 N.W.2d 215 (Wis. Ct. App. 1993).

[84] *Miyasato v. State,* 892 P.2d 200 (Alaska Ct. App. 1995).

[85] *People v. Patillo,* 6 Cal. Rptr. 2d 456 (Cal. Ct. App. 1992).

[86] *Bearden v. Georgia,* 461 U.S. 666, 103 S. Ct. 2064 (1983).

[87] *In re Robert M.,* 163 Cal. App. 3d 812, 209 Cal. Rptr. 657 (1985).

[88] *Beckner v. State,* 296 S.C. 365, 373 S.E.2d 469 (1988).

[89] *Nichols v. State,* 528 So. 2d 1282 (Fla. Ct. App. 1988).

[90] *State v. Labure,* 427 So. 2d 855 (La. 1983).

[91] See, *e.g. Fay v. Commonwealth,* 379 Mass. 498, 399 N.E.2d 11 (1980) ("anti-social" conduct impermissibly vague).

[92] *People v. Saucier,* 221 Ill. App. 3d 287, 581 N.E.2d 852 (1991).

[93] *Scroggins v. State,* 815 S.W.2d 898 (Tex. Ct. App. 1991).

[94] *State v. Jones,* 550 N.E.2d 469 (Ohio 1990).

[95] *State v. Cote,* 540 A.2d 476 (Me. 1988).

[96] *State v. Rasinski,* 464 N.W.2d 517 (Minn. Ct. App. 1990), *modified,* 474 N.W.2d 645 (1991).

[97] *Commonwealth v. Wood,* 300 Pa. Super. 463, 446 A.2d 948, 950 (1982).

[98] *State v. Boca,* 90 N.M. 280, 282 (1977) (citations omitted).

[99] *People v. Arvanites,* 17 Cal. App. 3d 1052, 95 Cal. Rptr. 493 (1971).

[100] *People v. Zaring,* 8 Cal. App. 4th 362, 10 Cal. Rptr. 263 (1992).

[101] See, *e.g., State v. Mosburg,* 786 P.2d 313 (Kan. App. 1989); *Rodriguez v. State,* 378 So. 2d 7 (Fla. Ct. App. 1979); *State v. Livingston,* 372 N.E.2d 1335 (Ohio App. 1976).

[102] *In re Mannino,* 122 Cal. App. 3d 953 (1971).

[103] *People v. King,* 267 Cal. App. 2d 814 (1968), *cert. denied,* 396 U.S. 1028 (1970).

[104] *State v. Haynes,* 423 N.W.2d 102 (Minn. Ct. App. 1988).

[105] *State v. Coreau,* 651 A.2d 319 (Me. 1994).

[106] *Griffin v. Wisconsin,* 483 U.S. 868, 874 (1987).

[107] See, *e.g., Commonwealth v. Pickron,* 535 Pa. 241, 634 A.2d 1093 (Pa. 1993) (search requires specific statutory or regulatory framework; *contra, Commonwealth v. Lafrance,* 402 Mass. 789 (1988) (state Bill of Rights found to require more than federal Bill of Rights.)

[108] N.H. Ct. R.A. Superior Ct. R. 107(h), discussed in *State v. Field,* 132 N.H. 760, 571 A.2d 1276 (1990).

[109] *United States v. Giannetta,* 909 F.2d 571, 575 (1st Cir. 1990); *United States v. Schoenrock,* 868 F.2d 289 (8th Cir. 1989).

[110] *State v. Burke and Roth,* 235 Mont. 165, 766 P.2d 254 (1988); *State v. Small,* 235 Mont. 309, 767 P.2d 316 (1989).

[111] See, *e.g., Anderson v. State,* 209 Ga. App. 676, 434 S.E. 2d 122 (1993); *People v. Bravo,* 43 Cal. 3d 600, 738 P.2d 336 (1987), *State v. Josephson,* 125 Idaho 123, 867 P.2d 993 (Idaho Ct. App. 1993).

[112] *Commonwealth v. Alexander,* 436 Pa. 335, 647 A.2d 935 (Pa. 1994).

[113] See, *e.g., State v. Sigler,* 236 Mont. 137, 769 P.2d 703 (Mont. 1989) (urine tests upheld); *State v. Finnegan,* 232 Neb. 75, 439 N.W.2d 496 (1989) (can be performed by any law enforcement agent); *United States v. Oliver,* 931 F.2d 463 (8th Cir. 1991).

[114] *People v. Miller,* 208 Cal. App. 3d 1311, 256 Cal. Rptr. 587 (1989).

[115] *United States v. Robinson,* 893 F.2d 1244 (11th Cir. 1990).

[116] *United States v. Clark and Jeffrey,* 918 F.2d 843 (9th Cir. 1990).

[117] *United States v. Stine,* 675 F.2d 69 (3d Cir. 1982), *cert. denied,* 458 U.S. 1110, 102 S. Ct. 3493 (1982).

[118] *Hamburg v. State* 820 P.2d 523 (Wyo. 1991).

[119] *Crowson v. State,* 552 So. 2d 189 (Ala. Crim. App. 1989).

[120] See, *e.g., People v. Hodgkins,* 194 Cal. App. 3d 795, 239 Cal. Rptr. 831 (1987). (Defendant given 10-year term for bad checks).

[121] *State v. Macy,* 403 N.W.2d 743 (S.D. 1987).

[122] See, *e.g., People v. Baum,* 251 Mich. 187, 231 N.W. 95 (1930).

[123] *State v. Mosburg,* 13 Kan. App. 2d 257, 768 P.2d 313 (1989).

[124] *People v. Gauntlett*, 134 Mich. App. 737, 352 N.W.2d 310 (1980), *modified*, 419 Mich. 909, 353 N.W.2d 463 (1984).

[125] *Downing v. State*, 593 So. 2d 607 (Fla. Dist. Ct. App. 1992).

[126] *People v. Johnson*, 44 Cr. L. 2015 (Ill. Ct. App. 1988).

[127] See, *e.g., Goldsmith v. State*, 490 So. 2d 123 (Fla. Dist. Ct. App. 1986).

[128] *State v. Bouldin*, 717 S.W.2d 584 (Tenn. 1986).

[129] See, *e.g., United States v. John Scher Presents Inc.*, 746 F.2d 959 (3d Cir. 1984); but see, *People v. Burleigh*, 727 P.2d 873 (Colo. Ct. App. 1986).

[130] *Commonwealth v. Crosby*, 390 Pa. Super. 140, 568 A.2d 233 (1990).

[131] *Jackson v. State*, 891 P.2d 70 (Wyo. 1995).

[132] *United States v. Ouaye*, 57 F.3d 447 (5th Cir. 1995); *United States v. Jalilian*, 896 F.2d 447(10th Cir. 1990); *cf. United States v. Mercedes-Merceded*, 851 F.2d 529 (1st Cir. 1988) (probation officer cannot determine whether an immigrant can reenter United States.)

[133] *Smith v. State*, 80 Md. App. 371, 563 A.2d 1129 (1989).

[134] *State v. Donovan*, 307 Or. 461, 770 P.2d 581 (1989).

[135] *Towers v. State*, 92 Md. App. 399, 607 A.2d 105 (1992).

[136] *In re Shannon*, 483 A.2d 363 (Md. Ct. App. 1984).

[137] *Fogle v. State*, 667 S.W.2d 296 (Tex. Crim. App. 1984).

[138] *People v. Butler*, 484 N.E.2d 921 (Ill. Ct. App. 1985); *White v. State*, 560 N.E.2d 45 (Ind. 1990).

[139] *Larson v. State*, 572 So. 2d 1368 (Fla. 1991).

[140] Rule 27.1, discussed in *State v. Jones*, 788 P.2d 1249 (Ariz. Ct. App. 1990).

[141] *Matter of Pedro*, 257 Cal. Rptr. 821, 209 Cal. App. 3d 1368 (1989).

[142] *People v. Thomas*, 577 N.E.2d 496 (Ill. Ct. App. 1991).

[143] *State v. Nelson*, 417 N.W.2d 814 (N.D. 1987).

[144] *People v. Peters*, 477 N.W.2d 479 (Mich. Ct. App. 1991).

[145] *State v. Duffy*, 562 A.2d 1036 (Vt. 1989).

[146] 18 U.S.C. § 3563(c) (1984); see also TEX. CODE CRIM. PROC. ANN. art. 42.12 § 6(a) (Vernon 1979; CONN. GEN. STAT. ANN. § 53a-30(a) (West 1994); N.Y. CRIM. PROC. LAW § 410.10(1) (McKinney 1994).

[147] See, *e.g., People v. Nazarian*, 541 N.Y.S.2d 262 (N.Y. App. 1989), *appeal den.*, 545 N.Y.S.2d 119, 543 N.E.2d 762; *Jacobsen v. State*, 536 So. 2d 373 (Fla. Dist. Ct. App. 1988).

[148] *Atkins v. State*, 546 N.E.2d 863 (Ind. Ct. App. 1989).

[149] *People v. Sorge*, 410 N.Y.S.2d 49 (N.Y. Sup. Ct. 1978).

[150] *People v. Bruce*, 102 Mich. App. 573, 302 N.W.2d 238 (1980).

[151] *People v. Howland*, 108 A.D.2d 1019, 485 N.Y.S.2d 589 (1985).

[152] See, *e.g., Malone v. State*, 571 N.E.2d 329 (Ind. Ct. App. 1991).

[153] 18 U.S.C § 3563(c) (1984); see also P.A. 77-2097, ILL. COMP. STAT. ANN. tit. 730, § 515-6-4 (Smith-Hurd 1991); N.J. STAT. ANN. § 2C.45-2(b) (West 1982).

[154] *People v. Graber,* 128 Mich. App. 185, 191, 339 N.W.2d 866, 869 (1983) (footnotes omitted).

[155] *Buckley v. Quincy Division of the District Court,* 395 Mass. 815, 817, 482 N.E.2d 511, 512 (1985) (quoting from *Burns v. United States,* 287 U.S. 216, 221 (1932)).

[156] *State v. Day,* 147 Vt. 93, 511 A.2d 995 (Vt. 1986).

[157] *People v. Dinger,* 554 N.E.2d 1376 (Ill. 1990).

[158] *State v Hardwick,* 422 N.W.2d 922 (Wis. Ct. App. 1988).

[159] *State v. Schafer,* 583 So. 2d 374 (Fla. Dist. Ct. App. 1991).

[160] See, *e.g., People v. Cookson,* 3 Cal. Rptr. 2d 176, 820 P.2d 278 (Cal. 1991); *Hewett v. State,* 588 So. 2d 635 (Fla. Dist. Ct. App. 1991).

[161] *State v. Stanford,* 786 P.2d 225 (Or. Ct. App. 1990).

[162] *Ledford v. State,* 375 S.E.2d 280 (Ga. Ct. App. 1988).

Chapter 4

Examples of Alternative Sentences

§4.01   Introduction

This chapter focuses on more examples of alternative sentences organized by type of offense and later by type of offender. Offenses run the gamut from homicides to housing code violations. Offenders range from little old ladies in San Francisco to hard-core drug addicts in the South Bronx, the place where presidential candidates go to decry the nation's worst example of urban decay.

All of the examples are drawn from real-life cases with actual sentences imposed in municipal, state and federal courts. If the cases were reported in the news media or were drawn from appellate case reviews, the names of offenders are used. If the cases were drawn from case files made known to the author, fictitious names are employed to safeguard the privacy of the parties involved. In either situation, the events and circumstances of the cases are factual. While this chapter will not go beyond presentation of the cases, several have come to stand for important principles later enunciated by appellate courts. These cases will be discussed in detail in subsequent chapters.

Finally, several of the sentences discussed in this chapter were later overturned. Nevertheless, the cases are presented because despite the later decision, they illustrate important issues or principles in alternative sentencing. Practices that may be barred in certain jurisdictions due to a particular law may, after all, be permissible in other jurisdictions. Further, while judges may be barred from imposing certain sanctions, defendants can volunteer to comply with them prior to sentencing, perhaps to impress the court with their contrition or sincere desire to make amends.

§4.02   Homicide Alternative Sentences

According to 1993 statistics, 19,600 offenders were imprisoned for manslaughter or non-negligent manslaughter.[1] The imposition of lengthy prison sentences for such crimes is not only authorized by statutes, but there would seem to be few alternatives. In the following cases, however, judges, often with the help of prosecutors, defense attorneys and probation officers, have come up with alternative homicide sentences.

Case #1 (California, 1982): Clark shoots his former lover's husband.

William Clark met his victim's wife two years previously through his work. The relationship became intimate. When Clark's wife found out, she threatened to tell the other woman's husband, David. Consequently, the other woman told him herself. But the air did not clear. Although the married couples stayed together, David would not let the matter drop. He threw it up in his wife's face repeatedly. They separated for periods of time and finally began to dissolve the marriage legally. He also conveyed threats through his wife to William.

Subsequently he tried twice to physically confront William, chasing after him when they both were in cars. Escaping David's initial attempts, William nevertheless bought a pistol for protection. He kept it under his car seat. At one point, the two families passed each other on the road. David shooed his family out of the car and went in pursuit. David beat William to his house. Upon the latter pulling up to the house, David left his vehicle and told William, "Your time is now." He reached into the car window and William fired. David died of the resulting bullet wound in his chest.

William Clark, convicted of involuntary manslaughter, could have been sentenced to prison for many years by Superior Court Judge Richard Sims. Instead, he considered the plight of the victim's family, specifically his four children, all under age 18. Placing Clark on probation, he ordered him to pay the victim's family $100 per month for the five years of his probation, adding up to $6,000.

The defendant appealed, arguing, in part, that the restitution order was improper in that it directed the payment of unliquidated damages to persons other than the direct victim. The appellate court upheld the restitution order, ruling, in part, that it "alleviated the tragedy underlying the offense" and "moreover, the condition served an additional purpose in reforming and rehabilitating the defendant by serving to make him aware of the damage which his actions caused to others."[2]

Case #2 (Michigan, 1981): Miller, battered woman, kills boyfriend.

Thirty-seven-year-old Judith E. Miller shot her 24-year-old live-in boyfriend, Richard Collins, three times, killing him. Convicted of second degree murder, Miller could have been sentenced by Circuit Court Judge Gary R. McDonald to 15 years in prison.

In presentencing hearings, Miller's attorney, Barbara Klimaszewski, presented testimony that her client suffered from "battered woman syndrome," being a woman prone to such abusive relationships. The court rejected incarceration and, instead, ordered the defendant to refrain from marrying or living with any man without the court's approval for the five years in which she would be under court supervision.[3]

Case #3 (California, 1979): Brown shoots husband to death.

Rebecca Brown, a 48-year-old nurse, mother of one child, fatally shot her husband, and was convicted of manslaughter. The presentence report prepared by probation informed the court that the defendant was not regarded as a high risk for repeat crimes. Nonetheless, Judge Stanley Golde sentenced her to one year's confinement, but not in prison or jail. He placed her instead on house arrest for a year as a condition of her probation. She was restricted to Alameda County and required to report to the local probation department each and every morning and evening, seven days a week—similar to the requirements for a work furlough from the local jail.

The sentence allowed her to continue her occupation as a nurse so that she could support and care for her minor child. Judge Golde claimed at the time that Ms. Brown's sentence was the first house arrest in the nation's history. The sentence was necessitated, in part, by the earlier passage of the state's Proposition #13, which severely restricted county correctional expenditures.[4]

Case #4 (Massachusetts, 1982): Dawson, drunk driver, kills his passenger who was his best friend.

A 20-year-old unemployed auto mechanic, Carl Dawson, killed his friend and car passenger. He went around a curve at 50 m.p.h., twice the speed limit. Confronted by an oncoming car, he braked. His reflexes were undoubtedly slowed by the beers he drank earlier and he lost control of the car. The other car's two passengers walked away. Police found Dawson cradling the body of his friend in his arms, pleading "Don't leave me Brian, don't."

Pleading guilty to vehicular homicide by reason of endangerment, Dawson was sentenced to 18 months in jail, 12 months short of the maximum, by Hampshire District Court Judge George Keady, Jr. The judge, however, suspended the sentence for four years. In lieu of the maximum fine of $3,000, he ordered $700 to cover the victim's funeral expenses. He also incorporated into his sentence a plan suggested by the Assistant District Attorney Charlotte Guyer and Probation Officer George Blake. The plan was also endorsed by the victim's parents and the local police chief. The defendant was ordered to address each of the nine local schools in the county on the dangers of drinking and driving.

At first Dawson was reluctant to comply with the order, but he was more reluctant to go to jail. "I'm only 20 years old, "he lectures his high school audiences, "and a big part of my life is ruined. . . ."[5]

Case #5 (New York, 1983): Davis, drunk driver, runs over woman in the presence of her grandson.

An inebriated upstate New Yorker, Donald Davis, a line foreman for a power company, struck and killed an elderly woman while he was driving. The accident and death were witnessed by her young grandson. Convicted of negligent homicide, the defendant was placed on probation for eight years. He was ordered to spend 14 weekends in jail and perform 1,250 hours of community work service. To comply with the sentence, Davis spent four nights a week rewiring lights for a local church, running Bingo games for the local volunteer fire department and other chores. "Work," he reported that "gnaws at you." In addition, he was ordered to accompany local ambulance crews and the Sheriff's Department to the scene of accidents during his probation. He was ordered to pay $4,000 toward a memorial fund for the education of the victim's grandson.

Perhaps the most onerous provision of his sentence was to meet the family of his victim. He learned, among other things, that his victim's son "hated my guts," and that the victim's husband of 45 years thought the sentence acceptable. "Better to make him pay for it instead of sitting in jail."[6]

Case #6 (North Carolina, 1984): Dr. Ornitz, drunk driver, leaves young family fatherless.

Dr. Robert Ornitz, a 40-year-old radiation oncologist, admitted to motor vehicle homicide. Drunk, he drove left of the center of the road, hitting head-on a station wagon containing a family of five. The father died of head injuries resulting from the accident. The wife suffered slight injuries; the doctor suffered a fractured pelvis and a broken jaw.

Superior Court Judge Coy E. Brewer placed Ornitz on probation for five years. To help the victim's family survive without their breadwinner, he ordered the defendant to pay $25,000 a year for thirty years, adding up to an eventual total of three-quarters of a million dollars. In addition, Ornitz was ordered to donate a pint of blood every two months for five years, a total of thirty pints. Defense attorney Wade W. Smith praised the sentence as "remarkable" for its fairness.[7]

Case #7 (Maryland, 1979): Arthur, drunk driver, wipes out his truck and kills all ten passengers.

Labeled the worst traffic accident in a decade, 19-year-old, inebriated Arthur crashed his pickup truck, killing all of his ten young friends in it. Convicted of ten counts of automobile manslaughter, his defense counsel hired the services of the National Center on Institutions and Alternatives, a dispositional advocacy group, to help develop an alternative sentence. County Court Judge Samuel W. Barrick imposed it, announcing that "ten lives have been lost in this case, and certainly the Court does not want to do anything that would ruin another one."

The defendant was ordered to spend the next three years performing three thousand hours of community work service in the same Baltimore Emergency Medical Unit where three of his friends died. Before he began the work, however, he was ordered to complete a 28-day inpatient alcohol treatment program, followed by weekly therapy sessions.[8]

Although the county attorney expressed outrage at what he perceived to be the leniency of the sentence, THE BALTIMORE SUN disagreed:

> What stronger deterrent is there than the deaths themselves and the fact that (the defendant) must live with these deaths for the rest of his life? If we wish to protect society from the dangers of reckless driving abetted by drugs and alcohol, what better guarantee than (his) clearly repentant attitude and the fact that he will be going into treatment instead of a prison where he almost certainly would be brutalized and rendered a far greater hazard to society?[9]

Case #8 (Florida, 1990): Florida girl smothers newborn.

A 17-year-old Florida girl smothered her newborn baby in a bathroom of a Jacksonville hospital in the spring of 1990. Originally charged with second degree murder, she could have faced from 12 to 22 years in prison.

The defendant had never told her parents she was pregnant. Her mother took her to the hospital when she complained of bleeding and pain. Once in the hospital she delivered her baby in the bathroom and then killed it.

The prosecution agreed to a reduction of charges to manslaughter and the defendant agreed to a split sentence of two years in prison followed by 10 years of probation. Explaining that he placed a "higher value on freedom than being concerned about a probationary condition," the defense lawyer and client accepted a number of conditions of probation. First, she must finish high school. Second, she must go to counseling. Third, she must receive education in birth control. Fourth, she must be on birth control for the 10 years of her probation.

Although objected to by civil rights and abortion opponent groups, the prosecutor supported the sentence, raising the question: "Who's going to take care of these babies? We've reached the point where citizens expect the courts to do it . . . We're starting to reach the point where the courts are responsible for anyone. It's one final step to have to supervise teenagers in sexual relationships they aren't ready to handle."[10]

Duval County Circuit Court Judge Lawrence Haddock's order did not specify what birth control the defendant must use. The defendant's lawyer suggested that the order of mandatory birth control was based on the defendant being single. If she were to get married, he advised that the judge would revise the condition.

§4.03   —Analysis of Homicide Alternative Sentences

Although all of the preceding cases differed—different defendants, different crimes, crimes committed in different communities with different laws, and different victims—an alternative sentence was imposed in each. These alternative sentences sought to accomplish the same goals as traditional sentences, including punishment, reparation, rehabilitation, incapacitation, deterrence and just deserts. However, they relied on something other than the use of traditional probation and long-term incarceration. They relied on an array of common components, usually specific, nontraditional probation conditions. Like the alternative sentences themselves, these individual components can address more than one sentencing goal. For example, the order of victim restitution is a common alternative sentencing component. It addresses not only reparation, but also offender rehabilitation. Repaying victims may teach offenders responsibility for their actions. At the same time, the restitution order may be as punitive as the stiffest fine. While the money from restitution orders goes to the victim and not the state, to the defendant's pocket there is no difference.

For ease of analysis, the various alternative sentencing components can be grouped in several major clusters. The first cluster includes alternative sentencing components that address reparation. These components include orders of cash restitution, charitable donations, direct victim services, victim-offender meetings and community work service. The second cluster includes alternative sentencing components that address rehabilitation. These include orders of mandatory treatment, ranging from outpatient to inpatient therapy or counselling, behavior-modifying drugs, and restrictions on behavior. The third cluster includes alternative sentencing components that address incapacitation. These include orders of intensive probation supervision, ranging from increased contact with a probation officer to electronic surveillance schemes, curfews and house arrest, as well as various treatment modalities, such as inpatient treatment, that rigidly restrict the offender's freedom of movement. These components also include alternative uses of traditional incarceration, including split sentences, periodic detention such as weekend sentences, shock sentences and use of correctional diagnostic institutions.

Inherent in all alternative sentencing components is punishment to one extent or another. Any time an offender is required to do something he would not otherwise do, whether it is reimbursing a victim or remaining locked up in his own home under house arrest, there is punishment, even if that is not the sentence's primary goal. In addition, inherent in many of these alternative sentencing components are financial sanctions. These financial sanctions include restitution, donations, treatment costs, court costs, forfeitures, bonds, as well as fines. As a result, the costs of an alternative sentence may exceed the maximum permissible fine allowed for the particular offense. Finally, the sentence seeks to prevent future crimes. In one case, the court sought to stop crimes against unborn victims.

1. Alternative Sentencing: Reparative Components

Reparative components of alternative sentencing require the offender to make up for his crime both directly to his crime victim (or victim's immediate family) or indirectly to the community at large. The most common reparative component is the ordering of cash restitution—usually, but not always, as a condition of probation. Examples of monetary restitution abound in the above examples. Clark was ordered to pay his homicide victim's children $100 a month for five years; Dawson was ordered to pay $700 for his motor vehicle homicide victim's funeral; Ornitz was sentenced to pay his victim's family $25,000 a year for 30 years.

In addition to cash restitution, defendants were also ordered to perform unpaid community work service. Community work service, also called "community restitution," is another common reparative component. Community work service orders were either prescribed in hours or by the task to be completed. Drunk driver Dawson was ordered, for example, to complete a series of speeches warning his peers about drunk driving. Davis was ordered, on the other hand, to perform 1,250 hours of community work service. Work sites may relate to the crime or the defendant's rehabilitation. Arthur, for example, was ordered to work at the hospital where some of his victims died.

Besides donating their labor, defendants were ordered to donate money and even blood as a form of restitution and community service. Donation orders form a third common reparative component of alternative sentencing. Davis, for example, was ordered to donate to a memorial fund established by the court for the victim's grandson's education. Ornitz was ordered to make a donation of his blood at the rate of one pint every two months for five years.

To better fashion reparative components, defendants are sometimes asked to meet with their victims. Not only do such confrontations strip away offender rationalization and allow the victims to express their feelings, they can facilitate the development of restitution, community work service or donation orders. In the Dawson case, the court proceeded only after the victim's parents had been consulted and approved the alternative sentence.

Victim-offender meetings can also form a reparative component of the alternative sentence. Davis was mandated as part of his sentence to meet with his victim's children and husband, unprotected by lawyers, courtroom procedures and rules of evidence.

2. *Alternative Sentencing: Rehabilitative Components*

Alternative sentencing rehabilitative components require the offender to change his behavior in order to prevent future crimes. The most common rehabilitative component is an order of mandatory treatment. Arthur, the drunk driver, was ordered into inpatient alcohol treatment to be followed by outpatient weekly therapy. Other rehabilitative components included orders of behavior modification. Judith Miller, a battered woman, was ordered not to live with or marry anyone without the court's approval. The young Florida girl was ordered to attend counseling. In addition, mandatory birth control would allow her to mature before she would again be faced with the responsibilities of bearing a child.

3. *Alternative Sentencing: Incapacitative Components*

Alternative sentencing incapacitative components require the defendant to either remain out of his community or be rigidly restricted within it but without resorting to long-term and expensive incarceration. Almost all of the above defendants were incapacitated somewhat as a result of their alternative sentences. By ordering the payment of restitution or the performance of community work service, defendants were required to work. Work is incapacitative. Every hour spent working is an hour off the streets. Further, community work service, as well as most private employment, is performed under the supervision of responsible adults. Arthur was ordered to work at a hospital where he would be supervised by health professionals. Davis was placed under the direct supervision of the local Sheriff's department in his work service.

Certain orders of treatment were also incapacitative. Placing drunk driver Arthur in an in-patient treatment center for 28 days, in addition to offering him rehabilitation, effectively incapacitated him for almost one month.

Other alternative sentencing incapacitative components were orders restricting offenders to nonjail-type facilities. Rebecca Brown was placed under house arrest for one year. The requirements of the order were equivalent to participation in the jail's work furlough program, except that the defendant, not the county, bore the cost of the defendant's stay.

Finally, the cases include examples of persons incapacitated through traditional methods of incarceration but employed in an alternative manner, such as the imposition of weekend sentences. Davis was ordered to spend 14 weekends in jail. This periodic detention allowed him both his days during the week to work to support himself and his evenings during the week to perform community work service.

In addition, all of these homicide alternative sentences were, in part, punitive. Although avoiding long-term incarceration, these sentences restricted defendants' liberties and required many to pay substantial monies to the state, the crime victim or the community. These financial sanctions ranged from several thousand dollars to almost one million dollars to be paid over 30 years.

Not only do these examples illustrate common alternative sentencing components, but equally important, they show various actors in the criminal justice system adopting slightly different roles. Victims became more active participants, no longer confining their role solely to that of being a passive witness who suffers in silence. The victims of both Davis and Dawson were brought directly into the sentencing process. In the Davis case, not only did they help to develop the sentence, but they were a part of its execution. Davis' victim-offender meeting was a mandated condition of the sentence.

Defense attorneys actively helped fashion an alternative sentence using community resources and then advocating the alternative sentence before the court. In drunk driver Arthur's case, the defense counsel hired an organization that specializes in putting together alternative dispositional packages for cases in which the defendant otherwise stands a good chance of incarceration. Similarly, the prosecutors and probation officers were involved in fashioning the details of these sentences. In the Dawson case, they consulted with the victim as well as the local police chief and presumably with the local high school principals to put together the disposition requiring Dawson to address local high school audiences on the perils of drunk driving. In fact, many of the new statutes that have emerged out of the victim rights movement now demand victim consultation in sentencing; some even require it in the plea bargaining process.

Finally, judges ventured into new, largely uncharted legal waters in mapping out these alternative sentences. Many of the states in which these sentences were handed down lacked at the time specific statutory or case law authorizing the imposition of restitution, community work service, house arrest, donations and more. Someone had to lead the way. Many of these judges chose to be in that number.

§4.04   Sexual Assault Alternative Sentences

According to 1993 statistics, 32,200 persons convicted of rape and another 84,600 convicted of other sexual offenses were imprisoned throughout the country.[11] From 1988 to 1992, state and federal prisons experienced a 37 percent increase in sex offender admissions. As a result, sex offenders accounted for more than 10 percent of all inmates. California's prisons alone housed more than 15,000 sex offenders.[12] Yet in the cases that follow, various courts have sentenced sexual offenders and rapists without resorting to long-term incarceration.

Case #1 (New Hampshire, 1985): Robert Litteer, Scout leader, sexually assaults two boys.

Robert Litteer, a 43-year-old Boy Scout leader, admitted to one count of rape and five lesser charges of sexual assault, all upon boys under the age of 13. Superior Court Judge William O'Neill sentenced the defendant to eight years in prison, but suspended the sentence for a year with the following conditions. Litteer must perform 1,000 hours of community work service, attend psychological counseling, pay for the victims' counseling, refrain from contact with minors, and, finally, abstain from drug or alcohol use.[13]

Case #2 (Michigan, 1984): Gauntlett molests stepchild.

Roger A. Gauntlett, III, great-grandson of W.E. Upjohn, founder of the pharmaceutical company bearing his name, was accused of repeatedly raping his stepdaughter until she ran away from home at age 14. After she left, Gauntlett was accused of turning his attentions to his 10-year-old stepson. As the result of a plea bargain, the second count of first degree criminal sexual conduct with the boy was dropped and he admitted to the first. He had faced from five to 15 years on each count.

Kalamazoo Circuit Court Judge John E. Fitzgerald originally proposed, in a conference with the attorneys, a year's commitment to the local jail, five years probation and the donation of $2,000,000 from the defendant's trust fund (believed to be in eight figures) to establish a rape counseling center. An assistant prosecutor leaked the proposed sentence to the victim's natural father, who launched a campaign against the deal, including writing 120 letters to religious and community leaders protesting the sentence for its "compelling inference" that the defendant's money and influence alone kept him out of jail. The resulting public uproar led the judge to disqualify himself from the case and it went to Judge Robert Borsos.

Remaining within the framework of the first judge's sentence, Judge Borsos reimposed the one-year split sentence, but replaced the donation with a $25,000 court fee and an order of mandatory treatment for five years, the treatment to consist of the injection of the drug Depo-Provera, commonly (and inaccurately) called a chemical castrator. Depo-Provera, ironically manufactured in this country by Upjohn, is marketed abroad as a female contraceptive, but has also been found to inhibit males' sexual drives. Banned generally by the F.D.A. as a suspected carcinogen, the drug has been used experimentally since 1966 in certain United States prisons for persons convicted of various sexual crimes. Gauntlett, however, was ordered to take the drug on an outpatient basis.

As will be discussed in more detail in a later chapter on such treatment alternatives, the court's order of mandatory Depo-Provera treatment was later overturned by an appellate court as unlawful under Michigan state law.[14]

Case #3 (Oregon, 1975): Sullivan rapes and sodomizes a female.

George E. Sullivan was tried and convicted of rape and sodomy before Circuit Court Judge Robert E. Jones. Subsequently the court's probation department recommended a maximum sentence of 10 years' probation, a $1,500 fine, restitution of $500 to the victim and 80 hours of community service. The judge, instead, imposed two concurrent 10-year sentences and suspended them for five years. In lieu of the fine, he ordered the defendant to pay the victim $3,000 at the rate of $75 per month. On appeal, the appellate court upheld the sentence, ruling that the restitution amount need not be restricted to limited out-of-pocket losses.[15]

Case #4 (Rhode Island, 1986): Paster convicted of second-degree child molestation.

Howard Paster, 36, was convicted of second-degree child molestation. Superior Court Judge Alice Gibney sentenced him to two years house arrest, ordering him to remain home except to go to work and Naval Reserve meetings. "He's going to be living in a fish bowl," the judge declared. "He cannot even stop for milk on the way home."[16]

Case #5 (Oregon, 1987): Child molester ordered to post warning sign on domicile.

Portland, Oregon District Court Judge Dorothy Baker sentenced Richard Bateman after he admitted to child molestation. The case involved a young child who had come to the defendant's door to ask for paper to recycle and had been pulled inside by the defendant and molested. The defendant had two previous convictions for the same behavior. Prosecutor Jill Otey characterized him as "an absolute predator on small children" and a "prolific sex abuser of small children." Imprisoned for the previous offense, he had refused treatment. The judge doubted his present amenability to treatment. She also doubted the state's ability to keep him incarcerated for any length of time given the prison overcrowding crisis and the resultant policy of early offender release.

The judge sentenced him to a split sentence, one year in jail followed by five years probation. With the prosecutor's support, she imposed the following conditions upon his release. He was ordered to refrain from alcohol or drugs, to attend counseling and to stay away from playgrounds and school grounds. In addition, in response to his neighbor's demands, he was ordered to move out of his neighborhood. However, to insure that his new neighbors were also protected, the judge went further.

"In a small town," she explained, "everyone would know . . . and [neighbors] could protect themselves. A problem in our society now is that we don't know each other and so we become vulnerable to criminals when we would not if we knew what they were." To rectify this, she ordered the defendant to post a sign with three-inch-high lettering on his new home to read: **"Dangerous Sex Offender No Children Allowed."** A similar sign was also ordered for his car because a previous offense had occurred in his car.

The defense attorney, joined by the local American Civil Liberties Union, announced their intention to appeal the sign condition.[17]

Eventually the appeal was heard after Mr. Bateman violated eight of the conditions of his probation, including absconding. By then the Appeals Court ruled that the legal challenge to the conditions themselves were too late to be heard and upheld Mr. Bateman's incarceration. In a concurring opinion, one justice argued that the challenged conditions were not cruel and unusual because the public had a right to know about Bateman and incidental humiliation and condemnation are properly part of criminal sanctions. Another justice, in a dissenting opinion, argued that he would consider the signs to be cruel and unusual pursuant to Oregon's Constitution.[18]

Case #6 (New Hampshire, 1991): Public apology required of ex-fireman child rapist.

Thomas Jache, 34, a former Londonderry fireman, faced 16 charges and a maximum sentence of 129 years for raping a 10-year-old boy. Instead, County Superior Court Judge Kenneth McHugh sentenced him to five to seven years, with two years suspended if he completed a sex offender treatment program. In addition, he was ordered to buy full-page ads in the *Manchester Union Leader* and *Lawrence* (Mass.) *Eagle* that contained his photo and admission of his guilt. The ad was also required to urge other sex abusers or victims of sex abuse to seek help.[19]

Case #7 (Massachusetts, 1992): Upon release, sex offender must reveal criminal past to all new girlfriends who have children or probation department will.

Convicted of sexually assaulting two girls he cared for in his day care business, Robert Shell was sentenced to 18 to 20 years in state prison after pleading guilty to 35 charges, including indecent assault on a nine-year-old girl and a three-and-a-half year-old girl and photographing them and others nude. He was also sentenced to 15 to 20 years, suspended.

One of the victim's mothers testified that her daughter was ever after afraid of Santa and would not open Christmas presents because Santa, like Shell, had a beard.

Superior Court Judge Wendie Gershengorn ordered the defendant, as a condition of probation, to inform any woman he dates who has children of his prior record. If he fails to do so, the probation department is directed to do it for him.[20]

Case #8 (Connecticut, 1995): School founder must donate $50,000 for sexual assault of student.

The founding president of a school for at-risk youths in Massachusetts was sentenced in Connecticut for sexually assaulting one of its students in her home. Thomas Bratter, 55 years old, was sentenced in the Litchfield Superior Court after admitting to second degree unlawful restraint. Placed on probation for three years, he was also ordered to make a $50,000 cash donation to a charity and perform 500 hours of community service.[21]

Case #9 (Wyoming County, New York, 1993): Child molester gets stiffer sentence outside than inside jail.

Campground operator Clyde Cox, 59, pled guilty to molesting five boys ages 10 to 12 at his campground in upstate New York. He had previous convictions and brief sentences for similar behavior in 1956 and 1972, also involving young boys. State Supreme Court Justice Glenn Morton accepted an agreed-upon sentenced hammered out by District Attorney David DiMatteo, after extensive consultation with the victims, their families, the Genessee County Sheriff's Office and a panel of respected community residents as well as the defendant's attorney, Norman Effman.

After his conviction, the defendant donated $1,000 to a foundation that helps victims of sexual abuse. He also performed 300 hours of community service. He sat down with a citizen panel made up of leading representatives of the small town (population 800) in which he lived and would serve his probated sentence. The panel consisted of 16 members, including two ministers and their wives, the general store manager, the fire chief and his wife, the school principal and others. The meeting lasted more than two hours and the panel heatedly challenged the defendant's minimization of the crime and his need for assistance. The defendant had himself been raped when he was 12 years old. The panel let the defendant know that they would be watching him upon his release from jail.

With the victims' support, the plea agreement included a six-month sentence in jail followed by five years probation. The probation included the following stringent conditions: (1) he must live in a specially constructed trailer in the middle of a field; (2) he must wear an electronic monitoring device for five years; (3) he must remain in his house except with permission granted one week in advance; (4) he must not be allowed within 50 feet of any child; (5) he must not possess any photos of children, even his grandchildren; (6) he must not have a camera or videotape equipment. To enforce these orders, he must allow probation officials to search him or his house at any time without prior notice. If he violates any of the above, he will be prosecuted as a felon and sentenced to state prison in lieu of the misdemeanor sentence imposed.

At the time of sentencing, some people protested the sentence as too lenient. The protest did not include any of the victims or their families. The boys did not want to testify at trial. The prosecutor described the sentence as safer than a longer jail sentence, noting the defendant's fear of further incarceration. The public defender praised the sentence as fair, noting it also included counseling for the offender, to "get a sick person help . . . (and) . . . at the same time, it absolutely minimizes any risk to the community." The prosecutor also explained that any alternative to the plea would mean a trial that required the victims to testify against their will. "Think about it," he said. " You're a 13- or 14-year-old boy—or even a 17-year-old boy— and you're going to take the stand to testify about these things before the only community you've known."[22]

§4.05   —Analysis of Sexual Assault Alternative Sentences

Again, the common components of alternative sentences are evident. Restitution was imposed in both the Litteer and Sullivan cases. Similarly, in each case the restitution went beyond out-of-pocket loss, and aimed at helping the victims overcome the emotional trauma caused by the crimes committed against them. The Oregon appellate court, which has gone further than most, ruled that although the restitution in such cases was "exceedingly difficult" to determine, the court could consider the mental anguish such crimes caused in making such orders.

In addition to monetary restitution to the crime victims, Litteer was ordered to perform 1,000 hours of community work service. Both the cash restitution and the hours of community work service form the retributive component of the alternative sentences.

Three cases illustrate a reformative component of alternative sentences. Litteer and Bateman were both ordered to undergo psychological counseling (coupled with specific behavioral conditions), avoid contact with minors and abstain from alcohol and other drugs. More dramatically, Gauntlett was ordered into a controversial behavior-modifying drug treatment program. The judge's intent, if not his understanding of the law, was clear. He ordered that if the defendant could not complete the chemical castration regime, he was to serve his full sentence in prison. In other words, the judge sought to incapacitate the man's sex drive, releasing the rest of him to go about his business. Although the use of Depo-Provera remains severely restricted in this country, mandatory treatment orders, including the use of behavior-controlling drugs, are becoming increasingly common in alternative sentences. Examples, which will be presented later, include ordering drug addicts to take methadone; alcohol abusers, disulfiram (commonly known as anabuse or antabuse); and manic depressives, who commit crimes while manic, lithium; and so on.

The Gauntlett and Paster cases provide examples of an incapacitative component of alternative sentencing. Gauntlett and Bateman were ordered to complete a split sentence. In lieu of long-term incarceration in the state's prison, both were ordered to spend a year in the county jail, followed by a probationary period. Paster was ordered confined to his own house for two years. While Litteer was not ordered under house arrest, he was restricted in his movements and activities. The former school committeeman and Boy Scout leader was barred from pursuing contact with minors during his probation.

The posting of warning signs on Bateman's home and car and the paid advertisements of the New Hampshire fire fighter also served to isolate these offenders and restrict their contact with unwary children. Similarly, the day care center operator was required to tell all women he met who had children, of his prior criminal past. This too will act to protect their unwary children.

Similarly, the requirement that the sex offender in upstate New York be confined to a trailer in the middle of a field, monitored by an electronic device, with probation offficers authorized to search him and his trailer at any time without a warrant and an informed citizenry on the lookout, also minimizes the offender's risk of abusing more victims.

These sentences for sex offenders also demonstrate other trends and measures involved in alternative, intermediate and probationary sentences. First, the signs, advertisements and oral warnings, monitored by probation officers, add elements of shame and humiliation to the sentences, reminiscent of the colonial pillory and practice of branding offenders. Resurrected in the 1980s, sentences such as these contemplated the now national movement to require sex offenders to register once they are released from incarceration (as will be discussed in Chapter 8). Massachusetts was one of the few states without such a register for sex offenders at the time of the sentencing of the day care operator. As a result, Judge Gershengorn's order was the only vehicle available to alert future victims as to his perhaps risky presence in the community, once released.

Second, the sentence in upstate New York not only required the offender to make a cash donation to a community charity for sex abuse victims and perform 300 hours of community service, but to meet with a citizen panel to help fashion his sentence. Such citizen panels are designed to allow for community participation in sentencing, especially because the offender will return to that community after any sentence. Equally important, they confront the offender with the impact of his crime on the community. In this case, the crime also had specific victims. But in some crimes there may be no such specific victims— only the community is victimized. Citizen panels for these crimes can include, for example, representatives of Mothers Against Drunk Drivers to confront drunk drivers even where no injury resulted from their drunken driving, parents of children killed by drug abuse for offenders convicted of possession and sale of drugs, parents of murdered children for offenders convicted of possession of firearms, and so on.

Finally, financial sanctions were contained in the orders of restitution imposed in the Litteer case to pay the costs of his victims' counseling and in the Sullivan case to pay the victim $3,000. In addition, Gauntlett was orderd to pay courts costs of $25,000 and Cox agreed to make a $1,000 donation for sex abuse victim treatment as well as perform 300 hours of community service. The school founder was ordered to make a $50,000 contribution to charity.

§4.06   Assault and Battery Alternative Sentences

According to 1993 statistics, 439,300 persons convicted of aggravated assault and almost one million convicted of lesser assaults were imprisoned throughout the country. Following are examples of such crimes and resulting sentences that did not contribute to the above numbers.[23]

Case #1 (Pennsylvania, 1979): Walton shoots rival for common law wife's affections, blinding him.

Achelohiym Walton shot Mancey Hamm with a shotgun, blinding him for life. The fight arose over Walton's former common law wife and mother of his children. In the early hours Walton surprised Hamm, who was with Walton's wife. He brought a shotgun and used it. Convicted of aggravated assault, recklessly endangering another person and two weapons offenses, probation officials recommended long-term incarceration. Circuit Court Judge Lois Forer, a national leader in the sentencing reform movement and author of *Criminals and Victims*, stated what she was trying to accomplish in rejecting this course of action:

> I would prefer to have him do something to make some slight atonement for society for the terrible wrong that he has done. The only thing I can think of having him do is to work and make some payment to Mr. Hamm other than sitting in jail and being an expense to the public.[24]

After ascertaining Walton's spotty work record, the Judge sentenced him to 19 years probation by sentencing the counts consecutively. During the course of those 19 years, she ordered him to pay Mr. Hamm $25 a week. Although the weekly contribution was small, the total would eventually add up to almost $25,000.

On appeal, the state's Supreme Court, in an important ruling, upheld the order, allowing restitution to go beyond easily calculated specific damages. The Philadelphia Bar Association's Victim Counseling Service filed an *amicus curiae* brief supporting the original sentence.[25]

Case #2 (New York, 1983): Piscitelli, a police officer, strikes handcuffed prisoner.

Vincent Piscitelli, a 38-year-old New York City police officer, struck a handcuffed prisoner on the head with his night stick in a Brooklyn Station House. State Supreme Court Judge John F. Hayes found him guilty of second degree assault. Instead of sentencing him to seven years in prison, he ordered him jailed weekends for one year.[26]

Case #3 (Arizona, 1977): Garner shoots victim in neck, paralyzing him.

Fred Garner and a group of youths were giving another young man, Everett Deemer, a hard time, yelling at him and generally abusing him. In the course of the abuse, Garner fired an air rifle at him; the bullet lodged in the victim's neck. An inch to either side and the victim would have been killed. Because the bullet could not be removed, Deemer was substantially incapacitated. Charged with assault with a deadly weapon, amended by agreement to aggravated battery, the defendant was found guilty.

The record presented by an insurance company to the court documented victim expenses of $2,600 which covered his medical bills. In its presentence report, the probation department recommended that the insurance company be reimbursed $1,800. The defendant had reported monthly earnings of $500. The Superior Court Judge placed Garner on probation for five years and ordered him to pay his victim $125 a month until a total of $6,000 was paid.

This also was appealed. Subsequently upheld, this case has become a leading case both in Arizona and around the country, as will be discussed in a later chapter.[27]

Case #4 (Massachusetts, 1990): Michael W., twice jailed, slices former companion's ear off with a broken beer bottle during a fight.

Twenty-one-year-old Michael W. was charged with assault and battery with a dangerous weapon, to wit, a beer bottle, a felony punishable in the District Court by up to two and one-half years in the house of correction. No stranger to court, having been incarcerated twice before, Michael readily admitted his guilt. During a double date, he had become jealous of the other fellow's attentions to his date. A fight erupted and Michael ended up attacking his companion with the beer bottle, broken earlier during the melee. The other man had to have 40 stitches. Michael had to have six to patch up his knee, having also been cut during the fight from the same beer bottle shards.

Despite his long prior record, this time he had managed to remain arrest-free since his last release from jail, 10 months earlier—a personal longevity record. The probation department reported to the court that Michael had maintained steady employment as an auto mechanic for more than six months. Further, he was apparently using his earnings to support his mother and younger siblings (there being no father in the picture). The victim, his former friend, was not anxious to see Michael in jail; however, he was anxious to receive reimbursement for the gap between his insurance and the plastic surgery costs for his ear, $1,000.

The Judge, Albert L. Kramer, a national alternative sentencing advocate, sentenced Michael to the house of correction for 18 months, but suspended that sentence for two years. The price for the suspension was weekly restitution payments of $60 and a total of 50 hours of community work service to be performed each and every Saturday until completed. Because he had already been on probation numerous times, the judge did not require him to see a probation officer. The probation department, however, was assigned the task of monitoring the weekly payments and performance of community work service (the latter assigned at a skating rink). By monitoring these conditions, the probation officer actually could maintain a tighter rein on the defendant than weekly office visitation, which is Massachusetts' most stringent mandated probation supervision.[28]

Case #5 (Oregon, 1991): Man with AIDS sentenced to refrain from sex after attack.

Alberto Gonzalez, sentenced for giving a woman AIDS after learning he had it himself, was ordered to six months house arrest. In addition, he was required to have no sexual contact with anyone during his five-year probationary period. He is believed to be the first man sentenced in Oregon for knowingly spreading AIDS.[29]

Case #6 (California, 1991): Norplant ordered for mother who beat children with belt.

Shortly after coming onto the market, Tulare County Superior Court Judge Howard Broadman, in Visalia, California, sentenced a woman convicted of beating her children with a belt to have a Nor-Plant device implanted in her for three years. Darlene Johnson, 27, a pregnant mother of four, was also sentenced to one year in jail and three years on probation. At the time, although she agreed to the condition, the defendant did not understand that the Norplant had to be surgically placed in her arm, her lawyer later revealed.[30]

The judge refused to rescind his order when the defense later asked the judge to change the NorPlant condition.[31]

§4.07   —Analysis of Assault and Battery Alternative Sentences

Similar to the previous cases, judges achieved their various sentencing goals in these assault and battery cases relying on the imposition of restitution to achieve reparation and weekend sentences to achieve incapacitation. In responding to the victim's needs, the courts carefully considered the earnings and ability of the defendants to pay. Although Walton will eventually pay almost $25,000 to his victim, the order was set at only $25 a week to insure that this marginally employed defendant could make the order each week. In the Garner and Michael W. cases, where the defendants' earnings were greater, the court ordered them to pay in monthly installments to insure that they could eventually come up with the full restitution orders. As these cases illustrate, alternative sentences, even those built around restitution orders, need not be confined to rich, white-collar defendants.

In the case of the New York police officer, the court was not concerned with the victim. Instead, the court incapacitated the defendant by imposing weekend sentences. By sentencing the police officer to jail, he would lose his position as a police officer. By sentencing him to weekends, not only did the court save the city money, but took into account the special dangers the former police officer would face mingling with the regular inmate population during the week. Offenders sentenced to weekends are usually segregated from more permanent residents.

Finally, in the last two cases, the court sought to incapacitate the offenders' criminogenic behaviors. The AIDS giver was ordered to refrain from sex and the pregnant child beater was ordered to refrain from having children by having Norplant implanted. While on probation, at least, if they obey their probationary conditions, the public will be protected.

§4.08   Arson Alternative Sentences

Although figures are not readily available for the number or percentage of incarcerated convicted arsonists, arson is an extremely serious crime. It is responsible for billions of dollars worth of property damage every year, not to mention personal injuries and deaths. Following are a variety of examples in which judges, despite the seriousness of this crime, imposed alternative sentences.

Case #1 (Massachusetts, 1981): Three youths set municipal ice skating rink on fire, causing $20,000 in damages.

A trio of teens broke into a municipal skating rink, just closed for the season. Once in, they tried unsuccessfully to fry a frozen pizza stolen from the concession stand, stole $17 from a cash box, drove the Zamboni machine until the huge ice tender had ingested yards of rubber matting and refused to go further and, finally, set fire to an oil drum whose oily smoke caked the ceiling with soot. Subsequently apprehended, the youths admitted having been well-lubricated with beer and valium chasers.

They were charged with larceny, wanton destruction of property (two counts) and arson, later reduced to willful burning in order to keep the case in the lower court. Rink officials put the damages at $20,000, the majority being for repainting the entire ceiling before the rink was to be reopened in the autumn. Serendipitously filmed for *60 Minutes,* the CBS cameras recorded the three rather grim-faced youths being sentenced by Quincy, Massachusetts Judge, Albert L. Kramer. In exchange for two suspended sentences of two years, imposed consecutively, the trio agreed to work for the next 14 weeks, five days a week, eight hours a day, repairing the damages they caused in the rink. In addition, they had to attend alcohol treatment as determined by the probation department.

All summer long the youths toiled at the rink under the direction of the ice rink officials and the supervision of the probation department. One's unexcused absences from his alcohol treatment program, which included weekly attendance at Alcoholics Anonymous meetings, resulted in his incarceration after a probation revocation hearing. The other two completed their work order and the rink reopened on time the following fall.[32]

Case #2 (Pennsylvania, 1972): Drunken Adeline sets landlady's apartment on fire.

Adeline, drunk, took revenge on her boyfriend who had previously knocked out her tooth. Soaking his sleeping body with kerosene, she set him on fire. Awaking none too soon, he managed to jump through a closed window to escape the flames, landing safely on the grass below. However, the top two floors of the apartment house were destroyed. The landlady could not afford to repair the house and lacked the wherewithal to sue—not that Adeline, an unemployed welfare recipient, had any resources anyway.

By the time Adeline appeared before Circuit Court Judge Lois Forer, she was not only reconciled with her boyfriend, but was engaged to be married. After a finding of guilt, a probation presentence report recommended probation with mandatory alcohol counseling. Judge Forer included restitution to the landlady in the sentence. With the help of her new husband, the restitution was paid and Adeline got a job to repay him. As a result, she was dropped from public assistance for the first time in her adult life.[33]

Case #3 (Georgia, 1983): McGill burns down future home to avoid leaving area of video arcade.

Eric McGill, an 18-year-old dropout, did not want to move. He especially did not want to leave the local video arcade where he spent all his time playing Pac Man. When his Aunt and Uncle put the family home up for sale, he hailed a cab to the new home and burned it down. Apparently he had burned another new home before. No one was hurt in either blaze.

Superior Court Judge Ben J. Miller placed him on probation, ordered him to pay for the damages he caused and banned him from playing video games for the course of his probation. In addition, he was ordered into counseling at the mental health center.[34]

Case #4 (Virginia, 1979): Three students burn down $4.5 million dollars worth of their high school.

Three youths, two aged 18 and one aged 19, lit a match one night and burned $4.5 million worth of their Fairfax City high school. All three were intoxicated at the time. Realizing that his clients faced substantial jail time, the defense attorney procured the services of the National Center for Institutions and Alternatives.

County Circuit Court Judge Lewis Griffith agreed with the defense. In lieu of jail, he sentenced all three, upon their admission of guilt, to pay $10,000 restitution each, at the rate of $1,000 a year. Also, each was ordered to complete 3,000 hours of community work service, the first at a group home for severely retarded, the second at a shelter house run by Catholic Charities, and the third at a Catholic

Youth Organization in the District of Columbia. All three, finally, were ordered to attend an alcohol abuse program monitored by the probation department.[35]

§4.09   —Analysis of Arson Alternative Sentences

These examples contain a few new alternative sentencing components worthy of special note. The skating rink trio were ordered to perform community work service like others, but they were ordered to repair the very damages they caused. This form of community work service is called "victim service" or "direct victim service." It is a common reparative component of alternative sentencing. Such orders are particularly appropriate where the defendants do not have the means to reimburse their victims monetarily. In this case, all three of the defendants together could not have paid for the rink's repair. They were, however, able to do the repair work substantially themselves, saving the taxpayers thousands of dollars.

The restitution order in the Fairfax high school case was only partial, approximately $4,470,000 short of the actual damages. Given the large amount, the court came up with what is known as a "symbolic" restitution order. For teenagers, however, $1,000 a year for three years may very well seem like a million. The youths were also ordered community work service to make up the difference. *The Washington Post*, praised the sentence:

> The aspect of the sentence that imposes a burden on the three arsonists seems reasonable and routine enough. The special aspect is the one that acknowledges their debt to and their continuing link with the community. . . . It is right that the treatment should recognize this link between perpetrator and community and should involve some actual as well as symbolic restoration of benefit to the community. This sentence addresses precisely the element of belonging the arsonists had abused.[36]

Finally, in all of the above cases, various forms of mandatory treatment were ordered, including alcohol counseling and mental health counseling. That the courts were serious about this aspect of the cases was demonstrated in the case of one of the ice skating rink arsonists. His failure to attend his AA meetings led to his being prosecuted by the probation department for violating the court order and his subsequent incarceration. While the order of restitution imposed against Adeline addressed reparation, it also forced Adeline to get a job. As a result, the restitution order ended up assisting in the defendant's rehabilitation. This provides another example of how one alternative sentencing component can address several different sentencing goals.

§4.10   Robbery, Burglary and Theft Alternative Sentences

According to 1993 statistics, 124,600 robbers, 264,600 burglars and more than one million thieves were imprisoned throughout the country.[37] Many, including the following, were not.

Case #1 (Indiana, 1978): Vietnam vet Palmer burglarizes a dozen homes.

Harry Fred Palmer, a Vietnam veteran, returning to Elkhart, Indiana, committed a dozen first degree home burglaries. By state law, Palmer should have received a minimum sentence of no less than 10 years in a state prison. However, Superior Court Judge William Bontrager suspended all but nine and one-half of them for five years, claiming his intention to give the defendant "a solid dose of maximum security and then bring him back while there was still time to work with him."

After seven months, Palmer was released on the condition that he meet with his 12 victims and make restitution satisfactory to them. The judge expressed his belief that rehabilitation without atonement was meaningless. Palmer's probation officer referred him to the Elkhart Victim Offender Reconciliation Program (VORP) which arranged the meetings. The restitution contracts included direct cash payments as well as victim services, including Palmer splitting one victim's family winter wood supply. Palmer convinced his former employers from whom he had stolen to rehire him so he could earn the money to repay them and other victims.

One victim was so impressed with Palmer's turnaround that he became a board member of Elkhart's VORP. He was Elkhart's Deputy Sheriff. Nonetheless, the prosecutor appealed Palmer's sentence and Palmer was resentenced, three years later, to the state prison for the remaining nine and one-half years. Palmer's former victims organized to press the Governor for clemency which was finally granted in 1982 on condition that Palmer complete an additional six months at a community-based work release center.[38]

Case #2 (Massachusetts, 1981): Bill B. breaks and enters homes of three elderly couples.

Already on probation for the attempted larceny of a motor vehicle, Bill B. was charged with five new separate misdemeanors, including two breaking and enterings in the nighttime with intent to commit felonies, burglary and possession of burglar's tools. The case had begun at 3:30 A.M. with an anonymous call to the Milton police, reporting several suspicious persons lurking about the upper middle class neighborhood. The police tracked Bill's footprints in the snow from the broken window of one house to another house where he and a codefendant were apprehended red-handed. Later Bill skipped bail and was incarcerated in Indiana for suspicion of breaking into a pizza parlor. He was released without trial after promising to return to Massachusetts, which he did.

In court, Bill finally admitted his guilt but introduced to the court his new employer, ironically, a former Boston police officer. The man now ran a security company and Bill had apparently begged him for a job as a parking lot attendant so that he could be employed when he faced sentencing. The employer related to the court how Bill had been the only person to show up after a particularly bad snow storm so he had hired him. Bill had been completely candid with the employer about his past and pending charges.

Although impressed, the court was still loath to release a man with such a record, despite his current enrollment in the workforce. District Court Judge Albert L. Kramer continued the case, inviting all three victims in his chambers, as well as the defendant's lawyer and his employer. He had the employer repeat the story to the three elderly couples who had not attended the original court hearing. Then he questioned each couple as to their losses. In the first two homes where the defendant had gained entry, losses were considerable, including broken windows, pried open chests, soiled carpets and missing jewelry. The third victim sustained no losses. Calculating repair and replacement costs, plus the time the victims spent in court and with the police, the judge set the damages at $700 for the first two sets of victims and $400 for the third.

The judge explained that he could not order both straight imprisonment and restitution, and even if he ordered restitution, the defendant would not be able to pay it immediately. Rather he would pay in small weekly installments out of his earnings at the parking lot. In addition, the judge said he would order, with the victims' and the defendant's consent, 21 days of community work service to be performed weekends to keep the defendant occupied seven days a week. The judge then committed the defendant to jail for several weekends for violating his existing probation. Whether he should then add a straight sentence of a year or so he left open to the victims. The three elderly couples opted for the alternative sentence, although one admitted later they really did not believe it would happen as the judge had outlined.[39]

Case #3 (Massachusetts, 1982): Fred C., former West Point cadet, steals mowing tractor.

Fred C., expelled from the United States Military Academy at West Point for violating the honor code for possessing a popcorn popper, was subsequently convicted and imprisoned for holding up a number of gas stations with shotguns. Fred served three years, mostly in solitary confinement for his own protection because the other inmates suspected him of being a snitch. Released, he established a lawn and gardening company which, unfortunately, he later equipped with a mowing tractor he stole from another company. The irate victim, discovering his tractor missing, had his employees track it down, printing and disseminating $200 worth of reward posters in the process. Eventually discovering it, they called the police who arrested Fred.

The judge sentenced Fred C. to a lengthy suspended sentence and ordered him to pay $1,090 to the victim, $625 immediately, the rest on an installment plan. In addition, Fred and his company were ordered to perform 200 hours of community work service in landscaping services. Not only did Fred receive no compensation for his work, but he had to pay his employees out of his own pocket.[40]

Case #4 (Oregon, 1986): Burglar apologizes in print and warns the public to pay heed.

"I, Tom Kirby," the *Newport News-Time* newspaper ad ran, "wish to apologize to the people of the City of Newport for all the problems I have caused. I know now what I did was selfish and wrong. I also realize that I have caused a lot of hardships on people that were my friends." Accompanying the ad was a mug shot of the defendant wearing a Mickey Mouse t-shirt. In bold print, the ad included the message: "Thomas E. Kirby was convicted of burglary first degree for burglarizing a residence in South Beach, Oregon on October 25, 1985. He has previously been convicted of burglary in Portland. He was placed on probation to the corrections division on March 7, 1986 and ordered to make restitution, pay a fine, perform community service and place this ad in the Newport News-Times apologizing for his conduct. At the time of his arrest, he was in a residence on Sam Creek Road in the Toledo/Newport area. Prior to this, he resided in Waldport."

In a box at the bottom of the ad, labeled Crime Stoppers Tip, was the following: "As the jails and penitentiaries fill up and as criminals remain in the community, be aware of which of your neighbors poses a threat to you and your family. Don't hesitate to call a person's probation officer or the police if you observe any suspicious activity on their part. Be aware of who has been convicted of crimes and who may be committing crimes in your neighborhood."

The total cost of the ad was $89.12. The Lincoln County District Attorney, Ulys Stapleton, defended the ads. "They're something," he explained, "a guy's mom's going to see. They let good old small town values break through the impersonality of sentencing." The idea for the ads originated with probation officer Carl Reddick.[41]

Case #5 (Massachusetts, 1992): House arrest and restitution ordered for thefts.

A hidden surveillance camera captured an employee of the Department of Transportation stealing a government computer, stuffing it in his duffel bag. A subsequent search of his house revealed that Richard Gridale, 39, had stolen other government property.

Pleading guilty to one count of theft, U.S. District Judge Mark Wolf sentenced him to three years probation with four months of home detention. He was also ordered to pay $2,772 in restitution to the Department of Transportation.[42]

Case #6 (Minnesota, 1995): Thief faces town from which she stole.

To support a gambling habit, Connie Eischens, 36, stole tens of thousands of dollars from her employer, a liquor store in Renville, Minnesota, population 1,315. She had been manager of the store for five years and spent the money on the slot machines in a state tribal casino. Rather than sentence her to a 10-year prison sentence, she was placed on probation for 10 years with the condition that she enter into mediation sessions with two City Council members, another Renville resident, the City Administrator, a probation officer and a mediator. Commenting on the mediation sessions, the City Administrator commented:

> Initially there was a lot of uneasiness, uncertainty. Some very pointed questions were asked both ways. I believe the mediation process . . . worked as it was supposed to . . . to get beyond that initial hurt and victimization and find someway to ease it all over.

Another participant, chairwoman of the council's Liquor Store Commitee, added:

> You show anger at times. It's still kind of hard to understand how someone could do something like this, (but) I know I have a better understanding of it all. Even if it makes you angry that this happened, she's still a person—you've got to look at it from that side too.

The sessions worked out agreements that the defendant would repay the city the $95,000 she stole at the rate of $9,500 per year for the next 10 years. The town estimated its losses at between $95,000 and $120,000. In addition, she would attend treatment for her gambling addiction and stay out of casinos. She would write a letter of apology to the town and do community work service.

The defendant, who had graduated from the local high school and was a church organist in the town, remarked that the mediation had been very difficult but allowed her to, in her words, "kind of get her life back to normal." The panel decided that she would not do her community service in Renville so that she could get on with her life. Concluded one participant:

> The way she responded, it was not an easy thing for her to go through, and I think if she wasn't remorseful, she wouldn't put herself through that.[43]

§4.11 —Analysis of Robbery, Burglary and Theft Alternative Sentences

These alternative sentences basically repeat earlier themes, but with a few interesting twists.

In the Bill B. case, the judge invited the victims to help him decide whether to impose an alternative sentence. This is another example of victims playing a more active role in alternative sentences. The victim's endorsement of the alternative sentence may have been influenced by the restitution order offered. The order itself went beyond strict out-of-pocket losses to include other kinds of expenses faced by the victims, including missed work and lost leisure time. In such a manner, even the elderly couple whose home was untouched received $400 in restitution.

Fred C. was ordered to perform community work service that took advantage of his particular skills and resources, namely of the fact that he ran a landscaping company. The probation department arranged that he work for the Weymouth Garden Club, which had him and his crew clean up the Abigail Adams Village Green, site of the first lady's birthplace. As the following letter received by the court testifies, the community work service order proved popular in the community:

> Mr. C., with his men, arrived at 8:30 A.M. and reported to the wrong location. They went to the Weymouth North Cemetery and when they did not find me went to work on shrubs that the town lacked funds to attend to. We finally made connections and he and his men moved to the Abigail Adams Green where I hoped a minimum amount of work could be accomplished. We discussed the jobs that needed attention and I had to leave for another commitment. At 7:00 P.M., I swung by to see what had been done to find him still at work. A visit this morning revealed a park in the best shape it has been since being completed. Shrubs are trimmed, walks cleared, gardens turned; bushes planted and all rubbish carted off. . . . Mr. C. was the most conscientious and cooperative person we have ever had. I do not know if it is possible but would like to recommend that he be given extra credit for time worked due to the exceedingly fine, cheerful job he did.[44]

Although involving more direct victims, Fred Palmer's victims also demonstrated their enthusiasm for their offender's alternative sentence. They lobbied the Governor for his early release after he was reimprisoned when the original sentencing judge's decision had been overturned by the state's highest court. As one of his victims freely confessed to the Governor, before he had met Fred and watched him work, "At first, I wished that I had been home (during the robbery) so that I could have shot him. It's just as simple as that."[45] For his part, Fred admitted that his meetings with his victims were not easy. "When I faced my victims it scared the living daylights out of me and it hurt. I done wrong."[46]

Both Palmer and the original sentencing judge, William Bontrager, were deeply affected by the case. Palmer became a member of a local church group and later, in prison, clerked for the prison chaplain and became involved in the Prison Fellowship ministry, founded by former Watergate conspirator Chuck Colson. Upon being overruled, Bontrager gave up his judgeship and set up a Christian mediation service within Elkhart. He later worked with the Christian Legal Society in Minnesota, and did consulting work for the Prison Fellowship.

The Kirby alternative sentence sought to make him apologize to the whole community for his misdeeds by taking out an ad in the local paper. Like the Bateman alternative sentence for child molestation, the sentence publicly labeled the defendant as a criminal, both as a form of public atonement and as a means to assist the public in protecting itself from future criminal violations by the defendant. The sentence also sought to punish the defendant through public humiliation in an ad even his "mom" might see.

Finally, almost the entire town of Renville, Minnesota was involved in holding Connie Eischens accountable for her crime. By requiring her to mediate her disposition with representatives of the town, her theft moved from coffee shop talk to face-to-face discussions. The whole town, in effect, not only made sure she would make up for her crime through restitution and work service, but helped restore its stability that was disturbed and threatened by her five years of theft from the liquor store. The process of mediation enabled the court to fashion a unique, effective and restorative sentence for the victimized town and the offender.

§4.12   Drug Offenses and Drunk Driving Alternative Sentences

According to 1993 statistics, slightly over one million drug offenders and more than 1.5 million drunk drivers were imprisoned throughout the country.[47] While those imprisoned for drug offenses has increased 1,156 percent since 1980, the following were not among them.

Case #1 (Massachusetts, 1981): Krutschewski imports 57,000 pounds of pot into Massachusetts.

It took Krutschewski and his colleagues six and one-half months to set up the deal to import $14 million worth of marijuana from Colombia. The crime was well-organized, involving Colombian drug brokers, a 20-man crew to ship the drugs, four smaller boats to off-load it, rental vans to deliver it on land and rental of several safe houses, including the famous Gloucester Glass House overlooking Folly Cove. Peter Krutschewski directed the off-loading with a walkie-talkie with military precision. In fact, as a Vietnam combat pilot he had won 55 medals, including two Bronze Stars, and two Distinguished Flying Crosses. Unlike the majority of pilots who completed the Army training with him, he had survived the war. Since the war he reported being addicted to danger.

Krutschewski pocketed half a million dollars and celebrated in Las Vegas where he proceeded to lose, then gain back, his fortune. (He has the ability to count cards.) He paid his gambling taxes, but six years later was apprehended for his role in the drug importation. In the interim, he turned legitimate, establishing an oil company that eventually struck oil in the lower peninsula in Michigan. Appearing before the Federal District Court in Massachusetts, he could claim to be a well-respected businessman, with a wife and daughter. Judge Walter Skinner, reviewing his past six years, expressed doubt that the incarceration the U.S. Attorney asked for would do much for the defendant. "I don't for a minute believe that incarceration will rehabilitate Mr. Krutschewski or that he needs it."[48] But the judge did not want him to profit from the crime either. He asked the defense to present him with an alternative sentence.

The defense came up with one. As the defendant's share of the oil company, originally derived from his ill-gotten gains, was $1.75 million, Krutschewski offered to give it back. He would donate it to a court-authorized drug program in yearly installments of $300,000. Explained the defendant, "I'm a homebody. All I want to do is come home at night to my wife and kid, and watch the news on television like everybody else."[49] He also offered to do 30 hours of community service with mental patients each week for four years.

Reminding a skeptical prosecution that, among others, the American Bar Association recommended alternative sentencing and that such sentences should not be restricted to "a little old lady who shoots migratory birds out of season," the judge pondered his sentence for several days. Finally, he rejected the defense offer and sentenced Krutschewski to 10 years in federal prison, which with parole became a minimal sentence of three years. He also ordered a $60,000 fine. "I conclude," he announced, "that the general deterrence effect of the suggested alternative disposition is not sufficiently strong." The judge also expressed concern over the speculative nature of the cash donation; it did not have "the element of certainty desirable in criminal disposition."[50] Krutschewski was imprisoned. Two months later, the judge modified the sentence, making

Krutschewski eligible for immediate parole and suggesting that the United States Parole Board should establish a national policy of leniency for imprisoned veterans traumatized by their combat experience. A Washington lawyer representing Vietnam veterans hailed Judge Skinner's action as a "step forward in clarifying . . . the obligation of the government to consider how extensively it should punish."[51]

Case #2 (Massachusetts, 1986): Peter F. possesses cocaine with intent to distribute.

Following an undercover operation, the narcotics squad of the District Attorney's office apprehended Peter F. in possession of a sufficient quantity of cocaine to charge him with possession with intent to distribute. Scheduled to appear before the lower court for a probable cause hearing, Peter's lawyer made a deal to plead if the prosecution reduced the charge to a misdemeanor possession charge. The defendant agreed to forfeit his new Trans Am and provide testimony against others. The prosecution accepted the deal as did Massachusetts Judge Lewis Whitman, conditioned upon a presentence report to be completed by the probation department.

In addition to the deal as set out, the court placed the defendant on a two-year suspended sentence with certain stipulations. First, the defendant must enroll and complete a 28-day inpatient drug treatment program, beginning with complete detoxification. Second, he must enter an outpatient weekly counseling program supplemented by attendance at two Narcotics Anonymous meetings per week for the course of his one-year probation. To insure drug abstinence, the defendant was also ordered to submit to periodic urine analysis arranged by the probation department. Shortly thereafter the defendant entered inpatient drug treatment and police narcotics agents began driving their new Trans Am for undercover work.[52]

Case #3 (California, 1981): Rathburn, grandmother, busted for selling pot.

Ms. Rathburn, a.k.a. Brownie Mary, a 64-year-old grandmother, baked and sold marijuana brownies out of her San Francisco kitchen. The prosecutor revealed that Brownie Mary's business retailed from $500,000 to $1 million per year. Superior Court Judge Thomas Dandurand placed her on probation and ordered her to perform 500 hours of community work service, baking for the Salvation Army soup kitchen.[53]

Case #4 (New York, 1987): Drunk driver must install breathtester in car.

Before James Donaldson can start his Oldsmobile Delta 88, he has to blow in a predetermined sequence into a device that analyzes his breath for alcohol. Only when the device determines his sobriety will the car's ignition engage. Sentenced for repeat drunk driving offenses, Mr. Donaldson was placed on three years probation and ordered to install the ignition interlock device in his car.

At least two manufacturers are currently marketing similar devices, which are now specifically authorized by legislation in six states.

Judge Michelle M. Morehouse from Oswego County, New York, ordered the device in lieu of license revocation or incarceration so that the defendant could attend court-ordered alcohol treatment. The defendant's wife did not drive and there was no public transit in the defendant's small town, 15 miles east of Lake Ontario. The defendant needed his car to travel to the VA hospital in Syracuse for medication. The cost of the device was reported to be $500 a year.[54]

Case #5 (Florida, 1986): Drunk driver's car must sport bumper sticker warning other motorists.

A Florida court routinely requires convicted drunk drivers to place a bumper sticker on their cars that reads: "Convicted D.U.I.—Restricted License." The Florida appellate court has upheld this condition.[55] Other family members were allowed to attach a Velcro strip over the sticker when they drove the car.

Case #6 (Oregon, 1985): Second offender drunk drivers sentenced to skid row.

Noting that jail cells in the state were as "precious as platinum," Multnomah County Judge Frank L. Bearden developed an alternative to the 48-hour jail sentence routinely handed down to repeat drunk drivers. Instead, he sentences them to probation for the same two-day period. But they spend their days on skid row, living and working with street alcoholics, doing service work in missions and eating in soup kitchens. For this privilege they must pay $80.[56]

Case #7 (Tennessee, 1985): Drunk driver ordered to forfeit car.

Arrested as a third offender drunk driver and for carrying a gun and resisting arrest, Sonny Bouldin eventually plead to first offense drunk driving. He was sentenced by Judge Charles Hastings of Warren County to 11 months and 29 days in jail to be served and fined $250. After six months, however, his sentence was suspended with two conditions. First, he was to attend AA weekly. Second, he was to forfeit his 1984 Cadillac during the period his license was revoked, which was two years. The judge ordered the car to be held in storage by the local police.

On appeal, the appellate court opined:

> At a time when our correctional facilities are literally bursting at the seams with inmates and, when, under mandate of federal courts, the legislative and executive branches of our government are wrestling with the problems of prison overcrowding and idleness in those facilities, it certainly behooves state trial judges to do what they can to alleviate the overcrowding. One way the third branch of government can do its part is by fashioning imaginative and innovative conditions of probation to allow eligible defendants the opportunity to serve the sentences "outside the walls," rather than needlessly confine nonviolent offenders. Innovative conditions of probation which are not "out of harmony" with the tone and tenor of our probation laws nor are "arbitrary," "capricious" or "palpably abusive of [the court's] discretion" and which meet the requirements of the ABA Standards should be employed and should withstand the scrutiny of appellate review.[57]

Case #8 (Florida, 1992): Drunk drivers ordered to copy obituaries of drunk driving victims.

Monroe County Judge William Ptomey requires drunk drivers convicted in his court to submit handwritten obituaries of the 27 children and adults who died in a fiery 1988 school bus crash in Kentucky. Each offender must obtain the list of obituaries and transcribe them for the court.

"You know, you have got to have a heart of stone to read that and not be moved by it. That was the effect it had on me, and I thought it would be a good thing to make persons guilty of drunk driving read what I had just read," commented the judge.[58]

Case #9 (Illinois, 1992): Leon Spinks, drunk driver, must attend Victim Impact Panel.

Leon Spinks, former Olympic gold medalist and heavyweight boxer, was convicted in DuPage County for his second drunk driving charge. He caused three vehicles to crash. He had no license and a blood-alcohol level of twice the legal limit in Illinois. He was placed on probation for two years, ordered to perform 40 hours of community work service and to attend a Victim Impact Panel.

§4.13   —Analysis of Drug Offenses and Drunk Driving Alternative Sentences

Two of these cases again illustrate incapacitative components of alternative sentencing. One employs an alternative use of incarceration and the other an alternative facility to incapacitate the offender.

Judge Skinner, in rejecting the alternative sentence promoted by the Krutschewski defense, created another. In lieu of long-term incarceration, the original sentence of 10 years, he created a "shock sentence," first sentencing Krutschewski to long-term incarceration, then revising it two months later to time served. Originally developed by Ohio jurists, the shock sentence is designed to provide the same deterrent impact of traditional sentencing by giving the defendant a taste of jail, but sparing him (and the taxpayers) the full course. Before his sentence was revised, the defendant had several months to realize that even his money could not buy his way out of jail. His period of incapacitation was short but deemed sufficient by the court, given his background and law-abiding behavior over the previous six years.

Peter F. presented a different background. He was drug-addicted. The court sought to incapacitate him until he detoxified. It did so, not with jail but with inpatient treatment to be paid for by the defendant. Then the court sought to keep his drug habit "imprisoned" by imposing stringent weekly counseling and NA attendance while monitoring urine tests to insure his being drug-free. The court gambled that as long as the defendant remained drug-free, he would remain crime-free. Use of Narcotics Anonymous or its equivalent for alcohol abusers, Alcoholics Anonymous, is a common element of alternative sentences containing a rehabilitative component.

Finally, both cases demonstrate how monetary sanctions may form a substantial part of alternative sentences. Krutschewski was ordered to pay a $60,000 fine and Peter F. was ordered to forfeit his Trans Am, valued in excess of $15,000.

The first example of drunk driving alternative sentences introduces modern computer technology to sentencing. The interlock device, which prevents a car from being started by a driver with alcohol on his breath, seeks to prevent the probationer from repeating his crime by altering his immediate environment. The second example uses public labeling, in this case a car bumper sticker, to both humiliate and help prevent offenders from reoffending. The final example illustrates the rehabilitative component of alternative sentencing. The exposure to street alcoholics is meant to serve as an object lesson to the drunk drivers of where their alcohol abuse may lead them.

The last two drunk driving sentences seek to bring the crime home to the offenders who may see the crime of drunk driving as victimless. Vicariously through copying the names of children killed by a drunk driver or meeting with a victim impact panel head-on, the defendants are confronted with the potentially lethal nature of their criminal conduct.

§4.14   Miscellaneous White-Collar Crime Alternative Sentences

According to 1993 statistics, a half-million people were imprisoned for fraud, forgery or embezzlement.[59] Undoubtedly, many other so-called white-collar criminals escaped imprisonment altogether because white-collar criminals traditionally are punished less severely than blue-collar criminals. The following white-collar offenders, however, while escaping long-term incarceration, did not escape meaningful imposition of some sanctions.

Case #1 (Indiana, 1982): Hayes, Vice President, embezzles $1.1 million from firm.

John Hayes embezzled $1.1 million from the firm he served as vice president. The prosecutor asked for the maximum sentence for the 37-year-old who had apparently gambled away most of the money by the time he was apprehended. Judge Margaret Arnow imposed a 10-year term, suspending all but three years. In lieu of jail, however, Mr. Hayes was required to reside in a community-based halfway house and perform community work service for a local gambler's assistance center. In addition, he was ordered to participate in counseling and to maintain employment. Upon release from the halfway house, he was placed on probation for five years and ordered not to gamble.[60]

Case #2 (New York, 1982): Weiss, Assistant Treasurer of Warner Communications, accepts bribes.

Solomon Weiss, Assistant Treasurer of Warner Communications, Inc., was convicted for accepting $170,000 in bribes for inducing Warner to buy 40,000 shares in a New York theater. New York Federal Court Judge Mary Johnson Lowe accepted defense counsel's plea that he receive an alternative sentence. In lieu of jail, he was ordered to complete five years of full-time, unpaid work at the Essex County New Jersey Division of Youth Services. His duties were to include accounting, fundraising and job counseling for unemployed youth. In addition, he was fined the maximum of $58,000 for seven counts of racketeering, fraud and perjury and ordered to forfeit to the government 14,000 shares of his Warner stock, then worth $353,827.[61]

Case #3 (Missouri, 1983): O'Brien, Bank President, misapplies money.

Missouri bank scion, Donald O'Brien, misappropriated funds from his bank to help his failing chicken business. Federal District Court Judge Scott O. Wright allowed O'Brien to donate $90,000 in the form of clothes, food, toys and heat to the 100 most needy families in rural McDonald County in lieu of incarceration.[62]

Case #4 (New York, 1987): Avol, slumlord, violates health, building, and safety code.

Dr. Milton Avol, a neurosurgeon who lives in Beverly Hills, was found to be repeatedly in violation of health, building and safety codes in regard to rat-infested apartments he owned. Finally, Municipal Judge Veronica Simmons McBeth sentenced him to a split sentence, 30 days in jail followed by 30 days suspended. However, she ordered him to spend the 30 remaining days in one of his own one-room apartments. The judge described one typical apartment as having "a torn, filthy mattress and a filthy hot plate . . . no screens on the windows and that's the only ventilation . . . the shower is totally corroded."[63]

Following two years of appeals, Dr. Avol began serving his sentence on June 25, 1987. After spending 15 days in jail, he was released to his preselected apartment. He was ordered to wear an electric monitor attached to his leg so that the probation department would be automatically alerted if he left the apartment in violation of the judge's order. He also had to pay a fine of $1,000 and reimburse the Department of Health another $1,000 for inspecting his apartments.

Dr. Avol told the press the sentence gave him a chance to catch up on his leisure reading.[64] His attorney indicated that the defendant was getting out of the landlord business.[65]

Case #5 (Florida, 1989): Stephen Smith defrauds investors in oil and gas exploration company for $20 million.

Florida Circuit Judge J. Tim Stickland sentenced Stephen L. Smith to a 15-year term and follow-up probation in lieu of a life sentence for defrauding investors of $20 million in his gas and oil exploration company. The judge could have sentenced him to 500 years for the 98 felonies he pled guilty to in March of 1989. Smith, 38, will serve his term in federal prison concurrent with a federal 10-year term imposed for an earlier case of defrauding a bank. In exchange for his plea, the state dropped 164 charges including racketeering and grand theft and security violations. The judge told the victims that he would not sentence more than the 15 years, but would require tough probationary terms. The terms included: (1) limiting his income to $30,000 a year; (2) not possessing personal property over $10,000; (3) not obtaining a loan, mortgage, credit cards or bank accounts; (4) mandatory giving of lectures on business ethics to graduate level business students at all state universities and to students at all Polk County High Schools in each of the 10 years of probation. The defendant was also ordered to appear in shirt sleeves so as not to appear to be a successful businessman; (5) perform 20 hours of community service among the poor each month for the first five years of probation; (6) not to own his own corporation; (7) be barred from consulting work with other businesses; (8) reimburse oil investors $5 million plus 12 percent interest; (9) hand-deliver refunds with a personal apology.

The defense announced it would appeal.[66]

Case # 6 (Minnesota, 1995): Attorney swindles elderly couple's life savings.

Through the transfer of funds to a personal business account and issuing false quarterly investment statements, the attorney, a longtime friend of the elderly couple, stole $250,000. In their mid-80s and in poor health, the victims lived at an extended care nursing home and intended to pay for their living expenses with the vanished trust. The theft forced them to begin to accept welfare.

Chief Judge Kevin Burke of Hennepin County District Court, Minnesota, was faced with a dilemma. He wanted the couple repaid. The prison sentence recommended by the prosecutor would make that impossible. Fearful that a court confrontation would further victimize the elderly couple, the judge went to their nursing home with a court reporter. The wife, the more alert of the two, revealed their greatest upset was being forced on welfare. They had a lot of pride and had always been on their own. Childless, they saved the money to pay for their retirement care. Assuring the couple that they need not hire their own lawyer, the judge promised to assist them. He arranged for a *pro bono* lawyer to assist in settling the offender's previous claim. The offender was involved in a legal case with potential significant economic benefit to him.

The judge sentenced the offender to pay restitution to the victims, to the client security fund after the victims were paid and an additional fine. The sentence also included 10 years probation during which the offender had to perform 200 hours of community service per year at a nursing home operated by the same company that operated the residence in which the victims lived. Said the judge:

> The punitive side of the sentencing is the community service work in the nursing home. I wanted him to see the people who were involved here. . . . At 88, the victim deserved to live the rest of her life with her pride.[67]

§4.15   —Analysis of Miscellaneous White-Collar Crime Alternative Sentences

Although all of the defendants were low-risk, white-collar criminals, none was allowed simply to write out a check for a maximum fine, often less than the ill-gotten gains, and be done with it. Befitting white-collar offenders, the monetary components of the cases tended to be substantial. Warner treasurer Weiss was ordered to forfeit more than $300,000 worth of shares in Warner Communications. In addition, his sentence deprived him of his normal earnings by requiring him to work full-time in an unpaid job for five years and he was assessed a fine of $58,000. Banker O'Brien was ordered to donate $90,000 to charity.

In addition, substantial incapacitation was involved in the alternative sentences, achieved both by alternative uses of prison and through commitments to facilities other than prisons. Vice President Hayes was incapacitated for three years in a halfway house, and was ordered to complete community work service and participate in counseling. While not incapacitated through a split sentence or a halfway house, Warner Assistant Treasurer Weiss was surely incapacitated through his work order, five years of full-time unpaid service at the New Jersey Youth Service Department. Perhaps most uniquely and most fittingly, slumlord Avol was incapacitated in his own slum property following a short split sentence in jail at the county's expense.

While these particular cases do not illustrate as specifically as other examples retributive components of alternative sentences, due to the lack of specific victims, they do present several examples of "community restitution" or community work service. As mentioned, Warner treasurer Weiss was sentenced to five years of such service.

Finally, at least one case also contains an example of a rehabilitative component of alternative sentences. Vice President Hayes, a compulsive gambler, was sentenced both to perform community service work for a local gambler's assistance center and to enter treatment. In addition, he was ordered to refrain from gambling while under court supervision. While the other offenders lacked so readily identifiable a treatment need as Hayes, the various community work service jobs were designed to impress upon them better modes of behavior in the future. Similarly, Dr. Avol's commitment to his own slum property was designed as an object lesson more forceful than any one-on-one counseling session could hope to drive home. Dr. Avol's sentence presents another example of the use of modern technology in alternative sentencing. An electronic monitoring device is attached to the defendant's leg and transmits a signal to a receiver attached to a telephone. If the signal is broken, the phone automatically informs a central computer that the defendant has left the premises. Instead of taking the defendant to jail, the technology takes the jail to the defendant. There are almost a dozen companies marketing these systems.

The alternative sentencing components contained in the sentences handed down against these white-collar defendants are the same as those used in sentences of other defendants. The only differences are found in the more numerous options available to the court in imposing such sentences against white-collar offenders. Given these defendants' backgrounds and work histories, it is easier to place them, whether it is in a community work service site or an alternative living arrangement. It is also easier to monitor them once they are placed. Payment of monies up front, for example, is much easier to monitor than small installment payments made over a number of years.

§4.16   High-Risk, Chronic Offender Alternative Sentences

Many jurisdictions provide special penalties for classes of chronic recidivists. A few impose mandatory life imprisonment for offenders convicted of as few as three separate felonies.[68] Others require four.[69] Some require that at least one of the prior felonies to be violent.[70] Still others give judges or juries discretion to impose a life sentence after three felonies.[71] While not mandating life sentences, the 1984 federal criminal code revision directed the United States Sentencing Commission in setting sentencing standards to "assure . . . a substantial term of imprisonment" for offenders with two or more prior federal, state or local convictions.[72]

In a landmark case, *Rummel v. Estelle,*[73] the United States Supreme Court upheld Texas' statute providing for mandatory life imprisonment with the possibility of parole for offenders convicted of a third felony. The case concerned William Rummel, who was convicted of felony theft for obtaining $120.75 by false pretenses (Mr. Rummel's third felony conviction). He had been convicted of fraudulently using a credit card to obtain $80 worth of goods in 1964 and in 1969 he had been convicted of forging a check for $28.36.

Rummel appealed, claiming the mandatory sentence to be so disproportionate to the crime as to constitute cruel and unusual punishment, proscribed by the Eighth and Fourteenth Amendments to the United States Constitution. The majority of the Court disagreed, ruling that the states had a legitimate interest in "dealing in a harsher manner with those who by repeated criminal acts have shown that they are incapable of conforming to the norms of society as established by its criminal law."[74]

In a similar case three years later, *Solem v. Helm,*[75] the Supreme Court heard a challenge to South Dakota's habitual offender law, which provided for mandatory imprisonment without parole. Abandoning the majority he helped form in the *Rummel* decision, Justice Blackmun joined with the previous dissenters and tipped the Court against South Dakota's law. The life sentence was judged to be disproportionate to the crime. In the instant case, the defendant had uttered a "no account" check for $100. Justice Powell, writing for the majority, took pains to explain that this decision did not overrule *Rummel,* as the Texas law allowed for parole. Nor did the majority suggest that fourth-time offenders may not constitutionally receive a mandatory life sentence if they are "heroin dealers or other violent criminals." In making its decision, the majority also noted that the mandatory life imprisonment ignored the offender's and the state's interest in rehabilitation:

> Helm, who was 36 years old when he was sentenced, is not a professional criminal. The record indicates an addiction to alcohol, and a consequent difficulty in holding a job. His record involves no acts of violence of any kind. Incarcerating him for life without possibility of parole is unlikely to advance the goals of our criminal justice system

in any substantial way. Neither Helm nor the State will have an incentive to pursue clearly needed treatment for his alcohol problem, or any other program of rehabilitation.[76]

Although the Supreme Court has upheld life sentences for certain categories of habitual offenders, given certain safeguards, it did not say that such a sentencing scheme was a very wise use of precious community resources or the only way to protect the state's interests. As the following cases illustrate, alternative sentences can and have been safely imposed for high-risk, chronic recidivists who make Rummel and Helm seem like crime novices. The alternative sentences are specifically tailored to fit these high-risk, low-skill offenders.

Case #1: "Turk" Brock is sentenced in Georgia as a "habitual criminal."

Pictured in a photograph for an article in the now defunct *Corrections Magazine,* Turk Brock appears to be a "good old boy," sporting a baseball cap and toting a baseball bat. But he has an extensive record, most recently having fled the state of Georgia to avoid imprisonment for being a habitual criminal. Returning to the state, he faced the court, presided over by Judge Charles Pannell, Jr. Already on probation for passing 11 bad checks, drunk driving and being a habitual violator, his latest probation infraction could mean three years and seven months in state prison. But the Judge, previously urged to divert inmates from the state's woefully overcrowded prison system, decided to give the state's new intensive probation supervision scheme its supreme test. He gave them Brock.

To abide by the sentence, Brock had to secure employment, pay restitution out of his earnings, do 132 hours of community work service, be home every night by 7:00 P.M. and find an acceptable member of the community to sponsor him and help insure his supervision in the community. To help the court see that Brock obeyed these conditions, the program assigned a team of two officers, one a probation officer, the other a surveillance officer. During the first week of his sentence, Brock was visited 12 times—unheard of under traditional probation supervision. Later the visits were reduced but came randomly, any hour of the day or night.

Within the first six months, Brock had been returned to court just once for missing a curfew. Judge Pannell, Jr. was so impressed that he allowed Brock to remain on intensive supervision rather than send him to prison. After completing his community service at a neighborhood recreation center, Brock was hired by the same center. His community sponsor, his no-nonsense girlfriend and a nurse, reported changes in the defendant, all for the better, after 20 years of abusing alcohol, petty crimes, assorted misdemeanors and loafing.[77]

Case #2: South Bronx drug addict is before the New York court for the twenty-fourth time.

Warren, an unemployed, drug-addicted, 31-year-old, stole a new pair of pants in order to support his infant child. Although not Post Office wall material, Warren had twenty-three prior arrests for drug offenses, other shoplifting charges and a sprinkling of more serious burglaries, robberies and assaults. For the latter, he had been sentenced to five years in state prison. Recently, he had been in and out of city jail for petty offenses like the current shoplifting charge. His last incarceration had been for 45 days.

This time, Warren was particularly anxious not to go back to jail. He was anxious to be home to care for his new baby because his common law wife, the mother of his child, was due to be admitted to the hospital to cope with her own drug addiction. Despite his desire to remain in the community, Warren did not present a particularly good risk for release. He was on methadone, trying to break a 15-year drug history. He had recently been released from an alcoholism detoxification center. He possessed absolutely no work history. Nonetheless, the New York Court, on the recommendation of the District Attorney, did not put Warren in jail. Instead, he was sentenced to perform 70 hours of community work service. If he performed it, the case would end. If he failed, he would go to jail. Warren was assigned to a work crew supervised by the VERA Institute, which was beginning a project in the South Bronx called the Community Service Sentencing Project.[78]

Warren's first day on the job was inauspicious. He failed to appear. Searching the neighborhood, VERA staff finally located him at his methadone clinic. Shocked, he admitted that he really did not think the whole sentence was for real. Convinced, he went to the Davidson Senior Citizens' Center. The seniors had been playing cards and eating their meals in filthy rooms, floors caked with dirt and wax, unwashed windows opaque with dirt, surrounded by dirty walls. Warren, joined by other offender crew members, went to work cleaning the Center. Invited by the seniors to join them in their midday meal (a boon for crew members like Warren who could not afford their own lunches or who were not organized enough to bring their own), seniors expressed their gratitude, as did the program director:

> When I heard those young men might be available to help me clean my center, I leaped at the opportunity. After all, the people in [the] program aren't much different from a lot of the people living right upstairs in this project. . . . With all the unemployment, why not give people a chance to do something useful? Maybe helping us out will make them feel better about themselves.[79]

At least some New York judges share the director's enthusiasm. Judge Joan Carey, Chief Administrative Judge of the Manhattan Criminal Court, called the VERA Project "constructive."

> There is a lot of optimism that maybe community service will cause some people to rethink their lives and not get involved in crime so quickly again. At the very least, it's more constructive than letting them sit in a jail cell.[80]

Judge Stephen Crane, interviewed for the same issue of *Corrections Magazine*, expressed his support:

> It's a punishment that's a repayment to society. It certainly doesn't make them commit any more crimes than they would if we sent them to jail. Instead of spending the taxpayers' money to lock them up, we can let them do something for the community.[81]

Case #3: St. Louis judges see to it that defendants who engage in high-risk behavior learn about AIDS.

Begun in July 1987, St. Louis' Municipal Court Judge James Sullivan began to order prostitutes and drug users to attend two successive weekday classes to learn about AIDS and to be tested for it if they so desired. Those who attend have all or part of their fines remitted and/or jail term reduced. The goal of the program is to insure that education and information about AIDS is provided to those who engage in high-risk behavior for contracting it.

The maximum crimes for the above offenses are $500 fines and no more than 90 days in jail. The classes talk about safe sex, clean needles and other AIDS countermeasures. The first class is held at the court house. The second is held in a public health facility. The costs of the program are borne by the Department of Public Health. In the first 15 months of the program, 260 defendants went through it. According to the instructors who teach the classes, feedback is positive. One woman convicted of prostitution told her instructor after her classes were completed that she had put the information to good use and increased her profits. She now provided condoms to her customers which she attached without using her hands.[82]

§4.17   —Analysis of High-Risk, Chronic Offender Alternative Sentences

Until this section, examples focused on alternative sentences that fit various offenses. The preceding were particularly tailored to fit high-risk, chronic offenders. Turk Brock and Warren resemble, in terms of prior record and presenting offenses, habitual offenders Rummel and Helm. In fact, Turk was convicted of being a habitual offender pursuant to Georgia's statute. Warren's shoplifting charge represented his twenty-fourth offense. Yet by careful tailoring of their alternative sentences, the courts fashioned realistic sanctions for these offenders without compromising the public safety and still avoided long-term incarceration.

The options in sentencing white collar, educated, talented former bank presidents, corporation treasurers and even grandmotherly marijuana bakers to alternative sentences were wide; none was likely to reoffend anyway. In contrast, these high-risk offenders presented a challenge to the court to find the appropriate alternative sentencing components. Uppermost in the court's mind had to be sentences that reduced the offender's risk of reoffending. In the examples, judges relied on community work service orders to incapacitate and control the offenders in the community. Warren was placed on a work crew, supervised by VERA (which actually hires ex-convicts as its crew supervisors). Turk Brock was placed in a local recreational agency, supervised by the court.

Equal in importance to the placement of Warren and Turk in community work service was strict monitoring of their activities. Two officers, as well as a community sponsor, checked Turk's activities and enforced restrictive conditions (community work service, curfews and employment). Although not assigned a probation officer, Warren was supervised at the community work services site by VERA. The first time he failed to show up for work, VERA staff went looking for him and brought him back to complete his court assignment.

By intensifying the supervision, imposing curfews and house arrest, tightly monitoring community work service placements, ordering restitution paid in small but consistent installments, mandating treatment and behaviorally specific conditions such as abstinence, committing defendants to periodic incarceration, requiring them to forfeit their ill-gotten gains, and more, courts can insure that alternative sentencing is not confined to Federal Judge Skinner's "little old ladies who shoot migratory birds out of season."

Finally, while petty drug users and common street walkers who parade through St. Louis' busy municipal courts may not seem like high-risk offenders requiring any more than a cursory glance by the criminal justice system, their high-risk behavior not only endangers them but many others. While more serious offenders may cost more in the short run, the attendant costs of AIDS to society is enormous in terms of money and human life. By efficiently linking these offenders with public health prevention programs, these municipal judges and circuit judges who also make referrals may be preventing criminal behaviors that cost lives.

§4.18   Fashioning Alternative Sentences

Just because a sentence may avoid or shorten otherwise long periods of incarceration does not make it a good alternative or intermediate sanction, unless the only criterion used is jail avoidance. In many cases, even alternative sentences that avoid incarceration initially may only set up offenders to still longer sentences in the future if they fail to, among other objectives, address the offenders' criminogenic behaviors.

On the other hand, the longest sentence possible may not be the best sentence. If not absolutely necessary to safeguard the community, specific victim or vindicate social norms, long-term incarceration is extremely wasteful of precious state resources. Although many may take momentary pleasure when a judge pronounces a long sentence against an offender who has done something odious, their pleasure might be dulled if the judge also spelled out the consequences of that same sentence. What would the reaction be, for example, to the following sentence? "In order to sentence you to 30 years for being a habitual thief (or third-time felon), the state will have to deny 30 poor young men and women tuition at the state university."

Simply put, like medicine, if aspirin will do the trick, it is bad policy to rush to radical surgery or other costly treatment. Similarly, if a shock sentence followed by serious probation sanctions will achieve the relevant sentencing goals, long-term incarceration may not be necessary or desirable. It might be far better to construct a sentence that also compensates the victim, provides service to the community, and sees to it that the offender leaves the criminal justice system a better, more capable citizen than when he entered it.

A common mistake is to reserve creative, community-based sanctions for exceptional, white-collar criminals alone. Ironically, traditional sentences may be more effective for this type of offender than those for whom they are usually reserved. A jail cell may not offer much deterrence to a career criminal practically raised in juvenile institutions, but it may provide the necessary trauma and shock to convince the middle class drug user or drunk driver that he must finally address his problems and the behaviors that landed him in jail.

Also, white-collar criminals can do more damage than most street criminals combined. For example, as an editorial in the *Patriot Ledger* declared, "Polluters Deserve Jail Time."

> The U.S. government and the states will be cleaning up after industrial polluters for a long time to come. Part of that cleanup should include holding individuals responsible for their crimes against other humans and the environment, and sending the culprits to jail. This week a federal judge in Boston did just that and we applaud him. The defendant sent to jail for 26 months was John Borowski of Carlisle, the 71-year-old head of a metal finishing company, who was found guilty of ordering workers to dump hazardous chemicals from plastic buckets into the town of Burlington's sewer system. . . . Knowingly threatening people's lives with toxic substances is no different from threatening them with a gun. And the punishment should be similar.[83]

In addition, United States District Court Judge Douglas P. Woodlock fined the defendant $400,000 and ordered his company to pay restitution in the form of insurance premiums to two employees injured in the illegal dumping. The defendant's lawyer objected, saying that the sentence would mean a literal death sentence and requested a fine of $20,000.

Courts rightly receive criticism for imposing alternative sentences that appear to provide more leniency for offenders because they are white-collar and middle class. For example, Wall Street's felonious financier Michael Milken's sentence, which replaced longer term incarceration with an order of 1,800 hours of community work service, was widely attacked. As one newspaper columnist railed at the time:

> The sentencing of Michael Milken to 1,800 hours of community service in each of three consecutive years is an outrage that ought to be revoked. . . . Milken joins Zsa Zsa Gabor, the goulash bimbo, and Marion Barry, the one-time old-lion/mayor, in the ranks of celebrities convicted of crimes and ordered by courts to perform community service instead of more ordinary punishments. . . .[84]

Courts also receive wide criticism when an alternative sentence appears designed to inflict extraordinary pain on particularly vulnerable defendants. A case in point is the reaction to various judges ordering female defendants to take Norplant as a condition of probation to stop them from having future children.

> Norplant is the most revolutionary contraceptive for women since the birth control pill. But its potential is being seriously undermined. In three states—Louisiana, Kansas and California—conservatives are trying to use it to control the lives of poor women. . . . [I]n a case still pending in California, a Tulare County judge . . . ordered the use of Norplant as a condition of probation for a woman convicted of child abuse.[85]

Alternative sentences may contain differing sentencing components that address various sentencing goals. The question remains, however: how do the parties involved in sentencing know which component or components to include in their alternative sentence? Because the selection of alternative sentencing components is so wide, imposing alternative sentences requires particular deliberation. Judge Urbom provides some insight into the process in his sentencing memorandum quoted at length earlier. As Judge Urbom illustrates, in fashioning alternative sentences, defense attorneys, prosecutors, probation officers and judges must consider the following five factors: the offender, the offense, the victim, the community at large and, more specifically, the individual court environment. The last factor is included because each sentence establishes a precedent the court must live with for years and cases to come.

Consideration of the Offender

In fashioning alternative sentences, all parties must first take a hard look at the offender. The most important consideration is whether he or she poses a high or low risk for recidivism or is likely to be dangerous.

The following cases, detailed earlier, supply some examples of alternative sentences addressing offender risk and dangerousness. In the first set of cases, the alternative sentence sought to find, isolate and control the behavior that seemed to underlie the offender's risk of future criminality.

Judith Miller suffered from battered woman's syndrome, going from one unhappy and violent relationship to another. To control this, the judge imposed specific conditions barring her from living with or marrying anyone who did not meet court approval.

Compulsive and chronic child sex offender Roger Gauntlett was ordered to take Depo Provera to impede his sex drive.

Drunk driver Arthur was ordered to complete a 28-day inpatient alcohol program, followed by weekly outpatient treatment to control his alcoholism.

Chronic gambler Hayes, who embezzled over one million dollars to satisfy his compulsion, was ordered to live in a halfway house for three years, to submit to treatment to cure his gambling and to refrain from gambling.

In these examples, the alternative sentences were designed to control the offenders within the community. One jurist, Massachusetts Justice Albert L. Kramer, refers to this as establishing a "community cell." Although these offenders present multiple behavior problems, conditions can be tailored to fit these high-risk offenders, also.

Habitual offender Turk Brock, who never took responsibility for his actions, was placed under intensive probation supervision, narrowly restricting his behavior 24 hours a day. Among other things, he was required to find full-time employment.

Vietnam veteran Fred Palmer was given a split sentence. Incarceration interrupted his crime spree. Stringent probation conditions, including the payment of restitution and completion of victim work service, helped stabilize him in the community. Meetings with all his crime victims broke down the rationalization of his behavior and helped him resettle in the community, even allowing him to make friends with people he had previously robbed.

Once conditions that mitigate future recidivism are imposed, the offender must be examined to determine his skills and resources, with an eye to imposing specific sentencing components. Offender incomes, for example, must be examined before restitution is assessed. Dr. Ornitz, a radiation oncologist, was obviously able to make larger payments than Achelohiym Walton, an unemployed, unskilled defendant, when it came to considering restitution orders. Therefore the court imposed $25,000 a year against the former and only $25 a week against the latter. Similarly, Warner Communications Treasurer Solomon Weiss possessed very specific skills as opposed to South Bronx drug addict Warren, who had no discernible skills at all. While the court could place the former in a government agency to do accounting work among other duties, it had to place the latter in rudimentary maintenance and cleaning work.

Consideration of the Offense

After considering the offender, all parties must examine the offense. In considering the offense, the most important consideration is its seriousness. If the offense is petty, other factors such as who the offender is or the victim is or where the crime was committed may take precedence. But if the crime is serious, its consideration overshadows these other factors.

The more serious the offense, obviously, the more substantial the alternative sentence. If petty theft in the South Bronx calls for 70 hours of community work service, then killing 10 people in Maryland obviously demands more. In the case of drunk driver Arthur, the court imposed 3,000 hours to be performed over a period of three years.

In addition to gauging the seriousness of the crime, the sentence must try to come to terms with what the offender did.

Drunk driver Davis killed an elderly grandmother. The alternative sentence tried to come to terms with this fact. To do this, the defendant was ordered to do a number of things in addition to spending weekends in jail. These included meeting with his victim's relatives and donating money to a scholarship fund in the name of the victim. Besides performing community work service, the defendant was also ordered to accompany the Sheriff's department to the scenes of all motor vehicle accidents during the course of his probation.

Police officer Piscitelli assaulted a handcuffed prisoner. Not only did he commit a crime, he abused his position in the community. This, more than the harm done to the victim, was the central issue the court strove to address. It committed him to jail on weekends for a year which led to his dismissal from the police department, preventing future abuses.

Consideration of the Victim

After reviewing the offender and the offense, all parties must next turn to the victim. Not all crimes have specific victims. Even in cases in which there are specific victims, they may not be as important as other factors. The victim in the police officer assault case, for example, did not weigh heavily in the sentence. Whether the victim assumes an importance depends upon several factors. How directly is the victim related to the offense or the offender? What is the nature of the victimization? If the victim shares some culpability for the conduct, such as the batterer in the Judith Miller case, he may be overlooked in the sentence. On the other hand, the victims in the various homicide cases were key considerations in the alternative sentences.

Drunk driver Davis was ordered to establish a trust fund as a memorial to his victim.

William Clark was ordered to support the children of his victim.

Drunk driver Dr. Ornitz was ordered to pay his victim's family $25,000 a year for 30 years.

In cases involving injury, property damage, or theft, the victim's losses are often considered in fashioning the sentence. Cases in which restitution to the victim was ordered as part of the alternative sentences include the cases of: Walton, ordered to compensate his blind victim for 19 years; Sullivan, ordered to pay for his victim's emotional trauma; Bill B., ordered to repay the three elderly couples he stole from and whose property he damaged; Fred Palmer, ordered to meet his victims and to arrange for restitution; and Dr. Avol, the slumlord, ordered to reimburse the Health Department for inspecting his apartments.

Besides being a recipient of restitution or direct victim services, victims may be involved in the sentencing process itself. This involvement may convince the court to impose the alternative sentence in the first place. This involvement may also figure into the alternative sentence. Before imposing the alternative sentence in the case of Bill, who burglarized the homes of three elderly suburban couples, the judge, for example, obtained the support of the victims. He carefully spelled out to them the options he had and what each option meant to them in terms of restitution. He made sure that they heard from the defendant's employer before they made their decisions. With their endorsement, the judge felt free to allow the offender to escape the lengthy jail sentence he otherwise certainly merited.

The Davis case provides another example of direct victim involvement. In this case the victim's relatives were involved both as recipients of the offender's donation and as confronters of the offender in a court-ordered, victim-offender meeting that was part of the sentence. Both the donation and the meeting were court-ordered conditions of the defendant's probation. The confrontation dramatically crushed any rationalization or illusions the defendant may have harbored about the impact of his crime. While the probation conditions did not make these victims love their victimizer any more, it did increase their appreciation of the alternative sentence. One would not expect the long-time husband of a victim killed by a drunk driver to support anything less than a maximum sentence, yet as a result of his confrontation with the offender, the victim's husband expressed his satisfaction and support of the alternative sentence.

Consideration of the Community

After consideration of the offender, the offense and the crime victims, parties must look to the location of the crime. The communities are important considerations in fashioning the alternative sentence. The degree to which the community is considered depends partly upon whether the crime received much public notice. Most crimes are both committed and tried in obscurity. A few, however, achieve public notoriety. As a result, the community in which the crime occurred must figure prominently in the alternative sentencing.

For example, Boston's South Shore is predominantly Catholic, predominantly working class, but the area's passion seems reserved for ice hockey. When three youths vandalized the hockey rink, causing $20,000 damage, the entire community was upset. In fashioning the sentence, the court addressed the community's main concern by insuring that the sentence would require that the rink be repaired in time for its reopening in the fall. Similarly, when drunk driver Dawson killed his best friend, the crime sent shock waves through the small rural communities in Western Massachusetts. In order to reassure the community, the victim's parents, the police chief, the district attorney, the probation officer and the judge worked together to provide an alternative sentence that touched the community deeply. The alternative sentence had Dawson address all of the local high schools on the dangers of drunk driving.

The community that was the site of the crime can also serve as the site of the alternative sentence. Banker O'Brien, for example, was required to donate $90,000 worth of aid to poor people in his rural Missouri community. A New Jersey youth agency was used in another instance as a community work service site, as was a senior citizen's project in the South Bronx, a garden in Weymouth, Massachusetts and a volunteer fire department in upstate New York.

Consideration of the Court Environment

Although not spelled out by explicit legislation, each court establishes standards for sentencing, precedents that defense, prosecution and probation officers rely on in plea bargaining and formulating sentencing recommendations. Some commentators have referred to these informal sentencing standards as the "going rates." Going rates are established for most common crimes. They may be court-wide or limited to a specific judge or prosecutor. Therefore, in formulating alternative sentences, the parties must be mindful of the type of sentences handed down in the past. If, in a certain court community, sexual offenders are usually sentenced to 40 years in prison, it will prove exceedingly difficult to win acceptance for an alternative sentence that lacks equivalent weight or punishment. This is what happened in the case of child sexual molester Roger Gauntlett. On appeal, the Michigan appellate court held that the alternative sentence "shocked the conscience" of the community for its leniency and ordered the defendant to be resentenced.

On the other hand, with proper attention to the weight or punitive content of the components of alternative sentences, courts can impose them even in the most serious cases. This most graphic example was the case of drunk driver Arthur, who killed 10 people. The court was able to fashion an alternative sentence that was within the going rates for that court. As evidence of this, not only did the judge impose the sentence over the objections of the prosecutor, but the newspaper went out of its way to praise the alternative sentence. While the going rates for various crimes change depending upon the court environment, alternative sentences that recognize and build alternative sentences of equal punitive content will have a better chance of being accepted.

Once the above set of considerations is made, the alternative sentence can be fashioned from a wide variety of available alternative sentencing components. The most common alternative sentencing components are detailed in the following chapters.

Notes

[1] Beck, A. and D. Gilliard (1995). *Prisoners in 1994*. BUREAU OF JUSTICE STATISTICS BULLETIN. Washington, DC: U.S. Department of Justice, August.

[2] *People v. Clark*, 130 Cal. App. 3d 371, 181 Cal. Rptr. 682 (1982).

[3] *Michigan Killer Accepts Sentence of Celibate Living.* NEW YORK TIMES, June 19, 1981.

[4] From Alameda Probation Case files.

[5] Richard (1983). *He Serves Sentence By Warning of Danger of Drinking, Driving.* BOSTON GLOBE, May 27.

[6] 3 Vorp Network News, November 1983.

[7] *Drunken Driving Term: Pay Widow for 30 Years.* NEW YORK TIMES, April 1, 1984.

[8] *Client Specific Planning: The Alternative Sentence.* 3 INSTITUTIONS ETC. August, 1980.

[9] *Editorial.* BALTIMORE SUN, December 13, 1979.

[10] Barringer (1990). *Sentence for Killing Newborn: Jail Term, Then Birth Control.* NEW YORK TIMES, November 11.

[11] Beck, A. and D. Gilliard (1995). *Prisoners in 1994,* BUREAU OF JUSTICE STATISTICS BULLETIN. Washington, DC: U.S. Department of Justice, August.

[12] *Incarcerated Sex Offenders Today Total Nearly 100,000* (1993). CORRECTIONS COMPENDIUM, November 1993.

[13] *Conditional Term Given Sex Offender,* BOSTON GLOBE, August 8, 1985.

[14] *People v. Gauntlett*, 134 Mich. App. 737, 352 N.W.2d 310 (1984), *modified,* 419 Mich. 909, 353 N.W.2d 463 (1984).

[15] *State v. Sullivan*, 24 Or. App. 99, 544 P.2d 616 (1976).

[16] *"Stay Home" Sentence Given Child Molester.* BOSTON GLOBE, June 8, 1986.

[17] Turner (1987). *Unusual Sentence Stirs Legal Dispute.* NEW YORK TIMES, August 21.

[18] *State v. Bateman*, 765 P.2d 249 (Or. Ct. App. 1988), *reheard,* 771 P.2d 314 (en banc 1989).

[19] *Ex-firefighter Must Admit Rape.* ASSOCIATED PRESS. April 5, 1991.

[20] Nealon, P. (1992). *Arlington Man is Sentenced for Sexual Assault of 2 Girls.* BOSTON GLOBE, Sept. 16.

[21] *Man Sentenced in Assault Case.* ASSOCIATED PRESS, July 22, 1995.

[22] Simon, P. (1993). *Molester Will Face Stiff Curbs After Jail.* BUFFALO NEWS, July 10; and remarks of Dennis J. Wittman, Director, Genesee Justice Program, Genesee County Sheriff's Department, Batavia, N.Y., at Restorative Justice Symposium, National Institute of Justice and Office for Victims of Crime, Washington D.C., Jan. 25, 1996.

[23] Beck, A. and D. Gilliard (1995). *Prisoners in 1994.* BUREAU OF JUSTICE STATISTICS BULLETIN Washington, DC: U.S. Department of Justice, August.

[24] *Commonwealth v. Walton,* 483 Pa. 588, 397 A.2d 1179 (1979).

[25] *Id.*

[26] *Ex Officer Gets Weekends in Jail.* NEW YORK TIMES, July 8, 1983.

[27] *State v. Garner,* 115 Ariz. 579, 566 P.2d 1055 (1977).

[28] From Quincy court case files.

[29] *Man Who Spread AIDS is Punished.* REUTERS, October 30, 1991.

[30] *Abuse Sentence: Contraceptive.* WASHINGTON POST, January 5, 1991.

[31] *Birth Control Order Upheld for Pregnant Child Beater.* ASSOCIATED PRESS, January 11, 1991.

[32] From Quincy District Court case files.

[33] Forer, L. CRIMINALS AND VICTIMS 22 (1980).

[34] *Arsonist Sentence: Ten Years Without Pac Man.* BOSTON GLOBE, November 19, 1983.

[35] *Client Specific Planning: The Alternative.* 3 INSTITUTIONS ETC. 3 (1980).

[36] *Editorial,* WASHINGTON POST, July 16, 1979.

[37] Beck, A. and D. Gilliard (1995). *Prisoners in 1994.* BUREAU OF JUSTICE STATISTICS BULLETIN. Washington, DC: U.S. Department of Justice, August.

[38] Umbreit, M. (1985). CRIME AND RECONCILIATION 21-34.

[39] From Quincy Court case files.

[40] *Id.*

[41] Muro (1987). *Stalking Justice in Oregon Town.* BOSTON GLOBE, January 16.

[42] *Duxbury Man Sentenced in Theft from Government.* PATRIOT LEDGER, May 28, 1992.

[43] Franklin, R. (1995). *City Uses "Restorative Justice" With Woman Who Stole to Gamble.* TWIN CITIES STAR TRIBUNE. In *Restorative Justice Newsletter* (Minnesota Department of Corrections, November).

[44] Letter from Chairman of the Weymouth Garden Club, Beautification Committee, North Weymouth Civic Association, Weymouth Conservation Commission, from Quincy Court Files.

[45] Umbreit, M. (1985). CRIME AND RECONCILIATION 26.

[46] *Id.*

[47] Beck, A. and D. Gilliard (1995). *Prisoners in 1994.* BUREAU OF JUSTICE STATISTICS BULLETIN. Washington, DC: U.S. Department of Justice, August.

[48] *United States v. Krutschewski,* 509 F. Supp. 1186 (D. Mass. 1981).

[49] *Id.*

[50] *Id.*

[51] Doherty (1982). *Judge Eases Sentence for Traumatized Viet Vet.* BOSTON GLOBE, March 11.

[52] From Quincy Court case files.

[53] Barach (1981). *Names and Faces.* BOSTON GLOBE, June 17.

[54] *Not Drunk? Tell it to the Car.* NEW YORK TIMES, August 6, 1987.

[55] *Goldsmith v. State,* 490 So. 2d 123 (Fla. Dist. Ct. App. 1986).

[56] *For Oregon Drunk Drivers, a Close-Up of Skid Row.* NEW YORK TIMES, December 30, 1985.

[57] *State v. Bouldin,* 717 S.W.2d 584 (Tenn. Ct. App. 1986).

[58] *Court Reporting,* MADDVOCATE 5:2, Fall, 1992.

[59] Beck, A. and D. Gilliard (1995). *Prisoners in 1994.* BUREAU OF JUSTICE STATISTICS BULLETIN. Washington, DC: U.S. Department of Justice, August.

[60] Hoetler (1982). *Make the Sentence Fit the Felon.* 21 JUDGES JOURNAL 48, 53 (Winter).

[61] *Third Warner Official is Sentenced in Scheme Involving Theater.* WALL ST. J., March 14, 1984.

[62] *Court Sentence Brings Food and Toys To Needy.* NEW YORK TIMES, December 23, 1983.

[63] *Landlord To Get Taste of Filth in His Apartments.* BOSTON GLOBE, June 19, 1985.

[64] *Slumlord "Seems to Like" Sentence.* BOSTON GLOBE, July 25, 1987.

[65] *Landlord Told to Begin Sentence: 30 Days in His Squalid Apartment.* NEW YORK TIMES, July 11, 1987.

[66] *$20 Million Fraud Brings Tough Probation Terms.* NEW YORK TIMES, June 4, 1989.

[67] Larson, C. (1995). *Shaping a Sentence Around Victim Concerns.* RESTORATIVE JUSTICE NEWSLETTER, Minnesota Department of Corrections (November).

[68] See, *e.g.,* W. VA. CODE § 61-11-18 (1984).

[69] See, *e.g.,* COLO. REV. STAT. § 16-130101(2) (Supp. 1985).

[70] See, *e.g.,* MISS. CODE ANN. § 99-19-83 (Supp. 1985).

[71] See, *e.g.,* D.C. CODE § 22-104a (1981); IDAHO CODE 519-2514 (1979).

[72] 28 U.S.C. § 994(i)(1) (Supp. 11 1984).

[73] *Rummel v. Estelle,* 445 U.S. 263, 100 S. Ct. 1133, 63 L. Ed. 2d 382 (1980).

[74] *Id.* at 276, 100 S. Ct. 1140, 63 L. Ed. 2d 392.

[75] *Solem v. Helm,* 463 U.S. 277, 103 S. Ct. 3001, 77 L. Ed. 2d 637 (1983).

[76] *Id.* at 297, n.22, 103 S. Ct. 3013, n.22, 77 L. Ed. 2d 653, n.22.

[77] Gettinger (1983). *Intensive Supervision: Can It Rehabilitate Probation?* 9 CORRECTIONS MAGAZINE 6-17 (April).

[78] VERA Institute Of Justice (undated). NEW YORK CITY COMMUNITY SERVICE SENTENCING PROJECT: DEVELOPMENT OF THE BRONX PILOT PROJECT.

[79] *Id.*

[80] Krajick (1982). *The Work Ethic Approach to Punishment.* 8 CORRECTIONS MAGAZINE 6, 19 (October).

[81] *Id.*

[82] HEAT Program Statistics, Parole and Probation Office, St. Louis Circuit Court, Municipal Division (undated). Interview with Program staff, November 11, 1988 by author.

[83] *Polluters Deserve Jail Time.* PATRIOT LEDGER, November 11, 1990.

[84] Wilson, D. (1990). *A Sentence that Should Insult Every Volunteer,* BOSTON GLOBE, Dec. 12.

[85] Denmark, S. (1991). *Birth Control Tyranny.* New York Times, October.

Chapter 5

Victims, Restitution and Alternative Sentences

§5.01   Victim Involvement in Sentencing

As the examples from the previous chapter demonstrate, victims can play an active role in the fashioning of alternative sentences. Victims can be involved as recipients of court-ordered restitution or donations and also as participants in victim-offender meetings ordered by the court. This new role for victims addresses a long-standing injustice in the criminal justice system. As noted by the Chairman of a Presidential Task Force on Victims of Crime, formed in 1982, at the beginning of President Reagan's first term:

> Somewhere along the way, the [criminal justice] system began to serve lawyers and judges and defendants, treating the victims with institutionalized disinterest.[1]

As a result of this disinterest, studies have documented that crime victims feel as victimized by the courts as they do by their offenders. To find out just how victims feel, a judicial task force in Pennsylvania commissioned a survey of every victim it could find listed in the state's juvenile court case files (7,365). The survey found widespread dissatisfaction with the courts and the court dispositions. Most victim anger focused on the judge in the particular case. The researcher posited the reason:

> Because victims do not know what is going on, do not understand the system, and do not know the outcome, their frustration and hostility is taken out on the judges.
>
> Judges are blamed for the lenient sentences and the general failure of the system. . . . The long range problem for the victim does not

appear to be the crime, but the treatment by the system. The system tends to feed the hostility and anger the victim has as a result of the crime. . . . Victims . . . seem to feel a dual victimization: they are a victim of the crime and a victim of the system.[2]

Just as dramatically, the survey found that the victims' feelings were generally positive when they were involved in and informed about the court process or received restitution. The moral of the Pennsylvania study, and others like it, is simple. Courts need not resort to Draconian sentences to increase victim satisfaction. The simple expedient of victim recognition, involvement and the ordering of restitution, all common components of alternative sentences, can substantially increase victim satisfaction with the system, the sentence and the judge.

§5.02   —The Historic Role of the Victim in Criminal Justice

The alienation of the victim from the criminal justice system is relatively recent. Since the first written criminal code, the Code of Hammurabi, chiseled on a diorite column in 2,100 B.C., the rights of victims were clearly preeminent in the criminal justice system. Foremost among these rights was the right of restitution. The Code held, for example:

> If a man has stolen an ox or a sheep or an ass or swine or a boat, if [it belongs to] . . . a god . . . [or] . . . a palace, he shall pay 30-fold. If [it belongs to] . . . a villein, he shall replace [it] 10-fold. If the thief has not the means of repayment, he shall be put to death.[3]

The Code even provided for the victim if the government was unable to apprehend the perpetrator.

> If the robber is not caught, the man who has been robbed shall formally declare whatever he has lost before a god, and the city and the mayor in whose territory or district the robbery has been committed shall replace whatever he has lost for him. If . . . [the victim is killed], the city or the mayor shall pay one maneh of silver to his kinfolk.[4]

Victim compensation legislation was not enacted in this country by Congress until 1984.

The Old Testament concept of *lex talionis*, an eye for an eye, was not established to exact bloody retribution, but to establish proportionality between the offender's punishment and the victim's losses. As in the Code of Hammurabi, restitution was provided for the victims of crime.

> If anyone sins and commits a breach of faith . . . through robbery, . . .
> he shall restore what he took by robbery . . . he shall restore it in full,
> and shall add a fifth to it, and give it to him to whom it belongs.[5]

Although present-day appellate courts are divided over the legality of providing restitution for "unliquidated," "punitive" or "general damages" in criminal cases, the Old Testament had no such problem.

> And if a man entice a maid that is not betrothed, and lie with her, he
> shall surely endow her to be his wife. If her father utterly refused to
> give her to him, he shall pay money according to the dowry of virgins.[6]

At the dawn of the Middle Ages, a fairly sophisticated system, called composition, was established, providing for pre-set restitution orders for both property loss and personal injury, much like the present-day worker's compensation laws. A *wer* was paid for homicides, the amount depending upon whether the victim was a nobleman or a serf. A *bot* was paid for injuries, the amount depending upon the injury. A molar, for example, was valued more highly than a front tooth. If a criminal defendant made his composition, further vengeance on the part of the victim was unlawful. Criminals were protected by the king if they paid their restitution. Otherwise they were "outside the law" and could be hunted by the victim with impunity.

However, as states became increasingly centralized under the rule of the king, a victim's rights and role in the criminal justice system began to decline. In addition to the wer and the bot, the king demanded a *wit*, a fee to the state for its role in administering the composition process. By the 12th century, wit payments increased dramatically with a proportional decrease in payments to the victim. Victims who demanded private payments directly from the offender were charged with the offense of *theftbote*, literally theft of the king's share of the offender's payment. Not only did the medieval "fines" replace restitution, but the adversaries in the case changed. Instead of the victim versus the offender, it became the state versus the offender.

By the reign of King Louis IX, the ascendancy of the state in sentencing was almost complete, as the following case illustrates:

> In 1256, a powerful French nobleman, known as Sire deCoucy,
> caught three young squires armed with bows and arrows poaching
> on his land. Summarily, he had them hanged. Whereupon King
> Louis sent his court officers off to arrest the Sire. In deference to the
> Lord's rank, he was not shackled as he awaited trial in the Louvre,
> which then housed a prison.
>
> The Sire demanded trial by combat, but the King insisted that
> there be a trial, notwithstanding deCoucy's wealth. DeCoucy was
> convicted and the King ordered him to be hanged. However, under
> enormous pressure from deCoucy's peers, fellow knights of the
> realm, the King relented, realizing his dependence upon deCoucy

and his fellow Lords for his royal treasury, depleted by his numerous crusades to reclaim the Holy Land.

Instead, he devised an alternative sentence. In lieu of death, he ordered that the Sire pay 12,000 livres. (One livre constituted one day's wages for a knight.) Although a small portion of this money went to endow a Mass to be said in perpetuity for the crime victims, the lion's share went to Louis himself to finance another crusade.[7]

Although known as Louis the Just, and later canonized by the Catholic Church, King Louis contributed to perhaps one of the greatest thefts in the annals of history, the theft by the medieval kings of victims' restitution. After more than 3,000 years of reparative justice, the bond between restitution and criminal justice was split apart. It was replaced with a variety of other sanctions including state fines, torture, flogging, banishment and, later, incarceration.

What little reparative justice survived the reach of the kings was wiped out by America's contribution to corrections, the penitentiary. With its development, first by Philadelphia's Quakers, and later New York's more utilitarian reformers, America's love affair with incarceration dominated the correctional field. In colonial Massachusetts, the punishment for theft was a session on the gallows with a rope around the neck, a whipping and treble damages payable to the victim. If the offender could not pay, he could work directly for the victim or a third party as an indentured servant. However, with the establishment of the Commonwealth's first prison in 1785, the courts began to imprison thieves, ignoring the victim. Finally, in 1805, the state amended its criminal code to eliminate treble damages to the victim and rely exclusively on imprisonment.[8]

Although interest in the victims waned, victims were not entirely forgotten. Some of the first probation statutes included specific language calling for victim restitution. As probation focused almost exclusively on rehabilitation, it, too, lost sight of the victim and restitution orders did not receive much attention.

New Zealand helped refocus attention on victims in 1964 when it became the first modern nation to resurrect part of Hammurabi's Code by providing for state-funded victim compensation. Within a year, both New York and California enacted similar legislation. Today the federal government and most states have such programs. Unlike restitution, victim compensation is paid by taxpayers and is available to eligible victims whether or not the offender has been convicted or even apprehended. Amounts and coverage are usually limited by statute. It is estimated that nationally there exists the potential for $150 million in victim claims, well in excess of present or expected expenditure levels for state-funded compensation programs.[9]

In the mid-1950s, a Hungarian refugee and former Professor of Criminology, Stephen Schafer, was commissioned by the British Home Office to study that nation's victim compensation programs. Schafer published *Compensation and Restitution to Crime Victims*,[10] generally acknowledged to be the first modern text focusing on crime victims. The influence of the text is revealed by the fact that it has been translated and published around the world. In it, Schafer departs from determinist crime theories, arguing instead that crime represents a conflict relationship, not a social or psychological aberration to be either treated or punished. The victim, he posits, as well as the criminal, could bear responsibility for the criminal offense. His work not only launched a new field of study called victimology, but a theory of sentencing that he called "punitive" or "correctional" restitution.

Unlike other criminal sanctions, he argues, restitution requires the offender to do something as opposed to having something done for or to him. It also requires the offender to maintain a personal relationship with the victim until that person's condition is restored, as much as possible, to its former state. By concentrating on the victim-offender relationship, "correctional" or "punitive" restitution promotes the offender's responsibility, seeks to resolve the conflict between the offender and the victim, and therefore promotes social harmony and a sense of community. The process personalizes the effect of the crime as well as the process of reparations.

Schafer argues that restitution offers more than a simple introduction of tort law into the criminal courts. He calls it a new "synthetic" justice, combining the concerns of criminal law for the offender and civil law for the victim. To enhance the sanction, Schafer proposes that restitution should constitute more than out-of-pocket loss. As the New Testament admonished: "And whosoever shall compel thee to go a mile, go with him twain," similarly the restitution order should go beyond mere damages.

The victim rights movement turned Schafer's and other theories into practice. The movement began in the early 1970s with the establishment of crisis intervention programs for victims, the invention of victim impact statements by West Coast probation officers and the opening of the first shelters for battered women. In 1974, the Justice Department began to fund victim-witness programs. By 1976, some 2,000 victim assistance projects throughout the country joined together to form the National Organization for Victim Assistance (NOVA). NOVA helped promote many of the victim rights and restitution laws on the books today. Mothers Against Drunk Driving (MADD), a NOVA affiliate, encouraged 33 states to reform their drunk driving legislation in the early 1980s. Congress joined the victim rights drive, passing the Victim and Witness Protection Act of 1982[11] and federal criminal recodification, called the Comprehensive Crime Control Act of 1984. A section of this Act created the first national victim compensation program.[12] The program is financed through a fine levied against offenders, forfeited bonds and collateral, and forfeitures from profits obtained by offenders from their crimes' notoriety. This latter provision is modeled after New York legislation passed when it appeared that the mass killer, "Son of Sam," might profit from his crime's notoriety by authoring a book on the subject.[13]

In addition to promoting specific pieces of legislation, the victim rights movement refocused the criminal justice system's attention on crime victims, reintroducing them as active participants. The Massachusetts victims' rights legislation, hailed by NOVA as model legislation, creates a state victims' assistance panel charged with funding victim and witness assistance programs across the state. The program is currently collecting over three million dollars a year through fine assessments. In addition to the Attorney General and several District Attorneys, the panel contains two crime victims, including Margaret Grogan, whose son was murdered. She brings to the panel her own experiences as a victim.

> I was like nothing in the courtroom. . . . I was never told when the trial would be. I never did get my son's things back. I didn't get to speak in the courtroom. I had no chance to tell anyone who John was, why it was so terrible that he was murdered, what it did to me.[14]

The long-term effect of the introduction of victims like Margaret Grogan into the criminal justice system is unknown at present. What is known, however, is that the reemergence of the victim has meant an increase in the use of restitution in the courts.

§5.03   —The Rise of Restitution

The federal government and an increasing number of states provide for restitution in criminal sanctioning as a victim right, regardless of whether the offender is placed on probation or incarcerated.[15] California voters amended their state's constitution in 1982 to provide:

> It is the unequivocal intention of the People of the State of California that all persons who suffer losses as a result of criminal activity shall have the right to restitution from the person convicted of the crimes for losses they suffer. Restitution shall be ordered from the convicted persons in every case, regardless of the sentence or disposition imposed, in which a crime victim suffers a loss, unless compelling and extraordinary reasons exist to the contrary.[16]

However, more states simply provide for restitution as a permissible condition of probation.[17] An increasing minority demand it for any probationary sentence or at least demand that the court consider it before imposing sentence.[18] Restitution is required in a few states for certain classes of crime: misdemeanors in Texas;[19] crimes that result in property damage in Missouri, Kentucky and Virginia;[20] and assorted specific crimes such as welfare fraud in other states.[21]

Restitution is also recognized in some states as a criterion in deciding whether to grant probation to a defendant.[22]

Even where restitution is not specifically authorized by statute, appellate courts have upheld its imposition. The District of Columbia Municipal Court of Appeals first allowed the practice in 1944.[23] State appellate courts eventually followed suit.[24]

The rationale for restitution differs in the various statutes. While in some it is declared a victim right, others define it as rehabilitative for the offender. In these latter states, restitution is generally not authorized in addition to commitment to jail. While many appellate courts are quick to point out that criminal restitution cannot usurp civil remedies, the convenience of criminal versus civil court collections is repeatedly noted by the courts in imposing restitution orders. All of the model sentencing proposals of the last several decades have endorsed the use of restitution in sentencing.[25]

The modern use of criminal restitution can be traced back to some of the early probation statutes. By the 1930s, 11 states as well as the federal probation statute imposed restitution as a condition of probation. Actual imposition of restitution appeared to be limited, and collection haphazard. Most historians credit the Minnesota Department of Corrections' creation of a Restitution House in 1972 as the breakthrough restitution program in modern corrections. It allowed property offenders early parole if they paid restitution. It represented the first attempt to systematically apply the idea of restitution to community-based corrections. Other correctional departments copied the Minnesota program, even as the original program was dissolved for lack of referrals. Governor Jimmy Carter opened Georgia's first restitution center in response to prison overcrowding. Texas began its program in 1984.

Other correctional institutions became interested in the concept of restitution. In the 1970s, the Justice Department, responding to a Congressional mandate to encourage restitution, launched a $35 million program to fund programs that tested restitution sanctions in lieu of incarceration. The Justice Department effort, both in adult as well as juvenile corrections, proved enormously successful. While a study found only 15 formal restitution programs among juvenile courts in 1976, seven years later it found that over one-half of the courts reported formal programs. In addition, 97 percent used restitutional dispositions on an *ad hoc* basis. An increase was also noted in adult courts. A 1980 survey found 50 formal adult restitution programs in courts around the country. Several years later, *Corrections Magazine* reported more than 100.

Many of the federally funded restitution programs also provided for "indirect" or "community" restitution, also known as community work service.

While restitution programs were encouraged by federal monies and the victim rights movement in the 1970s, other correctional and court programs focusing on the crime victim, known as Victim Offender Reconciliation Programs (VORP), also developed. VORP began in Kitchener, Ontario in the early 1970s. It evolved out of a single case in which several defendants were convicted of a series of crimes involving 22 different victims. While investigating the case, the probation officer decided there would be some therapeutic value in the two defendants confronting their victims. The Mennonite Central Committee, meanwhile, was searching for prison alternatives. They joined forces. Although skeptical, the judge of the case ordered the confrontations. In the company of the probation officer or the Mennonite volunteers, the two defendants located 20 of the victims, met them, and determined what they owed in restitution.

The partnership between the court and the Mennonites grew. Eventually the latter took over the program. They recognized the merit of having neutral, trained mediators conduct the victim/offender meetings. The first VORP in the United States was located in Elkhart, Indiana. It was formed in 1978 by a prison reform group called Prisoners and Community Together (PACT), made up of representatives of the Mennonite Central Committee, the United Methodist Church, the Christian Church (Disciples of Christ) and court probation officers. Elkhart's first felony case was Fred Palmer, presented in Chapter Four.

§5.04   —Victim/Offender Mediation

While only a handful of VORP programs existed in the 1970s, by the beginning of the 1990s, the number increased to over 100 in 26 states and Canada.[26] The programs have spread across the country although they are still concentrated in the midwest. A national resource center for VORP, originally established in Valparaiso, Indiana, moved to Orange, California in 1994, home of the largest juvenile VORP in the country, servicing over 1,200 offenders a year.[27] In addition, a Center for Restorative Justice and Mediation has been established at the University of Minnesota School of Social Work, "committed to the development of community-based restorative responses to crime and violence which strengthen community safety and social harmony."[28] Since the 1980s, mediation programs have taken off in Europe, too.

In most of the programs, local churches or community groups provide the volunteer mediators who organize the meetings between offenders and victims. The Oklahoma prison system also adopted a victim/offender mediation program as an adjunct to its shock sentencing program. Select offenders must meet with their victims and agree to a restitution plan, which is then submitted to the court. If the judge agrees, the long-term prison sentences are revoked and the inmates are released to fulfill their restitution obligations. The program was originally mandated by law until it was struck down as unconstitutional for violation of separation of powers. The program, however, was continued administratively by correction officials.[29]

In 1994, the American Bar Association's Criminal Justice Section endorsed victim/offender mediation dialogue programs. The ABA recommended that such programs be guided by 13 requirements, including, among others: (1) participation must be voluntary, on the part of both parties; (2) victims and offenders must be screened on a case-by-case basis; (3) face-to-face meetings should be encouraged; (4) follow up should be in place to insure agreements are monitored; (5) discussions in mediation are not admissible in either criminal or civil proceedings; and (6) mediators must be trained and reflect a cross section of the community.[30]

A body of research has developed over the past decade offering support for the effectiveness of such programs in both reducing recidivism and encouraging higher rates of restitution repayments. One of the more sophisticated studies looked at over 2,000 offenders who participated in programs in four states—New Mexico, Texas, Minnesota and California. It compared how they did versus a matched population of offenders who did not participate in victim/offender mediation programs. It found that restitution collection (agreed to in 95 percent of the mediations) in the experimental group exceeded that of the control group by 81 percent to 58 percent. Recidivism was lower, 18 percent versus 27 percent.

A survey of both victims and offenders participating in the programs indicated mutual support and satisfaction. Victims reported 79 percent satisfaction while offenders reported 87 percent. Victims found it fair at a rate of 83 percent compared to offenders at 89 percent. Victims reported their fear was reduced from 25 percent to 10 percent as a result of meeting their offenders.[31]

Many of the victim/offender mediation programs operate within the larger context of "restorative justice" theory.[32] Unlike traditional views of crime, this view emphasizes that crime is a violation of one person by another, rather than against the state. Encouraging victims and offenders to be directly involved in resolving the conflict, through dialogue and negotiation, is central to restorative justice. Resolving conflict for the future takes precedence over establishing blame for prior behavior.

Victim/offender mediations are not restricted to property or minor personal crimes. In 1994, a Rhode Island state prison hosted a series of mediation sessions between a mother and the inmate who murdered her son. The murderer, high on drugs, had murdered the victim in the course of a $10 robbery. Capturing the outcome of the mediation, a newspaper reporter described: "Eight days ago, Suzanne Molhan reached across a prison table and held the hand that fired the gun that killed her son." The article continued with the victim's explanation:

> "I never wanted Alfred (the murderer) to touch me, ever," says Molhan, a Rhode Island state health worker whose nine-year crusade to confront her son's killer led to her first meeting with Alfred Lemerick 21 months ago—and to changes in Molhan's own life that even she cannot fully fathom. "I still don't forgive him," she adds quickly, to answer the one question that haunts her wherever she goes. However, says Molhan, after discussing her son's death and Lemerick's upcoming parole hearing for more than an hour last week, "Alfred reached over to shake hands, and I responded automatically. He covered my hand in both of his, and I held his in mine. We said goodbye that way."[33]

The article concludes with a story of the tenth anniversary of her son's death. Mrs. Molhan received no phone calls or cards from any friend or relative who might have been inclined to share their sympathies with her that day. There was one card, however, that arrived not by mail but was read to her over the phone, by a Rhode Island prison official.

"Dear Sue," the card said, "I don't want you to think I have forgotten you, because I haven't. I know today is the 10th anniversary and I know you must be going through a tough time. I hope our mediation has made this anniversary date a little easier for you. I'm thinking of you. You're not alone." It was signed, simply, "Alfred."

As a result of the meetings, the victim reported how she could begin to allow herself to get on with her own life. The mediation had finally brought closure to the murder of her son.[34]

§5.05   —Restitution and the Criminal Justice System Today

As a result of their experience working and administering restitution programs in the 1970s and 1980s, select practitioners and researchers banded together to establish and promote a new generation of restitution programming in the 1990s. Unlike the current practice of establishing *ad hoc* programs attached to courts and corrections, they sought to integrate their programs into mainstream corrections as a core program element. Restitution, they argued, should not be seen as a stand-alone correctional program, but a philosophy of corrections. In short, they proposed a fundamental reformulation of the correctional mission itself, emphasizing goals of victim restoration and offender accountability. The legitimate activity of corrections, they argued, was not to do something *to* or *for* the offender, but require the offender to do for himself, specifically restoring his victim and the community he offended.

In 1988, three writers and researchers publicly issued this challenge to their peers in a landmark treatise published by the National Council of Juvenile and Family Court Judges.[35] They criticized traditional corrections and its exclusionary concentration on the offender, either rehabilitating him or punishing him, depending upon the political winds. In its place, they urged the adoption of a "balanced approach," concentrating on three core goals—community protection, accountability and competency development.

Whether it comes to judges at sentencing or the operation of correctional agencies, the "balanced approach" calls for a focus on the victim and the community as well as the offender. Specifically, it calls for sentences or correctional programs that require the offender to make the victim and the community at large as whole as possible and for the offender to leave the system more competent to be a productive citizen than when he or she entered it. And all of these goals must be realized while minimizing any risk that the offender may present to the public in the interim.

The publication was widely circulated, becoming the National Council's all-time most popular publication. A small but growing number of states have actually changed their juvenile statutes to incorporate the balanced approach into their laws. In 1995, for example, Pennsylvania redefined the mission of juvenile courts to "provide for children committing delinquent acts programs of supervision, care and rehabilitation which provide *balanced attention to the protection of the community, the imposition of accountability for offenses committed and the development of competencies to enable children to become responsible and productive members of the community* (emphasis added).[36]

The Justice Department paid attention also. The Office of Juvenile Justice and Delinquency Prevention replaced its much more massive efforts to promote individual restitution programs in the previous decades with a project out of Florida Atlantic University, begun in the early 1990s, the Balanced Approach and Restorative Justice Project (BARJ) was composed of a small group of restitution practitioners and researchers from across the country, joined by a pioneer in the VORP movement, to promote this broader concept of restitution sentencing. In addition to calling for a balanced approach, BARJ called for a new restorative paradigm of corrections.

The new paradigm built on the tenets of the balanced approach. Rather than defining crime as an offense against the state, it views crime as an act against another person and the community. Crime control, consequently, cannot be accomplished by the criminal justice system alone, but lies primarily in the community. Offender accountability is not the offender receiving punishment, but assuming responsibility and taking action to repair the harm he or she caused. Instead of depending on paid lawyers acting in proxy, parties to the crime should have direct involvement, and engage in dialogue and negotiation. The focus should be on problem solving, on offender obligations and what should be done rather than establishing blame and focusing on past actions. Restitution is one of the means of restoring both parties through reconciliation and restoration.[37]

BARJ established model programs in Florida, Pennsylvania and Minnesota and participated in conferences and workshops around the country promoting its mission. Though specifically funded for juvenile corrections, BARJ also applies to adult corrections. In the fall of 1995, the BARJ project was showcased to other federal justice agencies, including the National Institute of Corrections, the National Institute of Justice and the Office of Victims, which were interested in promotion of and research on restorative justice within their agencies. A national restorative justice symposium, sponsored by the U.S. Justice Department was held the following year.

Also in 1995, the National Organization for Victim Assistance, the oldest and largest victim advocacy group in North America, and the American Restitution Association, comprised of restitution practitioners and advocates, publicly supported the concept of restorative justice. The former endorsed what it called "restorative community justice."[38] The latter voted to change its name to the "Restorative Justice Association." In renaming itself, it released a new mission statement:

> The Restorative Justice Association believes that crime is an act of harm against victims and members of the community. We see criminal justice as a process which ensures that offenders repair this

harm, respond to victims compassionately, fairly and justly, and promotes safe and secure communities.[39]

The Prison Fellowship, a Christian prison reform group begun by Watergate conspirator Charles Colson, also endorsed restorative justice.

> We at Prison Fellowship have a vision we want to share with you: a vision for justice that reaches beyond mere crime and punishment. It's a vision based on ancient biblical principles and truths that are largely ignored but amazingly relevant to the crime crisis that is crippling our nation. Let us introduce you to what is called restorative justice, which opens doors to restored lives and community peace . . .[40]

In another example of current restitution practices, in the mid-1990s the Vermont corrections department adopted a new track for probationers called "Reparative Probation." After an intensive analysis of what the public wanted in its community corrections programs, the department determined that there was wide support for restorative justice. To implement it, the department asked for citizen volunteers to serve on newly established Reparation Boards to assist the courts in sentencing and supervising select offenders. Board members receive 20 to 30 hours in training.

Each board, one for each of the larger counties, shared boards for smaller counties, meets monthly to consider the cases of property offenders and others referred to them by the court. To refer an offender to the board, the court must have the consent of either the defense or prosecution lawyer, or both. The offender is found guilty but the sentence is deferred pending his or her participation in the reparative program developed by the board. Active offender participation usually runs between 90 days and six months. If the program is completed successfully, the offender's record of conviction is erased.

The board meets with the offender and the victim, sometimes together and sometimes separately. Lawyers may witness the proceedings but are not allowed to participate. The board can order victim/offender mediation, set restitution amounts if not already determined, order community work service, refer the offender to complete a course on decisionmaking or write a letter of apology to the victim. To assist the boards, several dozen mediators, both volunteers and correctional personnel, were trained throughout Vermont to perform victim/offender mediation when so requested. After the sentence is determined by the board, offenders must return to demonstrate that they have completed their assigned tasks.

For the most part, offenders do not receive traditional probation supervision. They are not required, for example, to report to probation officers as long as they are making their restitution payments on time. "Reparative Probation" in Vermont was established administratively. It is administered by a "Reparations Coordinator" in each of the major counties, funded by the state corrections department.[41] The department hopes to eventually divert 2,400 cases a year through straight reparations. Even in cases that involve prison sentences, the department of corrections has announced its determination to build restorative programming within these sentences as well. The goal is to restore victims of crime, have the offender make amends for his crime, learn about the impact of his crime and learn to avoid new offense behavior.[42]

The Minnesota Department of Corrections has similarly focused on implementation of restorative justice in that state, holding annual statewide conferences on restorative justice and establishing a specialized restorative justice initiative headed by a full-time Restorative Justice Planner.[43] Don Streufert actively assisted the department in developing its initiative. His daughter was raped and murdered and, as a result, he personally experienced that state's criminal justice system at its best and worst. After participating in several meetings with his daugher's murderer, he became committed to the concept of restorative justice. The department publishes the *Restorative Justice Newsletter.* Commissioner Frank Wood writes in its November, 1995 issue:

> Restorative justice is truly an exciting concept. It is not a passing fad or quick fix. It has been very rewarding for me to have participated with Mark Umbreit and Don Streufert as the department assisted them in facilitating and implementing their very bold restorative justice initiatives with the perpetrators of a senseless homicide. . . . The department is very encouraged by the statewide interest in and commitment to restorative justice. The list of community and criminal justice individuals and professional associations involved is extensive. . . . With this broad-based support, we are confident that restorative justice efforts will grow and continue to be implemented throughout the state.[44]

Even in the vast majority of jurisdictions that do not espouse a restorative justice philosophy or do not have a formal restitution program, restitution orders as part of sentences or correctional programs are routine. As the great growth in both statutory and case law reveals, restitution to crime victims is no longer confined to civil courts.

§5.06   Restitution Law: Federal

The 1984 federal code revision[45] provides that a court may order, in addition to the sentence imposed, that the defendant make restitution to any victim of the offense. It also provides that the defendant be ordered to provide restitution as a condition of probation. The latter is mandatory for felons if the court does not mandate the performance of community work service or payment of a fine.

The 1984 code revision also incorporates the language added by the 1982 Victim and Witness Protection Act.[46] It defines the restitution order in some detail. First, in cases of property damage or loss, it calls for the return of the property or payment in an amount equal to the value of the property on the date of its destruction, loss or damage, or its value at the time of sentencing, whichever is greater, less the value of the property returned. Second, in cases of bodily injury, it calls for payment in an amount equal to the necessary medical or other professional services and devices relating to physical, psychiatric and psychological care, including nonmedical care and treatment rendered "in accordance with a method of healing recognized by the law of the place of treatment." It also calls for payment for physical and occupational therapy and reimbursement for victim income lost by the victim as a result of the offense. Third, in cases in which the victim is killed, it calls for payment for funeral and related expenses to the victim's estate.

Uniquely, the code allows the offender to make restitution in services in lieu of money or make restitution to a person or organization designated by the victim or the estate. In other words, with the victim's consent, the offender can perform victim services or make a contribution to a third party in lieu of paying money directly to the victim or the victim's estate.

Except in the interest of justice, the court may not order restitution to a third party who has compensated the victim for his losses, such as insurance companies. If such restitution is ordered, the victim must receive his money first.

Money received by the victim is set off against any subsequent federal or state civil proceedings.

Restitution is due at the end of the probationary period, five years after the end of a term of imprisonment, or five years from the date of sentencing, if not ordered to be paid immediately or pursuant to an installment plan established by the court.

The statute goes on to detail that the court may revoke an offender's probation if he fails to make restitution payments. In so doing, it must consider the defendant's financial situation and ability to pay. The Act gives the victim the right to enforce the order "in the same manner as a judgment in a civil action." The victim is given the same standing as the probation department in enforcing the restitution order.

If there is any dispute as to the proper restitution order, the code provides that it shall be decided by the court, based on a preponderance of the evidence. The government is given the obligation to represent the victim's losses. The defense is given the obligation of demonstrating the offender's financial needs and the needs of his dependents.

Finally, the code provides that a conviction for the offense giving rise to the restitution order shall prevent the defendant from denying the essential allegations of the offense in any subsequent federal or state civil proceedings brought by the victim.

Although the Act has been been challenged numerous times, particularly regarding its intrusion into civil law, none of these challenges has been successful to date.[47]

Since it was enacted, Congress amended its original law in 1986, 1987, 1988, 1990 and again in 1994. The amendments are generally designed to clarify the original act and insure that victims receive their due. Several seek to reverse the effect of court rulings restricting the scope of permissible restitution. The amendments include a specific section allowing restitution to victims of an offense that involves as an element a scheme, a conspiracy or a pattern of criminal activity if they are directly harmed by the criminal conduct in the course of the scheme, conspiracy or pattern.[48] They also allow the court to order restitution as agreed to by the parties in a plea agreement.[49]

In terms of what is covered, a new section specifically authorizes the court "to reimburse the victim for lost income and necessary child care, transportation, and other expenses related to participation in the investigation or prosecution of the offense or attendance at proceedings related to the offense."[50]

Congress also required that before the court may bypass restitution because determining it would involve complex and prolonged proceedings, it must find that the former outweighs the "need to provide restitution to any victims."[51] Previously, the court could forego restitution if the imposition of it would "unduly complicate or prolong the sentencing process."

Finally, a new section was added to penalize offenders who do not pay. Section (i) requires a federal agency to immediately suspend all federal benefits provided by the agency to the defendant, and shall terminate his or her eligibility for more, upon receipt of a certified copy of a written judicial finding that the defendant is delinquent in making restitution as imposed.

As of 1994, the federal code also provides for mandatory restitution for specific crimes such as telemarketing fraud and certain crimes against women.[52] In regard to the latter crimes, restitution includes the costs incurred by the victim for attorney's fees, plus any costs incurred in obtaining a civil protection order as well as temporary housing and child care expenses.[53] Because the restitution is mandatory, the court is directed to ignore the economic circumstances of the defendant in determining the restitution, but to take it into account when determining "the manner in which and the schedule according to which the restitution is to be paid."[54]

The law has also withstood more recent challenges that Congress, in effect, created a civil judgment in establishing criminal restitution orders but deprived the defendants of their right to a jury determination of the amounts owed.[55]

Circuits have split in regard to the nature of the hearing to order restitution as either a separate sentence or condition of probation. The issue that concerns them the most is the statutory obligation of the sentencing court to consider the defendant's ability to pay in determining whether restitution should be ordered and whether payment should be full or in part.

The Third Circuit uses its supervisory power to require district courts "to make specific findings as to the factual issues that are relevant to the application of the restitution provisions of the [Act]."[56] The Second Circuit declines to require such specific findings, requiring only that the district judge "consider" the factors listed in the Act, which include the victim's loss as well as the offender's financial resources and circumstances.[57] The Second Circuit ruled that a requirement for such findings would interfere with the court's exercise of discretion. Because in the case before it, the district judge did not consider all of the factors listed in the Act in determining restitution, it remanded the case for a further hearing on restitution, rejecting the district judge's ruling that consideration of the defendant's ability to pay should be put off until the defendant fails to comply with the court's order. At that time, the Second Circuit noted the court must again consider the factors listed in the Act which bear on the defendant's ability to pay. Unlike the determination of the initial order, the victim's losses are not listed among the factors to be considered at that time.

The Seventh Circuit requires explicit findings when the judge does not impose restitution, or orders only partial restitution.[58] The United States Supreme Court has ruled that when the judge decides not to order restitution, he or she must consider the same statutory factors required when he or she does.[59] Other circuits do not require specific findings as long as the court documents that it considered all the statutory factors mandated for consideration.[60] The First Circuit, for example, excused a judge from making open court findings on the defendant's ability to pay when ordering restitution so long as the judge made *implicit* findings or otherwise evinced considerations of those factors.[61]

Most of the circuits allow the court to rely on the probation presentence report in which the factors have been addressed by the probation officer.[62] For example, the Seventh Circuit upheld a $5 million restitution for a fraud scheme because the record revealed that the presentence report considered the net worth of each of the defendants ($16,945 and $11,642) as well as the fact that neither had dependents and one was working toward a degree in computer engineering. The judge also said that he ordered the restitution so that if the defendants were later able, they would have to pay.[63]

However, if the judge's order conflicts with the content of the presentence report, the court must justify its order on the record. In one example, the presentence report indicated that the defendant had both a negative net worth and monthly cash flow yet the court made no attempt to tie the defendant's finances, financial needs and earning ability to the amount of restitution ordered.[64]

The circuits agree that the court, not the probation officer, must determine the restitution order. The court may rely on the probation officer's input, but cannot delegate its responsibility to the officer.[65] Further, the judge must impose the restitution order at sentencing and not leave it open-ended for another time.[66]

The court's decision to impose or not impose restitution lies within its discretion and absent a showing of abuse is not appealable.[67] The victim does not have standing to appeal if the court does not order restitution or orders only partial restitution.[68]

In regard to the content of the restitution order, the circuits differed on how far the courts could go until the United States Supreme Court set some basic parameters in a 1990 decision. In that decision, it rejected earlier liberal interpretations of some of the circuits, which had upheld restitution orders that went beyond the amount as it related to the offense of conviction if there were significant links between the crime and similar misconduct to justify it. In a unanimous decision, Justice Marshall wrote that Congress intended to compensate victims only for losses caused by the conduct underlying the offense for which the criminals were *convicted*. He rejected the argument that plea bargaining might lead to the dismissal of charges that led to legitimate victim losses.

> (A)lthough a plea agreement does operate to limit the acts to which a court may order the defendant to pay restitution, it also ensures that restitution will be ordered as to the count or counts to which the defendant pleads guilty pursuant to the agreement. The essence of a plea agreement is that both the prosecution and the defense make concessions to avoid potential losses. Nothing in the statute suggests that Congress intended to exempt victims of crime from the effects of such a bargaining process.[69]

The Ninth Circuit, the same year, further clarified that Congress had not intended to give courts the power to forfeit the offender's ill-gotten gains. Rather, the aim of the federal restitution statute is to compensate the victim.[70] Nor may the court go beyond the items listed in the statute. It may not, for example, order restitution for pain, suffering or mental anguish. As a result, the Eleventh Circuit rejected a $500,000 order designed to compensate a raped and sodomized female prison guard's suffering from post-traumatic stress disorder as a result of the defendant's crime.[71] Similarly, a court could not order restitution for psychiatric treatment for an IRS employee traumatized by tax protesters' bombings because the statute specifically calls for counseling costs when the victim suffered physical, as well as emotional injury.[72]

In another case, however, another circuit upheld the order that the defendant pay for the victim's airfare to see her parents. The court held that the support and comfort of her family were important elements in her care and treatment for the psychological trauma created by the sexual assault that resulted from the defendant's crime for which he was convicted.[73]

At least one circuit has rejected restitution for what it terms "consequential damages." These include costs such as attorney and investigatory fees expended to recover property relevant to the offense.[74]

Although Congress amended the statute to allow courts to impose restitution generally agreed to in a plea, several circuits have insisted that the order not exceed the amount charged in the offense of conviction even if agreed to. In short, parties to a plea agreement cannot increase the statutory powers of the sentencing judge to authorize restitution by simply agreeing to it.[75] A defendant convicted of fraud, for example, could not be made to pay restitution in excess of the losses the government proved were a result of her criminal acts, even though she agreed she would pay up to $25 million. Her agreement, the court ruled, did not absolve the government of its burden to prove that losses included only those caused by her criminal acts.[76]

But if the defendant agrees to pay restitution as determined by the court or pay restitution for full losses of all victims identified in the indictment, the court may order more restitution than that covered in the count or counts to which the defendant pled guilty.[77]

The circuits have also explored what constitutes "a scheme, conspiracy or pattern of criminal activity" for which the court may order restitution. The Sixth Circuit, for example, found that the theft of two cars did not qualify.[78] Where the court orders restitution pursuant to this section, it may be broad. The Fifth Circuit, for example, refused to limit the court to losses caused by specific misrepresentations of the defendants, but allowed it to consider the entire amount lost by investors as a result of the criminal scheme. In short, any actions taken pursuant to the scheme had to be considered conduct that was the basis of the offense of conviction.[79] Similarly, the Ninth Circuit gave the court authority to order, as a condition of probation, the defendant to pay restitution to all victims of his fraud scheme, not just those who happened to receive the mailings that were subject of his guilty plea.[80]

Interest on losses may be included in the restitution orders.[81] The interest can include either post- or pre-judgment losses.[82]

Victims entitled to receive federal restitution awards must be either those whose suffer direct losses or those who compensate them for their direct losses caused by the crimes as specified by the evidence. The government's costs of prosecuting the case, and even lost "buy" money spent in investigating it are judged to be regular agency expenses and not losses subject to restitution orders.[83] The government, however, may receive restitution when it is the direct victim of a crime.

For example, the government was considered a victim for purposes of receiving restitution when a juror's misconduct resulted in a mistrial requiring a new trial. Upon conviction, the juror was ordered to pay the government over $40,000 for lost salaries and time of prosecutors and DEA witnesses.[84] Similarly, an inmate who killed a fellow inmate could be ordered to pay for the government's autopsy of the victim, funeral and burial even though the defendant had the audacity to state that he actually saved the government the cost of the victim's future incarceration.[85]

Other cases have upheld restitution to various government agencies, including the IRS when, for example, Leona Helmsley, self-styled New York hotel queen, was ordered to pay back taxes. Other federal agencies awarded restitution include the Federal Savings and Loan Insurance Corporation and the Department of Labor,[86] to name a few.

In an example of impermissible restitution to indirect victims, the Second Circuit did not allow a court to order a defendant convicted of a drug conspiracy to pay restitution to a fund that would be used for medical treatment, rehabilitation and restitution to persons injured by drug addiction in the 1980s. The problem was that the victims who would benefit from this fund could not be tied into the specific crime for which the restitution was ordered.[87] Nor could a court order restitution to unnamed victims of a conspiracy.[88]

Although courts must consider a defendant's ability to pay restitution, they may still order it even when the defendant is legally determined to be indigent.[89] Poor defendants have been ordered to pay rather rich restitution orders. In considering the ability to pay, courts have been creative and extremely optimistic. For example, an armed bank robber was ordered to pay restitution of $13,000 even though he had no assets, no real employment history and faced 20 years in prison followed by five years of supervised release. The judge ruled that it was possible for the prisoner to pay the first $10,000 through prison industries and while he was engaged in that he could also earn a degree, which would improve his chances of obtaining a job upon his release. The court noted that the scenario was not beyond the realm of objective reasonable possibility.[90]

Other rationales approved include the fact that payment is spaced out in installments and not due until the offender is released from prison.[91] Others include the fact that the defendant might inherit money or write a best-seller based on his crime.[92] Another court found that the defendant not only had a degree in petroleum engineering but had successfully managed supermarkets and his mail fraud scheme revealed him to have imagination and skills of persuasion that might be applied to legal endeavors.[93]

Another circuit upheld an order even though the defendant was not only indigent, but according the presentence report, had liabilities of over one million dollars and no remaining assets. Nevertheless, restitution was upheld because the defendant had concealed assets in a corporate bankruptcy case, had received the benefit of a fraud and he had education, experience and had the ability to obtain high earnings once out of jail.[94]

However, some Circuits have ruled, the court must find some assets or earnings potential or possibility of payment of restitution that constitutes more than a mere chance. Moreover, the defendant must be able to comply without undue hardship on his family.[95] Some assets of the defendants are restitution-proof. Convicted of wire fraud, the Fourth Circuit did not allow the court to attach the defendant's Employee Retirement Income Security Act (ERISA) fund for restitution. These funds are protected by statute and may not be assigned or alienated.[96]

Of course, one of the reasons appellate courts can be permissive in regard to restitution orders being made against indigent offenders is that just because the order is made does not mean it can be enforced during the statutory period of five years. Defendants who fail to pay cannot be revoked if on probation if they make a *bona fide* effort to pay or if they are unable to pay.[97]

Finally, if there are codefendants, they may be ordered to pay joint and several. In other words they are each responsible for the full amount if the other does not pay his or her share.[98] If charged with a conspiracy, each co-conspirator, similarly, can be ordered to pay for the whole enterprise, not just for their specific role in it.[99]

§5.07   Restitution Law: State

State restitution laws vary. As a rule, they are not as comprehensive as the federal laws. Most are not specific as to who may receive restitution, what they may receive and for which offenses they may receive it.

In regard to who may receive restitution, most state laws simply refer to "aggrieved parties" or "victims of the offense," as in the federal code. North Carolina law defines victims as "individuals, firms, corporations, associations or other organizations, and government agencies, whether federal, state or local," but bars restitution to third parties such as insurance companies.[100] Some states allow for restitution to such indirect victims.[101] Where statutes are silent, courts have not ruled consistently on whether indirect victims are eligible for restitution.[102] Common indirect victims include insurance companies, medical facilities, police and fire departments, persons who put up fidelity bonds and even prosecutors.

Courts allowing restitution to insurance companies, like a Virginia appellate court, reason that by paying the victim, they stand in place of the victim and may in the name of the victim pursue a civil claim against the third party. As such, the insurance carrier may also be an aggrieved party.[103] Even though Michigan state restitution law refers to victims as "persons,"[104] its appellate courts have ruled that insurance companies qualify.[105] Similar rulings have been made in Arizona, Utah and Michigan.[106] Faced with a state statute that failed to define "victim" at all, Vermont's Supreme Court reached an opposite conclusion, barring restitution to insurance companies.[107]

Idaho state law specifically defines the victim, entitled to receive restitution to include "any health care provider who has provided medical treatment to the victim if such treatment is for an injury resulting from the defendant's conduct, and who has not been otherwise compensated for such treatment by the injured victim."[108] Pursuant to this law, an appellate court ruled that Blue Cross was not entitled to restitution because it was not a health care provider, but an insurer who was not a victim under state law. Illinois law specifically requires defendants convicted of domestic battery to pay restitution to any domestic violence shelter where the victim lived because of her abuse. The amount of restitution shall be the actual expenses of the shelter in providing for housing and other expenses.[109]

Absent statutory authority, jurisdictions have split regarding whether the government can be considered a victim and recover, for example, "buy" money used to apprehend the offender. An Illinois appellate court suggested that for a drug enforcement agency seeking to recover buy money in that state, the court would have to order a fine or forfeiture, not restitution.[110] A Minnesota appellate court similarly held that the state drug task force could not be considered a victim within the meaning of that state's law.[111] The Alaska Supreme Court allows its recovery through restitution orders as do the Supreme Courts of North Carolina and Nevada.[112] An appellate court in Wisconsin also allowed it even though the state may not be a "victim," the order was reasonable and appropriate.[113] Similarly, Florida allowed the costs of pretrial investigation to form the basis of a restitution order.[114]

Some statutes specifically authorize restitution to be awarded to dependents in homicide cases. For example, an Arizona statute defines the victim to include "the surviving dependent of a person who has suffered injury or pecuniary loss resulting from the crime of the accused."[115] A Maine law authorizes it for family members who are dependents of the deceased victim.[116] Where the law is silent, state appellate courts have split.[117] Those that refuse to allow awards to victim's dependents allow restitution only for the victim's funeral and burial expenses.

The Mississippi Supreme Court, although it upheld a $10,000 restitution award to the victim's family and $3,000 for funeral expenses, did not allow for a continuing restitution support order of $100 per month for the minor child. The Court ruled that the child was living with the mother and a new husband who could support him.[118]

Most state laws limit restitution to "specific," "actual," "liquidated," or "easily ascertainable" losses. Several states limit restitution to property damage; some add medical costs; but most simply speak of "economic" loss.[119] Oklahoma's statute speaks of "economic detriment suffered by the victim consisting of medical expenses actually incurred, damages to real and personal property and any other out-of-pocket expenses reasonably incurred as a direct result of the criminal act of the defendant." It adds that "no other elements of damages shall be included."[120] Pain and suffering and punitive damages awarded in civil actions are generally excluded.[121]

A few states, however, are more permissive. The North Carolina law is the broadest, defining restitution as "such losses and damages as ordinarily recovered by civil action."[122] Similarly, Alabama's statute allows for pecuniary damages that may be recovered against a defendant in a civil action.[123] Washington, harkening back to ancient law, provides in certain cases that restitution shall be twice the offender's gain or the victim's loss.[124] Nevada includes indirect damages.[125] Louisiana law provides that victims may be compensated for loss and inconvenience in addition to any monetary loss or medical expenses.[126]

Absent legislation, appellate courts have generally ruled against broader interpretations of restitution orders. They are concerned about criminal courts intruding too much into the domain of civil law. The Michigan Court of Appeals explains:

> Criminal and civil liability are not synonymous. A criminal conviction does not necessarily establish the existence of civil liability. Civil liability need not be established as a prerequisite to the requirement of restitution as a probation condition; such restitution for personal injury, therefore, generally should be more limited in scope than civil damages. . . . (W)e believe that restitution should encompass only those losses which are easily ascertained and measured, and which are a direct result of the defendant's criminal acts.[127]

Minnesota's highest court holds simply: "If the legislature intended the term (restitution) to be used more loosely, as a form of punitive damages, it should have used some other word or made its particular use of the word clearer."[128]

Notwithstanding this, a minority of appellate courts interpret the statutes more broadly. An Oregon appellate court judge, reacting to his court's decision that allowed restitution for pain and suffering, lamented in his dissent that "the majority approved joinder of questions of criminal liability with questions of liability for civil damages for trial, but then does not allow a trial on civil liability."[129] Other appellate courts in Washington, Nebraska, Arizona and Pennsylvania have upheld similar civil-type orders. A Washington appellate court approved a $1,500 award for a beating victim, based on that state's probation statute authorizing probation conditions "which bear a reasonable relation to the defendant's duty to make reparations, or as tend to prevent the future commissions of crime."[130] Nebraska's highest court allowed a restitution order compensating a victim for pain and suffering pursuant to the state's restitution statute calling for "reparations as the court determines to be appropriate for the loss or damage caused by the crime."[131] In upholding the $6,000 order in the *Garner* case detailed earlier, the Arizona Court of Appeals rejected the notion that restitution must be limited to liquidated or easily measured damages.[132] Finally, the Pennsylvania Supreme Court upheld Judge Forer's restitution order in the *Commonwealth v. Walton* case, discussed in Chapter 4, in which the court ordered the defendant to pay $25 a week for nineteen years, even though the state was without a restitution statute at the time. In a subsequent case, the court reviewed appellate decisions from other states allowing broad awards, and agreed with them even though it noted that Pennsylvania's statute, effective after *Walton,* was more specific than those in other states.[133]

Although the Washington Restitution Statute[134] disallows "intangible losses," an appellate court refused to bar restitution for the counseling costs of the victim. Because the psychological damage to the child sexual abuse victim may last a lifetime, counseling, it held, was commonly recognized as an essential part of the recovery process.[135] A Colorado appellate court allowed the victim to receive restitution for the reward paid by the victim of the burglary. It held that the statute requires restitution for actual damages sustained. In the case, the trial court rightfully concluded that the reward constituted part of those actual costs and its payment would not have been necessary but for the actions of the defendant and his cohorts.[136] An Iowa appellate court allowed restitution in the amount of the employer's expectant profits from the sale of the merchandise that was stolen by the defendant rather than the actual worth of the property in question.[137]

Most appellate courts agree that defendants who fail to protest restitution orders at the time that they are imposed usually lose the right to contest them later.[138] Further, defendants who offer to pay certain amounts of restitution as part of a plea bargain may not later be able to contest the amounts as unauthorized by statute or claim inability to pay.[139]

Statutes vary in regard to acts for which victims may receive restitution. At the narrowest, the offender must be convicted of the specific offense for which the restitution is ordered.[140] As a result, restitution may not be ordered for the crime of leaving the scene, for example, notwithstanding the victims' injuries. In one such case, the Michigan Supreme Court ruled:

> Criminal charges must be specific, and proved beyond a reasonable doubt. . . . Here the criminal has been convicted of one charge, but his freedom from incarceration . . . is related to another act (negli-

gence resulting in harm to the victim), precedent in time, with respect to which neither criminal charges nor civil complaint has been made.[141]

Similarly, restitution may not be ordered for complaints that are dismissed or on which the defendant was acquitted. Even where statutes defining restitution do not specify offenses for which the defendant was convicted, many appellate courts have construed these statutes narrowly. As a result, if a defendant is accused of passing a series of bad checks but pleads or is found guilty of a set amount, the court may not order restitution for all of the bad checks.[142]

However, there are a number of exceptions. The defendant admits his culpability for the restitution on the dismissed or other acquitted charges. The defendant agrees to pay restitution for these charges as part of a plea bargaining arrangement. The court specifically finds sufficient evidence of the offender's culpability, notwithstanding the dismissal or acquittals.

The rationale for allowing restitution pursuant to plea bargains for dismissed counts was spelled out by a Michigan appellate court.

> Every trial judge accepts plea agreement convictions to lesser offenses . . . and hears the defendant admit the greater or completed criminal conduct. Crime should not be profitable. . . . If a judge cannot require restitution of a loss he knows has occurred, he may decide against probation.[143]

The key is that there must be on the record acknowledgment from the defendant that he does indeed owe the money before the order is made.[144] For example, the amount to be ordered can be read into the record before the defendant agrees to the plea bargain.[145] The Montana Supreme Court similarly upheld restitution for uncharged offenses for which the defendant was granted immunity. Nonetheless, the court found that the defendant could be ordered restitution for these charges because of the plea bargain. Although the plea did not indicate for which burglaries and thefts restitution would be ordered, the presentence report clearly set forth the total amount of restitution owed for 11 charged offenses and six uncharged offenses to which the defendant admitted.[146]

The Arizona Supreme Court spelled out the exact nature of such an agreement in that state: (1) a specific dollar amount of restitution is set forth in the plea agreement; (2) a defendant states in court that he agrees to pay that dollar amount; or (3) the defendant pleads guilty after being warned by the trial judge that a specific dollar amount may be ordered. Notwithstanding this, the Arizona Supreme Court upheld a restitution order pursuant to a plea bargain in which the full, specific amount of restitution was not agreed to. But the court found that the defendant did know that restitution would cover all lost property. And, because the plea was advantageous to the defendant, the court held he *would have* agreed to it had he known the specific restitution order. As a result, the defendant was not allowed to appeal the sentence at a later time.[147]

The North Dakota Supreme Court refused to invalidate a restitution order for damages caused by a car even when it was invalid under that state's restitution statute because it was not related to the criminal act of leaving the scene because the defendant agreed to pay under a plea agreement.[148] An Illinois appellate court, for the same reason, refused to overturn a restitution award to a prosecutor even though the prosecutor did not meet the legal standard for being a victim under state law. Again, the defendant had agreed to the order as part of the plea bargain.[149]

A number of states, including Michigan, Illinois and California, go further. Even if the defendant is convicted of a crime with a specified dollar limit, the court may order restitution in an amount that exceeds that limit. For example, although the defendant was convicted of criminal damage to property below $150, the restitution order was $200. In this case, the Illinois Appellate Court held that "[t]he question of damages related only to the court's exercise of its power to place defendant on probation."[150] Similarly, an Oregon appellate court allowed for restitution even though the defendant was convicted of attempted theft. It held that "the fact that defendant's conviction is for an attempt to commit theft would not preclude the court from conditioning probation upon restitution of the amount actually taken, even though a larger amount."[151] Other appellate courts have also ruled that restitution orders may exceed the court's civil jurisdiction.[152]

No appellate courts have gone further than California's in allowing restitution for crimes for which the defendant was not convicted. In one case, an appellate court upheld a court order adding a $7,000 restitution obligation to a second victim, eight months after imposition of the disposition, which included an order of restitution for only $821 to the first victim.[153] In another case, the Supreme Court of California upheld an order of restitution for a charge from which the jury had acquitted the defendant.[154] Although the court held that the acquittal would normally have meant no restitution, in the instant case additional circumstances were developed in the unusually prolonged probation hearing conducted by the meticulous trial judge. The trial court found that the restitution order was justified "because the defendant had shown the same type of dishonesty in regard to the disposition of those funds (he was acquitted of stealing) as he had demonstrated in the proved theft."[155] In a later opinion, the California court cautioned that "absent extraordinary circumstances, probation for a defendant may not be conditioned on restitution sums involved in purported crimes of which he was acquitted."[156]

Similarly, the state top court upheld restitution for parked cars damaged by a defendant convicted of leaving the scene. The court ruled that striking and damaging cars was an element of the crime of leaving the scene and therefore valid. Regarding arguments that restitution should only be for the direct result of the crime of conviction, such a limitation, it argued, would call into question various other probation conditions that are indisputably proper such as conditions relating to association, taking of fingerprints, employment, and costs of probation services. These too would not pass such a test.[157]

Almost all jurisdictions agree that the judge must make the final restitution order.[158] He may not delegate the task to probation or some other third party. However, probation or other third parties may conduct the research and recommend the restitution amount for the court's consideration.[159] The restitution order must be founded on some factual basis. The recommendation of an amount in a presentence report based on hearsay and unverified reports has been rejected as an inadequate basis for making the determination.[160] If the defendant disagrees with the amount, the court is generally required to have a hearing, giving the defendant a chance to present evidence and refute the victim's claims. A few jurisdictions require the restitution to be based on a preponderance of the evidence.[161] A handful of states, including Kentucky, Missouri and Tennessee, call for juries to be impaneled to determine restitution amounts.

The South Dakota Supreme Court is more typical. It ruled, for example, that while the defendant has a due process right to an adversarial hearing before restitution is required, the defendant has no greater procedural protections than those normally employed at sentencing. All that is required is that the defendant be given a meaningful opportunity to be heard. While the court did require the judge to provide written findings of fact in support of the order, it rejected a dissenting justice's call for a formal hearing with sworn witnesses, a right of cross-examination and proof such that the court is "reasonably satisfied" that the damages have been proven.[162]

A Louisiana appellate court requires even less. It ruled that the death of the victim was a sufficient basis within itself for the establishment of a $25,000 restitution order. No hearing was required because the statute only mandates that the amount be determined by the court.[163]

In determining restitution orders, the court must consider the offender's ability to pay. Some state statutes and appellate courts require the court to examine an offender's resources prior to the imposition of the restitution order.[164] Even if the defendant claims poverty at the time of sentencing, some appellate courts have allowed the court to base the order on future earnings. As the Michigan Court of Appeals held "[i]n deciding what is reasonable, the court should be optimistic that probation and the defendant will both work."[165] All jurisdictions, however, must examine an offender's ability to pay before punishing him for nonpayment. The United States Supreme Court ruled in 1983 that to automatically revoke an indigent's probation due to his inability to pay restitution violates the Fourteenth Amendment.[166]

In *Bearden v. Georgia,* the defendant had been placed on probation and ordered to pay a $500 fine and $250 in restitution, the first $200 due immediately and the remaining $550 within four months. The defendant paid the first installment but failed to pay the second. He had lost his job shortly after being placed on probation and had been unable to obtain another despite his sincere efforts. Nonetheless, his probation was subsequently revoked and he was committed. In the opinion for the majority, Justice O'Connor based the decision on previous cases involving nonpayment of fines in which the court had ruled that indigents could not be incarcerated unless nonpayment was found to be willfull. The majority pointed out, however, that the court was not helpless in enforcing its restitution orders. It could extend payments, reduce the amounts, or impose community service alternatives. Then if the court found that these alternatives did not fulfill the punishment and deterrence goals of the sentence, it could impose an alternative sentence of incarceration, but only as a last resort.

> If, upon remand, the Georgia courts determine that petitioner did not make sufficient bona fide efforts to pay his fine, or determine that alternative punishment is not adequate to meet the State's interests in punishment and deterrence, imprisonment would be a permissible sentence. Unless such determinations are made, however, fundamental fairness requires that the petitioner remain on probation.[167]

The minority worried that in suggesting that the defendant could be eventually incarcerated for his nonpayment, the majority failed to take into account the fact that he had made partial payment of the order. The sentence, they reasoned, should therefore be proportional to the unmet portion of the defendant's sentence.

Consistent with *Bearden,* even indigent probationers may be held accountable for their nonpayment if they do not try to find work in order to earn money to meet their obligations. A Florida appellate court upheld a revocation in which the probationer failed to file two monthly reports with his probation officer, each of which was to contain a list of employers to whom the probationer had applied for work.[168] The very sacrifice a probationer may have to make in order to pay restitution is looked upon with approval by at least one state supreme court:

> In many instances, however, it will be necessary for defendant to make substantial sacrifices in order to make restitution to the victims of his crime. This is not an obstacle to an order requiring such restitution. Rather, where sacrifice is necessary, the probationer or parolee may learn to consider more carefully the consequences of his acts and thereby strengthen the offender's sense of responsibility. Thus, an order of restitution may properly require additional or alternative employment, a reduction of expenses, and even a temporary change in lifestyle in order to achieve that sense of responsibility which signals efforts of effective rehabilitation. . . . The rehabilitative goal is defeated only when the payments ordered by the court are so unreasonable in view of the defendant's financial circumstances and ability to work that, despite good faith efforts, the defendant cannot hope to comply.[169]

Some appellate courts have put the onus squarely on the defendant to prove his inability to pay.[170] A defendant cannot be released from payment if court finds they transferred assets to his wife to avoid payment.[171] The New Jersey Supreme Court ruled it a willful violation for a defendant who failed to pay because the court determined that the defendant gambled, drank and smoked, rather than paying restitution and the judge was convinced that the defendant did not look for work.[172]

There are some things courts can do to see that defendants adhere to their restitution orders. One appellate court, for example, allowed for the execution of a note and second deed of interest on property owned by the defendant.[173] But there are some things courts cannot do. One appellate court, for example, ruled that the court cannot put a lien on workers' disability to pay restitution when it is the only means of income for the defendant. Nor could probation seize the defendant's retirement accounts and sell his automobile and firearms.[174]

In 1990, the United States Supreme Court ruled that criminal restitution orders may be discharged in civil bankruptcy proceedings pursuant to Chapter 13 of the Bankruptcy Code.[175] Earlier in a 1986, the Court had ruled that restitution orders were non-dischargeable under Chapter 7 of the Bankruptcy Code.[176] The Court, in a seven-to-two decision, held that if Congress had not wanted to exempt restitution debts from bankruptcy proceedings, it could have explicitly written it into the law as it did in Chapter 7 bankruptcy cases. The minority argued that Congress had not intended to allow for such discharges.

At least one jurisdiction has ruled that the restitution obligation does not abate with the defendant's death.[177] Another ruled that it does.[178]

In some jurisdictions, if the restitution amount is agreed to by the defendant as part of plea negotiation and adopted by the court, the defendant may not expect later claims of indigency to absolve him of the obligation to make payment. The reason is because as a result of the original plea bargain, the victim may have foregone civil remedies. As a result, the court cannot consider lack of funds a defense for revocation because there is no alternative measure to guarantee the state's interest.[179] However, others are concerned that indigents not be penalized for their poverty, even if they agreed to pay at sentencing.[180]

If there are codefendants, each may be ordered an equal share of the order, an unequal share of the order based on his relative culpability[181] or each may be ordered to pay "jointly and severally."[182] In the latter case, each is responsible for the full amount, whether or not the codefendant pays his share. This gives each codefendant an interest in the other's performance.

Only Wisconsin's Supreme Court has expressed concern that criminal restitution not be used for the collection of a debt. It has held that if the probationer lacks the capacity to pay and has demonstrated a good faith effort during probation, failure to make restitution cannot be "cause" for extending probation.[183]

Where restitution is ordered in lieu of or in addition to other penalties, even after the defendant's probationary period may have run out, the order is enforceable as a civil judgment. A Vermont statute allows for restitution to be ordered as a term of probation with restitution as its only condition, whether or not any other sentence or disposition is imposed.[184] However, even where it is mandatory, the criminal judge cannot leave the order's determination up to the civil courts.[185]

§5.08   Restitution Collection and Practice

The ever-growing collection of statutory and case law regarding restitution reflects its increased use as a criminal sanction over the past several decades. Although national statistics are not regularly kept regarding restitution collections, the smattering of statistics that are maintained suggest broad and increasing use. The rate of collection, however, varies markedly among jurisdictions.

Despite Congress' intent to promote restitution orders in federal sentences, studies indicate that between 1988 and 1991, restitution was still ordered in less than one-half of the sentencing involving identifiable victims, such as embezzlement or robbery. In 1992, the federal courts established the United States Courts National Fine Center which became fully operational in 1995. The centralized agency receives and tracks payments of restitution and fines. It also provides accounting support and issues monthly notices to offenders who owe money. If a defendant defaults in payment, it notifies appropriate federal agencies including the requisite U.S. Attorney for prosecution.[186] However, the national center was abandoned in early 1996, because the task was found to be too complicated for one agency to handle.

According to a national survey of a sample of 20 state probation and parole agencies, conducted in 1990 for the National Institute of Justice, total restitution collected was almost $55 million ($54,837,288) that year.[187] Another study of felons sentenced in 32 counties across the country in 1992 reveals that in 1986 these courts sentenced 79,043 felons. Twenty-nine percent were ordered to pay restitution, with an average order of $3,400. The collection rate was 54 percent. Based on this sample, the study reveals that felons across the entire country were ordered to pay approximately $295 million in restitution, of which $159 million was actually paid.[188]

Other studies reveal varying collection rates. Utah probation documents a 66 percent collection rate, for example, among its juvenile offenders ordered to pay $500,000 in 1990.[189] On the other hand, another study found the mean collection rate in Cook County (Chicago) over three years, 1982-1984, averaged only 34 percent.[190] In 1994, Cook County probation collected $1.6 million. In that same period, probation in Massachusetts, a state with an equivalent population to Cook County, collected more than $10 million.[191]

Some probation departments report that collections have decreased as a result of more serious offenders being placed on probation, coupled with a lack of adequate procedures to collect the money. In many probation departments, the collection of restitution is simply an additional supervisory task. In others, sometimes by statute, offenders' payments go to pay fees and fines before they go to compensate victims.

Some departments maintain special collection units. Minneapolis probation maintains a separate restitution unit within its Department of Court and Field Services. The unit determines restitution as well as the payment schedule of defendants. It also enforces the payments. Offenders are given until the end of their probation to pay (one year for misdemeanants and two years for more serious misdemeanants). In 1988 the unit monitored 2,800 cases with awards amounting to more than $400,000. One study indicated the mean collection rate to be 50 percent.[192]

In Brooklyn, New York, the Victim Service Agency collects restitution in all non-probated misdemeanors (including deferred prosecution, diversion and filed cases). Offenders have from four to 10 months to pay. The staff consists of five full-time employees and collected more than $1 million in 1989.[193]

Studies indicate that collection rates have to do with both the character and circumstances of the offenders as well as the policy and procedures of the agency seeking to collect the money. Collection rates can be increased significantly through serious efforts to secure payment. These include such measures as reminder letters, phone calls and threats of court action.[194] Other studies reveal several common strategies used to increase collections:

> (1) Use money collections as one criterion for evaluating probation officers (Texas); (2) Tighten criteria for recommended money waivers and reductions in fees to the court (Texas, Oregon); (3) Work with judges to reduce the number of waivers granted by the courts (Texas); (4) Grant no waivers at sentencing, instead, grant waivers only after the offenders have been on probation 90 days and have shown that they truly cannot pay (Texas, Yakima County, Washington); (5) work with judges to have probationers pay their restitution before they make other payments; (6) Take over collection responsibilities from the clerk of courts or other offices that have no incentive to monitor and enforce collections (Oregon, Yakima County, Washington); (7) Install an automated system for recording collections and issuing overdue letters (Texas, Oregon, Yakima County, Washington); and (8) Require probationers who are in arrears to perform community work service unless they resume payments (Texas, Yakima County, Washington).[195]

To determine restitution, courts generally rely on three methods: (1) judicial fiat, (2) insurance claim and (3) victim/offender meetings.

The first method, also called the convenience model, describes a judge ordering the amount based on courtroom testimony, the plea agreement, the presentence report, victim allocution or the like. The court must be confident, however, that if the defendant objects to the determination, there has been enough evidence presented to sustain the court's order. The court must also consider the defendant's finances. This is necessary both in making the initial determination of the restitution amount and the plan of payment.

The second method is similar to the way policyholders make a claim on their insurance. The victim is asked to document his losses. Generally the victim is asked to bring in bills for cleanup, repair or replacement, if the damage was to property. If the losses were sustained as the result of personal injury, the victim is asked to bring in medical bills, documentation of missed work and so on. If the jurisdiction is concerned about how much of the losses are covered by insurance, the victim may also be asked to bring in his insurance coverage and claims. This method is particularly appropriate if the victim is not present at the hearing or if the exact costs of the crime are not fully realized at the time of the sentencing.

There are several problems with this method. First, it puts the onus on the victim, who may be unable to accomplish the task, especially if the crime resulted in injury or emotional distress. Second, certain losses may not be readily documented. If an item is stolen, the victim may not have a recent appraisal of its worth. Nor may it be possible to obtain an appraisal for an item that is not available for inspection. Third, the replacement cost of an item may be much higher than the actual value of the stolen or destroyed item. For example, a victim's used car may provide perfectly satisfactory transportation for the victim despite its nominal book value. To replace it with an equivalent reliable vehicle may cost the victim far more than the value of the stolen or destroyed car.

The third method puts the offender and the victim together and permits them to work out an agreement satisfactory to both sides. If such an agreement results, this method obviates the paperwork of getting cost estimates. Victim/offender meetings, if well-structured and monitored, can result in more than simple restitution agreements. They allow the victim to express his feelings directly to the offender, often breaking down the latter's rationalization of the crime. They may also help resolve the conflict between the parties that led to the crime in the beginning or that resulted from the crime. As previous cases have illustrated, they can be part of the offender's alternative sentence.

Summaries of several victim/offender meetings from the Quincy, Massachusetts District Court, highlighted in a Justice Department restitution training manual, demonstrate the powerful impact such meetings can have on victim and offender alike.

Case #1: Two sisters assaulted[196]

Two sisters were assaulted and beaten with a wooden table leg by a former family friend. The victims nervously shifted about in their chairs as they sat across the table from the offender. While describing the events that led to this face-to-face confrontation, one pointed at the offender and shouted angrily, "If you didn't drink so much, you wouldn't be in so much trouble. None of this would have happened."

The offender muttered under his breath, "Just get on with it." The victims explained that they all had been at their mother's home. The offender began drinking. He began to push one, then the other sister. They asked him to leave. Angered, he picked up the table leg and swung, missing his intended target but hitting the other sister in the face.

"You broke her nose—just look at her," one sister demanded in a loud voice. "You did some job on her—she had to have surgery because of you—you could have killed her."

Squirming in his seat, the offender, obviously very uncomfortable, cleared his throat. "O.K., what can I do now? I've gotten into enough trouble to last a long time. Look what happened to me—I face jail if I don't pay you—I got to go to drunk school."

Instantly, the victim who had been more severely injured responded sharply. "Listen, don't try to make me feel guilty. I could have sent you straight to jail—but I didn't want to. I know you have a drinking problem, but you'll have to pay for what you did to me. I hope it teaches you a lesson."

"O.K.," he responded, "you know I'll pay—let's not fight anymore. Do you have the bill here; can I see it?"

Together they worked out a satisfactory weekly payment schedule ensuring that the $660 restitution would be paid. After the offender left the room, one sister admitted, "I was kind of scared sitting down with him, but it worked out better than I thought it would. It's a good idea—putting all the cards on the table at one time. Now he knows he has to be responsible for what he did and either shape up or face the consequences."

Case #2: Hit and run driver[197]

A 65-year-old man, a concertmaster for the Shubert Theatre, driving home from work on a cold, snowy, winter night, became the victim of a hit-and-run driver. This elderly gentleman was trapped in his car for over three hours until help arrived.

During the face-to-face meeting, the victim spoke quietly, describing his experience. As he related more and more about the case, his voice grew stronger and his anger and frustration over what happened to him clearly came through.

The young offender, 17 years old, stared at the ground, had little eye contact with the victim, and said very little. "You know," the victim addressed him, "I have a grandson about your age. I don't understand how anyone could leave someone in the way you left me. What if I were seriously hurt or dying? As it was, I banged my head and was very confused for a few minutes. Do you realize how awful it was for me to be alone and have to wait such a long time for help?"

At this time the offender, a strong, muscular fellow, looked up at his victim, tears in his eyes. "Believe me, I haven't stopped thinking about that night. I haven't been able to sleep through a night since then. I thought I really hurt you very badly. Did you know that I got out of my car and ran to see you, but you looked dead! There was a big bang on the side of your head. I panicked and ran away. I'm sorry. I should have stayed to help or at least called someone from a phone booth. I'll pay you whatever you say. Whatever you want. I'm glad you're alive."

The older man stared at the offender a few seconds. He stood up and extended his arm. "It's O.K., son, we all make mistakes," he said while shaking the young man's hand, "You just have to learn to be responsible for them. I don't want anything from you except what it actually cost me. Two hundred dollars is what I had to pay so that's what I think is fair. What do you think?"

One week later the victim called the court to thank the staff for the $200 check he had received from the offender. "I really didn't expect anything like what happened during that meeting. I was so mad at that kid, I could have killed him. Now I feel that he made up for what he did. You people are on the right track."

Unlike court hearings, victims confront their offenders directly. The offenders are unshielded by lawyers, rules of evidence and courtroom etiquette. The real impact of the crime can be better conveyed in such a setting. Research indicates the powerful results of such victim/offender meetings. According to detailed analysis sponsored by the Justice Department, of the national restitution programs involving more than 17,000 juvenile offenders across the nation from 1977 to 1979, offenders who participated in victim/offender meetings had a consistently higher rate of victim restitution repayment.[198] In addition, they had a lower recidivism rate. The research was controlled for all variables, including seriousness of the offense, offender record, amount of restitution ordered, etc. Not only offenders are affected. Consider the Elkhart, Indiana Deputy Sheriff, victimized by Vietnam veteran Fred Palmer, who not only campaigned for Palmer's release from the state penitentiary, but became head of his local Victim Offender Reconciliation Program.

Once the victim and offender reach agreement as to the restitution amount, the judge must ratify it for the record.

Once the restitution amount is determined, the court must establish a specific plan of payment if the offender cannot pay the entire amount at once. Unless otherwise specified by the court, the restitution is not due until the expiration of the probationary sentence. Unless the offender is extremely responsible, he is likely to forget about it until the probationary period is about to end and then be unable to pay. It is far more prudent to require installment payments until the full amount is paid. This also enables the court or the prosecutor to monitor the payments and bring back nonpayers before the arrearage mounts too high.

Federal studies of restitution reveal that the overwhelming majority of offenders, both adults and juveniles, ordered to pay restitution will comply with their orders if they are allowed to pay in installments and are monitored by probation officials or other program staff. This holds true regardless of the seriousness of the offense, the seriousness of the offender's past record or whether or not the offender is employed at the time of disposition.[199] Out-of-pocket losses for most reported crime in this country is not very large. According to the Justice Department, nearly one-half of all losses from personal crimes are valued at less than $50 per victimization, and only 15 percent result in losses of $250 or more. Almost 40 percent of losses from household crimes are valued at under $50 with only 16 percent above $500. Only one of every 10 violent crime victims incurs medical expenses. Of those who do, 38 percent suffer losses below $249 and only 26 percent suffer losses of more than $250. The most costly crimes are motor vehicle thefts, with 86 percent of the victims suffering losses of $500 or more.[200]

If the victim has refused to meet the offender to determine restitution at the time of disposition, once restitution is paid in full, he may be more agreeable. This will allow the other benefits of such meetings to occur. It will also help "close" the restitution aspect of the case. If the offender is unable to arrange a meeting, the final payment to the victim could be accompanied by a letter of apology from the offender. Such a final meeting or letter will help insure that the restitution experience is personalized.

§5.09   Summary

An American psychologist theorized that restitution "contains the best features of punishment (deterrence, justice) and of clinical treatment (recognition of psychological basis of behavior; returning good for evil)." He goes on to say that restitution is a form of "psychological exercise, building muscles of the self, developing a healthy ego."[201]

Whether for healthy ego development or victim compensation, restitution harkens back to pre-modern law systems in which criminal acts were viewed as conflict between the offender and the victims. Restitution provides the defendant with the opportunity to pay back his victim and become better integrated into the community. According to a British criminologist, the use of restitution as an alternative sentence is "[w]iser in principle, more reformatory in its influence, more deterrent in its tendency and more economic to the community than the modern practice.[202] For all of these reasons, an American criminologist has labeled it "a sanction for all seasons."[203]

For the defense, the chance to involve the victim in the sentencing process and the offer of restitution may be paramount in convincing the court to impose an alternative sentence. If the victim is reconciled with the defendant, or at least not demanding that the defendant be locked up and the key thrown away, it is easier for the court to also show compassion or leniency. Initial research of some of the early victim rights legislation, including laws that increased victim participation in the sentencing process, have documented no increase in sentence severity.

> Attorneys frequently object to increased victim participation because they assume such involvement is synonymous with harsher penalties, retribution, obstruction and delay. There is no evidence to support these assumptions; the evidence that exists suggests the contrary. . . . This may suggest that the victims' primary concern is how they are treated, not what punishment the defendant incurs.[204]

For prosecutors, as for defense counsel, victim involvement in sentencing and restitution orders allows them to address the needs and concerns of the victim while still being mindful of the need to engage in plea negotiations, husband precious correctional and court resources and insure that justice is done.

For the court, victim involvement in sentencing and restitution orders helps restore a sentencing system that has too long ignored crime victims. In addition, victim participation in victim/offender mediation offers the court a powerful means of breaking down offender rationalization, an efficient means to settle complicated and conflicting restitution claims, as well as a method of resolving underlying victim/offender conflict which the court has neither the time nor the means to address.

Notes

[1] PRESIDENT'S TASK FORCE ON VICTIMS OF CRIME (1982). FINAL REPORT VI (1982).

[2] D. Hinrichs (1981). REPORT ON JUVENILE CRIME VICTIM PROJECT ATTITUDES AND NEEDS OF VICTIMS OF JUVENILE CRIME 56.

[3] Cook (1961). *The Code of Hammurabi 2100 B.C.* In R. Nice (ed.), TREASURY OF RULE OF LAW 25.

[4] *Id.* at 27.

[5] *Leviticus* 6:1-5.

[6] *Exodus* 22:16-17.

[7] Tuchman, B. (1978). A DISTANT MIRROR, 12-13.

[8] Gittler (1984). *Expanding The Role of the Victim in a Criminal Action: An Overview of Issues and Problems.* 11 SYMPOSIUM PEPPERDINE L. REV. 133-134, n.56.

[9] New York State Crime Victims Board (1983). ESTIMATES OF POTENTIAL VICTIM RECOVERIES FROM RESTITUTION IN NEW YORK STATE (unpublished). Quoted in Hudson (1984). *The Crime Victim and the Criminal Justice System: Time for a Change.* 11 SYMPOSIUM PEPPERDINE L. REV. 46.

[10] S. Schafer (1970). COMPENSATION AND RESTITUTION TO CRIME VICTIMS, SECOND EDITION.

[11] VICTIM AND WITNESS PROTECTION ACT OF 1982, 18 U.S.C. § 1503 (1982 & Supp. 11, 1984).

[12] COMPREHENSIVE CRIME CONTROL ACT OF 1984, Pub. L. No. 98-473,1984 U.S. CODE CONG. & AD. NEWS (98 Stat.) 1837, 2170 (to be codified at 42 U.S.C. § 1401).

[13] N.Y. EXEC. LAW § 632-a(1) (McKinney 1982) (similar legislation has been adopted in other states including Alabama, Arizona, Arkansas, Georgia, Idaho, Illinois, Indiana, Kentucky, Massachusetts, Minnesota, Montana, Nebraska, Oklahoma, South Carolina, Tennessee, Texas and Washington).

[14] DeValle (1984). *The Victim Witness Law: A New Approach.* BOSTON GLOBE, July 16.

[15] 18 U.S.C. §§ 3556, 3663, 3664 (Supp. 11, 1984) (effective Nov. 1, 1986); See, *e.g.,* ALA. CODE §§ 15-18-65 to -78 (1982 & Supp. 1985); ARIZ. REV. STAT. ANN. § 43.2350-59 (Supp. 1985); FLA. STAT. ANN. § 775.089 (West Supp. 1986); HAWAII REV. STAT. § 706-605 (1)(e)(Supp. 1984); MD. ANN. CODE Art. 27 § 640(g)(1), (2) (1992); ME. REV. STAT. ANN. tit. 17A, §§ 1321-1330 (1964 & Supp. 1985-1986); MISS. CODE ANN. §§ 99-37-1 to -23 (Supp. 1985); N.J. STAT. ANN. § 2C:43-3 (West 1982); N.Y. PENAL LAW § 60.27(1) (1987); OHIO REV. CODE § 2929.11 (Supp. 1986); OR. REV. STAT. §§ 137.103, 137.106, 137.109 (1985); S.D. CODIFIED LAWS ANN. § 22-61 (Supp. 1995) (felonies); VT. STAT. ANN. tit. 28, § 252(b) (1986). *Cf. State v. Holmes,* 379 N.W.2d 754 (Neb. 1986) (in which a divided court held that restitution was a civil or administrative penalty, not a criminal sanction; therefore, it did not constitute double jeopardy for the trial court to impose a $2,700 restitution order against a drug offender already sentenced to two years in prison.)

[16] CAL. CONST. art. 1, § 28 (B).

[17] See, *e.g.,* ALASKA STAT. § 12.55.100(a)(2) (1980); CONN. GEN. STAT. ANN. § 53a-30(a)(4) (West 1985); ILL. ANN. STAT. ch. 38, § 1005-6-3(b)(9) (Smith-Hurd Supp. 1985); MICH. COMP. LAWS ANN. § 771.3 (West 1982 & Supp. 1985).

[18] See, *e.g.,* COLO. REV. STAT. § 16-11-204.5 (Supp. 1985); LA. CODE CRIM. PROC. ANN. art. 895.1 (West Supp. 1986).

[19] TEX. CODE CRIM. PROC. art. 42.13, § 6(a)(8) (Vernon Supp. 1986).

[20] Defendant must restore property or make restitution: KY. REV. STAT. § 431.200 (1985); MO. ANN. STAT. § 546.630 (Vernon 1983); VA. CODE § 19.2-205.1 (Supp. 1985).

[21] See, *e.g.,* PA. STAT. ANN. tit. 62, § 48(c)(Supp. 1985).

[22] See, *e.g.,* ARK. STAT. ANN. § 41-1201 (2)(f)(1977); Ohio Rev. Code § 2951.02 (B)(9) (Anderson Supp. 1985); See also *Garski v. State,* 75 Wis. 2d 62, 248 N.W.2d 425 (1977).

[23] *Basile v. United States,* 38 A.2d 620 (D.C. Mun. App. 1944). Compare an earlier state appellate court decision in which it was held "[h]owever equitable it may seem that the victim of the transaction should be paid money which he was induced to part with by fraudulent representations, there is no provision in the law of our state for hanging over the head of a convicted criminal the threatened enforcement of an imposed sentence for the purpose of coercing him to pay a debt." *Ray v. State,* 40 Ga. 145, 146, 149 S.E. 64, 65 (1929).

[24] See, *e.g., State v. Bretz,* 185 Mont. 253, 605 P.2d 974 (1979), *reh'g denied,* 444 U.S. 1104, 100 S. Ct. 1073, 62 L. Ed. 2d 791 (1979); *Commonwealth v. Walton,* 438 Pa. 588, 397 A.2d 1179 (1979).

[25] See, *e.g.,* MODEL PENAL CODE § 301.1 (2)(h) (Proposed Official Draft 1962); ABA STANDARDS RELATING TO PROBATION, § 3.2 (c)(viii)(Approved Draft 1970).

[26] Umbreit, M. and B. Coates (1992). VICTIM-OFFENDER MEDIATION: AN ANALYSIS OF PROGAMS IN FOUR STATES OF THE U.S. Minneapolis, MN: Citizens Council Mediation Services.

[27] The Victim Offender Mediation Association is located at 777 S. Main St. Suite 200, Orange CA 92668, and the local program is the St. Vincent De Paul Center for Community Reconciliation.

[28] Headed by Dr. Mark Umbreit, the Center's address is 386 McNeal Hall, 1985 Buford Avenue, St. Paul, MN 55108.

[29] Laws 1983, ch. 70, § 1 (22 O.S. Supp. 1984 § 995 *et seq.*), struck down in *Swart v. State,* 720 P.2d 1265 (Okla Crim. 1986).

[30] 1994 AMERICAN BAR ASSOCIATION REPORT ON MEDIATION/DIALOGUE PROGRAMS, April, 1994.

[31] Umbreit, M. and B. Coates (1992). VICTIM-OFFENDER MEDIATION: AN ANALYSIS OF PROGRAMS IN FOUR STATES OF THE U.S. Minneapolis, MN: Citizens Council Mediation Services.

[32] See, *e.g.,* Galaway, B. and J. Hudson (eds.) (1996). RESTORATIVE JUSTICE: INTERNATIONAL PERSPECTIVE. Monsey, NY: Criminal Justice Press; M. Umbreit (1994). VICTIM MEETS OFFENDER: THE IMPACT OF RESTORATIVE JUSTICE AND MEDIATION. Monsey, NY: Criminal Justice Press.

[33] Kahn, J. (1994). *Making Peace with a Murderer.* BOSTON GLOBE, January 20.

[34] The mediator was Dr. Mark Umbreit, University of Minnesota Center for Restorative Justice and Mediation.

[35] Maloney, D., D. Romig and T. Armstrong (1988). JUVENILE PROBATION: THE BALANCED APPROACH. 39:3. Reno, NV: National Council of Juvenile and Family Court Judges.

[36] Special Session No. 1 of 1995, Senate Bill 100 (amending §§ 6301 et. seq. of Title 42 of PENN. CON. STAT.

[37] Bazemore, G. (1995). BALANCED AND RESTORATIVE JUSTICE FOR JUVENILES: A NATIONAL STRATEGY FOR JUVENILE JUSTICE IN THE 21ST CENTURY. Fort Lauderdale, FL: Florida Atlantic University.

[38] *National Victim Group Endorses Restorative Justice.* BALANCED AND RESTORATIVE JUSTICE UPDATE, Summer 1995, p. 2.

[39] *Restorative Justice Association Formed.* BALANCED AND RESTORATIVE JUSTICE UPDATE, Summer 1991, p. 4.

[40] *Beyond Crime and Punishment, Restorative Justice* (1991). Prison Fellowship, Washington D.C.

[41] Interview with Herb Sinkinson, Reparations Coordinator for Chittendon County, Vt., October 25, 1995.

[42] Remarks of John Gorczyk, Commissioner of Corrections, Vermont, Restorative Justice Symposium, National Institute of Justice and Office of Victims of Crime, Washington D.C., January, 25, 1996.

[43] Occupied by Kay Pranis as of 1996.

[44] Wood, F. (1995). *Restorative Justice Implementation in Minnesota is a Key Focus of State Department of Corrections.* RESTORATIVE JUSTICE NEWSLETTER, November.

[45] 18 U.S.C. § 3556, 3663, 3664 (Supp. 1984) (effective Nov. 1, 1986).

[46] 18 U.S.C. § 3663-64 (effective Nov. 1, 1986).

[47] See, *e.g., United States v. Keith,* 754 F.2d 475 (9th Cir. 1985), *cert. denied,* ___ U.S. ___, 106 S. Ct. 93, 88 L. Ed. 2d 76 (1985); *United States v. Palma,* 760 F.2d 475 (3d Cir. 1985); *United States v. Florence,* 741 F.2d 1066 (8th Cir. 1984); *United States v. Brown,* 744 F.2d 905 (2d Cir. 1984); *United States v. Sutterfield,* 743 F.2d 827 (11th Cir. 1984).

[48] 18 U.S.C. § 3663(a)(2) (1994).

[49] § 3663(a) (3).

[50] § 3663 (b) (4).

[51] § 3663 (d).

[52] 18 U.S.C. § 2327 (1994) (telemarketing); 18 U.S.C. § 2248, 2259 (1994). (Safe Streets for women).

[53] 18 U.S.C. § 2248(b)(3)(C,E) (1994).

[54] 18 U.S.C. § 2248 (b)(4)(B,C) (1994).

[55] See, *e.g., United States v. Murphy,* 28 F.3d 38 (7th Cir. 1994).

[56] *United States v. Palma,* 760 F.2d 475, 480 (3d Cir. 1985).

[57] *United States v. Atkinson,* 2d Cir. No. 85-1336 (4/18/86).

[58] *United States v. Arvanitis,* 902 F.2d 489 (7th Cir. 1990).

[59] *Hughey v. United States,* 110 S. Ct. 1979, 495 U.S. 411, 109 L. Ed. 2d 408 (1990).

[60] See, *e.g., United States v. Patterson,* 809 F.2d 244 (5th Cir. 1987); *United States v. Hairston,* 888 F.2d 1349 (11th Cir. 1989).

[61] *United States v. Savoie,* 985 F.2d 612 (1st Cir. 1993).

[62] See, *e.g., United States v. Molen,* 9 F.3d 1084 (4th Cir. 1993), *cert. denied,* 114 S. Ct. 1649 (1993).

[63] *United States v. Boula,* 997 F.2d 263 (7th Cir. 1993).

[64] See, *e.g., United States v. Plumley,* 993 F.2d 1140 (4th Cir. 1993), *cert. denied,* 114 S. Ct. 279 (1993).

[65] See, *e.g., United States v. Clark,* 957 F.2d 659 (9th Cir. 1992); *United States v. Albro,* 32 F.3d 173 (5th Cir. 1994).

[66] *United States v. Prendergast,* 979 F.2d 1289 (8th Cir. 1992), *appeal after remand,* 4 F.3d 560 (1993).

[67] See, *e.g., United States v. Murphy,* 28 F.3d 38 (7th Cir. 1994); *United States v. Lavin,* 27 F.3d 40 (2d Cir. 1994), *cert. denied,* 115 S. Ct. 453, 130 L. Ed. 2d 362 (1994).

[68] *United States v. Johnson,* 983 F.2d 216 (11th Cir. 1993); *United States v. Grundhoefer,* 916 F.2d 788 (2d Cir. 1990).

[69] *Hughey v. United States,* 110 S. Ct. 1979, 495 U.S. 411, 109 L. Ed. 2d 408 (1990).

[70] *United States v. Salcedo-Lopez,* 907 F.2d 97 (9th Cir. 1990).

[71] *United States v. Husky,* 924 F.2d 223 (11th Cir.), *cert. denied,* 502 U.S. 833, 112 S. Ct. 111, 116 L. Ed. 2d 81 (1991).

[72] *United States v. Hicks,* 997 F.2d 594 (9th Cir. 1993).

[73] *United States v. Keith,* 754 F.2d 1388 (9th Cir. 1985), *cert. denied,* 106 S. Ct. 93, 474 U.S. 829, 88 L. Ed. 2d 276.

[74] *United States v. Mullins,* 971 F.2d 1138 (4th Cir. 1992).

[75] See, *e.g., United States v. Young,* 953 F.2d 1288 (11th Cir. 1992); *United States v. Braslawsky,* 913 F.2d 466 (7th Cir. 1990).

[76] *United States v. Patty,* 992 F.2d 1045 (10th Cir. 1993).

[77] See, *e.g., United States v. Arnold,* 947 F.2d 1236 (5th Cir. 1991); *United States v. Marsh,* 932 F.2d 710 (8th Cir. 1991); *United States v. Soderling,* 970 F.2d 529 (9th Cir. 1992).

[78] *United States v. Clark,* 957 F.2d 248 (6th Cir. 1992).

[79] *United States v. Stouffer,* 986 F.2d 916 (5th Cir. 1993), *cert. denied,* 114 S. Ct. 115, 126 L. Ed. 2d 80 (1994).

[80] *United States v. Hammer,* 967 F.2d 339 (9th Cir. 1992).

[81] See, *e.g., United States v. Simpson,* 8 F.3d 546 (7th Cir. 1993): *United States v. Kress,* 944 F.2d 155 (3d Cir. 1991) (post judgment), *cert. denied,* 112 S. Ct. 1163, 117 L. Ed. 2d 410 (1991).

[82] See, *e.g., United States v. Patty,* 992 F.2d 1045 (10th Cir. 1993); *United States v. Rochester,* 898 F.2d 971 (5th Cir. 1990).

[83] See, *e.g., United States v. Salcedo-Lopez,* 907 F.2d 97 (9th Cir. 1990); *Ratliff v. United States,* 999 F.2d 1023 (6th Cir. 1993).

[84] *United States v. Hand,* 863 F.2d 1100 (3d Cir. 1988).

[85] *United States v. House,* 808 F.2d 508 (7th Cir. 1986).

[86] See, *e.g., United States v. Hemsley,* 941 F.2d 71 (2d Cir. 1991), *cert. denied,* 112 S. Ct. 1162, 117 L. Ed. 2d 409 (1991); *United States v. Smith,* 944 F.2d 618 (9th Cir. 1991), *cert. denied,* 112 S. Ct. 1515, 117 L. Ed. 2d 651 (1991); *United States v. Fountain,* 768 F.2d 790 (7th Cir. 1985), *cert. denied,* 475 U.S. 1124, 106 S. Ct. 1647, *modified,* 732 F.2d 1338 (1985).

[87] *United States v. Casamento,* 887 F.2d 1141 (2d Cir. 1989), *cert. denied,* 110 S. Ct. 1138, 493 U.S. 1081, 107 L. Ed. 2d 1043 (1989), *aff'd,* 926 F.2d 1311 (1990).

[88] *United States v. McHenry,* 952 F.2d 328 (9th Cir. 1991).

[89] See, *e.g., United States v. Rice,* 945 F.2d 40 (2d Cir. 1992); *United States v. Brandon,* 17 F.3d 409 (1st Cir.), *cert. denied,* 115 S. Ct. 80, 130 L. Ed. 2d 34 (1994); *United States v. Owens,* 901 F.2d 1457 (8th Cir. 1990).

[90] *United States v. Williams,* 996 F.2d 231 (10th Cir. 1993).

[91] See, *e.g. United States v. Narvaez,* 995 F.2d 759 (7th Cir. 1993).

[92] *United States v. Logar,* 975 F.2d 958 (3d Cir. 1992).

[93] *United States v. Morrison,* 938 F.2d 168 (10th Cir. 1991).

[94] *United States v. Blanchard,* 9 F.3d 22 (6th Cir. 1993).

[95] See, *e.g., United States v. Patty,* 992 F.2d 1045 (10th Cir. 1993); *United States v. Piche,* 981 F.2d 706 (4th Cir. 1992), *cert. denied,* 113 S. Ct. 2356, 124 L. Ed. 2d 264 (1992).

[96] *United States v. Smith,* 47 F.3d 681 (4th Cir. 1995).

[97] See, *e.g., United States v. Payan,* 992 F.2d 1387 (5th Cir. 1993).

[98] See, *e.g., United States v. All Star Industries,* 962 F.2d 465 (5th Cir. 1992), *cert. denied,* 113 S. Ct. 377, 121 L. Ed. 2d 288.

[99] See, *e.g., United States v. Brewer,* 983 F.2d 181 (10th Cir. 1993), *cert. denied,* 113 S. Ct. 2348, 124 L. Ed. 2d 257 (1993).

[100] N.C. GEN. STAT. § 15A-1343(d)(1983). (Amended in 1985: "[N]o third party shall benefit by way of restitution . . . as a result of the liability of that third party to pay indemnity . . . but . . . payment of indemnity . . . does not prohibit or limit in any way the power of the court to require the defendant to make complete and full restitution . . . to the aggrieved party for the total amount of damages or loss caused by the defendant.") Upheld, *State v. Maynard,* 339 S.E.2d 666 (N.C. App. 1986).

[101] See, *e.g.,* OR. REV. STAT. § 137.103(4) (1985) (restitution to any party suffering pecuniary damages as a result of the defendant's crime).

[102] See, *e.g., People v. Crago,* 24 Misc. 2d 739, 204 N.Y.S.2d 774 (1960) (in which the court allowed restitution to the embezzled union fund, but not the insurer of the bank that had repaid the embezzled funds); *People v. Daugherty,* 104 Ill. App. 3d 89, 432 N.E.2d 391 (1982) (insurance company not a victim within the meaning of Illinois statute). But *cf., People v. Calhoun,* 145 Cal. App. 3d 568, 193 Cal. Rptr. 394 (1983); *State v. Flores,* 513 S.W.2d 66 (Tex. 1974); *State v. Yost,* 232 Kan. 370, 654 P.2d 458 (1982) (in which the courts held that by reimbursing the victims, the third parties had stepped into the victims' shoes).

[103] *Alger v. Commonwealth,* 19 Va. App. 252, 450 S.E.2d 765 (1994); see also *People v. Foster,* 18 Cal. Rptr. 2d 1 (1993) (state statute permits restitution to insurance company).

[104] MICH. COMP. LAWS ANN. §780.751 *et. seq.* (West 1994).

[105] *People v. Washpun,* 438 N.W.2d 305 (Mich. Ct. App. 1989).

[106] See, *e.g., State v. Merrill,* 665 P.2d 1022 (Ariz. Ct. App. 1983); *State v. Stayer,* 706 P.2d 611 (Utah 1985); *People v. Bond,* 297 N.W.2d 620 (Mich. Ct. App. 1980).

[107] *State v. Webb,* 559 A.2d 658 (Vt. 1989) (pursuant to Vt. Stat. Ann. tit. 13, §7043 (Supp. 1994).

[108] Idaho Code § 19-5304(1).

[109] Ill. Ann. Stat. ch. 38, § 1005-5-6(b) (1996).

[110] *People v. Evans,* 122 Ill. App. 3d 733, 461 N.E.2d 634 (1984), *cert. denied,* 488 N.E.2d 295 (1984).

[111] *State v. Murray,* 529 N.W. 2d 453 (Minn. Ct. App. 1995).

[112] See, *e.g., Gonzales v. State,* 608 P.2d 23 (Alaska 1980); *State v. Stallings,* 316 N.C. 535, 342 S.E.2d 519 (1986); *Igbinovia v. State,* 895 P.2d 1304 (Nev. 1995).

[113] *State v. Connelly,* 143 Wis. 2d 500, 421 N.W.2d 859 (Wis. Ct. App. 1988).

[114] *Cuba v. State,* 362 So. 2d 29 (Fla. Dist. Ct. App. 1978).

[115] Ariz. Rev. Stat. Ann. § 13-4201(4)(1989).

[116] Me. Rev. Stat. Ann. tit. 17-A, §§ 1322-1324 (West 1983).

[117] See, *e.g., People v. Catron,* 678 P.2d 1 (Colo. Ct. App. 1983) (victim's minor children were not direct aggrieved party pursuant to statute); *State v. Brown,* 263 Mont. 223, 867 P.2d 1098 (1994); *contra, People v. Clark,* 130 Cal. App. 3d 371, 181 Cal. Rptr. 682 (1982) (allowed for minor children); *People v. Wager,* 129 Mich. App. 819; 342 N.W.2d 619 (1983) (loss resulting from death included income contributed by the decedent who was the family breadwinner.): *State v. Young,* 63 Wash. App. 324, 818 P.2d 1375 (1991) (rest for child support of victim's son. Court further held that insurance to victim's son need not be credited against such payments.)

[118] *Butler v. State,* 544 So. 2d 816 (Miss. 1989).

[119] See, *e.g.,* Ark. Stat. Ann. § 41-1203(2)(h) (1977) (actual loss); Ohio Rev. Code Ann. § 2951.02(c) (Anderson Supp. 1985) (property damage for misdemeanors only).

[120] Okla. Stat. Ann. tit. 22, § 991(f)(3) (1986).

[121] See, *e.g.,* Wash. Rev. Code Ann. § 13.40.020.(17) (Cum. Supp. 1987) ("easily ascertainable damages for injury or loss of property, actual expenses incurred for medical treatment for physical injury . . . shall not include reimbursement for damages for mental anguish, pain and suffering, or other intangible losses;" discussed in *State v. Morse,* 45 Wash. App. 197, 723 P.2d 1209 (Wash. App. 1986).

[122] N.C. Gen. Stat. 515A-1343(d) (1983).

[123] Ala. Code 515-18-66 (1982).

[124] Wash. Rev. Code Ann. § 9A.20.030(1) (Supp. 1986) (Court may order in lieu of a fine, restitution up to double the victim's loss from the crime's commission); see also Utah Code Ann. § 76-3-201(3)(a)(Supp. 1985) (in addition to any other sentence, court may order restitution up to double the amount of pecuniary damages).

[125] Nev. Rev. Stat. § 209.4825 (1985) (victims include those suffering damages indirectly resulting from criminal conduct).

[126] La. Code Crim Proc. Ann. Art 895.1 (A), (B), (5) (West Supp. 1995).

[127] *People v. Heil,* 79 Mich. App. 739, 748-49, 262 N.W.2d 895, 900 (1977).

[128] *State v. Fader,* 358 N.W.2d 42, 48 (Minn. 1984).

[129] *State v. Sullivan,* 24 Or. App. 99,105, 544 P.2d 616, 619 (1976) (J. Schwab, dissenting). *Sullivan* was overruled later in the year by *State v. Stalheim,* 275 Or. 683, 552 P.2d 829 (1976), in which the court cited the *Sullivan* dissent and found that Oregon's restitution statute, Or. Rev. Stat. § 137540(10), permitted restitution or reparation to the victim only and limited recovery to amounts that were readily measurable.

[130] *State v. Morgan,* 8 Wash. App. 189, 504 P.2d 1195 (1973).

[131] *State v. Brehrens,* 204 Neb. 785, 285 N.W.2d 513 (1979).

[132] *State v. Garner,* 115 Ariz. 579, 566 P.2d 1055 (Ariz. Ct. App. 1977), relying on *Shenah v. Henderson,* 106 Ariz. 399, 476 P.2d 854 (1970).

[133] *Commonwealth v. Balisteri,* 329 Pa. Super. Ct. 148, 478 A.2d 5 (1984).

[134] Wash. Rev. Code Ann. § 13.40.020 (17) (West 1983).

[135] *State v. Landrum,* 66 Wash. App. 791, 832 P2d 1359 (1992).

[136] *People v. Dillingham,* 881 P.2d 440 (Colo. Ct. App. 1994).

[137] *State v. Ihde,* 532 N.W.2d 827 (Iowa Ct. App. 1995).

[138] *Commonwealth v. Walton,* 483 Pa. 588, 397 A.2d 1179 (1979); *State v. Garner,* 115 Ariz. 579, 566 P.2d 1055 (Ariz.Ct.App. 1977).

[139] See, *e.g., State v. Steele,* 100 N.M. 492, 672 P.2d 665 (N.M. Ct. App. 1983) (in which the court ruled that the defendant was bound by his plea agreement to pay restitution of $50,000 whether or not the amount was authorized by state law); *cf., Doherty v. State,* 448 So. 2d 624 (Fla. Dist. Ct. App. 1984) (in which the court upheld a plea based on the defendant's waiver of his right to have the state prove his inability to pay restitution).

[140] Fla. Stat. Ann. § 947.181(1) (West 1985) (restitution ordered for offense for which parolee was imprisoned unless the commissioner finds reasons to the contrary).

[141] *People v. Becker,* 349 Mich. 476, 481, 84 N.W.2d 833, 835-836 (1957); *cf., Bowling v. State,* 479 So. 2d 146 (Fla. Dist. Ct. App. 1985) (in which the court ruled that while restitution must bear a significant relationship to the convicted offense, it need not be a necessary element of the offense, upholding a restitution order resulting from an automobile accident caused by the probationer even though he was convicted of failure to stop and render aid).

[142] See, *e.g., People v. Mahle,* 57 Ill. 2d 279, 312 N.E.2d 267 (1974); *cf., United States v. Elkin,* 731 F.2d 1005 (2d Cir. 1984) (in which the court ruled restitution under the federal statute may include only the specific crime charged for which the defendant is convicted). Contra, *Jones v. State,* 480 So. 2d 163 (Fla. Dist. Ct. App. 1985) (though defendant was convicted of receiving stolen items, restitution ordered for costs arising from burglary as damages bore "a significant relationship" to the convicted offense.)

[143] *People v. Gallagher,* 55 Mich. App. 613, 223 N.W.2d 92 (1974); see also Iowa Code Ann. 910.1(3) (West Supp.1985) (restitution is authorized for the convicted offense and "any other crime . . . admitted or not contested by the offender"); Utah Code Ann. § 76-3-201(3)(a) (Supp. 1985) (restitution authorized for other criminal conduct admitted by defendant to sentencing court); *cf., Phillips v. United States,* 679 F.2d 192 (9th Cir. 1982) (in which the court ruled that the defendant "agreed to make restitution for crimes for which he was not convicted); *State v. Reese,* 124 Ariz. 212, 603 P.2d 104 (Ariz. Ct. App. 1979); *People v. Quinonez,* 735 P.2d 159 (Colo. 1987); *Lee v. State,* Md. Ct. Spec. App. No. 161, 499 A.2d 969 (1985) (in which the court upheld restitution on the basis of an indictment count that had been *nolle prosequi,* but in which the defendant agreed to make restitution or acknowledged his liability for it).

[144] See, *e.g.*, *State v. Wilson*, 459 N.W.2d 457 (S.D. 1990).

[145] *State v. Gerard*, 57 Wis. 2d 611, 205 N.W.2d 374, 378-80, *app. dismissed*, 414 U.S. 804, 94 S. Ct. 148, 38 L. Ed. 2d 40 (1973).

[146] *State v. Blanchard*, 889 P.2d 1180 (Mont. 1995).

[147] *State v. Grijalba*, 157 Ariz. 112, 755 P.2d 417 (1988).

[148] *State v. Steinolfson*, 483 N.W.2d 182 (N.D. 1992).

[149] *People v. Lawrence*, 206 Ill. App. 3d 622, 565 N.E.2d 322 (1990).

[150] *People v. Tidwell*, 33 Ill. App. 3d 232, 277, 338 N.E.2d 113, 117 (1975).

[151] *State v. Foltz*, 14 Or. App. 582, 585, 513 P.2d 1208, 1210 (1973).

[152] See, *e.g.*, *State v. Scherr*, 9 Wis. 2d 418, 101 N.W.2d 77 (1960) (power to determine restitution does not depend on the civil jurisdiction of the court, which in this case was limited to $200).

[153] *People v. Miller*, 256 Cal. App. 2d 348, 64 Cal. Rptr. 20 (1967).

[154] *People v. Lent*, 15 Cal. 3d 481, 541 P.2d 545, 124 Cal. Rptr. 905 (1975).

[155] *People v. Richards*, 17 Cal. 3d 614, 624, 552 P.2d 97, 103, 131 Cal. Rptr. 537, 543 (1976) discussing *Lent*, 15 Cal. 3d 481, 541 P.2d 545, 124 Cal. Rptr. 905 (1975).

[156] *Id.*

[157] *People v. Dailey*, 286 Cal. Rptr. 772 (Cal. 1991).

[158] See, *e.g.*, *Commonwealth v. Seminko*, 297 Pa. Super. Ct. 418, 443 A.2d 1192 (1982) (trial court's obligation to determine restitution is not delegable); *People v. Fuller*, 57 N.Y.2d 152, 441 N.E.2d 563, 455 N.Y.S.2d 253 (1982) (in which the court ruled that while the sentencing court may order probation to act as factfinder and submit a report that the court may accept or reject for restitution, it may not delegate the power to determine the restitution); *accord, People v. Good*, 287 Mich. 110, 282 N.W. 920 (1938) (in which the court ruled that not only must the sentencing court determine the restitution amount, but also the payment plan) *State v. Johnson*, 711 P.2d 1295 (Hawaii 1985); *Contra, State v. Stinson*, 424 A.2d 327 (Me. 1981) (in which the court upheld trial judge's delegation to probation the task of determining the restitution order within strict parameters established by the court).

[159] See, *e.g.*, ILL. REV. STAT. ch. 38, § 1005-5-6 (1981) ("A presentence hearing shall be held to assess the financial capacity of the defendant to make restitution as well as determine the amount and conditions of payment at the court's discretion").

[160] See, *e.g.*, *United States v. Watchman*, 749 F.2d 616 (10th Cir. 1984) (in which the court held that Congress intended the determination of restitution to require, if necessary, a special hearing, but more than generalities contained in the presentence report).

[161] See, *e.g.*, *Commonwealth v. Nawn*, 391 Mass. 1, 474 N.E.2d 545 (1985) (in which the court required a hearing in which the defendant has a chance to cross-examine the victim as to the restitution, the judge may consider the defendant's ability to pay, and the Commonwealth must prove the amount by a preponderance of the evidence).

[162] *State v. Tuttle*, 460 N.W.2d 157 (S.D. 1990).

[163] *State v. Schmidt*, 558 So. 2d 255 (La. Ct. App. 1990).

[164] See, *e.g.,* ARIZ. REV. STAT. ANN. § 13-603(C) (Supp. 1985) (court must consider the "economic circumstances of the convicted person"); MICH. COMP. LAWS ANN. § 771.3(5)(a) (West Supp. 1985) (court must take into account "financial resources" of probationer and the "nature of the burden" that restitution payments will impose, with "due regard to his other obligations" and amount is not to exceed what probationer is able to pay during the term of probation); *State v. Farrell,* 676 P.2d 168 (Mont. 1984) (in which court ruled that a restitution hearing requires a meaningful inquiry into the defendant's finances); *accord, State v. Lack,* 98 N.M. 500, 650 P.2d 22 (1982) (in which the court held that the defendant must have an opportunity to challenge his ability to pay restitution order).

[165] *People v. Gallagher,* 55 Mich. App. 613, 619, 223 N.W.2d 92, 95 (1974); *cf. State v. Wilson,* 150 Ariz. 602, 724 P.2d 1271 (Ariz. Ct. App. 1986) (even when statute requires the court to consider the defendant's economic circumstances at disposition, this is unworkable if defendant is incarcerated because court cannot predict future finances. Holds that court may ignore the question and defendant may petition the court upon release for hearing to reconsider his economic circumstances).

[166] *Bearden v. Georgia,* 461 U.S. 660, 103 S. Ct. 2064, 76 L. Ed. 2d 221(1983).

[167] *Id.* at 674, 103 S. Ct. 2074, 76 L. Ed. 2d at 234.

[168] *Chappell v. State,* 429 So. 2d 84 (Fla. Dist. Ct. App. 1983); *cf. People v. Cottrell,* 141 Ill. App. 3d 364, 95 Ill. Dec. 858, 490 N.E.2d 950 (1986) (employment made a condition of probation); *People v. Hodgkins,* Cal. Ct. App. 5th Dist. No. F007169 (9/9/87) (seek and maintain employment); *Hoffman v. State,* 711 S.W.2d 151 (Ark. 1986) (failure to search for work outside of car sales and purchase of $17,000 car supported finding that nonpayment of restitution was "inexcusable").

[169] *Commonwealth v. Wood,* 300 Pa. Super. 463, 468, 446 A.2d 948, 950 (1982).

[170] See, *e.g., Brown v. State,* 10 Ark. App. 387, 664 S.W.2d 507 (1984) (in which the court found that the mere fact of unemployment was not enough to demonstrate indigency where defendant offered no evidence of search for work or living expenses); *State v. Young,* 21 N.C. App. 316, 204 S.E.2d 185 (1974) (defendant should offer evidence of inability to make payments); *contra, Depson v. State,* 363 So. 2d 43 (Fla. Dist. Ct. App. 1978) (court must make affirmative finding that defendant is able to pay).

[171] See, *e.g., People v. Modjeska,* 553 N.Y.S.2d 216 (N.Y. Sup. App. 1990).

[172] *State v. Townsend,* 222 N.J. Super. 273, 536 A.2d 782 (1988).

[173] *People v. Neptune,* 866 P.2d 176 (Colo. Ct. App. 1993).

[174] *Green v. State,* 631 So. 2d 167 (Miss. 1994).

[175] *Pennsylvania Department of Public Welfare v. Davenport,* 495 U.S. 555, 110 S. Ct. 2126, 109 L. Ed. 2d 588 (1990).

[176] *Kelly v. Robinson,* 479 U.S. 36, 107 S. Ct. 353, 93 L. Ed. 2d 216 (1986).

[177] *State v. Christensen,* 866 P.2d 533 (Utah 1993).

[178] *People v. Peters,* 205 Mich. App. 312, 517 N.W.2d 773 (1994).

[179] *United States v. Johnson,* 767 F. Supp. 243 (S.D. Ala. 1991); see also *People v. Tharp,* 577 N.E.2d 492 (Ill. App. 1991) (by accepting plea, waived right to raise inability to pay later).

[180] *State v. Dye,* 715 S.W. 2d 36 (Tenn. 1986) (*Bearden* court made no suggestion that its reasoning depended upon the procedure by which the restitution came to be).

[181] See, *e.g., United States v. Anglian,* 784 F.2d 765 (6th Cir. 1986) (may be proportional based on individual culpability).

[182] See, *e.g., State v. LaCasce,* 512 A.2d 312 (Me. 1986); *Morrison v. State,* 181 Ga. App. 440, 352 S.E.2d 622 (1987).

[183] *Huggett v. State,* 83 Wis. 2d 790, 266 N.W.2d 404 (1978); upheld in *State v. Davis,* 127 Wis. 2d 486, 381 N.W.2d 333 (1986); *contra, Sherer v. State,* 486 So. 2d 1330 (Ala. App. 1986) (probation automatically extended as long as restitution unpaid).

[184] VT. STAT. ANN. tit. 13, §7043 (Supp. 1994).

[185] *People v. Johnson,* 780 P.2d 504 (Colo. 1989).

[186] Tobolowsky, P. (1993). *Restitution in the Federal Criminal Justice System.* JUDICATURE 77:90.

[187] Parent, D. (1990). RECOVERING CORRECTIONAL COSTS THROUGH OFFENDER FEES. Washington DC: National Institute of Justice.

[188] Langan, P. and M. Cunniff (1992). RECIDIVISM OF FELONS ON PROBATION, 1986-1989. Washington DC: Bureau of Justice Statistics.

[189] Butts, J. and H. Snyder (1992). RESTITUTION AND JUVENILE RECIDIVISM. Washington, DC: Office of Juvenile Justice and Delinquency.

[190] Davis, R. (1992). *Who Pays?* PERSPECTIVES, Spring.

[191] RESTITUTION REPORT, January 1995, Office of the Commissioner of Probation, Boston, MA.

[192] Davis, R. op. cit.

[193] *Ibid.*

[194] *Ibid.*

[195] Finn, P. and D. Parent (1992). MAKING THE OFFENDER FOOT THE BILL, A TEXAS PROGRAM, October. Washington DC: National Institute of Justice.

[196] Bazemore, G., A. Klein, A. Schneider and P. Schneider (1985). *Program Models,* GUIDE TO JUVENILE RESTITUTION 53-54; A. Schneider (ed.), RESTITUTION EDUCATION, SPECIALIZED TRAINING & TECHNICAL ASSISTANCE PROGRAM. Washington, DC: U.S. Department of Justice 84-JS-AX-K045.

[197] *Id.*

[198] Griffith, W., A. Schneider, P. Schneider and M. Wilson (1982). TWO-YEAR REPORT ON THE NATIONAL EVALUATION OF THE JUVENILE RESTITUTION INITIATIVE: AN OVERVIEW OF PROGRAM PERFORMANCE. Washington, DC: U.S. Department of Justice, 77-NI-99-0005 & 79-NJ-AX-0009.

[199] *Id.*

[200] Bureau of Justice Statistics (1985). *Criminal Victimization in the United States, 1983.* A NATIONAL CRIME SURVEY REPORT 7. Washington, DC: U.S. Department of Justice.

[201] Egash (1975). *Beyond Restitution Creative Restitution.* RESTITUTION IN CRIMINAL JUSTICE 90-101.

[202] Harding, J. (1982). VICTIMS AND OFFENDERS 16.

[203] Armstrong, T. (1980). *Restitution, A Sanction For All Seasons* (paper delivered to Fourth National Symposium on Restitution and Community Service Sentencing, Minn.).

[204] Kelly (1984). *Victim's Perceptions of Criminal Justice.* 11 SYMPOSIUM PEPPERDINE L. REV. 15, 21.

Chapter 6

Community Work Service and Alternative Sentences

§6.01   Introduction to Community Work Service

As previously illustrated, community work service can be ordered for sentences for different types of crimes. Usually ordered as a condition of probation, the orders may stand alone or be in addition to other conditions. Unlike orders of monetary restitution, there need not be a direct crime victim. Community work service may be ordered as a means of keeping the offender occupied in the community as a form of incapacitation. The unpaid work ordered may or may not be related to the crime. Work sites vary, and are usually confined to nonprofit or public agencies. Offenders can be ordered to perform work individually or as part of a work crew, often supervised directly by court or probation staff. Work assignments may require skilled or unskilled labor. Orders may be for full-time work, a certain number of hours per week or weekend work only. Alternatively, the offender may be ordered to work until he completes a specifically assigned task. In some cases, offenders can be ordered to work directly for the crime victim, either repairing the damages caused or compensating the victim through general unpaid labor. In these cases, the order is generally referred to as "victim service."

Like restitution, community work service deprives the offender of his leisure and makes him help others rather than being the recipient of help. Community work service is also often referred to as "community restitution" or "symbolic restitution." While an individual crime may not have a specific crime victim, all crime costs the community in terms of police, prosecution, defense costs and so on. Unlike restitution, the number of hours ordered is not commensurate with the victim's loss, but with the seriousness of the offense. Some jurisdictions allow unpaid fines, costs and other court-ordered monies to be worked off through community work service. The rationale for community work service varies depending upon the case and point of view as described by the British Home Office:

> To some, it would simply be a more constructive and cheaper alter-native to short sentences of imprisonment; by others it would seem as introducing into the penal system a new dimension with an emphasis on reparation to the community; others again would regard it as a means of giving effect to the old adage that the punishment should fit the crime; while still others would stress the value of bringing the offender into close touch with those members of the community who are most in need of help and support. . . . These dif-ferent approaches are by no means incompatible.[1]

The rise in popularity of community work service is primarily due to the tangible benefits it offers to the community, as well as to the offender and to the court, as described by the Michigan Department of Corrections:

> Imposition of community services penalties recompensates the com-munity through humane and productive punishment of the offender. Needy groups, organizations or individuals who utilize the services of the offender benefit from the free service provided. The communi-ty is also given the opportunity to become involved in the criminal justice system and assist in the reintegration of the offender. Taking advantage of the skills and services offenders can provide, rather than imposing what is seen as the harshness of prison or leniency of probation, is a notion that makes sense to most in the community who examine the matter.[2]

Community work service may teach offenders basic work skills and disci-pline, especially if the offenders have never worked in a job before. The work placement may also influence an offender's subsequent behavior. An alcohol-abusing offender, for example, who is placed in a detoxification center may learn through the experience the need to stop abusing alcohol.

While at least one agency that supervises and places court-referred offend-ers for community work service reports that a substantial minority volunteer to continue work after their court-ordered hours are completed, this is not always the case.[3] New York City began a city-wide community work service program called the New York Sanitation Alternative Sentencing Program. The program found, however, that the majority of offenders, presented with the alternative, preferred jail.[4] A study of offenders in Great Britain found that the majority preferred community work service over fines or probation, finding the sanction more understandable and, surprisingly, helpful to them.[5]

Community work service has been endorsed by the American Bar Associ-ation whose interest in it began in 1976 when a delegation from the association toured Europe to find correctional innovations suitable to introduce to the United States. The delegation decided that the British community service order sentence was the single innovation most likely to be successfully transplanted to the United States.

§6.02   Development of Community Work Service

Although idle drunkards were made to chop wood in colonial Boston's Public Common and chain gangs built much of the interstate highway system in the south, modern community work service traces its roots to California in the mid-1960s. The first orders involved female traffic offenders who could not pay their fines in Alameda County. Municipal judges were reluctant to jail them due to the hardship it would cause them and their families. An intermediary placement agency received the offenders from the court and placed them in community agencies. By 1976, over 4,500 offenders were placed in Alameda County (Oakland) alone. The court found that 80 percent of the offenders completed their hours, providing the community over a 500,000 hours of free labor.[6]

The idea spread across California, then Oregon, and then across the country. Referrals expanded beyond traffic offenders.

The Supreme Court helped promote community work service by prohibiting courts from incarcerating indigent defendants for their nonwillful failure to pay fines in *Tate v. Short*.[7] Several states, such as Delaware, had already enacted laws providing for community work service for unpaid fines for indigent offenders. The Delaware law provided that defendants report to the department of correction for work on public work projects.[8] When first enacted, the law is reported to have reduced the adult prison population by 105 inmates in less than five weeks. The Supreme Court ruling gave other jurisdictions the impetus to develop similar alternative work programs.

In 1983, the Supreme Court extended the principle of *Tate* to cover unpaid restitution by indigent defendants.[9] The Court ruled, however, that courts were not helpless in enforcing payment. Among other things, the Court specifically noted that courts could order community service. One state has enacted a statute that provides that the unpaid fines and restitution may be converted to "day fines" to be worked off as community service.[10] The "day fine" varies, depending upon the defendant's financial resources.

Impetus for community work service also came from overseas, specifically Great Britain. While American courts largely experimented with community work service on an *ad hoc* basis, Britain established community work service as a specific sentence in 1972 for adults over 17. Orders ranged by statute from 40 to 240 hours. Work was monitored by probation although these offenders were not on probation. An early Home Office study found that violent, addicted and alcoholic offenders completed their orders as well as nonviolent offenders. The key lay in placing the offender in the right work situation. As a result of its findings, the Home Office urged expanding the use of the sanctions. By 1980, over 22,000 British offenders were being sentenced to community work service. Judges began to impose community work service more frequently than probation. While not all offenders ordered community service were prison-bound, Home Office studies concluded that almost one-half of the offenders sentenced to community work service were so sentenced instead of being incarcerated.

New York officials traveled to Great Britain in 1976 to examine the British system. Upon their return, they established New York City's first community work service program for offenders who otherwise would be jail-bound. The program is administered by VERA, the same agency that pioneered bail reform. Orders are standardized at 70 hours. Sample cases from the program have been discussed previously in the examination of high-risk offenders receiving alternative sentences. Initial studies reveal that, similar to the British program, the VERA program has served in many cases as an alternative to incarceration. Participants averaged more than eight prior arrests and four convictions; 42 percent were arraigned on felony charges; and 34 percent had been sentenced to jail for the offense immediately prior to the offense for which they were sentenced to the VERA community work program.[11] The VERA program has served as a model for similar programs around the country.

The impetus for community work service also came from the millions of dollars the Justice Department disbursed in the 1970s for pilot restitution programs across the country. As mentioned, although these funds were to develop restitution programs, the definition was loose, including "community restitution," which is community work service. Along with providing specific jurisdictions with program money, the Justice Department had a series of monographs published on the subject. In the foreword to one of the monographs, the head of the National Institute of Corrections reflected the Department's enthusiasm for the sanction, writing that community work service "holds great promise for American Corrections."[12]

As important as any of the other forces promoting community work service orders was the enactment of drunk driving laws, which contained specific provisions for community work service. Community work service has been established as an alternative to short-term jail sentences for drunk drivers in more than 20 states. It is used in most other states as an additional sanction to jail, fine and license suspension. In addition, a number of states have programs whereby incarcerated offenders can reduce their sentences by performing community service. Use of community work service as an alternative sentence has been encouraged by the report of the President's Commission on Drunk Driving issued in 1983. The Highway Safety Act of 1984 provides that one qualification for federal incentive funds shall be the enactment of a state law that requires two days of jail or 100 hours of community work service for first-offender drunk drivers.[13]

In 1982 in New Jersey, as a result of drunk driving legislation that provides that second offenders may substitute 30 days of community service for 90 days in jail and third offenders may reduce a 180-day sentence to 90 days if they perform 90 days of community work service, statewide programs were funded from the Administrative Office of the Courts. By the following year, the state reported 20 local programs enrolling almost 10,000 offenders who performed almost one million hours of work. Convicted felons were assigned in numbers second only to drunk drivers.[14] Each year, California judges sentence more than 10,000 defendants to complete between 10 and 15 million hours of service. The majority are sentenced for drunk driving, but the community work service orders are not limited to them. When police rounded up prostitutes during the campaign to protect them from the Hillside Strangler, the United Way reported "a whole parade of (prostitutes) here for about a week. We sent them to convalescent homes, where they could feed people, wheel them around and talk to them. They turned out to be pretty good, too."[15]

Finally, jail overcrowding has contributed to the growth of community work service orders. A number of sheriffs specifically provide for weekend community work service crews made up of offenders in lieu of weekend jail sentences. In upstate New York, the Genessee County Sheriff established one of the first such programs administered by a law enforcement agency. The Sheriff was elected on a platform opposing the building of a new, expanded jail facility. To make good his campaign, once elected he worked with the courts to substitute community service work for jail time. He reports that his department's community work program has supervised offenders completing 15,000 hours of work, saving the county the equivalent of paying for 2,500 days of jailing offenders, or $75,000.[16]

In 1983, the Administrative Office of the New Jersey Courts published a national directory of community service programs. It found that all 50 states reported having such programs within their jurisdictions, although Alabama, Kentucky, Mississippi, Nevada, Rhode Island and South Carolina reported programs only for juvenile offenders. Most of the programs were administered by probation departments. The directory revealed that all jurisdictions reported ordering community work service whether or not there existed specific statutory authority for the orders.[17]

Community work service orders are also frequently imposed in federal courts. The orders were championed by the Chief Justice of the District Court in Memphis, Tennessee. Judge Brown extolled their use in the *Federal Probation Journal,* writing in 1977:

> The advantages of such a program of work without pay appeared to me to be obvious and I could foresee no disadvantages. . . . Certainly there is plenty of public and charitable work to be done that is not being done in every city and town in America. We recommend this program to all courts throughout the land.[18]

Other federal judges have adopted the practice of ordering community work service. Massachusetts District Court Judge Joseph Tauro has written that he thinks "it should be one of the alternatives considered in every case."[19]

There is a growing evangelical movement to promote community service orders in lieu of incarceration. The chief sponsor is Charles Colson, former Watergate co-conspirator, and current director of the Prison Fellowship Project.

Although most community work service programs are either operated or contracted by courts, probation, sheriff, correctional agencies or other agencies also operate them. For example, the District Attorney in Detroit, John O'Hair, won plaudits in the *New York Times* in 1988 for the community work service program he initiated. Begun as a small pilot program, by 1988 he had over 2,000 offenders a year wearing orange vests and cleaning litter from highways leading to and from the city seven days a week. The *Times* noted:

> It is also unusual for a prosecutor to take the lead in such a project. District Attorneys usually prefer to campaign for more jails . . . [B]ut obsessive belief in jails as the only meaningful punishment corrodes justice where jails can't possibly contain all who need punishing.[20]

Finally, community work service orders are being incorporated into intensive probation supervision programs to incapacitate the offenders in the community. An example of this was presented earlier in regard to Turk Brock's participation in Georgia's intensive supervision program. Dissatisfied with traditional probation, Florida's legislature created the Community Control Program. Supervised by "Control Officers," offenders in this program must also complete a specified number of hours of community work service.

§6.03   Community Work Service Law

Making offenders perform unpaid labor was specifically allowed in the Thirteenth Amendment to the United States Constitution:

> Neither slavery nor involuntary servitude, except as punishment for a crime whereof the party shall have been duly convicted, shall exist within the United States, or any place subject to their jurisdiction.[21]

Like restitution, the use of community work service developed without specific statutory authority, but rather as a permissible rehabilitative condition of probation.

In the federal system, appellate courts relied on the broad language authorizing probation to uphold community work service orders.[22] The Second Circuit found that community work service served both as a crime deterrent as well as a symbolic form of restitution.[23] The Third Circuit declared that it helped "reinstate (the defendants) in society," integrating them in "a working environment" and inculcating "a sense of social responsibility."[24]

Like other probationary conditions, federal courts have ruled that the community work service order must be reasonable. The Ninth Circuit held impermissible an order of three years of full-time community service for an offender convicted of defrauding the government, because it left inadequate time for paid employment and substantially interfered with the defendant's ability to maintain his normal family life.[25] The federal sentencing guidelines recommend that community work service orders not exceed 400 hours.

Most state appellate courts have followed the same course. The Florida District Court of Appeals, cited with approval the trial judge's hope that community work service would be rehabilitative by encouraging the offender's empathy with the needy clientele of the public agency in which the offender was ordered to perform her work.[26] The Wisconsin Court of Appeals held that community work service orders may be appropriately punitive. It ruled, however, that the work service in the case in question, namely that a psychiatrist, convicted of theft, be made to live in India for three years while providing nursing or pediatric services for poor children, went too far.[27] Most other state appellate courts have also upheld reasonable community work service orders.[28]

New York's appellate court, alone, has held community work service orders to be unlawful without specific statutory authority.[29] While the court held that the defendant could not be ordered to perform the community work service, his continued performance of the same would "undoubtedly inure to his benefit vis-à-vis his conduct evaluation by the probation department."[30] As a result of this decision, when VERA and the City of New York decided to establish their community work service sentencing program, representatives lobbied the state legislature to enact legislation authorizing community work service for misdemeanants.[31]

In 1983 the United States Supreme Court suggested that courts could require offenders to perform "some form of labor or public service" if they could not afford to pay fines or restitution.[32]

Like New York, many jurisdictions have enacted specific legislation authorizing community work service as a condition of probation. Many of the drunk-driving laws enacted at the beginning of the 1980s contain provisions for the performance of community work service. Nine states require first offenders to perform community work service or offer it as an alternative to jail with hours ranging from eight to 100.[33] Another 15 mandate from seven and one-half to 30 days of community work service for second offenders.[34]

The first state community work service statute was passed in New Hampshire in 1977. It is limited to offenders convicted of property destruction or unauthorized entry.[35] It allows for 50 hours of service to be performed under the supervision of the city or town in which the offense occurred. Many of the more recent statutes simply authorize community work service as a condition of any probationary sentence.[36] New Jersey law provides that the future performance of community service be considered by the court at sentencing as a mitigating circumstance.[37] While the Washington legislature abolished probation in establishing its comprehensive sentencing guidelines, it provides for community work service sentences for certain categories of crimes.[38] Florida law provides for community work service orders in addition to any other punishment.[39] Louisiana provided by statute in 1990 that judges may sentence offenders to community service in lieu of imprisonment in whole or in part if the defendant has no prior felony record, the offense calls for imprisonment of 30 years or less, the court imposes a period of court-approved community service of *not less than two nor more than five years*, and the judge writes why he chose service over incarceration. Offenders performing community service under the above provisions are supervised as probationers. If revoked, they are not allowed to receive credit for time spent doing the community service or for the time elapsed during suspension of the sentence.[40]

While some of the statutes authorizing community work service specify what type of work is to be performed, most simply state that the service shall be "public" or "community." Mississippi's statute refers to community work service as "restitution to society."[41] Kentucky's statute specifies how monetary restitution may be converted to work "for or on the behalf of" the victim. The court, it directs, shall determine the number of hours of work necessary by applying the then-prevailing federal minimum wage to the total amount of monetary damage caused by or incidental to the crime.[42] Several states provide that the order shall be consistent with the offender's "employment and family responsibilities." Most are silent as to who is supposed to administer the orders. A few delegate the task to correctional departments, county governments or probation departments. Ohio's statute spells out that the responsibility lays with the agency in which the offender is placed. Before being placed, the offender is required to pay a reasonable fee to procure a policy of liability insurance to cover the service period.[43]

Congress enacted legislation in 1982 providing for the performance of "restitution in services" if the victim or the victim's estate consents.[44] Two years later it provided for community work service as a mandatory condition of felony probation if the offender is not ordered to pay restitution or a fine. It is discretionary for misdemeanants.[45]

§6.04   Insurance and Liability

Despite much discussion in the field concerning possible liability if offenders ordered to perform community work service injure themselves or others, actual suits involving offenders performing community work service have been very few and far between. The Justice Department's juvenile restitution initiative, which followed 17,000 offenders who were ordered to perform community work service or restitution in jurisdictions across the country found no liability claims arising from program participants.

The National Center for State Courts completed a telephone survey in 1982 of formal community work service programs. It found that programs handled liability for injury in one of four ways: (1) enabling legislation that specifically addresses liability issues; (2) the program carried its own liability insurance; (3) the "employing" organization maintained its own insurance; or (4) offenders were required to waive program liability.[46]

Some states specifically provide by statute that offenders performing community work service are state employees and therefore are covered by state worker's compensation.[47] Wisconsin limits liability to $25,000 for any organization accepting offenders assigned to community work service.[48] Several national insurance companies provide coverage for community work service programs. One company, Corporate Insurance Management, provides a specific policy designed for such programs, called "Court Referred Alternative Sentencing Volunteer Insurance Program." The policy covers accident insurance, death and dismemberment. The American Home Assurance Company, the Integrity Insurance Company and Travelers Insurance Company are also reported to cover programs in various parts of the country. Most charitable agencies that accept volunteers already have insurance coverage for volunteers. If the offender understands that the performance of community work service is voluntary, that he can choose another equivalent correctional alternative, that any injury sustained by the offender in service permits the defense of *volenti non fit injuris,* then he cannot claim damages when he consents to the activity that caused the damages. Ohio requires offenders to pay a fee for liability insurance.[49]

The problem of the offender in service injuring a third party is defined by individual state tort law and insurance practices. An offender performing community work service is regarded as an independent contractor, responsible for his own torts. However, because most have few financial resources, persons injured by them would probably sue the organization for whom the offender is working. Illinois law restricts the liability of county employees for offenders' tortious acts.[50] The United States Supreme Court has upheld state tort immunity laws.[51] The doctrine of judicial immunity insulates the judge from any liability arising out of the exercise of his discretion in ordering community work service. Because probation staff perform a quasi-judicial duty in carrying out the judge's order, they too can argue similar immunity.[52]

A Georgia appellate court addressed the legal fallout in a 1991 decision in regard to what must be a community work service administrator's worst nightmare. A defendant ordered to do community work service, who had signed a waiver assuming liability for any injury sustained as a result of doing community work service, was killed during its performance. A skilled heavy machinery operator, he was put to work in a local landfill. His decedents sued. The court gave a summary judgment to the county. On appeal, the appellate court noted that the waiver established a complete defense to any claims of negligence. However, an exculpation provision did not relieve the county for liability for willful or wanton conduct. Insofar as the claim was for reckless and conscious indifference on part of the county, summary judgment was ruled improper. Because it was not apparent that the county's insurance covered liability for such misconduct, it was an error for the court to grant summary judgment to this aspect of the plaintiff's claim.[53]

The state is, of course, no less vulnerable if the offender is incarcerated and subject to prison violence, participates in work release, works in a prison industry or is furloughed or paroled.

§6.05   Community Work Service in Practice

Examples of Creative Community Work Service Programs and Placements

Restorative Justice Corps: Deschutes County, Oregon juvenile and adult probation departments have joined together to form an innovative community correctional agency under the leadership of one of the pioneers in correctional reform, Dennis Maloney. The agency is built around an exciting community work service program called the Restorative Justice Corps. The Corps provides community supervision of both adult and juvenile offenders while overseeing their community work orders. About 2,000 offenders perform over 60,000 hours of work each year.

The Corps engage in sophisticated community service projects including construction of a homeless shelter for 70 families, cutting and distributing free firewood to housebound elderly, as well as conservation work in the area's many forests. Treated solely as liabilities in most communities, Maloney's offenders work themselves into substantial community assets. In fact, a plaque memoralizing the community members who donated money for the shelter also contains the names of the offenders who completed more than 1,000 hours of their community work service building the shelter. The Corps is paid by the federal and county government for much of its work, bringing in $267,000 in 1994. The payments go both to meeting 85 percent of the program's operating budget and paying many of the victims of the offenders owed restitution.

The Corps, through paid staff and community mentors, provides enough structure that only 20 percent of the offenders fail to complete their work assignments.[54]

Community Restoration Crew: Across the country, the Dakota County, Minnesota probation department, directed by Mark Carey, in collaboration with the county sheriff and local police chiefs, has established another innovative community work service program. Building on prior accomplishments, in 1994 they established the Community Restoration Crew. The Crew, made up of offenders ordered to community work service, are made available to victims of crime to clean up or repair damages caused by the crimes. In other words, whether or not the offender is ever caught, victims can at least get help in cleaning up the mess criminals often leave behind. And who better to do it than other offenders trying to clean up their own act?[55]

Two White Cross Burners Rebuild Black Church: Judge Milton Wharton of St. Clair County, Illinois ordered two whites convicted of burning a cross at the home of a black man to help rebuild a 125-year-old black church that was destroyed by fire in an unrelated attack. The victim of the cross burning was quoted as saying that "I didn't spend 20 years in the military to have five clowns burn a cross in my yard." Two white juveniles were ordered to complete 100 hours each at the New Bethel AME Church, destroyed for the second time in six months. The two adults were ordered to spend holidays in jail and do the community service when out.[56]

Graffiti artist paints over past works: A 20-year-old university graffiti artist, using the moniker "Exakto," was sentenced to six months house arrest and ordered to spend 600 hours painting over his extensive prior works sprayed over the neighborhood abutting his university in Boston's Allston Brighton area. Arrested and pleading guilty to 24 felony counts of defacing property, the sentence required the defendant to drop out of school for the electronically monitored house arrest portion of the sentence. Area residents praised the sentence, hoping it would discourage future graffiti in their neighborhoods.

One resident told the *Boston Globe*, "That kid was part of an organized attempt to desecrate the streets of Boston, and it turned into an ego trip for him. I hope we can use this to explain to everyone that ruining property is not a misdemeanor but a felony." The defendant told the press that he knew people's property was getting ruined but he did not think anyone would care. During the offender's court dates, at least a dozen residents of the neighborhoods where most of the graffiti appeared attended the proceedings. The defendant was the first suspected graffiti vandal arrested in Boston as the result of a court-issued search warrant.

Said the Suffolk County District Attorney Ralph Martin, "It is gratifying to see a crime of this nature taken seriously." The defendant announced that it was the last time he would do graffiti without legal permission. He had been arrested once before for defacing property and sentenced to 80 hours of community work service.[57]

Community work service orders are not difficult to put into effect. There are three basic steps. First, the order must be determined. Second, a placement where the offender can perform the work must be secured. Third, the order must be monitored and enforced.

Determining Community Work Service Orders

Generally, orders are determined commensurate with the seriousness of the crime. Some jurisdictions have developed a formal grid based on both the offender and the offense to establish specific orders. See the example from the Dallas County Juvenile Department on the following page.[58] Other jurisdictions correlate work service hours with fines and jail time, generally providing that eight hours of community work service is the equivalent of one day's wages at minimum wage or one day in jail.[59] Finally, some jurisdictions are guided substantially by what the crime victim may recommend to the court. If the victim is not inter-

Dallas County Juvenile Department
Community Service Restitution Behavior Grid

Assignment of CSR hours	Minimum community service (24-50 hours)	Moderate community service (51-100 hours)	Maximum community service (101-150 hours)
Maximum assigned	50 hours	100 hours	150 hours
In school full-time	–4 hours	–5 hours	–5 hours
Working	–4 hours	–5 hours	–10 hours
Extracurricular activities— includes sports, counseling, etc.	–4 hours	–5 hours	–5 hours
No prior record	–4 hours	–10 hours	–15 hours
All of the above	–4 hours	–5 hours	–10 hours
Total CSR hours			

This behavior grid has been developed to help determine the number of Community Service Restitution hours appropriate for each client. The Probation Officer is instructed to start with the appropriate maximum number of hours and subtract hours for exhibited positive behavior:

a) *Minimum Community Service* should be used for youth on informal adjustment or 6-month probation.

b) *Moderate Community Service* should be used for youth ages 10 to 14 years on 1-year probation.

c) *Maximum Community Service* should be used for youth ages 15 to 17 years on 1-year probation or suspended commitment.

---

ested in having the defendant work directly to repair the damages the crime caused, the victim may suggest alternative service work in the community. Instead of determining the number of hours to be performed, the court may also assign the offender a specific task to be completed. Such work assignments are commonly limited to repairing or cleaning up property damaged by the offender.

Like restitution orders, the court must determine the number of hours to be performed, but it may delegate the work schedule to the probation department.[60] Based on the offender's work schedule, courts usually order a certain number of hours to be performed daily or weekly, or simply order that the defendant work each weekend until the order is completed. In certain circumstances, the order may be open-ended. The court may order the offender to do community work service until the offender obtains paid employment. In all cases, the schedule must be reasonable, based on the defendant's work schedule and family obligations.

Placements

Once the order is established, including the rate of completion, the offender must be placed in a suitable worksite. Worksites are usually restricted to government agencies or private, nonprofit agencies. Some jurisdictions administer formal programs that take care of placing offenders in community agencies or in program work crews that perform community service. However, placements may be suggested to the court by individual offenders or their defense attorneys at the time of disposition. Offenders may volunteer to work at hospitals, libraries, public cemeteries, the Red Cross, religious institutions, parks, police departments and so on.

The key to successful completion of community work service orders is placement. Offenders should not be placed at worksites that require skills they do not possess. Many programs report that offenders do best at sites where they work helping other people, although other programs report that certain offenders do better if placed at animal shelters, removed from contact with other people. Australia, which utilizes community work service orders extensively in sentencing, has placements overseen by a committee that includes a labor union member, a community representative and the Chief Probation Officer. Some programs seek to match a defendant's skills with work assignments. Others specifically reject this approach, preferring to treat all offenders alike when it comes to work assignments. Still others seek to make the placement therapeutic for the offender. As examples presented demonstrate, compulsive gamblers can be ordered to work at a gambler's rehabilitation center and alcoholics can be ordered to work at alcoholism treatment facilities.

The responsibility for placement can be put on the shoulders of probation staff, the district attorney's office, a community agency or the offender. If delegated, the court should provide specific guidelines so that parties know exactly what kind of work qualifies for community work service. Given this task, many offenders go to local religious leaders to secure volunteer work. Some courts without formal programs simply provide the offender with a list of community agencies that welcome volunteers.

Monitoring and Enforcing Orders

The onus for monitoring community work service orders can be put on probation or equivalent staff or the offender. The latter is particularly common if the offender also secures his own work assignment. The offender must bring to court periodic proof of the volunteer work or proof of its completion. A letter from the agency director where the offender volunteered is usually acceptable. Some courts provide forms for such agency personnel to fill out.

A community service program in Saskatchewan, Canada provides a unique solution to monitoring. Offenders are provided with a short list of worksites. Each site is given community service tokens with which they "pay" offenders for a specified number of hours worked. The offender then turns in the token to the court to demonstrate the number of hours worked.

If an offender fails to perform community work service as ordered, he should be brought back to court immediately rather than waiting until the end of the probationary period. In such a manner, quick corrective action can be taken before the offender reaches the point where he cannot possibly fulfill the court's order. In assessing the offender's failure, attention must be given to whether the failure is caused by the defendant's unwillingness to perform the service hours or by his lack of ability. If the latter is the reason, the defendant must be assisted. Worksites may be changed or instruction may be given to the offender to enable him to complete the assignment.

§6.06   Summary

Community work service orders provide the courts with an extremely effective and available sentencing alternative. Unlike more traditional probation conditions, which are based on the offender refraining from doing something negative such as committing a new crime, community work service orders require the offender to do something positive. They are easily measured and enforced. The sanction is almost excuse-proof, because indigency is not a bar to its completion. In fact, unemployed offenders have more time to complete work service hours. The same studies of offenders who were ordered to pay monetary restitution have found that offenders, notwithstanding the seriousness of the offense or the offender's record, consistently complete community work service orders at a high rate. Further, there is consistently enthusiastic public support for such sentences. Not only does the public understand that the offender is being required to make up for the crime, it actually sees the results in terms of repainted fire hydrants, cleaned beaches, dusted library books and so on. A judge, running for re-election in Rochester, New York on the Democrat and Conservative tickets, actually ran on a community work service platform. His television ad focused on a park bench surrounded by litter. A voice announced: "When people do this to our parks, one judge makes them clean it up." As the voice continues, the camera pulls back to first reveal a rake pushing the debris across the screen. Then it reveals the judge standing behind the park bench looking on sternly, his arms folded across his chest. The judge won re-election.

For defense, federal judge Joseph Tauro advises of the efficacy of advocating community work service orders rather than simply pleading mercy at the time of sentencing:

> The lawyer's responsibility is to focus the judge's attention on *this particular* defendant—that *this* defendant is salvageable—that it would be in the public's best interest for *this* defendant to be given the opportunity to redeem himself by a voluntary program of public service, rather than by making mailbags in Atlanta. During the past ten years, I have often imposed public service sentences, either under terms of straight probation or combined with short jail terms. These public service sentences have been imposed in all types of cases, including bookmaking, controlled substances, tax evasion, and embezzlement. The type of crime is never controlling. The character, record and potential of the defendant are the significant factors.[61]

For prosecutors, community work service offers a significant sanction that is easily quantifiable. It may be increased in proportion to the seriousness of the crime or the record of the offender.

For the court, community work service offers a supervised, behaviorally specific sanction.

Notes

[1] Advisory Council on the Penal System (1970). *Non-Custodial and Semi-Custodial Penalties*, In J. Harding, VICTIMS AND OFFENDERS 21 (1982).

[2] Michigan Bureau of Field Services (undated). *New Programs in Probation Supervision* (Department of Corrections).

[3] Harris, K. (1979). COMMUNITY SERVICE BY OFFENDERS 9. National Institute of Corrections, U.S. Department of Justice (the Solano, California program reported that 47 percent of its offenders who successfully completed their assignments worked more hours than ordered).

[4] Anderson (1984). *Cells Over Brooms.* NEW YORK TIMES, October 10.

[5] Thorvalson (1980). *Does Community Service Affect Offenders' Attitudes?* In Hudson, J. and B. Galaway (eds.), VICTIMS, OFFENDERS AND ALTERNATIVE SANCTIONS.

[6] Beha, J., K. Carlson, and R. Rosenblum (1977). SENTENCING TO COMMUNITY SERVICE. Washington, DC: Institute of Law Enforcement and Criminal Justice, U.S. Department of Justice, JLEAA-030-76.

[7] *Tate v. Short,* 401 U.S. 395, 91 S. Ct. 668, 28 L. Ed. 2d 130 (1971).

[8] 57 DEL. LAWS ch. 198 (1970) (current version at DEL. CODE ANN. tit. 11, § 4105 (Supp. 1984)).

[9] *Bearden v. Georgia,* 461 U.S. 666, 103 S. Ct. 2064, 76 L. Ed. 2d 221 (1983).

[10] KAN. STAT. ANN. § 21-4610 (3)(k) (Supp. 1985).

[11] VERA Institute of Justice (1981). THE NEW YORK COMMUNITY SERVICE SENTENCING PROJECT AND ITS UTILITY FOR THE CITY OF NEW YORK 3-5.

[12] Breed (1979). *Foreword.* In K. Harris, COMMUNITY SERVICE BY OFFENDERS. Washington, DC: National Institute of Corrections, U.S. Department of Justice.

[13] Highway Safety Act of 1984, Pub. L. No. 98-363, 98 Stat. 435, 438 (codified as amended at 23 U.S.C § 408(e)(3) (Supp. II 1984).

[14] New Jersey Administrative Office of the Courts (1984). Community Service Update, Spring.

[15] Krajick (1982). *Community Service: The Work Ethic Approach to Punishment.* 7 Corrections Magazine 6.

[16] Genessee County Sheriff's Department (undated). Community Service Restitution.

[17] New Jersey Administrative Office of the Courts (1983). Community Service Directory for Interstate Compact Transfers.

[18] Brown (1977). *Community Service as a Condition of Probation.* 41 Federal Probation 7.

[19] Tauro (1983). *Sentencing: A View From The Bench.* 9 New Eng. J. Crim. & Civil Confinement 323, 330.

[20] *Detroit's Benign Chain Gangism.* New York Times, May 4, 1988.

[21] U.S. Const. amend. XIII, §1.

[22] See, *e.g., Higdon v. United States,* 627 F.2d 893 (9th Cir. 1980); *United States v. Chapel,* 428 F.2d 472 (9th Cir. 1970).

[23] *United States v. Arthur,* 602 F.2d 660 (4th Cir.), *cert. denied,* 444 U.S. 992, 100 S. Ct. 446, 62 L. Ed. 2d 373 (1979).

[24] *United States v. Restor,* 679 F.2d 338 (3d Cir. 1982).

[25] *Higdon v. United States,* 627 F.2d 893 (9th Cir. 1980).

[26] *Fillastre v. State,* 387 So. 2d 400 (Fla. Dist. Ct. App. 1980).

[27] *State v. Dean,* 111 Wis. 2d 361, 330 N.W.2d 630 (Wis. Ct. App. 1983).

[28] See, *e.g., Cogburn v. State,* 264 Ark. 173, 569 S.W.2d 658 (1978); *People v. Ford,* 95 Mich. App. 608, 291 N.W.2d 140 (1980); *Fogle v. State,* 667 S.W.2d 296 (Tex. Crim. App. 1984).

[29] *People v. Mandell,* 50 A.D.2d 907, 377 N.Y.S.2d 563 (1975).

[30] *Id.*

[31] See N.Y. Penal Law § 65.10(2)(h) (McKinney Supp. 1986).

[32] *Bearden v. Georgia,* 461 U.S. 666, 103 S. Ct. 2064, 76 L. Ed. 2d 221 (1983).

[33] Ariz. (8 hrs.); Colo. (48 hrs.); Fla. (50 hrs.); Hawaii (72 hrs.); Kan. (100 hrs.); La. (96 hrs.); Nev. (48 hrs.); Or. (80 hrs.); Utah (48 hrs.).

[34] Ala. (20 days); Colo. (7.5 days); Ga. (10 days); Ill. (10 days); Ind. (10 days); La. (30 days); Minn. (10 days); Mo. (10 days); N.J. (30 days); N. Dak. (10 days); Or. (10 days); S. Car. (10 days); Utah (10 days); Vt. (10 days).

[35] N.H. Rev. Stat. Ann. § 651:2 (VI-a) (Supp. 1983).

[36] See, *e.g.,* Alaska Stat. § 12.55.055 (1984) (as a condition of a suspended sentence or in addition to a fine or restitution); Hawaii Rev. Stat. § 706-605(1)(f) (Supp. 1984) (as a condition of probation or as a sentencing alternative); P.A. 77-2097 and P.A. 79-1334, as amended, Ill. Ann. Stat. ch. 38, 55 1005-6-3(b)(9), 3.1(c)(10) (Smith-Hurd Supp. 1986) (as a condition of probation, conditional discharge or deferred judgment); Mich. Comp. Laws § 771.3(2)(e) (Supp. 1986) (condition of probation); Ohio Rev. Code Ann. § 2951.02(H) (Supp. 1987) (as a condition of probation for misdemeanants); Okla. Stat. Ann. tit. 22, 5991a(A)(1)(a), (B) (1986) (as a con-

dition of probation and suspended sentence, except for three or more felony convictions); TEX. CODE CRIM. PROC. ANN. art. 42.12 § 10A(d)(1)((5) (Vernon Cum. 1987) (establishes ranges of community service orders from 320 to 1,000 for first degree felony to 24 to 100 for Class B misdemeanor).

[37] N.J. STAT. ANN. § 2C:44-1(b)(6) (West Supp. 1985).

[38] WASH. REV. CODE § 9.94A.380 (Supp. 1986).

[39] FLA. STAT. ANN. § 775.091 (West Supp. 1986).

[40] LA. CODE CRIM. PROC. ANN. Art. 893.4 (West Supp. 1995).

[41] MISS. CODE ANN. § 47-747(4) (Supp. 1985).

[42] KY. REV. STAT. § 533.030 (3) (1986).

[43] OHIO REV. CODE ANN. § 2951.02(H) (Supp. 1985).

[44] Act of Oct. 12, 1982, Pub. L. No. 97-291, § 5(a), 96 Stat. 1253 (codified as amended at 18 U.S.C. § 3579(b)(4) (1982) (redesignated as § 3663 effective Nov. 1, 1986).

[45] Act of Oct. 12, 1984, Pub. L. No. 98-473, tit. II, § 3563(a)(2), (b)(13) (Supp. II 1984) (effective Nov. 1, 1986).

[46] National Center for State Courts (1982). COMMUNITY SERVICE SENTENCING LIABILITY ISSUES (October).

[47] See, e.g., MINN. STAT. ANN. § 3.3739 (West Supp. 1986).

[48] WIS. STAT. § 971-38(2) (1985).

[49] OHIO REV. CODE ANN. § 2951.02(g) (Supp. 1994).

[50] P.A. 80-710, as amended, ILL. ANN. STAT. ch. 38, § 204(a)(i)(d) (Smith-Hurd Supp. 1986).

[51] See *Martinez v. California,* 444 U.S. 277, 100 S. Ct. 553, 62 L. Ed. 2d 481 (1980), *reh'g denied,* 445 U.S. 820, 100 S. Ct. 1285, 63 L. Ed. 2d 606 (1980).

[52] *Id.*

[53] *Turner v. Walker County,* 408 S.E.2d 818 (Ga. Ct. App. 1991).

[54] Conversation with Dennis Maloney, Director of Deschutes County Community Corrections, Jan. 9, 1995, Bend, Oregon.

[55] Conversation with Dakota County Community Corrections Director, Mark Carey, November, 1994, Dakota County, Minnesota.

[56] *Two Whites Ordered to Aid Black Church.* BOSTON GLOBE, December 18, 1988.

[57] McPhee, M. (1996). *Graffiti Draws House Arrest.* BOSTON GLOBE, Jan. 28.

[58] Schneider, A. (1985). GUIDE TO JUVENILE RESTITUTION 31.

[59] Accord, *Brown v. State,* 508 So. 2d 776 (Fla. Dist. Ct. App. 1987) (each hour of community service shall be credited against costs at a rate equivalent to minimum wage pursuant to § 27.3455(1)(1985)).

[60] See, e.g., *People v. Butler,* 137 Ill. App. 3d 704, 484 N.E.2d 921 (1985) (in which the court ruled that it "would be impossible for the court to detail in its probation order every aspect that would lead to successful completion of the public service requirement.")

[61] Tauro (1983). *Sentencing: A View From The Bench.* 9 NEW ENG. J. OF CRIM. & CIVIL CONFINEMENT 323, 329-330 (Summer).

Chapter 7

Monetary Sanctions Other Than Restitution and Alternative Sentences

§7.01   Introduction

In addition to restitution, there are other monetary sanctions that can form all or part of an alternative sentence. These include fines, court costs, various fees, bonds, forfeitures, support payments and cash donations. Some are usually imposed as a condition of probation. Others can be in addition to any other sentence. Monetary sanctions cost the system practically nothing and add to the public coffers. They add little to the burden of corrections and probation departments. They allow the offender to remain in the community, to work, and to support his family. They avoid negative stigmatization that may occur with incarcerating the offender or placing him on probation.

The specific rationale for each monetary sanction varies. Court costs, fines, donations, and forfeitures can share a rationale similar to restitution. In jurisdictions where appellate courts have ruled that "drug buy" money spent by narcotics agents could not be recouped through restitution orders, they have ruled that such costs could be recouped by the state through the imposition of court costs or forfeitures.[1] Donations can be ordered as a symbolic restitution, such as the educational trust fund Davis was ordered to donate to in the name of his victim for her grandson, which was described in Chapter 4. Forfeitures, like restitution, can insure that the crime does not pay, even though the state, not private individual victims, receive the forfeited goods or money. Unlike restitution, amounts are based on the defendant's gain, not strictly the victim's loss.

213

Support payments, on the other hand, either reimburse the state for welfare costs supplied to the defendant's family or require the defendant to support his family in an amount set by the court after the defendant has been convicted of having failed to support his family previously.

Fines, particularly, as well as other monetary sanctions (depending upon the context in which they are imposed) are punitive. Like community work service orders, they are usually based on the seriousness of the offense. While fines compensate the community, they are not based on the actual costs of the crime. Most laws contain preset minimum or maximum amounts that can be ordered. Although fines are not usually thought of as rehabilitative, some jurisdictions allow them to be imposed as a condition of probation. Bonds, in the sense that they tie up a defendant's capital, are also punitive. They are generally required to be posted by the defendant in contemplation of certain behavior. If the defendant fails to perform as ordered, the bonds are forfeited. Such bonds are often called "performance bonds" or "peace bonds."

Costs and fees are more like civil assessments levied against the defendant to reimburse the state or locality for the actual expenses associated with the crime or the defendant's rehabilitation. They generally go beyond the actual costs of the crime itself, covering the costs of prosecution, defense, if the defendant is indigent and receives public counsel, trial and the defendant's subsequent treatment or supervision. In some jurisdictions, up to one-third of the probation department's budget comes from the imposition of probation supervision fees. In the National Highway Traffic Safety Administration recommendations to the states, it is urged that "maximum efforts" be made to make drunk driver treatment programs self-sufficient through fees paid by the offenders themselves.[2]

No matter whether the defendant is ordered to pay restitution, fines, fees, forfeitures, costs or bonds, to his pocket there is no difference. All require him to give up money. Donations, costs, forfeitures, fees, nonsupport orders and restitution orders may actually exceed the maximum permissible fine set by the legislature.

All monetary sanctions are difficult to enforce if the offender is indigent. The high correlation between unemployment and crime makes this a substantial problem. For this reason, the American Bar Association is on record opposing the broad use of fines, costs, probation supervision fees and performance bonds. It does not believe that the criminal courts should be in the revenue-raising business. It does support the imposition of support payments for nonsupporting family heads.[3] The Model Penal Code endorses the use of bonds as they expand the court's sentencing options and guarantee payments even if the offender absconds.[4]

The Supreme Court has laid down strict guidelines for enforcing such orders against indigent defendants. Fortunately, the imposition of community work service in lieu of such payments insures the court that all defendants will be able to either pay or work off monetary orders.

§7.02   Current Use of Monetary Sanctions

Fines and other monetary sanctions, while used extensively in American courts, are not generally used as an alternative to custodial sentences as they are in European courts. A study conducted by the VERA Institute reveals that fines are widely used as criminal sanctions throughout the United States. They are not confined to traffic offenses and minor ordinance violations. Although a great deal of state revenue results from their imposition, few courts have reliable information on how fines are used or enforced. Despite the fact that fines are routinely assessed against offenders with limited means, courts uniformly report success in collections. High collection rates are associated with strict enforcement policies and payments on installments.[5]

Generally, fines are not used extensively as an alternative to either incarceration or probation. If used in cases of any discernible seriousness, their use is as an add-on to other sanctions. This contrasts sharply with the use of fines in Western Europe where it is used extensively as a sole penalty and is used widely with repeat offenders. In Germany, for example, fines are used in 80 percent of all criminal cases.[6] As perhaps the premier capitalistic country in the world, one might expect fines to play a larger role in our criminal justice system.

The use of fines as an alternative sanction is inhibited by several factors. First, statutes often provide for the imposition of fines in addition to imprisonment. The imprisonment, however, provides no means for the inmate to work to pay off the fine.

Second, statutes are inconsistent and outdated in establishing fines. In Massachusetts, the maximum fine for assault with intent to murder is $1,000. The maximum fine for assault and battery on a police officer is five times as much. The maximum fine for lewd and lascivious cohabitation at $300 is more than the maximum fine for leaving the scene of an accident, which is only $200.

Judge Lois Forer writes of how inappropriately fines are used in cases of white-collar crime. She cites the case of a Philadelphia councilman convicted of receiving and making illegal payments amounting to $312,000. Yet the fine was only $6,050.[7] Cases such as this are not rare. In Massachusetts, elected officials cannot work as lobbyists for one year after they leave office. The maximum fine for violating this conflict-of-interest law is only $1,000. The last person prosecuted for this violation had made over $30,000 in commissions during the forbidden period of work.

Third, courts have been slow to adjust to the Supreme Court's ban on automatically imposing jail terms for indigent offenders who cannot pay their fines. Before *Tate* and *Williams*,[8] nonpayment of fines was a major cause of imprisonment in the United States. A study conducted by a Presidential commission in 1967 found that, in Washington D.C., 19 percent of misdemeanants were fined during a certain period.[9] Of these, 47 percent were jailed for nonpayment. Similarly, 60 percent of the inmates in Philadelphia's jail had been committed for nonpayment. Over 26,000 inmates in New York City's jails in 1970 were there for nonpayment. After *Tate* and *Williams,* courts no longer had this option.

While fines traditionally accounted for the lion's share of monies assessed against offenders, in the last several decades there has been an explosion in other monetary costs assessed against offenders. In addition to fines, a majority of states authorize courts to impose costs. As of 1987, 11 states imposed surcharges on fines and seven others allowed various penalty assessments. As of 1980, only 10 states provided for the assessment of probation supervision fees. By 1990, that number increased to 28. By 1991, 21 states also collected parole fees. While a few abandoned supervision fee assessments due to poor collections, more and more offenders are being assessed multiple monetary obligations. Twenty-six different fees alone have been identified in courts across the country today.[10]

Texas is an example of one of the highest fee-collecting probation systems in the country. Probationer fees actually provide for one-half of the state's $90.6 million operating budget for basic probation services. The $45.7 million collected annually exceeds the total operating budgets of most probation departments. Florida also collects substantial fees, $15.6 million annually, or about one-third of its probation budget. Other states collect much less, but have substantially reduced operating costs. For example, while Alabama collects $2.7 million, that represents more than 30 percent of its annual probation budget. Arkansas collects $369,559, or 27 percent of its budget. Other states vary, with Colorado, Kentucky and Virginia having the lowest collections, covering less than four percent of their respective budgets.[11]

Generally, the amount of money collected has more to do with the collection rate than the amount ordered by the court or imposed by law. Texas collections, for example, increased from $11.4 million in 1980 to $45.6 million in 1988. The increase of 300 percent occurred despite the fact that the total caseload increased only 125 percent. An 85 percent collection rate against misdemeanants and 60 to 65 percent rate against felons were responsible for the increased collections.[12]

A survey that reached 71 percent of probation and parole agencies across the country, released in 1990 for 1988, reported collections of $191,919,786 nationwide, broken down as follows: (1) correctional fees: $80.2 million; (2) restitution: $55 million; (3) fines: $40 million; (4) costs: $12 million; (5) victim compensation: $4.6 million; and (6) attorney fees: $500,000. As the above figures document, fees now surpass fines as the largest costs collected from offenders. In the above survey, agencies reported an average collection rate of 45.8 percent. Ten percent of the agencies reported accepting credit card payments and 60 percent accepted personal checks.[13]

Massachusetts' probation collections in 1994 provide another example of monies assessed against offenders. In that year, probation collected $44.6 million from offenders, mostly probationers. The largest amount, slightly over $10 million, was in support. Although support collections are no longer handled by criminal courts in the state, these collections represent old criminal orders that are diminishing each year. Slightly less than $10 million was paid out in restitution, followed by $8.4 million in fines, $5.4 million in costs, $2.3 million in victim/witness fees, $1.7 million in reduced counsel fees, $2.2 million in drunk driving fees and $4.3 million in probation supervision fees. The victim/witness fees go to a special fund to pay for advocates in the offices of the various district attorneys in the state. The above figures do not include fines, fees and costs, which are paid directly in court when assessed. In these cases, they are paid directly to the Clerk of Courts and are not included in the probation statistics. For some reason, the state trial court does not report these collections in its annual report.[14]

§7.03   Monetary Sanction Laws

Fines

Fines may be imposed in addition to other criminal sanctions, including imprisonment, or as a condition of probation. While the former is subject to enforcement in either civil courts or in contempt proceedings, the latter is enforced through probation revocation hearings. Not all probation statutes authorize fines as a condition of probation. Those that do often allow the imposition of costs, also.[15] Federal law allows for the imposition of fines for both felony and misdemeanor probation, requiring it in the former case if the court does not impose either restitution or community work service.[16]

Some appellate courts have upheld the imposition of fines as a condition of probation absent specific statutory authority.[17] When imposed as a condition of probation, the amount is usually controlled by the statute defining the particular crime. Other appellate courts have specifically rejected the imposition of fines as a condition of probation, absent statutory authority.[18]

The revised federal criminal code specifies a number of factors the court must consider in imposing fines, including the nature of the defendant, the seriousness of the crime and so on. It also requires the court to consider the burden the defendant may face from the imposition of restitution orders. Other factors are included for corporations, such as the size of the organization, and any actions it took to discipline employees responsible for the crime.[19]

Costs and Fees

Costs and fees can be ordered as conditions of probation. They may also be assessed much like a civil assessment of expenses necessitated by the defendant's actions either in regard to the crime, its prosecution and defense or its aftermath, including the defendant's supervision.[20] Few state statutes spell out specific amounts that may be ordered either by the court or as a condition of probation. Nevertheless, appellate courts have uniformly upheld their imposition.[21]

The amounts imposed must relate to the actual costs incurred by the offender, tempered by his ability to pay. Exactly what may be covered by costs and fees depends upon the jurisdiction. Appellate courts have split on whether extradition costs may be covered.[22] They have split on costs for jury fees, prosecution and criminal investigation.[23]

Some states specifically authorize recoupment of defense fees by statute.[24] The United States Supreme Court has ruled that such counsel recoupment statutes are constitutional as long as the offender has or attains the ability to pay.[25] Some appellate courts have forbidden the practice, absent legislative authorization.[26] An Ohio appellate court, in approving an assessment to cover the costs of court-appointed lawyers, held that the practice would encourage the offender to accept responsibility for his misdeeds and enhance his self esteem.[27]

The United States Supreme Court upheld a special assessment in federal courts of $25 for misdemeanants and $50 for felons in 1990.[28] The fees go to a national victim fund. The provisions had been challenged as constituting a revenue bill, which did not originate in the House of Representatives as is required by the federal Constitution. The Supreme Court held that because the provision raises revenue for a particular government program, it did not constitute a revenue bill that must originate in the House. Previously, the Ninth Circuit had held because the provisions were not designed to punish offenders, they were revenue bills.

As mentioned, the use of probation and other correctional fees has grown over the past two decades. Usually these fees are assessed monthly and are determined on a sliding scale. When first imposed in Alabama, the fees were challenged as imposing "imprisonment for a debt" and creating a penal sanction and grounds for subsequent revocation that bear no relationship to the valid purposes of probation. While the challenge was rejected, the suit did lead to the establishment of income guidelines promulgated to determine fee assessments in that state.[29] Supervision fees were also challenged in Pennsylvania as violating the separation of powers. The state high court held that they were permissible because they were administrative in nature, not intended as punishment.[30]

Finally, the federal guidelines also authorize federal courts to impose an additional fine amount that is at least sufficient to pay the costs to the government of any imprisonment, probation or supervised release.[31] Circuits have split on its validity. The Third Circuit found it invalid.[32] The Seventh Circuit found the guideline a permissible exercise of the Sentencing Commission authority.[33] The Second Circuit has agreed with the latter.[34]

Absent specific legislative authority, several appellate courts have ruled against such fees.[35]

Other common fees include treatment fees. Drunk drivers are frequently assessed such fees. Many states have other victim-related assessments like the federal government. At least one appellate court has allowed the costs of preparing a presentence report to be assessed against the defendant.[36] Other states assess the costs of home confinement programs. Florida's extensive home confinement program charges offenders $30 per month and collects 97 percent of the costs charged.[37]

Forfeitures

The rationale for forfeitures is spelled out, in part, in a Fifth Circuit decision:

> Congress found the traditional criminal sanctions of imprisonment and fine wanting in the effort against infiltration by organized crime. Incarcerating individuals could remove them from the operation of victimized organizations. So long as those individuals retained or could transfer economic leverage over the organizations, however, removing them to prison often resulted only in the rule by proxy or in the promotion of junior members of organized crime.[38]

Since that decision, federal forfeiture statutes have been significantly broadened to include other major criminals, drug dealers and so on. The 1984 code recodification contains a section titled the Comprehensive Forfeiture Act of 1984.

The United States Supreme Court upheld in 1995 the power of the federal prosecutor to take possession of all assets of a criminal who agrees to give them up as part of a guilty plea, even property and money that was obtained legally. In an eight-to-one decision, the Court said that the offender can agree to forfeit everything in exchange for sentence reductions. In this case, the drug trafficker gave up $400,000 including a childhood coin collection and savings account as part of his plea. He was sentenced to 20 years rather than 50.[39]

A number of states also have forfeiture statutes. Depending upon how broadly the statute is drawn, items subject to forfeiture vary. Pursuant to New York's forfeiture statute, the Brooklyn District Attorney created headlines by forfeiting the motor vehicles of certain repeat drunk drivers. The law, modeled on federal statutes, allows for the forfeiture of assets gained from the crime as well as "instrumentalities" used to commit the crime. While the law (enacted in 1984) covers felonies only, certain repeat drunk drivers may be prosecuted as felons in New York.[40]

While defendants may agree to certain forfeitures as part of a plea arrangement, absent statutory authorization, the court does not have broad authority to order forfeiture of the defendant's property.[41] On the other hand, the Pennsylvania Supreme Court ruled that while the state's probation statute did not allow for forfeiture, the common-law principles on forfeiture of contraband supply authority for the state to deprive a defendant of a motor vehicle he operated under the influence of alcohol. As the instrumentality used in the commission of a crime, the defendant's car was ruled to be derivative contraband which is forfeitable at the discretion of the judge. The judge, however, must take thorough and careful consideration of the effects of the forfeiture on the defendant and his family before depriving him of his vehicle.

Charitable Donations

There are different forms of charitable donations ordered or approved in courts. They can be in the form of service, material things or money. Service was discussed in the previous chapter. The most common material donation is blood. Ordering offenders to donate blood became so popular in courts that the American Red Cross had to officially urge courts to refrain in the 1980s in light of the growing concern over the spread of HIV-infected blood. Spokespersons from the Red Cross announced that donations of blood through court order would not be used in blood transfusions. The practice was also challenged as constituting a cruel and unusual punishment and was heard by the Ninth Circuit. The court held that because probation is not a punishment, the argument could not apply.[42] Several justices, in concurring opinions, argued that the pint of blood order invaded "the physical person in an unwarranted manner and [is] void on its face."[43]

Jurisdictions have split regarding the legality of requiring cash donations. Various federal circuits have ruled that it is not a valid condition because it is unauthorized by statute. Unlike restitution, such donations are not earmarked for the "aggrieved" victim. They are not fines because they do not go to the state.[44] Congress, however, has specifically authorized donations if the victim or the victim's estate so consents.[45] The statute specifically refers to donations as "restitution to a person or organization designated by the victim or the estate." The victim, not the court, picks the recipient.

State courts have split on charitable donation orders. Some simply state, like the federal circuits, that it is unauthorized by state statute.[46] Others allow for it as consistent with the broad discretion given judges to fashion conditions of probation. A Colorado appellate court, for example, held that the donation was reasonably related to the rehabilitation and education of the offender and also met the best interests of the public.[47] An Indiana appellate court not only allowed for a $40,000 donation to a university foundation where the offender had stolen from the same university but upheld the requirement that the defendant not declare a tax deduction for the "contribution."[48] In the instant case, the judge imposed a slightly larger fine but stated he would waive it if the offender made the contribution.

In the same state, several drunk drivers agreed as part of a plea bargain to donate $1,000 each to charities of their choice. Later, they challenged the donations. The appellate court ruled that it was too late to challenge the condition because they had already agreed to them as part of their plea negotiations.[49]

Finally, federal courts have revisited the role of donations in sentencing when a United States District Court reduced the sentence of a convicted drug conspirator because he had been a generous benefactor of a small North Carolina town, donating air conditioning to the local elementary school, among other things. The defendant had submitted a report by the National Center on Institutions and Alternatives (discussed in § 2.05) that had persuaded the judge to disregard the sentencing recommendations contained in the presentence report provided by probation. The judge departed three levels downward.

On appeal, the Fourth Circuit rejected the departures based on the charitable donations. The court held that Congress' intent in creating the sentencing guidelines was to rest sentences upon the offense committed, not upon the offender. The statutory factors listed for downward departures do not include any that look to the characteristics of the offender. Further, the court is not to consider the offender's socioeconomic status and his community ties only if considering probation. Even if the court were to include the latter in this case, the court ruled, it would be inappropriate.

> It would be ironic if the judicial system were to reward [the offender] with a lower sentence because he was a successful drug dealer rather than an unsuccessful one. Such an approach to sentencing would create perverse incentives for those involved in criminal enterprises. Moreover, to allow any affluent offender to point to the good his money has performed and to receive a downward departure from the calculated offense level on that basis is to make a mockery of the guidelines. Such accommodation suggests that a successful criminal defendant need only write out a few checks to charities and then indignantly demand that his sentence be reduced. The very idea of such purchases of lower sentences is unsavory, and suggests that society can always be bought off, even by those whose criminal misconduct has shown contempt for its well-being.[50]

Child Support

Many statutes include child support as a condition of probation no matter why the offender is on probation. Some appellate courts have upheld the condition, even absent specific statutory authorization. For example, a District of Columbia appellate court found that a judge could impose child support for the illegitimate child of a drug offender because it related to his need for comprehensive rehabilitation contemplated by the statute. Even though payment is a civil obligation, it comports with the general probation provision to obey the law. In the instant case, however, the case was returned because the trial court erred in setting the exact amount to be paid.[51]

On the other hand, an Arizona appellate court ruled that, absent legislative authority, a court could not generally order child support for offenders. The court went on to point out that child support is within the province of the civil court with its own unique procedures, which were not followed by the criminal court in that case. Imposing child support payments without regard to these procedures constitutes a denial of due process.[52]

As nonpayment of child support is increasingly handled in civil courts, rather than criminal courts, it may become more difficult for appellate courts to include child support payments ordered by criminal courts as a condition of probation in the future. Before, when nonpayment was generally treated as a crime, payment obligations could be included under the general "obey all laws" provision of probationary statutes. Some state domestic abuse restraining orders provide for temporary support payments to be made by the abuser to the victim. While violation of these restraining or protective orders is a crime in 35 states, generally violation of the support orders is considered civil or criminal contempt.[53]

Bonds

Some jurisdictions require probationers to post bonds in cash or surety against future probation violations. Bonds are authorized by statute in a handful of states.[54] Federal statutes provide for bonds to be imposed to preserve property subject to forfeiture.[55] Some states allow bonds for specific reasons such as insuring the defendant's presence at a court hearing.[56] Others have not allowed them without explicit statutory authority.[57]

§7.04   Monetary Sanction Payment

The major problem with fines and other costs assessed against offenders is collecting them. Most offenders are not wealthy, especially if their ill-gotten gains are forfeited before they are tried for the crime. Obviously, a monetary sanction is not a sanction, if the offender does not have to pay it. There is also an element of unfairness about monetary sanctions. While on the surface it seems reasonable that two people who commit the same offense should receive the same monetary assessment, the impact will be very different if one is wealthy and the other is destitute. The impact on the former may be negligible and on the latter quite enormous (unless he pays nothing, in which case it is even more negligible for the latter than the former). The assessment of court-ordered monies in this country aggravates the inherent limitations of monetary sanctions.

Day Fines

The fines imposed throughout this country are called "flat" fines. Defendants, sentenced to pay fines, are sentenced to pay set amounts established by statute. While often there is a range set, not less than a certain amount nor more than another amount, courts usually set the amount based on the seriousness of the crime. As a result, the same fine for two different offenders may have two very different effects, depending upon the resources of each offender. For example, the impact of a $100 fine on a poor offender will be much more punitive than the same fine assessed against a millionaire. Because fines are limited by statute and affect offenders unequally, rarely are sentences in this country built solely around the imposition of the fine.

In most other Western nations this is not the case. Fines are the sole punishment in the majority of criminal cases, including serious offenses. In Germany, for example, 80 percent of all offenders are fined as their sole penalty.

The reason fines are used so much more is that European countries do not rely on flat fines, but a concept called *day fines.*

Invented in Finland in 1921, day fines are proportional to each defendant's individual income or wealth. Defendants are not sentenced to pay a specific amount. Instead, they are ordered to pay a certain number of day fines, based on the seriousness of the crime. A minor crime may call for a two-day fine, a more serious crime may call for a 20-day fine. The defendant, then, must pay the equivalent of one day's income for each day fine. For the poorer defendants, a day's income may be $50. For a millionaire, it may be $4,000. As a result, each defendant pays the same proportion of their income for the same crime. The actual amounts vary accordingly.

Nonpayment is punishable by the number of day fines not paid. If a defendant fails to pay three day fines, he is subject to three days in jail.

While this country has had little experience with day fines, community work service orders, which are fairly common, are somewhat similar. Each day a defendant is forced to do community work service, he is deprived of earning his normal daily income. As a result, rich offenders "lose" the same proportion of their income as poorer defendants. In addition, because the number of hours or days of community work service is not as tightly limited by legislation, the judge is more able to assess community service based on the seriousness of the crime. Of course, unlike day fines, the defendants pay their debt through a donation of labor rather than money.

Kansas alone has adopted day fine language in its statute, if not the same program as that used throughout Europe. It provides that the court may include as a condition of probation that "the defendant perform services under a system of day fines whereby the defendant is required to satisfy fines, costs, or reparations or restitution, by performing services for a period of days determined by the court on the basis of ability to pay, standard of living, support of dependents and other factors."[58]

VERA Institute, a correctional reform agency located in New York City, introduced day fines to this country, developing a pilot program in Staten Island, New York for misdemeanants in 1988 with some federal Justice Department funds. While constrained by state law limiting misdemeanor fines to a maximum of $1,000, VERA got judges and prosecutors to agree to impose fines in lieu of other punishments on a day fine basis as much as possible. VERA established a table for the number of day fines to be imposed for 71 common crimes. The number of day fines ranged from 5 to 120 days. The judges then multiplied this number by two-thirds of each defendant's net income. The judge then subtracted for each dependent. The result is the daily rate for each day fine.

Staten Island was chosen because most offenders were employed. Judge Michael Brennan, one of the three Staten Island judges, told the *Times* why he endorsed the day fines pilot program.

> To keep someone in jail costs at least $100 a day, so it makes sense to deprive a person of their disposable income for ten days rather than putting them in jail. It would have the same effect as a cell while saving the taxpayers a tremendous amount of money.[59]

VERA vigorously enforced the fine payments, scheduling installment payments where necessary, sending out due letters, putting liens against property for unpaid fines and attaching wages.

The *New York Times* endorsed the program enthusiastically.

> The concept offers promise for overworked American courts and city jails. For the most part, American courts have not used fines as aggressively or imaginatively as European courts. Judges tend to assume that a thief won't be able to pay a fine except by way of more thievery, or that he won't feel punished; or that overworked court administrators won't follow up to make sure the fine gets paid. Better, they reason, send the offender off to 30 days in jail. Yet jail is often an expensive, even dangerous option. . . . In Sweden and West Germany, day fines constitute more than 70 percent of all criminal sanctions. Administrators in both nations believe the day-fine system has had a major impact in reducing prison populations. To the extent it can do that in New York, it deserves enthusiastic support.[60]

The immediate impact of the Staten Island program was to increase the use of fines. In addition, fine totals increased 20 percent, from an average of $205.66 to $257.85. If richer defendants' fines had not been limited to $1000 by state law, the average fine would have been much higher, at $440.83. The fine revenues generated by the court increased from $82,000 to $94,000. The court not only maintained a high collection rate at 71 percent but the number of defendants who failed to pay anything was greatly reduced, from 22 percent to six percent.[61] VERA researchers noted that criminal fines in New York have not been increased for 30 years. They suggest that the program would be better but for artificially low fines set by state law.

After establishing the Staten Island day fine program, VERA introduced the concept to Maricopa County (Phoenix), Arizona in 1991. Unlike Staten Island, in the first ten months of the Arizona Day Fine program, the average fine was $1,000, ranging from $60 to $12,325.[62] In 1992, Connecticut courts implemented day fines in a pilot program in Bridgeport through its Alternative Sanction Program after receiving a grant from the Justice Department. The first three defendants in Bridgeport included two shoplifters and one drug felon.[63] Similar grants were given to start programs in Des Moines, Iowa and Portland, Oregon.

Money Collection

Whether the fine is a day fine or a flat fine, it will serve little constructive purpose if not collected. Collection is the Achilles' heel of court monetary sanctions. While many jurisdictions do a creditable job of collecting fines from people who, almost by definition, are not disposed to pay them, more jurisdictions do not. A Virginia state study, for example, found that 20 percent of all fines and costs assessed against misdemeanants in district courts were not paid in that state. Sixty percent of felons in circuit courts did not pay. But other surveys document payments as high as 90 percent. Harris County (Houston), Texas collects between 85 and 90 percent and the Montgomery Court of Common Pleas in Pennsylvania had a collection rate of 93 percent.[64]

Experts who have studied the various jurisdictions report that the reason for low collections has much to do with the courts and relatively little to do with the wealth of the defendants.

> Many judges and administrators appear reluctant to recognize that courts are responsible for fine collection. Judges seem to have the attitude that their job is to impose sentences, but not to be involved in seeing that they are carried out.

Judges may be used to having the executive branch (usually a Department of Corrections) carry out their orders and are untrained in administering correctional programs themselves. In addition, because the money does not usually go to the court itself, there may be little incentive to see that the monies are paid. The fines mandated may also be unrealistic. For example, in Illinois, the legislature requires drug offenders to be fined not less than the full street value of seized drugs.[65]

Experts document similar techniques to improve collections: (1) requiring payment in installments; (2) allowing for the use of credit cards; (3) computerizing recordkeeping systems; (4) telemarketing; and (5) hiring private collection agencies to collect the fines. The Tacoma, Washington court has used telemarketing since 1984. During the first two years of operations, the court expended $26,000 and took in $375,000. The court then hired a full-time private collection agency. The Washington state legislature in 1987 authorized courts to assess the costs of these private collection agencies to the offenders. A study in 1988 compared three collection systems: (1) court orders alone; (2) third-party billing; and (3) licensed collection agency. The court collected the least, the third-party billing system collected more than twice what the court collected and the private collection agency collected more than three times what the court collected.[66]

In 1990, the Massachusetts District Courts hired a temporary team to go after unpaid fines and costs in 18 local courts. For a costs of $100,000, the team collected $6 million.[67] Subsequently, the state legislature enacted legislation in 1995 to develop a private collection program to take over collections in the state's largest district courts. The program is overseen by the executive, rather than the judicial branch of government.

Texas has become a model for the collection of probation fees. In 1990, Texas collected 90 percent of all such fees ordered from misdemeanants and 65 percent of those ordered from felons. This was accomplished mainly because the state legislature enacted several statutes deliberately calculated to encourage local probation departments to see that fees are ordered and, once ordered, collected. According to researchers, the most important incentive passed in Texas was allowing local departments to keep a proportion of the fees collected, even if they collect more than they spent that year. The greater the proportion of the local budget that is based on probation fees, the greater the percentage of fees the department is allowed to keep. In addition, the fees can be spent as the local department sees fit, including salaries, operating expenses, new staff, program contracts and so on.

To give departments added incentive, the legislature increased the monthly fees from $15, set in 1965 to $40 in 1985. In 1987, it also established minimum fees of $25 a month for the poorest probationers and made it more difficult for judges to waive them.

In 1986, seven Texas counties collected more than 80 percent of their budgets through fees. On the other hand, three counties recovered less than 40 percent. Most collect between half and 69 percent of their budgets through fees. While offender populations may vary, the difference in fee collections is generally attributed to individual department efforts and policies. What appears to make a difference is: (1) linking fee collections to staff performance; (2) giving priority to fees over fines and other court ordered costs; (3) instituting a strong no-waiver policy; and (4) enforcing payments strictly (including ten days of community work service for each missed payment in one county).

Technological innovations have also encouraged collections in Texas. The larger departments have automated routine accounting functions allowing departments to automatically mail statements to probationers each month. The letters are timed to arrive when offenders receive government benefit checks and wages. In addition, probationer officers receive statements each month of who on their caseloads paid that month. Probationers also receive warning letters if they miss three payments.

Despite fears, the increased collection of fees has not decreased state contributions to probation budgets. However, some probation officers complain that they have become fee collectors, concentrating on this to the exclusion of other issues. Some probationers stop reporting because they are behind on payments and are afraid to come in to see their probation officers. Administrators counter that fee collection is good casework, furthering the goals of helping probationers stay on the straight and narrow. They cite a direct correlation between fee payment and probation compliance. In several counties, including Dallas and Harris, probation departments have added job readiness and training programs to specialized caseloads in high unemployment areas of the counties. And the increased revenues have allowed departments to develop specialized programs for sex offenders and other risky probationers.[68] Study of the Texas collections also indicates that increased fee collection does not result in decreased fine and other collections.[69]

Punishing Nonpayers

Ultimately collection rates for fines, fees and assorted costs have to do with the ability of the offender to pay and the penalties for nonpayment. It is generally conceded that unrealistic amounts assessed against indigent offenders is an exercise in futility. With the proliferation of fines, fees and costs, although individual fines, fees and costs may be reasonable, when they are added together the totals due can add up quickly. Even if fines are limited by statute, the total costs assessed against the offender may exceed that amount if the court adds various user fees, court costs, restitution, forfeitures and the like.

For example, a typical drunk driver in many states will be assessed a fine, a fine surcharge, court costs, probation fees, urine testing fees, drunk driving program assessment plus the actual cost of the drunk driving education program mandated by law, not to mention a public counsel fee (assessed, for example, against *indigent* defendants who have a public attorney appointed in Massachusetts). This does not include ongoing support obligations that may also be assessed. While the fine is limited by statute and is usually no more than several hundred dollars, the actual costs the probationer is required to pay the court and related agencies typically reaches several thousand dollars.

To control overall monetary obligations imposed against offenders, the court may want to aggregate them and compare them with what a day fee would be, given each offender's financial circumstances. If the equivalent day fee is excessive, given either the offender's overall circumstances or the seriousness of the offense, the court may want to reconsider its total package of monetary orders.

As total costs mount, the question of the defendant's ability to pay correspondingly becomes more important. The United States Community Services Administration determines the poverty threshold annually. By law, for example, Massachusetts defines indigent as a person whose income, after taxes, is 125 percent or less of the current poverty threshold as determined below.[70]

The following table applies in all states except Alaska and Hawaii.

Size of Family	125% of Poverty Threshold
1	$ 9,338
2	$12,538
3	$15,738
4	$18,938
5	$22,138
6	$25,338
7	$28,538
8*	$31,738

*For family units with more than eight members, add $3,200 for each additional family member.[71]

Some jurisdictions insist that the court assess the ability of the offender to pay before ordering various monetary sanctions. For example, Michigan's statute authorizing the payment of restitution and costs as a condition of probation provides that "[t]he court shall not require a probationer to pay restitution or costs unless the probationer is or will be able to pay them during the term of probation."[72] In 1988, the Florida Supreme Court allowed, for the first time, indigent defendants to challenge excess monetary orders at the time of their imposition, as opposed to waiting until they were charged with their nonpayment.[73] As a result, the trial court must hold a hearing on the defendant's ability to pay before assessing costs against indigent defendants. In the instant case, the defendant had been charged $5,000 in costs, which was ruled improper.[74] Similarly, Minnesota and California put the onus on the state to determine the offender's ability to pay prior to assessment of costs.[75] In Oregon, the court must assess the offender's ability to pay before it assesses certain victim costs, because they must be paid within 90 days of imposition.[76]

On the other hand, in many jurisdictions, ability to pay does not come up until the order is enforced. Then all courts have a constitutional obligation to consider the offender's ability to pay. For example, the First Circuit approved the assessment of special costs against an indigent offender because there was no indication that the court intended to collect the money so long as the offender remained indigent.[77] In other words, assessing monies against indigents is all right as long as the court does not try to collect from them.

As the above decision alludes, assessed payments can be delayed pending employment or made payable in small installments. As a United States Supreme Court Justice remarked in *Williams v. Illinois:* "The deterrent effect of the fine is apt to derive more from its pinch of the purse, than the time of payment."[78] In addition to delaying payment or making payments due on an installment plan, the court can make the defendant pursue other means to meet payment demands. For example, a Texas appellate court upheld requiring a defendant who missed any payments to: (1) file income and expense statements showing money received and spent during the default months; and (2) if employed less than 150 hours during a given month, file a statement detailing his efforts to secure employment during that month. These conditions, the court ruled, contributed significantly to the offender's rehabilitation.[79] A federal circuit similarly upheld a revocation for a defendant's failure, among other things, to report termination of his employment and his failure to produce a copy of his personal income tax return as instructed by his probation officer.[80]

Enforcing payment of monetary sanctions differs depending upon the specific monies ordered. In some jurisdictions, the nonpayment of costs must be handled differently from the nonpayment of fines. In the leading New Jersey case on the subject, the state's Supreme Court held that fines are a form of punishment.[81] Therefore, the court could exact punishment for nonpayment. However, costs were imposed to collect a debt. Therefore, unless the defendant contemptuously failed to pay, the court was without authority to punish the defendant for nonpayment.

The federal code gives the government broad power to collect a fine. Within 10 working days after a fine is determined to be delinquent (30 days past due), the Attorney General shall notify the person whose fine is delinquent. Within 10 working days after a fine is determined to be in default (90 days past due), the Attorney General shall notify the defaulter that the entire unpaid balance, including interest and penalties, is due within 30 days. Upon a determination of willful nonpayment, interest may be imposed on the remaining balance at one percent per month beginning the 31st day after sentencing for nonpayment. Also, a penalty sum equal to 10 percent of the delinquent portion of the fine shall be charged, subject to waiver for good cause.[82] An unpaid fine is considered a lien in favor of the government upon all property belonging to the person fined. Defendants may not declare bankruptcy to avoid payment.[83] Finally, nonpayers can be sentenced to jail if nonpayment is found to be willful or if "in light of the nature of the offense and the characteristics of the person, alternatives to imprisonment are not adequate to serve the purposes of punishment and deterrence."[84] Willful nonpayers can be sentenced to pay a fine not more than twice the unpaid balance or $10,000, whichever is greater, or imprisoned not more than one year, or both.[85]

States generally lack this enforcement mechanism provided for in the federal code. If costs, fees or other monies are ordered as a condition of probation, they may then be enforced like any other probationary condition, usually by contempt proceedings or probation revocations. By statute, nonpayers of probation fees in California may not be prosecuted in criminal courts.[86] Civil penalties may be imposed and are not tied to the defendant's terms of probation. Probation revocations are discussed in detail later.[87] Like the enforcement of restitution orders, the burden to prove inability to pay rests with the state in some states and the defendant in others.[88]

Although there are no comprehensive studies that reveal how successful courts are in collecting assorted fines, costs and other fees, a National Institute of Corrections survey found that "the overall average collection rate (for probation fee assessments) . . . appears to be about 60 percent."[89]

Example of Court Enforcement of Monetary Order

In what was believed to be the first sentence under the three-year-old federal "deadbeat dad" law, the U.S. District Court in Michigan sentenced a surgeon to reside in prison for one year while keeping his job, to pay the $220,000 in support he owed his 11-year-old daughter in Worchester, Massachusetts. Convicted in February 1995, the surgeon displayed, according to the court, a lack of candor regarding his financial resources. His attorney asserted that the surgeon had paid for his daughter's insurance, but the court found that the father had failed to alert his daughter that his medical insurance covered her.

The prosecution had recommended six months in jail. The judge rejected this in favor of a sentence he called "more severe and more enforceable." After the first year, the defendant could be sentenced again for contempt if he failed to keep up on his payments. The ex-wife called the judge's sentence "creative" and was elated. Over the past six years, the defendant had violated court-ordered payments in Michigan and Georgia. At one point, he had actually changed jobs to reduce his income so his court-ordered payments would be reduced. By his own admission, he was paying $2,225 in legal fees a month to fight the court-ordered payments. Eventually, the mother had to move home to Georgia to find full-time employment and send her daughter to live with her grandmother in Massachusetts.[90]

§7.05   Summary

Too often courts think only of fines when they think of monetary sanctions. Often the maximum permissible fine is too small to provide a sanction commensurate with the seriousness of the offense. On the other hand, the court often believes the maximum fine is beyond the reach of a poor or unemployed offender, so there is little point in imposing it. There is an answer to both problems within the alternative sentencing arsenal.

First, monetary sanctions include more than fines. If the court seeks to punish a defendant through his pocketbook, it can impose costs to cover certain trial expenses, fees for necessary treatment, restitution for victim losses, forfeitures against defendant gains, support payments and donations where permissible, as well as make the defendant post a bond for his future performance. Such orders add up to substantial monetary penalties. They also require offenders to go to work to pay them. Work is not only rehabilitative, it is incapacitative. For every hour defendants are on the job, that is one hour away from troublesome peers, bars or street corners. Payment by mandatory installments allows even poor defendants to eventually pay large amounts. By placing defendant Walton's probationary sentences [on and after each other], Justice Forer was able to extend his probation for 19 years, allowing him time at 25 dollars a week to pay almost $25,000 to his permanently blinded victim. If the defendant is not working at the time of the imposition of the monetary sanction, large financial orders may inspire him or her to get a job.

A second problem is presented by indigent defendants. Although the Supreme Court articulated in its rulings that nonwillful nonpayers may not simply be tossed in jail, courts are not powerless to enforce monetary orders. They may extend payments, order payments on installments or make offenders perform community work service.

Faced with mandatory community work service orders, many defendants will work extremely hard to obtain real employment so that they may at least receive compensation for their work, even if much of that goes to making court-ordered payments. Many courts have noted that offenders who claim inability to pay based on indigency suddenly find the necessary money when told to report to community work service. They either possess resources that they did not reveal to the court or they are in fact employed but work "off the books," i.e., the employer does not report their wages to the government. For offenders who legitimately cannot afford to pay, community work service orders provide a penalty equivalent to that of their wealthier peers. If courts adopt the day-fine concept in calculating total monetary sanctions, they can insure that all defendants, notwithstanding their financial status, are given proportional punishment.

Monetary sanctions offer defense attorneys bargaining chips to be used in obtaining alternative sentences. They offer the defense and the court substantial punishment, but avoid incarceration. For the same reason, they offer the prosecution a punitive sentence that avoids the high cost of incarceration, allows for easier case clearance through plea bargaining, and brings in revenue to the local or state governments, the crime victims and the defendant's dependents, who might otherwise have to depend upon welfare for support. For the court, they offer a creative, flexible and fair sanction without increasing prison overcrowding.

Notes

[1] See, *e.g., State v. Zaruba,* 306 N.W.2d 772 (Iowa 1981) (court allowed court imposition of costs to cover drug buy money); *People v. Evans,* 122 Ill. App. 3d 733, 461 N.E.2d 634 (1984) (court barred restitution for drug buy money but suggested the imposition of fines or forfeiture). But *cf. Commonwealth v. Mourar,* 504 N.E.2d 197 (Pa. Super. 1986) (sentencing could properly order restitution of buy money to Bureau of Drug Control as "victim" of drug offense); *State v. Stalling,* N.C. Sup. Ct. No. 652A85 (5/16/86), *affirming* 79 N.C. App. 375, 335 S.E.2d 344 (1985) (drug buy money was not part of the agency's normal operating expenses and therefore could be assessed against the defendant).

[2] National Highway Traffic Safety Administration (1986). THE DRUNK DRIVER AND JAIL: RESOURCE MATERIALS 229 (DOT HS 806 765 Jan.).

[3] Standards Relating to Probation, § 3.2(c)(ii) & (d), (e), (f) (1970).

[4] MODEL PENAL CODE § 301.1(2)(k) (Proposed Official Draft 1962), *accord,* STANDARDS AND GOALS, CORRECTIONS 578 (Nat'l Advisory Commission on Crim. Just. 1973) (which also endorses the use of bonds).

[5] Hillsman, S., J. Sichel and B. Mahoney (1984). FINES IN SENTENCING—A STUDY OF THE USE OF FINES AS A CRIMINAL SANCTION— EXECUTIVE SUMMARY (VERA NCJ 96334).

[6] Hillsman, S., B. Mahoney, G. Cole and B. Auchter (1987). *Fines as Criminal Sanctions.* RESEARCH IN BRIEF. NIJ (September).

[7] Forer, L. (1980). CRIME AND VICTIMS.

[8] See discussion of these cases at § 6.02.

[9] The President's Commission on Law Enforcement and Administration of Justice (1967). TASK FORCE REPORT: THE COURTS 18.

[10] Mills, J. (1992). *Supervision Fees: APPA Issues Committee Report.* PERSPECTIVES *16:4* (Fall).

[11] Parent, D. (1990). RECOVERY OF CORRECTIONAL COSTS THROUGH OFFENDER FEES. Washington, DC: National Institute of Justice (June).

[12] Finn, P. and D. Parent (1992). MAKING THE OFFENDER FOOT THE BILL, A TEXAS PROGRAM. Washington, DC: National Institute of Justice (October).

[13] Parent, D. (1990). RECOVERY OF CORRECTIONAL COSTS THROUGH OFFENDER FEES. Washington, DC: National Institute of Justice (June).

[14] *Annual Report on the State of the Massachusetts Court System, Fiscal Year 1994,* Supreme Judicial Court, Boston, Mass. 1995.

[15] See, *e.g.,* KAN. STAT. ANN. § 21-4610(3)(g) (Supp. 1986) (fines or costs); TEX. CODE CRIM. PROC. ANN. art. 42.12, § 6(a)(8) (Vernon Supp. 1986) (fines and costs); VT. STAT. ANN. tit. 28 § 252 (fines only).

[16] 18 U.S.C. § 3563(b)(2) (Supp. II 1984) (effective Nov. 1, 1986).

[17] See, *e.g., State v. Rugon,* 355 So. 2d 876 (La. 1977); *cf. Brown v. State,* 559 P.2d 107 (Alaska 1977) (in which the court ruled that the language allowing for the imposition of a fine as a condition of probation allowed it to be imposed even if the statute upon which the defendant was convicted provided for no fine).

[18] See, *e.g., State v. Ayala,* 95 N.M. 464, 623 P.2d 584 (Ct. App. 1981) (deals with costs).

[19] 18 U.S.C. § 3572(a) (Supp. II 1984) (effective Nov. 1, 1986).

[20] See, *e.g., People v. Teasdale,* 335 Mich. 1, 55 N.W.2d 70 (1952) (the court listed "normal operating costs" to include salaries of police and prosecutors, expenses of operating a courtroom and a variety of expenses tangential to the specific apprehension and prosecution of the offender).

[21] See, *e.g., People v. Robinson,* 253 Mich. 507, 235 N.W. 236 (1931); *Commonwealth v. Ferguson,* 201 Pa. Super. 649, 193 A.2d 657 (1963); *State v. Kluesner,* 389 N.W.2d 370 (Iowa 1986) (restitution, court costs, attorney fees or public defender costs, if appointed, mandatory, even if judgment deferred pursuant to statute).

[22] See, *e.g., People v. Burnett,* 86 Cal. App. 3d 320, 150 Cal. Rptr. 126 (1978) (extradition covered within general costs of prosecution and cannot be charged to the defendant). But see *State v. Balsam,* 130 Ariz. 452, 636 P.2d 1234 (Ariz. Ct. App. 1981) ($853 in extradition costs allowed to be assessed).

[23] Compare *Giddens v. State,* 156 Ga. App. 258, 274 S.E.2d (1980), *cert. denied,* 450 U.S. 1026, 101 S. Ct. 1733, 68 L. Ed. 2d 220 (1981) (in which court allowed costs for witness fees, the court reporter, bailiff fees and the gathering of evidence) and *State v. Welkos,* 14 Wis. 2d 186, 109 N.W.2d 889 (1961) (in which the court allowed fees, as well as the costs of the audit conducted pursuant to the investigation); *United States v. Vaughn,* 636 F.2d 921 (4th Cir. 1980) (in which criminal investigation expenses were not allowed); *State v. McCarthy,* 259 Minn. 24, 104 N.W.2d 673 (1960) (in which the court allowed prosecution costs but not jury fees).

[24] See, *e.g.,* TEX. CODE CRIM. PROC. ANN. art. 42.12, § 6(a)(11) (Vernon Supp. 1986).

[25] *Fuller v. Oregon,* 417 U.S. 40, 94 S. Ct. 2116, 40 L. Ed. 2d 642 (1974).

[26] See, *e.g., United States v. Turner,* 628 F.2d 461 (5th Cir. 1980), *cert. denied,* 451 U.S. 988, 101 S. Ct. 2325, 68 L. Ed. 2d 847 (1981) (in which the court held that the relevant federal probation law failed to authorize recoupment).

[27] *State v. McLean,* 87 Ohio App. 3d 392, 662 N.E.2d 87 (1993).

[28] *United States v. Munoz-Flores,* 863 F.2d 654, *cert. granted,* 110 S. Ct. 48, 107 L. Ed. 2d 17, *rev'd,* 110 S. Ct. 1964, 109 L. Ed. 2d 384 (1990).

[29] Decree, *Tinker v. Ussery,* Ala. Cir. case # 203-060 (1977) reported in Department of Transportation, *The Drunk Driver and Jail: Resource Materials,* 5 at 237, 240 (DOT HS 806 765 Jan. 1986).

[30] *Commonwealth v. Nicely; Commonwealth v. Williams,* 536 Pa. 144, 638 A.2d 213 (1994).

[31] U.S.S.G. § 5E1.2(i).

[32] *United States v. Spiropoulos,* 976 F.2d 155 (3d Cir. 1992).

[33] *United States v. Turner,* 998 F.2d 534 (7th Cir), *cert. denied* 114 S. Ct. 639, 126 L. Ed. 2d 598 (1993).

[34] *United States v. Leonard,* 37 F.3d 32 (2d Cir. 1994).

[35] See, *e.g., State v. Haynes,* 53 Or. App. 850, 633 P.2d 38 (1981); *cf. State v. St. Clair,* 177 W. Va. 629, 355 S.E.2d 418 (W. Va. 1987) (no charges for room and board in jail although by statute allowed to charge for costs of prosecution).

[36] *Tovar v. State,* 777 S.W.2d 481 (Tex. App. 1989)

[37] *Community Control: House Arrest: A Three Year Longitudinal Report* 16. Florida Department of Corrections, Probation and Parole Services (Jan. 1987).

[38] *United States v. Rubin,* 559 F.2d 975, 991 (5th Cir. 1977).

[39] *Libretti v. United States,* 516 U.S. ___, 116 S. Ct. ___, 133 L. Ed. 2d 271 (1995).

[40] N.Y. CIV. PRAC. R. § 1310 et. seq. (Consol. Supp. 1985).

[41] See, *e.g., State v. Bouldin,* 717 S.W.2d 584 (Tenn. 1986) (court may not forfeit car of drunken driver as not specifically authorized by statute).

[42] *Springer v. United States,* 148 F.2d 411, 415 (9th Cir. 1945).

[43] *Id.* at 416.

[44] See, *e.g., United States v. Missouri Valley Construction Company,* 741 F.2d 1542 (9th Cir. 1984); *United States v. John Scher Presents, Inc.,* 746 F.2d 959 (3d Cir. 1984); *United States v. Haile,* 795 F.2d 489 (5th Cir. 1986).

[45] 18 U.S.C. § 3579(b)(4) (1982) redesignated as § 3663 (effective Nov. 1, 1986).

[46] See, *e.g., State v. Theroff,* 33 Wash. App. 741, 657 P.2d 800 (1983); *Luby v. State,* 648 So. 2d 308 (Fla. Dist. Ct. App. 1995); *People v. Sullivan,* 529 N.Y.S.2d 311 (N.Y. Sup. App. 1988).

[47] *People v. Burleigh,* 727 P.2d 873 (Colo. Ct. App. 1986).

[48] *Campbell v. State,* 551 N.E.2d 1164 (Ind. Ct. App. 1990).

[49] *Ratliff v. State; Heavrin v. State,* 596 N.E.2d 241 (Ind. Ct. App. 1992).

[50] *United States v. McHan,* 920 F.2d 244 (4th Cir. 1990).

[51] *Brown v. United States,* 584 A.2d 537 (D.C. App. 1990); see also *State v. Garner,* 54 Wis. 2d 100, 194 N.W.2d 649 (1972).

[52] *State v. Garibaldi,* 802 P.2d 1030 (Ariz. Ct. App. 1990).

[53] See, *e.g.,* MASS. GEN. L. ch 209A (1995).

[54] See, *e.g.,* ARK. STAT. ANN. § 41-1203(2)(1) (1977); CONN. GEN. STAT. § 53a-30(a)(6)(1985); N.Y. PENAL LAW § 65.10(2)(j) (McKinney Supp. 1986), WASH. REV. CODE § 9.95.210(4)(Supp. 1986).

[55] 18 U.S.C. § 1963(e)(1) (Supp. II 1984).

[56] See, *e.g., People v. Hubble,* 81 Ill. App. 3d 560, 401 N.E.2d 1282 (1980).

[57] See, *e.g., Logan v. People,* 138 Colo. 304, 332 P.2d 897 (1958).

[58] KAN. STAT. ANN. § 21-4610(3)(k) (Supp. 1990).

[59] Brozan, N. (1988). *In Staten Island Court, Each Is Fined to Fit His Means.* NEW YORK TIMES, Sept. 17.

[60] *Criminal Fines, By the Day.* NEW YORK TIMES, August 30, 1988.

[61] Winterfield, L. and S. Hillsman (1993). *Staten Island Day Fine Project.* RESEARCH IN BRIEF. Washington, DC: National Institute of Justice (January).

[62] McCarthy, P. (1992). *Fitting Penalty to Crime.* BOSTON GLOBE, May 24.

[63] *Ibid.*

[64] Cole, G. *Fines Can Be Fine—and Collected.* JUDGES JOURNAL 28:1 (Winter).

[65] *Ibid.*

[66] *Ibid.*

[67] Murphy, S. (1990). *Collecting Fines Seen as Crucial.* BOSTON GLOBE, November 8.

[68] Finn, P. and D. Parent (1992). *Making the Offender Foot the Bill: A Texas Program, Program Focus.* Washington, DC: National Institute of Justice (October).

[69] Parent, D. (1990). *Recovering Correctional Costs Through Offender Fees.* Washington, DC: National Institute of Justice (June).

[70] MASS. GEN. LAWS ANN. ch 261, § 27A (1994).

[71] OMB FEDERAL POVERTY INCOME GUIDELINES, Annual Revision, Effective April 6, 1995.

[72] MICH. COMP. LAWS ANN. § 771.3 (5)(a) (West Supp. 1986).

[73] *Harriel v. State,* 520 So. 2d 271 (Fla. 1988); *Mays v. State,* 519 So. 2d 618 (Fla. 1988).

[74] *Camp v. State,* 536 So. 2d 369 (Fla. Dist. Ct. App. 1988).

[75] See, *e.g., Foster v. State,* 416 N.W.2d 835 (Minn. App. 1987); *People v. Greco,* 240 Cal. Rptr. 804 (Cal. Ct. App. 1983).

[76] *State v. Wetzel,* 765 P.2d 835 (Or. App. 1988).

[77] *United States v. Rivera-Velez,* 839 F.2d 8 (1st Cir. 1988).

[78] *Williams v. Illinois,* 399 U.S. 235, 265, 90 S. Ct. 2018, 2034, 26 L. Ed. 2d 586, 606 (1970).

[79] *Tovar v. State,* 777 S.W.2d 481 (Tex. Ct. App. 1989).

[80] *United States v. Lindo,* 52 F.3d 106 (6th Cir. 1995).

[81] *State v. DeBonis,* 58 N.J. 182, 276 A.2d 137 (1971).

[82] 18 U.S.C. § 3611-3615 (Supp. II 1984) (effective Nov. 1, 1986).

[83] *Id.* at § 3612(a), (e), (f).

[84] *Id* at § 3614 (a), (b).

[85] *Id.* at § 3615.

[86] CAL. PENAL CODE § 1203.1b (West Supp. 1982).

[87] See Chapter 10, *infra.*

[88] See, *e.g., McCowen v. State,* 703 S.W.2d 787 (Tex. Ct. App. 1985); *Hill v. State,* 718 S.W.2d 751 (Tex. Ct. App. 1985) (defendant must prove by a preponderance of the evidence that he is unable to pay); *contra, State v. Duke,* 699 P.2d 576 (N.M. 1985), Depson v. State, 363 So. 2d 43 (Fla. Dist. Ct. App. 1978) (onus is on state to make affirmative finding that defendant is able to pay).

[89] U.S. Department of Justice (1986). FEES FOR PROBATION SERVICES 15 (N.I.C. FZ-4 Jan).

[90] Rakowsky, J. (1995). *Surgeon Sent to Prison in Child-Support Case.* BOSTON GLOBE, November 2.

Chapter 8

Mandatory Treatment and Alternative Sentencing

§8.01   Introduction

While other alternative sentencing components focus on both the offense and the offender, alternative mandatory treatment sanctions focus almost exclusively on the latter. The offense, however, may be an indicator of the offender's treatment needs. For example, courts may assume that there is a high probability that defendants convicted of drunk driving have an alcohol abuse problem. In other cases, the offense may not reveal whether the offender suffers from alcoholism, drug addiction or a similar problem. As has been demonstrated by the factors found to correlate to recidivism, a substantial number of offenders suffer substance abuse problems—alcohol, drugs or both. Unless these treatment needs are met, repeat criminal behavior is likely. Mental illness per se does not strongly correlate with criminal behavior.

Most experts agree that incarceration does not cure these underlying problems. The 1984 federal criminal code revision contains language acknowledging the "inappropriateness of imposing a sentence to a term of imprisonment for the purpose of rehabilitating the defendant or providing the defendant with needed educational or vocational training, medical care, or other correctional treatment."[1] Incarceration may only prevent repeat offenses while the defendant is in prison. Notwithstanding this, many correctional experts and the public at large have lost faith in treatment or "rehabilitation" of offenders. The medical model of corrections, which holds that defendants are "sick" but can be "cured" by counseling, is dismissed by some as naive and by others as subversive.[2] Much of the disillusionment with rehabilitation comes from the almost exclusive use by correction officials of traditional psychological counseling. Such counseling is usually predicated on the client establishing a relationship of

235

trust with his therapist, developing rational insight into his behavior and changing that behavior. Unfortunately, these ingredients are frequently missing in treating offenders. First, most enter treatment only because they are forced to by the court. Insight into behavior is impossible to obtain if the client is drunk or high on drugs. If a therapeutic relationship with a counselor is established, statistics reveal that before the healing process has time to take place, the majority of offenders who are going to recidivate will have already done so.

Courts usually rely on probation officers to serve as the counselors of first, and often last, resort. They are expected to assume the roles of both social worker and police officer. As noted by correctional historian David Rothman, the position of the probation officer becomes untenable. "The probation officer is the ultimate reflection of the failure of the idea in American corrections that you can guard and treat at the same time. . . . It's a patently absurd notion."[3] In most probation departments, contact between probation officer and probationer is reduced to perfunctory periodic office visits.

Reviewing correctional studies conducted over the last decade, James Q. Wilson, a noted criminologist, concludes that treatment of certain offenders is actually counterproductive. "Treating such persons—at least by means of verbal therapy—apparently," he writes, "makes society worse off." Such offenders learn only how to manipulate their counselors, obtain early release and generally "con" the system.[4]

For these and other offenders, there are more appropriate treatment modalities, specifically mandatory treatment based on behavior modification. This theory of treatment holds that the best way to change behavior is to concentrate on behavior and not attitude change. If a person is forced to change behavior, eventually his attitudes will also change, insuring long-term behavior change. Behavior-controlling drugs, such as Depo-Provera, methadone or Antabuse, are sometimes used to insure requisite behavior change. The role of the probation officer becomes that of enforcer of the behavior change. Courts are specifically geared to provide the system with incentives and disincentives necessary to modify behavior. Courts, with their threat of incarceration and other punishments, are in a better position to treat alcoholism, drug addiction, compulsive gambling, chronic criminal sexual behaviors such as pedophilia, domestic violence and other established patterns of criminal behaviors than are voluntary treatment facilities and programs.

First of all, if a client can voluntarily enter treatment, he can voluntarily leave it, too. Typically, perhaps the majority of persons suffering with these behaviors voluntarily enter treatment because the negative consequences of their behaviors become oppressive. Their abused wives threaten to leave them; the doctor informs them that they will die of liver disease; their victim threatens to call the police and expose them and so forth. However, once the immediate crisis has passed, the offenders pronounce themselves cured and leave treatment. The addicts return to their vials, needles or bottles; the sexual offenders return to their prey; the gamblers to the tables.

This is not the case with compulsory treatment. Long after the precipitating crisis (usually the arrest and conviction) is over, the court order remains. If effectively enforced, courts can insure that offenders stay in treatment, forcing at least short-term behavior change. If the behavior can be changed long enough, the offenders' lifestyles begin to accommodate the changes. Eventually attitudes adjust and the old behavior is not only changed, but abandoned as undesirable by the offenders.

While most offenders lack the requisite insurance to pay for most treatment programs, especially costly insight mental health services, fortunately some of the most successful programs for offenders are free. They include self-help groups such as Alcoholics Anonymous (AA), Narcotics Anonymous, Gambler's Anonymous, Parents Anonymous and so on. These self-help groups can provide necessary tools, support and encouragement for offenders to change their behavior.

There have been some legal challenges raised against mandatory participation in AA. Some have argued that such orders violate the Establishment Clause of the Constitution. Part of the tenets of AA is a belief in a "higher power" that is commonly interpreted to mean God. A third-offense drunk driver, for example, challenged mandatory attendance at AA, claiming that as an atheist, participation in AA violated his rights. Upon reviewing AA, one U.S. District Court noted repeated references to "God" in the twelve steps of the AA recovery program. Therefore, the court held that although there was no intent, the order impermissibly, in effect, established a state-sponsored religion. In addition to declaratory relief, the plaintiff was awarded $1 in nominal damages.[5] Fortunately, there is an explicitly non-religious self-help program for alcoholics called Rational Recovery, which has over 80 chapters nationwide. Another court decision upheld mandatory participation at AA or similar programs because the defendant could choose Rational Recovery, rather than AA if the latter's religious tenets were found to be objectionable.[6]

(While the court must be wary at requiring participation in a program deemed to constitute a religion, the reverse is not true. The court may order a defendant to attend a treatment program that prevents her from attending church, especially where she had both suggested and consented to the treatment program initially.[7])

Although groups like AA insist on the anonymity of their members, most will cooperate in certifying attendance of court-ordered participants. The central governing body of AA addresses this question in its national literature:

> All of us sober in AA know to get well we really had to want it for ourselves—eventually, if not at first. We could not stay sober just because we were required to for somebody else.
>
> Yet, in every real sense, every single AA member is at first "sentenced" to AA—if not by the court, then by employer, family, friends, doctor, or counselor, or by his or her own inner suffering. We would not come to AA until we had to, in some way.

> So in AA we are not concerned about who or what first sends the alcoholic to us, or how. Our responsibility is to show AA as such an attractive way of life that all newcomers who need it soon want it . . .
>
> In most cases, the group secretary is happy to sign or initial a slip furnished by the court saying so and so was at the such and such meeting on a particular date.[8]

Numerous studies have found that, rather than hinder recovery, mandatory treatment has a higher success rate than voluntary treatment in many of these areas. There are many significant, real-life demonstrations of the efficacy of forced treatment. Various extensive pretrial release programs, for example, have found that by mandating abstinence enforced by drug testing, rearrest rates can typically be cut in half compared to pretrial offenders released who do not maintain abstinence or report for testing.[9] A government review of one such program led experts to conclude that given the relationship between drug use and crime, crime could be cut through such programs.

On the other end of the correctional spectrum, another study of prisoners released in New York and Washington found that those released after spending time in an inpatient treatment center for drugs were two times more likely to avoid re-arrest within three years of release than parolees released directly to the streets. Other parolees released with mandatory testing and outpatient treatment were also two times more likely to avoid re-arrest than those released with no mandatory treatment conditions. The director of the research study concluded: "You use the leverage of the criminal justice system to get somebody into treatment—a combination of criminal justice system and treatment. That is the ticket." The Justice Department announced, after reviewing the study, it would release $1 million to duplicate the program elsewhere. As a reporter covering the story concluded, "In many ways, the trend represents a return to the rehabilitation of offenders, an idea that was popular in the 1960s . . . "[10]

Researchers examining such findings have concluded that despite long-standing beliefs that rehabilitation efforts aimed at substance abusing offenders are relatively ineffective, and more recent evidence that clients with extensive criminal involvement before treatment tend to exhibit poorer outcomes than persons without such a history, "significant research results indicate that correctional drug treatment programs can have a substantial effect on the behavior of chronic drug-abusing offenders."[11]

In June, 1994, the Rand Corporation released a study indicating that treating cocaine addicts is seven times more cost effective than domestic drug enforcement. The report concluded that the annual cocaine consumption could be reduced by one percent by adding $24 million to the treatment budget. To reach a comparable outcome, more than $246 million would need to be added to the domestic law enforcement budget and $366 million for international interdiction costs. Rand researchers estimated that out of the current $13 billion spent on cocaine control in the United States, only $1 billion goes to treatment.[12]

In his widely hailed study of alcoholism, George Vaillant explains the theory behind compulsory treatment for substance abusers. His research found that "the most important single prognostic variable associated with remission among alcoholics who attend alcohol clinics is having something to lose if they continue to abuse alcohol."[13] The discriminate use of and threat of incarceration can provide the motivation to begin the recovery process. As Chicago gangster Al Capone admonished, "you get further with a kind word and a gun, than a kind word alone." Or as former President Lyndon Johnson used to say, "if you have them by the short hairs, their hearts and minds will follow!"

Because mandatory treatment programs insist on immediate behavior change, society is protected from the negative consequences of the offender's addiction, alcoholism, spouse battering, sexual compulsion etc. If monitored strictly by probation, the moment the offender slips, he or she is returned to court for further controls to insure public protection. Blood, urine, saliva, hair, polygraph, penile plethysmograph and other tests are routinely available to test against continued alcohol use, drug use, restricted contact with minors or other persons, deviant sexual fantasies and other forbidden behaviors.

The treatment of alcohol and drug abuse requires additional emphasis. Addiction and substance abuse play a role in many other dysfunctional and criminal behaviors. First, it is now clear that vast numbers, probably most offenders arrested for serious crimes in urban areas, are drug abusers. A study of 2,000 men arrested in 12 cities found that 50 percent to 75 percent tested positive for illicit drug use between June and November 1987. Rates of positive tests ranged from 53 percent in Phoenix to 79 percent in New York City. Other cities were as follows: Portland, Oregon 70 percent; Houston 62 percent; Indianapolis 60 percent; San Diego 75 percent; Ft. Lauderdale 65 percent; District of Columbia 77 percent; Chicago 73 percent and New Orleans 72 percent. If marijuana was not included rates dropped in some jurisdictions, from 60 to 25 percent in Indianapolis. However, in the District of Columbia they only dropped from 77 to 74 percent. Cocaine rates varied from 11 percent in Indianapolis to 63 percent in New York City. Heroin fluctuated from two percent in Ft. Lauderdale to 26 percent in New York City. The overall use of drugs found, according to the then-Director of the National Institute of Justice was "higher than suspected." Prior estimates of drug-using offenders was only 20 percent based on post-arrest studies.[14]

Second, not only is there a significant correlation between crime and substance abuse, but studies specifically find a particular link between violent crime and certain substance abuse, especially alcohol abuse. Alcohol is involved in more than 66 percent of the nation's homicides, 50 percent of rapes and up to 70 percent of sexually aggressive acts against children and adults.[15] A succession of studies have documented a correlation between alcohol and drug abuse and domestic violence.[16]

Third, while alcohol and other substances may not cause any of the above behaviors (with the exceptions of the alcohol/drug addiction), they may worsen them in many cases. In addition, most experts agree that offenders will not respond to treatment and intervention as long as they continue to get high on drugs and alcohol. Any controls or insights they gain in treatment will be lost as soon as they lose control under the influence. For this reason many jurisdictions that mandate batterer treatment also mandate concurrent alcohol and drug treatment.[17]

Vaillant has documented that many persons diagnosed as sociopathic and even psychotic are simply suffering from alcoholism. Sustained sobriety will eradicate their sociopathic and even psychotic symptoms.

In addition to intervention programs aimed at extinguishing certain behaviors, a new type of programming has been developed, replacing standard mental health type counseling programs. In their place, cognitive skill training programs are increasingly being offered to offenders. Based on extensive analysis of the common elements of programs that actually worked to change offenders' behaviors, researchers discovered that the single most significant predictor of offender success was participation in programs that altered how they thought. Studies have been conducted which show that programs that systematically alter how offenders make decisions can reduce recidivism and other negative behaviors.[18]

Cognitive-based programs attack the faulty beliefs and reasoning that lead offenders to make poor choices. They seek to replace the offender's hedonism, which constantly opts for instant gratification, by a higher level of reasoning. They also seek to increase the offender's empathy for others. One of the pioneering theorists in the field defined various levels of moral development, with hedonism being the lowest level and acting out of moral principles as the highest level.[19] Cognitive programs accomplish a higher level of functioning by confronting the offender's personal beliefs, attitudes and behaviors and how he evaluates his relationships and associations. In effect, the offender is given the opportunity to restructure his identity and personality.

A cognitive program, called Moral Recognition Therapy (MRT) for drug offenders was first introduced in institutional corrections in 1985 in Memphis, Tennessee. The program quickly expanded to cover drunk drivers and other offenders. The program spread to Oklahoma's prisons where it soon covered not only all inmates but those released under supervision. Its massive implementation in that state means that inmates, offenders in community corrections, parole or probation all have access to standardized rehabilitation programming which allows for treatment continuation when the offender moves from one security level or institution to another. Other MRT programs exist in Washington state and Montana. MRT has also expanded its program to treat sex offenders, domestic violence perpetrators, school dropouts and others.[20]

Another cognitive skills development program, Reasoning and Rehabilitation, is also in place. In 1991, the Colorado Judicial Department incorporated it in a large pilot demonstration project for substance abusers. As of the winter of 1992, it operated in the majority of the state's 22 judicial districts. Its first application, however, was in 1985 in Canada. It then spread to Great Britain and Spain. The program operates in conjunction with other treatment approaches.[21]

Batterers' treatment programs, pioneered in Duluth, Minnesota, Quincy, Massachusetts and Seattle, Washington, also employ cognitive-behavioral treatment as well as psychosocial education programs to stop perpetrators of domestic violence. In fact, a number of jurisdictions prohibit traditional mental health counseling, couple counseling or other alternative treatments for batterers, finding them ineffective, or even dangerous.[22] Similarly, standard treatment programs for sex offenders also employ cognitive behavior programs aimed at confronting the offender's cognitive distortions, denials and rationalizations.

Traditional drug treatment programs have also had a revival of sorts because many jurisdictions have established drug courts. One of the first was established in Miami, Florida in the late 1980s. The court was targeted to drug users and its mission was to provide for therapeutic jurisprudence, or drug treatment, for abusers.[23] Miami uses both traditional counselors and acupuncturists. The latter were used particularly to help abusers detox from their drug of choice. In the past seven years, almost 7,000 offenders have gone through the Miami drug court.

In 1990, Oakland, California established another drug court. Offenders are required to attend group counseling, acquire GEDs and obtain employment as well as report periodically to the court. In the past five years, more than 4,000 offenders have been treated in this court. In 1991, a drug court was established in Portland, Oregon, using both acupuncture and counseling. Since then, drug courts have been promoted by the Justice Department. The 1994 Omnibus Crime Bill included money to help establish drug courts.

§8.02   Diagnosis

In order to impose effective mandatory treatment, courts must first diagnose the offender's problems. The offense may provide evidence of the problem, as mentioned. Addiction to certain drugs, such as heroin, is usually obvious. Compulsive sexual deviance or gambling may also be obvious. If the underlying reason for the offender's chronic criminal behavior is unclear, presentence reports may also help. Experts may be brought in to assist the court. However, if the offender suffers from alcoholism, diagnosis may be extremely elusive. More than one-half of the alcoholics seen by physicians are undiagnosed. Psychiatrists share a similarly dismal record. They often overlook the disease, concentrating on its symptoms, which often include depression, marital breakups and unemployment. As Vaillant describes, "would-be helpers recognize only stereotypic alcoholic drinkers. Different social groups regard alcohol abuse differently, and individual use and abuse patterns differ. The observer's own belief system and patterns of alcohol use may interfere with his appraisal of others."[24] Also, unlike most people seeking treatment, alcoholics are adept at concealing overt signs of intoxication and their denial of alcoholism is often convincing. In order to diagnose alcoholism, courts or their agents must adopt single-minded attention to the possibility of the disease, even in its early stages. As a noted physician has written, "Teaching and supervised experience in alcoholism has been so vague and disorganized that clinicians often fail to pursue the hypothesis that the patient has alcoholism. In contrast, the alcoholism expert may verify the diagnosis after a brief exchange with a patient."[25]

The failure of the criminal justice community to diagnose the alcoholism of many of the men and women who pass through it is profound. A Justice Department study of state prison inmates found that as much as one-quarter of inmates drank more than four ounces of ethyl alcohol every day for the year prior to their last arrest. Although it may be assumed that most of these prison inmates had substantial involvement with both the juvenile and adult criminal justice systems prior to incarceration, almost none of these inmates had ever been exposed to an alcohol treatment program.[26]

There are several tests that have been developed to assist in the diagnosis of alcoholism. The CAGE test, able to be administered by any probation officer, defense lawyer or other individual, is the simplest. It consists of four questions:

1. Have you ever felt the need to *cut* down?
2. Have you ever felt *annoyed* by criticism of your drinking?
3. Have you ever had *guilt* feelings about drinking?
4. Have you ever taken a morning *eye-opener*?

Validated tests include the Michigan Alcoholism Screening Test (MAST), developed in the late 1960s, consisting of 25 questions calling for yes or no answers, the Mortimer-Filkins test, which measures the problems associated with alcoholism, specially developed by courts to identify problem drinkers (not copyrighted) and the MacAndrews Scale, which is a subscale of the Minnesota Multiphasic Personality Inventory (MMPI), widely used in mental health agencies to measure personality.

Often, careful review of the defendant's prior record will indicate alcohol abuse. Prior convictions for relatively less serious crimes like disorderly conduct, drunk driving, leaving the scene of an automobile accident and simple assault, may all indicate an alcohol problem.

There are also a vast array of clinics, institutions and experts of varying competencies available to diagnose the problems of offenders. Some specifically offer evaluation services for court-referred clients. In many jurisdictions, probation officers are trained to make similar determinations or refer offenders to experts who will. Many jurisdictions provide various in-patient diagnostic institutions for defendants to aid the court in sentencing. As discussed in Chapter 2, these facilities are administered by both correctional and other human service agencies and are available to assist the court in diagnosing a defendant's treatment needs.

Many psychologists and psychiatrists without special training fail to accurately diagnose an offender's problems with drugs or penchant for illegal and inappropriate sexual partners, etc. because they dismiss the presenting behavior as a *symptom* of an underlying problem, not the problem itself.

There is also evidence that compulsive gambling is widespread among offenders, but is rarely diagnosed. A rare study of inmates in the District of

Columbia in 1967, for example, found that 56 percent of armed robbers, 14 percent of drug addicts, 70 percent of assaultive drinkers and a majority of burglars could be classified as inveterate gamblers. A more recent 1985 National Institute of Justice study similarly found that 30 percent of all prisoners studied showed clear signs of pathological gambling, 10 to 15 times higher than one would expect to find in the population at large. The study concluded that many offenders suffered multiple addictions, including gambling. It also concluded that a similar proportion of gamblers probably existed in probation caseloads, undiagnosed.[27] If these two studies are accurate, evaluations of offenders must also assess offender gambling behavior in addition to everything else.

A recently developed tool, now available outside the laboratories of the FBI, is hair testing. One and one-half inches of a strand of hair can reveal every drug ingested by the owner from the week before the strand was cut to three months earlier. It takes about a week for a drug to enter the hair, where it will remain for the life of the hair. As a result, unlike urine, blood or saliva tests, which reveal only current use, hair tests give a retrospective screen. With the exception of marijuana, the hair tests reveal the average monthly quantity in nanograms of each drug used. Hair tests do not reveal alcohol use. Although more expensive than single-screen urine tests, for example, hair tests can replace even more expensive clinical evaluations.

Although newly marketed, at least one court has ruled that the hair test meets the requisite standards for admissibility as reliable scientific evidence. The ruling was based on the Federal Rules of Evidence, which require courts to determine the admissibility of novel scientific evidence by balancing the "relevance, reliability and helpfulness of the evidence against the likelihood of waste of time, confusion and prejudice."[28] The standard is close to the *Frye*[29] standard, developed in case law, which requires general acceptance in the scientific community. Using either standard, the court found extensive scientific writing testifying to hair test reliability and acceptance in the field of forensic toxicology. The decision cites a comparison of hair and urine tests conducted by the Justice Department, which concluded that the hair tests were more accurate.[30] Also, the court noted that hair analysis has been used to detect the presence of metals and nutrients for almost 20 years. (Lord Peter Wimsey used it to detect arsenic in a victim's hair in the 1930s.) While a great deal is not known regarding how the drugs are incorporated into the hair, that does not affect the reliability of the test findings. The actual analysis of the drugs in the hair is based on radio immunoassay, an effective and accurate method of detecting the presence of various compounds, including narcotics.[31]

At least three companies offer commercial hair testing. They are Psychemedics of Cambridge, Massachusetts, American Toxicology Institute of Las Vegas and New Jersey-based Barringer Instruments Inc. Many companies offer urine testing. Urine tests are available for alcohol use. Alcohol stays in the urine longer than in the breath so detection is a bit more revealing. However, unlike other drugs, small amounts of alcohol pass through the system relatively quickly. Testing will not reveal much past use, only current use. For this reason, alcohol testing, like any testing, must be random and periodic to reveal continuing use.

Often relied upon, but the worst source of accurate information on drug and alcohol use, is the offender himself. Studies have documented, for example, that only one-half of all arrestees in the District of Columbia and New York City interviewed for drug use between 1984 and 1987 who tested positive for drugs admitted to drug use. Even though they knew they would be tested, they did not believe the test would reveal their use, they lied on principle, or their self-denial of use convinced them that they would test negative for use. Almost as bad for making accurate assessments are probation officers, who are expected to know better. The same study revealed that even regarding offenders on intensive case-loads, which means above-average contact with the probation officer, the probation officer significantly underassessed use as revealed by drug testing.[32]

The moral is clear. In terms of drug assessment, there is no substitute for testing.

Finally, modern technology has added to the tools available to evaluate certain sexual offenders. Again traditional psychological testing is of little or no value in predicting who will re-commit a sex crime or determining which sex offender is the least dangerous and which is the most dangerous. A penile plethysmograph, on the other hand, can measure sexual arousal for various stimuli, either visual or oral. It can reveal whether the person on whom it is attached is attracted to children, for example, sex with violence, and so on.

Relatively new to the market, the plethysmograph has met some legal challenges in federal courts. It has withstood challenges that it impermissibly compromises offenders' Fourth and Fifth Amendment rights. Such infringements are generally permissible as described in § 3.04. The same decision also found that the plethysmograph met standards for scientific acceptability because it was recognized as a legitimate instrument utilized by treatment centers including the one to which the defendant was required to be treated.[33] The Vermont Supreme Court addressed a similar challenge that sex offender treatment that required masturbation therapy and use of a penile plethysmograph conflicted with the offender's religious beliefs. The Court found the program was not overly restrictive of the defendant's liberty and autonomy and was permissible.[34]

Similarly, one of the pioneers in sex offender research, Dr. Gene Abel, has developed a computer-driven physiologic test that he claims measures sensory response that "measures deviant sexual interests, including sexual interest in children of various ages and sexual violence against adult men and women."[35] Unlike the plethysmography, the test is not as invasive, bypassing the need for penile measurements and nude slides typically used in sex offender testing. The test became available in 1995.

Some courts and programs use polygraph tests, especially to monitor sex offender truthfulness in treatment. Courts have split regarding the reliability of polygraph testing *per se*. Some have found it to be a scientifically reliable instrument. Others do not. An example of the former was discussed in § 3.04. In a contrary finding, a Florida appellate court objected to a polygraph test being used to enforce a sex offender's probation on two grounds. The polygraph was not reliable and its use constituted an improper delegation to a machine. The defendant has no ability to confront and cross-examine a machine's "evidence."[36] An Oregon appellate court let stand conditions of sex offender treatment that included mandatory polygraph testing even though the defendant challenged that statements he made using the polygraph constituted a denial of his Fifth Amendment rights. In upholding the condition, the court focused on the right of the state to insist that the probationer answer questions truthfully as long as it did not forbid him from invoking his privilege against self-incrimination.[37]

§8.03   Treatment

Treatment may be either on an outpatient or inpatient basis. Inpatient treatment programs run the gamut from hospital-based, short-term programs, to residential non-hospital treatment programs that run in excess of a year. Frequently, hospital facilities are necessary to detoxify drug-addicted or alcoholic offenders before other longer term treatment is possible. If the offender is less in need of treatment than a supportive environment, there are halfway houses for drug abusers, compulsive gamblers, the emotionally disturbed, alcoholics and so on.

Many varieties of outpatient treatment are offered. Many medical, psychiatric and social service agencies offer one-on-one outpatient counseling on a periodic basis. Group counseling is also offered. There are a variety of self-help treatment groups for common categories of offenders. Alcoholics Anonymous (AA) meetings are open to the public. Almost every community in the country has an AA chapter. Listings of meetings are usually available from a central office listed in the telephone book. Narcotics Anonymous, modeled after AA, is also widely available, as is Gamblers Anonymous. There is even a group for compulsive sexual deviants called Sex and Love Addicts Anonymous (SLAA), formed a decade ago. SLAA is a fellowship of men and women struggling to control sexual compulsions or emotional dependencies. It follows the 12-step program of AA. Many members report drug or alcohol addiction, and that they grew up in alcoholic homes.

Offenders, usually on an outpatient basis, can be treated with a variety of behavior-modifying drugs. Methadone is prescribed as a legal substitute for heroin. The drug, naltrexone hydrochloride, marketed by Dupont as "Trexan," blocks the effects of opiate use, preventing a "high." Disulfiram, commonly known as Antabuse, is a chemical blocker of alcohol. Persons on anabuse become extremely ill if they continue to ingest alcohol. Depo-Provera is used experimentally in certain prisons as a chemical sex suppressant to enable chronic sexual offenders to resist their sexual compulsions. Lithium and other drugs are prescribed to control the erratic behavior swings among manic depressives who often pose a threat to the public or themselves during manic swings. With the exception of Depo-Provera, all of these chemical therapies have won widespread endorsement in the medical and treatment communities.

Depo-Provera is still experimental as a sex depressant. Although legally prescribed both in Europe and just recently in the United States as a female contraceptive, it has just begun to be used in this country for sexual offenders. Some research has been ongoing at Johns Hopkins University Hospital in Baltimore. At least one sexual offender agreed to receive weekly injections of the drug as part of a plea bargain that allowed him to remain in the community under probation supervision for 10 years. The defendant had been convicted of two rape-related charges in 1983.

Some judges have bypassed chemical castration and ordered surgical castration for sexual offenders. A Circuit Court Judge in South Carolina offered three defendants, convicted of brutally raping a 23-year-old woman, either castration, receiving Depo-Provera or imprisonment for 30 years. Subsequently, the state supreme court ruled that castration constituted a cruel and unusual punishment. The defendants were each resentenced to 30 years in prison.[38] A Texas judge in 1992 also offered to lighten a sentence if the defendant would submit to castration. The issue became moot with the judge withdrew from the case after a furor arose over his offer. The judge was re-elected the following year with the highest percentage of votes of any judge that year in the entire state.[39]

Legislation was introduced in Texas to allow prisoners to be castrated with their consent in 1995 following one inmate's plea that he be castrated. Imprisoned child molester Larry McQuay, declaring himself to "still be a monster," requested castration to help him control his lust for children. He argued that removal of his testicles would drain 90 percent of the male hormone testosterone from him and free him of his sexual impulses.

Critics point out that 30 percent of castrated men can still maintain the ability to have sexual intercourse. However, studies in Europe suggest that recidivism has been cut substantially through castration. Meanwhile, McQuay is scheduled for release in 1996.[40]

Treatment orders need not be confined to one modality or another. Alcoholic offenders, for example, may be ordered to complete a standard 28-day inpatient program, followed by weekly outpatient counseling, supplemented by several meetings of AA per week, with a condition of mandatory abstinence accompanying the treatment orders. A defendant could also be ordered to take anabuse to assist him in maintaining sobriety. Mandatory treatment conditions of probation need not stand alone, either. They can be in combination with other probationary conditions that assist in the defendant's behavior modification. The same defendant may also be ordered to complete 100 hours of community work service in an alcohol detoxification center, to be performed weekends. Such a community work service order will expose the offender to a graphic illustration of the perils of excessive drinking. He will see the suffering that alcoholism causes. In addition, the order will subtract from free time normally spent in a bar or lounge.

In coordinated, integrated sentences, treatment does not stand alone, independent of the rest of the offender's sentence or conditions of probation. Rather, the treatment program is incorporated into an overall intervention program that begins literally when the offender is first arrested. As a result, additional "treatment" conditions are tailored to change the environment of the offender to lessen his opportunity to engage in his problematic behavior. In effect, these additional conditions support and reinforce the offender's treatment.

In the following three subsections, examples of overall treatment/intervention programs will be described for three typical groups of problematic, high-risk offenders: (1) sex offenders; (2) drunk drivers and (3) perpetrators of domestic violence.

1. Sex Offenders

According to the FBI's Uniform Crime Report for the United States, in 1989 there were 251,310 persons arrested for sex crimes, about one-seventh of one percent of all those arrested that year. The largest portion, one-half, were arrested for prostitution. In addition, almost 40,000 were arrested for rape and 104,000 for miscellaneous sex crimes, including indecent exposure, indecent assault and the like. While most of the prostitutes are female, other sex offenders are 10 times more likely to be male when it comes to rape and 100 times more likely when it comes to other crimes. Between 1980 and 1989, sex crimes increased by 42.1 percent and rape increased by 17.2 percent. Overall crime was up 27.7 percent.[41]

Victimization reports suggest that many more sex crimes occur than the arrests alone would indicate. One-third of females report being sexually molested or raped by the age of 18, according to at least one study. Others place the figure from 10 to 60 percent. Other studies reveal that boys are molested at a rate from three to 31 percent.[42]

One of the reasons for the relatively low arrest rate and the high victimization rate reported obviously may have to do with the low reporting rate of these crimes. But it also has to do with the large number of victims per individual sex offender. In a landmark study, researchers secured federal certificates of confidentiality to allow 561 identified sex offenders (admitted or convicted) to reveal their actual victim count.[43] They reported an astounding 291,737 pedophilic acts involving 195,407 victims/participants. Within this number, the researchers identified two groups of offenders. The first, with fewer victims, were "situational" offenders. They acted impulsively, in stressful situations or when the opportunity presented itself. The second, with a much larger number of victims, were "preferential" offenders. They acted compulsively in a predatory fashion.

For example, child molestations numbered from one to 10 for the situational offenders. But for the preferential it numbered from 23 to 282. The same was true for other sexual behaviors. For obscene telephoning, for example, the first group committed an average of 30 calls, the second 136. Exhibitionism among the first was 51 versus 505 for the second group. Rape was one for the first and seven for the second group. Child relatives were more likely to be abused, averaging 36 to 45 separate victimizations. Nonrelative victims were likely to be abused only one or two times.

Despite common belief, sexual offenders do not only engage in one form of sexual offenses. Child molesters also engage in adult rape. Rapists also engage in indecent exposure crimes and so on.

According to a 1987 American Bar Association study, the primary response to sex crimes with child victims is a probationary sentence. The study looked at such cases in Trenton, New Jersey, Fairfax County, Virginia and Santa Cruz, California. It found of 159 such cases, four-fifths received probation. The most common condition of that probation was court-mandated treatment. This was ordered in 89 percent of the cases. A follow-up study, published in 1990, consisting of a telephone survey of 100 representative county probation departments around the country, sought to discover what the typical probationary sentences looked like.

Fewer than one-half of the departments supervising these offenders had any special guidelines, protocols or regulations for dealing with these sex offenders. Rather, they were supervised as one of generally too many cases on high caseloads. Only one-quarter of the departments had specialized units for supervising child sex abuse offenders. The average probationary period was from three to five years. Most were ordered to participate in psychological counseling. Also, many were ordered to stay away from their victims. Public mental health programs were utilized most often although private counselors were also used. Fewer than one-quarter of the probation officials reported that treatment ordered was "good" for either the offenders who were indigent or those who could afford to pay. Most departments, however, had no standards by which to rate or evaluate treatment programs used.

Surveys mailed to state probation officials found similar concerns, with most being even more pessimistic about the quality of treatment facilities and staff training available for these cases.

Four model programs were also studied in Travis County, Texas, Salt Lake City County, Utah, Vermont, and St. Joseph County, Indiana. This analysis found that most sex offenders reached probation via plea bargains, rather than trials. This may explain the numbers of sex offenders given probationary sentences. Often, prosecutors are reluctant to go to trial with child victims, especially the younger victims. Jail overcrowding was also mentioned in the study as another reason for use of probation. In the model programs, supervision ranged from two to 10 years. Supervision was intense, ranging from residential halfway house stays to frequent personal contact with offenders, family members and employers. Three of the four sites maintained specialized caseloads. All offenders were required to sign waivers of confidential information, giving probation officials access to their treatment records.

None of the sites had written policies regarding treatment standards. Treatment was not recommended for offenders who were in denial. Treatment approaches ranged from very confrontational therapy to holistic "support" therapy. Reoffenses were not common, but officials were quick to admit that the probationers probably posed long-term risks, despite their probationary supervision.

As a result of the study and analysis of the four model sites, the American Bar Association published standards which include: (1) establishment of specialized, reduced caseloads for sex offenders; (2) intense supervision by specially trained probation personnel; (3) close coordination with treatment agencies that meet standards established for such specialized treatment and so on.[44]

Since the study and American Bar Association standards, much progress has taken place in the field of probation.

The first step in fashioning a coordinated treatment/intervention program for sex offenders as suggested by the American Bar Association, is to identify sex offenders. The research indicates that the case actually brought before the court probably represents only a fraction of the offender's criminal sexual activities. To determine the true extent of his behavior, it is necessary to interview his victims, the police and so on. The worst source of information will come from the perpetrator himself. Sex offenders characteristically deny and minimize their behavior. These are the principle psychological defense mechanism these offenders use. Untrained therapists can easily be fooled. The offenders usually present themselves as severely depressed and suffering low self-esteem, grist for the therapist's mill. As a result, the untrained therapist will immediately go to work to lift the offender's depression and self-esteem. The therapists, however, will fail to ask a simple question. Why do we want sex offenders to be undepressed and have high self-esteem? Perhaps their depression will at least motivate them to change their behavior. In fact, their depression and low self-esteem may be a result of the *arrest* that led them to the therapist in the first place. Neither caused them to commit their crimes.

For this reason, once identified, correctional experts advise that sex offenders be sent to specialized sex offender treatment programs, or therapists who understand this type of offender. Although there is no national licensing authority for sex offender therapists, there is a national Association for the Treatment of Sexual Abusers (ATSA), based in Oregon. Unlike generic therapists, ASTA members must be committed to community protection and safety. "Community safety takes precedence over any conflicting consideration, and ultimately is in the best interests of the offender." They believe that treatment can be aided by criminal investigation, prosecution, and court orders for treatment. They hold that without external pressure, many sexual offenders will not follow through in treatment. Internal motivation improves prognosis, but is not a guarantee of success. "Nor may members make claims regarding the efficacy of treatment that exceed what can be reasonably expected and supported by empirical literature."

The specific treatment recommended is long-term, comprehensive, offense-specific treatment.

> Currently, cognitive-behavioral approaches that utilize sexual offender peer groups and drug intervention appear to be the most effective and best evaluated methods. Self-help or time limited treatment should be used only as an adjunct to comprehensive treatment. Each offender will have an individual plan that identifies the issues, intervention strategies, and goals of treatment. This plan should outline expectations of the offender, his family (when possible), and support

systems. Treatment contracts should include provisions to avert high risk situations. Contracts should be re-assessed periodically. Progress, or lack thereof, should be clearly documented in treatment records. . . . Progress in treatment must be based on specific, measurable objectives, observable changes, and demonstrated ability to apply changes in relevant situations. For most offenders, progress requires changes in the offender's behavior, attitudes, social and sexual functioning, cognitive processes and arousal patterns. These changes should demonstrate increased understanding of deviant behavior, victim sensitization, and ability to see and apply help. . . . When a treatment provider determines that an offender is not making the changes necessary to reduce his risk to the community, the provider has an ethical obligation to refer the client to a more comprehensive treatment program and/or the judicial system.[45]

ASTA also advises that if the client's denial continues after a suitable trial period, he should be terminated from treatment. In regard to technology, the group advises that "polygraphs and plethysmography should not replace other forms of monitoring but may improve accuracy when combined with active surveillance, collateral verifications, and self report." Aversion therapy requires client consent.

The treatment itself should cover the following 10 areas: arousal control; cognitive thinking; relapse prevention; improving primary relationships, couples/family therapy; increasing social competence; support systems; victim empathy; biomedical approaches (anti-androgens, antidepressants etc. may give clients greater control over excessive fantasy and compulsive behavior); follow-up treatment.

Common treatments include masturbatory satiation with the aim of making deviant thoughts, fantasies and images repulsive. In another technique, covert sensitization, the molester is taught to identify thoughts, feelings and situations that tend to make him aroused. He is then asked to imagine the steps leading to his deviant acts, along with the worst consequences, such as being imprisoned. Ammonia aversion is a variant on this method. In psychosocial rehabilitation, offenders are taught to express themselves more directly, relate more effectively with others, correct their misconceptions about sexuality and be more sexually responsive to adult partners. Surveillance and monitoring are very crucial parts of the treatment. People close to the offender must learn to identify the signs of relapse. Long-term follow up is essential. Treatment, in effect, never ends, it just becomes less frequent.

Sex offenders are also usually ordered to abstain from drugs and alcohol.

A survey released in 1995 of a dozen studies utilizing control and experimental groups of sex offenders found, on the average, that treated sex offenders repeated offenses 19 percent of the time, compared to untreated offenders, who on the average committed another crime 27 percent of the time. Researchers at Kent State University in Ohio found that cognitive-behavioral therapy, designed to change the offender's thinking and behavior, and hormonal treatments, intended to reduce testosterone levels and lower sexual arousal, were significantly more effective than behavioral conditioning alone. Treating adolescent sexual offenders is the most effective time to reduce recidivism.[46]

In terms of related conditions of probation, there are several. The Maricopa County, Arizona Probation Department provides a comprehensive list of conditions for sex offenders. It was identified by the National Association of Probation Executives as a model program in its *Executive Exchange* newsletter. The first set of conditions relates to contact with children.

1. You shall not initiate, establish, or maintain contact with any male or female child under the age of 18 nor attempt to do so except under circumstances approved in advance and in writing by your probation officer.

2. Notwithstanding any court order to the contrary, you shall not reside with any child under the age of 18 or contact your children in any manner unless approved in advance and in writing by your probation officer.

3. You shall not enter onto the premises, travel past, or loiter near where the victim resides except under the circumstance approved in advanced and in writing by your probation officer. You shall have no correspondence, telephone contact, or communication through a third party.

4. You shall not go to or loiter near school yards, parks, playgrounds, arcades, or other places primarily used by children under the age of 18 without permission of your probation officer.

5. You shall not date or socialize with anybody who has children under the age of 18 without the permission of your probation officer.

The second set relates to mandatory treatment.

6. You shall actively participate in sex offender treatment and remain in such treatment at the discretion of the supervising officer.

7. You shall submit to any program of psychological or physiological assessment at the direction of the probation officer, including the penile plethysmograph and/or the polygraph, to assist in treatment, planning and case monitoring.

8. You shall allow the therapist to disclose to the court information about your attendance and progress in treatment.

Other behavior conditions include:

9.   You shall register with the Sheriff of the County in which you reside as a sex offender within 30 days of sentencing.

10.   You shall reside at a place approved by your probation officer.

11.   You shall abide by any curfew imposed by your probation officer.

12.   You shall not possess any sexually oriented material as deemed inappropriate by treatment staff, nor patronize any place where such material or entertainment is available.

13.   You shall be responsible for your appearance at all times. This includes the wearing of undergarments and clothing in places where other persons may be expected to view you.

14.   You shall not hitchhike or pick up hitchhikers.

15.   You shall not utilize "900" telephone numbers without permission of the supervising probation officer.

16.   You shall not operate a motor vehicle alone without specific written permission of the probation officer unless accompanied by an adult approved by the probation officer.

17.   You shall abide by all terms and restrictions of the family reunification procedure mandated in writing by the supervising officer.

The vast majority of states now have specific statutes requiring certain sex offenders to register with police or some sort of centralized registry. While only six states had such laws in 1984, by 1996 all but Massachusetts had such registries. Most apply to convicted felons only. At least one state, Illinois, requires that certain sex offenders must submit specimens of their blood to a state agency for genetic marker indexing. In such a manner, the offender's DNA may be matched with specimens taken in future criminal investigations of sex crimes to see if he is responsible.[47]

Because these mandatory registries are of recent origin, they cannot be enforced retroactively against sex offenders already in the criminal justice system. However, by imposing offender participation in a sex offender registry as a condition of parole, eligible sex offenders can be forced to register even though they cannot be forced to pursuant to the law mandating the registry itself. For example, Louisiana law requires inmates convicted of sex offenses to register with local sheriffs within 30 days of their release. A sex offender, imprisoned before the law went into effect, was so ordered. The order was appealed. A state appellate court approved this special condition because the order was a condition of parole, not the statute. The court went on to provide that if the parolee refused to register, his parole could be revoked.[48]

2. Drunk Drivers

Much progress has been made in the national campaign against drunk driving. In 1980, 28,000 people were killed by drunk driving. By 1990, the number was down to 22,420. The percentage of people killed by drunk drivers out of all motor vehicle fatalities dropped from 56.8 percent to 49.3 percent. The credit for this success is due to many sources. The national decline in the speed limit probably helped. Mothers Against Drunk Driving probably helped as well. There were two chapters in 1984 and 400 chapters in 1990. In part because of MADD, the criminal justice system became much more actively involved—arresting, prosecuting and aggressively sentencing drunk drivers. More drunk drivers are being incarcerated and many more are being forced into treatment. Twenty-four states now mandate alcohol evaluation for treatment for drunk drivers. Rather than being viewed as a motor vehicle offense, drunk driving is being perceived as a drinking offense.[49]

However, the criminal justice response varies tremendously state by state. In Massachusetts, for example, first offenders must complete a 26-week counseling program and attend meetings of Alcoholics Anonymous. Second offenders must complete a two-week minimum-security inpatient program with required followup. Third-time offenders must go to jail for at least 180 days. License loss is a minimum of 45 days for first offenders, six months if they refuse to take a Breathalyzer test and 45 days for testing 0.1 or higher. Second offenders lose their license for a minimum of six months before they can obtain a day license and third-time offenders for at least two years.[50]

In Georgia, on the other hand, reports reveal that treatment is the exception, not the rule, for drunk drivers. As of November 1991, out of 5.4 million licensed drivers in the state, records found that 17,532 had five or more drunk-driving convictions. The vast majority of first-time offenders were allowed to plea *nolo contendere* with no license loss. In 752 of the worst cases, judges mandated treatment in only 13 cases, confiscated cars in only four cases, although it would have been legal to do so in 600 cases.[51]

Originally developed by the Federal Highway Safety Administration, many courts refer drunk drivers to Alcohol Safety Programs, which are short-term education programs to demonstrate the unwise combination of drinking and driving. The underlying assumption of these programs is that drunk drivers are primarily social drinkers who had one too many. Studies found these programs to be ineffective. Many revealed that these programs actually increase the probability of reoffenses.[52]

The problem is that the underlying assumption of these programs is erroneous. The average drunk driver, even a first offender, did not have one too many. They had several six packs too many. They are not social drinkers, but abusive drinkers who have already built up a tolerance for alcohol use, just as any drug abuser develops a tolerance for his or her drug of preference. Ironically, those offenders most able to appear sober may be those who are the most serious abusers who drink the most. Because of tolerance, they hold their liquor much better than a social drinker who has not built up tolerance. As a result, abusive drinkers may appear and act less drunk with the same amount of alcohol in their system.

The idea that a first offender is an unlucky social drinker defies probability. The level of enforcement means that the average drunk driver will drive drunk up to 2,000 times before he or she is caught once. Therefore, a person who drives drunk only occasionally is not likely to be arrested, ever.[53]

It stands to reason that programs aimed at teaching awareness among social drinkers may not be very relevant, much less effective among abusive drinkers or alcoholics. Effective programs must aim, instead, to stop the abusive drinker from drinking. Generally, controlled drinking programs are found to be ineffective.

George Vaillant suggests that four elements must be addressed in the healing process of alcoholics. First, the patient must be offered a nonchemical substitute dependency for alcohol; second, there must be some external control to remind the patient that even one drink will lead to negative consequences; third, the patient's social and medical damage caused by alcoholism must be repaired; fourth, the patient's self-esteem must be restored. Vaillant goes on to suggest that Alcoholics Anonymous addresses these four elements most consistently for most persons suffering from alcoholism. Finally, Vaillant concludes that it is easier to walk with two crutches rather than one. Combinations of treatment, "such as group therapy and renewed church attendance and disulfiram and vocational rehabilitation may be employed to provide all four therapeutic components."[54] Similar treatment strategies may prove efficacious for drug addicts.

In addition to "treatment," effective intervention may be enhanced with other behavioral conditions supporting that treatment. Drug and alcohol testing is, of course, indicated. Deprived of alcohol, many offenders will simply switch to other drugs such as cocaine or marijuana. If nothing else, it is more difficult for police to arrest for and prosecutors to prove driving under the influence of other drugs because they are undetected by Breathalyzers.

In addition to anabuse which makes people sick who drink, a new drug was introduced in the 1990s to help drinkers refrain. Naltrexone has been found to be an effective medication to address alcoholism. In research backed by the National Institute on Alcohol Abuse and Alcoholism (NIAAA) at the University of Pennsylvania, it was determined that the drug cut relapse rates by 50 percent. Those taking the drug reported less cravings for alcohol compared to those taking a placebo. The NIAAA recommends, however, given the incomplete testing of the drug, that naltrexone be given only by doctors knowledgable in addiction treatment and that the drug be given in conjunction with traditional treatment.[55]

Most states require license loss for varying periods. Unfortunately, license loss is only effective if enforced. Government studies indicate that from 60 to 80 percent of drunk drivers operate without licenses.[56] For this reason, by 1990, 11 states had either allowed for or mandated that courts order offenders to install special devices in their cars that do not allow them to drive while intoxicated. They include California, Texas, Kansas, Maryland, Washington, Michigan,

Idaho, Oregon, Ohio, Iowa and New York. For example, California law mandates ignition interlock devices be installed in cars of certain persons convicted of drunk driving.[57] The driver must blow into the device before the ignition will occur. If any measurable alcohol is detected, the car will not start. The failed test will be coded and revealed at periodic inspections also ordered with the device. The device costs the motorist several hundred dollars to install and maintain.

Like many technological innovations enthusiastically embraced by corrections, the interlock devices are not foolproof. First, the offender can operate another car without the device. Second, in many systems, they can simply have someone else who is sober start the car for them as the following case tragically reveals:

> San Marcos, Texas—Gregory Cook decided to take his two daughters to breakfast, starting up the car after one of the girls apparently blew into a Breathalyzer device that had been installed to keep him from driving drunk. About a half-hour after they set out Sept. 25, the car skidded into a waste water treatment pond, drowning Cook and the girls. On Thursday, a grand jury indicted the youngsters' mother . . . for not stopping the girls from riding with their intoxicated father.[58]

In addition to the misogyny this case reveals, it also underscores the problem of trying to change the offender's environment (i.e., his car) as opposed to trying to change the offender's behavior (i.e., his alcoholism).

The device is also used without specific statutory language in Pennsylvania and Indiana.[59]

Other jurisdictions allow for the forfeiture of the drunk driver's car. A Pennsylvania appellate court, for example, found that the court had the power under common law to forfeit instruments used in the commission of a crime as contraband.[60] Still others allow the offender to keep and drive his car but require them to attach bumper stickers. Bumper stickers notify passing motorists that the driver is a convicted drunk driver and to report erratic operations to a probation number.[61] Appellate courts in both Florida and New York have upheld such bumper stickers, as discussed in §3.04.[62]

Judge Jeffrey Gunther of the Sacramento Municipal Court pioneered the condition ordering drunk drivers, among other things, to visit local morgues. The visits started in 1985. The practice spread to 24 judges throughout California and Des Moines, Iowa by 1988. The following year, California passed legislation that allows people under 18 to be sentenced to visit coroners' offices and emergency rooms.[63]

3. Perpetrators of Domestic Violence

Violence against women by their male partners or husbands is widespread. Research suggests that from two to three million women are assaulted by male partners each year in the United States and that 21 to 34 percent of all women will be assaulted by an intimate male during adulthood. Almost two million are severely assaulted, i.e., punched, kicked, choked, beaten, threatened with gun or knife or had a gun or knife used against them.[64] While women also hit their male partners, the level of injury or violence that leads to criminal justice involvement is almost exclusively male.

For centuries this behavior was not only tolerated but sanctioned by common law as a husband's right. After it was made illegal, the criminal justice system's failure to intervene continued this sanctioning on a *de facto* basis until the 1980s. As a result of the women's movement, dramatic law suits against police such as *Thurman v. Torrington*,[65] (in which police failed to enforce restraining orders or arrest for repeated domestic assaults) jurisdictions have begun to arrest male batterers in larger and larger numbers, prosecutors to prosecute them even against the wishes of reluctant or terrified victims, and judges to sentence them.[66] California, for example, in the wake of the O.J. Simpson verdict, passed and the Governor signed into law legislation banning that state's huge diversion program for perpetrators of domestic violence, mandating instead their prosecution.[67] Effective January 1, 1996, the new law should result in tens of thousands of wife/partner assaulters being prosecuted for the first time in that state.

Perpetrators of domestic violence are no longer seen primarily as mentally ill, the victims of masochistic or provocative wives, enmeshed in a dysfunctional family system and so on, but as perpetrators of crimes. The crimes usually charged are assault or threats, although batterers, in their effort to dominate and intimidate their victims, may be brought into court on a number of charges including cruelty to pets, malicious damage and child maltreatment. The pets killed are family pets; the property destroyed belongs to the partner; the child is used as an instrument to get to the mother or was injured trying to protect his or her mother.

Studies have found that, notwithstanding common notions, most batterers resemble the vast majority of other criminals. Not only do they commit criminal acts, but they have extensive criminal histories for a variety of offenses, including, in a majority of cases, drug and alcohol use. About one-half have records of violence, and that violence is against males as well as females. Only a minority come to court with no other criminal history.[68] (The criminal justice system, however, is probably skewed toward persons with criminal histories. Men who live in affluent neighborhoods are less likely to have arrest records even if they, too, abuse their wives or partners.) The biggest difference that distinguishes male batterers is that their behavior is still not universally recognized as a serious crime. Offenders receive a certain amount of encouragement from the culture and general sexism of society as well.

Notwithstanding the devastating effect of domestic violence, the thousands of women murdered, not to mention the hundreds of thousands of children traumatized by viewing domestic violence each year, the major response to domestic violence has been on the civil side of the court. Beginning in Pennsylvania in 1976, by 1995 all states and the District of Columbia had passed legislation allowing abused women to come to court to obtain civil injunctive relief for their abuse. Courts issue protective or restraining orders barring the abusers from continued abuse. In this regard, judges can order the offenders typically to vacate their family households, stay away from the victim, have no contact with her, pay child support and give up immediate custody of their children. Several dozen also allow the court to order the abuser into batterer treatment programs.

While these civil injunction programs represented a significant improvement for women who were effectively barred from the criminal side of the court by police refusal to arrest their abusers, it would be unheard-of for courts to identify violent criminals in any other area of the law and restrict their response to civil action only. It would be strange indeed, for example, for a court to be notified of a bank robbery and respond by issuing an order for the bank robber to refrain from robbing that bank again. But because the crime takes place within the family, authorities are reluctant to do more in most domestic violence cases brought to their attention.

However, over a dozen states have enacted mandatory arrest legislation, most commonly when the police have probable cause to believe the man has violated the injunctive order. As a result, many domestic violence cases began to reach the courts in the 1990s and perpetrators are being sentenced increasingly for their criminal behavior. As with drunk drivers and sex offenders, common standards are evolving regarding the sentencing and treatment of domestic abusers.

Although probation departments are just beginning to be involved in supervising perpetrators of domestic violence, a number are beginning to develop specific programs. The American Probation and Parole Association, the national membership organization for probation and parole officers throughout North America, published a manual in 1996 suggesting model programming in this and other areas of family violence (it also includes elder and child abuse). Among other things, the manual emphasizes the need for close coordination between probation and batterers' treatment programs, which must reinforce the goal of probation in these cases. The goal is specifically identified as victim safety.

In regard to treatment, one of the pioneers proposes that the goals of treatment must be to increase the abuser's responsibility for his behavior; develop behavioral alternatives to battering; increase constructive expression of all emotions and develop listening skills and anger-control mechanisms; decrease isolation of the batterer and develop a personal support system; decrease the batterer's dependency on and control of the victim; and increase his understanding of family and social facilitators of wife beating.[69]

The principles of treatment are, first, that spouse abuse is a crime, not a disease or mental disorder. It is learned behavior, under the control of the batterer. Treatment should be mandatory. The goal of the treatment is to halt the battering behavior. Further, group treatment is indicated over individual treatment, and the abuser should pay for it.[70]

One of the most imitated treatment programs for batterers was developed in Duluth, Minnesota and comes complete with 26 weeks of videotapes for participants to analyze and discuss each week.[71] Increasing numbers of jurisdictions have instituted standards for such treatment, mandating similar programs, barring couples counseling, mental health counseling or anger management counseling programs.[72] All of the latter have been found to be either ineffective or counterproductive in dealing with batterers. Studies have found that almost one-half of batterers, for example, have stalked their victims who have physically separated from them prior to the abuse incident that led the victims to request restraining orders.[73] Given this, it is hard to dismiss their behavior as an example of a bad temper or dysfunctional family relationship or mental illness.

Although there is debate in the field, optimal treatment time is believed to be from one to three years, although most jurisdictions provide considerably less. California, by law, provides for 52 weeks of weekly counseling. Most treatment standards include alcohol and drug evaluations and concurrent or prior treatment if indicated.[74]

In addition to such treatment programs, a number of behavioral conditions of probation have been formulated. Quincy Court, located in Massachusetts and recognized as a national model in probation in domestic violence cases, has developed a list of such conditions.[75] First, conditions must reinforce the primary court aim in these cases, which is victim safety. Therefore, the first group of conditions are protective:

1. Incorporation of civil restraining order provisions. By incorporating the civil conditions, even if the abuser successfully terrifies or seduces the victim into dropping her restraining order, they cannot be changed without court approval.

2. Forfeiture of all weapons. A number of jurisdictions mandate such forfeiture upon conviction or even the issuance of restraining order.

3. Intensive probation supervision.

4. Submit to warrantless searches and seizures

5. Electronic monitoring, including reverse monitoring in which the abuser wears the radio transmitter and the victim's phone has the receiver so that if he approaches within 500 yards of her phone, it automatically informs the supervisor that he has approached the victim.

6. Cooperate with child protection workers.

Conditions should also be punitive to reinforce the criminal nature of the behavior.

7. Incarceration as condition of probation or split sentence.

8. Non-custodial loss of liberty, such as curfew, or home confinement (if living apart from victim).

9. Fine.

10. Community work service.

Financial conditions are also indicated.

11. Child and family support so victim is not forced to return to the abuser out of financial necessity.

12. Restitution for injuries and property damage even if the abuser and victim continue to live together to reinforce that she still has rights. Restitution to any domestic shelter that housed the victim as a result of the offender's abuse.

13. Her attorney fees for related probate action.

14. Counseling costs both for the partner and the children exposed to the violence. Studies have indicated that the mere viewing by children of domestic violence is as traumatizing as being a victim of abuse.

15. Other court assessments.

Finally, treatment conditions include:

16. Attendance, active participation in and successful completion of batterers' treatment program.

17. Alcohol and drug treatment and/or drug testing for required abstinence.

The success of treatment and overall intervention programs can be increased with good monitoring and strict enforcement, as will be discussed subsequently. However, there is no proven, foolproof treatment for addiction, sexual offenders, compulsive gamblers, domestic abusers and so forth. These behaviors are not well understood nor is their eradication easily accomplished. These behaviors are not uniform among all offenders. As Vaillant writes, for example, in regard to alcoholism, there are probably as many "isms" as there are alcoholics. Different offenders may respond to different programs or combinations of programs. Successful treatment probably is helped by early diagnosis and intervention as well as flexible, multi-modality approaches. Then, too, it may be that some of these offenders cannot be treated or supervised safely in the community. Finally, whether they work or not, serious intervention programs can at least screen out offenders who have no intention or ability to change their behaviors.

One thing is known—if the courts do not intervene, many of these behaviors will become worse and injure more victims as well as the defendants themselves.

§8.04   Mandatory Treatment Laws

Mandatory treatment is specifically provided for in federal and many state probationary statutes. The federal code provides for discretionary conditions, including sobriety ("refrain from excessive use of alcohol") and abstinence from drugs ("any use of narcotic drug or other controlled substance"), as well as various treatment modalities ("undergo available medical, psychiatric, or psychological treatment, including treatment for drug or alcohol dependency, as specified by the court, and remain in a specified institution if required for that purpose").[76]

State statutes similarly authorize psychiatric treatment, participation in community-based residential programs, or treatment specifically for alcohol and drugs.[77] Some statutes mandate counseling or treatment for specific categories of offenders. Idaho, for example, mandates evaluation and treatment for domestic violence offenders. Further, if the defendant does not make a good faith effort to provide the court with the evaluation, the court may consider such behavior as an aggravating circumstance in sentencing.[78]

Absent statutes, treatment conditions have generally been upheld as reasonable conditions of probation if they meet the general criteria outlined in § 3.04. Mandated treatment has withstood a number of legal challenges, including charges that it violates an offender's right to privacy.[79] Because the treatment is mandatory, the offender cannot expect the same doctor-patient privilege that exists in other treatment contexts. For example, a sex offender charged with violating his probation argued that the probation department could not use information gathered from his psychologist therapist because that was protected by the doctor-patient relationship. The court declared that the probationer, in effect, waives any such privilege by participating in court-ordered treatment. The court went on to say that it was only common sense that if treatment is a condition of probation, the court and the probation officer must have some means of determining whether the defendant is in compliance, Further, the required disclosure frustrates neither the intent nor design of the treatment condition.[80]

Another sex offender maintained that his failure to complete a court-ordered treatment program was based on the unreasonable requirement that he sign an information release form. The Supreme Court of Maine ruled that the refusal to sign was a clear violation because the information was necessary for treatment. Therefore even though the probationer never refused to enter the treatment program *per se*, his refusal to sign the release could lead to his revocation of probation.[81]

In a related case, involving a court-referred program, a hospital-based treatment program refused to release information on a probationer, citing its obligation to protect confidential patient information. A New York court disagreed. The information requested, it held, was not to investigate a new crime, but was solely for purposes of determining offender compliance with treatment. Because there was no other way to get the information, and the public interest outweighed injury to the patient, the court ordered the hospital to comply with a subpoena for *in camera* inspection of the patient records.[82]

Mandatory in-patient treatment has also withstood challenges from probationers. For example, after pleading guilty to possession of an unregistered firearm, a defendant was given a three-year suspended sentence. He was ordered, among other things, to admit himself to a hospital for 60 days where he was required to submit to psychiatic treatment, including forced medication. Upon release, the probationer was required to bring his medical records from the treatment with him to probation. He actually spent more than 60 days in the hospital but was eventually released to outpatient treatment. The treatment included monthly injections of Haldol (from 150 mg to 25 mg). The treating doctor noted ominous changes in the probationer as the dosage was decreased. The probationer denied need for treatment, hallucinated and became threatening. The court held a hearing and amended his conditions to require additional inpatient treatment to insure proper medication. The probationer refused and his probation was revoked and he was sentenced to one year in jail followed by strict supervision.

The defendant appealed, arguing that his probation had not been conditioned on hospitalization beyond the original 60 days. The appellate court disagreed, holding that "proper psychiatric treatment" included such a possibility, thus the probationer had fair notice that probation might mean further inpatient treatment. As a result, even though there was no allegation that the defendant violated his probationary conditions, the court could mandate inpatient treatment even after the initial probationary sentence was ordered.[83] Previously, the same defendant had threatened the life of then-Secretary of State George Shultz but had been found incompetent to be tried. He was diagnosed as paranoid schizophrenic.

Inpatient treatment orders can include persons who are not diagnosed as suffering from a psychiatric problem. For example, they have also been upheld for a defendant convicted of burglary and assault. In one example, the offender was ordered to enter and complete inpatient treatment for alcoholism, followed by aftercare which included a halfway house, counseling, AA attendance and monitored Antabuse if necessary.[84]

An appellate court in Alaska, on the other hand, refused to uphold mandatory inpatient treatment conditions for a drunk driver. The probationer originally received a 60-day sentence, 40 days suspended. Upon release, he was required to complete an alcohol evaluation and comply with recommended treatment. The treatment program subsequently recommended inpatient treatment. The defendant asked the court for modification of the treatment. The court refused. On appeal, the appellate court found the inpatient requirement to be the functional equivalent of imprisonment and was too onerous a condition. Further, the appellate court said that the sentencing court could not delegate such a sentencing decision to a third-party treatment program.[85]

There has been concern shown in several appellate decisions that mandatory inpatient stays be based on medical, not court mandates. Some are concerned that stays not exceed that provided in civil commitment laws. For example, when a defendant was ordered not to leave a mental hospital without the court's approval, an appellate court ruled that such an order placed the court's opinion above the doctor's opinion and contravened that state's mental health laws governing voluntary commitments.[86] These cases concern probationers with mental illness. The same concerns have not generally been raised in regard to inpatient treatment programs designed to treat drug abusers and the like.

There have been virtually no limits placed on outpatient treatment.

Despite some earlier cases suggesting that it was unreasonable to demand abstinence for alcoholics,[87] abstinence conditions are uniformly allowed.[88] A California Court of Appeals, for example, rejecting the holdings of an earlier case, rejecting its logic in a sharply worded opinion:

> We feel societal interests, and indeed, the interests of defendants seeking rehabilitation through probation, require the court to have flexibility in imposing probation conditions which tell the kleptomaniac he must refrain from pilfering his local 7/11, the pyromaniac he may not burn his neighbor's house, and the addict-burglar he must keep the needle out of his anatomy.[89]

The United States Supreme Court has suggested that it would be appropriate for a court to revoke a chronic drunk driver's probation if he were unable to refrain from drinking and driving regardless of culpability.[90]

Mandatory use of chemical treatment has generally been upheld if found to meet the standard probation criteria. In 1983, Oregon passed legislation initiating a pilot program in which drugs could be used to "inhibit the psychological or physical inclination toward forcible sexual compulsion." The law specifically authorizes the use of Depo-Provera for those convicted of rape.[91] Earlier, in Michigan, the mandatory use of Depo-Provera for a sex offender was found to be unreasonable, because at the time it was not approved by the FDA, much less proven as an effective sexual depressant. Also, the court noted that its availability was limited.[92]

In a 1936 case involving a syphilis-infected rapist, a California court upheld forced sterilization. The court held that if the defendant objected, he did not have to accept the probationary sentence to begin with.[93] However, more recently, the South Carolina Supreme Court struck down as cruel and unusual punishment surgical castration of three convicted rapists.[94] Ironically, over 30 years later, the California probationer who had been sterilized was re-arrested for another sexual assault.

As with other conditions of probation, the court itself must order the treatment condition, except where probation is given that authority by statute. Vermont has such a statute, as previously described in § 3.04. Arizona provides for similar delegation by its Rules of Criminal Procedure.[95] However, even without statutory authority, the judge does not have to be as specific in setting treatment conditions as in setting exact monetary conditions. A series of cases indicates that most appellate courts will allow the sentencing court to delegate some of the specifics necessary to implement the broad treatment order. The court can also allow the treatment program to set its own rules that the offender, in turn, must then follow to be in compliance with the judge's overall treatment order.

For example, a Michigan appellate court ruled it was all right to delegate to the treatment program behavioral rules for the probationer's participation. The court held that requiring the probationer to abide by these rules simply provided a structure within which his probation and rehabilitation could proceed to successful conclusion.[96]

Regarding delegation to probation, a Connecticut appellate court allowed a state judge to order a sex offender to either in- or outpatient treatment as determined by the probation officer. The officer picked a program that the probationer attended for one day then quit. The offender then chose his own program with a doctoral student who charged no fee. The other program charged $25 per session. The probation officer moved to revoke the probation. The probationer challenged that the delegation to probation was unlawful. The appellate court upheld the revocation, declaring it a proper delegation.[97] An Indiana judge, in a like situation, ordered a child molester to attend counseling as determined by probation. The probation officer referred the offender to several programs. When the offender failed to attend the second program, his probation was revoked. The offender claimed illegal delegation in selecting the treatment program. The appellate court ruled that it was up to the offender and the officer to find a satisfactory program inherent in the judge's order of counseling and therapy for the offender to overcome his problems. The probationer's nonattendance was, therefore, a blatant violation of probation.[98]

Once a probationer is referred to treatment, the problem remains, however, how does the court insure that the offender gets better?

§8.05 Enforcing Mandatory Treatment

Like any other alternative sentence, intermediate sanction or condition of probation, mandatory treatment must be monitored and enforced in order to be effective. First, access to offenders' treatment records must be secured. As discussed in the previous section, offenders do not enjoy the same rights of privacy as other persons participating in treatment programs or counseling.

Enforcement of attendance alone, however, is not enough. For most forced treatment programs to be successful, the offender has to actively participate. To do so, he must not be in total and adamant denial of the behavior that brought him to treatment. This is a particular problem regarding the treatment of sex offenders. One of the hallmarks of sex offenders, as discussed, is denial of their problematic behavior. ("She asked for it and didn't look like a child.") But such denial is not limited to sex offenders. Domestic abusers typically minimize their abuse or project blame on their victims or otherwise rationalize their behavior. ("Your Honor, I was only trying to stop her from disturbing the neighbors with her screaming" . . . which is why the defendant was convicted of strangling his partner at two a.m.) Drug and alcohol abusers also deny their addiction. ("I can stop anytime, I did it once.")

Courts have the right to expect more than mere occasional attendance at treatment programs, according to an increasing number of appellate decisions. Montana's Supreme Court allowed for a probationer's revocation based on poor attitude, hostility to staff, missed meetings coupled with the staff determination that he was not amenable to treatment and a risk to reoffend.[99] Utah's Supreme Court similarly allowed for revocation based on the sex offender's failure to make adequate progress in treatment and failure to cooperate in treatment.[100]

Appellate courts have upheld probation revocations where the defendant entered required treatment but failed to participate cooperatively with the treatment program. The Texas Court of Criminal Appeals held that the defendant's mere appearance and physical entry into a prescribed drug treatment program did not satisfy the condition that he "participate in all prescribed treatment programs" at the facility.[101] The Minnesota Court of Appeals upheld a probationer's revocation even though he participated in the prescribed treatment program but proved, according to the experts there, "unamenable" to treatment. Convicted of intrafamilial sexual abuse, the defendant was ordered to complete a sex offender outpatient treatment program. Staff at the program subsequently terminated him due to the following: his attempt "to terminate his parental rights" toward the victim, his resistance to completing program requirements, his combativeness, his "paranoid posture, and his minimization of the effect of his crime." All of the above, the staff held, demonstrated the defendant's unamenability to treatment.[102]

The Illinois Appellate Court held that a sex offender's release could be revoked for violating the "spirit," if not the letter, of the court's order. The defendant and another party had followed in their car a party of young women and had tried to entice them into the car. The defendant's specific conditions included that he live with his sister, maintain a sunset-to-sunrise curfew, participate in all local mental health programs, report three times a month, take any medication prescribed and comply with any other conditions set up by the director of the mental health clinic.[103] The North Dakota Supreme Court upheld the revocation of a drunk driver who left an inpatient treatment program. He had been ordered to be evaluated for chemical dependency and abide by the results. The evaluation recommended inpatient treatment. He entered but was later discharged because treatment staff concluded that he was "not serious" about confronting his problem and changing his behavior. At the revocation hearing, the probationer testified that he did not believe that he needed inpatient treatment but would undergo other treatment depending upon what it was. Interpreting treatment to mean more than physical presence, the court revoked the defendant's probation. "To adopt [the probationer's] argument that physical presence per se constitutes compliance," the Court ruled, "elevates form over substance."[104]

Probationers who refuse to sign waivers of confidentiality can be revoked for consequently not attending treatment. For example, the Wyoming Supreme Court allowed for a revocation when the probationer decided that such a waiver violated his constitutional rights and refused to sign it. Because of his refusal, he was barred from entering the treatment program. Both the probation officer and the defendant's attorney had warned him what would happen if he refused to sign his treatment contract, which was required before he could attend the sex offender group program.[105]

Other appellate courts have upheld revocations of sex offenders who refuse to admit their guilt once in treatment, even though they had admitted their guilt in their court plea. For example, the Colorado Supreme Court allowed for the revocation of an offender who refused to admit his guilt in treatment who had earlier pled to the offense. In reversing an earlier appellate decision, the court argued: "A contrary result would encourage a sex offender to avoid cooperation in any evaluation procedure in hope of achieving a denial of admission and thus never having to participate in such a program." In the case, the defendant also demonstrated a lack of candor, missed an appointment and so on.[106]

Another example involved a defendant who, after five visits with his psychotherapist, still refused to admit to the offense for which the treatment was ordered. The court, in affirming his revocation, noted that "it is apparent that the defendant failed to follow the recommendation of treatment when he refused to admit his involvement in the offense, an action directly contrary to the stipulation made at his plea of guilty for which the court placed him on supervision." The court went on to explain that the defendant's denial frustrated the purpose of his court supervision of developing treatment through counseling. The high court distinguished this case from an earlier one in which the defendant similarly did not admit his offense. But in that case the defendant's denial was caused by a mental defect, which included his inability to remember his offense at all.[107]

The New Hampshire Supreme Court also allowed for revocation for failure to participate in treatment after the defendant was found unamenable to treatment because of his refusal to admit to the underlying sex offense. The court emphasized that the offender had been on notice that his denial would lead to revocation.[108] In a similar situation in which the court ruled the other way, the North Dakota Supreme Court ruled that the defendant had not been clearly warned that his denial would lead to his revocation. In fact, the trial judge had stated on the record that the defendant did not have to change his mind that he was innocent to receive the sentence and treatment condition.[109] Similarly, sex offenders who enter an *Alford* plea (while not admitting guilt, the defendant chooses to allow the state to proceed with sentencing) may not be judged in violation of their probation when they later refuse to admit to their crimes in treatment.[110]

Finally, Montana's Supreme Court has gone so far as to hold the revocation of a sex offender for failure to admit his guilt in treatment, after having been found guilty, to be unconstitutional because it penalized him for invoking his privilege against self-incrimination. The court expressed concern that the defendant still might have grounds to challenge his conviction in the future. Therefore, unless he is offered use immunity, he could not be sent to prison for refusing to surrender his privilege. Faced with the same situation, except that the defendant had pled no contest originally, Vermont's Supreme Court ruled that the defendant had waived his privilege. Therefore, he could be required to discuss in treatment the sex crime for which he was convicted.[111]

Some appellate courts require the sentencing judge to be very precise in what it is they are requiring of the offender regarding treatment participation and cooperation. For example, a Florida appellate court refused to allow the revocation of a sex offender who refused to admit to the charges against him. The reason was the court order stated only that he was to "submit" to counseling, which, it ruled, he satisfied by going for eight weeks before he was terminated for refusal to admit to the charges. The order did not state that he was to "admit to" the underlying charges or that he must "complete" the program. The court contrasted this case with another in which revocation was upheld. In the other case, the defendant had been ordered to "complete" the treatment. When the defendant was terminated for refusal to admit he had a sexual problem, he was revoked and the court upheld the revocation. He was not required to admit to the underlying charge itself.[112]

Courts, however, have been leery of requiring probationers to admit to sexual misconduct not already covered by the crimes for which they were sentenced to treatment. The Arizona Supreme Court, for example, did not uphold a revocation when a sex offender was required to take a polygraph regarding any criminal conduct. In the case, the court ruled that the sentencing court had failed to offer the probationer use immunity if he participated in the polygraph testing program. Even though the defendant had not contested the polygraph order at sentencing, the court found its requirement in this case to be unconstitutional.[113] Similarly, the federal district court in Vermont would not allow that state to revoke a probationer for refusal to admit to sexual intercourse with his stepdaughter even though his refusal to admit was called a stumbling block to treatment. The problem was that the admission would have provided evidence against the probationer for a new crime. Therefore his subsequent refusal to admit and resulting revocations approved by that state's supreme court was overturned.[114]

Similarly, a Wisconsin appellate court ruled that a probationer had no right to refuse to answer questions regarding a crime for which he was already convicted and his probation could be revoked for his refusal to answer. He could not, however, be revoked for refusing to answer questions about other criminal behavior that could be used against him.[115] Reaching an opposite conclusion, an Ohio appellate court ruled that a prison inmate has no such right if he participates in a prison sex offender treatment program. The inmate had argued that his refusal to participate was based on his choice not to abandon his Fifth Amendment right against self-incrimination which, in turn, imposed upon him certain due process losses related to the denial of parole. The court, however, ruled that the inmate was not compelled to participate in the program to begin with, so the issue of the Fifth Amendment compulsion was not encountered. Of course, his failure to participate may negatively influence the parole board later.

In enforcing treatment orders, courts face the additional problem of those who do cooperate, but fail to find an adequate treatment facility or fail to get better. Judges are faced with a dilemma. The recognition of the need to treat many addicted offenders clashes with society's demand for protection, especially from addicted offenders. Treatment capability is lacking in most jails. On the other hand, a bed in a state jail or prison is usually available but a bed in an inpatient treatment facility may not. Even if available, there is no guarantee that the offender will not be released for outpatient treatment or released outright because the therapist decides that he is not amenable to treatment. Similarly, if an offender needs outpatient treatment, he may never receive it because of lack of motivation, lack of insurance, refusal by the treatment facility to accept the referral, etc.

If the defendant fails to receive treatment, the court may be unsure of where the fault lies for the failure. Many probation officers mistakenly believe that they should not bring the offender back to court unless he willfully fails the court's orders. Unfortunately, while the probation officer is wondering what to do, the offender frequently provides additional cause for revocation of probation. He commits another crime. A comprehensive Massachusetts study of probation recidivists reveals that one-third of probationers who commit new crimes while on probation do so within the first month and almost 90 percent do so within six months.[116]

Emerging case law, however, suggests that probation officers and judges need not be reluctant to bring these cases forward for probation revocation, even if the failure to enter treatment cannot be shown to be willful on the probationers' part. Despite the expansion of due process rights to probationers as typified by *Morrissey*[117] and *Gagnon*,[118] it appears that probation may be revoked for nonwillful treatment failures.

The requirement to establish fault prior to the court's right to impose sanctions first arose in the area of fines. In *Williams*[119] and *Tate*,[120] the Supreme Court ruled that nonpayment of fines must be found to be willful in nature before the court can move to penalize the defendant for nonpayment. This principle was further extended to cases involving restitution. In *Bearden v. Georgia*,[121] the Supreme Court ruled that an indigent probationer could not be incarcerated for failure to pay restitution, absent evidence and findings that the defendant was proven responsible for the failure:

> But if the probationer has made all reasonable efforts to pay the fine
> or restitution, and yet cannot do so through no fault of his own, it is
> fundamentally unfair to revoke probation automatically without con-
> sidering whether adequate alternative methods of punishing the
> defendant are available.[122]

The Court went on to emphasize that, at least in the cases of indigents who
cannot pay court-ordered monies, there are ample alternatives open to the state,
including extending the due date or directing the defendant to complete "some
form of labor or public service." The majority concluded that the indigent's probation could be revoked for his nonwillful failure to pay "[o]nly if alternative
measures are not adequate in a particular situation to meet the State's interest in
punishment and deterrence. . . ."[123]

Although this principle leaves an opening for punishing a probationer for a
nonwillful payment violation "if alternative measures are not adequate," in practice it has been widely ignored, the common belief being that revocations for
such nonwillful violations violate the decision. However, in this same decision,
the majority included a footnote that is becoming increasingly noted:

> We do not suggest that, in other contexts, the probationer's lack of
> fault in violating a term of probation would necessarily prevent a
> court from revoking probation. For instance, it may indeed be reck-
> less for a court to permit a person convicted of driving while intoxi-
> cated to remain on probation once it becomes evident that efforts at
> controlling his chronic drunken driving have failed.[124]

The Court distinguished mere nonpayment of fines and restitution, however,
from drunk driving. It noted that, unlike drunk driving, indigency was itself no
threat to the safety or welfare of society.

Both independent of *Bearden* and in light of it, a flow of state appellate
court decisions has begun to create case law specifically upholding the principle
that probation revocations are valid even in the absence of a defendant's willful
failure to abide by his probationary terms. A California appellate court, for
example, specifically citing the *Bearden* footnote, stated "[w]e are not suggesting that, in other contexts a court would be prevented from revoking probation
because of the lack of fault in violating a probation condition."[125] The court
went on to recite the same example of the hypothetical chronic drunk driver.

Other state appellate courts have actually upheld such nonwillful revocations. For example, the Illinois Appellate Court heard the case of a probationer,
convicted of aggravated battery, who, after an initial revocation hearing, was
ordered to participate in an inpatient treatment program for drug and alcohol
abusers.[126] Subsequently the offender was returned to court because he was
unable to gain admission to a suitable program. It appears that the programs
found him unamenable to treatment based on past experience. As a result, the
sentencing court revoked his probation and committed him to prison.

The defendant appealed, claiming that he had not engaged in any willful violation of the court order. The Illinois Appellate Court disagreed:

> While the probationer's culpability in violating the conditions of his or her probation ordinarily occupies a preeminent position among the factors considered in determining whether probation should be revoked, an approach to the probation revocation question which regards this factor as the sole touchstone of whether a probation violation has occurred ignores the fact that circumstances other than conduct chargeable to the probationer may frustrate the purposes of probation.[127]

The court noted that probation has two purposes, first, rehabilitation of the defendant and second, protection of the public. It concluded that "[w]hen the varied purposes of probation are fully considered, it becomes readily apparent that nonculpable conduct on the part of a probationer may frustrate the goals of a probationary sentence."[128]

Other courts have made similar rulings. A Minnesota appellate court upheld a nonwillful revocation of a drug offender ordered to participate in a specific residential treatment program. Unfortunately, the program no longer had a contract with the county to take court referrals. The court, therefore, revoked the probation and incarcerated the probationer. On appeal, the appellate court ruled:

> The sentencing court was within its discretion in revoking appellant's probation where the facilities contemplated in the sentencing alternative became unavailable. Any other rule might force sentencing judges to be unreasonably cautious in ordering probation, lest the probation plan fall through, as it did here.[129]

On the other hand, an Ohio appellate court refused to uphold revocation of a burglar who was ordered to successfully complete a specific drug treatment program. The defendant was subsequently terminated from the program because his problems were too extreme to be dealt with in the program. The court held that the termination was based on the program's failure, not the offender's. Therefore there could be no revocation for a nonwillful departure from the terms of the probation by the defendant. A dissenting judge would have allowed "no fault" terminations of probation as inherent under the court's power to modify, reconsider or suspend sentences as appropriate.[130]

The Illinois Appellate Court found that the only reason the appellant was given a probationary sentence was so that he could obtain inpatient treatment. His inability to gain admission into two such programs rendered him without inpatient treatment. The evidence was clear that the defendant was not receiving the treatment ordered; therefore, notwithstanding the refusal by the treatment programs to admit the defendant the sentencing court was held to be within its discretion to revoke the sentence.[131]

The Wisconsin Supreme Court, facing a similar treatment failure, also allowed the offender to be incarcerated, but via a different route.[132] The appellant had been ordered to admit himself voluntarily into a specific mental hospital for treatment upon his conviction for lewd and lascivious behavior. He had exposed himself to two children while impersonating a police officer. However, after being interviewed for placement, he was denied admission. The probation officer then sought to have the defendant's probation revoked. The sentencing court ruled that there was no probable cause for such a revocation. The state then filed a motion for reconsideration of the sentence. Ruling that the probationer's rejection from the treatment facility represented a "new factor," the sentencing court modified the sentence and incarcerated the defendant.

The defendant appealed, claiming the state had no authority to request that his sentence be modified and the court's resentencing constituted double jeopardy. The Wisconsin Supreme Court held that the sentencing court had the power to modify probation to include incarceration because the "primary condition" had become "unachievable, thereby circumventing the intent behind the grant of probation."[133] The court also found that the sentence modification did not violate the defendant's double jeopardy rights. His legitimate expectations were not defeated by his subsequent incarceration because the sentencing court had made it clear that it had specifically rejected outpatient counseling prior to placing him on probation.

> We also conclude that the defendant's inability to gain admission to (the mental hospital) should not serve as an opportunity for him to remain on probation without any sort of constraints on his behavior, particularly on his sexual impulses.[134]

Many decisions allow for nonwillful revocations in special circumstances, namely where the defendant is found to be a threat to public safety. For example, a Utah appellate court allowed a sex offender to be revoked when he was kicked out of treatment for failure to make satisfactory progress. Experts found his mental problems entrenched, coupled with a manipulative personality. In addition, the probationer was unable to get an erection, which was needed to measure his treatment progress. The probationer claimed he tried to participate constructively in treatment. On appeal, the court could not determine whether the probationer was at fault for his termination from treatment. Nonetheless the court ruled that fault is not necessary in all cases when the probationer presently threatens the safety of society. In the instant case, the court found no such threat.[135]

In a more convoluted case, the Hawaii Supreme Court reached the same conclusion. The probationer was convicted of sexually assaulting his 10-year-old daughter. One of the conditions was to remain drug-free. The probationer then went on to assault a member of his family and was convicted of drunk driving. At his revocation, the judge ordered him to attend a residential drug treatment program until clinically discharged. Thereafter, the program found out he was a sex offender and refused to admit him. The court then determined that the probationer was *dangerous* and likely to repeat his sexual offense and jailed him. On appeal, the supreme court held that the court properly considered the defendant's termination from the treatment program, even though the termination did not result from any willful act of the defendant. However, the court also found that the probationer had not been given notice of other factors that the court considered in the revocation hearing so the case was remanded.[136]

Finally, an Ohio appellate court allowed for a probationer's revocation for a new crime committed while he was insane. The court held that, sane or insane, the welfare and safety of society outweigh the interest of the probationer who violated his probation.[137] Other jurisdictions have also looked at the issue of violations of probation committed by probationers judged to be insane. Although their violations are, in effect, nonwillful, many courts have also allowed them to be the basis of revocations. The Fourth Circuit, for example, held that because probation violations may be for noncriminal acts, there is no standard for determining whether the probationer is sane. Nor could the court find that *Bearden*[138] stands for a broad rule against revoking probation for involuntary violations. Moreover, the fact that probation is violated may be sufficient proof that probation is not serving the purpose for which it was granted.[139] Idaho's appellate court agrees, holding that the defendant's instability and inability to work with probation leaves the trial court no alternative but to revoke his probation.[140]

But not all courts agree. A New York court ruled that because revocations must be based on knowing acts by the probationer, insanity constitutes a defense to a probation violation. The court noted that even though the standard of evidence is less for a revocation, if the defendant is insane beyond a reasonable doubt, he is also insane by a preponderance of the evidence, the standard for revocations in New York.[141]

In an analogous area concerning the enforcement of probationary conditions requiring defendants to abstain from alcohol, appellate courts also seem to be moving away from the notion of culpability as an essential condition for probation revocations. In 1965, for example, the United States Court of Appeals for the Seventh Circuit ruled in *Sweeney v. United States*[142] that it was unreasonable to revoke a chronic alcoholic's probation for his failure to abstain from alcohol use. The offender's alcoholism, the court held, may have "destroyed his power of volition and prevented his compliance with the condition."[143] Since that time, however, there has been a swing in the other direction. A spate of appellate court decisions have considered the Seventh Circuit's reasoning and rejected it.

For example, the Oregon Supreme Court considered the same question several years later and came to the opposite conclusion:

> Whether the forbidden conduct is the product of illness or of a character disorder, the protection of society and the efficacy of probation both are jeopardized if probation does not include at least an attempt to cause the person to discontinue the kind of conduct which resulted in his conviction. In testing the reasonableness of conditions imposed

as part of a probation plan, it is necessary to bear in mind the various purposes sought to be served by probation as a substitute for penitentiary custody. The freedom of the individual is only one of the desiderata. Rehabilitation and public safety are others.[144]

The court went on to note that "[i]f an offender cannot be placed on probation on the condition that he refrain from doing acts dictated by his particular character disorder, the use of probation will be sharply curtailed."[145]

Similarly, the California Court of Appeals rejected the logic of *Sweeney* in a sharply worded opinion:

> We feel societal interests, and indeed, the interests of defendants seeking rehabilitation through probation, require the court to have flexibility in imposing probation conditions which tell the kleptomaniac he must refrain from pilfering his local 7/11, the pyromaniac he may not burn his neighbor's house, and the addict-burglar he must keep the needle out of his anatomy.[146]

The Wyoming Supreme Court upheld a revocation for alcohol consumption even though the alcoholic probationer claimed his drinking was beyond his control. The court found that it was well settled in that state that it is not fundamentally unfair to allow probation violations when the probationer's conduct is beyond his control and such conduct creates a threat to society.[147] In the instant case, however, the court found the consumption to be willful anyway.

Although the Supreme Court of Idaho agreed with the logic of *Sweeney* that one could not find a violation of probation without culpability, it prescribed a different remedy with the same result. Similar to the previously discussed Wisconsin decision, it held that if a court finds that compliance with the condition of abstinence is impossible but determines such compliance fundamental to proper probation, it may properly revise its sentence to imprisonment:

> Thus, upon discovering a probationary condition to be impossible of performance by a particular probationer, the judge may determine whether such condition is fundamental and whether the probationer is still, though unable to perform the condition, a fit subject for probation. After sound determination that a probationer could not possibly perform a fundamental condition of his probation, the judge has discretion to remove probation and pronounce sentence.[148]

Other decisions have allowed no-fault revocations as a matter of course. Ordered to stay away from his victim, the probationer claimed the contact was initiated by the victim. His revocation was upheld because all contacts was forbidden, not merely willful contact.[149]

Of course, there are some decisions that have come down clearly on the other side. In a 1985 assault case,[150] a Kentucky defendant was placed on probation on condition that he commit himself to a mental hospital and remain there until discharged. The admitting psychiatrist instead sent the probationer to out-patient treatment, deciding that course of treatment more appropriate. The probationer reported faithfully to this treatment. When the probation authorities learned that the probationer was an outpatient, they moved for revocation of his probation. The appellate court ruled that the defendant had done everything reasonably within his power to comply and reversed the revocation. Interestingly, the appellate court relied on *Bearden,* noting ". . . it is fundamentally unfair to deprive him of his liberty for reasons beyond the appellant's control, that is because the hospital's admitting physician did not believe he needed the treatment anticipated by the court."[151]

Although state court decisions vary, it is becoming clear that the increased use of probation as an alternative to incarceration for serious offenders in need of treatment should increase the number of appellate cases in this area. With the pressure to expand intensive forms of supervision to include these more serious offenders, normally jail-bound, there will be a corresponding pressure that supports the revocation of nonculpable probationers who prove unamenable to treatment, especially if they pose an increased threat to the public safety. Such decisions, if they continue along the course suggested here, may subject a new class of probationers to a loss of liberty. This may very well be the price paid for opening up probation to serious offenders in need of treatment.

§8.06   —Alcohol and Drug Testing

While an offender is in treatment, it is imperative that he be monitored for compliance with treatment-related orders proscribing drug or alcohol use, mandating drugs such as lithium for certain manic depressives who commit crimes while in their manic stages, barring contact with specific individuals, such as children for pedophiles, and the like. Because so many treatment programs involve requirements of abstinence, mandatory drug and alcohol testing is common. Tests are not only performed in treatment centers, but probation officers often perform them in the field. The technology is such that accurate tests can be performed by the probation officer using a drop of the defendant's urine or saliva on a premixed chemical slide. The results are known within seconds.

As a result of the extensive use of drug testing, there has developed over the past several decades extensive law regarding the legality and requirements of drug testing of probationers. Some states, like Louisiana, require weekly urine testing for drug offenders placed on probation.[152] Although the Hawaii Supreme Court in 1984 found that such testing subjected probationers to illegal searches if they were conducted without a reasonable suspicion of drug use,[153] it reversed itself in 1991. In the latter case, the court allowed for such testing, concluding that urinalysis did not force the probationer to cede almost his entire privacy interest. Instead, conducted in a reasonable manner, the tests were no more intrusive than necessary, even if not based on reasonable suspicion.[154] Other state supreme courts have followed suit.[155]

Drug testing has also been generally upheld without specific statutory authorization. The Montana Supreme Court, for example, ruled that in light of *Griffin,* testing need be based only on reasonable suspicion. Further, although the probation officer had no specific reason to suspect the probationer of drug use, the court ruled the probation officer was authorized to insist on the test because he felt "the rehabilitation process could not begin until [the probation officer] was certain the defendant was free from drugs." [156]

Other courts, including federal appellate courts, have upheld required tests even if not specifically imposed by the court as a condition of the defendant's probation. In one example, the federal probation officer told his probationer to submit to a urine test because the defendant appeared to be on drugs as determined by the fact that he remained unemployed in poor financial conditions and police were suspicious that he had participated in a home burglary and more. Three tests came back positive for drugs. The court revoked the probation. On appeal, the Ninth Circuit held that probation officers are authorized to use all suitable methods not inconsistent with the conditions imposed by the court, to improve their charges and stay informed of their charges' activities. As a result, probation officers could order the test without court authorization as they were merely enforcing the courts' orders for the defendants to stay out of trouble. While it would have been preferable for the probation officer to ask the court to modify the conditions of probation to require mandatory testing, in this case, the court concluded that due process did not require that prior notice be given of the techniques through which noncompliance would be detected. The court also noted that the urine tests also were less intrusive than inspecting the defendant's home, which was part of the probationer's court-ordered conditions. [157]

Challenges to drug testing have generally followed those raised against searches in general. However, as the above cases illustrate, courts have generally found that urine tests are less intrusive than other types of searches so they have been more apt to approve their use.

Because such tests involve securing bodily fluids from the defendants, other legal criteria must be met in administering the tests, securing the samples, analyzing them and reporting the results to the court. First and foremost, the chain of custody must be maintained so that the ultimate test results can be certified to be from the sample actually secured by the tester from the correct defendant. On-site testing, in which the results can be determined in minutes, limits the possibility of sample mix-ups or inability to prove chain of custody. The burden on proving the chain of custody falls on the probation officer or proponent of the test results. Proof requirements, however, are less for revocation hearings than criminal trials.

Second, the testing process must meet scientific standards for accuracy. There have been a number of cases upholding the standard immunoassay methods used to detect drugs in most on-site drug testing programs. [158] Many decisions do not require alternative backup or confirmatory tests for positive results. [159]

If the sample is sent to a laboratory to determine drug content, most courts allow for the printed results to be admitted as evidence of either use or no use.

For example, the Fifth Circuit abandoned its rationale in a 1980 case and found that hearsay was admissible in revocation cases that balanced the probationer's interest in confronting witnesses against him versus the government's good cause for denying confrontation. Regarding drug reports, the court went on to find them to be regular reports from companies whose business it was to conduct such tests and the government had an interest in minimizing the difficulty and expense of procuring witnesses for revocation hearings.[160] Another circuit, in similarly allowing such written reports, remarked that in its experience, formal testimony rarely leads to any admissions helpful to the party challenging the evidence.[161] In a related case, the Fifth Circuit ruled that the offender had better avenues to challenge the laboratory results than confronting the lab technician. He could request a retest by a different lab. He could produce evidence challenging the testing procedures or methods. He could present evidence that medication caused an erroneous result.[162]

However, probation officers must be prepared, if challenged, to offer proof that the laboratory reports are accurate. Some courts have demanded, absent a showing of good cause, a representative of the laboratory to present the evidence in court. In one such case, the Tennessee Supreme Court was concerned because the defendant challenged the positive test by asserting that he had used Advil, an over-the-counter medication, and the Advil use contaminated the results. The defendant presented a scientific article backing up his claim. The other side presented no rebuttal witnesses from the laboratory that made the finding of illicit drug use.[163]

The probation officer can be a sufficient vehicle through which the lab report is introduced into evidence, but he or she must demonstrate its reliability.[164] For example, do the reports come in a form that meets the requirements of the business record exception to the hearsay rule? Do they demonstrate the qualifications of the personnel and analysis method employed? Do they show the reliability of the results and answer any questions regarding chain of custody?[165]

The Hawaii Supreme Court found, however, substantial prejudice and fundamental error for a court to deny the defendant the opportunity to retest the sample by his own laboratory. In the instant case, when the defense made the request he was told the sample was not maintained. In fact, the sample was kept for six months. The state's failure to give him access to the sample violated principles of justice and fundamental fairness. Without the sample, the defense was reduced to cross-examining the probation officer, who knew little about the test. The revocation was reversed.[166]

Positive results from a drug test may prove two different violations of probation. First, it may prove that the defendant failed to remain drug free as may have been specifically ordered by the court. Second, it may prove drug possession. Several appellate courts, both state and federal, have found the presence of drugs in a person's system to constitute ample evidence that the person is guilty of the crime of possession of a drug.[167] On the other hand, a New Mexico appellate court ruled that a positive drug test alone is insufficient to prove possession of a controlled substance.[168] But if, in addition to the test, the probationer admits to use and asks for assistance in dealing with his or her drug problem, the court may infer drug possession.[169]

In a related case, the probation officer tried to use evidence of a single positive drug test to prove that the probationer had violated the condition that he must avoid vicious habits. The appellate court found that a single positive test did not indicate a habit.[170]

A defendant's refusal to submit to a test upon request has been held sufficient evidence for probation revocation.[171] In a Texas case, for example, the probationer was asked to give a sample twice. He claimed he could not, then left rather than wait to try again. The revocation of his probation was upheld.[172] In a similar case in Illinois, a probationer at first refused to submit to a urine test. He was taken back before the judge, who explained his obligation. Subsequently he was again before the judge for failing to give a sample. He had been given from 3:00 P.M. to 7:00 P.M. and four different opportunities to urinate. The judge found his nonperformance to constitute a willful refusal to cooperate. On appeal, the appellate court noted that the defendant had had no trouble urinating the day before. His inability to perform, as raised by the defense, was dismissed as mere speculation.[173]

Many programs require probationers to pay for their own tests. On-site single-screen drug tests are relatively inexpensive, one or two dollars per test. If the tests are performed randomly, different drugs can be tested for each time, which reduces overall costs. For example, one week heroin is tested for, the next time it is cocaine, and so on. Otherwise, each separate test costs an additional one or two dollars. Some kits test for multiple drugs with the same sample. These tests are proportionately more expensive.

Random testing also reduces the number of tests needed to reasonably guarantee that the probationer does not use drugs. As most drugs stay in the offender's system for several days, a random test that averages once a week should serve as a pretty good indicator of the offender's continued use pattern.

Probably as a response to increasing use of drug testing for employment, a cottage industry has developed for products purporting to "beat" drug tests. Most of these products simply encourage water consumption to dilute urine so that urinary drug concentrations may temporarily fall below the test cutoff levels. Some other products do affect immunoassay tests but not radio immunoassay tests. Some of the products sold do create false negatives for certain drug use, but also increase false positives for other drug use. These products do not influence hair tests. As products develop to defeat drug tests, commercial urine tests will probably become more sophisticated in detecting the use of these products.

Example of Probation Department Drug Testing Program

The Quincy Probation Department, located south of Boston, Massachusetts, performs almost 10,000 drug tests per year. To insure randomness, all probationers ordered into testing are given a color and are required to call a special telephone message each evening after 4:00 P.M. The message announces which color will be tested the next day. If the color matches, the probationer is required to report by 5:00 P.M. the next day for testing. The colors allocated correlate with the offender's risk of continued drug use or dangerousness perceived if the defendant uses drugs. For example, perpetrators of domestic violence or sexual offenses are given colors that average five or six within a 30-day period. Run-of-the-mill low-risk drug users are given a color that is called no more than once a month, and so on.

Among hundreds of probationers tested in 1995, on average more than a third tested positive for an illicit drug (mostly marijuana and cocaine) or alcohol. Interestingly, the highest positive rates were produced by perpetrators of domestic violence, not multiple drunk driving offenders.[174] Offenders are charged for the cost of the testing, prompting Court Probation Officers to refer to the program as the "Piss and Pay Program."

§8.07   Summary

Unless an offender is to be sentenced for his natural life, public safety demands that treatment issues be addressed. The simple passage of time does not extinguish the potency of alcohol or drug addiction, or compulsive sexual or gambling behavior. Deprived of alcohol for 10 years, an alcoholic begins exactly where he left off with the first drink. On the other hand, rehabilitation has proven unsatisfactory, even dangerous, as a sole aim of sentencing. To dismiss it entirely, however, is to condemn the public as well as classes of offenders to a painful cycle of crime. Mandatory treatment offers the courts a realistic sentencing alternative. It allows the court to address rehabilitation in the context of control. Studies suggest that it works. A survey of the available research through the mid-1970s, commissioned by the Justice Department, concluded:

> These results, and numerous others, challenge the assumption that treatment must be voluntary in order to be successful. We feel that the evidence is sufficiently strong to lay aside this "red herring" so that more important issues can be pursued.[175]

If the offender fails to respond to treatment, incarceration is always available. If the offender is monitored strictly, the court can act before the offender slips back into criminal behavior.

For the defense attorney, a realistic mandatory treatment plan, with or without other alternative sentencing elements, offers the court a sentence that addresses offender risk and/or dangerousness. Treatment may also be considered a mitigating factor in sentencing. Minnesota has comprehensive and strict sentencing guidelines spelling out specific punishment ranges based on the offense and offender type. Yet an appellate court there has ruled that a sentencing court could depart from the guidelines and impose probation in lieu of a sentence of 43 months imprisonment based on the defendant's treatment. In the specific case, the offender was convicted of sexual conduct in the first degree. Both the probation officer completing the presentence report and the court psychologists agreed that the offender was amendable to treatment. The latter recommended deviation from the guidelines.[176] Some courts give credit for inpatient treatment against jail time, although this is not required.

For the prosecutor, mandatory treatment alternatives enable the state to recommend sentences that will compel the offender to address the behavior that underlies his crime. Although offenders may deny any alcohol, drug or other problem, the prosecutor, in consultation with the police, often is in the position to know the truth. As Vaillant explains, "the point to be made is that in any intractable habit, willpower is inferior to behavior modification."[177]

For the judge, mandatory treatment alternative sentencing allows the court to get at the root of much crime while safeguarding the public. Despite the well-documented link between alcohol and other drug abuse and crime, adequate treatment intervention has been largely absent in corrections. A survey conducted by the Justice Department revealed that almost 25 percent of all state inmates admitted to daily abusive drinking (i.e., four or more ounces of ethanol) for the year prior to their imprisonment, revealing "an alcohol problem of staggering size." Yet the same study found very few of these offenders had ever received any treatment for alcoholism.[178] Nor would most of them receive any treatment while incarcerated. Yet without such treatment, according to most researchers, inmates are much more likely to reoffend upon release. The Rand Corporation found that the major difference between "normal" inmates in state prisons and the extremely high-risk recidivists labeled "violent predators" was drug and alcohol abuse.[179]

Judges must be particularly cognizant of the treatment needs of offenders, especially because other segments of the criminal justice system, as well as the social service system may ignore them. The challenge for judges is all the greater because past performance indicates failure to address the issue of adequate treatment even in regard to so obvious a population as convicted drunk drivers. For this reason, the National Transportation Safety Board has called for the training of judges in the sentencing of drunk drivers. Unfortunately, corrections has not responded to the need for offender treatment. It is up to judges to impose individualized mandatory treatment plans utilizing existing community resources, and to see that these plans are strictly monitored and enforced.[180]

Notes

[1] 28 U.S.C. § 994 (k) (Supp. II 1984).

[2] See, e.g., J. Wilson (1975). THINKING ABOUT CRIME (in which he argues that treatment is ineffective in preventing crime); American Friends Service Committee (1971). STRUGGLE FOR JUSTICE (in which it is argued that treatment threatens offenders' civil liberties).

[3] Quoted in Krajick (1980). *Probation: The Original Community Program.* 6 CORRECTIONS MAGAZINE 6, 11 (December).

[4] Wilson (1981). *"What Works?" Revisited: New Findings on Criminal Rehabilitation*, PUBLIC INTEREST 3, 8-9 (Spring).

[5] *Warner v. Orange County Probation Department*, 870 F. Supp. 69 (S.D.N.Y. 1994).

[6] *O'Connor v. State of California*, 855 F. Supp. 303 (S.D. Cal. 1994).

[7] See, *e.g., State v. Van Winkle*, 889 P.2d 749 (Kan. 1995).

[8] General Services Office, *A.A. Guidelines, Cooperating with Courts, A.S.A.P. and Similar Programs*, 4 (6M-5/82(R).)

[9] See, *e.g.,* Wish, E., M. Toborg and J. Bellassai (1988). IDENTIFYING DRUG USERS AND MONITORING THEM DURING CONDITIONAL RELEASE. Washington, DC: National Institute of Justice.

[10] Kerr, P. (1988). *Drug Testing as Way to Reduce Prison Overcrowding.* NEW YORK TIMES, Jan. 19.

[11] Anglin, M.D. and Y. Hser. (1990). *Treatment of Drug Abuse*. In Tonry, M. and J.Q. Wilson (eds.), DRUGS AND CRIME. Chicago, IL: University of Chicago.

[12] *Substance Abuse Treatment,* PERSPECTIVES 20:1. Winter 1996.

[13] Vaillant, G. (1983). THE NATURAL HISTORY OF ALCOHOLISM 191.

[14] Kerr, P. (1988). *Crime Study Finds High Use of Drugs at Time of Arrest.* NEW YORK TIMES, Jan. 22.

[15] Califano, J. (1982). THE 1982 REPORT ON DRUG ABUSE AND ALCOHOLISM (reported in M. Lipske, CHEMICAL ADDITIVES IN BOOZE 71-73); accord, Bureau of Justice Statistics (1985). PRISONERS AND ALCOHOL (U.S. Dep't of Justice) (More than one-half of the jail inmates had been drinking before violent crime, including 68% convicted of manslaughter, 62% assault, 49% murder or attempted murder).

[16] See, *e.g.,* Klein, A. *Reabuse in a Population of Court-Restrained Male Batterers.* In Buzawa, E. and C. Buzawa (eds.) (1996). DO ARREST AND RESTRAINING ORDERS STOP DOMESTIC VIOLENCE? Newbury Park, CA: Sage Publications.

[17] See, *e.g., Massachusetts Guidelines and Standards for Certification of Batterers' Intervention Program.* Mass. Department of Public Health, Boston, Ma. pursuant to Ch. 403 § 16, Acts of 1990.

[18] See, *e.g.,* Gendreau, P. and R.R. Ross (1987). *Revivification of Rehabilitation: Evidence from the 1980s.* JUSTICE QUARTERLY, 3, 349-407.

[19] Kohlberg, L. (1980). *The Cognitive-Development Approach to Moral Education.* In Erickson, V.L. and J. Whiteley (eds.), DEVELOPMENTAL COUNSELING AND TEACHING. Monterey, CA: Brooks/Cole.

[20] Little, G.L., K.D. Robinson, K.D. Burnette and E.S. Swan (1995). *Rehabilitation Effectiveness Through Moral Recognition Therapy.* ALTERNATIVES TO INCARCERATION 1, pp. 24-26.

[21] Fogg, V. (1992). *Implementation of a Cognitive Skills Development Program.* PERSPECTIVES (Winter) pp. 24-26.

[22] See, *e.g.,* Adams, D. (1988). *Treatment Models for Men who Batter.* In K. Yllo and M. Bograd (eds.), FEMINIST PERSPECTIVES ON WIFE ABUSE, 175-199. Newbury Park, CA: Sage Publications; Ganley, A. (1989). *Integrating Feminist and Social Learning Analysis of Aggression: Creating Multiple Models for Intervention with Men who Batter.* In P.L. Casear and L.K. Hamberger (eds.), TREATMENT OF MEN WHO BATTER. New York, NY: Springer; E. Pence and M. Shepard (1988). *Integrating Feminist Theory and Practice.* In K. Yllo and M. Bograd (eds.) FEMINIST PERSPECTIVES ON WIFE ABUSE, 282-299. Newbury Park, CA: Sage Publications.

[23] Lehman, J. (1995). *The Movement Towards Therapeutic Jurisprudence.* NJC ALUMNI, 10:3, pp. 13-18, Spring.

[24] Vaillant, G. (1983). THE NATURAL HISTORY OF ALCOHOLISM 295.

[25] Clark, W. (1981). *Alcoholism: Blocks to Diagnosis and Treatment.* 71 AMERICAN JOURNAL OF MEDICINE 275, 277.

[26] Bureau of Justice Statistics (1983). PRISONERS AND ALCOHOL. Washington, DC: U.S. Department of Justice.

[27] Gabina, B. and S. Stein (1983). *Gambling Research and Education Programs, Center for Addiction Studies, Harvard Medical School and Cambridge Hospital,* reported in HARVARD JOURNAL 24:1, March 1989.

[28] *In re Agent Orange Prod. Liab. Litig.,* 611 F. Supp. 1223,1242 (E.D.N.Y. 1985), *cert. denied,* 487 U.S. 1234, *affirmed,* 818 F.2d 187.

[29] *Frye v. United States,* 293 F. 1013, 1014 (D.C. Cir. 1923).

[30] Baumgartner, Baer, Hill and Blahd (1986). HAIR ANALYSIS FOR DRUGS OF ABUSE IN PAROLE/PROBATION POPULATIONS. Final Report, Washington, DC: National Institute of Justice.

[31] *United States v. Medina,* 749 F. Supp, 59 (E.D.N.Y. 1990).

[32] Wish, E., *et al.* (1986). *Estimating Drug Use in the Intensive Supervision of Probation: Results of Pilot Study.* FEDERAL PROBATION, December.

[33] *Walrath v. United States,* 830 F. Supp. 444 (S.D. Ill. 1993).

[34] *State v. Emery,* 156 Vt. 364, 593 A.2d 77 (1991).

[35] Letter from G. Abel, July 28, 1995.

[36] *Hart v. State,* 633 So. 2d 1189 (Fla. Dist. Ct. App. 1994).

[37] *State v. Tenbusch,* 131 Or. App. 634, 886 P.2d 1077 (1994).

[38] *State v. Brown,* 326 S.E.2d 410 (S.C. 1985).

[39] Canellos, P. (1995). *In Texas, Molester Pleads for Castration.* BOSTON GLOBE, July 14.

[40] *Ibid.*

[41] FBI UNFORM CRIME REPORTS. Washington, DC: Bureau of Justice Statistics. 1989.

[42] Dodd, M. (1991). PROFESSIONAL NOTES: A NEWSLETTER ADDRESSING MENTAL HEALTH CONCERNS, 1:1 January.

[43] Abel, G., I.V. Becker, M. Mittleman, J. Cunningham-Rathner, J.L. Rouleau and W.D. Murphy (1987). *Self-Reported Sex Crimes of Nonincarcerated Paraphiliacs.* THE JOURNAL OF INTERPERSONAL VIOLENCE, 2:1, pp. 3-25.

[44] Smith, B., S. Hillenbrand and S. Goretsky (1990). THE PROBATION RESPONSE TO CHILD SEXUAL ABUSE OFFENDERS: HOW IS IT WORKING? Chicago, IL: American Bar Association.

[45] Jensen, S. (ed.) (undated). THE ATSA PRACTITIONER'S HANDBOOK. Lake Beaverton, OR: Association For the Treatment of Sexual Abusers.

[46] *For Sex Criminals, Therapy Held to Help.* BOSTON GLOBE, November 1995, reporting on study appearing in JOURNAL OF CONSULTING AND CLINICAL PSYCHOLOGY.

[47] ILL. COMP. STAT. ANN. tit. 720, § 515-4 (West 1993), upheld in *Jones v. Murray,* 962 F.2d 302 (4th Cir. 1992), *cert. denied,* 113 S. Ct. 472, 121 L. Ed. 2d 378 (1992); *Doe v. Gainer,* 642 N.E.2d 114 (Ill. 1994).

[48] *State v. Sorrell,* 656 So. 2d 1045 (La. Ct. App. 1995).

[49] MADDVOCATE 4:2 Winter 1991.

[50] MASS. GEN. L. ch. 90, § 24d (1994).

[51] National Committee Against Drunk Driving (1992). *Recidivism Problem Uncovered in Georgia.* NETWORK NEWS NOTES 7:2, p. 4. Summer.

[52] Foon, A.E. (1988). *The Effectiveness of Drinking-Driving Treatment Programs: A Critical Review.* THE INTERNATIONAL JOURNAL OF THE ADDICTIONS, 23, pp. 151-174.

[53] Kramer, A. (1986). *Sentencing the Drunk Driver: A Call for Change.* ALCOHOL TREATMENT QUARTERLY.

[54] G. Vaillant (1983). THE NATURAL HISTORY OF ALCOHOLISM 300-302.

[55] (1995). *Naltrexone Stems Alcoholism.* ALTERNATIVES TO INCARCERATION 1:4 (Fall).

[56] Hinds, M. (1988). *Judges Turn to Ignition Locks to Ground Drunk Drivers.* NEW YORK TIMES, Dec. 12.

[57] CAL. VEHICLE CODE, Art. 4, § 23235 *et. seq.* (West Supp. 1996).

[58] *Drunken Dad Drives Girls into Pond: Mom Charged.* LEXINGTON HERALD-LEADER, Nov. 12, 1994.

[59] Hinds, M. (1988). *Judges Turn to Ignition Locks to Ground Drunk Drivers.* NEW YORK TIMES, Dec. 12.

[60] *Commonwealth v. Crosby,* 390 Pa. Super 140, 568 A.2d 233 (1990).

[61] See, *e.g.,* (1985). *Scarlet Bumper, Humiliating Drunk Drivers.* TIME MAGAZINE, June 17.

[62] See, *e.g., People v. Letterlough,* 613 N.Y.S.2d 687 (N.Y. Sup. App. 1994) (upheld bumper sticker that read: "Convicted DWI.").

[63] Wilson, D. (1988). *Drunken Drivers Visit the Morgue.* NEW YORK TIMES, September 21.

[64] Cited in Browne, A. (1993). *Violence Against Women by Male Partners.* AMERICAN PSYCHOLOGIST, 48: 10, pp. 1077-1087, October.

[65] *Thurman et al. v. City of Torrington,* 595 F. Supp. 1521 (D. Conn. 1984).

[66] Buzawa, E. and C. Buzawa (1992). DOMESTIC VIOLENCE: THE CHANGING CRIMINAL JUSTICE RESPONSE. Westport, CT: Auburn House.

[67] S.B. 169, amending Penal Code § 1203.097, repealing ch. 2.6 of Title 6 Part II.

[68] See, *e.g.,* Klein, A. (1996). *Do Restraining Orders Work?* In E. Buzawa and C. Buzawa (eds.), DO ARREST AND RESTRAINING ORDERS WORK? Newbury Park, CA: Sage Publications.

[69] Ganley, A. (1981). COURT-MANDATED COUNSELING PROGRAMS FOR MEN WHO BATTER: A THREE DAY WORKSHOP FOR MENTAL HEALTH PROFESSIONALS. Washington, DC: Center for Women Policy Studies.

[70] *Ibid.*

[71] Pence, E. and M. Shepard (1988). *Integrating Feminist Theory and Practice: The Challenge of the Battered Women's Movement.* In K. Yllo and M. Bograd (eds.), FEMINIST PERSPECTIVES ON WIFE ABUSE, 282-299. Newbury Park, CA: Sage Publications.

[72] See, *e.g.,* COLORADO STANDARDS FOR THE TREATMENT OF DOMESTIC VIOLENCE PERPETRATORS (1989).

[73] Ptacek, J. (1995). DISORDER IN THE COURTS: JUDICIAL DEMEANOR AND WOMEN'S EXPERIENCE SEEKING RESTRAINING ORDERS. Ann Arbor, MI: University Microfilms International.

[74] See, *e.g., Massachusetts Guidelines and Standards for Certification of Batterers' Intervention Programs.* Mass. Dep't of Public Health, pursuant to ch. 403 § 16, Acts of 1990 (revised 1995).

[75] Klein, A. (1992). SPOUSAL/PARTNER ASSAULT: A PROTOCOL FOR THE SENTENCING AND SUPERVISION OF OFFENDERS. Swampscott, MA: Production Specialties Inc.

[76] 18 U.S.C. § 3563(b)(8), (10) (Supp. II 1984) (Effective Nov. 1, 1986).

[77] See, *e.g.,* CONN. GEN. STAT. ANN. § 53a-30(a)(2) (West 1985) (medical, psychiatric treatment, possible institutionalization); P.A. 77-2097, as amended, ILL. ANN. STAT. ch. 38, § 1005-6-3(4) (Smith-Hurd Supp. 1986) (medical, psychological, pyschiatric, alcohol/drug treatment); N.D. CENT. CODE § 12.1-32-02(1)(g) (1985) (commitment to an appropriate licensed public or private institution for treatment of alcoholism, drug addiction or mental disease or defect); TEX. CODE CRIM. PROC. ANN. art. 42.12, 55 6(a)(15), 6(b)(2) (Vernon Supp. 1986) (psychological treatment, treatment for drug or alcohol dependency).

[78] IDAHO CODE § 18-918 (1996).

[79] See, *e.g., United States v. Stine,* 675 F.2d 69 (3d Cir. 1982), *cert. denied,* 458 U.S. 1110, 102 S. Ct. 3493, 73 L. Ed. 2d 1373 (1982) (privacy); *cf. United States v. Nolan,* 932 F.2d 1005 (1st Cir. 1991) (defendant claimed psychiatric treatment violated religious freedom).

[80] *Crowson v. State,* 552 So. 2d 189 (Ala. Crim. App. 1989).

[81] *State v. Smith,* 573 A.2d 384 (Me. 1990).

[82] *People v. Silkworth,* 538 N.Y.S.2d 692 (N.Y.C. Crim. Ct. 1989).

[83] *United States v. Gallo,* 20 F.3d 7 (1st Cir. 1994).

[84] *State v. Ford,* 218 Mont. 215, 707 P.2d 16 (1985).

[85] *Hester v. State,* 777 P.2d 217 (Alaska Ct. App. 1989).

[86] See, *e.g., State ex rel. Candella v. Director, Marcy Psychiatric Center,* 88 Misc. 2d 44, 387 N.Y.S.2d 978 (Sup. Ct. 1976).

[87] See, *e.g., Sweeney v. United States,* 353 F.2d 10 (7th Cir. 1965)

[88] See, *e.g., Sobata v. Williard,* 247 Or. 151, 427 P.2d 758 (1967); *State v. Sullivan,* 197 Mont. 395, 642 P.2d 1008 (1982); *Hernandez v. State,* 704 S.W.2d 909 (Tex. Ct. App. 1986); *Wickham v. Dowd* 914 F.2d 1111 (8th Cir. 1990) (refused to review case in which known alcoholic who violated condition of probation by drinking and then sentenced to 20 years constituted cruel and unusual punishment).

[89] *People v. Mitchell,* 125 Cal. App. 3d 715, 719-720, 178 Cal. Rptr. 188, 190 (1981).

[90] *Bearden v. Georgia,* 461 U.S. 660, 668, n.9, 103 S. Ct. 2064, 2070-71, n.9, 76 L. Ed. 2d 221, 230, n.9 (1983).

[91] S. 284, 62d Leg. Reg. Sess. 1983 OR. LAWS 487.

[92] *People v. Gauntlett,* 134 Mich. App. 737, 352 N.W.2d 310 (1984), *modified,* 419 Mich. 909, 353 N.W.2d 463 (1984).

[93] *People v. Blankenship,* 16 Cal. App. 2d 606, 61 P.2d 352 (1936).

[94] *Brown v. State,* 326 S.E.2d 410 (S.C. 1985).

[95] ARIZ. R. CRIM. PROC. § 27.1, discussed in *State v. Jones,* 788 P.2d 1249 (Ariz Ct. App. 1990).

[96] *People v. Peters,* 191 Mich. App. 159, 477 N.W.2d 479 (1991).

[97] *State v. DeMasi*, 34 Conn. App. 46, 640 A.2d 138 (1994).

[98] *Lind v. State*, 550 N.E.2d 823 (Ind. Ct. App. 1990).

[99] *State v. Stangeland*, 233 Mont. 230, 758 P.2d 776 (1988).

[100] *State v. Jameson*, 800 P.2d 798 (Utah 1990).

[101] *Ott v. State*, 690 S.W.2d 337 (Tex. Crim. App. 1985).

[102] *State v. Hemmings*, 371 N.W.2d 44, 47 (Minn. Ct. App. 1985); *cf. State v. Muhlenhardt*, 403 N.W.2d 638 (Minn. 1987) (defendant first refused to fill out application for admission, then told interviewer he did not need program; probation revoked).

[103] *People v. Davis*, 127 Ill. App. 3d 49, 468 N.E.2d 172 (1984).

[104] *State v. Orseth*, 359 N.W.2d 852, 859 (N.D. 1984).

[105] *Leyba v. State*, 882 P.2d 863 (Wyo. 1994).

[106] *People v. Ickler*, 877 P.2d 863 (Colo. 1994).

[107] *People v. McGuire*, 200 Ill. App. 3d 146, 576 N.E.2d 391 (1991), *distinguished from, People v. Prusak*, 558 N.E.2d 696 (Ill. Ct. App. 1990).

[108] *State v. Woveris*, 138 N.H. 33, 635 A.2d 454 (1993); see also *State v. Smith*, 812 P.2d 470 (Utah App. 1991).

[109] *Morstand v. State*, 518 N.W.2d 191 (N.D. 1994); see also *State v. Hodges*, 798 P.2d 270 (Utah Ct. App. 1990) (defendant not told that progress would be rated by treatment staff).

[110] *People v. Walters*, 627 N.Y.S.2d 289 (N.Y. Const. Ct. 1995).

[111] *State v. Gleason*, 576 A.2d 1246 (Vt. 1990).

[112] *Bell v. State*, 643 So. 2d 674 (Fla. Dist. Ct. App. 1994), *distinguished from, Archer v. State*, 604 So. 2d 561 (Fla. Dist. Ct. App. 1992).

[113] *State v. Eccles*, 179 Ariz. 226, 877 P.2d 799 (1994).

[114] *Mace v. Amestoy*, 765 F. Supp. 847 (D. Vt. 1991), *overturning State v. Mace*, 154 Vt. 430, 578 A.2d 104 (1990).

[115] *State v. Carrizales*, 528 N.W.2d 29 (Wis. App. 1995).

[116] Cochran, D., M. Brown and R. Kazarian, EXECUTIVE SUMMARY OF RESEARCH FINDINGS FROM THE PILOT COURT RISK/NEED CLASSIFICATION SYSTEM, REPORT #4. Massachusetts Office of the Commissioner of Probation.

[117] *Morrissey v. Brewer*, 408 U.S. 471, 92 S. Ct. 2593, 33 L. Ed. 2d 484 (1972).

[118] *Gagnon v. Scarpelli*, 411 U.S. 778, 93 S. Ct. 1756, 36 L. Ed. 2d 656 (1973).

[119] *Williams v. Illinois*, 399 U.S. 235, 90 S. Ct. 2018, 26 L. Ed. 2d 586 (1970).

[120] *Tate v. Short*, 401 U.S. 395, 91 S. Ct. 668, 28 L. Ed. 2d 130 (1971).

[121] *Bearden v. Georgia*, 461 U.S. 666, 103 S. Ct. 2064, 76 L. Ed. 2d 221 (1983).

[122] *Id.* at 668-669, 103 S. Ct. at 2070, 76 L. Ed. 2d at 230.

[123] *Id.* at 672, 103 S. Ct. at 2074, 76 L. Ed. 2d at 233.

[124] *Id.* at 668, n.9, 103 S. Ct. at 2070, n.9, 76 L. Ed. 2d at 230, n.9.

[125] *In re Robert M.,* 163 Cal. App. 3d 812, 209 Cal. Rptr. 657 (1985).

[126] *People v. Davis*, 123 Ill. App. 3d 349, 462 N.E.2d 824 (1984).

[127] *Id.* at 353, 462 N.E.2d 827.

[128] *Id.*

[129] *State v. Thompson,* 486 N.W.2d 163 (Minn. Ct. App. 1992).

[130] *State v. Bleasdale,* 69 Ohio App. 3d 685, 90 N.E.2d 43 (1990).

[131] *Cf. State v. Bennett,* 35 Wash. App. 228, 301, 666 P.2d 390 (1983), citing *State v. Giraud,* 68 Wash. 2d 176, 179 P.2d 104 (1966) ("Where an implied condition of probation cannot be met because of subsequent events, and that condition was the essential assumption underlying the grant of probation, the court may revoke probation.").

[132] *State v. Sepulveda,* 119 Wis. 2d 546, 350 N.W.2d 96 (1984).

[133] *Id.* at 556, 350 N.W.2d 101.

[134] *Id.* at 568, 350 N.W.2d 107.

[135] *State v. Hodges,* 798 P.2d 270 (Utah Ct. App. 1990).

[136] *State v. Wong,* 73 Haw. 81, 829 P.2d 1325 (1992).

[137] *State v. Bell,* 66 Ohio App. 3d 52, 583 N.E.2d 414 (1990).

[138] Discussed in § 5.07.

[139] *United States v. Brown,* 932 F.2d 342 (4th Cir. 1991).

[140] *State v. Fife,* 115 Idaho 879, 771 P.2d 543 (Idaho Ct. App. 1989).

[141] *People v. Jarfas,* 540 N.Y.S.2d 137 (Supt. Ct. Queens 1989).

[142] *Sweeney v. United States,* 353 F.2d 10 (7th Cir. 1965).

[143] *Id.* at 11.

[144] *Sobota v. Williard,* 247 Or. 151, 152-153, 427 P.2d 758, 759 (1967); accord, *Upchurch v. State,* 289 Minn. 607,184 N.W.2d 607 (1971).

[145] *Sobota v. Williard,* 247 Or. at 153, 427 P.2d at 759.

[146] *People v. Mitchell,* 125 Cal. App. 3d 715, 719-720, 178 Cal. Rptr. 188, 190 (1981).

[147] *Kupec v. State,* 835 P.2d 359 (Wyo. 1992).

[148] *State v. Oyler,* 92 Idaho 43, 47, 436 P.2d 709, 713 (1968).

[149] *State v. Pease,* 233 Mont. 65, 758 P.2d 764 (1988), *cert. denied,* 488 U.S. 1033, 109 S. Ct. 845 (1988).

[150] *Keith v. Commonwealth,* 689 S.W.2d 613 (Ky. Ct. App. 1985).

[151] *Id.* at 615.

[152] LA. CODE CRIM. PROC. ANN. art. 902(C) (West 1984).

[153] *State v. Fields,* 67 Haw. 268, 686 P.2d 1379 (1984).

[154] *State v. Morris,* 72 Haw. 67, 806 P.2d 407 (1991).

[155] See, *e.g., State v Finnegan,* 232 Neb. 75, 439 N.W.2d 496 (1989).

[156] *State v. Sigler,* 236 Mont. 137, 769 P.2d 703 (1989).

[157] *United States v. Duff,* 831 F.2d 176 (9th Cir. 1987).

[158] See, *e.g., Spence v. Farrier,* 807 F.2d 753 (8th Cir. 1986); *Lahey v. Kelly,* 518 N.E.2d 924 (N.Y. App. 1987); *People v. Walker,* 164 Ill. App. 3d 133, 517 N.E.2d 679 (1987).

[159] See, *e.g., Jensen v. Lick,* 589 F. Supp. 35 (D.N.D. 1984); *Vasquez v. Coughlin,* 499 N.Y.S.2d 4612, 118 A.2d 897 (Sup. Ct. App. 1986); *Peranzo v. Coughlin,* 850 F.2d 125 (2d Cir. 1988); *In re Johnston,* 109 Wash. 2d 493, 745 P.2d 864 (1987).

[160] *United States v. Kindred,* 918 F.2d 485 (5th Cir. 1990), abandoning *United States Caldera,* 631 F.2d 1227 (5th Cir. 1980); see also *United States v. Penn,* 721 F.2d 762 (11th Cir. 1983).

[161] *United States v. Bell,* 785 F.2d 640 (8th Cir. 1986).

[162] *United States v. McCormick,* 54 F.3d 214 (5th Cir. 1995).

[163] See, *e.g., State v. Wade,* 863 S.W.2d 406 (Tenn. 1993).

[164] *United States v. Kindred,* 918 F.2d 486 (5th Cir. 1990).

[165] *Taking Shortcuts in Drug Use Revocations May Create Problems.* Community Corrections Report, May/June, 1994.

[166] *State v. Ouelnan,* 70 Haw. 194, 767 P.2d 243 (1989).

[167] See, *e.g., Moore v. Commonwealth,* 109 Pa. Commw. 142, 530 A.2d 1011 (Pa. Commw. 1987); *United States v. Granderson,* 969 F.2d 980 (11th Cir. 1992) (one positive test proved possession of cocaine).

[168] *State v. McCoy,* 116 N.M. 491, 864 P.2d 307 (N.M. App. 1993), *reversed on other grounds by State v. Hodge,* 882 P.2d 1 (N.M. 1994).

[169] *State v. Ware,* 118 N.M. 703, 884 P.2d 1182 (1994).

[170] *Bolieu v. State,* 779 S.W.2d 489 (Tex. Ct. App. 1989).

[171] See, *e.g., People v. Holzhauser,* 144 Ill. App. 3d 153, 494 N.E.2d 272 (1986) *aff'd,* 519 N.E.2d 879.

[172] *Clay v. State,* 710 S.W.2d 119 (Tex. App. 1986), relying on *Macias v. State,* 649 S.W.2d 150 (Tex. 1983).

[173] *People v. Hood,* 204 Ill. App. 3d 895, 562 N.E.2d 394 (1990).

[174] Crossman, H. (1996). *Drug Testing Results, 1995.* Quincy, MA: Quincy Probation Report.

[175] Carlson, E., E. Parks and H. Allen (1978). Critical Issues in Adult Probation, The State of Research in Probation 64. Washington, DC: National Institute of Law Enforcement and Criminal Justice, U.S. Department of Justice.

[176] *State v. Case,* 350 N.W.2d 473 (Minn. 1984); see also *State v. Dobbins,* 221 Neb. 778, 380 N.W.2d 640 (1986) (inpatient treatment permissible mitigating factor despite prosecutor's objections).

[177] Vaillant, G. (1983). The Natural History of Alcoholism 191.

[178] Bureau of Justice Statistics (1983). Prisoners and Alcohol. Washington, DC: U.S. Department of Justice.

[179] The Rand study is discussed in § 2.06.

[180] At least one state's supreme court has held that the failure of responsible state parole officials to mandate abstinence for a parolee with a history of violence when drunk subjected them to liability for the parolee's subsequent murder of three individuals, *Neakok v. Division of Corrections,* 721 P.2d 1121 (Alaska 1986).

Chapter 9

Incapacitation and Alternative Sentences

§9.01   Introduction

The traditional way to incapacitate an offender is to put him in prison. There are other, vastly cheaper ways. Offenders can be incapacitated in their own homes, largely at their own expense. In what is usually called "house arrest" or "home confinement," offenders are ordered to remain in their homes in lieu of prison. Tight surveillance in the community also serves to confine the offender's freedom of movement. Formal programs to accomplish what Judge Albert Kramer has named "community cells,"[1] are generally achieved through intensive probation supervision.

Incapacitation, full or partial, both protects the community and punishes the offender. Correctional researchers from Rand suggest that the crime rate could be reduced if certain high-risk recidivists were "selectively incapacitated." Most street crimes are committed by young men who eventually outgrow their criminal careers. Incapacitation for relatively short periods may achieve the utopian wishes of Shakespeare: "I would there were no age between ten and three and twenty, or that youth would sleep out the rest, for there is nothing in between but getting wenches with child, wronging the ancientry, stealing, and fighting." By offering alternatives to prisons and jails, the offenders are spared the corrupting and negative influences of traditional incarceration. Incapacitation of offenders may also assist in their rehabilitation. As previously illustrated, offenders can be effectively incapacitated in inpatient treatment facilities or confined in therapeutic halfway houses or the like.

In addition to confining an offender to a residence or providing tight surveillance in the community, partial incapacitation can be obtained by requiring offenders to maintain jobs, either by ordering employment or making employment necessary by ordering monetary sanctions, or requiring the performance of community work service. Daily toil keeps the offender occupied and usually results in nightly sleep. In New South Wales, Australia, a unique prison workshop facility is only open during the night. Offenders are sentenced to work there into the early morning hours. They are then released during the day, the time when it is relatively difficult to commit crimes without easy detection, and the state saves housing, feeding and clothing costs.

With a little creativity, the court can construct a similar stricture for the offender, using the various alternative sentencing options available to it. In addition to those already detailed, house arrest and curfews offer the court valuable alternatives.

§9.02   House Arrest/Electronic Monitoring

Common in the military system and used extensively in other countries, especially in regard to so-called political prisoners, house arrest is becoming more and more popular among state and federal judges. Judge Golde of Contra Costa County, California claims to have been among the first to impose a sentence of house arrest. More recently, New York Federal District Court Judge Weinstein has introduced it to the federal courts in New York. He asked federal probation staff to devise comprehensive rules and regulations to govern the sanction. The specific sentence involved a woman convicted of racketeering and conspiracy. She was among nine defendants charged with defrauding 19 insurance companies during a 10-year period by filing inflated and bogus accident claims. She was also convicted of obstruction of justice for encouraging two witnesses to lie to a grand jury. Instead of sentencing her to 50 years in prison and imposing a $56,000 fine, Weinstein placed her on probation for five years and ordered her to serve two years under house arrest.[2]

In December of 1983, a 28-year-old carpenter from Key Largo, Florida became the first person in the history of the state, and one of the first in the nation, to be sentenced to electronic house arrest. An electronic monitor was attached to his leg. If he ventured more than a certain number of yards from another monitor attached to his phone, the electronic impulse would inform a central computer whose printout would record the violation for the court. Several different companies market electronic monitoring devices used to enforce house arrest orders, including Advanced Signal Concepts, Behavioral Systems Southwest, BI Incorporated, Contrac, Controlec, Inc., Corrections Services, Inc., Cost Effective Monitoring System, Guardian Alternative Technologies, Hitek Community Control Corp., Innovative Security Systems, Inc., Life Science Research Group, Inc., Luma Telecon Sales Division, Monitech Systems, Inc., Trak-Tech, Inc. and Voxtron.

On February 15, 1987, a federal study identified 53 electronic house arrest programs in 21 states, monitoring almost 1,000 offenders.[3] In addition to specific electronic monitoring programs, usually administered by or contracted by state or local court or correctional agencies, several of the companies that manufacture the equipment will monitor, for a fee, individuals sentenced in jurisdictions without programs. The companies maintain long distance telephone lines that are, in effect, plugged into the defendant's electronic device. If the defendant leaves his home, a company computer is activated and the company notifies the requisite court or correctional official of the violation. Such an arrangement enables courts to sentence individuals to electronic confinement even if the jurisdiction in which they are sentenced has no such program.

Since 1985, a number of states have passed legislation authorizing home confinement as a condition of probation or as an alternative sentence.[4] Some have specifically authorized electronic monitoring of these defendants.[5] In one case involving enforcement of home confinement that was electronically monitored, the court upheld it as a condition of probation but cautioned that "more in-depth scientific and technical testimony may be necessary in a case where a defendant charged with a violation has not made an admission or in an instance where there is an issue of credibility pertaining to a claimed admission."[6]

The Contra Costa County, California probation department established a house arrest pilot project in the early 1980s to address overcrowding in its adult detention facility in Martinez. Lacking exotic electronic gadgets, it developed the following rules defining house arrest:

> (1) Unless specifically authorized and approved by the Probation Officer, you are to remain in your house of residence during the entire period of home detention; (2) If authorized to be away from your place of residence by the Probation Officer, you are to only go to those places and at the times authorized by him/her; (3) You are specifically directed not to engage in, participate in, or attend any parties, celebrations, or social gatherings at your place of residence; (4) You must have prior approval from the Probation Officer to have visitors in your place of residence. This approval will specify the hours you may have visitors; and (5) You must allow the Probation Officer into your place of residence upon his/her demand, at any time of the day or night.[7]

If the court desires only partial incapacitation, offenders may be allowed to work during the day and be confined to their homes only during the evening and night. Curfews are imposed to secure nightly confinement. If the defendant lacks a suitable home environment, courts may confine him in an alternative facility. Due to prison overcrowding, courts have confined Nashville, Tennessee drunk drivers in a school auditorium, Los Angeles offenders in local police lock-ups for a $75 fee (rather than county facilities), and at least one Arkansas female offender in a Holiday Inn. Many statutes specifically authorize offenders to reside in places other than their homes.[8]

Many probation statutes provide that probationers may be required "to attend or reside in a facility established for the instruction, recreation, or residence of persons on probation."[9] Some provide that the probationer may be required to reside in specific facilities.[10] Others specify residence at "a community residence" operated by various private and public agencies.[11]

The growth of electronic monitoring since the mid-1980s has been significant. From 95 defendants wired in 1986, the number grew to almost 6,500 by 1989 on a daily basis.[12] Most were monitored for property crimes (31%), followed by drugs (22%) and major traffic offenses (17%). Only slightly more than 10 (11.8%) were for crimes against persons. Still, this represented an increase for such defendants.

A survey found the number of defendants wired increased to 49,150 by 1992, scattered throughout 1,443 different jurisdictions around the country. In that same year, sales of electronic monitoring equipment and services topped more than $13 million.[13] Over 67,000 electronic monitors were in use in 1995.[14]

House arrest or home confinement, usually monitored electronically, is currently used at many stages in the sentencing process. It is used as a condition of pretrial release or bail. It is used as a condition of a toughened probation or as an intermediate sanction in lieu of jail. Finally, it is used as a condition of early release from prison or as a condition of a toughened parole.

In the federal system, home confinement was specifically approved as a condition of pretrial release, but not as a form of detention in a 1986 Third Circuit decision.[15] It is also used in the federal system as an alternative to traditional probation and supervised release or for sentences that are made outside the guidelines for exceptional cases.[16] The U.S. District Court of Nebraska took the early lead in developing a comprehensive home confinement program in conjunction with defense attorneys and the Nebraska Center on Sentencing Alternatives. The program recruits volunteer work sites that also house the federal offenders. The defendants perform community service at the host sites and pay for their room and board at a rate of from $100 to $200 a day. The program is monitored by a retired law enforcement officer if the offenders can afford to pay. Indigents are monitored by the probation department.

Example: Florida Community Control Program

On a state level, Florida has taken the lead with its Community Control, established in 1985.[17] The program is an intensive supervision program in which offenders are placed under house arrest when not in specifically approved activities. They are also urine tested and must pay back victim restitution and perform community work service. Between 1983 and 1987, Florida's program held 17,952 offenders in home confinement. Early evaluations revealed that the vast majority, 80 percent, completed their period of confinement successfully. Less than six percent escaped. Of the 20 percent who failed the program, almost two-thirds did so by not meeting the program requirements of drug abstinence or abiding by curfew restrictions. Only a third committed new crimes while in the program.[18]

By 1993, another 12,000 offenders were sentenced to the Florida Community Control Program. A comparison of graduates of state prison and Community Control found that the former had a higher conviction rate for new offenses than the latter after 18 months, 24.3 percent versus 19.7 percent. Even the drug addicts sentenced to Community Control experienced lower reconviction rates than those sent to prison, 11 percent to 27 percent. Of course, the 10 percent of Community Control offenders who violate the program for dirty urines and the like were resentenced to prison, which skews the samples in the former's favor. The Florida program costs $6.49 per offender per day, compared to $2.19 for probation and $39.05 for prison. Almost all offenders in the program pay for their participation.[19] Researchers estimate that a slight majority of Community Control participants (54%) represented prison diversion. The remainder probably would not have been imprisoned anyway. Still, the program also represents one of the largest prison diversion programs in the country.

As of 1987, a study identified 31 formal home confinement programs throughout the country.[20] That number increases each year. Numerous other jurisdictions also use electronic monitoring both for individual offenders and as parts of intensive supervision programs. At least one state supreme court has declared that offenders have no right to resist wearing an electronic monitor if they want to remain on intensive probation supervision instead of going to prison.[21]

Electronic Monitoring Lawsuits

Despite the tremendous growth and use of house arrest/electronic monitoring, enthusiasm has been tempered by problems that have arisen. In the Chicago area alone, for example, two suits have been brought, alleging that defendants have escaped their electronic confinement and gone on to murder people. Neither of the systems employed included tamper-proof features to signal if the equipment is removed by the offender sentenced to wear it. Another suit filed in Miami, Florida, alleges that over 2,000 of the monitoring devices have broken down due to technical flaws. Suits have been brought both against the manufacturers of the equipment and those who administer the home confinement programs.

The equipment manufacturers uniformly argue that their equipment is being used inappropriately. It is not suited for violent offenders to begin with. They also argue that the sites fail to use the equipment properly.

In the largest award to date, $3 million was awarded the estate of Marvin Cheeks, a Chicago fire fighter and brother of NBA star Maurice Cheeks of the Philadelphia 76ers. In October of 1992, Marvin Cheeks was killed by a gang whose members included Darryl Clemons, a convicted armed robber and burglar who had recently escaped from his electronic confinement. The suit alleged that the county had contracted with an agency to run its electronic confinement program that was ill-equipped to properly administer the program. As a result, it failed to take proper precautions to ensure its effective performance. The Cook County Sheriff argued that the incident represented an isolated case among 40,000 cases on the program since its inception in 1988. It was revealed that 120 other offenders had also cut off their monitors over the past seven years and had not been recaptured.

In December of 1994 another suit in Lake County, Illinois was filed by the estate of an 11-year-old babysitter. Following the suit, the judges of the county announced that they were abandoning the program entirely.

Other notable cases include parolees on electronic confinement who went on to rape or murder. In some of the cases, the parolee had removed the equipment on them. In others they were arrested with the equipment still attached to them. In a 1990 case, a convicted car thief confined to his apartment and monitored electronically lured a man to his apartment and shot him. The day before, he had ordered a pizza and robbed the deliveryman.[22]

A new generation of technology is in the making. In 1995, the Justice Department gave Westinghouse $500,000 to develop a prototype second generation system that can track an offender's whereabouts over a wide area, such as a city. The system is to be tested in Pittsburgh. Technology is also being developed to combine electronic monitoring with other testing technologies so that in addition to monitoring presence, the systems will measure bodily fluids to detect drug use or sexual urges.[23]

The best technology in the world, however, cannot prevent its inappropriate and unsafe use. Perhaps one of the worst applications of home confinement/electronic monitoring is the confinement of perpetrators of domestic violence to their homes with their victims. Electronic monitoring can reveal an offender's violation of his confinement or removal of his monitoring equipment. It cannot stop him from doing either. And, if the monitoring units are not themselves monitored 24 hours a day, in many cases such violations will not be discovered until 8:00 A.M. or 9:00 A.M. the next day. By then the scent may be cold, even if the program has the resources to pursue the violator. Offenders who represent an unacceptable threat to others should not be released on home confinement, no matter how they are monitored.

The American Bar Association Criminal Justice Section has promulgated standards for home confinement/electronic monitoring although it neither approves or disapproves of its use. The standard is mainly concerned that such confinement be used appropriately as the *least restrictive alternative* consistent with the protection of the public and the gravity of the offense, not as an "automatic" adjunct to regular supervision. Further, no one should be barred from participation in such a program because of lack of funds. The ABA goes on to define different levels of confinement, beginning with curfew (usually evening hours), home detention (be at home except for work, treatment or other approved activities) to home incarceration (remain at home 24 hours a day).

The ABA also cautions against the adoption of technology without study, fearing unintentional consequences and undesired effects.[24]

Notwithstanding its use as an alternative to prison, most jurisdictions that have addressed the matter by statute or case law agree that home confinement is not legally equivalent to imprisonment. Confinees do not get credit against prison time if they are subsequently resentenced to prison. A federal offender, for example, convicted of passing counterfeit money, was sentenced to 10 months imprisonment followed by two years of supervised release. She sought credit for the seven months she was under house arrest with electronic surveillance, arguing that she had, in effect, already been imprisoned and deserved credit for it. She pointed out that under the guidelines, a federal offender sentenced to less than six months may do so under home confinement. Thus it was a denial of equal protection for her to be denied credit for the seven months she spent so confined. The Ninth Circuit disagreed.[25] It ruled that all of the circuits addressing the issue agreed that home confinement with electronic monitoring is not "official detention."[26] It dismissed her second claim, citing a Tenth Circuit ruling denying such credit.[27]

The Nebraska Supreme Court ruled that the state's statute requiring credit for time spent in *custody* did not include time spend in home confinement subject to electronic monitoring. An offender in jail or prison, the court held, does not enjoy unrestricted freedom of activity and association within their homes like those under home confinement. Because it was far less onerous, no credit was granted for time spent under home confinement.[28]

Other courts agree with Nebraska's Supreme Court.[29] A California appellate court also disallowed credit for time spent under house arrest even though California does give credit for time spent in drug rehabilitation programs, halfway houses and other such programs.[30] As will be discussed in § 10.08, a number of other states, like California, do grant credit for time spent in inpatient or residential programs other than formal jails and prisons. As in California, the difference appears to be that these confinements are not in the defendant's own home. Because home confinement is not equivalent to imprisonment, at least one state, Connecticut, does not allow those who leave to be charged with the crime of escape as defined by that state's laws.[31]

The Louisiana statute creating home incarceration as a sanction in lieu of imprisonment for certain misdemeanors and felonies specifically bars credit for time served under home incarceration in the event of revocation and sentence to imprisonment.[32]

§9.03   Intensive Supervision

There are a number of different models for intensive supervision programs across the country. Many use electronic monitoring, require urine testing and include home confinement to differing degrees. Some also require performance of community work service and payment of restitution to crime victims. Most are operated by probation and parole agencies. Some are run by private contractors. Some are specifically created by statute, others by specific conditions of probation or parole.

Intensive supervision programs have developed for various reasons. Some address the simultaneous problems of unacceptably high recidivism rates of traditional probation on the one hand and overcrowded prisons on the other. Both issues are, of course, very real. A widely circulated study of felons on traditional probation supervision between 1986 and 1980, for example, found that recidivism was 43 percent for another felony within three years.[33] At the same time, by 1991, 36 state correctional systems were operating either under court order or consent decrees to reduce prison overcrowding. Still other intensive supervision programs are specifically constructed to provide courts with intermediate sanctions between prison and traditional probation/parole.

For all these reasons, between 1980 and 1990, every state in the Union adopted some form of an intensive supervision program for select offenders.[34] As of 1993, studies estimated that 120,000 offenders were in intensive supervision programs across the country.[35]

The first generation of intensive supervision programs emphasized the level of surveillance provided. Their main difference with traditional supervision revolved around the intensity of face-to-face contact with the offender. It was assumed that intensity of supervision correlated with lowered risk of recidivism. Reviewing correctional research in the 1970s, a proponent of these early programs, James Q. Wilson concluded that frequency of contact was more important than the content of that contact.

> (Studies imply) that how strictly the youth were supervised, rather than what therapeutic programs were available, had the greatest effect on the recidivism rate. . . . [I]f one measures offense frequency, some kinds of programs involving fairly high degrees of restrictiveness and supervision may make some differences.[36]

The degrees of intensive programs varied greatly, from multiple daily contacts reinforced by electronic monitoring to weekly face-to-face contact or less. Although more intrusive than traditional supervision, no offenders successfully challenged the imposition of these programs in lieu of traditional supervision.[37]

Georgia created the first such program as a result of prison overcrowding crisis in 1981. The program has been described in § 3.01. New Jersey provided another early example that also is flourishing today. Its program is for select offenders released from prison early. Surveillance standards include 20 contacts per month, 10:00 P.M. to 6:00 A.M. curfews, employment within 90 days, 16 hours of community service per week and maintenance of a community sponsor. Another example can be found in Arizona. That state's intensive probation supervision program requires that a team of a probation officers and one or two surveillance officers have visual contact with a caseload of from 25 to 40 offenders four times a week and weekly contact with each offender's employer. In addition, offenders are subject to tests for drugs and alcohol use. They must secure employment or participate in community work service six days a week.

However, a study of intensive programs in nine states reported in 1993 that although each claimed to be "intensive," the average offender was seen less than two hours a month and had only two drug tests per month.[38]

Jurisdictions do not need formal programs to provide intensive supervision for select offenders. All the judge or parole board has to do is fashion such program components as individual conditions of the offender's release. For example, random telephone calls or home visits by the supervising officer can substitute for electronic monitoring, or police can be asked to visit the house periodically.

Results of Intensive Supervision Research

To test the effectiveness of intensive supervision programs, the National Institute of Justice evaluated a demonstration project funded by the Bureau of Justice Assistance. It involved 14 programs in nine states (Contra Costa, Ventura and Los Angeles, CA; Seattle, WA; Atlanta, Macon and Waycross, GA; Santa Fe, NM; Des Moines, IA; Winchester, VA; Dallas and Houston, TX; Marion County, OR and Milwaukee, WI). The study ran from 1986 to 1991, involving a total of 2,000 offenders. Rand did the evaluation. All sites had matched control offenders with which to compare results.

All but two of the sites were established as enhanced probation/parole programs. Two were established for prison diversion. The offense for which the offender was referred had to be nonviolent. Several programs concentrated on drug offenders.

The general conclusion of the massive study was as follows:

> Most notably, [the evaluations] suggest that the assumptions about the ability of ISPs to meet certain practical goals—reduce prison crowding, save money, and decrease recidivism—may not have been well founded and that jurisdictions interested in adopting ISPs should define their goals carefully. Other study findings indicate that ISPs were most successful as an intermediate punishment, in providing closer supervision of offenders and in offering a range of sentencing options between prison and routine probation and parole.[39]

The study found that there was no relationship between surveillance level and recidivism. For example, the Seattle program saw offenders face-to-face 3.4 times per month. In Macon, Georgia they were seen 16.1 times per month. Yet both jurisdictions had arrest rates in the 40 percent range (46% and 42% respectively). It is difficult, of course, in this research to separate the effects of surveillance from other program aspects.

The programs, however, were uniformly more onerous than traditional probation/parole supervision regimens.

Evidence also suggests that some offenders may view ISPs as even more punitive and restrictive of freedom than prison. Among offenders at the Oregon site, 25 percent who were eligible for prison diversion chose not to participate. The reason may be that Oregon's crowded prisons made it unlikely that anyone sentenced to one year would serve the full term, while offenders assigned to ISPs could be certain of a full year of surveillance in the program. As prisons become more crowded and length of sentences decreases, ISPs may come to seem increasingly punitive to offenders.[40]

Regarding recidivism, ISP participants were not subsequently arrested less often, did not have a longer time to failure, nor were they arrested for less serious crimes than the control group members. Both recidivated in the 30 percent range (37% and 33%). Of course, because of the intensity of surveillance, it was probably much more likely that the ISPs would be arrested than their control member peers. Given this, equivalent arrest rates may mean, in fact, higher crime rates among the control population. Reflecting this tighter supervision, technical violations among the experimental population was 65 percent versus only 38 percent for the control group. Increased drug testing among the experimental group accounted for one-third of all the technical violations.

A little less than a one-quarter of the ISPs were sent or returned to prison for failing the program. Only 15 percent of the control group went to prison. This means that if the ISP population is drawn from existing probation/parole caseloads and not prison divertees, ISP may actually increase prison populations.

ISP offenders participated much more in drug treatment programs, employment, community work service and restitution payment than their peers in the control group. While treatment was not high in either groups, 43 percent of the experimental group participated in drug treatment compared to only 22 percent of the control population. Half of the ISP participants were employed versus 43 percent of the control group. ISP participants also paid restitution at a rate four times greater than the control group (12% versus 3%).

Combining Intensity and Treatment

The study did find a difference in recidivism regarding IPS participants who were required to participate in drug treatment and those in the control group who were not. Those who received any counseling for drugs or alcohol, held jobs, paid restitution and did community service were 10 to 20 percent less likely to recidivate than those who did not. The study concluded that overall outcomes might have been even more positive had a greater proportion of the offenders participated in treatment. Although about one-half of the offenders were identified as having drug problems, many were not required to undergo or were offered treatment of any kind. About one-third of all participants rearrested were arrested for drugs.

The newest generation of intensive supervision programs emphasize treatment as well as increased surveillance. Some have suggested that these programs be called "Intensive Rehabilitation Programs" to mark the new orientation.[41] The new generation of programs is based on extensive research that suggests, as did the review above, that correctional treatment programs work. In a study of 443 studies with control groups, Mark Lipsey found that 64 percent reported reductions in favor of the treatment group. The average reduction was 10 percent. Further, when the content of the treatment was broken down, reductions in recidivism reached as high as 18 percent.[42]

Supervision and treatment programs, other researchers have suggested, can reduce recidivism from 25 to 80 percent with an average of 40 percent if they possess the following characteristics: (1) Intensity: occupies 40 to 70 percent of the offender's time from three to nine months; (2) Behavioral treatment: behaviorism to cognitive social learning strategies; (3) Reduction of criminogenic needs, such as drug use, as opposed to treatment of self-esteem or depression; (4) Strict but fair enforcement; (5) Therapist trained to deal with offender population; (6) Program structure that disrupts criminal network; and (7) Advocacy and brokerage of services.

Characteristics that exemplified programs that do not work include programs that: (1) target need factors not predictive of criminal behavior (anxiety, self-esteem, depression); (2) programs that target low-risk offenders; (3) traditional psychodynamic and Rogerian nondirective therapies (talking cures, good relationship with client as primary goals, unraveling the unconscious, gaining insight as major goal, resolving neurotic conflicts and self-actualizing, externalizing blame to parents, staff, victims, society, ventilating anger); and (4) medical model approaches (diet change, pharmacological, plastic surgery, subcultural and labeling approaches).[43]

The empirical evidence, according to researchers promoting the new generation of ISPs is decisive "without a rehabilitation component, reductions in recidivism are as elusive as a desert mirage."[44]

Day Reporting Centers

A variant of intensive supervision programs are day reporting programs invented in Great Britain and first copied in the United States in Massachusetts in 1987. There are now more than 100 such centers across the country in 20 different states. They are run by parole, probation, sheriffs and correctional departments, but mostly probation. Like intensive supervision programs they are used in a variety of contexts for different offender populations at different stages of sentencing. In Chicago, the probation department found that the majority of its probationers came from the same 10-block area, so it established a day reporting center in that neighborhood, called Project Safeway. Centers also exist in smaller towns such as Valparaiso, Indiana.

A typical program may resemble the Metropolitan Day Reporting Center operating in Boston, Massachusetts by a private nonprofit agency, Crime and Justice Foundation, under contract to the County Correctional Department. Offenders in the program must check in to the center in person according to an approved schedule. They must submit an itinerary, in advance, to include location, names and telephone numbers for all activities when they are outside the Center. They must call the center at scheduled times, up to three to five times a day. They must be available for random calls or visits at home or other locations listed on their itineraries. They must participate in all activities as planned and as stipulated in the contract with the center, submit to random drug tests each week and comply with a curfew.[45]

§9.04   Intermediate Sanctions, Incarceration Without Jail

Over the past 15 years a number of states have enacted laws creating intensive supervision programs and day reporting programs like the one described above, not as a condition of probation or parole, but as an intermediate sanction to which offenders can be directly sentenced. For example, in 1983 the Maine legislature created a new sentence of intensive supervision. The sentence consists of the following stringent conditions: curfew, travel restrictions, searches without warrants and probable cause; no drug use or alcohol use, urinalysis, breath testing, or other chemical tests without probable cause; notification to any law enforcement officer of his status as "prisoner on intensive supervision" if stopped; and notification to the intensive supervision officer within 12 hours of any contact with law enforcement.[46]

Vermont also created a "supervised community sentence" in the early 1990s in which offenders can be sentenced to what is essentially an intensive supervision program. The difference being, if they violate the conditions of the program, instead of going back to a judge for a revocation hearing and possible further sentencing, they are brought back to the parole board for possible incarceration. Before the creation of this vehicle, offenders were furloughed to equivalent supervision. Now they can be directly sentenced to it. It is open to felons only. The average time an offender is supervised on community sentence is six months. Typical program content for a drug abusers, for example, might include three one and one-half hour sessions each week for intensive drug treatment including AA and treatment groups led by a probation officer and a therapist. Non-drug abusers would meet twice a week for three hours per session. To be eligible, the offender must be sentenced with the agreement of the judge and a defense or prosecution attorney.[47] The program has reportedly saved millions of dollars in jail costs statewide.

In New Jersey, offenders in its Intensive Supervision Program (ISP), although supervised by probation officers, similarly are not defined as probationers. They are not placed on intensive supervision by the sentencing judge, but by a review board that screens eligible nonviolent felons in prison. The review board includes citizens who are not state employees. Once released to the program, intensively supervised offenders who fail the program are brought to a three-judge panel that determines whether they go back to prison. The panels are specially organized just to review ISP participants. In effect, New Jersey has created a new class of offenders under correctional control who are neither parolees nor probationers, but intermediate sanction supervisees.

Certain programs such as Day Reporting Centers or Electronically Monitored House Arrest programs may be run by prison or jail authorities. Legally, offenders participating in these programs are still considered inmates. If they violate the rules of these programs or abscond, they are simply returned to prison or charged with escape from prison. Although offenders may be required to act like probationers or parolees in similar programs in similar settings, they are still inmates under the direction of the prison authorities, not the court or the parole board.

Whether such hybrid intermediate sanction programs that look like intensive probation or parole, but are not, are allowed to bypass the requirements of formal revocation hearings before they return offenders to prison remains an open question. In a recent United States Supreme Court case, the Court seemed to liberalize exemptions from such hearings. The Court ruled in June of 1995 in *Sandin v. Conner*[48] that not all inmates have liberty interests in custody decisions that require due process hearings. Such hearings are only necessary when the freedom "loss" is an atypical and significant departure from the expected parameters of a prison sentence. However, in interpreting this decision, the Tenth Circuit ruled that Oklahoma prisoners released on its Pre-Parole Conditional Supervision Program, an intermediate sanction somewhere between a work furlough and parole, were entitled to revocation hearings before removal from the program back to prison. The court ruled that there is a federal liberty interest in remaining in the program and therefore *Morrissey* applies.[49]

Many of the comprehensive alternative to prison intermediate sanction programs are, in effect, repackaging and renaming probation and parole programs, but placing them in a different legal context. Whether appellate courts will treat these programs differently than probation/parole programs in terms of revocation hearings, due process requirements and so forth remain to be seen. Time and offender lawsuits will tell.

§9.05   Alternative Uses of Incarceration

Not only does this country have one of the highest rates of incarceration, but its sentences are generally longer than those in other countries. The average incarceration is 21 months in the United States compared to three in Sweden and less than a month in the Netherlands.[50] The American Bar Association has long advocated that, with few exceptions, a maximum sentence be five years and "only rarely ten."

> There is general agreement among most who have recently studied
> the patterns of sentencing in this country that the average sentence to
> prison is for a term in excess of what can reasonably be justified and
> that there are far too many long-term commitments.[51]

Long term imprisonment can institutionalize the offender, making him less able
to cope legally in the real world. Increased length of incarceration does not correlate with decreased recidivism.[52]

For this reason, a number of jurisdictions have developed alternatives to
long-term incarceration, trying, in effect, to get more "bang for their incarceration buck." Even long-term incapacitation increasingly includes sentences that
follow up periods of incarceration with strict community-based sanctions and
supervision. Often the length of imprisonment is not as important as the fact of
imprisonment, even for a relatively short period.

Judges can construct alternative sentences that take advantage of the powerful message of incarceration and still avail themselves of the myriad other
sentencing options by keeping the incarceration part of the sentence reasonably
short, followed by probation or intermediate sanctioning programs. By imposing what are called "split sentences," the judge decides the offender's sentence,
not the parole board. Often this means that the court can impose stricter supervision in the community than may be available with traditional parole programs.
Other jurisdictions have developed specific release programs for offenders
following periods of incarceration.

The split sentence may be authorized in one or more ways. First, the court
may suspend the imposition or execution of the sentence in part and place the
defendant on probation after serving the designated period of confinement.
Second, the court may impose a period of imprisonment as a condition of probation. Third, the court may modify or reduce a sentence within a specified
period and release the offender under probation supervision. Fourth, the court
may commit an offender, prior to sentencing, to a state or other diagnostic facility for diagnosis and sentencing recommendations. Fifth, the court may re-sen-
tence an offender who is already serving time to a period of probation.

Split sentencing has won the endorsement of the American Bar Association.[53] Only three states, Minnesota, South Dakota and South Carolina, do not
provide statutory authority for split sentencing. Notwithstanding the lack of
such statutory authority, split sentences are common in South Carolina. The
Federal Code has provided for split sentences since 1958. The revised code
enacted in 1984 enhances probation supervision for inmates given split sentences. It provides that any sentence may provide a requirement that the defendant be placed on a term of supervised release after imprisonment. The terms
are prescribed as not more than three years for a Class A or B felony, two for a
Class C or D felony and one for a Class E felony or misdemeanor. Offender
supervision is provided by the federal probation service.[54]

Partial Commitments

The most common split sentence is obtained through partial commitments imposed at the time of sentencing. The incarceration part of the disposition is part of the sentence. The defendant knows exactly how long he will be incarcerated. Partial commitments are authorized in many state statutes. When challenged, they have been upheld.[55]

Incarceration as a Condition of Probation

After partial commitments, the second most common split sentence is obtained through the imposition of a relatively short period of incarceration as a probationary condition. California led the way, adopting this condition in 1927. Other states followed suit. Some of the statutes establish the specific lengths of such commitments.[56] Jurisdictions without specific statutory authority have split on whether to allow incarceration as a condition of probation.[57] Following adverse rulings, Texas and a half-dozen other states enacted legislation allowing for the condition.

In a Florida case, the state's supreme court ruled that the period of incarceration as a condition of probation could not exceed one year.[58] In an Idaho case, the state's supreme court ruled that an inmate who escaped while serving time as a condition of probation could not be charged with the crime of escape, as he was not sentenced to jail, but he could be charged with violating his probation.[59]

Both the American Bar Association and the Model Penal Code endorse incarceration as a condition of probation, although the latter recommends periods of commitment not to exceed 30 days.[60]

Shock Probation

Imposing a lengthy term of incarceration and later reducing it within a set period is another method of obtaining a split sentence. This method is often called "shock sentencing" or "shock probation." The exact terms and rules governing the sentence modification vary from jurisdiction to jurisdiction. To be a true shock, the defendant must believe he has been committed to a lengthier sentence, then be brought back and released after receiving a taste of prison.

The shock sentence was pioneered by judges in Ohio who successfully lobbied for legislation originally aimed at enabling them to amend imposed sentences if new information came to their attention or if upon reconsideration they thought the sentence too harsh. It was passed in 1965.[61] It allowed judges to resentence offenders within 30 to 60 days of incarceration and release them on probation. The practice was not known as shock sentencing until a Dayton, Ohio newspaper later coined the term in describing it. In 1976, the Ohio legislation restricted the judges' authority, excluding offenders convicted of violent crimes.

The chief of the Ohio Adult Parole Authority listed the following purposes for shock sentences:

1. A way for the courts to impress offenders with the seriousness of their action without a long prison sentence.

2. A way for the courts to release offenders found by the institution to be more amendable to community-based treatment than was realized by the courts at the time of sentence

3. A way for the courts to arrive at a just compromise between punishment and leniency in appropriate cases.

4. A way for the courts to provide community-based treatment for rehabilitatable offenders while still observing their responsibilities for imposing deterrent sentences where public policy demands it.

5. A way to afford the briefly incarcerated offender protection against socialization into the inmate culture.[62]

Kentucky created the sentence in 1972, followed by more than a dozen other states.[63] As mentioned earlier, select inmates sentenced to prison in Oklahoma may have their sentences revised within 120 days of being sentenced. The revision is based, among other things, on the inmate's participation in a victim/offender mediation program administered by the Oklahoma Department of Corrections.[64]

Sentences may also be revised pursuant to state statute or rule for other reasons, such as to correct illegal sentences. In the federal code, sentences may be reduced on motion of the government if the defendant substantially assists in the investigation or prosecution of another person who has committed an offense.[65]

Commitment to a Diagnostic Facility

As previously described in the discussion of presentence reports, offenders may be confined in diagnostic facilities predisposed to aid the court in sentencing. These facilities may be correctional, mental health or other institutions. In some states, correctional diagnostic centers are used to screen candidates for probation.

Intermittent Sentences

Split sentences can also be obtained through the use of intermittent sentences. Intermittent sentences are usually, but not exclusively, weekend sentences. They may also stand alone, without the imposition of probation. Increasingly popular, intermittent sentences are a hybrid, splitting the difference between incarceration and release, allowing the offender to maintain employment, family ties, schooling and so on and suffer incarceration on a periodic but sustained basis.

New York City Federal Judge Jack B. Weinstein is credited with introducing weekend sentences more than a decade ago. Vermont adopted this sentence across the state. Judges reported that young offenders especially did not pick up new bad habits from other inmates, unlike those sentenced to straight jail time. Inmates find the weekend confinements particularly onerous. Unlike straight time, they find it difficult to adjust to the jail environment, because they are out during the week.

Periodic or intermittent sentences are specifically authorized in more than a dozen states.[66] It is authorized as a condition of probation in the Federal Code.[67] At least one jurisdiction, Florida, has upheld intermittent incarceration without specific statutory authority.[68] Intermittent sentencing has been endorsed by the American Bar Association, among others.[69]

Boot Camps

Designed to maximize the impact of incarceration, especially on young and initial offenders, prison boot camps have taken corrections by storm. Begun in Georgia and Oklahoma in 1983, by early 1990 there were 21 such camps in 14 states and another dozen pending.[70] By 1993, there were 67 boot camps in 27 states and one in the Federal Bureau of Prisons.[71] Thirteen state programs and the federal program admit women. Another eight have been developed just for juveniles. New York has the largest number of beds dedicated to boot camps, 1,500, followed by Georgia with 800 and Michigan with 600. All in all, there are well over 7,000 beds devoted to boot camp programs across the country. Given that the average length of stay is 107 days, that means potentially 23,000 offenders could go through existing boot camps each year if all are filled all twelve months of the year.

Boot camps are patterned after military basic training. Offenders usually must spend from 90 to 180 days in camp. The camps are characterized by a demanding daily schedule complete will drills and workouts and exacting discipline. Boot camp prisoners typically get up early, exercise and march before most inmates leave their cells. Most must work during the day, followed by still more drills and workouts. After dinner, many receive treatment, then lights are out and the routine begins again early the next morning. Many boot camps are introducing more treatment and educational services within their programs in addition to the military training activities. While many question the relevance of three months of military training for inmates, the camps have proven extremely popular among the public, striking a deep chord in American corrections.

Inmates leaving the boot camps graduate to different programs depending upon the jurisdiction. In slightly over one-half of the states, the offenders return to regular supervision. Forty-two percent of the states return boot camp graduates to specific intensive supervision programs. New York developed a specific aftercare program that includes work, drug treatment and counseling. The newest program, as of 1993, was California's, located at San Quentin. Following 120 days of boot camp, inmates are required to live at a nearby naval station for 60 days. During that time, they may leave the base to work. Upon release from the base after two months, they are intensively supervised in the community for an additional four months.

Many inmates do not make it through boot camp and are returned to regular incarceration or to the court for further sentencing. Termination rates depend upon the specific programs and run from eight to 50 percent. Georgia's termination rate for its 90 days program is nine percent while New York's 180-day program termination rate is 31 percent. States where terminations are determined by judges have the lowest termination rates.[72]

Boot camps have a robust future in American corrections. Talking to the American Correctional Association, U.S. Attorney General Janet Reno announced in 1995 that 40 communities nationwide would receive more than $20 million in federal aid to fund more boot camp programs. Over one-half of the money is earmarked for juvenile offenders.[73] Ironically, initial studies of the camps have failed to differentiate their results versus traditional incarceration.[74]

§9.06　Summary

Alternative uses of incarceration and alternative methods of incapacitation, together or alone, avoid the often irreversible adverse effects of long-term incarceration as well as its exorbitant costs. Equally important, they allow the court to still hold the defendant accountable by ordering other alternative sanctions, including restitution for the crime victim, community work service, other monetary sanctions such as support orders, cash donations, fines, rehabilitation costs and mandatory treatment. Short-term incarceration as part of a longer split sentence or intermittent sentencing saves precious correctional resources while allowing the court to sentence the offender to prison. The split sentence and sentences that employ alternative methods of incapacitation, such as house arrest and saturation surveillance in the community, do not compromise the court's ability to incarcerate the offender the moment he fails to merit his release.

While it is perhaps naive to believe that a short shock sentence will scare a defendant straight, it may, at least, convince the offender to take his probationary segment of the sentence (including its specific conditions) seriously. The commitment part of the sentence may also mobilize family members, friends and employers to take the offender in hand, something a straight probationary sentence would not accomplish.

Prison overpopulation will not go away. Despite the tremendous prison-building boom of the 1980s and early 1990s, everywhere prisons are overcrowded. Currently, more than 30 states are in court accused of operating unconstitutionally crowded facilities. The short-term solution will continue to be more double bunking and emergency early release programs. Neither promise more than temporary solutions at best. The long-term solution has to be the use of hard-headed, strictly enforced alternative sentences. For serious offenders, alternative uses of incarceration may prove to be one key. For these and others, alternative forms of incapacitation will also prove essential. The federal Bail Reform Act of 1983, for example, demands that the court not release offenders unless reasonably assured of the public safety. Yet the Third Circuit upheld the release on bail of a defendant charged with racketeering involving threats of violence because the judge had imposed, as a condition of that release, house arrest and severance of union ties.[76]

For defense attorneys, sentences that incapacitate without incarceration offer sentencing options even for dangerous offenders in need of treatment, restraint and control. The defense can show the court that public safety can be addressed *and* his defendant can be spared lengthy incarceration. Often, if the defendant has been already held without bail, or a bail he cannot afford to pay, awaiting trial, the defense attorney may argue that the defendant has already received the commitment portion of a split sentence. While the reflex reaction in American corrections to equate punishment with incarceration alone should be resisted by defense attorneys, the defense may find it necessary to accede to the demand for incarceration. Where the seriousness of the offense, the offender's past record, or the court's habitual sentencing practices demand incarceration, alternative uses of incarceration, split and intermittent sentences offer defense attorneys realistic sentencing options to propose to the court which minimize lengthy incarceration. In such situations, the court is often more concerned that the offender be sentenced to jail than how long he is sentenced.

For prosecutors, alternative sentences that incapacitate without incarceration allow the court to impose the array of alternative sentencing components that address victim, offender and community needs while providing for offender control in the community. Alternative uses of incarceration allow the prosecutor to send a powerful message of deterrence to the public as well as the offender, yet avoid investing all sentencing options in one basket of long-term incarceration. Further, both sentencing alternatives allow the prosecutor to save precious correctional resources for offenders for which there are no feasible alternatives.

For judges, incapacitation without incarceration and alternative uses of incarceration offer important partial solutions to the escalating problem of prison and jail overcrowding. To the extent that they can relieve overcrowding, sentencing judges can also relieve the increasingly common burden thrust upon appellate judges, forced by unconstitutional overcrowding, to administer entire correctional departments to insure constitutional corrections. Sentencing judges can either choose to ignore this problem and pass it on to their peers on appellate benches or they can seek to become part of the solution and impose sentences that utilize alternatives to incarceration and incapacitate offenders without the use of incarceration.

Notes

[1] See Kramer (1986). *Sentencing the Drunk Driver: A Call for Change.* ALCOHOL TREATMENT QUARTERLY (Special edition); Kramer (1983). *Foreword,* 9 NEW ENG. J. CRIM. & CIVIL CONFINEMENT 319-322.

[2] Rangel (1985). *She's A Prisoner In Her Own House.* PATRIOT LEDGER, Sept. 24.

[3] Schmidt (1987). THE USE OF ELECTRONIC MONITORING BY CRIMINAL JUSTICE AGENCIES (National Institute of Justice, Discussion Paper, 2-87).

[4] See, *e.g.,* P.A. 77-2097, as amended, ILL. STAT. ANN. ch. 38, § 1005-63(b)(10)(i), (ii) (Smith-Hurd Supp. 1986) (home confinement as condition of probation); S.C. CODE ANN. § 24-21-430(9)(10)(11) (Law Coop. Cum. Supp. 1986) (conditions of probation may include curfew, house arrest, intensive surveillance "but not by electronic means"); 1985 OR. LAWS CH. 818 (special condition may include restriction of probationer to own residence not to exceed one year or one-half the period of maximum confinement, if non-violent offender); UTAH CODE ANN. § 77-181(5)(f) (Cum. Supp. 1987) (home confinement as condition of probation).

[5] See, *e.g.,* KY. REV. STAT. § 532.200-250 (Cum. Supp. 1986) (such device must be "minimally intrusive" and not monitor "visual images, oral or wire communications"); 1987, R.I. PUBLIC LAWS, § 12-193 (community confinement in lieu of incarceration if not convicted of felony within five years; also provides for intensive supervision and term of imprisonment; may use electronic monitoring).

[6] *People v. Ryan,* 510 N.Y.S.2d 828,134 Misc. 2d 343 (Dist. Ct. 1987).

[7] Information supplied by Contra Costa County Probation Department.

[8] 18 U.S.C. § 3563(b)(12) and (14) (Supp. II 1984) (effective Nov. 1, 1986) ("reside at, or participate in the program of, a community corrections facility for all or part of the term of probation" and "reside in a specified place or area"); FLA. STAT. ANN. § 948.03(d) (West 1985); KAN. STAT. ANN. § 21-4610(i) (Supp. 1985); TEX. CODE CRIM. PROC. ANN. art. 42.12, § 6(a)(7) (Vernon Supp. 1986).

[9] COLO. REV. STAT. § 16-11-204(2)(c) (1978); PA. STAT. ANN. tit. 42. 59754(5) (Purdon 1982).

[10] N.Y. PENAL LAW § 65.10(2)(i) (McKinney Supp. 1986).

[11] FLA. STAT. ANN § 948.01 (10) (1985) (probationer or community controllee may be required to reside in agency of the Department of Corrections or the Department of Health and Rehabilitative Services or an agency owned or operated by the Salvation Army or any public or private entity).

[12] Renzema, M. and D. Shelton (1990). *Use of Electronic Monitoring in the United States: 1989 Update.* NIJ REPORTS 22 (Nov.-Dec.).

[13] *Electronic Monitoring Market Continues to Expand,* JOURNAL OF OFFENDER MONITORING, UPDATE. (Summer 1992).

[14] *Electronic Bracelets Flawed, Suit Claims,* 81 A.B.A. JOURNAL 30, 1995.

[15] *United States v. Traitz,* 807 F.2d 322 (3d Cir. 1986).

[16] 18 U.S.C. § 3553 (b) (1994).

[17] FLA. STAT. ANN. § 948.10 (West Supp. 1995).

[18] Hofer, P. and B. Meierhoefer (1987). HOME CONFINEMENT, AN EVOLVING SANCTION IN THE FEDERAL CRIMINAL JUSTICE SYSTEM, Federal Judicial Center.

[19] Wagner, D. and C. Baird (1993). *Evaluation of the Florida Community Control Program,* NCJ (January).

[20] Hofer, P. and B. Meierhoefer (1987). HOME CONFINEMENT, AN EVOLVING SANCTION IN THE FEDERAL CRIMINAL JUSTICE SYSTEM, Federal Judicial Center.

[21] *State v. Kelly,* 644 A.2d 454 (Me. 1994).

[22] Johnson (1990). *Convict in Home Custody is Charged in a Killing.* NEW YORK TIMES, Dec. 2.

[23] Christianson (1995). *Defective Electronic Equipment May Lead to Further Criminal and Civil Liability.* COMMUNITY CORRECTIONS REPORT, July/August.

[24] ABA CRIMINAL JUSTICE SECTION STANDARDS, HOME CONFINEMENT.

[25] *Fraley v. United States Bureau of Prisons,* 1 F.3d 924 (9th Cir. 1993).

[26] *United States v. Edwards,* 960 F.2d 278 (2d Cir. 1992); *United States v. Insley,* 927 F.2d 185 (4th Cir. 1991); *United States v. Wickman,* 955 F.2d 592 (8th Cir. 1992) (en banc); *cf. United States v. Zackular,* 945 F.2d 423 (1st Cir. 1991) (district court erred, allowed time spent under house arrest to be credited as official detention).

[27] *United States v. Woods,* 888 F.2d 653 (10th Cir. 1989), *cert. denied,* 494 U.S. 1006, 110 S. Ct. 1301, 108 L. Ed. 2d 478 (1990).

[28] *State v. Muratella,* 240 Neb. 567, 483 N.W.2d 128 (Neb. 1992).

[29] See, *e.g., People v. Ramos,* 133 Ill. 2d 152, 561 N.E.2d 643 (1990); *State v. Pettis,* 149 Wis. 2d 207, 441 N.W.2d 247 (1989); *State ex rel. Moomau v. Hamilton,* 184 W. Va. 251, 400 S.E.2d 259 (1990).

[30] *People v. Reinertson,* 223 Cal. Rptr. 670 (Cal. Ct. App. 1986).

[31] *State v. Lubus,* 216 Conn. 402, 581 A.2d 1045 (1990).

[32] LA. CODE CRIM. PRO. ANN. art. 894.2 (I) (West Supp. 1995).

[33] Langan, P. and M. Cuniff (1992). *Recidivism of Felony Probationers, 1986-1989.* SPECIAL REPORT. Washington DC: Bureau of Justice Statistics (Feb.).

[34] General Accounting Office (1990). INTERMEDIATE SANCTIONS: THEIR IMPACTS ON PRISON CROWDING, COSTS, AND RECIDIVISM ARE STILL UNCLEAR. Gaithersburg, MD: General Accounting Office.

[35] Camp, G. and C. Camp THE CORRECTIONS YEARBOOK: PROBATION AND PAROLE. South Salem, NY: Criminal Justice Institute.

[36] Wilson, J. (1981). *What Works? Revisited: New Findings on Criminal Rehabilitation.* PUBLIC INTEREST 3, 13-16 (Spring).

[37] See, *e.g.,* Mellinger v. Idaho Department of Corrections, 114 Idaho App. 494, 7567 P.2d 1213 (1988) (parole).

[38] Petersilia, J. and S. Turner (1993). *Evaluating Intensive Supervision Probation/Parole: Results of a Nationwide Experiment.* RESEARCH IN BRIEF. Washington DC: National Institute of Justice (May 1993).

[39] Petersilia, J. and S. Turner (1993). *Evaluating Intensive Supervision Probation/Parole: Results of a Nationwide Experiment.* RESEARCH IN BRIEF. Washington DC: National Institute of Justice (May).

[40] *Ibid.* 5.

[41] See, *e.g.,* Gendreau, P., F. Cullen and J. Bonta (1994). *Intensive Rehabilitation Supervision: The Next Generation in Community Corrections?* FEDERAL PROBATION 58:1 p. 72-78 (March 1994).

[42] Lipsey, M. (1992). *Juvenile Deliquency Treatment: A Meta-Analytic Inquiry into the Variability of Effects.* In T. Cook, H. Cooper, D. Cordray, H. Hartmann, L. Hedges, R. Light, T. Louis and F. Mosteller (eds.), META-ANALYSIS FOR EXPLANATION, 83-127. New York, NY: Sage Foundation.

[43] See, *e.g.,* Gendreau, P., F. Cullen and J. Bonta (1994). *Intensive Rehabilitation Supervision: The Next Generation in Community Corrections?* FEDERAL PROBATION 58:1 p. 72-78 (March 1994); D. Andrews and J. Bonta (1994). THE PSYCHOLOGY OF CRIMINAL CONDUCT. Cincinnati, OH: Anderson.

[44] Gendreau, *et. al. op. cit.* p. 77.

[45] Interview with John Larivee, President of the Crime and Justice Foundation, May, 1995.

[46] ME. REV. STAT. ANN. tit. 17-A, § 1264(2)(A)-(G) (1983).

[47] Interview with H. Sinkinson, October 25, 1995.

[48] *Sandin v. Conner,* 115 S. Ct. 2293 (1995).

[49] *Harper v. Young,* 644 F.3d 563 (10th Cir. 1995).

[50] Dolescal, E. (undated). *Median Time Served by Prison Inmates.* JUST THE FACTS. American Institute of Criminal Justice.

[51] STANDARDS RELATING TO SENTENCING ALTERNATIVES AND PROCEDURES 56 (Approved Draft 1968).

[52] See, *e.g.,* Beck (1987). BUREAU OF JUSTICE STATISTICS, RECIDIVISM AMONG YOUNG PAROLEES. Washington DC: U.S. Department of Justice (May).

[53] *Id.* at § 24(a).

[54] 18 U.S.C. § 3583(a),),(b)(1-3) (Supp. II 1984) (effective Nov. 1, 1986).

[55] See, *e.g., Commonwealth v. Nickens,* 259 Pa. Super. 143, 393 A.2d 758 (1978) (in which the court upheld the first use of partial commitment despite the appellant's argument that it was inconsistent with the purpose of sentencing and without historic precedent).

[56] See, *e.g.,* ARIZ. REV. STAT. ANN. § 13-901(F) (Supp. 1985) (one year in county jail); COLO. REV. STAT. § 16-11-202 (1978) (90 days for felony); IND. CODE ANN. § 35-38-2-2(c),(d) (Burns 1985) (within the period of probation, 60 days if intermittent).

[57] See, *e.g., State v. Chvirko,* 23 Conn. Supp. 355, 183 A.2d 629 (1962) and *Tabor v. Maxwell,* 175 Ohio 373, 194 N.E.2d 856 (1963) (upholding the condition). *Contra, Boyne v. State,* 586 P.2d 1250 (Alaska 1978); *People v. Pickett,* 16 Ill. App. 3d 166, 305 N.E.2d 551 (1973) (overruling the condition).

[58] *Villery v. Florida Parole and Probation Commission,* 396 So. 2d 1107 (Fla. 1981).

[59] *State v. Rocgue,* 104 Idaho 445, 660 P.2d 57 (1983).

[60] STANDARDS RELATING TO SENTENCING ALTERNATIVES AND PROCEDURES 74-80 (Approved Draft 1968); MODEL PENAL CODE § 301.1(3) (Proposed Official Draft 1962). But see PRESIDENT'S COMMISSION ON LAW ENFORCEMENT AND ADMINISTRATION OF JUSTICE, CORRECTIONS 43-35 (1976) (arguing that incarceration defeats the aims of probation).

[61] 1965 OHIO LAWS 131 v 684, codified as OHIO REV. CODE § 2947.061 (Supp. 1986).

[62] Allen, H. and C. Simonsen (1981). CORRECTIONS IN AMERICA 161; see also, J. Scott (1974). PIONEERING INNOVATIONS IN CORRECTIONS: SHOCK PROBATION AND SHOCK PAROLE 41.

[63] See, e.g., TEX. CODE CRIM. PROC. ANN. art. 42.12. §§ 3e(a), 3f(a) (Vernon Supp. 1986) (within 60 to 180 days for felonies and 10 to 90 for misdemeanors).

[64] Described in § 5.04.

[65] FED. R. CRIM. P. 35 (b).

[66] See, e.g., MASS. GEN LAWS ANN. ch. 279, § 6A (West 1981) (limited to first-time incarcerations); MICH. COMP. LAWS ANN. § 771.3(2)(a) (West Supp. 1986) (imprisonment at such time or intervals consecutive or nonconsecutive within probation period but not more than 12 months); OR. REV. STAT. § 137.520(2) (1985) (court may order sheriff to arrange for prisoner to continue his employment); WIS. STAT. ANN. §973.09(4) (West 1985) (county jail between hours of employment not to exceed a year, defendant to pay costs).

[67] 18 U.S.C. § 3563 (a)(11) (Supp. II 1984) (effective Nov. 1, 1986) (remain in the custody of the Bureau of Prisons during nights, weekends or other intervals of time, totaling no more than the lesser of one year or the term of imprisonment authorized for the offense . . . during the first year of the term of probation).

[68] State v. Williams, 237 So. 2d 69 (Fla. Dist. Ct. App. 1970).

[69] See STANDARDS RELATING TO SENTENCING ALTERNATIVES AND PROCEDURES § 2.4 (a) (1968); PRESIDENT'S COMMISSION ON LAW ENFORCEMENT AND ADMINISTRATION OF JUSTICE, CORRECTIONS 28 (1967).

[70] Byrne, J., A. Lurigio and J. Petersilia (1992). SMART SENTENCING. Newbury Park, CA: Sage Publications.

[71] Cowles, E. and T. Castellano (1995). Boot Camp Drug Treatment and Aftercare Intervention: An Evaluative Review. NIJ RESEARCH REPORT, July, citing a 1993 American Correctional Association Report.

[72] MacKenzie, D. (1993). Boot Camp Prisons in 1993. NATIONAL INSTITUTE OF JUSTICE JOURNAL. Washington DC: U.S. Department of Justice (November).

[73] Fed Awards $20 million for Boot Camps. ALTERNATIVES TO INCARCERATION 1:4, Fall 1995.

[74] Byrne, J., A. Lurigio and J. Petersilia (1992). SMART SENTENCING. Newbury Park, CA: Sage Publications.

[75] Specter (1984-1985). Making America's Cities Safer: Reforming the Criminal Justice System. 9 PERSPECTIVES 17, 20 (Winter).

[76] United States v. Traitz, 807 F.2d 322 (3d Cir. 1986).

Chapter 10

Enforcing Alternative Sentences

§10.01   Introduction

No matter what alternative sentence or intermediate sanction is imposed by the court, whether it includes restitution to victims, house arrest, mandatory treatment, urine testing, cash donations, electronic monitoring or more, it will only be as effective as its enforcement. Unenforced sanctions jeopardize any sentence, undermining its credibility and potential to address serious sentencing concerns, including victim protection, offender accountability and offender rehabilitation or public safety. Unenforced alternative sentences and intermediate sanctions are like sentences to prisons with cell doors that do not lock and perimeter gates that slip open. The moment the word gets out that the alternative sentence or intermediate sanction is unmonitored is the moment the court loses another sentencing option.

Alternative sentences and intermediate sanctions are enforced equivalently with one basic exception. Generally, alternative sentences are conditions of probation, enforced by probation officers. Intermediate sanctions are often, although not uniformly, specific sentences created by statute, enforceable by parole authorities. Violations of the former are returned to court for further sentencing. Violations of the latter are returned to the parole board or its equivalent for imprisonment. In either case, however, the powers of probation and parole officers are very similar. The hearings afforded probation and parole violators are analogous.

§10.02   Monitoring Alternative Sentences and Intermediate Sanctions

The criminal justice system pays an enormous amount of money to monitor incarcerated offenders. However, similar offenders who are allowed to remain on the streets are often virtually ignored. If just a portion of the resources that went into institutional corrections went to community-based correctional monitoring, there would be no problem insuring that offenders complied with their alternative sentences. Unfortunately, such is not the case. A national news magazine reported that, as of 1980, the Justice Department maintained a roster of 18,000 federal offenders who owed almost $100 million in unpaid fines and forfeitures. Included in this group was G. Gordon Liddy, who owed $35,000 in fines for Watergate-related crimes.[1]

Victims all too often find that the restitution that judges awarded them in court never reaches them. In recognition of this, Congress enacted legislation in the federal system giving victims the right to sue offenders civilly for unpaid restitution, as they would for an unpaid civil award.[2] Most state laws do not provide for this last-resort measure for victims seeking court-ordered restitution payments.

Even the minimal supervision provision of traditional probation is wanting in many major metropolitan areas of the country. According to a 1980 audit by the Comptroller of the City of New York, almost one-half of the mandatory office visits by probationers were not kept. More than 70 percent of probationers violated the terms of their probation an average of 4.7 times. Yet little was done about these violations. In one-third of the cases in which probationers failed to report, the court was not even notified. In another 10 percent, it took six months for the court to be notified.[3]

However, examples of effective monitoring of alternative sentences and intermediate sanctions abound, proving their possibility. A preliminary report of the Florida Community Control program, the community-based saturation surveillance program that includes mandatory community work service orders, curfews, restitution and house arrest, found that not only did assigned officers meet the required 28 offender contacts per month, they exceeded them on the average by 14 contacts per offender.[4] The Justice Department found adequate monitoring in 65 restitution and community work service programs it funded around the country. As a result, the programs could report consistently high completion rates of court orders, averaging over 80 percent. Further, this high completion rate occurred in both major metropolitan centers such as Washington, D.C. and rural areas such as Waterloo, Iowa.[5]

Serendipitously, alternative sentences and intermediate sanctions are relatively easy to monitor. They are generally finite, based on easily measurable behavior, as opposed to things impossible to measure such as positive attitude changes and the like. Either the offender pays the monetary sanction or does not, remains drug free or not, remains in the house in a house arrest situation or not, completes community work service or not. The onus for monitoring compliance can be placed on a third party or, often, the offender's shoulders. Offenders ordered to complete a specified number of community work service hours can bring into the court a certified report testifying to their compliance. Or the court or its agent can contact the work site to ascertain compliance. Victims owed restitution can be contacted to determine that amounts are paid or the court can require payments to be processed through it so that records can be obtained. Many of the intensive probation supervision programs require offenders to recruit reliable third parties to vouch for their continued good behavior in the community. Similar third parties can be recruited by the defense lawyer or the court to assist in efforts to monitor the offender.

Good alternative sentences and intermediate sanctions have built-in monitoring capability.

§10.03   Contracting Conditions

In order to insure proper monitoring, the provisions of the alternative sentence should be reduced to a written contract spelling out specifically what the defendant is required to do and when. The contract should be behaviorally specific. Rather than admonish the defendant that he is "not to associate with persons of bad character," for example, the contract should specify "not to associate with the following co-defendants." The co-defendants should then be listed. If the sentence contains a monetary sanction, the contract should state what is due and how the payments should be made, for example, "$300 in restitution is to be paid at the rate of $25 a week commencing this date and paid each week until the entire amount is paid." Community work service orders should have similar deadlines and installment requirements.

The contracts should also specify what tolerance, if any, will be allowed for nonperformance. It may contain a provision that reads: "I understand that if I miss two weekly payments I will reappear before the court for further sentencing." Contracts may also contain penalty clauses, increasing sanctions automatically if certain deadlines are not met. "I understand that if I fail to complete 50 hours of community work service by November 15, an additional 10 hours will be added to my order."

The court or the agency or person monitoring compliance should maintain simple ledgers tracking the defendant's performance. If the defendant is ordered to pay money, the ledger should record each payment as it comes in. The regular disbursement to the victim should be similarly recorded. If the defendant is under house arrest and the confinement is monitored through random house calls, each call should be logged into a ledger by date and time. Similarly, if the offender is ordered to remain drug and alcohol free, each random urine, blood or saliva test result should be logged into a ledger by date. The ledgers should reveal at a glance whether the offender is in compliance with the order. These may be used either as evidence or notes to refresh the memory of the monitor in any subsequent hearing.

If the probationer is ordered into mandatory treatment, release forms should be executed prior to entrance into the treatment program. This will allow the treatment program to release information to the court, ascertaining the probationer's attendance and progress.

If the defendant fails in his compliance, the monitor should alert the defendant directly and the parties responsible for enforcing the sentence. Successful completion depends upon speedy action at the first signs of noncompliance. If nothing is done, the arrearage or noncompliance might increase to the point where the situation is no longer remediable. If the defendant is in a mandatory treatment program for alcoholism, drugs or compulsive behavior, slips tend to be progressive and call for even stricter controls and monitoring.

§10.04   The Role of Probation/Parole Officers

In most cases, it falls to probation and parole officers to monitor alternative and intermediate sanctions. Although what the offenders are required to do may be different, the role of monitoring them doing it is traditional for probation and parole officers. New York's probation statute, for example, provides that, among other things, probation officers are "to keep informed concerning (the probationer's) conduct, habits, associates, employment, recreation, and whereabouts. . . ."[6] The revised Federal Code similarly provides that the probation officer is to "keep informed concerning the conduct, conditions and compliance with any condition of probation, including the payment of a fine or restitution of each probationer under his supervision and report thereon to the court placing such person on probation and report to the court any failure of a probationer under his supervision to pay a fine in default within 30 days after notification that it is in default so that the court may determine whether probation should be revoked. . . ."[7]

Power of Arrest

To fulfill their monitoring duties, officers have considerable powers. First and foremost, they can arrest offenders whom they have reasonable suspicion to believe are not doing what they are supposed to be doing. For example, the New Jersey Supreme Court said it was not unconstitutional for probation officers to arrest probationers for *any* violation, even if the violation does not constitute a violation of any law. Probationers, like parolees, have a special status, one outside standard constitutional guarantees.[8] Regarding their caseloads, officers have greater arrest powers than regular law enforcement officials.

Power to Require Reporting

Second, officers can insist that the offenders report to them or vice versa at any reasonable time or on a periodic basis. The federal code, much like that of most states, provides that the probationer must "permit a probation officer to visit him at his home or elsewhere as specified by the court. . . ."[9] Also, like many state codes, the federal code provides that probationers must "answer inquiries by a probation officer and notify the probation officer promptly of any change in address or employment."[10] Like some state laws, the probationer must also "notify the probation officer promptly if arrested or questioned by a law enforcement officer. . . ."[11]

The Florida District Court of Appeals, for example, has specifically ruled that the probationer's failure to follow routine reporting instructions is enough to require revocation. One missed visit made up 24 hours later, however, where there was evidence of confusion was not, in and of itself, enough for revocation.[12]

Although responding to rumors that a probationer had marijuana plants growing in his house, the probation officer had every right to demand that the probationer admit him to his house based on state law authorizing the probation officer to conduct home visits.[13] In the instant case, the probation officer brought with him two police officers. The appellate court ruled that the probationer had every right to deny entrance to the two police officers, but not the probation officer. A home visit, the appellate court concluded, does not constitute a search.[14]

In some jurisdictions, police act as supplemental probation/parole monitors. In Long Beach, California, for example, police are provided with a list of area adults on probation. They are encouraged to make random and unannounced visits to probationer's homes and places of employment. If violations are found, they notify probation officers.[15] In Quincy, Massachusetts, probation disseminates to police the pictures and *modus operandi* of all sex offenders on probation where they live and work if different from where they were arrested. In addition, conditions of their probation, such as no contact with children, are included so that police can report any probation violations. If similar crimes occur, the police can use the probationer's photo in a photo array to either eliminate or identify him as a suspect.[16]

Implied in the federal code and explicitly inserted in some by state statute, probationers must not only answer questions regarding their status asked by officers, but they must answer truthfully. Probationers can even be called as witnesses at revocation hearings to testify against themselves as long as they are not required to admit guilt to a new crime in some jurisdictions.[17] A Michigan appellate court, on the other hand, disagrees, ruling that unless the probationer agrees to take the stand, the court cannot insist that he answer questions.[18]

The Eleventh Circuit provides several examples that are instructive of the power of probation and parole officers. In the first, a probationer invoked his Fifth Amendment right against self-incrimination when his probation officer asked him to account for $25,000 income reported on his tax return. The probationer's tax return raised the officer's suspicion that the probationer was engaged in unlawful money smuggling activities—a clear violation of his probation. When the probationer failed to report these activities completely and truthfully according to the terms of his probation, he committed a probation violation.

The court ruled that although the probationer had a right to invoke his right not to incriminate himself, the probation department had a right to revoke his probation for refusing to answer or using his silence "as one of a number of factors to be considered by the finder of fact" in deciding whether one of the conditions of probation had been violated. The issue is not an invocation of the privilege, but failure to report. Further, relying on a First Circuit case,[19] the court went on to find that "there is no question that the failure to comply with reporting requirements is a serious violation . . . and that alone is enough for revocation."[20]

In a parole case, a federal parolee lied to his parole officer regarding his employment. Charged and convicted under 19 U.S.C. § 1001, which prohibits the willful falsification of statements made to an administrative agency, the court upheld his conviction even though he had not been read his *Miranda* rights. The court found that the parolee's lies were designed to frustrate the parole board.[21]

Conditions may also be imposed that make it easier for the officer to determine the truthfulness of the offender under supervision. By statute, for example, California probationers' convicted of drunk driving are required to submit to a breath test whenever stopped by a police officer. Unlike non-probationers who are stopped, they are not allowed to refuse to submit to the test. The Idaho Supreme Court allowed evidence against a sex offender obtained by a polygraph test required by probation. While the court did not rule on the reliability of the evidence (because the probationer did not question it), it upheld the revocation based, in part, on the negative polygraph results.[22]

Other courts have ruled on the reliability of polygraphs and have found them acceptable in the context of revocation hearings, if not criminal trials. The Florida District Court of Appeals, sitting *en banc,* disagreed with prior decisions, barring such evidence. In that case, the court found that the judge had set forth substantial findings indicating her reasoning for imposing the polygraph condition. The judge ordered that the defendant, a sex offender, submit to a polygraph test at least once every six months for the first two years and then once every year thereafter. The polygraph examiner was to ask the defendant only two questions: "Have you been alone with a child?" Have you had any manner of sexual contact with a child?" The sentencing judge explained:

> The Court imposes the special condition based on research which
> shows that this is a valid and effective deterrent to reoffend and is
> both valid and effective in dealing with denial . . . [which is] . . . cru-
> cial in dealing with evaluation of rehabilitation of sex offenders . . .

> in large part because sex crimes, particularly with children, are
> secret crimes as to which it is very difficult to make an effective
> [probation order to insure] detection or an effective way to monitor
> whether we are having a violation of either the Community Control
> (Florida's intensive supervision program) or the probation.[23]

While the above case involved a sex offender, other courts have upheld
polygraphs used to monitor burglars[24] and drug offenders.[25] Oregon approves of
polygraphs as a condition of probation by statute.[26]

Further, officers can use non-Mirandized confessions against probationers
in revocation hearings that are not allowed in new criminal trials. For example,
the Massachusetts Supreme Judicial Court allowed a probationer's revocation to
be based on such a confession even though the confession had not been allowed
to be used against him at trial which consequently resulted in a hung jury. Subsequently, the probation officer used the confession at a revocation hearing
based on the same, new criminal behavior.[27]

The Supreme Court of Vermont visited this issue in a 1992 case involving a
sex offender ordered, among other things, not to use drugs. In a routine office
visit, he told his probation officer in response to a question that he had smoked
marijuana. In a subsequent meeting, he told the probation officer he smoked
once a week to once a month. Later he said he smoked one to two joints a day.
The probation officer successfully moved to revoke his probation based on the
defendant's admission to him of marijuana use.

Even assuming that his status as a probationer forced him to answer his
probation officer and that a refusal to answer under a claim of self-incrimination could be grounds to revoke probation, the state supreme court still stated it
would uphold the revocation. After all, the confession was used in a revocation,
not a new criminal proceeding. If probationers were allowed to withhold
information from their probation officers, the core purpose of probation would
be undermined, the court concluded. The court went on to add that, absent
Miranda rights being given, the confession cannot be used in a new criminal
trial. But:

> [t]o require a probation officer to explicitly assure a probationer that
> any statements made will not be used against a probationer in a
> criminal proceeding to make them admissible in a revocation pro-
> ceeding is an overtechnical use of the law for no apparent purpose.[28]

In 1984, the United States Supreme Court ruled on a case in which the probationer, in response to his probation officer's interrogation, confessed to a murder. The probation officer had not warned the probationer previously of his
Miranda rights. The confession was used against him at a subsequent criminal
trial (not probation revocation). The Court upheld the confession's use, rejecting
the argument that mandatory probation visits and the requirement that probationers answer questions truthfully put the probationer, in effect, in a custodial
situation.[29]

Of course, probation officers may not obtain non-Mirandized confessions from probationers if they happen to be in the cell block at the time or if they knowingly circumvent the accused's rights to have counsel present in a confrontation between the accused and an agent of the state. The Supreme Court of Washington, for example, ruled it impermissible for a probation agent to advise a probationer he should confess his crime in order to gain admission to treatment, even though the probation officer knew the probationer was appealing the conviction of first degree murder. The probationer did not confess at first but later contacted the probation officer to return to talk to him.[30]

Power to Search

Third, as discussed in § 3.04, probation and parole officers may also conduct reasonable searches of probationers/parolees without a warrant. As the Minnesota Supreme Court noted, in its ruling upholding warrantless searches by probation officers, it is in the defendant's ultimate interests that a probation officer be able to fulfill his mission:

> [I]t might be added that putting onerous restrictions on the ability of the probation officer to protect the public interest may actually deter courts from a judicious use of probation in the future in a marginal case. A court's uncertainty as to the ability of a probation officer to supervise his probationers closely may tip the balance when it comes to sentencing.[31]

Even in Massachusetts, where the state supreme court refused to follow the United States Supreme Court in *Griffin*[32] (which allows warrantless searches by probation officers) because the state constitution's Bill of Rights were drawn more strictly than the federal Bill of Rights, that high court proposed drug testing as a less invasive alternative.

Drug and alcohol testing also help officers monitor their offenders' behavior as discussed in § 8.05.

Given the leeway allowed probation and parole officers in supervising offenders, coupled with the resources necessary for monitoring them in the community, there is little reason that even complicated and demanding alternative and intermediate sanctions cannot be monitored successfully.

§10.05 Revoking Probation or Parole

Revoking probation or parole is the basic mechanism used to enforce violations of alternative sentences or intermediate sanctions. The only exception might include special offender status such as an unconfined inmate reporting to, for example, a day reporting center. If the offender violates conditions of the day reporting center program or absconds, he may be treated as a prison escapee. Upon apprehension, he is simply returned to prison from which he was never legally released to begin with.[33]

Probationers or parolees may be brought back for a revocation hearing based on two classes of violations—new crime violations or technical violations, any other condition such as reporting, abstinence from drug use, program participation and the like. Most statutes specify that probation officers are authorized to file probation violation charges before the court. A dozen mention other officials, usually prosecutors. Probationers may be summoned to court to face revocation or may be arrested and brought to court. If arrested, generally, they have a right to bail. Several states, however, require that they be held without bail pending the hearing.[34]

Where a probation officer filed a motion to revoke probation even though not authorized to do so specifically by statute, an Indiana appeals court refused to reverse the subsequent revocation. The court was concerned when the petition should be filed, not by whom it should be filed.[35] In another case, another appellate court upheld the judge himself filing the petition to revoke. In the case above, the probationer was still in prison and had not been assigned a probation officer yet. The violation involved a jail infraction. As a result, when the judge was informed, the judge filed the petition to revoke the defendant's probation. The Alabama appellate court allowed the judge to conduct the hearing and revoke the probation without probation involvement.[36]

Before the due process revolution of the Warren Court, probation and parole were considered an act of grace that could be given and taken away with equal ease, especially the latter. The probationer or parolee had few due process rights to contest his or her revocation. No hearing was even required. However, this all changed in the early 1970s.

First, in *Mempa v. Rhay*,[37] the Supreme Court ruled that probationers were entitled to attorneys in certain cases when sentences were imposed. Then, in *Morrissey v. Brewer*,[38] the Court ruled that a parolee had basic due process rights. These included the right to a hearing before his parole could be revoked. The hearing need not be formal, the Court ruled, but must be based on verified fact. It must consist of two parts, a preliminary hearing to be conducted by an independent hearing officer and a final hearing before the parole board. The preliminary hearing was required to be held relatively quickly so that the parolee did not languish in prison awaiting the full hearing on whether his parole should be revoked permanently. Upon a finding of probable cause, the parolee must be given a more extensive final hearing.

The Court specified the format of the hearings. The parolee must be given notice specifying the violations alleged. The parolee was given the right to appear at the hearing, give evidence and cross-examine adverse witnesses to a limited degree.

On the heels of *Morrissey*, the Supreme Court ruled in *Gagnon v. Scarpelli*[39] that these same rights applied to probationers even though the hearing would take place before a judge, not a lay board. The Court also held that if the probationer maintained his innocence and the defense were complicated, a lawyer should be appointed for the probationer.

A number of state statutes spell out the standards for probation revocations based on these rulings. Some specify notice requirements, time frames to be followed, character of the hearings and so forth. Other states with no such statutes, or statutes enacted before the Supreme Court set its parameters, rely on state case law to define the revocation process. In almost all cases, the process is designed to be reasonably efficient and informal. After all, the hearings are not criminal proceedings, but civil or quasi-civil in nature. The standard of proof is not, in most instances, beyond a reasonable doubt, but the civil standard of a preponderance of the evidence.

Some states allow revocations if the fact finder is "reasonably satisfied." These include Rhode Island, South Dakota, Alabama, Montana and at least one federal circuit ruling.[40] In Connecticut the standard was once "reliable and probative," but was changed to a preponderance of the evidence in 1994.[41]

Notice

Generally, probationers are required to receive prior written notice of the alleged violations of their probation. Failure to give notice, however, has been ruled not to be fatal for a subsequent revocation. The Illinois Supreme Court, for example, ruled that where the record showed that the defendant and his attorney were present for the state's petition to revoke the probation and where the attorney fully participated and cross-examined government witnesses and never objected to the hearing on grounds of lack of notice, there was no prejudice shown and even if no notice had been given, the court refused to reverse the revocation.[42] Similarly, an Arkansas appellate court ruled that as long as oral notice was given, if no objection is raised, the lack of written notice required by state statute constitutes harmless error.

On the other hand, Louisiana demands a warrant or summons for a revocation hearing to be accompanied by a supporting affidavit, sworn to under oath before a revocation hearing may go forward.[43]

The content of the notice is of concern to appellate courts, also. Generally, it must be specific enough so the probationer knows what he is being accused of violating. To this end the notice must include what the alleged violation is, where it occurred and when or during what time period. In upholding a revocation based on three allegations, the Massachusetts Supreme Judicial Court found two of them to be impermissibly vague.

1. During the term of probation, you have violated criminal laws of the United States and of the Commonwealth, any ordinance of a municipality of said Commonwealth or the criminal law of the United States.

2. You have engaged in an anti-social conduct which shall furnish good cause for the Court to believe that the probationary order should be revoked in the public interest.

The third allegation passed muster and allowed the court to uphold the revocation.

3. You have failed to pay restitution in the sum of $26,028.41 and court costs in the sum of $8,000 as submitted by the plan dated March 10, 1978.[44]

Counsel

Many states hold that probationers have an absolute right to counsel at revocation hearings. Florida, for example, requires counsel for revocation hearings but not parole hearings.[45] The federal probation statute also provides for the right to counsel.[46] The failure of judges to appoint counsel for indigent offenders constitutes reversible error.[47] So does failure to allow time for probationers to secure their own counsel or for counsel to prepare their defense.[48] If the probationer waives his right to counsel, the waiver must be knowing and intelligent, not based on a promise from the probation officer.[49] Nor may the waiver be allowed if the revocation judge fails to inform the probationer what his possible sentence is if probation is revoked.[50]

On the other hand, other jurisdictions hold that the need for counsel is at the discretion of the judge, to be decided on a case-by-case basis. While there is no absolute right, counsel may be necessary if the defendant insists that he is innocent or wishes to offer mitigation, which makes his revocation inappropriate.[51]

Not only may counsel be required, but the counsel has to be competent—at least in California, where an appellate court remanded a case because it was concerned that the defense attorney's failure to help his client gain admission into drug treatment may have hurt the probationer in qualifying for possible reinstatement on probation.[52]

Hearing

Although the original United States Supreme Court decisions talked about both a preliminary and final hearing, in most cases appellate courts now require only one hearing. Back when the Supreme Court made its ruling, most defendants were incarcerated pending their revocation hearing. Now many are not. As a result, the courts are less worried about defendants spending time in prison while waiting for allegations against them to be proven. If defendants are not held pending their revocation hearing, or are being held on unrelated matters, appellate courts do not require both a preliminary and final hearing.

There are two parts to a revocation hearing. First, the fact finder must find that the defendant violated his conditions. Second, the fact finder must decide what to do about it. In some jurisdictions, like Hawaii, the court in a probation revocation hearing must decide if the violations are "substantial" enough to warrant incarceration. As will be discussed in § 10.08, some courts require new presentence investigation reports at this stage and defendants are allowed the right of allocution.

Discovery

Because formal rules of evidence do not apply in revoking probation or parole in most jurisdictions, usually the defense has no right of discovery.[53] However, consistent with basic concepts of fairness, given that revocation may lead to loss of liberty, many appellate courts have found it reversible error when discovery was not allowed in specific cases. For example, an Arizona appellate court found pre-hearing discovery to be desirable where the defense wanted to depose the probation officer, because it held that its defense was based on improper actions of the probation officer. In this case, the probation officer had refused to talk to the defense.[54]

On the other hand, although the Arkansas Supreme Court gives the defense the right of discovery in revocations, it held, in at least one case, that the court's failure to allow the same constituted harmless error where no prejudice to the defense resulted.[55]

Federal hearings are governed by Federal Rule of Criminal Procedure 32.1(a)(2)(B), which requires the right of discovery. Again, in a case in which the government failed to provide copies of the probation officer's records and notes to the defense, the Ninth Circuit upheld the revocation because the government did not introduce the requested records and only referred to them in cross-examination.[56] The court ruled that the government's failure violated neither the rules of criminal procedure nor due process.

Timeliness

Generally, the revocation must occur within a reasonable period after the allegations have been made. Originally, the United States Supreme Court was concerned that they be held quickly so offenders did not languish in jail. Because many probationers are not incarcerated pending revocations, the concerns now may be to proceed quickly on the part of the government to protect the public safety. In any event, the defendant must be given reasonable time and notice.

The decision to petition for revocation is within the discretion of the state. At least one appellate court has ruled that if it withdraws its petition, that does not preclude it refiling it at a later time.[57] Similarly, federal circuits and others have upheld states that move to revoke, then withdrew their motions when their witness did not show. When the witness was secured later, the state moved again to revoke. The defendants' claim that the state's action constituted double jeopardy was rejected.[58] At least one state appellate court, however, held that it was wrong to allow a second parole revocation after the first one was reversed on appeal.[59]

The Florida District Court of Appeals has ruled that a defendant's right to a speedy trial does not apply to revocation proceedings.[60] On the other hand, an Ohio appellate court has ruled that the state must proceed with the hearing with due diligence pursuant to *Gagnon*.[61] If the probationer voluntarily absents himself, the court may proceed with a revocation hearing without him or her.[62] The Connecticut Supreme Court, for example, upheld a revocation that was conducted after the probationer absented himself and went to another state where he was incarcerated.[63] Subsequent incarceration, before the hearing has commenced, however, does not count as a voluntary absence.[64]

Most jurisdictions agree that defendants may be revoked for conduct that occurs after they were sentenced but *before* they are released on probation. Most of the federal circuits have ruled similarly, interpreting 18 U.S.C. § 3653 (West 1985) as allowing revocation prior to commencement of probation.[65] As one stated in its rationale in such circumstances: "[T]he power to revoke probation permits the correction of a sentence based on an erroneous assumption that a defendant would benefit from lenience." Where a defendant displays tendencies indicating that he is unworthy of the opportunity for rehabilitation, the court saw no reason for restricting the judge's ability to revoke probation to the period before the beginning of a defendant's probationary sentence.[66]

Appellate courts allow for conduct, such as rule infractions committed while the offender is incarcerated before being released to probation on a split sentence to form the basis of a violation of probation.[67] Crimes committed within custody also count.[68] They also allow for new crimes committed or discovered after sentencing but before commencement of probation.[69] They allow for parole violations to be considered if the parole precedes the probationary period.[70] Finally, they have upheld violations of a dirty urine sample found when the defendant reported for drug treatment before his probation began or for other rule infractions in a residential program.[71]

The following facts represent one of the few cases in which an appellate court ruled that revocation was *not* allowed for pre-probation misconduct. After convicting the offender of burglary, the trial court continued the case so the defendant could be evaluated for drug addiction. The evaluation revealed that the defendant was an addict. He was sentenced to concurrent imprisonment and probation under the supervision of a treatment facility. When he appeared for booking at the jail, cocaine was found on him. New criminal charges were filed. The defendant was returned to court for revocation. Notwithstanding the new violations, the defendant was recommended for treatment again. The court, instead, committed him. On appeal, the Illinois appellate court ruled that the defendant was entitled to resentencing because he should have been given the opportunity to begin therapy for his drug addiction.

Perhaps the reason this jurisdiction's path is so different from most others is the emphasis in Illinois state law promoting secure treatment for drug addicts. As described earlier, an Illinois appellate court similarly disallowed bumper stickers for drunk drivers, citing legislative intent that drunk drivers receive treatment, not the punishment represented by mandatory bumper stickers.

On the other side of the coin, appellate courts are very much divided regarding violations that occur after the period of probation is over. For example, pursuant to federal statute, probationary periods run for five years. What happens if the probationer absconds and does not reappear until the sixth year or spends a year during that period in jail for another offense? The majority of federal circuits allow the time period when the probationer is unavailable to be "tolled," not counted toward the five-year limit.[72]

Many states have followed suit.[73] However, some appellate courts demand that courts make an effort to proceed with revocation hearings, even if the defendant is imprisoned on unrelated charges. In other words, the court must try to arrange for the prison to be brought to answer the revocation charges in a timely manner.[74] The standard is usually defined as "reasonable effort." In determining whether the effort has been reasonable, the Iowa Supreme Court has determined, for example, that it will look at four factors: (1) the state's diligence in attempting to serve the warrant; (2) the reason behind the delay in executing the warrant; (3) the conduct of the probationer that is frustrating service of the warrant; and (4) the prejudice suffered by the probationer resulting from any delay.[75]

In jurisdictions that demand such efforts to serve warrants, the onus is on the state to show it tried to serve its warrant. Absent any showing, if the offender is not brought to court after seven months or more after the hearing was scheduled, the case must be dismissed.[76] The Fifth Circuit has similarly addressed the issue of delayed revocation after the legal term of probation has ended. It ruled that such delayed hearings are allowable if the government made a "good faith effort" to proceed and no prejudice against the defendant was caused by the delay.[77] Other jurisdictions are not very demanding, recognizing that they cannot expect "spit and polish efficiency."[78]

Generally, the revocation notice must be sent out before the probationary period has ended. New Jersey mandates this in its law.[79]

Some courts, on the other hand, demand that the hearing be completed before the probation is officially terminated.[80] According to an Ohio appellate court, that state's statutory language is clear, even if the defendant absconds, the plain language of the law precludes revocation after the probationary term is over.[81] The Wyoming Supreme Court also ruled that revocations could not take place after the term had expired.[82] Responding to that decision, the state legislature passed legislation specifically allowing for such revocations if they commence within 30 days after the probation term expires.

Massachusetts appellate courts allow revocations to proceed after the defendant's probation has been officially terminated if, after termination, the court discovers that the offender committed a new offense while on probation before the case was terminated. The appellate court ruled that in such cases the probation was, in effect, terminated in error and the probationer may be brought back for revocation.[83]

Written Findings

Although the United States Supreme Court included written findings as part of the minimum due process in revocation proceedings, many jurisdictions have let this slide by. Usually they allow for the transcript of the proceedings themselves to qualify as the written findings, where they clearly spell out the judge's reasons and the evidence relied upon.[84] Others demand the findings be written out as literally required by law or the Supreme Court decisions.[85] The remedy, however, for failing to write up the required findings may not be reversal of the revocation, but remanding the case for the judge to finish the job.[86]

In a recent federal parole case, the Fifth Circuit ruled that the failure of the federal parole board to provide written findings of its decision to revoke a defendant's parole constituted "harmless error."[87] The court held that "the clarity of the testimony and the quality of the documentary evidence are sufficient to enable us to review the district court's implicit conclusions."

The Judge

Many jurisdictions require the same judge that heard the original case to also sit at the revocation if practical.[88] Other jurisdictions are silent on the matter. At least one requires that if the judge is not the judge that heard the original case, the state must prove by a preponderance of the evidence that the probationer before the revocation judge is, in fact, the same as the defendant placed on probation by the original judge.[89] In busy jurisdictions, the sentencing judge is not likely to remember the case anyway. If he does, he is not deemed to be prejudiced even though he obviously knows of the defendant's prior conviction.

No matter which judge sits on revocation, even though it is not technically a criminal proceeding, his or her role is prescribed. He or she still sits as a neutral fact finder, not a party to the surrender. The "prosecution" of the revocation is up to the state, whether represented by the probation officer or the prosecutor. It is not up to the judge. As a result, one appellate court has ruled that the judge may not interrogate the defendant, which would violate the judge's role as a fact finder.[90] Similarly, a Michigan appellate court ruled that a judge exceeded his authority and invaded the prosecutor's discretion when it dismissed the prosecution's petition to proceed with the revocation prior to a trial on new charges.[91]

Another judge was overruled when he refused to allow the probationer to speak on his own behalf or offer evidence.[92] Nor may judges turn the revocation hearing into a summary contempt hearing.[93] With few exceptions, contempt hearings may not be used to proceed with violations of probation.[94] Illinois specifically allows for contempt proceedings as a sanction for probation violations pursuant to state law[95] but an Illinois appellate court suggests that contempt is best suited for enforcement of conditions alone.[96]

§10.06   Evidence of Violation

Violations may involve specific terms and conditions imposed by the court or statute, or criminal conduct. Both *Morrissey* and *Gagnon* emphasize that revocation hearings should be flexible enough to consider evidence that may not be legal in full criminal trials. These cases talk about including as evidence letters, affidavits and other such material. Defendants do not have the same right of confrontation as in criminal trials either. Generally, for good cause, the revoking court may rely, to varying degrees, on hearsay.

The Seventh Circuit illustrates these parameters in *Egerstaffer v. Isreal.*[97] Probation was revoked based on the defendant's involvement in a new crime, robbing a man at gunpoint, possessing drugs and refusing to account for his activities at a certain date. The probationer appealed, claiming that his revocation was based on hearsay and other evidence, including his probation officer's notes, that should have been suppressed because they violated his Fourth and Fifth Amendment Rights. The court ruled that hearsay was permissible. Although the probationer was admittedly deprived of an opportunity to confront the witnesses against him, the court found "good cause" for their absence. The witness, also the victim in the case, was incapacitated after a fall. The court found the probation officer's notes, which contained statements made by the defendant, to be reliable. They were also corroborated by other witnesses. The revocation was upheld.

In another situation, in which the evidence used included a police report of a codefendant's allegations against the probationer, the Eighth Circuit ruled there was no good cause for the codefendant to be produced at the revocation.[98]

The Massachusetts Supreme Judicial Court has gone as far as any appellate court, allowing a revocation based on two police reports of separate incidents of drunk driving. The probation officer read the police reports into the record. Based solely on these reports, the probation was revoked. The court ruled that the two reports were credible, particularly because it is a crime for a police officer to file a false report. There was good cause not to require the arresting officers to present the evidence themselves because they worked outside the county in which the revocation hearing took place and the burden to them and their departments outweighed the probationer's right to confrontation. In the same decision, the court suggested other good cause to excuse witnesses may be cases of sexual assault in which it may represent too much of a "trauma" for victims to have to testify before grand juries, criminal trials *and* revocation hearings. "Society," it went on to state, "has an interest in not adding probation revocation hearings to that list."[99] The court did add that where hearsay is the only evidence, the indicia of reliability must be "substantial."

The defendant in the Massachusetts case appealed to the United States District Court, claiming that his federal constitutional rights were violated.[100] The United States District Court found no such violation, citing a number of cases including an Eight Circuit case that upheld a revocation based on a probation officer presenting a police report of an arrest. In that case, as in the Massachusetts case, the appellate court found that the police report was reliable, containing the defendant's name and an accurate physical description of him.[101]

The Connecticut Supreme Court calls for hearsay that has rational and probative force. In one case, the probation officer had testified that she saw two police arrest reports with affidavits sworn by the victims and she had telephoned one of the victims to confirm same. The revocation was allowed.[102]

As in the Massachusetts case, a California appellate court may have also recognized the special needs of a child sexual assault victim by upholding a revocation in which the child's father testified for his child. Although in the instant case, the court found that the father's testimony was based on the child's excited utterances to him. Given this, the appellate court ruled that the revoking court had no requirement to find that the actual witness, the child, was not available to testify. Interestingly, the child had testified in a similar case involving another person the year before.[103]

The Kansas Supreme Court reversed a trial court's dismissal of a revocation in which the trial court, among other things, erroneously refused to allow a revocation based on hearsay evidence in the form of an affidavit and a lab report, regarding a drug test.[104]

Some state codes specifically exempt revocation hearings from the state rules of evidence.[105]

On the other hand, a few states specifically have ruled that revocations may not be based solely on hearsay evidence.[106]

Various appellate courts have allowed probation officer records to be considered business records, admissible in both revocation hearings and criminal trials.[107] Treatment records have also been admitted as both reliable hearsay and as business records.[108] One appellate court ruled that a jail infraction report prepared for the prosecution did not constitute a business record and therefore was not admissible in a revocation.[109]

The Fifth Circuit, ruling in a federal parole revocation case, allowed revocation based solely on the hearsay testimony of his parole officer regarding the defendant's firing by his employer, a laboratory report on drug test results and hearsay from a confidential informant. In upholding the evidence, the court held that there was sufficient indicia of reliability of the evidence to justify its admission, relying specifically on the employer's hearsay testimony (unchallenged by the defendant) and the laboratory reports (which were specifically challenged). The court instructed the defendant that rather than demand his right to confrontation, he should have subpoenaed the lab technicians himself, requested a re-test or otherwise found evidence to challenge the reliability of the testing methods or obtained independent evidence to support his claim as to the erroneous nature of the lab results. In other words, given the good reason to spare the government the expense and inconvenience of bringing in the lab technicians, the defendant had other avenues to challenge the results.[110]

The Vermont Supreme Court allowed evidence when a Vermont probation officer testified that a probation officer in another state told him that the probationer had not been located at the address given. As a result, that state had returned his probation supervision to Vermont. The court said the evidence really was not hearsay, it was direct testimony about an act performed by the other state.[111] The same allowances are made for admissions against interest.[112]

Generally, illegally obtained evidence may be used in revocation hearings. Exclusionary rules do not apply if the police officer securing the evidence illegally did not secure it specifically for use in a revocation hearing.[113] All but one federal circuit agree,[114] and only a few states have not followed suit.[115] Voters in California, by state referendum, require such evidence to be used if not ruled unconstitutional.[116]

Most recently, the Kansas Supreme Court ruled that illegally obtained evidence may be used even if the police officer obtaining it knew the defendant was on probation, except where the police officer's conduct is so egregious that the need for police deterrence outweighs the court's need for the information in question. [117]

Similarly, appellate courts have allowed non-Mirandized confessions rejected in criminal courts to be used in revocations. For example, courts have allowed confessions to be used even absent evidence of voluntary and intelligent waivers of the confessor's constitutional rights.[118]

New Criminal Conduct

If the offender engages in new criminal conduct, his probation may be revoked before trial for and conviction of that conduct in most jurisdictions.[119] Most typically, the probation officer must show by a preponderance of the evidence that the probationer engaged in conduct that violated municipal, state or federal law. Nor does it matter whether the probation department fails to comply with its obligation to commit probation conditions to writing if the violation is a new crime.[120]

The criminal conduct alleged does not have to be charged conduct. In other words, the probationer does not have to have been arrested and charged with the conduct in order for it to be alleged as a violation of probation. On the other hand, the probation department may also proceed with revocation for new crimes already disposed of, whether or not the offender was convicted or found not guilty[121] or whether the case was dismissed, or *nolle prossed*.

If the offender was legally convicted of a subsequent offense, the revoking court does not need the facts behind the conviction,[122] but the conviction must be final, not on appeal.[123] If the revocation was based on a new conviction, the offender may not relitigate the basis for the new conviction.[124] Even if the offender is found to have committed a lesser included offense than that alleged in the violation hearing, that is enough to warrant revocation in another jurisdiction.[125] Uncounseled convictions may also be used for the basis of revocation, although they may not be used for sentence enhancement in sentencing proceedings.[126]

A minority of appellate courts are concerned that the revocation for new crimes not compromise the probationer's full rights afforded at the subsequent criminal trial by affording the prosecutor a fishing expedition to gain evidence for the upcoming trial,[127] or coerce self-incriminating testimony from the probationer.[128] A Maryland appellate court found other reasons to express concern with revocations held before trials on the alleged criminal violations.

> We cannot leave this issue without making known our disapproval of the State's conduct in these proceedings. Our focus is upon its attempt to use these violation proceedings as a substitute for a criminal prosecution. We suspect that this approach was chosen because probation violation proceedings require less by way of proof and formal procedures than do criminal trials. . . . We suspect that the State had no intention of proceeding with those criminal charges, either because it could not prove them or it did not wish to invest the time or effort to do so. The State is required to be fair. Fundamental fairness requires that, if the State does not intend to proceed criminally or is unable to prove the criminal charges, it should not proceed in another forum where less is required.[129]

Courts with these concerns have suggested different remedies. First, they have advised or mandated that revocation hearings for new crimes follow trials for those crimes. Jurisdictions have done this through both case law[130] and statute.[131]

Second, they have ordered that if the revocation precedes the trial, use immunity should be granted to the probationer if he takes the stand in his own defense.[132] If this occurs, anything the probationer testifies to cannot be used against him at a subsequent trial so that he need not fear self-incrimination. The testimony is only admissible at the subsequent trial for purposes of impeachment or rebuttal if the probationer chooses to testify again. Prior testimony may also be entered if it is so clearly inconsistent that it reveals to the trier of fact the probability that the probationer committed perjury at either the trial or previous revocation hearing. Several courts have also required that the probationer be informed of his right to testify with use immunity at revocation hearings before trials.

Third, still other courts have allowed revocations to precede trials but ruled that if they do, due process requires hearsay to be barred as well as other evidence usually allowed at revocation hearings.[133]

Fourth, some invoke the doctrine of collateral estoppel to say that if the revocation is unproved, the state may then not proceed to prosecute the charges that were the basis of the revocation.[134] However, most appellate courts addressing this matter disagree.[135]

Again, most jurisdictions dismiss these concerns. They find that such revocations only impose sentences that are already pronounced.[136] While they may put probationers in the predicament of whether to testify, they do not violate his constitutional rights because revocations are not part of criminal prosecutions with their full panoply of rights.[137] Further they acknowledge that the state has an interest in public protection against persons who may not be suitable for probation supervision.[138] It may also be added that in most jurisdictions, the revocation proceedings are initiated by probation, not prosecution officials.

All but one of the federal circuits have allowed revocations to precede trials. The exception is the Third Circuit.[139] In fact, the Fifth Circuit not only held that the court did not have to postpone its revocation hearing until after a new trial, but the revocation court had no authority to grant the probationer use immunity.[140]

§10.07   Sentencing Revocations

After the judge finds the defendant in violation of probation, the second part of the hearing begins, determining disposition. In most jurisdictions, pursuant to either statute or case law (or unchallenged practice), the judge may sentence the defendant as originally available to the court for the crime for which he was placed on probation. Most states follow the federal code, allowing the court to "continue (the probationer violator) on probation, with or without extending the term or modifying or enlarging the conditions or revoke the probation and require him to serve any other sentence available."[141] The period of incarceration may exceed the period of probation.

If the probationer is already on a specific sentence, he may be sentenced for that specific term, but not more. Often, he may be required to serve less time, with the balance further suspended and the defendant placed back on probation. A few states, like New Mexico and Massachusetts, however, require the court to either place the offender back on probation or incarcerate him for his full term.[142] In West Virginia, the probationer must be incarcerated if the new violation is a felony.[143] If a federal defendant violates the conditions of his supervised release, the court may either revoke the supervised release and return the defendant to prison, or modify and extend the supervised release, but it may not do both.[144]

Generally, the prosecution (usually the probation officer) is not bound by its original plea bargain because the probation violation presents a change of circumstances that releases the prosecution from its initial agreement regarding sentencing.[145]

Vermont, on the other hand, mandates that the court not incarcerate the probationer even after a violation is found, unless the court finds that incarceration is necessary to protect the community, provide treatment or is demanded by the seriousness of the violation.[146] Similarly, a Maryland appellate court suggests that revoking courts consider the probationer's various problems, the strains on the penal system and the proper objectives of criminal sanctions and fashion a sentence, in the instant case, more suitable to the defendant and the community.[147]

In another Maryland case, a defendant on probation for drugs was later convicted of larceny and possession charges. His probation was revoked. An appellate court remanded the case because it could not determine from the record whether the revoking court had considered whether other actions were more appropriate to protect society and improve the probationer's chances of rehabilitation. In this case, the defendant had admitted to the new charges, and entered a drug rehabilitation program with the assistance of his employer. During that period he lived in a recovery house for several months and had been steadily employed for 11 years.[148]

More typically, if jurisdictions require anything, like the Minnesota Supreme Court, they simply require that the sentencing court find that the "need for confinement outweighs the policies favoring probation."[149]

What constitutes a substantial enough violation to warrant imprisonment is obviously decided on a case-by-case basis and differs from one jurisdiction to another. It is agreed, however, that once a violation is found, the defendant must be given the opportunity to present evidence that the violation does not warrant imprisonment and/or suggest alternative sentences for the court to consider. The United States Supreme Court, however, has ruled that the revoking court does not have to make specific findings in sentencing probation violators to imprisonment.[150] In *Black v. Ranamo*, the probationer argued that his rights were violated by the failure of the court to consider alternatives to his imprisonment prior to revoking his probation and stating the reasons for not considering the alternatives. Both the district and circuit agreed. The Supreme Court did not.

The Supreme Court ruled that as long as the violation was proven, there was no violation of the due process clause of the Fourteenth Amendment, even if the court failed to note on the record that it had considered alternatives to incarceration and rejected them before incarcerating the defendant for the violation. In other words, automatic revocations of probation or parole upon a finding of violation are permissible. The only exception is in regard to revocation for failure to pay court-ordered monies due to indigency. In such cases, the Court requires the revoking court to consider alternatives before ultimately revoking the nonpayer's probation.[151]

If the defendant fails to argue to mitigate his violations or suggest alternatives to incarceration, it is not incumbent for the revoking court to do it for him. Due process is satisfied if the defendant is provided the opportunity to do so. In short, the onus is squarely on the defendant, not the court. The Ninth Circuit refused, for example, to overturn a revoking court's refusal to grant the probationer a continuance to prepare arguments for alternative dispositions, ruling that he had ample opportunity during the course of the hearing.[152]

Appellate courts have remanded or overturned cases for failure of the revocation court to either provide written findings or state clearly on the record that the violation found was substantial enough to justify incarceration. Violations questioned include cases in which the only violation was travel outside the country without permission,[153] or a single violation of a general ban on association with persons convicted of felonies,[154] or failure to go to 20 job interviews when the probationer went to 15 and received 4 job offers.[155]

On the other hand, failure to report, alone, although a technical violation, has been held to constitute a serious enough violation to warrant incarceration.[156]

In states that require presentence reports prior to sentencing, they are also required for sentencing revocations.[157] If defendants are given the right of allocution, that right also applies in revocation sentencing hearings[158] unless specifically omitted by statute or rule.[159] Federal circuits have, however, split on this issue.[160]

Once the court has found a violation, allowed the defendant to present evidence in mitigation of the violation as well as to suggest alternative dispositions and received any required presentence reports, the court must then sentence the probationer. Here, too, state and federal requirements differ.

In the federal system, the sentence following revocation cannot be based on the probation violation conduct. The language of the federal code calls for sentencing that was available at the time of the initial sentencing. Obviously at that time the court could not know of the violation conduct for consideration in imposing its original sentence. However, the court may "reconsider its original decision not to depart (from the sentencing guidelines) in light of the defendant's subsequent actions."[161]

In the federal system, if the offender is on supervised release, there are three grades of violations, each of which calls for a different degree of punishment.[162] Grade A violations arise from conduct that constitutes an offense punishable by a term of imprisonment exceeding one year that is a crime of violence or drugs or involves firearms or a destructive device or any offense punishable by more than 20 years. A grade B violation consists of conduct constituting any federal, state or local offense punishable by a term of imprisonment exceeding one year. A grade C violation is conduct constituting an offense punishable by one year or less, or a violation of any other condition of release.

For example, filing a false report with a probation officer can constitute a grade B violation, not a C violation. So ruled the Eighth Circuit in considering such a case when the defendant failed to report, for example, a new arrest or questioning by police. The court said the conduct constituted the crime of perjury.[163]

Some states also specifically bar the revocation judge from considering the violation conduct in sentencing.[164] However, the violation conduct can be considered in assessing the probationer's potential for rehabilitation.[165] Similarly, one appellate court specifically approved of the revocation judge relying on the probation officer's opinion regarding incarceration because an important consideration is whether the probation officer is able to assist the probationer's rehabilitation. On that, the probation officer may be considered an expert.[166] Probation officers making revocation recommendations are standard practices in many jurisdictions.

The concern is that probationers not be punished twice, once for the original crime for which they were placed on probation and again for the violation of the probation. For example, if the defendant is given probation for a relatively minor crime like shoplifting, it would be unfair when revoking his probation for a subsequent probation violation to impose a very severe sentence because his probation conduct was so bad. No matter how badly he behaved on probation, his punishment must be for the crime of shoplifting, even if the violation is murder. The appropriate time to punish him for the probation conduct behavior is after a new trial regarding that behavior if the behavior is criminal in nature. However, the revocation judge is free to sentence the defendant to the legal maximum sentence for shoplifting.

A handful of states limit the amount of time a probation violator may be sentenced following revocation. Some suggest specific alternative sentences such as 30 days (North Carolina), 60 days (Washington)[167] or six months (Georgia). Generally these limitations have been specifically imposed by legislators worried about prison overcrowding and related expenses. In addition, there may be some fear that revocations are used as a back door to incarcerate defendants. Because the standards for revocation are lower than the standards for convictions, prosecutors may convince defendants to plea bargain, offering them probationary sentences, realizing that the very first time they violate the conditions of that probation they can be more easily incarcerated.

Credit

As probationary terms become increasingly punitive and restrictive, they have increasingly come to resemble jail sentences. Yet, if violated, in the vast majority of jurisdictions, probationers seldom receive credit for any conditions successfully completed or fulfilled. For example, two probationers are required to pay $5,000 restitution for auto theft. One pays, one does not. Both commit new crimes and are revoked. Both can be sentenced equivalently even though one, at least, complied at least partially with his probation, and one did not. While the revoking judge can take the probationer's conduct into account in sentencing the probation violation, there is no requirement that the judge give specific credit for specific positive probation compliance. The same pertains to other conditions of probation successfully completed, including often residential treatment, time spent under house arrest etc., even though the probationer's liberty may have been severely restricted as a condition of probation. If subsequently revoked, the court need not give the defendant credit for time spent in such facilities or programs.

The United States Supreme Court recently reversed a Third Circuit decision giving credit to a defendant who had spent six months between his arrest and his guilty plea in a halfway house in the technical custody of the Pretrial Services Agency.[168] While confined, the defendant was only allowed to leave the halfway house once, for medical treatment. The Third Circuit had found the confinement was "jail-like" and gave the defendant credit for time served. The Supreme Court, however, in reviewing the language of the federal statute, ruled that credit could only be given for "official detention," in a facility operated by the Bureau of Prisons. Therefore there could be no credit for time spent in a community treatment center, no matter what the conditions of that confinement were. Because this decision revolves around the wording of the federal code, it does not cover similar circumstances in the states.

Only a relatively few state court decisions have led to different results, however. Most, like Florida's Supreme Court, do not require the trial court to give credit for time served on probation.[169] Courts have even split on whether probationers may receive credit for time actually spent in jail when jailed as a condition of probation. Oregon's Supreme Court has, for example, ruled that time spent in jail as a condition of probation must be credited toward an eventual sentence of incarceration.[170] Wisconsin's has not, finding that probation is not a sentence, so time spent in jail as a condition of probation cannot be credited against time spent in jail as part of a sentence.[171]

Some appellate courts have gone out of their way to differentiate probation conditions from jail, no matter how onerous they are. The Supreme Court of Florida, for example, held that if jail is the result of a probation condition, as long as it is less than one year, it does not constitute punishment. It explained:

> A sentence and probation are discrete concepts which serve wholly different functions. Imposed as a sentence, imprisonment serves as a penalty, as a payment of defendant's "debt to society." Imposed as an incident of probation, imprisonment serves as a rehabilitative device to give the defendant a taste of prison.[172]

One wonders if the distinction is perhaps lost on all but the most astute inmates after the first few months.[173]

Similarly, credit for time spent under home detention has been denied because it does not fall within the legal meaning of "custody" in Wisconsin[174] or was not sufficiently restrictive to constitute "custody" as understood in Nebraska.[175] Colorado's Supreme Court refused to provide credit for a certain private residential community placement even though it involved substantial restrictions, but the offender was allowed to leave for interstate travel.[176] Wyoming's Supreme Court, on the other hand, allowed credit for a certain community corrections program in which residents who leave may be charged with the crime of escape.[177] Nevada's allowed credit for residential drug treatment,[178] and Vermont's for time spent in a residential alcohol facility.[179] New Jersey's holds that credit must be given when a program is so confining as to be substantially equivalent to custody in jail or in a state hospital.[180] While California has given credit for time spent in drug programs, halfway houses and other such programs, it denies it for time spent in home detention.

> Being confined to one's home, subject to electronic monitoring, with the freedom to engage in employment and probation-related activities, is far less onerous than being imprisoned.[181]

The decision to grant credit or not, at least in Arizona, revolves around three considerations: (1) the legal definition of custody in the statutes; (2) a case-by-case examination of the restrictiveness of the program or closeness to custody; and (3) whether the program was a condition of the sentence or probation.[182]

Finally, even though a defendant may not automatically receive credit for time spent in restrictive placements or the like, time spent in such facilities may be a factor to be considered by the trial judge in sentencing. If the judge fails to consider this, the case may be remanded.[183]

Sentencing probation violators, especially those guilty of technical violations, is extremely important in enforcing alternative sentences. Many defendants given alternative sentences, especially ones with stringent conditions that are monitored tightly, will fail and be brought back to court. They may miss restitution payments, or fail to show up for community work service, or take drugs, or violate any number of conditions of their alternative sentence. In the interest of public safety or justice, some should be committed to long-term incarceration. However, many more may be redeemable with shorter sentences. The court must consider why the defendant failed his probation. Was the failure a matter of inability to comply or unwillingness to comply?

If the probationer is unable to comply, then it is encumbent upon the court to impose alternative conditions that help the probationer comply. If the probationer is unable to maintain sobriety in the community, the court might consider requiring the use of anabuse or inpatient treatment in a treatment facility, followed by residency in a halfway house. If the probationer is unable to meet weekly payment plans, the court might consider altering the payment plan and extending the final payment date.

If the probationer is unwilling to comply, the court has at its disposal a unique resource unavailable to the whole panoply of treatment programs, jail. Short-term shock sentences may be all that is necessary to convince the defendant that the court is serious about the alternative sentence. A weekend in jail, a short split sentence or intermittent commitment may make the probationer realize that he is not going to be let off the hook. Eventually, the court is going to demand that the restitution be paid, the community work service be completed, sobriety be maintained and so on. Judge Albert L. Kramer has termed this method of enforcing alternative sentencing "tourniquet sentencing."[184] Like a tourniquet, the penalty for noncompliance is increased incrementally until the offender complies. Another judge has termed the same approach "progressive discomfiture." Only the few states that restrict revocation sentences to full term incarceration prevent the court from utilizing "tourniquet sentencing."

With such an approach, courts have been able to achieve high alternative sentence completion rates with serious, chronic offenders. Frequently, the "tourniquet" has to be twisted only once or twice before the defendant completes his conditions successfully. If the alternative sentence promises the victim restitution or the community work service, this method helps assure that the promise will be kept. Alternative sentences are more than simply a test of the offender's willingness and ability to comply. They are a commitment on the court's part that the offender shall exercise a certain responsible behavior in the public's interest whether he wants to or not. If a court finds that those given alternative sentences never have to be brought back to court for violations, either the court's orders are not being monitored or the court is restricting its alternative sentences to low-risk offenders whose behavior is in little need of alteration.

The idea of incremental penalties is intrinsic to alternative sentencing. It allows the court to think of penalties other than all-or-nothing incarceration. It allows the development of a sentencing matrix that spans a range of penalties from community work service to long-term incarceration. Such a matrix has been developed by the Delaware Sentencing Reform Commission under the direction of that state's former Republican Governor, Pierre S. du Pont, a lawyer and then second-term governor.

The Commission was created in response to prison overcrowding. As the Governor frankly stated, the state had simply found that it could no longer build its way out of the problem of overcrowding. When he had been sworn in as Governor in 1977, three percent of the state budget went to corrections. The state had just completed a brand-new, state-of-the-art prison that was supposed to handle the state's needs through the 1990s. By his second term, the Governor found that corrections accounted for seven percent of the state budget and two more prisons had to be built. A third was on its way. Despite the cost, the Governor would have been willing to continue the state's traditional correctional system if he felt it was working, but he did not.

> Despite the great cost, and the promise of more increases to come, the present system might be largely acceptable if it were working properly. But it isn't. We traditionally rely on incarceration as the primary method of punishing criminals, but—as numerous studies have demonstrated—there is no evidence that higher incarceration rates have any impact on the crime rate. For one thing, prison overcrowding limits whatever chances exist for success in rehabilitation programs.[185]

To address the problem, the Governor proposed a fundamental reform of the state's sentencing system.

> In my judgment, a fundamental reshaping of the approach to corrections is not only in order, it is feasible and imperative. As a start, we must begin to view punishment in terms of certainty rather than severity. The criminal justice system is undermined when men and women are sentenced to probation when they should go to jail, or are released from jail on probation when they ought to remain behind bars. The answer that overcrowding forces these compromises is not acceptable when other answers are available. We must provide sentencing options between the extremes of probation and prison.[186]

Responding to the Governor's challenge, the Sentencing Commission developed a matrix that stresses accountability of the offender to the state and the victim as well as the accountability of the correctional system to the state and the victim. The matrix is based on the tenet that the offender should be sentenced to the least restrictive (and least costly) sanction available, consistent with public safety. Once sentenced, the offender can move up or down the matrix, depending upon his behavior. The matrix has ten levels of accountability. Each level contains four grades of restrictions: (1) mobility in the community; (2) amount of supervision; (3) special conditions covering such things as employment, travel, curfews, associates and so on; and (4) financial obligations. The level of restrictions runs from unsupervised probation to maximum security imprisonment.

To illustrate, a hypothetical drug offender, with a minimal record but unstable employment, might be sentenced to Level II, which includes supervised probation for two years, with restrictions on place of residence, association and travel to high drug/crime areas of the city. He might also be assessed a $10 monthly probation supervision fee. If the offender does well, he could move down the matrix to Level I. This would entail unsupervised probation and no fees, but may include continued bans on travel. If the offender does poorly, he could be moved to Level III with increased supervision, a nightly curfew and increased fees. The matrix gives the offender a clear incentive to comply with his sentence. Equally important, it gives the judge options other than prison when probation is violated. Having the use of these options will increase the certainty of appropriate, proportional punishment.

After analyzing the state's offender population, the commission found that 70 percent could be sentenced within Levels I to III, see Chart 13.

> Analysis showed that many in prison could be released if the programs were available to restrict their activities properly and closely supervise their rehabilitation. That analysis also showed that many in probation were undersupervised. Many of these men and women clearly needed to be moved into a middle level where they would be subject to stronger, more restrictive programs.[187]

While the Delaware sentencing scheme requires substantial legal and correctional restructuring, judges can develop their own scheme, using many of the alternatives discussed. In enforcing these sentences, they can structure their penalties accordingly.

§10.08   Current Practice

Examples of Revocations

Today's tabloid headlines provide several examples of probation revocations for some infamous probationers, enjoying their "15 minutes of fame."

> **Divine Brown,** aka Estella Thompson, a Hollywood prostitute, got her 15 minutes of fame when she was arrested and sentenced for a six-month suspended sentence for lewd conduct with a famous movie star "john," Hugh Grant. Sentenced to pay a fine of $1,350, take an AIDS test and complete an AIDS Awareness Education Program and perform five days of community work service, Ms. Brown returned to court on November 2, 1995 for noncompliance. She

failed to do her community service or attend the AIDS classes. Her probation was revoked and she went to jail.[188]

John Wayne Bobbit got his 15 minutes of fame after being partially (but temporarily) dismembered by his wife. Subsequently, he received a five-month sentence for beating up a subsequent girlfriend, a topless dancer. He spent a month in jail with the remainder suspended with probationary conditions that included batterer's treatment. Shortly before Christmas 1995, his probation was revoked after the judge found that he had skipped too many domestic violence treatment sessions. Mr. Bobbit argued in vain that a learning disability made him unable to concentrate at the sessions. He was sentenced to the four remaining months in jail.[189]

Rapper Tupac Shakur was sentenced to 15 days in jail and 45 days of community service—including 15 days on a road crew— for conviction of one count each of battery and assault in Los Angeles. On January 23, 1996, he was ordered jailed for violating his probation

Delaware Sentencing Commission
Sentencing Options Chart[190]

Restrictions	Level I	Level II	Level III	Level IV
Mobility in the community	100 percent (unrestricted)	100 percent (unrestricted)	90 percent (restricted 0-10 hours/week)	80 percent (restricted 10-30 hours week)
Amount of supervision	None	Monthly written report	1-2 face-to-face/month; 1-2 weekly phone contacts	3-6 face-to-face/month; weekly phone contact
Privileges withheld or special conditions	100 percent (same as prior conviction)	100 percent (same as prior conviction)	1-2 privileges withheld	1-4 privileges withheld
Financial obligations	Fine, court costs may be applied (0- to 2-day fine)	Fine, court costs, restitution (supervisory fee may be applied: 1- to 3-day fine)	Same (increase probation fee by $5-10/month; 2- to 4-day fine)	Same (increase probation fee by $5-10/month; 3- to 5-day fine)
Examples (Note: many other scenarios could be constructed to meet the requirements at each level)	$50 fine, court costs; 6 months unsupervised probation	$50 fine, court costs, restitution; 6 months supervised probation; $10 monthly fee; written report	Fine, court costs, restitution; 1 year probation; weekend community service; no drinking	Weekend community service or mandatory treatment 5 hours/day; $30/month probation fee; no drinking; no out-of-state trips

by not completing the work crew assignment on California roads. Judge Gregory Alarcon had given Shakur until then to complete his work. A hearing was set for February 14 to determine if his probation should be revoked. In the interim, bail was set at $52,000.[191]

Probation/Parole Revocation and Prison Commitments

The last major examination of probation and parole violators was conducted for the calendar year 1991 and was released in 1995 by the United States Justice Department.[192] The study did not examine all probation or parole revocations, only those in which the offender was sentenced to prison. As a result, the study does not tell us anything about violators who were *not* sentenced to prison. By definition, this means the study leaves unaddressed a profile of misdemeanants whose probation or parole is revoked. By definition, these offenders, even if sentenced, would go to local correctional institutions, not state prisons.

Nonetheless, the study reveals several major consequences of probation and parole revocation. First, it reveals how well probation and parole protect public

Level V	Level VI	Level VII	Level VIII	Level IX	Level X
60 percent (restricted 30-40 hours/week)	30 percent (restricted 50-100 hours/week)	20 percent (restricted 100-140 hours/week)	10 percent (90 percent of time incarcerated)	Incarcerated	Incarcerated
2-6 face-to-face/week; daily phone contact; weekly written reports	Daily phone contact; daily face-to-face; weekly written reports	Daily onsite supervision 8-16 hours/day	Daily onsite supervision 24 hours/day	Daily onsite supervision 24 hours/day	Daily onsite supervision 24 hours/day
1-7 privileges withheld	1-10 privileges withheld	1-12 privileges withheld	5-15 privileges withheld	15-19 privileges withheld	20 or more privileges withheld
Same (pay partial cost of food/lodging/supervision fee; 4- to 7-day fine)	Same as Level V (8- to 10-day fine)	Same as Level V (11- to 12-day fine)	Fine, court costs, restitution payable upon release to Level VII or lower (12- to 15-day fine)	Same as Level VIII	Same as Level VIII
Mandatory rehabilitation skills program 8 hours/day; restitution; $40/month probation fee; no drinking; curfew	Work release; pay portion of food/lodging; restitution; no kitchen privileges outside mealtime; no drinking; no sex; weekends home	Residential treatment program; pay portion of program costs; limited privileges	Minimum-security prison	Medium-security prison	Maximum-security prison

safety. As President Gerald Ford reportedly said in response to a question: "How are we doing? On a scale of one to 10, I would say, not so good." Second, it reveals how revoked probationers and parolees contribute to prison overcrowding.

Thirty-five percent of state prison inmates in 1991 were convicted of a new offense while they were either on probation or parole. Another 10 percent were sent to prison for technically violating their probation or parole. Twenty-six percent of the 162,000 probation violators incarcerated were technical violators and 20 percent of the 156,000 parole violators incarcerated were technical violators. The balance all committed and were convicted of new crimes.

Not surprisingly, the vast majority of the technical violators also self-reported committing new crimes for which they were arrested but not convicted of while under supervision. Notwithstanding their new arrests, they were *not* revoked in three-quarters of the cases for new criminal behavior but rather for violating other conditions of their supervision. These included not reporting (34 to 37%), failing drug tests (10%), failing to attend counseling (5%), leaving the jurisdiction without permission (8 to 14%), possession of a weapon (1 to 2.5%), failure to pay various court ordered monies (3 to 12%) and so on.

Between the revoked probationers and parolees, they committed 13,200 murders, 12,900 rapes, 19,200 assaults and almost 40,000 robberies, all while under supervision, based on the new offenses that resulted in their revocations. The average time the revoked probationers spent on probation was 17 months and for parolees 13 months. Probation and parole violators comprised 30 percent of the prison population for violence, 56 percent for property crimes, 41 percent for drug offenses and 85 percent for public order offenses. The high rate of the later can probably be attributed to the fact that ordinarily public order offenses do not result in imprisonment, unless the offender is already on supervision for a more serious crime.

The data for the study was based on interviews with 13,986 inmates in 277 different state prisons.

One of the reasons so many probationers and parolees failed to straighten out their lives is that they continued to abuse drugs while on supervision. In addition, little was done that worked to keep them away from firearms. The majority of violators, 55 percent, reported drug use in the month before the crime that sent them to prison was committed. Forty-one percent reported daily drug use but only two percent reported being revoked for failing drug tests. Twenty percent said they committed their new crime for drug money. Their use was evenly divided between cocaine and pot for probationers and heroin and pot for parolees. One-third reported being high at the time of their new crime. Although felons are not allowed to possess firearms, 21 percent of the violators reported having firearms. And three-quarters of those who had them used them to commit the crime that sent them to prison. Only one percent of them were revoked for firearms possession.

In other words, despite legal prohibitions against drug use and firearms possession, these bans were unenforced in most cases until the offender committed a new crime. Then they were enforced incidental to the new offense.

Between 1975 and 1991, probationers and parolees entering state prisons increased from 18,000 to 142,000, twice the growth of new offenders committed directly from courts. The proportion of violators within prisons has increased from 17 percent in 1974 to 45 percent in 1991. Earlier studies, cited in the report, document that this expands upon a trend that began in the 1920s when violators only comprised five percent of the total prison population.

In other words, much of the present-day overcrowding in state prisons can be attributed to recycled probation and parole violators, not to increased numbers of new offenders being arrested. This suggests, as many have noted, that prison overcrowding cannot be addressed successfully unless and until this particular population is controlled.

The demographics of probation and parole violators is slightly different. Probationers are a little younger, with a median age of 27 versus 31 for parolees. The median age of nonviolators in prison is also 31. Probationers, perhaps being younger, are less likely to be married, 36 percent versus 45 percent, with nonviolator inmates the most likely to be married at 49 percent. Only 10 percent of either are female.

The nonviolators in prison had less criminal history than either the probation or parole violators. One-half of the nonviolators had past period(s) of probation. One-half were in prison for the first time. By definition, all of the parolees had been in prison before. In addition, 20 percent of the probationers had previously served jail time as part of their probationary sentence.

In addition, 27 percent of the probationers reported having been on probation three or more times before. Forty-three percent of the parolees had been in jail or prison three or more times before.

The average sentence served by parole violators was 63 months. Probation violators served an average of 49 months.

Confirming the danger of some probationers or parolees, the study also found that probationers and parolees accounted for 22 percent of the law enforcement officers murdered between 1988 and 1992. In 1992, alone, 38 percent of all individuals arrested for murder whose cases were disposed of in urban courts were on probation, parole or some form of correctional supervision at the time (including bail). The violence committed by violators is perhaps not surprising since 43 percent of the probationers and 50 percent of the parolees were being supervised for a crime of violence. However, violators who committed new crimes did not necessarily repeat the crimes for which they were already on supervision, with one exception. The majority (58% probationers to 60% parolees) on supervision for drug offenses committed new drug offenses.

Confirming the necessity for probation and parole to supervise domestic violence cases and sexual assault cases, of all the murders committed by violators, one-half were committed against victims known by the violator, 14 percent of assaults were committed against family spouses/partners. In addition, 47 percent of the rapes were against boys and girls under the age of 18.

The above study is revealing. Although it does not describe the average probationer or parolee, it does reveal that the average probation or parole violator sentenced to prison is a serious offender with a substantial prior record. Failure to supervise offenders for drug use and firearms possession means a continued threat to the public safety. Mandating testing is not enough. Drug use violators must be controlled before they commit a new crime. Similarly, banning firearms is not enough. Officers must search offender's homes and persons to insure that they do not actually possess them or have ready access to them.

If the probation and parole officers were, in fact, drug testing and monitoring these offenders for firearms possession in this study and returning them to court or the parole board, then the various courts and parole boards were consistently turning a deaf ear and releasing these violators back to the streets. Of course, the study does not reveal whether this is the case because it only looked at violators who were sentenced to prison.

Revocation practices are diverse among courts within the same state, much less between states and the federal courts. Some courts rarely enforce criminal, much less technical violations of probation. Some jurisdictions, including much of the state of California, "bank" large quantities of misdemeanant probationers, leaving them virtually unsupervised. Some send the most trivial violators to jail. Others intensively supervise large numbers of offenders, aggressively enforcing multiple behavioral and other conditions of probation. Almost one-half (40%) of all intensive supervision offenders in New Jersey, for example, are returned to prison for violating their supervision. Most are resentenced for technical violations.[193] The same is true in North Carolina, where 90 percent of the 10,000 inmates committed for probation violations committed technical violations until the legislature amended the law to restrict revocation sentencing.[194] Obviously, the more offenders are required to do, the more conditions they could violate.

It is also clear that if nothing is done to remove probationers or parolees from supervision until they are convicted of new offenses, probation and parole fail to prevent crime. Even if their supervision is then revoked, the revocation is often superfluous because the new crime will see them incarcerated anyway. The result is what prompts many to charge that probation and parole are the equivalent of surrender. The *Reader's Digest*, in discussing probation, for example, titled its article "When Criminals Go Free." In bold print, it captioned the article:

> Each day our courts "punish" dangerous felons by releasing them on probation. The result? Thousands of new crimes.[195]

George Lardner Jr., the father of a young woman murdered in Massachusetts by her ex-boyfriend, who was on probation for assaulting and stalking a prior girlfriend, expounds on the dangers of probation in his book, *The Stalking of Kristen,* released in late 1995.[196] When alerted to the probationer's continued violence by a new victim, the probation officer redoubled her efforts to get him into an inappropriate treatment program, ignoring the obvious threat to the new victim.

On the other hand, there are other probation and intermediate sanction programs that rigorously supervise and enforce their charges, reducing risk to the community. These include many cited in this text, including the Florida Community Control Program, the New Jersey Intensive Supervision Program and more.

Notes

[1] *Flouting Fines.* TIME MAGAZINE, March 24, 1980.

[2] 18 U.S.C. § 3580 (h) (1982) (redesignated § 3664 effective Nov. 1, 1986) ("An order of restitution may be enforced by the United States or a victim named in the order to receive the restitution in the same manner as a judgment in a civil action.")

[3] Office of the Comptroller of the City of New York (1981). AUDIT REPORT ON THE FINANCIAL AND OPERATING PRACTICES AND PROCEDURES OF THE NEW YORK CITY DEPARTMENT OF PROBATION, July 1 to April 30, 1980.

[4] Florida Department of Corrections (1984). PRELIMINARY REPORT ON COMMUNITY CONTROL (Probation and Parole Services).

[5] Griffith, W., A. Schneider, P. Schneider and M. Wilson (1982). TWO YEAR REPORT ON THE NATIONAL EVALUATION OF THE JUVENILE RESTITUTION INITIATIVE: AN OVERVIEW OF PROGRAM PERFORMANCE. Washington, DC: U.S. Department of Justice, 77-NI-99-0005 and 79-NJ-AX-0009.

[6] N.Y. EXEC. LAW § 257(4) (Consol. Supp. 1985).

[7] 18 U.S.C. § 3603(g) (Supp. II 1984) (effective Nov. 1, 1986).

[8] *State v. Hyman,* 236 N.J. Super. 298, 565 A.2d 1086 (1989).

[9] 18 U.S.C. § 3563(b)(17) (1994).

[10] *Id.* at (18).

[11] *Id.* at (19).

[12] *Haynes v. State,* 440 So. 2d 661 (Fla. Dist. Ct. App. 1983); *Goley v. State,* 584 So. 2d 139 (Fla. Dist. Ct. App. 1991).

[13] OR. REV. STAT. 137.540(21) (1993).

[14] *State v. Altman,* 97 Or. App. 462, 777 P.2d 696 (1989).

[15] Petersilia, J. (1988). *Probation Reform.* In J. Scott and T. Hirschi (eds.) CONTROVERSIAL ISSUES IN CRIME AND JUSTICE, Vol. 1. Newbury Park, CA: Sage Publications.

[16] *Domestic Abusers Can't Abuse This System.* INSTANT EVIDENCE VIII, Fall/Winter, 1994.

[17] See, *e.g., State v. Sites,* 231 Neb. 624, 437 N.W.2d 166 (1989); see also *State v. Heath,* 343 So. 2d 12 (Fla. 1977); *Wilson v. State,* 621 P.2d 1173 (Okla. Crim. App. 1980); *Beller v. State,* 597 P.2d 338 (Okla. Crim. App. 1979).

[18] *People v. Manser,* 172 Mich. App. 485, 432 N.W.2d 348 (1988).

[19] *United States v. Morin, a.k.a. Video,* 889 F.2d 328, 332 (1st Cir. 1989).

[20] *United States v. Robinson,* 893 F.2d 1244 (11th Cir. 1990).

[21] *United States v. Lamberti,* 847 F.2d 1531 (11th Cir. 1988), *cert. denied,* 488 U.S. 970, 109 S. Ct. 501 (1988).

[22] *State v. Travis,* 125 Idaho 1, 867 P.2d 234 (1994).

[23] *Cassamassima v. State,* 657 So. 2d 906 (Fla. Dist. Ct. App. 1995).

[24] *Patton v. State,* 580 N.E.2d 693 (Ind. Ct. App. 1991).

[25] *State v. Flores-Moreno,* 866 P.2d 648 (Wash. App.), *review denied,* 879 P.2d 292 (1994) (to determine new drug use only).

[26] OR. REV. STAT. § 137.540(2)(b).

[27] *Commonwealth v. Vincente,* 405 Mass. 278, 540 N.E.2d 669 (1989); see also *Cleveland v. State,* 557 So. 2d 759 (Fla. Dist. Ct. App. 1990).

[28] *State v. Steinhour,* 158 Vt. 299, 607 A.2d 888 (1992).

[29] *Minnesota v. Murphy,* 465 U.S. 420, 104 S. Ct. 1136, 79 L. Ed. 2d 409 (1984), *reh'g denied,* 104 S. Ct. 1932, 80 L. Ed. 2d 477 (1984).

[30] *State v. Sargent,* 111 Wash. 2d 641, 762 P2d. 1127 (1988).

[31] *State v. Earnest,* 293 N.W.2d 365, 369 (Minn. 1980).

[32] *Griffin v. Wisconsin,* 483 U.S. 868, 107 S. Ct. 3164, 97 L. Ed. 2d 709 (1987).

[33] Discussed in more detail in § 9.04.

[34] See, *e.g.,* N.J. STAT. ANN. § 2C:45-3(a)(3) (West 1982) (provides for no bail when probationer summoned or arrested for new crime, based on probable cause, while on probation); upheld in *State v. Garcia,* 193 N.J. 334, 474 A.2d 20 (1984).

[35] *Malone v. State,* 571 N.E.2d 329 (Ind. Ct. App. 1991).

[36] *Patterson v. State,* 572 So. 2d 508 (Ala. Crim. App. 1990).

[37] *Mempa v. Rhay,* 389 U.S. 128, 88 S. Ct. 254,19 L. Ed. 2d 336 (1967).

[38] *Morrissey v. Brewer,* 408 U.S. 471, 92 S. Ct. 2593, 33 L. Ed. 2d 484 (1972).

[39] *Gagnon v. Scarpelli,* 411 U.S. 778, 93 S. Ct. 1756, 36 L. Ed. 2d 656 (1973).

[40] *In re Lamarine,* 527 A.2d 1133 (R.I. 1987); *State v. Herrlein,* 424 N.W.2d 376 (S.D. 1988); *Powell v. State,* 485 So. 2d 379, 381 (Ala. 1986); *State v. Lange,* 237 Mont. 486, 775 P.2d 213 (1989); *United States v. Crawley,* 837 F.2d 291 (7th Cir. 1988).

[41] *State v. Villano,* 35 Conn. App. 520, 646 A.2d 915 (1994).

[42] *People v. McCracken,* 159 Ill. 2d 463, 639 N.E.2d 1270 (1994).

[43] *State v. Johnson,* 592 So. 2d 821 (La. Ct. App. 1991).

[44] *Fay v. Commonwealth,* 379 Mass. 498, 382 n.49, 399 N.E.2d 11, 14 n.49 (1980).

[45] *State v. Hicks,* 478 So. 2d 22 (Fla. 1985).

[46] 18 U.S.C. § 3006A(a)(1)(C) (1994).

[47] See, *e.g., Bradford v State,* 550 N.E.2d 1353 (Ind. Ct. App. 1990); *People v. Clark,* 157 Ill. App. 3d 371, 510 N.E.2d 1256 (1987).

[48] *Commonwealth v. Faulkner,* 718 Mass. 352, 38 N.E.2d 1 (1994); *State v. Marceaux,* 520 So. 2d 1203 (La. Ct. App. 1988).

[49] *State v. Bateman,* 296 S.C.2d 367, 373 S.E.2d 470 (1988); *Salley v. State,* 306 S.C. 213, 410 S.E.2d 921 (1991).

[50] *State v. Smith,* 18 Conn. App. 368, 558 A.2d 257 (1989).

[51] See, *e.g., Jones v. State,* 560 A.2d 1056 (Fla. Dist. Ct. App. 1989); *State v. Conlin,* 49 Wash. App. 593, 744 P.2d 1094 (1987).

[52] *In re Cotton,* 284 Cal. Rptr. 757 (Cal. Ct. App. 1991).

[53] *State v. Gedutis,* 653 A.2d 761 (Vt. 1994).

[54] *Kanuck v. Meehan,* 165 Ariz. 282, 798 P.2d 420 (Ariz. Ct. App. 1990).

[55] *Bond v. State,* 298 Ark. 630, 770 S.W.2d 136 (1989).

[56] *United States v. Tham,* 884 F.2d 1262 (9th Cir. 1989), cited in *United States v. Donaghe,* 924 F.2d 940 (9th Cir. 1991).

[57] *People v. Cagle,* 780 P.2d 12 (Colo. Ct. App. 1989).

[58] *United States v. Miller,* 797 F.2d 336, 340 (6th Cir. 1986); *Jonas v. Wainwright,* 779 F.2d 1576, 1577 (11th Cir. 1986), *cert. denied,* 479 U.S. 830, 107 S. Ct. 115 (1986); *State v. Eckley,* 34 Or. App. 563, 567-568, 579 P.2d 291 (1978).

[59] *Snajder v. State,* 74 Wis. 2d 303, 313, 246 N.W.2d 665 (1976).

[60] *Hall v. State,* 512 So. 2d 303 (Fla. Dist. Ct. App 1987).

[61] *State v. Carreker,* 39 Ohio App. 3d 112, 529 N.E.2d 951 (1987).

[62] See, *e.g., State v. Kasper,* 152 Vt. 435, 566 A.2d 982 (Vt. 1989); *People v. Smith,* 202 Ill. App. 3d 606, 560 N.E.2d 399 (1990).

[63] *State v. Durkin,* 219 Conn. 629, 595 A.2d 826 (1991).

[64] See, *e.g., People v. Liming,* 183 Ill. App. 3d 960, 539 N.E.2d 871 (1991).

[65] See, *e.g., United States v. Williams,* 15 F.3d 1356 (6th Cir. 1994), *cert. denied,* 115 S. Ct. 431, 130 L. Ed. 2d 344 (1994); *United States v. James,* 848 F.2d 160 (11th Cir. 1988); *United States v. Daly,* 839 F.2d 598 (9th Cir. 1988); *United States v. Camarata,* 828 F.2d 974 (3d Cir. 1987), *cert. denied,* 108 S. Ct. 1036, 98 L. Ed. 2d 1000 (1988); *United States v. Yancey,* 827 F.2d 83 (7th Cir. 1987), *cert. denied,* 108 S. Ct. 1239, 99 L. Ed. 2d 437 (1988); *United States v. Taylor,* 931 F.2d 842 (11th Cir. 1991), *cert. denied,* 112 S. Ct. 1191, 171 L. Ed. 2d 433 (1991).

[66] *United States v. Fryar,* 920 F.2d 252 (5th Cir. 1990), *cert. denied,* 499 U.S. 981, 111 S. Ct. 1635, 113 L. Ed. 2d 730 (1990).

[67] See, *e.g., State v. Jacques,* 554 A.2d 193 (R.I. 1989) (two jail infractions); *State v. Ashley,* 772 P.2d 377 (Minn. App. 1989).

[68] See, *e.g., United States v. Ross,* 503 F.2d 940 (5th Cir. 1974).

[69] *Williams v. State,* 560 A.2d 1012 (Del. 1989).

[70] See, *e.g., Grant v. State,* 654 P.2d 1325 (Alaska Ct. App. 1982).

[71] See, *e.g., United States v. Davis,* 828 F.2d 968 (3d Cir. 1987), *cert. denied,* 484 U.S. 1069, 108 S. Ct. 1036 (1987).

[72] See, *e.g., Nicholas v. United States*, 527 F.2d 1160 (9th Cir. 1976) (time spent in jail tolled); *United States v. Martin*, 786 F.2d 974 (10th Cir. 1986).

[73] See, *e.g., O'Shea v. State*, 683 P.2d 286 (Alaska App. 1984) (imprisonment for unrelated offense tolled); *People v. Pewretsky*, 44 Colo. App. 270, 616 P.2d 170 (1980); *Catlin v. State*, 569 A.2d 210 (Md. Spec. App. 1990) (absconded and periods of imprisonment tolled); *State v. Vaughn*, 105 Or. App. 518, 805 P.2d 733 (1991) (any warrants tolled).

[74] See, *e.g., People v. Young*, 228 Cal. App. 3d 171, 278 Cal. Rptr. 7684 (1991).

[75] See, *e.g., Barker v. States*, 479 N.W.2d 275 (Iowa 1991).

[76] *Langston v. State*, 800 S.W.2d 553 (Tex. Crim. App. 1990) (waited 7½ months to bring defendant in for revocation hearing).

[77] *United States v. Fisher*, 895 F.2d 208 (5th Cir. 1990), *cert. denied*, 495 U.S. 940 (1990).

[78] *Commonwealth v. Baillargeon*, 28 Mass. App. 16, 545 N.E.2d 1182 (1989) (citing *People v. Diamond*, 245 N.W.2d 809 (Mich. Ct. App. 1976).

[79] N.J. STAT. ANN. § 2C:45-3c (West 1982), interpreted in, *State v. DeChristino*, 235 N.J. Super 291, 562 A.2d 236 (1989).

[80] *Keller v. Superior Court*, 22 Ariz. App. 122, 524 P.2d 956 (1974).

[81] *State v. Jackson*, 565 N.E.2d 848 (Ohio App. 1988); *State v. Green*, 757 P.2d 462 (Utah 1988).

[82] *Lackey v. State*, 731 P.2d 565 (Wyo. 1987).

[83] *Commonwealth v. Sawicki*, 369 Mass. 377, 339 N.E.2d 740 (1975).

[84] See, *e.g., People v. Moss*, 213 Cal. App. 3d 532, 261 Cal. Rptr. 651 (1989); *United States v. Barth*, 899 F.2d 199 (2d Cir. 1990), *cert. denied*, 111 S. Ct. 953, 112 L. Ed. 2d 1042 (1990).

[85] See, *e.g., Roberson v. State*, 572 So. 2d 1323 (Ala. Crim. App. 1990).

[86] See, *e.g., Ex Parte Helton*, 578 So. 2d 1379 (Ala. 1990).

[87] *United States v. McCormick*, 54 F.3d 214 (5th Cir. 1995).

[88] See, *e.g.,* MD. ANN. CODE of 1957, § 4-346(c) (1992), discussed in, *Peterson v. State*, 73 Md. App. 459, 534 A.2d 1353 (Md. Spec. App. 1988), *vacated*, 553 A.2d 672 (1989); *Smith v. State*, 598 P.2d 1389 (Wyo. 1979).

[89] *McCowan v. State*, 739 S.W.2d 652 (Tex. Ct. App. 1987).

[90] *Ratliff v. State*, 546 N.E.2d 309 (Ind. Ct. App. 1989).

[91] *People v. Williams*, 186 Mich. App. 606, 465 N.W.2d 376 (1990).

[92] *Peltier v. State*, 119 Idaho 454, 808 P.2d 373 (1991).

[93] *People v. Boucher*, 179 Ill. App. 3d 823, 535 N.E.2d 56 (1989).

[94] See, *e.g., Alfred v. State*, 758 P.2d 130 (Alaska Ct. App. 1988).

[95] ILL. COMP. STAT. tit. 730 § 515-6-4 (1993).

[96] *People v. Gallinger*, 191 Ill. App. 3d 488, 548 N.E.2d 78 (1989).

[97] 726 F.2d 1231 (7th Cir. 1984).

[98] *United States v. Zentgraf*, 20 F.3d 906 (8th Cir. 1994).

⁹⁹ *Commonwealth v. Durling,* 407 Mass. 108, 551 N.E.2d 1193 (1990).

¹⁰⁰ *Durling v. Chairman, Massachusetts Parole Board,* 789 F. Supp. 457 (D. Mass. 1992).

¹⁰¹ *United States v. Pattman,* 535 F.2d 1062, 1063 (8th Cir. 1976).

¹⁰² *State v. Carey,* 228 Conn. 487, 636 A.2d 840 (Conn. 1994).

¹⁰³ *People v. Lusk,* 218 Cal. App. 3d 386, 267 Cal. Rptr. 146 (1990).

¹⁰⁴ *State v. Yura,* 250 Kan. 198, 825 P.2d 523 (1992).

¹⁰⁵ See, *e.g.,* Ohio R. Evid. 101(C).

¹⁰⁶ See, *e.g., Swackhammer v. State,* 808 P.2d 219 (Wyo. 1991); *Barnett v. State,* 194 Ga. App. 892, 392 S.E.2d 322 (1990); *Chasteen v. State,* 652 So. 2d 319 (Ala. Crim. App. 1994); *Commonwealth v. Davis,* 586 A.2d 914 (Pa. 1991).

¹⁰⁷ See, *e.g., Adams v. State,* 521 So. 2d 337 (Fla. Dist. Ct. App. 1988).

¹⁰⁸ *State v. Fuller,* 308 Md. 547, 520 A.2d 1315 (1987); but see *People v. Styles,* 573 N.Y.S.2d 541, 175 A.D.2d 961 (N.Y. Supp. 1991) appeal denied, 582 N.Y.S.2d 83, 79 N.Y.S.2d 923, 590 N.E.2d 1211 (1992) (although the discharge report does not meet the business exception rule, it is admissible but is insufficient in and of itself to form basis of revocation).

¹⁰⁹ *Layton v. Peronek,* 803 P.2d 1294 (Utah Ct. App. 1990).

¹¹⁰ *United States v. McCormick,* 54 F.3d 214 (5th Cir. 1995).

¹¹¹ *State v. Pennington,* 649 A.2d 513 (Vt. 1994).

¹¹² See, *e.g., Falasco v. Pennsylvania Board of Probation and Parole,* 104 Pa. Commw. 321, 521 A.2d 991 (1987).

¹¹³ See, *e.g., Carson v. State,* 21 Ark. App. 249, 731 S.W.2d 237 (1987); *Jackson v. State,* 34 Ark. App. 4, 804 S.W.2d 735 (1991); *Commonwealth v. Olsen,* 405 Mass. 491, 541 N.E.2d 1003 (1989); *Payne v. Robinson,* 207 Conn. 565, 541 A.2d 504 (1988), *cert. denied,* 488 U.S. 898, 109 S. Ct. 242 (1988); *State v. Turner,* 257 Kan. 19, 891 P.2d 317 (1995).

¹¹⁴ See *e.g., United States v. Finney,* 897 F.2d 1047 (10th Cir. 1990), *contra, United States v. Workman,* 585 F.2d 1205, 1211 (4th Cir. 1978).

¹¹⁵ See, *e.g., Adams v. State,* 153 Ga. App. 41, 264 S.E.2d 532 (1980); *State v. Burkholder,* 12 Ohio 3d 205, 466 N.E.2d 176, *cert. denied,* 469 U.S. 1062, 105 S. Ct. 545 (1984); *Michaud v. State,* 505 P.2d 1399 (Okla. Crim. App. 1973).

¹¹⁶ Proposition # 8, discussed in *People v. Piloto,* 207 Cal. App. 3d 518, 255 Cal. Rptr. 16 (1989).

¹¹⁷ *State v. Turner,* 257 Kan. 19, 891 P.2d 317 (1995).

¹¹⁸ See, *e.g., United States v. Segal,* 549 F.2d 1293 (9th Cir.), *cert. denied,* 431 U.S. 919 (1977); *People v. Hardin,* 245 N.W.2d 566 (Mich. Ct. App. 1976); *Nelson v. State,* 66 Md. App. 304, 503 A.2d 1357 (1986); *State v. Johnson,* 17 Conn. App. 226, 551 A.2d 1264 (1988).

¹¹⁹ See, *e.g., State v. Yura,* 250 Kan. 198, 825 P.2d 523 (1992) (error for revocation judge to not allow for hearing prior to conviction of new offense alleged).

¹²⁰ See, *e.g., State v. Kunkel,* 455 N.W.2d 213 (N.D. 1990); *State v. McGinnis,* 243 N.W.2d 583 (Iowa 1976); *State v. Austin,* 295 N.W.2d 246 (Minn. 1980).

¹²¹ See, *e.g., Commonwealth v. Holmgren,* 421 Mass. 224, 565 N.E.2d 577 (1995); *Justice v. State,* 550 N.E.2d 809 (Ind. Ct. App. 1990).

[122] *Patterson v. Commonwealth,* 12 Va. App. 1046, 407 S.E.2d 43 (1991).

[123] *State v. Coates,* 528 So. 2d 595 (La. Ct. App. 2d 1988); *cf.* if rely on conviction that is later appealed and defendant is acquitted, collateral estoppel keeps state from revoking probation again, *Commonwealth v. Royster,* 524 Pa. 333, 572 A.2d 683 (1990).

[124] See, *e.g., Carson v. State,* 751 P.2d 1317 (Wyo. 1988).

[125] *Greer v. State,* 783 S.W.2d 222 (Tex. Ct. App. 1989).

[126] *Baldasar v. Illinois,* 446 U.S. 222 (1980); *State v. Canady,* 391 S.E.2d 248 (S.C. 1990).

[127] See, *e.g., McCracken v. Corey,* 612 P.2d 990, 996 (Alaska 1980).

[128] *State v. Begins,* 147 Vt. 295, 514 A.2d 719, 722 (Vt. 1986).

[129] *Fuller v. State,* 64 Md. App. 339, 495 A.2d 366, 373 (1985), *modified,* 520 A.2d 1315 (1987).

[130] See, *e.g., State v. Begins,* 514 A.2d 719,711 (Vt. 1986).

[131] See, *e.g.,* HAW. REV. STAT. § 706-628(1) (repealed 1985); COLO. REV. STAT. § 16-11-206(3) (1986).

[132] See, *e.g., People v. Coleman,* 13 Cal. 3d 867, 533 P.2d 1024, 120 Cal. Rptr. 384 (1975); *State v. Phabsomphons,* 50 N.W.2d 876 (Minn. Ct. App. 1995).

[133] See, *e.g., Fuller v. State,* 64 Md. App. 339, 495 A.2d 366 (1985), *modified,* 520 A.2d 1315.

[134] See, *e.g., State v. Chase,* 588 A.2d 120 (R.I. 1991).

[135] *Lucido v. People,* 272 Cal. Rptr. 767, 792 P.2d 1223 (Cal. 1990), *cert. denied,* 111 S. Ct. 2021, 114 L. Ed. 2d 107 (1990) (reserve trial process as the exclusive forum for the determination of guilt or innocence); *State v. Nash,* 817 S.W.2d 837 (Tex. Ct. App. 1991); *People v. Johnson,* 191 Mich. App. 222, 477 N.W.2d 426 (1991).

[136] *State v. Watts,* 221 Mont. 104, 717 P.2d 24 (1986).

[137] *Dail v. State,* 96 Nev. 435, 610 P.2d 1193 (1980).

[138] *Commonwealth v. Kates,* 302 A.2d 701, 707-08 (Pa. 1973); *State v. Cyganoski,* 21 Wash. App. 119, 584 P.2d 426, 428 (1978).

[139] *United States v. Bazzano,* 712 F.2d 826 (3d Cir. 1983) (en banc), *cert. denied,* 465 U.S. 16778, 104 S. Ct. 1439 (1983).

[140] *United States v. Thevis,* 665 F.2d 616, *reh'g denied,* 671 F.2d 1379, *cert. denied,* 456 U.S. 1008, 102 S. Ct. 2300, 73 L. Ed. 2d 1303; *United States v. Herbst,* 641 F.2d 1161 (5th Cir. 1981), *cert. denied,* 454 U.S. 851, 102 S. Ct. 292 (1981).

[141] 18 U.S.C. §3565 (Supp. II 1984).

[142] N.M. STAT. ANN. § 244.05(3) (West Supp. 1986); *Commonwealth v. Holmgren,* 421 Mass. 224, 565 N.E.2d 577 (1995) (largely ignored in practice because the offender has no reason to appeal shorter sentences and the probation departments that initiate the revocation have no standing to appeal.)

[143] W. VA. CODE § 62-12-10 (Supp. 1995)

[144] *United States v. Behnezhad,* 907 F.2d 896 (9th Cir. 1990).

[145] See, *e.g., State v. Richmond,* 896 P.2d 1112 (Kan. Ct. App. 1995).

[146] VT. STAT. ANN. tit. 28 § 303 (1986).

[147] *Baynard v. State,* 318 Md. 531, 569 A.2d 652 (Md. Ct. App. 1990).

[148] *Dopkowski v. State,* 87 Md. App. 466, 590 A.2d 173 (1991), *modified,* 620 A.2d 1185, citing *Wink v. State,* 317 Md. 330, 563 A.2d 414 (1989).

[149] *State v. Austin,* 295 N.W.2d 246, 250 (Minn. 1980).

[150] *Black v. Romano,* 471 U.S. 606, 105 S. Ct. 2254, 85 L. Ed. 2d 636 (1985).

[151] *Bearden v. Georgia,* 461 U.S. 660, 103 S. Ct. 2064, 76 L. Ed. 2d 221 (1983).

[152] *United States v. Wende,* 925 F.2d 1472 (9th Cir. 1991).

[153] *United States v. Barth,* 899 F.2d 199 (2d Cir. 1990), *cert. denied,* 112 L. Ed. 2d 1042 (1990).

[154] *State v. Tardo,* 636 So. 2d 911 (La. 1994).

[155] *Molina v. State,* 520 So. 2d 320 (Fla. Dist. Ct. App. 1988).

[156] *United States v. Babich,* 785 F.2d 415 (3d Cir.), *cert. denied,* 479 U.S. 833 (1986); *cf. People v. Bell,* 579 N.E.2d 1154 (Ill. App. 1991) (failure to comply with one term enough to justify revocation).

[157] See, *e.g., Commonwealth v. Carter,* 336 Pa. 275, 485 A.2d 802 (1984); *Dodd v. State,* 686 P.2d 737 (Alaska Ct. App. 1984); *People v. Simpson,* 579 N.Y.S.2d 698 (N.Y. Sup. App. 1992); *People v. Walker,* 517 N.E.2d 679 (Ill. Ct. App. 1987).

[158] See, *e.g., People v. Perez,* 521 N.Y.S.2d 798 (N.Y. Sup. App. 1987).

[159] See, *e.g.,* VT. R. CRIM. PROC. 32(a) (required at sentencing but not revocation).

[160] *United States v. Barnes,* 948 F.2d 325 (7th Cir. 1991) (mandatory), *contra, United States v. Coffey,* 871 F.2d 39 (6th Cir. 1989).

[161] *United States v. White,* 925 F.2d 284 (9th Cir. 1990); *United States v. Smith,* 907 F.2d 133, 135 (11th Cir. 1990); *United States v. Von Washington,* 915 F.2d 390, 391 (8th Cir. 1990).

[162] SENTENCING GUIDELINES § 7B1.1

[163] *United States v. Grimes,* 54 F.3d 489 (8th Cir. 1995).

[164] See, *e.g., People v. Bogan,* 540 N.E.2d 1135 (Ill. App. 1989) (court may review violation conduct to assess potential for rehabilitation); *State v. Baylass,* 114 N.J. 169, 553 A.2d 326 (1989), *cert. granted,* 563 A.2d 807, 563 A.2d 821, 563 A.2d 842 (1989); *State v. Robinson,* 556 A.2d 342 (N.J. 1989) (revocation not aggravating factor in sentencing).

[165] *People v. Bogan,* 85 Ill. App. 3d 129, 540 N.E.2d 1135 (1989) (court may review violation conduct to assess potential for rehabilitation).

[166] *Hendly v. State,* 783 S.W.2d 750 (Tex. App. 1990).

[167] Nor can the court aggregate violations to exceed 60 days (*State v. McDougal,* 120 Wash. 2d 334, 841 P.2d 1232 (1992).

[168] *Reno v. Koray,* 115 S. Ct. 2021, 132 L. Ed. 2d 46 (1995).

[169] *Olsen v. Florida,* 654 So. 2d 304 (Fla. 1995).

[170] *Holcomb v. Sutherland,* 321 Or. 99, 894 P.2d 457 (1995).

[171] *Wisconsin v. Avila,* 532 N.W.2d 423 (Wis. 1995).

[172] *Villery v. Florida Parole and Probation Commission,* 396 So. 2d 1107 (Fla. 1981) (citations omitted).

[173] Klein (1989). *Should You Send a Probationer Back to Jail . . . .* JUDGES JOURNAL, Winter.

[174] *State v. Swadley,* 190 Wis. App. 2d 139, 526 N.W.2d 778 (1994).

[175] *State v. Jordan,* 485 N.W.2d 198 (Neb. 1992); see also *People v. Ramos,* 561 N.E.2d 643 (Ill. 1990).

[176] *People v. Hoecher,* 822 P.2d 8 (Colo. 1991).

[177] *Yellowbear v. State,* 874 P.2d 241 (Wyo. 1994).

[178] *Grant v. State,* 99 Nev. 149, 659 P.2d 878 (1983); see also *Maus v. State,* 311 Md. 85, 532 A.2d 1066 (1987).

[179] *In re McPhee,* 141 Vt. 4, 442 A.2d 1285 (1982).

[180] *State v. Reyes,* 207 N.J. 126, 504 A.2d 43 (1986).

[181] *People v. Reinertson,* 178 Cal. App. 3d 320, 223 Cal. Rptr. 670 (1986).

[182] See, *e.g., State v Reynolds,* 170 Ariz. 233, 823 P.2d 681 (1992).

[183] See, *e.g., Maus v. State,* 311 Md. 85, 532 A.2d 1066 (1987).

[184] Kramer (1986). *Sentencing the Drunk Driver: A Call For Change.* ALCOHOL TREATMENT QUARTERLY (Special Edition).

[185] DuPont (1984). *Expanding Sentencing Options: A Governor's Perspective.* NATIONAL INSTITUTE OF JUSTICE REPORTS 186 (July).

[186] *Id.*

[187] *Id.*

[188] *Divine Brown to Serve Sentence.* BOSTON GLOBE, Nov. 2, 1995.

[189] *Back to Jail for Mr. Bobbitt.* REUTERS, Dec. 21, 1995.

[190] DuPont (1984). *Expanding Sentencing Options: A Governor's Perspective.* NATIONAL INSTITUTE OF JUSTICE REPORTS 186 (July).

[191] *Rapper Shakur Ordered Jailed.* REUTERS, Jan. 23, 1996.

[192] Cohen, R. (1995). *Probation and Parole Violators in State Prisons, 1991, Special Report,* Bureau of Justice Statistics. Washington, DC: U.S. Justice Department (August).

[193] Conversation with ISP supervisor, Richard B. Talpey, Trenton, New Jersey, November 15, 1995.

[194] *North Carolina Implements Justice Fellowship Inspired Guidelines.* JUSTICE REPORT 11:1 (Winter 1995).

[195] Bidinotto (1993). *When Criminals Go Free.* READER'S DIGEST, March.

[196] Atlantic Monthly Press, New York, N.Y.

Chapter 11

Evaluating Alternative Sentences

§11.01   Introduction

When all is said and done, when the clerk has finished reading the formal disposition into the record, the parties have left the courtroom, the judge has adjourned to his lobby and the attorneys to their respective offices, the question remains, do alternative sentences work? Rigorous evaluation of alternative sentences, like that of sentencing in general, is difficult if not impossible. Either the existing research is nonexistent or it is compromised by the difficulty in conducting social research, with its multitude of uncontrolled and often uncontrollable variables. However, there exists a smattering of studies that suggest the efficacy of distinct components of alternative sentences.

§11.02   Does Victim Satisfaction Increase?

A major factor involved in alternative sentences is involvement of the victim both in the process of sentencing and in the sentence itself, most commonly as the recipient of court-ordered restitution. Does such involvement increase victim satisfaction? Once ordered, will victims actually receive restitution from the offender?

While individual cases obviously vary, the general answer to both questions is an emphatic "yes." Victim satisfaction does increase as a result of alternative sentences that involve them both in the process and in the disposition. Specifically, victim involvement, including just being informed of the case's progress through the court, or the awarding of restitution, increases victim satisfaction with the criminal justice system as well as victim perception of the fairness of the court.

The exhaustive survey of crime victims in Pennsylvania found that victims were generally unhappy with the courts and criminal justice system, with the exception of police work.[1] That unhappiness was reversed if they were informed about their cases or were ordered restitution. Further, their happiness increased in proportion to the amount of restitution ordered and subsequently received from the defendant.

The Pennsylvania findings were duplicated by a study of victims of adult offenders conducted in one of the busier district courts in Massachusetts, called the Quincy Division.[2] In the Quincy study, researchers created an experimental design consisting of a control group who were not invited to participate in the sentencing process, nor specially informed about their case's progress through the courts, nor awarded restitution as part of the disposition. Two other randomly selected groups of victims were also established. One was kept informed of their cases' progress and invited to participate in the sentencing process. Members of this group were invited to testify at disposition or send in a victim impact statement and a statement of opinion form. The second group was specifically ordered restitution as part of the disposition.

The victims who participated in either aspect of the experimental program perceived the quality of justice meted out by the court as "being better than those victims who were in the control group." Victims who received restitution tended to rate the court more positively than those who did not. Further, they viewed it as "more just" than their peers who did not receive restitution.

The findings from Pennsylvania and Massachusetts are not intuitively difficult to understand. It stands to reason that victims will better appreciate the court process if they are informed and involved in it. It also stands to reason that they will be positively influenced if ordered restitution. Beside the financial impact, the fact that the offender has to return something to them helps right the imbalance inherent in their original victimization. As one practitioner has so aptly described: "it is not so much the goods taken, but the taking of the goods that affects the victim."

There is anecdotal but increasingly plentiful evidence that even severely affected victims can be reconciled with their offenders. Victim Offender Reconciliation Programs are flourishing across the country, truly representing a grassroots movement of concerned religious and community activists working in concert with enlightened criminal justice practitioners. It is true that there are times when these programs experience bitter frustrations. One program reports a meeting it induced after much careful preparation between an offender, convicted of manslaughter, and the wife of his victim. As a result of the meeting, the victim's pain and suffering did not cease, but she was able to begin the slow process of rebuilding her life, finding a renewed peace within herself. For the defendant, too, the meeting's effects were profound. Nonetheless, the court sentenced the defendant to five to 15 years imprisonment without considering the victim's feelings or the breakthrough the meeting had effected. The program, however, pledged to continue its work:

> There will be a day of reconciliation between many more victims and offenders. And there will be a day when those rendering "Justice" will see that reconciliation is the issue which brings inner peace not only to the victim and the offenders but a sense of lasting peace to the entire community.[3]

The question remains, even if victims appreciate involvement and orders of restitution, will they then be paid by the defendant? If not, is not the court setting them up for a second victimization? This concern is particularly relevant because a significant majority of offenders tend to be young, unemployed and indigent. As a judge explained at a symposium on alternatives to incarceration sponsored by New York University in 1983:

> In New York County approximately 68 percent of the defendants cannot make $500 bail. . . . Given such a situation, how can we meaningfully talk about restitution? Restitution, in an environment such as New York City, with the kind of cases that come before me, is simply a Pollyanna solution.[4]

However, the available research suggests that offenders, including hard-core offenders from severely disadvantaged backgrounds, complete their restitution orders at a consistently high rate, well over two-thirds.[5] The largest restitution research project ever commissioned by the Justice Department, involving more than 17,000 offenders, mostly in their late teens, documented an even better nationwide average payment rate of 86.2 percent of cases closed over the two years of its study. Completion rates were uniformly high, differing only 11 percent between offenders from high to low income levels, 13 percent between first and multiple offenders and seven percent between whites and minority offenders. In fact, the completion rate never fell below 75 percent in any court studied around the country, including Washington, D.C., Quincy, Massachusetts (whose court has a 25 percent caseload from the poorer neighborhoods of contiguous Boston), Charleston, South Carolina and other urban areas.

Some experts posit that the surprisingly high completion rates documented by the Justice Department studies is due in part to the assumption of capability on the part of the judges, probation and program personnel who ordered, collected and enforced the restitution orders.

> Cultivating the perception among (offenders) that they possess the capability to achieve important goals will increase the likelihood these offenders will strive to meet the expectations posed for them. The tendency toward dependency and passivity must be eliminated as much as possible from the mind sets of [offenders] participating in restitution programs.[6]

High payment rates are also due to several other factors. Losses and injuries tend to be limited in the first place. In the second, unlike bail, the entire restitution amount need not be paid in one lump sum, but in installments over a period of time.

§11.03   Will Offenders Complete Community Work Service and Other Affirmative Orders?

In addition to payment of restitution, common alternative sentences require offenders to complete a number of affirmative tasks, including paying fines, costs, forfeitures, bonds, support, donations and fees as well as completing community or victim work service. Will such orders be completed? Particularly, will offenders complete court-ordered community work service? This is of great concern, as orders of community work service are often the court's last resort in providing alternative sentences to indigent offenders who cannot pay monetary orders.

Again, studies suggest the answer to be "yes" to both questions. The same studies that document high restitution payment rates document similarly high completion rates for community work service. While those who were ordered to work between one to 16 hours had the highest completion rates (over 95 percent), those ordered up to 1,000 hours had a completion rate of 75 percent.[7]

There are so many potential sites where defendants may be ordered to perform community work service that it is almost impossible to imagine a court being unable to place an offender. Despite concerns often expressed by courts and others over liability and accidents opening the court to lawsuits and liability, a survey of community work service programs across the nation conducted by the Hawaii courts' administrative office found virtually no such problems in any jurisdiction.[8]

Although relatively new on the alternative sentencing scene, programs experimenting with electronic home confinement report a uniformly high compliance rate. One federal survey found compliance averaging 90 percent, ranging from a low of 70 percent to programs reporting no failures at all.[9] Whether offenders respond because they like the attention the sanction affords, fear apprehension or because of the exotic equipment itself (many offenders only vaguely understand what the electronic equipment can and cannot do), or whether the wrist and leg monitors serve as the superego the defendants have failed to internalize, the sanction appears to keep offenders in their homes, out of trouble.

§11.04   Will Alternative Sentences Prevent Recidivism?

Most criminologists suggest that at least one legitimate aim of sentencing is to deter offenders from reoffending. Do alternative sentences offer such deterrence?

This question is difficult to answer for a number of reasons. There is little agreement as to what constitutes recidivism. There is little research to suggest what the base rate of recidivism is, which is necessary to compare the rate of recidivism of those who receive alternative versus non-alternative sentences. Some studies suggest that two-thirds of state inmates reoffend upon release.[10]

Does this mean that if only 50 percent of those with comparable crimes and backgrounds given alternative sentences reoffend, alternative sentences prevent recidivism? Finally, there is almost no research involving an experimental design that has tested alternative sentences to document recidivism rates.

Notwithstanding the above, the Justice Department did fund six national experimental sites in which random groups of teenage offenders were given "traditional" sentences versus others who were released with orders of restitution and/or community/victim work service.[11] In none of the sites did the offenders receiving the alternative sentence recidivate at a higher rate than those who did not. In five of the experiments, the offenders in the experimental sites had lower recidivism rates. Unfortunately, the "traditional sentences" were not limited to incarceration, but included regular probation supervision, mental health counseling and the like. Interestingly, the experiment found that the offenders who were ordered only to perform community work service or pay restitution as opposed to performing community work service or paying restitution plus submiting to probation supervision had lower rates of recidivism than their peers. Perhaps this confirms the inherent reformative and/or deterrent power of these restitution/work alternative sentencing components.

A research project in Britain may shed some light on the efficacy of community work service as an alternative sentence. Although the project did not study recidivism per se, it measured how various sentences were understood by those who received them. The results were surprising. It compared the attitudes of offenders who were sentenced to pay fines, placed on probation supervision for counseling or ordered to perform 240 hours of community work service. The researcher found that the offenders found the community work service sentence to be more helpful and fair than either fines or probation. He concluded:

> Community service speaks . . . to the root values the criminal law is supposed to represent. The offender would seem able, at least to some degree, to apprehend that, and it would seem important that the courts and correctional administrators also fully apprehend its significance and its promise for criminal justice practice.[12]

Whether offenders' positive attitudes toward community work service translate into lower recidivism remains to be tested.

Other studies suggest that increased supervision in the community reduces recidivism. James Q. Wilson found in his review of the literature that the intensity of supervision, rather than the quality of treatment, was essential in reducing recidivism.[13] If true, not only does this research speak for intensive probation supervision but for any alternative program that involves frequent contact and close supervision, including curfews, working to pay back money or complete community work service, mandatory attendance at Alcoholics Anonymous meetings and more.

Of 13,012 offenders released under shock probation in Ohio from 1966 to 1979, only 1,389 or 10.6 percent were reinstitutionalized.[14]

Vigorous enforcement of alternative sentences can lessen recidivism. If an offender is brought back to court for technical violations, *i.e.,* failure to abide by special conditions, the court has an opportunity to act before a new crime is committed. A Massachusetts study reveals that there is a high correlation between technical probation violations and recidivism.[15] Therefore, an offender's performance of his alternative sentence components can alert the court as to which offenders may safely remain free in the community and which it had better incapacitate either in the community or in jail.

There are no magic bullets in sentencing, no guarantees that any specific sentence works all the time with all offenders. Research into offender risk suggests that certain factors mitigate recidivism. Therefore, sentences that successfully produce those factors will be more successful than sentences that do not. Sentences that stop drug and alcohol abusers from drug use and drinking, that make unemployed offenders go to work, alter attitudes of offenders who are indifferent to their victims, are more apt to prevent recidivism. There is no evidence that alternative sentences are less able to address these factors than long-term incarceration. There is some evidence that they are better able to address them. After finding that recidivism among prisoners was higher than that of a matched group of probationers (53 percent of prisoners charged with new crimes versus 38 percent of probationers), Rand researchers concluded that as long as imprisonment is assumed to be the only means of incapacitating high-risk felons, the system will not get the greatest return possible in public safety from the resources available for corrections. They suggest community-based programs that provide for intensive supervision, including home confinement, sentences of community work service and other alternative sentences.[16]

Although most of the studies of alternative sentencing, intermediate sanctions and other programs that do not utilize long-term incarceration cited in the preceding chapters point to positive results, they are limited to specific offenders in specific, local jurisdictions, engaged in specific, localized programs. Because of the problem of having true random control groups to compare offenders sentenced one way versus another, even the largest, most comprehensive studies can only suggest that one program is superior to another.

Nonetheless, such suggestions can be fairly impressive. The Connecticut Alternative to Incarceration Program (discussed in Chapter 1), for example, has been rigorously studied, comparing arrest and incarceration rates of thousands of offenders sentenced to AIP across the entire state with those not so sentenced. The study found that 10 percent of the offenders released to AIP pretrial were arrested for a new crime pending their trial. That compares to 26 percent of offenders released without AIP participation. After the pretrial period, only six percent of AIP participants were incarcerated. This compares to 28 percent for non-AIP offenders. And one year after initial sentencing, 24 percent of AIP subsequently recidivated versus 30 percent for non-AIP offenders who had been incarcerated. While the latter difference may not seem very dramatic, it means that not only did AIP participants do marginally better than non-AIP participants, but they did so at one-fifth the cost. Not only did they save the taxpayers the high cost of their incarceration, but in AIP, they completed 200,000 hours of community service (1993 to 1994). They also freed up slots in state prison so that the state had the resources to increase the length of incarceration for more dangerous offenders from 13 percent of their full sentence in 1990 to 55 percent in 1995 (for those sentenced to two years or more).[17]

On the other hand, although widely popular, studies have not found such positive results with boot camps. Early studies of boot camp graduates versus comparable offenders who did not participate in boot camps found no difference in terms of subsequent recidivism. Such studies have been completed in Georgia (1989), Florida (1989), New York (1989) and Louisiana (1991).[18] But it should be noted that the boot camp graduates did no worse. The next generation of boot camps, which include more aftercare and supervision, may fare better. As mentioned in the research on intensive supervision programs reported in §9.03, while the first generation of programs proved ineffective, the second generation did much better.

§11.05   Will the Community and Judges Accept Alternative Sentences?

Many defense and prosecution attorneys are understandably reluctant to recommend alternative sentences, believing that the court will categorically reject such recommendations. There is substantial evidence, however, that courts are becoming increasingly receptive to alternative sentences. Indeed, what may be deterring wider acceptance is the very reluctance of attorneys to suggest them in the first place. According to an article in the *National Law Journal,* acceptance is growing:

> While alternative sentencing for minor offenders has won wide acceptance over the last five years, it recently has been spreading quickly for more serious offenses in both the violent and white-collar categories. . . . Criminal justice experts predict that once more lawyers start developing innovative sentencing packages, the movement will escalate even more rapidly, and that creative sentencing might someday be a necessary part of a successful trial strategy.[19]

The same article goes on to describe the major stumbling block to the growth of alternative sentencing—the lack of training defense attorneys receive to deal effectively with the sentencing process. As a result, according to Jerome Miller, lawyers treat a guilty client like doctors treat a terminal patient. If proposed, however, the journal article concludes that judges are accepting alternative sentences beyond most lawyers' wildest expectations.

The same journal has endorsed alternative sentences in an editorial:

> We hope the legal community takes advantage of the groups that spe-
> cialize in creating such alternative sentences, as well as others in the
> profession who have successfully used such sentences in the past. By
> proeeeding with caution, lawyers and judges utilizing such proce-
> dures could play a major role in reshaping the concept of punishment
> in this country.[20]

It should also be noted that a number of alternative sentence components
were "invented" from the bench, including weekend sentences, shock sentences and house arrest, among others. Other components are widely employed
by courts in all jurisdictions.

Especially where they are elected, judges must reflect to some extent the
values and sentiments of the general public when it comes to sentencing. Surveys have found deep public support for typical alternative sentencing components. In the deep south, researchers found overwhelming support for monetary
restitution, community work service and direct victim service, even from citizens who were dissatisfied with the criminal justice system overall.[21] The Edna
McConnell Clark Foundation commissioned a study of public attitudes about
crime and punishment. It found that "Americans support alternatives to incarceration because they believe that prisons have failed to instill attitudes and values that prepare inmates for jobs after their release."[22] Alternatives discussed
included restitution, community work service, fines, mandatory treatment for
drug and alcohol abuse, intensive probation, halfway houses and mandatory
employment, school attendance or job training. Confronted with the estimated
$50 billion price tag of building enough prisons to house inmates already incar-
cerated in overcrowded facilities, or nearly $1,000 in taxes per typical Ameri-
can family, the public is even more inclined to support alternatives.[23]

Mark Cannon, Administrative Assistant to the Chief Justice of the United
States Supreme Court, has also cited evidence of widespread public support:

> The logic of alternative sentencing is so powerful that tough-minded
> commentators—such as William Buckley and Paul Harvey, who
> have never been accused of being soft on crime—have endorsed
> alternative punishment for nonviolent offenders.[24]

Alternative sentences have won the support of many newspapers. A Gannett
newspaper in Rockland, New York, for example, endorsed alternative sentences
with enthusiasm, not only because they relieve prison overcrowding, but
because they are better. The paper read that with them "some sweat is extract-
ed" and with them comes a "realization that crime does not pay." It went on to
read that "that message does not always get through to the person sitting in a
jail cell, twiddling his thumbs." [25]

Genessee County Sheriff W. Douglas Call ran and won in an upstate New
York county on a platform of alternative sentencing. His programs, which
measure success by the number of offenders kept out of jail, are popular in
what the *Wall Street Journal* labeled the "conservative Republican . . . stretch

of farmland between Rochester and Buffalo."[26] All but four of the county's 34 judges use the sheriff's alternative sentencing programs. Their use has enabled the county to cancel the former sheriff's plan for a new, $5 million, 60-bed jail facility.

Proponents can take heart in the editorial praise even controversial alternative sentences have won in the past, including the Fairfax, Virginia school arson case and the Maryland drunk driving multiple homicide cases presented earlier. While individual alternative sentences handed down from time to time have been roundly criticized, on the whole the public, as well as the bench, seems receptive to alternative sentences. Whether or not a specific alternative sentence is accepted by a specific court at a specific time depends upon the circumstances of the case, including how well the sentencing alternative is promoted in court.

Delaware provides an instructive example of an entire state accepting a correctional scheme that relies on alternative and intermediate sentencing. Further, the reforms in Delaware were actively promoted by state politicians and criminal justice administrators. Described in Chapter 10, the Delaware sentencing reform program has survived its original sponsors. In 1991, Governor Castle, the second governor to support the program, explained how the program began and survived.

> Any Governor, mayor, or county executive can tell you that [intermediate sanctions and the problem of obtaining community acceptance for them] remain politically and publically sensitive issues. People expect government to protect them. They do not want government proposing programs that put unrehabilitated criminals back into their communities. The pressure thay can bring to bear against these programs is difficult to overcome. . . .

> The average person in Delaware annually pays $1,000 in State personal income tax. It would take the total State collected from 215 Delaware residents to pay for just 1 prisoner for only 1 year. Tell people that and you not only get their attention and anger, but you get their interest in perhaps doing things differently. . . .

> Once you open people's minds to the "prison-only" problem, you must convince them that viable alternatives do exist that still protect their personal safety. Never lose sight of the fact that this is a very personal and human issue. Show people that there are programs . . . where violent or habitual felons are assured prison beds only because [others] are being punished in other meaningful ways. . . .

> Our breakthrough came when we concluded that the solution was not putting more offenders in larger prisons, but that the structure of our system was inadequate. *We wanted to sentence smarter, not just tougher* (emphasis added). And it did not make sense to have such a gross dichotomy—offenders either in prison or out on the street under general probation. . . .

> To accomplish [our] goals, we began our work by establishing, by legislative act, a Sentencing Accountability Commission. It served as a forum for our target publics to study intermediate sanctions, debate them, and search for specific programs to create. . . . With representation from all facets of criminal justice, the Commission developed a defined continuum of sanctions based on the degree of supervision and control that needed to be exercised over each offender. We then went directly to our public opinion leaders—legislators on criminal justice committees, prominent judges, and others—and educated them, answered their questions, and made them part of the process.
>
> During this process we were able to hear concerns in a controlled environment and prepare the case for the general public. And by making the leaders part of the process, we gained some of our strongest and most effective advocates. . . .
>
> With a program supported by the three branches of government and key community groups, we were able to implement a public awareness strategy designed to mobilize public support for our new initiatives.

With public support, Delaware was able to build on its new sentencing matrix over the years. While prison growth increased by 15.8 percent in Maryland, 22.4 percent in Virginia, 22.3 percent in New Jersey, 25.8 percent in New York, to name a few, Delaware's prison population increased during the same five-year period by only 5.8 percent. The Governor attributes this trend to the manner in which Delaware judges and other members of the criminal justice community have embraced the matrix system of sentencing that relies on intermediate sanctions for eligible offenders. As a result, by 1991, the state had almost 1,000 offenders on intensive supervision at a cost of $2,300 per offender. If only one-half of them were true prison diversions, that would represent a program savings of $5.4 million per year, contributing to a total savings of $8 million if other intermediate sanctions, such as halfway houses, were also included.

The Governor concluded:

> By carefully developing sensible sentencing policies and a wide range of sanctions, and implementing an aggressive public education initiative, we have held offenders accountable to the public and the legal system and have held ourselves accountable to the public. . . . Always remember that while this is an issue of public concern, it is within your power to make it an issue of public interest and support as well. . . . Remember that it is people's perception of their personal safety as well as allocation of their hard-earned money that you must address. . . . And finally, remember that it is people, your community members, whom you must make your partners in solving and preventing future correction problems.[27]

§11.06   The Future of Alternative Sentences, Intermediate Sanctions and Probation

The country is at a crossroads in corrections and criminal sentencing. The present retributive justice emphasis, with its demonization of criminals and emphasis on their removal to high-security correctional institutions, threatens to bankrupt the country, state by state, county by county, and create an enduring criminal/correctional class, closely associated with race, class and ethnic groupings. If the country stays this course, alternative sentencing, intermediate sanctions and probation will continue. But they will revolve around greater community-based surveillance programs and application of high-tech enforcement devices and the like. Probation will continue to fade and alternative legal structures will be developed to house intermediate sanction programs.

The emerging alternative revolves around a more restorative system of justice, integrating many of the sanctions and sentences described in the preceding chapters. Under this system, corrections and criminal sentencing will focus in a more balanced way on criminals, victims and the community, with a goal of restoring each, as much as possible, to function as productively as possible. With such a system, alternative, intermediate and probationary sentences will replace or supplement the either/or dichotomy of current corrections, which either imprisons offenders or lets them go with minimal sanctions while largely ignoring the consequences of their crimes on victims and the community at large.

If institution of a restorative justice system is to occur, the traditional processing of criminal cases will also change. Victims and the community will become more involved in practice, rather than just on paper, as is now the case in most jurisdictions. Rather than limit judicial discretion with determinate sentencing or increase it with indeterminate sentencing, the judges' role will transform, giving more discretion to victims and citizens' panels to fashion more indivdualized sentences. These new actors will be more concerned with meeting the exigencies of each case and all parties involved than simply clearing cases to maintain a clean court docket.

If such a system is to work, probation will also necessarily be transformed. Probation's single-minded focus on and commitment to the offender, which has helped to make probation largely irrelevant to crime and justice in America, will change. Probation will no longer serve primarily as an inducement to facilitate plea bargaining, failing to address the public's rage and frustration over its mounting fear of crime. Probation's myopic vision will broaden beyond the offender. Its mission will be to see that justice is done, victims are served, and the community is protected.

Ask any probation officers today and they will tell you their "client" is the probationer. Whether they want to rehabilitate him, limit the risk he presents to the public or "trail him, nail him and jail him," their focus on the client is steadfast. Experts have assisted them in this course. The National Institute of Corrections, for example, has provided resources for probation nationwide to promote risk classification of offenders. Through risk assessments, probation can better, more scientifically identify the offenders who are more likely to re-offend than those who will not, based on shared characteristics.

It does not matter what the offender has done, who he has traumatized or hospitalized, the impact of his crime on society at large—these are only incidentally relevant in determining the risk the offender presents for reoffense. If he or she is at high risk, probation commits disproportionate resources his way. They may be strictly surveillance or rehabilitation resources, but they flow to the highest-risk offenders. Conversely, the low-risk offenders are "banked" in large caseloads, safely ignored, regardless of what they did, who they did it to and what the impact of their crimes was on the community at large.

Touted as a redemptive reform for probation, what risk classification does, as probation programs before it, is continue probation's focus on the offender to the exclusion of everything else. It has too often allowed probation to become, in effect, a haven for offenders to escape the negative consequences of their own criminal behavior. Like a child's game of tag, once offenders reach probation's "home base," they are "safe," not to be tagged by anyone else, not a revengeful victim, an outraged society or distraught family members. It is *not* that they have secured a "get out of jail free card," although many have. (Studies suggest that even when rearrested, the vast majority of probationers are allowed to remain on probation.[28]) It *is* that they have secured an "ignore the consequences of your crime and the exigencies of justice" card. These offenders are indeed "home free."

Before probation, before risk management, before all this, offenders had to answer directly to their victims. What they did, they had to undo if possible, or pay dearly. Under Hammurabi's Code, the world's first written criminal code, for example, if a person stole a cow, he or she had to pay it back, with interest. The obligation was to the victim. The power relationship reversed between victim and offender, with the victim ascending to the top. Up until the middle ages, restorative justice predominated. Then, with the rise of the king, the state became more active. It insisted on its share of the restitution pie, converting victim restitution to the state's fine. After all, the king also deserved compensation for arresting, prosecuting and holding the offender accountable. As the king's share increased, the victim's share diminished until it vanished. The victim had to pursue his or her claim without state assistance in civil court. He or she had to sue the offender.

Thanks to the victim rights movement of the 1970s and 1980s, the criminal justice system gives lip service to victims' rights, but little else. Victim/witness advocates have proliferated in police and prosecutors' offices. Often they really function as investigators at best and roadblocks at worst, to keep pesky victims away from busy officers and prosecutors. But probation has not even pretended to offer any victim services or special attention. After it monitors the offenders' payments of other supervision fees (which may come back to probation as in Texas) and fines (which go to the state), probation often has to ask courts to remit restitution orders (to victims) as uncollectable.[29] After all, how can the current system expect poor, drug addicted, illiterate offenders to do anything but steal the money necessary to repay their victims anyway? Especially when most of their disposable income is being spent on their drug habit. Studies suggest that most felony probation officers fail to drug test offenders under probation supervision or revoke those who are tested and fail.[30]

If restorative justice takes root, one of probation's principal clients will be, in fact, the victim. One of the measurements used to judge its service to the victim will be restitution ordered *and* collected. One of probation's concerns will be service to the victim. In the current system, most probation officers do not even know who the victim is, unless it is a name on the police officer's report or perhaps a nagging restitution claimant who just does not understand why the judge's order of restitution was just so much window dressing, not to be taken seriously.

Payment of restitution will mark the beginning of the case, not the end. Currently, restitution payment often has been reduced to any other payment made, such as a fine or court cost. A check is mailed from the central office to the victim. As far as the offender is concerned, he might as well be paying a fine. Except in limited jurisdictions, there is no direct confrontation with the victim. No apology. No recitation of lessons learned. No expression of remorse. And no reconciliation and often no peace nor resolution for the victim. Yet probation, in cases in which the money is paid, claims yet another success story, another debt paid, no matter that the lion's share of the debt was paid by the insurance company or that the victim, in effect, was made to give the offender an interest-free loan for the amount of time between crime and final repayment. No matter that everyone else will also pay in terms of higher insurance premiums. As explained in Chapter 5, many states currently forbid repayments to insurance companies who repay victims for their losses and injuries.[31] So little is the present system's regard for the principal probation client, the victim, the criminal jutsice system rushes to declare victory before the battle has even been joined. Victory is claimed when the restitution is paid or the offender is sentenced to jail, whether or not it is paid.

And restitution collection and payment is only the beginning. Every day, across the country, women are murdered by their husbands or boyfriends, current or former. Every week thousands of abusers are placed on probation for injuring and terrorizing the victims they do not kill. Most are sentenced for simple misdemeanor assaults or violations of restraining orders. What do probation officers do? They see the offender, except in jurisdictions that cannot be bothered to supervise misdemeanants. They may also make the abuser enter treatment. And they set up a potential homicide because they ignore a primary probation client, the victim. How can they protect the victim if they do not even know who she is? The task is simply impossible without this knowledge.

George Lardner Jr.'s indictment of probation in his chronicle of his daughter's murder by a Massachusetts probationer makes this clear.[32] Probation's mission, in this, as with most cases, was to make the offender enter treatment, not to protect his daughter or anyone else from the probationer. When informed, for example, that the probationer was abusing a new victim, probation's response was to intensify its pressure to get him into treatment, an inadequate program at that.

In cases such as these, if the probation officer has time to have periodic contact with *anyone,* it should be the *victim,* not the *offender.*

In addition to the victim, probation's next principal client will be the community. The community is also the victim of crime. To them, too, is owed "client-hood." It is fear of crime that makes citizens prisoners in their homes and prey to every demagogue proposing an easy solution to crime offered at every election year cycle. Probation will serve them by educating them that crime occurs in the community and must be confronted by the community. The solution to crime lies within the community. Like it or not, all must be involved.

How will probation serve the community as a "client?" Probation will do so on several levels, broad and narrow. On a broader level, probation will have a significant community crime prevention role, a role that cannot be performed as well or effectively by police or other criminal justice agencies. Probation will build on limited, current experiences outlined below.

> —**Drunk Driving:** Every year, tens of thousands of Americans are killed and more injured by drunk drivers. After the damage is done, probation is typically charged with seeing the drunk drivers, often putting them into treatment programs of varying competencies. Meanwhile, the carnage goes on and the community grieves more victims. Probation, if it only recognizes its legitimate client, the community, can do so much more. All it has to do is examine its caseload of drunk drivers. Probably most were served at a licensed establishment before they got into their motor vehicles. If they had not been over-served, which is often explicitly illegal in most state codes,[33] by definition, they would not have been drunk when they subsequently drove. Probation can pinpoint that small minority of establishments that serve most of the drunk drivers.
>
> Probation can either wait until people drive drunk and pick up the pieces later, or it can choose to stop drunk driving at the source. It is a bit like attacking yellow fever, either chase after the thousands of individual disease-carrying mosquitoes or dry up the swamps in which they breed. Unfortunately, probation has chosen the former strategy exclusively.
>
> As a result of probation activities in Massachusetts, drunk driving bars are now targeted. Licensing boards are provided with the names of each bar that served a drunk driver before his or her arrest. Happy hours, which probation documented to generate disproportionate numbers of drunk drivers, are now a thing of the past by state law.
>
> —**Serving Warrants:** Consider arrest warrants. Local police are inundated with court and probation arrest warrants. Warrants are issued for everyone who fails to pay a fine or show for the least serious complaint or revocation hearing. Police often make a valiant but

necessarily short-lived effort to serve these warrants. As a result, in most cases the warrant is served *after* the offender has been arrested for still another offense. Most warrants are eventually served, especially if the offender is an active, chronic offender. The problem is that this system does little to protect the community at large from the offenders and even less to protect vulnerable victims. It does not take much genius to guess, for example, where most domestic abusers on warrants will end up and what they will be doing when finally apprehended.

Yet probation continues to dump its warrants into this vast warrant pool. Few departments have the resources or training to serve their own warrants. Even if they did, apprehension of fugitives takes more than bulletproof vests and special warrant teams. It takes community cooperation. Probation is ideally suited to solicit that cooperation. All it takes is a commitment to community and victim as vital probation clients . . . and a snapshot or two. In Quincy, Massachusetts, just south of Boston, all probation fugitives who represent a threat to a specific victim or the community (this includes all sex offenders and domestic abusers) find a copy of their probation snapshot in the local newspaper.

More than a year after the program was initiated, the apprehension rate tops 80 percent.[34] The majority of probation violators are arrested as a result of citizen-supplied information to the probation department. Citizens see a probation system committed to their safety. They also see, literally, the faces of crime in their community. As Pogo observed so many years ago, "they see the enemy and it is we." It is not what they see on television news—racial and ethnic minority drug addicts.

On a narrower level, probation can see that offenders make up for their conduct to the community. The most obvious means is community work service, putting offenders to work for the community through donation of their labor as detailed in Chapter 6. Community work service does not have to mean picking up litter in the park. As described, in Bend, Oregon, the Deschutes County probation officers have formed a comprehensive community work service program called the Restorative Justice Corps. Offenders in the Corps have built 70-bed shelters for the homeless, stocked firewood for the county's impoverished elderly and much more. Rather than be seen as liabilities to the community, probation has made these offenders into substantial community assets. Not only does this serve the community, but it makes offenders see themselves as positively transformed. Reflecting its commitment to its community client, the Deschutes County probation officers have renamed themselves "community correction officers."[35]

In Vermont, other probation officers have abandoned their desks and joined with their fellow citizens to see that the community is also served in each and every probation disposition. They assure community satisfaction because they have recruited the community to serve on sentencing and probation panels that actually determine how the offender will restore peace to the community, which his or her offense threatened or disrupted.[36] Ultimately, protecting the community begins with being part of it. In fact, probation officers who work with the citizen panels call themselves "reparations coordinators."

Allegheny's juvenile probation department provides another excellent example of a true community-based restorative probation program. Its Community Intensive Supervision Program (CISP) operates out of five neighborhood centers located in five of Pittsburgh's worst slums. High-risk juveniles report to the centers every day after school. At the center, they are drug tested. They complete their homework, assisted by computerized tutoring programs. They also perform a great deal of community service in their neighborhoods. In the summer of 1995, they cleared a vacant lot and planted a community garden that fed area shelters. They actually made money registering area voters. Victims were paid with the profits. Each night the high-risk juveniles are escorted home and monitored electronically until the cycle repeats itself the next day. The probation department has, in effect, built a "community cell" for some of its worst delinquents. Although they protect the community as well as most "cells," the "community cells" do not isolate the offenders at great public cost.[37]

Many agencies claim to be community-based, but more than a name change is required. To do community probation, like community policing, officers have to get out into the community, work with the community and serve it, not their own bureaucratic and institutional needs. This means that measurements used to determine success will need to be changed. The number of persons on supervision will not be as important, for example, as the number of women enabled to leave or remain with their abusers in peace, or the hours of community service performed, or restitution paid to victims of crime. The latter, not the former, more accurately measures probation's success with two of its primary clients, the victim and the community.

Finally, the offender also will remain a probation client, but not more or less than the victim and the community. These three clients will be treated in balance.[38] If one or two are served to the exclusion of the others, probation will be considered out of balance.

Serving offenders will mean holding them accountable to their victims and the community. Probation will see that offenders are better, more capable citizens when they leave probation than when they came. Probation will force them to change criminogenic behaviors, such as alcoholism and other addictions detailed in Chapter 8. Probation will insist on abstinence and testing for substance abuse regularly and randomly. Every dirty specimen will be a call to action. Probation will not serve as a haven for drug users to continue their use insulated from its criminal consequences. After all, every probationer who tests positive for an illicit drug has violated the primary condition of probation, namely, not to commit new offenses. Even occasionally obtuse appellate court judges understand that testing positive for drugs is ample evidence of illegal drug possession.[39]

Too frequently, in the current, largely retributive system, probation's supervision develops the wrong competencies in offenders. It teaches them how to successfully manipulate and lie. By the end of their regimen of probation supervision, coupled by traditional mental health treatment, the probationer has learned how to look his or her probation officer directly in the eye and say sincerely that everything is fine since the last visit, blithely ignoring his or her arrest the night before in another jurisdiction. Meanwhile, the court-referred "therapists" work to increase the probationer's low self-esteem and alleviate his or her "depression." What probation and the courts fail to ask themselves is "why do we want criminals to have high self-esteem and not be depressed?" Perhaps, if left alone, they might at least be motivated to change their ways.[40]

A balanced probation department within a restorative justice system, one that sheds its preoccupation with offenders to the exclusion of the community and the victim, will find that it serves more than offenders, but justice itself. Then probation will offer a real sentence to the community, victims and offenders alike. Rather than simply offer a palliative to induce pleas, a probationary sentence will not only offer a vehicle for alternative as well as intermediate sanctions but also serve as a superior alternative to other criminal sanctions for many offenders *and* a solution to the problem of crime and fear of crime in our communities.

Incarceration will not dissappear but will serve as a last resort to either motivate recalcitrant offenders who are unwilling to make up for their offenses or to protect the public from dangerous predators. But even in regard to the latter, these offenders will be put to work to repay their victims and will be encouraged to make up for the harm they have caused.[41] Corrections will become more than three meals a day and lifting weights, marking time while waiting for release.

Notes

[1] Hinrichs, D. (1981). REPORT ON THE JUVENILE CRIME VICTIMS PROJECT: ATTITUDES AND NEEDS OF VICTIMS OF JUVENILE CRIME.

[2] Skelskis, A. (1980). VICTIM SERVICE PROGRAM: AN EVALUATION (unpublished thesis, Brown University).

[3] Whittman (1984). *Genessee County*. 3 VORP NETWORK NEWS.

[4] Fried (1983-1984). *Responses.* 12 N.Y.U. REV. L. & SOC. CHANGE 199, 200.

[5] Griffith, W., A. Schneider, P. Schneider and M. Wilson (1982). TWO YEAR REPORT ON THE NATIONAL EVALUATION OF THE JUVENILE RESTITUTION INITIATIVE: AN OVERVIEW OF PROGRAM PERFORMANCE. Washington, DC: U.S. Department of Justice, 77-NI-99-0005 & 79-NJ-AX-0009.

[6] Mahoney (1983). *The Role for Restitution in Rehabilitation Skill Development.* In T. Armstrong, M. Hofford, D. Mahoney, C. Remington and D. Steenson. RESTITUTION: A GUIDEBOOK FOR JUVENILE JUSTICE PRACTITIONERS. National Council of Juvenile and Family Court Judges.

[7] Griffith, W., A. Schneider, P. Schneider and M. Wilson (1982). TWO YEAR REPORT ON THE NATIONAL EVALUATION OF THE JUVENILE RESTITUTION INITIATIVE: AN OVERVIEW OF PROGRAM PERFORMANCE. Washington, DC: U.S. Department of Justice, 77-NI-99 0005 & 79-NJ-AX 0009.

[8] Westlake, R. (1979). THE COMMUNITY SERVICE SENTENCING PROGRAM IN HAWAII.

[9] Schmidt (1987). THE USE OF ELECTRONIC MONITORING BY CRIMINAL JUSTICE AGENCIES 11 National Institute of Justice Discussion Paper, Department of Justice, February.

[10] Bureau of Justice Statistics (1985). EXAMINING RECIDIVISM. Washington, DC: U.S. Department of Justice.

[11] Schneider, A. (1986). *Restitution and Recidivism of Juvenile Offenders: Results From Four Experimental Studies.* CRIMINOLOGY.

[12] Thorvaldson (1980). *Does Community Service Affect Offenders' Attitudes?* In J. Hudson (ed.), VICTIMS, OFFENDERS, AND ALTERNATIVE SANCTIONS.

[13] Wilson (1981). *"What Works?" Revisited: New Findings on Criminal Rehabilitation.* PUBLIC INTEREST 3-17.

[14] Farmer (1981). *Letter to the Editor.* 25 INTERNATIONAL JOURNAL OF OFFENDER THERAPY AND COMPARATIVE CRIMINOLOGY 75-76.

[15] Brown, M. and D. Cochran (1984). EXECUTIVE SUMMARY OF RESEARCH FINDINGS FROM THE MASSACHUSETTS RISK/NEED CLASSIFICATION SYSTEM, REPORT #5, 3942 (Mass. Office of the Commissioner of Probation).

[16] Petersilia, J., S. Turner and J. Peterson (1986). PRISON VERSUS PROBATION IN CALIFORNIA. Santa Monica, CA: Rand, R-3323 NIJ, July.

[17] Remarks of Hon. Aaron Ment, Chief Court Administrator, Connecticut, before Massachusetts Probation Conference, Randolph, MA, May 11, 1995.

[18] MacKenzie, D. and D. Parent (1992). *Boot Camp Prisons for Young Offenders.* In Byrne, J., A. Lurigo and J. Petersilia (eds.), *Smart Sentencing.* Newbury Park, CA: Sage Publications.

[19] Middleton (1984). *Sentencing: The Alternatives.* NATIONAL LAW JOURNAL (April 23).

[20] *Id.* at 12.

[21] Gandy and Galaway (1980). *Restitution as a Sanction for Offenders: A Public's View, 89-100 Victims.* In Hudson, J. and B. Galaway (eds.), OFFENDERS AND ALTERNATIVE SANCTIONS.

[22] Doble, J. (1987). CRIME AND PUNISHMENT: THE PUBLIC'S VIEW 4 (June).

[23] *Id.*

[24] Cannon, M. (1984). *Developing a Rational Corrections Policy in an Environment of Hardening Public Attitudes Against Criminals.* (paper delivered to Ethics and Public Policy Conference, Washington, DC March 30).

[25] *Seek Alternatives to Jail Sentences.* ROCKLAND JOURNAL-NEWS, June 16, 1984.

[26] Taylor (1983). *Instead of Jail, One County in New York Imposes Sentences of Work, Reparations, or House Arrest.* WALL STREET JOURNAL, December 23.

[27] Castle, M. (1991). *Alternative Sentencing: Selling it to the Public.* NATIONAL INSTITUTE OF JUSTICE RESEARCH IN ACTION, September.

[28] Revocation of probation did not occur upon arrest, but after conviction. If offenders were arrested, but not convicted, revocations for the criminal conduct did not occur, *ibid.*

[29] For this reason, Pennsylvania enacted legislation in 1995 making it impossible for judges to terminate a juvenile's probation until the restitution is paid or the order becomes a civil debt and follows the offender throughout his life. Act 12 of Special Session No. 1 of 1995-HB 18(136).

[30] In the sample of more than 300,000 felony probationers and parolees who were revoked in 1991, only a tiny fraction were either drug tested or sent to prison for failure to abstain from drug use, even though 55 percent of the violators reported using drugs in the month before they committed new crimes while under supervision. In fact, 20 percent reported committing new crimes to secure drugs, in *ibid.*

[31] See, *e.g.,* VERMONT STAT. ANN. tit. 13 § 7043; N.C. GEN. STAT. § 15A-1343(d) (1983) (amended in 1985) ("No third party shall benefit by way of restitution").

[32] Lardner, G. Jr. (1995). THE STALKING OF KRISTEN. New York, NY: Atlantic Monthly Press.

[33] See, *e.g.,* MASS. GEN. LAWS ch. 138, § 98 (no service to intoxicated patrons).

[34] Tatz (1995). *Quincy Court Pleased with Most Wanted Program.* PATRIOT LEDGER, August 4 and 5.

[35] Director Dennis Maloney's Corps were featured in a *USA Today* editorial, "Answer to Kid Crime: Restorative Justice Corps," Feb. 22, 1995.

[36] See Chapter 5.

[37] The name "community cell" was first proposed by Hon. Albert L. Kramer, described in A. Klein (1988). ALTERNATIVE SENTENCING. Cincinnati, OH: Anderson Publishing Co.

[38] The "balanced approach" was originally developed and championed for juvenile corrections by D. Maloney, D. Romig and T. Armstrong. *Juvenile Probation: The Balanced Approach.* JUVENILE AND FAMILY COURT JOURNAL, 39:3. National Council of Juvenile and Family Court Judges, Reno, NV 1988; the theory has been built upon and melded with victim-oriented advocates by Bazemore, G. and M. Umbreit (1995). BALANCED AND RESTORATIVE JUSTICE FOR JUVENILES. Ft. Lauderdale, FL: The Balanced and Restorative Justice Project, Florida Atlantic University.

[39] See, *e.g., Moore v. Commonwealth,* 530 A.2d 1011 (Pa. Commw. 1987); *United States v. Grunderson,* 969 F.2d 980 (11th Cir. 1992).

[40] Characteristics of programs that do not work include targeting noncriminogenic needs such as anxiety, self-esteem or depression; traditional psycho-dynamic and Rogerian nondirective therapies, etc. See, *e.g.,* P. Gendreau, F. Cullen and J. Bonta (1994). *Intensive Rehabilitation Supervision, the Next Generation in Community Corrections?* FEDERAL PROBATION, 58:1 (March), described in Chapter 9.

[41] For example, they can meet with their victims as described in § 5.04 to alleviate victim fears and help their victims put their victimization behind them.

Chapter 12

Alternative Sentencing Checklists

§12.01   Fashioning Alternative Sentences

Before a defense attorney, prosecutor or probation officer recommends an alternative sentence, or a judge imposes one, he should first consider who the offender is, what he has done and who, if anyone, was injured or suffered as a result of the crime. In addition, he should analyze the community in which the offense occurred and the court in which the defendant will be sentenced. The following checklist is designed to raise pertinent questions, covering all of the above sentencing considerations.

Considering the Offender

1. Does the offender represent a high risk for recidivism?

   ____ What was his age at first offense?
   ____ How many prior convictions has he had?
   ____ Does he rationalize his criminal behavior?
   ____ Does he abuse alcohol or drugs?
   ____ Has he lived at the same address for the past year? Held a job or attended school for the past year?
   ____ Is he part of a stable family?

371

2. Will he be exposed to the same environment in which the crime took place after sentencing?

    ____ Will he have access to a weapon?
    ____ Will he remain with the same peer group?
    ____ Will he be employed?
    ____ Will he receive necessary treatment?
    ____ Will he have access to drugs and/or alcohol?
    ____ Will he have access to the crime victim?

3. Does he have a history of violent crimes?

4. Does he suffer a compulsive behavior problem such as gambling or sexual deviance?

5. What resources does the offender possess that might contribute to the alternative sentence?

    ____ Does the offender have any special skills or talents to contribute to public service?
    ____ Does the offender have the ability to pay restitution, fees, costs, fines, donations or other monetary assessments?
    ____ Is he employable or able to work?
    ____ Is the offender interested in receiving treatment for any crime-related behavioral problems?
    ____ Is the offender able to remain drug/alcohol free?
    ____ Does the offender have a stable residence in which he may reside during a period of house arrest?
    ____ Did or will the offender apologize to the crime victims (if any), offer to pay restitution or otherwise make up for the crime?

Considering the Offense

6. How serious was the offense?

    ____ Was it a property crime? A crime against persons?
    ____ Was there an identifiable victim or victims?
    ____ Was anyone injured or killed?
    ____ How serious were the losses suffered by the victims? Society at large?
    ____ Did the crime receive major media attention? Major police or prosecutorial attention?
    ____ Did the crime represent a breach of public trust?

Considering the Victim

7. How seriously did the crime victim or victims suffer as a result of the crime?

    ____ Were the crime victims directly or indirectly affected?

_____ How large were victim losses or injuries?

_____ Was the victim covered by insurance? What was the deductible? Did the victim's rates increase because of the claim?

_____ Did the victim suffer non-monetary losses such as trauma, mental anguish and/or depression? Loss of work and/or leisure time?

_____ Is the victim afraid of the offender?

8. Did the offender know the victim prior to the crime?

9. Did the victim share culpability for the crime?

10. Did the victim have a chance to participate in the court case?

_____ Was the victim invited to attend the hearing? Testify? Speak at disposition? Report his losses to the court? Ask for restitution?

_____ Did the victim meet with the defendant?

_____ Does the victim want restitution?

_____ Is the victim willing to reconcile with the offender? Inform the court that he is not looking for the defendant's incarceration?

Considering the Community

11. Was the public informed about the crime by the media?

12. Was the general public especially victimized, inconvenienced or outraged by the crime?

13. Can the offender do something to make up for the crime in the community in which it occurred?

_____ Can the offender work at the site of the crime?

_____ Can the offender serve the citizens most adversely affected by the crime?

_____ Can the offender make a contribution or donate something to the community?

14. Can the offender promise to leave the community or stay out of a specified area within it?

Considering the Court

15. How has the court handled similar cases in the past?

_____ Does the prosecutor desire to try the case? Engage in plea bargaining? Make an example of the defendant?

_____ What is the "going rate" for this type of crime in the court?

_____ How have offenders with similar criminal records fared in the court?

_____ Is the judge particularly sympathetic or unsympathetic to this type of crime or criminal?

16. Will there be a full presentence report?

_____ Will the probation officer accept contributions and assistance from the defense and prosecution?

_____ Does the presentence include a victim impact statement? A statement of opinion from the victim?

_____ Does the presentence include an alternative disposition plan?

17. Will the court allow for a full dispositional hearing?

_____ Does the court rely on psychiatric and other related expert evaluations in sentencing? Diagnostic commitments?

_____ Will the court allow for a private presentence report to be presented?

_____ Is defendant allocution mandated? Allowed?

_____ Will the victim be invited to speak at disposition?

18. Is there appellate review of the sentence?

§12.02   Considering Victim Involvement and Restitution

After considering the offender, the offense, the victim, the community and the court, those involved in sentencing should consider the victim as a possible *participant* in the sentencing process, one who may influence the judge's decision. In addition, parties to sentencing should consider how the victim may fit into the sentence itself, most commonly as a recipient of restitution.

Involving the Victim

1. Does the jurisdiction maintain a victim compensation fund for the victim of the specific crime and the specific losses or injuries incurred?

2. Do victims have a right to participate in the court case?

_____ Do victims have a right to participate in plea bargaining?

_____ Are victims notified of the hearing date?

_____ Are victims given the opportunity to testify? Make a statement of opinion at disposition (allocution)? Present a statement of their losses or injuries?

_____ Are victims allowed to file a victim impact statement?

3. Is the victim willing to meet with the defendant or the defendant's representative?

4. Did the victim suffer out-of-pocket losses? Other damages?

5. Does the victim desire restitution?

6. Does the jurisdiction have access to a victim/offender mediation program (VORP)? Any trained mediators who may be willing to facilitate such a meeting?

7. Is the victim willing to accept in-kind or non-monetary work service in lieu of cash restitution?

8. Is the victim willing to suggest to the court what community work service, how many hours of community work service and where the defendant should perform it in lieu of direct restitution?

Restitution

9. Is restitution authorized as an independent remedy? As a condition of probation?

10. Is restitution mandatory or discretionary?

11. Is restitution limited to specific offenses?

12. Is restitution a legally recognized criterion in sentencing?

13. Is restitution limited only to the offense for which the offender is convicted?

    —— May restitution be ordered for behavior for which the defendant admits culpability for but for which he was not convicted?
    —— May restitution be ordered for uncharged or unconvicted behavior the defendant does not admit liability for but for which the court finds him responsible?
    —— Did the defendant make any commitments regarding restitution or responsibility as part of the plea bargain accepted by the court prior to sentencing?

14. What expenses may the restitution order include?

    —— Is restitution limited to out-of-pocket losses only?
    —— May restitution cover "civil-type" costs?

15. To whom may restitution be ordered?

    —— Is restitution limited to the direct crime victims?
    —— May restitution be ordered to indirect victims (insurance companies) or government agencies (drug "buy money")?
    —— May restitution be ordered to dependents of homicide victims?

16. Does the victim have an independent right of enforcement of the restitution payment?

17. How is restitution determined?

    —— Is the amount determined from evidence presented by the police, the prosecutor or the victim or his advocate?

_____ Is the legwork delegated to the probation department following sentencing? If so, how is the final order imposed by the court?

_____ Is the victim required to document losses?

_____ Are victims and offenders allowed or encouraged to meet to agree on the restitution order?

18. If contested, what is the standard of evidence necessary for the restitution order?

19. What are the standards for a hearing before the order may be set?

_____ Must the order be set by the judge? By a jury?

20. Does the defendant lose his right to appeal the restitution determination if he fails to protest at the time of determination?

21. What are the standards for determining the defendant's ability to pay?

_____ Must the defendant's ability to pay be considered at the time of disposition? At the time of collection?

_____ Is the onus on the defendant to prove his indigency? On the government?

22. How is restitution apportioned among co-defendants?

_____ Is restitution ordered "jointly and severally"?

_____ Is restitution ordered equally among co-defendants?

_____ Is restitution proportioned based on individual co-defendants' culpability?

23. How is the restitution to be paid?

_____ Is it to be paid in one lump sum at a certain date?

_____ Is it to be paid in periodic installments?

24. Does the jurisdiction provide any services to assist indigent or unemployed offenders?

_____ Are there job training programs?

_____ Are there employment programs?

_____ Does the jurisdiction maintain a formal restitution program?

25. How is the restitution order monitored?

26. How is the order enforced?

_____ Does failure to pay constitute contempt? A violation of probation?

_____ What are the usual penalties imposed for such failures?

§12.03   Considering Community Work Service

Whether or not there exists a specific crime victim or victims, all crimes cost the community at large. Whether defendants have money or not, most are able-bodied. Therefore, those involved in sentencing should consider community work service as a complete or partial sentencing alternative.

1. Is community work service authorized by statute?

    ____ Is community work service authorized as a condition of probation?
    ____ Is it authorized as an independent remedy?
    ____ Is it authorized in lieu of monetary payments?
    ____ Is it authorized in lieu of a license loss? Incarceration?

2. Are defendants allowed to "work off"—through the performance of community work service—certain court-ordered monetary obligations? If so, at what rate?

3. Is community work service recognized in mitigation of punishment?

4. Is community work service limited to certain specific offenses?

5. Are community work service orders defined in any way?

    ____ Are the number of orders specified?
    ____ Is the type of work specified?
    ____ Is the work site specified?

6. Will the court delegate to the defense, prosecutor or a third party the type of work to be performed? The placement? The work schedule?

7. Must the court consider the defendant's work schedule and family obligations in determining the order?

8. Does the jurisdiction administer or refer to a formal community work service program?

    ____ Does the court maintain a list of authorized work sites?
    ____ May the offender recruit his own work site? Arrange for court notification of compliance?

9. Does the work site or the referral agency where the work service is performed have adequate accident and liability insurance?

    ____ Is the offender performing work service considered a state employee?
    ____ Does the offender's own insurance policy, if any, cover him for community work service performance?

10. Are the order, the work to be performed and the work schedule reasonable?

11. How is the community work service to be monitored?

12. Is failure to perform the order a violation of probation? Contempt of court?

    ____ What are the usual sanctions for nonperformance of community work service?

§12.04   Considering Monetary Orders

Monetary penalties have traditionally served as an alternative to incarceration. In addition to fines, there are many other costs that may be imposed that parties to sentencing should consider.

1. May fines, costs, special fees (victim compensation fees, etc.), bonds and forfeitures be ordered as a condition of probation? An independent remedy?

2. Are probation fees, treatment fees, and family support orders authorized as a condition of probation?

3. Are the orders limited by law at time of disposition? At collection?

    ____ Must the jurisdiction consider the offender's ability to pay at the time of disposition? Collection?

4. What are the jurisdiction's standards for determining indigency?

5. May court costs or fees cover jury fees? Rendition costs? Drug "buy money?" Counsel recoupment? Prosecutorial costs? Bailiff fees? Presentence investigation report costs? Jail costs (when ordered as a condition of probation)? Supervision costs? Treatment costs? Special programs (*i.e.* drunk driving schools)?

6. What is the total cost of all monetary orders including restitution?

    ____ Does the defendant have the ability to pay?
    ____ Does the payment schedule consider all monies due?
    ____ Is there an order in which individual assessments must be paid?
    ____ May certain payments be worked off through community work service?

7. How are payments monitored?

8. Does the jurisdiction have programs to assist unemployed or indigent defendants?

    ____ Are there employment programs available?
    ____ Are there financial counseling programs available?

9. Does non-payment constitute contempt? A violation of probation?

    ____ What are the usual sanctions for non-payment?

§12.05   Considering Mandatory Treatment

If the defendant suffers from particular crime-related diseases, compulsions or behavior disorders, parties to sentencing should consider ways to address these problems in fashioning the alternative sentencing. Drug addiction and alcoholism usually correlate with a risk of reoffending and therefore must be controlled if the court is to consider imposing an alternative sentence.

1. Does the defendant's record indicate a pattern of alcohol abuse? Drug abuse? Compulsive gambling? Sexual deviance? Other behavior dysfunction?

   ____ Was the criminal behavior isolated and idiosyncratic?
   ____ Was the criminal behavior provoked by unique environmental factors?

2. Do the jurisdiction's prisons offer diagnostic service (prior to disposition) and treatment (post-disposition)?

   ____ Do the jurisdiction's mental hospitals provide diagnostic services for indigent defendants?

3. Does the court maintain a list of qualified experts to evaluate the defendant and recommend needed treatment? Is the probation department qualified to determine the defendant's treatment needs? If so, will the department be given the opportunity through a presentence investigation report or the like?

4. What other diagnostic and treatment facilities or services are available in the community on an inpatient basis? Outpatient basis?

5. Is treatment a standard condition of probation?

   ____ Are urinalysis, blood or saliva tests standard conditions of probation?
   ____ Is commitment to a state or private treatment facility a standard probation condition?
   ____ Is abstinence from drugs and/or alcohol a standard condition of probation?
   ____ Are there other standard conditions that control the defendant's behavior (i.e., restrictions on associations, residency, entering licensed establishments, gun ownership or driving privileges, etc.)?
   ____ If not standard conditions, will the court consider imposing them?

6. What self-help groups are available (i.e., Alcoholics Anonymous, Narcotics Anonymous)?

7. What facilities or practitioners are available to prescribe behavior-controlling drugs (i.e., Antabuse, methadone, Trexan, Depo-Provera)?

8. Is the mandatory treatment reasonably related to the crime?

   ____ Is it related to the defendant's rehabilitation?
   ____ Is it related to the public safety?
   ____ Are the orders "doable?"

9. Do inpatient treatment orders exceed the jurisdiction's civil commitment provisions?

10. How is the treatment monitored?

    ____ What is the standard of evidence necessary for the court to admit the results of scientific tests employed to monitor the defendant (i.e., urine, blood, saliva)?

11. May the jurisdiction revoke a defendant's probation for not being "amenable" to treatment? Failure to get better?

12. Do violations of treatment orders constitute violations of probation? Contempt?

13. What are the usual sanctions for treatment failures?

§12.06   Considering Incapacitation

Incarceration may be inevitable in certain situations. Parties to sentencing, however, can seek to lessen the length of incarceration through alternative uses of incarceration, namely the use of short, split or intermittent sentences. In addition, parties should explore alternative methods to incapacitate the defendant in the community.

Incapacitation Without Jail

1. Is house arrest or imposition of a curfew a standard condition of probation? If not, will the judge consider imposing them?

2. Does the jurisdiction administer a house arrest or curfew enforcement program?

_____ Do local police and/or the probation department have the resources to monitor house arrest and curfews through random telephone calls? Home visits? Pass-bys by sector patrol cars? Electronic surveillance? Does the defendant have a telephone?

3. Does the jurisdiction maintain special facilities, other than jails and prisons, for offender residency?

_____ Are there halfway houses in the community for offenders?
_____ Does the offender have responsible relatives to live with?

4. Is intensive probation supervision authorized by statute?

5. Does the jurisdiction maintain an intensive supervision program?

_____ Does the probation department have the resources to provide intensive supervision?
_____ Is there a reliable person willing to "sponsor" and monitor the offender in the community for the courts?
_____ Is the defendant willing and able to volunteer to do community work service in the community on weekends or on a set schedule?
_____ Does the offender have the ability to pay the costs of his intensive supervision?

Non-Traditional Uses of Incarceration

6. What is the state of local or state correctional facilities?

____ Are local or state correctional institutions overcrowded?

____ Are they currently being, or have they been, sued for unlawful or unconstitutional overcrowding?

____ Are they presently under court order to reduce overcrowding?

____ Is there an emergency overcrowding program to release offenders early to relieve overcrowding? Will the defendant's incarceration result in the release of another, more serious offender?

7. Does the law authorize split sentences? Shock sentencing? Motions to revise and revoke? Incarceration as a condition of probation? Temporary commitment to a diagnostic institution? Intermittent sentence?

8. How long may the defendant be incarcerated as a condition of probation?

____ Where may the offender be ordered to serve the sentence?

9. If incarcerated, when may the offender petition for revision or revocation of the commitment? When may the court, on its own motion, revise and revoke the commitment?

____ How long must the offender serve before being eligible for release on shock probation (if available)?

10. How long may the offender be on probation (or "supervised release" in the federal system) after a period of incarceration?

11. Did the defendant already in effect serve a split sentence by being held without bail or a bail he could not raise, before disposition of the case?

§12.07   Considering Enforcement of Alternative Sentences

Once the alternative sentence has been imposed, the responsibility of monitoring and enforcing it must rest on someone's shoulders. The task usually falls to probation officers, but defense attorneys and prosecutors may also be involved. Judges may establish standards for probation departments and must also sit on probation revocation hearings or contempt proceedings. While monitoring and enforcing alternative sentences may seem irrelevant to their imposition, judges may be reluctant to impose an alternative sentence that seems to be unenforceable. Further, if alternative sentences are not enforced, judges will find it more difficult to impose them in the future.

Monitoring Alternative Sentences

1. How is the alternative sentence to be monitored?

2. Are the conditions of the alternative sentence specific, clear, reduced to writing and understood by the defendant?

    ____ Do the conditions have due dates where necessary?

3. Has the defendant signed a release form so that treatment and/or other information may be released to the court?

4. What is the probation department authorized to do to monitor the alternative sentence?

    ____ Will the probation officer see his probationer periodically in the probation officer's office? At the probationer's place of work? At the probationer's home?
    ____ Is the probationer ordered to keep the probation officer informed about his whereabouts? Employment? Living arrangements? Travel? Police contacts (i.e., new arrests)?

5. Does the probation department have the authority to make reasonable warrantless searches of the probationer? The probationer's car? The probationer's residence?

    ____ May the probation department delegate this right to police agents?

6. Does the probation department have the authority to demand that the probationer reveal information concerning another crime the probationer may have committed?

Revoking Probation

7. Does the statute define the amount of notice required before a revocation hearing may be scheduled?

8. May the probationer be summoned to appear?

    ____ If arrested, does the probationer have a right to bail?

9. May a person other than a probation officer be authorized to charge the defendant with a violation of probation?

    ____ Who "prosecutes" the revocation case?

10. Does the probationer have the right to an attorney?

11. Does the notice of violation meet minimum standards?

    ____ Are the charges specific?
    ____ Do they cover only court-ordered, lawful probation conditions?

12. Is a preliminary hearing required?

13. What is the standard of evidence necessary for a finding of violation?

    ____ May the probationer be found in violation based solely on hearsay evidence?

    ____ What are the accepted standards for admissibility of scientific evidence?

    ____ To what extent must witnesses be called to prove the allegations against the defendant?

14. May the defendant be held in violation for a new crime for which he has not been convicted beyond a reasonable doubt?

15. Must the violation be "substantial" to justify revocation?

16. Was the defendant given the opportunity to call witnesses and present evidence to rebut allegations against him and/or in mitigation of punishment?

Sentencing Violators

17. Is the court limited to either maintaining the current probation or incarceration?

    ____ May the court impose any sentence originally available to the court at sentencing?

    ____ Is the length of possible incarceration specified?

18. Is a presentence report mandated before sentencing may take place?

19. Are there available alternative sanctions to long-term incarceration, notwithstanding the violation?

    ____ Are there incremental sanctions available to increase pressure to secure the defendant's compliance with court orders, i.e., additional orders of community work service?

    ____ Further monetary assessments? Mandatory treatment, including inpatient (if the defendant was previously receiving outpatient treatment)? Behavior modifying restrictions, including drugs, curfews, house arrest, increased reporting? Shock or other short split sentences?

Evaluating Alternative Sentences

20. Is the alternative sentence as agreed upon by the prosecutor or offered by the judge more or less onerous than the ultimate sentence that the court would likely impose?

Bibliography

Books and Journals

Abel, G., I.V. Becker, M. Mittleman, J. Cunningham-Rathner, J.L. Rouleau and W.D. Murphy (1987). *Self-Reported Sex Crimes of Nonincarcerated Paraphiliacs.* THE JOURNAL OF INTERPERSONAL VIOLENCE, 2:1, pp. 3-25.

American Bar Association (1968). STANDARDS RELATING TO SENTENCING ALTERNATIVES AND PROCEDURES (Approved Draft).

American Friends Service Committee (1971). STRUGGLE FOR JUSTICE.

American Institute of Criminal Justice, JUST THE FACTS (undated).

Andrews, D. and J. Bonta (1994). THE PSYCHOLOGY OF CRIMINAL CONDUCT. Cincinnati, OH: Anderson Publishing Co.

Anglin, M.D. and Y. Hser (1990). *Treatment of Drug Abuse.* In Tonry, M. and J.Q. Wilson (eds.), DRUGS AND CRIME. Chicago, IL: University of Chicago, 393-460.

ANNUAL REPORT ON THE STATE OF THE MASSACHUSETTS COURT SYSTEM, FISCAL YEAR 1994, Supreme Judicial Court, Boston, Mass. 1995.

Armstrong, T., M. Hofford, D. Maloney, C. Remington, and D. Steenson (1983). RESTITUTION: A GUIDEBOOK FOR JUVENILE JUSTICE PRACTITIONERS. National Council of Juvenile and Family Court Judges.

Augustus, J. (1939). A REPORT ON THE LABORS OF JOHN AUGUSTUS.

Banks, J., E. Carlson, J. Dahl, J. Debro, K. Kirkpatrick and L. Varnon, IMPROVED PROBATION STRATEGIES (National Institute of Law Enforcement and Criminal Justice, U.S. Department of Justice 1978).

Baird, S., R. Heinz and B. Bemus (1979). A TWO-YEAR FOLLOW-UP REPORT, THE WISCONSIN CASE CLASSIFICATION/STAFF DEPLOYMENT PROJECT.

Baird, S., D. Holien and A. Bakke (1986). FEES FOR PROBATION SERVICES (U.S. Department of Justice NIC FZ-4).

Baumgartner, Baer, Hill and Blahd (1986). HAIR ANALYSIS FOR DRUGS OF ABUSE IN PAROLE/PROBATION POPULATIONS, Final Report. Washington DC: National Institute of Justice.

Bazemore, G. (1995). BALANCED AND RESTORATIVE JUSTICE FOR JUVENILES: A NATIONAL STRATEGY FOR JUVENILE JUSTICE IN THE 21ST CENTURY. Fort Lauderdale, FL: Florida Atlantic University.

Bazemore, G. and M. Umbreit (1995). BALANCED AND RESTORATIVE JUSTICE FOR JUVENILES, The Balanced and Restorative Justice Project. Ft. Lauderdale, FL: Florida Atlantic University.

Beck (1987). RECIDIVISM AMONG YOUNG PAROLEES, Bureau of Justice Statistics. Washington DC: Department of Justice.

Beck, A. and D. Gilliard (1995). PRISONERS IN 1994, BUREAU OF JUSTICE STATISTICS BULLETIN. Washington, DC: U.S. Department of Justice, August.

Beha, J., K. Carlson and R. Rosenblum (1977). SENTENCING TO COMMUNITY SERVICE. Washington, DC: National Institute of Law Enforcement and Criminal Justice, U.S. Department of Justice J-LEAA-030-76.

Berman (1983). *Meeting the Goals of Sentencing: The Client Specific Plan.* 9 NEW ENG. J. CRIM. & CIVIL CONFINEMENT 331-342.

BEYOND CRIME AND PUNISHMENT, RESTORATIVE JUSTICE (1991). Washington, DC: Prison Fellowship.

Brown (1977). *Community Service as a Condition of Probation.* 41 FEDERAL PROBATION 7.

Brown, M. and D. Cochran (1984). EXECUTIVE SUMMARY OF RESEARCH FINDINGS FROM THE MASSACHUSETTS RISK/NEED CLASSIFICATION SYSTEM, REPORT #5 (Mass. Office of the Commissioner of Probation).

Browne, A. (1993). *Violence Against Women by Male Partners.* AMERICAN PSYCHOLOGIST, 48:10, pp. 1077-1087, Oct.

Bureau of Justice Statistics (1985). CRIMINAL VICTIMIZATION IN THE UNITED STATES, 1983, A NATIONAL CRIME SURVEY REPORT. Washington, DC: U.S. Department of Justice.

_____ (1985). Examining Recidivism (U.S. Department of Justice).

_____ (1983). PRISONERS AND ALCOHOL (U.S. Department of Justice).

_____ (1984). PRISONERS IN 1984 (U.S. Department of Justice).

_____ (1984). PROBATION AND PAROLE, 1983 (U.S. Department of Justice).

_____ (1985). PROBATION AND PAROLE, 1984 (U.S. Department of Justice).

_____ (1983). PROSECUTION OF FELONY ARRESTS (U.S. Department of Justice).

_____ (1983). REPORT TO THE NATION ON CRIME AND JUSTICE, THE DATA (U.S. Department of Justice).

_____ (1984). SENTENCING PRACTICES IN 13 STATES (U.S. Department of Justice).

Butts, J. and H. Snyder (1992). RESTITUTION AND JUVENILE RECIDIVISM. Washington, DC: Office of Juvenile Justice and Delinquency Prevention.

Buzawa, E. and C. Buzawa (1992). DOMESTIC VIOLENCE: THE CHANGING CRIMINAL JUSTICE RESPONSE. Westport, CT: Auburn House.

Byrne, J., A. Lurigio and J. Petersilia (1992). SMART SENTENCING, Newbury Park, CA: Sage Publications.

California Probation, Parole, and Correctional Association (1984). THE POWER OF PUBLIC SUPPORT.

Camp, G. and C. Camp (1984). THE CORRECTIONS YEARBOOK.

Carlson, E., E. Parks and H. Allen (1978). CRITICAL ISSUES IN ADULT PROBATION—THE STATE OF THE ART. Washington, DC: National Institute of Law Enforcement and Criminal Justice, U.S. Department of Justice.

Carter, R., PRESENTENCE REPORT HANDBOOK (1978). (National Institute of Law Enforcement and Criminal Justice, U.S. Department of Justice).

Castle, M. (1991). *Alternative Sentencing: Selling it to the Public.* RESEARCH IN ACTION, Washington, DC: National Institute of Justice, Sept.

Chaiken, J. and M. Chaiken (1982). VARIETIES OF CRIMINAL BEHAVIOR (Rand, R-2814-NIJ).

Christianson, S. (1995). *Defective Electronic Equipment May Lead to Further Criminal And Civil Liability.* COMMUNITY CORRECTIONS REPORT, July/August.

Clark (1981). *Alcoholism: Blocks to Diagnosis and Treatment.* 71 AMERICAN JOURNAL OF MEDICINE 275-286.

Client Specific Planning: The Alternative Sentence. 3 INSTITUTIONS ETC. (August 1980).

Cochran, D., M. Brown and R. Kazarian (1981). EXECUTIVE SUMMARY OF RESEARCH FINDINGS FROM THE PILOT COURTS RISK/NEED CLASSIFICATION SYSTEM, REPORT #4 (Mass. Office of the Commissioner of Probation).

Cohen, N. and J. Gobert (1983). THE LAW OF PROBATION AND PAROLE.

Cohen, R. (1995). PROBATION AND PAROLE VIOLATORS IN STATE PRISONS, 1991, SPECIAL REPORT. Washington, DC: Bureau of Justice Statistics, U.S. Justice Department (August).

Cole, G. (1989). *Fines Can Be Fine—and Collected.* JUDGES JOURNAL 28:1 (Winter).

COMMUNITY CONTROL: HOUSE ARREST: A THREE YEAR LONGITUDINAL REPORT, 16, Fla. Department of Corrections, Probation and Parole Services (Jan. 1987).

Court Reporting. MADDVOCATE 5:2, Fall, 1992.

Cowles, E. and T. Castellano (1996). BOOT CAMP DRUG TREATMENT AND AFTERCARE INTERVENTION: AN EVALUATIVE REVIEW. NIJ Research Report, July.

Criminal Justice Institute (1994). CORRECTIONS YEARBOOK: PROBATION AND PAROLE 1994.

Crossman, H. (1996). *Drug Testing Results, 1995.* Quincy Probation Report, Quincy, MA.

Cunniff, M. (1987). *Sentencing Outcomes in 28 Felony Courts in 1985.* Bureau of Justice Statistics. Washington, DC: U.S. Department of Justice.

Davis, CRIME VICTIMS: LEARNING HOW TO HELP THEM (N.I.J. Reports, No. 203, May/June).

Davis, R. (Spring, 1992). *Who Pays?* PERSPECTIVES. Lexington, KY: American Probation and Parole Association.

Deegan, P. (1995). *Community Corrections for the Year 2010: All Corrections is Local: Building Partnerships for Public Safety, II.* THE IARCA JOURNAL ON COMMUNITY CORRECTIONS, VII:1, September.

Dodd, M. (1991). PROFESSIONAL NOTES: A NEWSLETTER ADDRESSING MENTAL HEALTH CONCERNS, 1:1 January.

Dolescal, E. (undated). *Median Time Served by Prison Inmates.* JUST THE FACTS, American Institute of Criminal Justice.

Domestic Abusers Can't Abuse this System. INSTANT EVIDENCE VIII, Fall/Winter 1994.

DuPont, P. (1984). EXPANDING SENTENCING OPTIONS: A GOVERNORS PERSPECTIVE, NIJ Reports 4 (July).

Egash, *Beyond Restitution—Creative Restitution.* RESTITUTION IN CRIMINAL JUSTICE (Hudson ed. 1975).

Electronic Bracelets Flawed, Suit Claims. 81 A.B.A. JOURNAL 30 (1995).

Electronic Monitoring Market Continues to Expand. JOURNAL OF OFFENDER MONITORING, UPDATE. (Summer, 1992).

FBI UNIFORM CRIME REPORT. Washington, DC: Bureau of Justice Statistics, 1989.

Fed Awards $20 Million for Boot Camps. ALTERNATIVES TO INCARCERATION 1:4 (Fall, 1995).

Federal Poverty Income Guidelines, Annual Revision. Washington, DC: Office of Management and Budget (Effective April 6, 1995).

Finn, P. and D. Parent (1992). MAKING OFFENDER FOOT THE BILL: A TEXAS PROGRAM, PROGRAM FOCUS, NIJ (October).

Florida Department of Corrections (1984). PRELIMINARY REPORT ON COMMUNITY CONTROL (Probation and Parole Services).

Fogel, D. (1975). WE ARE THE LIVING PROOF: THE JUSTICE MODEL FOR CORRECTIONS.

Fogg, V. (1992). *Implementation of a Cognitive Skills Development Program.* PERSPECTIVES (Winter) pp. 24-26.

Foon, A.E. (1988). *The Effectiveness of Drinking-Driving Treatment Programs: A Critical Review.* THE INTERNATIONAL JOURNAL OF THE ADDICTIONS, 23, pp. 151-174.

Forer, L. (1980). CRIMINALS AND VICTIMS.

Frankel, M. (1972). CRIMINAL SENTENCES.

Franklin, R. (1995). *City Uses "Restorative Justice" With Woman Who Stole to Gamble.* Twin Cities STAR TRIBUNE, reprinted in RESTORATIVE JUSTICE NEWSLETTER, Department of Corrections, Minnesota, Nov.

Fried (1983-1984). *Responses.* 12 N.Y.U. REV. L. & SOC. CHANGE, 199.

Friedman, L. (1993). CRIME AND PUNISHMENT IN AMERICAN HISTORY, New York, NY: Basic Books

Gabina, B. and S. Stein (1989). *Gambling Research and Education Programs, Center for Addiction Studies, Harvard Medical School and Cambridge Hospital.* Reported in HARVARD JOURNAL 24:1, March.

Galaway, B. and J. Hudson (eds.) (1996). RESTORATIVE JUSTICE: INTERNATIONAL PERSPECTIVE, Monsey, NY: Criminal Justice Press.

Gandy and Galaway (1980). *Restitution as a Sanction for Offenders: A Public's View.* In J. Hudson and B. Galaway (eds.), VICTIMS, OFFENDERS, AND ALTERNATIVE SANCTIONS.

Ganley, A. (1981). COURT-MANDATED COUNSELING PROGRAMS FOR MEN WHO BATTER: A THREE DAY WORKSHOP FOR MENTAL HEALTH PROFESSIONALS. Washington, DC: Center for Women Policy Studies.

Gendreau, P. and R.R. Ross (1987). *Revivification of Rehabilitation: Evidence from the 1980s.* JUSTICE QUARTERLY, 3, 349-407.

Gendreau, P., F. Cullen and J. Bonta (1994). *Intensive Rehabilitation Supervision, the Next Generation in Community Corrections?* FEDERAL PROBATION, 58:1, March.

General Accounting Office (1990). INTERMEDIATE SANCTIONS: THEIR IMPACTS ON PRISON CROWDING, COSTS, AND RECIDIVISM ARE STILL UNCLEAR. Gaithersburg, MD: GAO.

General Services Office (undated). A.A. GUIDELINES, COOPERATING WITH COURTS, A.S.A.P. AND SIMILAR PROGRAMS, 4 (6M-5/82(R).

Genessee County Sheriff's Department, COMMUNITY SERVICE RESTITUTION (undated).

Gilliard, D. and A. Beck (1995). THE NATION'S CORRECTIONAL POPULATION TOPS 5 MILLION. Bureau of Justice Statistics, DOJ, August 27.

Gittler (1984). *Expanding the Role of the Victim in a Criminal Action: An Overview of Issues and Problems.* 11 Symposium Pepperdine L. Rev. 7-182.

Goldfarb, R. and L. Singer (1973). After Conviction.

Gordon, F. (1993). *Literacy Programs for Those on Probation: Do They Make a Difference?* 32 Judges Journal 2 (Winter).

Greenwood, P. and A. Abrahamse (1982). Selective Incapacitation (Rand, R-2815-NIJ).

Greenwood, P. and S. Turner (1987). Selective Incapacitation Revisited. Washington, DC: Rand, National Institute of Justice (March).

Griffith, W., A. Schneider, P. Schneider and M. Wilson (1982). Two-Year Report on The National Evaluation of the Juvenile Restitution Initiative: An Overview of Program Performance (U.S. Department of Justice 77-NI-99-0005 # 79-NJ-AX-0009).

Grinnell (1917). *Probation as an Orthodox Common Law Practice in Massachusetts Prior to the Statutory System.* 2 Mass. L. Q.

Harding, J. (1982). Victims and Offenders.

Harris, K. (1979). Community Service by Offenders (National Institute of Corrections).

Harris (1983-1984). *Strategies, Values, and the Emerging Generation of Alternatives to Incarceration.* 12 N.Y.U. Rev. L. & Soc. Change 141-170.

Hillsman, S., B. Mahoney, G. Cole and B. Auchter (1987). *Fines as Criminal Sanctions.* Research in Brief, NIJ (September).

Hillsman, S., J. Sichel and B. Mahoney (1984). Fines in Sentencing—A Study of the Use of Fines as a Criminal Sanction—Executive Summary (VERA NCJ 96334).

Hinrichs, D. (1981). Report on Juvenile Crime Victim Project Attitudes and Needs of Victims of Juvenile Crime.

Hofer, P. and B. Meierhoefer (1987). Home Confinement, an Evolving Sanction in the Federal Criminal Justice System. Federal Judicial Center.

Holt, N. (1995). *California's Determinate Sentencing: What Went Wrong?* Perspectives, Summer.

Hoelter (1982). *Make the Sentence Fit the Felon.* 21 Judges Journal 48 (Winter).

Hudson (1984). *The Crime Victim and the Criminal Justice System: Time for a Change.* 11 Symposium Pepperdine L. Rev. 23-63.

Huskey, B. (1995). *The Future of Community Corrections: A National Perspective.* The IARCA Journal on Community Corrections, VII: 1 (September).

Incarcerated Sex Offenders Today Total Nearly 100,000. Corrections Compendium, CEGA Services, Inc., Nov. 1993.

Jensen, S. (ed.) (undated). The ATSA Practitioner's Handbook. Lake Beaverton, OR: Association For the Treatment of Sexual Abusers.

Judges Complying: First Statistical Analysis by U.S. Sentencing Commission Finds Guidelines Working Well. Corrections Digest, 20:40 (7/12/89).

Kelly (1984). *Victims' Perceptions of Criminal Justice.* 11 Symposium Pepperdine L. Rev. 15-23.

Klein, A. (1996). *Reabuse in a Population of Court-Restrained Male Batterers.* In Buzawa, E. and C. Buzawa (eds.), Do Arrest and Restraining Orders Work? Newbury Park, CA: Sage Publications.

_____(1992). SPOUSAL/PARTNER ASSAULT: A PROTOCOL FOR THE SENTENCING AND SUPERVISION OF OFFENDERS. Swampscott, MA: Production Specialties Inc.

_____(1989). *Should You Send a Probationer Back to Jail . . .* JUDGES JOURNAL, Winter.

Klein (1982). *Earn-it.* 21 JUDGES JOURNAL 38 (Winter).

Klein, Schneider, Bazemore and Schneider (1985). *Program Models.* In Schneider, A. (ed.) GUIDE TO JUVENILE RESTITUTION 21-65; Restitution Education, Specialized Training & Technical Assistance Program, U.S. Department of Justice 84-JS-AX-KO45).

Kohlberg L. (1980). *The Cognitive-Development Approach to Moral Education.* In Erickson, V.L. and J. Whiteley (eds.), DEVELOPMENTAL COUNSELING AND TEACHING, Monterey, CA: Brooks/Cole. pp. 10-26.

Kramer (1983). *Foreword.* 9 NEW ENG. J. CRIM. & CIVIL COMMITMENT 319- 322.

Kramer (1986). *Sentencing the Drunk Driver: A Call for Change.* ALCOHOL TREATMENT QUARTERLY (Special Edition).

Kramer, A. (1986). *Sentencing the Drunk Driver: A Call for Change.* ALCOHOL TREATMENT QUARTERLY.

Langan, P. and M. Cuniff (1992). *Recidivism of Felony Probationers, 1986-1989.* SPECIAL REPORT. Washington, DC: Bureau of Justice Statistics (Feb.).

Lardner, G. Jr. (1995). THE STALKING OF KRISTEN. New York, NY: Atlantic Monthly Press.

Larson, C. (1995). *Shaping a Sentence Around Victim Concerns.* RESTORATIVE JUSTICE NEWSLETTER. Department of Corrections, Minnesota (Nov.).

Lehman, J. (1995). *The Movement Towards Therapeutic Jurisprudence.* NJC ALUMNI, 10:3, pp. 13-18, Spring.

Lemert, E. (1993). *Visions of Social Control: Probation Considered.* 39 CRIME AND DELINQUENCY, 447

Lipsey, M. (1992). *Juvenile Delinquency Treatment: A Meta-Analytic Inquiry into the Variability of Effects.* In T. Cook, H. Cooper, D Cordray, H. Hartmann, L. Hedges, R. Light, T. Louis and F. Mosteller (eds.), META-ANALYSIS FOR EXPLANATION, 83-127, New York, NY: Sage Foundation.

Lipske, M. (1982). CHEMICAL ADDITIVES IN BOOZE.

Little, G.L., K.D. Robinson, K.D. Burnette and E.S. Swan (1995). *Rehabilitation Effectiveness Through Moral Recognition Therapy.* ALTERNATIVES TO INCARCERATION 1, pp. 24-26.

MADDVOCATE 4:2, Winter 1991.

Maloney, D., D. Romig and T. Armstrong (1988). JUVENILE PROBATION: THE BALANCED APPROACH. 39:3, National Council of Juvenile and Family Court Judges, Reno, NV.

MacKenzie, D. (1993). *Boot Camp Prisons in 1993.* NATIONAL INSTITUTE OF JUSTICE JOURNAL. Washington, DC: U.S. Department of Justice (November).

MacKenzie, D. and D. Parent (1992). *Boot Camp Prisons for Young Offenders.* In Byrne, J., A. Lurigo and J. Petersilia (eds.), SMART SENTENCING. Newbury Park, CA: Sage Publications, 103-122.

Martinson (1974). *What Works? Questions and Answers About Prison Reform.* PUBLIC INTEREST 22-54 (Spring).

MASSACHUSETTS GUIDELINES AND STANDARDS FOR CERTIFICATION OF BATTERERS' INTERVENTION PROGRAMS, Mass. Department of Public Health, Boston, MA. (revised 1995).

Maurer, M. (1992). AMERICANS BEHIND BARS: ONE YEAR LATER. Washington, DC: The Sentencing Project, Feb.

_____ (1990). YOUNG BLACK MEN AND THE CRIMINAL JUSTICE SYSTEM: A GROWING NATIONAL PROBLEM. Washington, DC: The Sentencing Project (Feb.).

McAnany, P., D. Thomson and D. Fogel (eds.) (1984). PROBATION AND JUSTICE.

McDonald, W. (1983). PLEA BARGAINING: THE ISSUES AND THE PRACTICE. Washington, DC: National Institute of Justice, U.S. Department of Justice.

Michigan Bureau of Field Services, NEW PROGRAMS IN PROBATION SUPERVISION (undated, Department of Corrections).

Mills, J. (1992). *Supervision Fees: APPA Issues Committee Report.* PERSPECTIVES 16:4 (Fall).

Monohan, J. (1981). THE CLINICAL PREDICTION OF VIOLENT BEHAVIOR.

Naltrexone Stems Alcoholism. ALTERNATIVES TO INCARCERATION 1:4 (Fall, 1995).

National Center for State Courts, COMMUNITY SERVICE SENTENCING LIABILITY ISSUES (Oct. 1982).

National Highway Traffic Safety Administration (1985). ALCOHOL AND HIGHWAY SAFETY STUDY 1984: A REVIEW OF THE STATE OF KNOWLEDGE (DTNH22-83-P-05062).

_____ (1986). THE DRUNK DRIVER AND JAIL RESOURCE MATERIALS (DOT HS 806 765).

National Organization for Victim Assistance (1984). VICTIMS' RIGHTS AND SERVICES. A LEGISLATIVE DIRECTORY.

NETWORK NEWSNOTES 7:1, MADD (Spring, 1992).

New Jersey Administrative Office of the Courts (1983). COMMUNITY SERVICE DIRECTORY FOR INTERSTATE COMPACT TRANSFERS.

New Jersey Administrative Office of the Courts (1984). COMMUNITY SERVICE UPDATE (Spring).

New York Division of Probation, 1981 ANNUAL REPORT (undated).

Nice, R. (ed.) (1964). TREASURY OF RULE OF LAW.

North Carolina Implements Justice Fellowship Inspired Guidelines. JUSTICE REPORT 11:1 (Winter 1995).

Office of the Comptroller of the City of New York, AUDIT REPORT ON THE FINANCIAL AND OPERATIONAL PRACTICES AND PROCEDURES OF THE NEW YORK CITY DEPARTMENT OF PROBATION, JULY 1 TO APRIL 30, 1980 (1981).

O'Leary, V. and T. Clear (1984). DIRECTIONS FOR COMMUNITY CORRECTIONS IN THE 1990s. Washington, DC: National Institute of Corrections, U.S. Department of Justice.

Parent, D. (June, 1990). RECOVERING CORRECTIONAL COSTS THROUGH OFFENDER FEES. Washington, DC: National Institute of Justice.

Partridge, A., A. Chaset and W. Eldridge (1983). THE SENTENCING OPTIONS OF FEDERAL DISTRICT JUDGES (Federal Judicial Center).

Pence, E. and M. Shepard (1988). *Integrating Feminist Theory and Practice: The Challenge of the Battered Women's Movement.* In Yllo, K. and M. Bograd (eds.), FEMINIST PERSPECTIVES ON WIFE ABUSE, 282-299. Newbury Park, CA: Sage Publications.

Petersilia, J. (1988). *Probation Reform*. In Scott, J. and T. Hirschi (eds.), CONTROVERSIAL ISSUES IN CRIME AND JUSTICE. VOL 1. Newbury Park, CA: Sage Publications.

Petersilia, J. and S. Turner (1993). *Evaluating Intensive Supervision Probation/ Parole: Results of a Nationwide Experiment*. RESEARCH IN BRIEF. Washington, DC: National Institute of Justice (May).

Petersilia, J., S. Turner, J. Kahan and J. Peterson (1985). GRANTING FELONS PROBATION (Rand, R-3186-NIJ).

Polisky (1981). *Introduction*. AMERICAN CORRECTIONAL ASSOCIATION DIRECTORY OF PROBATION AND PAROLE.

President's Commission on Law Enforcement and Administration of Justice, CORRECTIONS (1976).

President's Commission on Law Enforcement and Administration of Justice, Task Force, THE COURTS (1976).

President's Task Force on Victims of Crime, FINAL REPORT (1982).

Proband, S. (1995). *Corrections Leads State Appropriations Increases for '96*. Denver, CO: National Conference of State Legislatures, quoted in OVERCROWDED TIMES, October.

PROBATION AND PAROLE 1990, NCJ-125833, November 1991.

Prosecution of Felony Arrests. Bureau of Justice Statistics. Washington, DC: U.S. Department of Justice, 1983.

Ptacek, J. (1995). DISORDER IN THE COURTS: JUDICIAL DEMEANOR AND WOMEN'S EXPERIENCE SEEKING RESTRAINING ORDERS. Ann Arbor, MI: UMI.

Recidivism Problem Uncovered in Georgia. NETWORK NEWS NOTES 7:2, p. 4., National Committee Against Drunk Driving, Summer, 1992.

Renzema, M. and D. Shelton (1990). *Use of Electronic Monitoring in the United States: 1989 Update*. NIJ REPORTS 22 (Nov./Dec.).

REPORT TO THE NATION ON CRIME AND JUSTICE, SECOND EDITION. Bureau of Justice Statistics. Washington, DC: U.S. Department of Justice, 1988.

RESTITUTION REPORT, January 1995. Boston, MA: Office of the Commissioner of Probation.

Rolph, J. and J. Chaiken (1987). IDENTIFYING HIGH RATE SERIOUS CRIMINALS FROM OFFICIAL RECORDS. Washington, DC: Rand, National Institute of Justice, April.

Rothman, D. (1981). THE DISCOVERY OF THE ASYLUM.

Schafer, S. (1970). COMPENSATION AND RESTITUTION TO CRIME VICTIMS (2nd ed.).

Schneider, A. (ed.) (1985). GUIDE TO JUVENILE RESTITUTION 31. Washington, DC: U.S. Department of Justice.

Schneider (1986). *Restitution and Recidivism of Juvenile Offenders: Results From Four Experimental Studies*. CRIMINOLOGY.

Scott, J. (1974). PIONEERING INNOVATIONS IN CORRECTIONS. SHOCK PROBATION AND SHOCK PAROLE.

SEEKING JUSTICE. New York, NY: Edna McConnell Clark Foundation, 1995.

Shine, C. and M. Mauer (March 1993). DOES THE PUNISHMENT FIT THE CRIME? DRUG USERS AND DRUNK DRIVERS, QUESTIONS OF RACE AND CLASS. Washington, DC: The Sentencing Project.

Silberman (1983). *Criminal Violence*. CRIMINAL JUSTICE 291-93.

Skelski, A. (1980). VICTIM SERVICES PROGRAM: AN EVALUATION (unpublished thesis, Brown University).

Smith, B., S. Hillenbrand and S. Goretsky (1990). THE PROBATION RESPONSE TO CHILD SEXUAL ABUSE OFFENDERS: HOW IS IT WORKING? Chicago, IL: American Bar Association.

Smith (1983-1984). *Will the Real Alternatives Please Stand Up?* 12 N.Y.U. REVIEW OF LAW AND SOCIAL CHANGE 171-197.

Substance Abuse Treatment. PERSPECTIVES 20:1 (Winter, 1996).

Taking Shortcuts in Drug Use Revocations May Create Problems. COMMUNITY CORRECTIONS REPORT, May/June 1994.

Tauro (1983). *Sentencing: A View From the Bench,* 9 NEW ENG. J. CRIM. & CIVIL CONFINEMENT 323-330.

Texas Adult Probation Commission, EXPLANATION OF THE PRESENTENCE REPORT FORMAT (undated).

THE PRESENTENCE INVESTIGATION REPORT (U.S. Department of Justice 1978).

Thorvalson (1980). *Does Community Service Affect Offenders' Attitudes?* VICTIMS, OFFENDERS AND ALTERNATIVE SANCTIONS (J. Hudson & B. Galaway eds.).

Tobolowsky, P. (1993). *Restitution in the Federal Criminal Justice System.* JUDICATURE 77:90.

Tuckman, B. (1978). A DISTANT MIRROR.

Umbreit, M. (1994). VICTIM MEETS OFFENDER: THE IMPACT OF RESTORATIVE JUSTICE AND MEDIATION. Monsey, NY: Criminal Justice Press.

_____ (1985). CRIME AND RECONCILIATION.

Umbreit, M. and B. Coates (1992). VICTIM OFFENDER MEDIATION: AN ANALYSIS OF PROGRAMS IN FOUR STATES OF THE U.S. Minneapolis, MN: Citizens Council Mediation Services.

Vaillant, G. (1983). THE NATURAL HISTORY OF ALCOHOLISM.

VERA Institute of Justice, THE NEW YORK CITY COMMUNITY SERVICE SENTENCING PROJECT DEVELOPMENT OF THE BRONX PILOT PROJECT (1981).

VERA Institute of Justice, THE NEW YORK COMMUNITY SERVICE SENTENCING PROJECT AND ITS UTILITY FOR THE CITY OF NEW YORK (1981).

Victim Appearances at Sentencing Under California's Victim Bill of Rights. RESEARCH IN BRIEF. Washington, DC: National Institute of Justice (August, 1987).

Wagner, D. and C. Baird (1993). *Evaluation of the Florida Community Control Program.* NCJ, Jan.

Westlake, R. (1979). THE COMMUNITY SERVICE PROGRAM IN HAWAII.

Wilson, J. (1981). *What Works? Revisited: New Findings on Criminal Rehabilitation.* PUBLIC INTEREST 3, 13-16 (Spring).

Wilson (1981). *"What Works?" Revisited: New Findings on Criminal Rehabilitation.* PUBLIC INTEREST 3-17 (Spring).

Wish, E. (1986). *Estimating Drug Use in the Intensive Supervision of Probation: Results of Pilot Study.* FEDERAL PROBATION, Dec.

Wish, E., M. Toborg and J. Bellassai (1988). IDENTIFYING DRUG USERS AND MONITORING THEM DURING CONDITIONAL RELEASE. Washington, DC: National Institute of Justice.

Winterfield, L. and S. Hillsman (1993). *Staten Island Day Fine Project.* RESEARCH IN BRIEF, National Institute of Justice (Jan.).

Wood, F. (1995). *Restorative Justice Implementation in Minnesota is a Key Focus of State Department of Corrections.* RESTORATIVE JUSTICE NEWSLETTER, Nov.

Young Black Americans and the Criminal Justice System: Five Years Later (1995). Washington, DC: The Sentencing Project.

Newspapers and Magazines

Abuse Sentence: Contraceptive. WASHINGTON POST, January 5, 1991.

Anderson, D. (1991). *A World Leader, in Prisons.* NEW YORK TIMES, March 2.

————— (1991). *Probation, Georgia Style.* NEW YORK TIMES, July 17.

Anderson (1984). *Cells Over Brooms.* NEW YORK TIMES, October 10.

Answer to Kid Crime: Restorative Justice Corps. USA TODAY, Feb. 22, 1995.

Arsonist Sentence: Ten Years Without Pac Man. BOSTON GLOBE, Nov. 19,1983.

Back to Jail for Mr. Bobbitt. REUTERS, Dec. 21, 1995.

Baquet, D., M. Gottlieb and E. Shipp (1991). *Slaying Casts a New Glare on Law's Uncertain Path.* NEW YORK TIMES, June 25.

Barach (1981). *Names and Faces.* BOSTON GLOBE, June 7.

Barringer, F. (1990). *Sentence for Killing Newborn: Jail Term, Then Birth Control.* NEW YORK TIMES, Nov. 11.

Bass, A., P. Nealon and D. Armstrong (1994). *The War on Domestic Abuse.* BOSTON GLOBE, Sept. 25.

Birth Control Order Upheld for Pregnant Child Beater. ASSOCIATED PRESS, January 11, 1991.

Blackmore (1980). *Treatment? There's No Treatment Going on Here.* CORRECTIONS MAGAZINE 13 (December).

Blumenthal (1985). *New Focus on Jail Alternative.* NEW YORK TIMES, Feb. 23.

Bohlen, C. (1989). *Probation Agency Faces a Double Burden.* NEW YORK TIMES, January 8.

Butterfield, F. (1995). *New Prisons Cast Shadow Over Higher Education.* NEW YORK TIMES, April 12.

Canellos, P. (1995). *In Texas, Molester Pleads for Castration.* BOSTON GLOBE, July 14.

Conditional Term Given Sex Offender. BOSTON GLOBE, August 8, 1985.

Court Sentence Brings Food and Toys to Needy. NEW YORK TIMES, Dec. 23, 1983.

Criminal Fines, By the Day. NEW YORK TIMES, August 30, 1988.

Denmark, S. (1991). *Birth Control Tyranny.* NEW YORK TIMES, Oct.

Detroit's Benign Chain Gangs. NEW YORK TIMES, May 4, 1988.

DeValle (1984). *The Victim Witness Law: A New Approach.* BOSTON GLOBE, July 16.

Divine Brown to Serve Sentence. BOSTON GLOBE, Nov. 2, 1995.

Doherty (1982). *Judge Eases Sentence for "Traumatized" Viet Vet.* BOSTON GLOBE, March 11.

Drunken Dad Drives Girls into Pond: Mom Charged. LEXINGTON HERALD-LEADER, Nov. 12, 1994.

Drunken Driving Term: Pay Widow for 30 Years. NEW YORK TIMES, April 1, 1984.

Duxbury Man Sentenced in Theft from Government. PATRIOT LEDGER, May 28, 1992.

Editorial. BALTIMORE SUN, Dec. 13, 1979.

Editorial. ROCKLAND JOURNAL-NEWS, June 16, 1984.

Editorial. WASHINGTON POST, July 16, 1979.

Ex-firefighter Must Admit Rape, ASSOCIATED PRESS, April 5, 1991.

Ex-Officer Gets Weekends in Jail. NEW YORK TIMES, July 8, 1983.

Flouting Fines. TIME MAGAZINE, March 24, 1980.

For Oregon Drunk Drivers, A Close-Up of Skid Row. NEW YORK TIMES, December 30, 1985.

For Sex Criminals, Therapy Held to Help. BOSTON GLOBE, November 9, 1995.

Gavzer, B. (1995). *Life Behind Bars.* PARADE MAGAZINE, August 13.

Gelb, A. (1991). *Scales of Justice Tip Toward Drunks.* ATLANTIC JOURNAL AND CONSTITUTION, Nov. 5.

Gettinger (1983). *Intensive Supervision. Can It Rehabilitate Probation?* CORRECTIONS MAGAZINE 6 (April).

Granelli (1983). *Presentence Reports Go Private.* NATIONAL LAW JOURNAL, May 2.

Grunwald, M. (1995). *Texas May Find Surplus of Cells a Fugitive Fix.* BOSTON GLOBE, Nov. 12.

Hicks, J. (1993). *Accord Made to Cut Staff for Probation.* NEW YORK TIMES, January 29.

Hinds, M. (1992). *Feeling Prisons' Costs, Governors Weigh Alternatives.* NEW YORK TIMES, August 7.

Hinds, M. (1988). *Judges Turn to Ignition Locks to Ground Drunk Drivers.* NEW YORK TIMES, Dec. 12.

Johnson, D. (1990). *Convict in Home Custody is Charged in a Killing.* NEW YORK TIMES, Dec. 2.

Kahn, J. (1994). *Making Peace with a Murderer.* BOSTON GLOBE, January 20.

Kerr, P. (1988). *Crime Study Finds High Use of Drugs at Time of Arrest.* NEW YORK TIMES, Jan. 22.

Kerr, P. (1988). *Drug Testing as Way to Reduce Prison Overcrowding.* NEW YORK TIMES, Jan. 19.

Kerr, P. (1988). *New Court in New York Succeeds in Cutting Backlog of Drug Cases.* NEW YORK TIMES, Feb. 6, 1988.

Krajick (1982). *Community Service: The Work Ethic Approach to Punishment.* CORRECTIONS MAGAZINE 6 (October).

Krajick (1980). *Probation, The Original Community Program.* CORRECTIONS MAGAZINE 6 (December).

Kulis (1983). *Profit in the Private Presentence Report.* 7 PERSPECTIVES 5 (Fall).

Kuttner, R. (1995). *State Should "Get Real" On Perverse Asset-Seizure Law.* BOSTON GLOBE, Dec. 11.

Landlord to Get Taste of Filth in His Apartments. BOSTON GLOBE, June 19,1985.

Landlord Told to Begin Sentence: 30 Days in His Squalid Apartment. NEW YORK TIMES, July 11, 1987.

Larson, C. (1995). *Shaping a Sentenced Around Victim Concerns.* RESTORATIVE JUSTICE NEWSLETTER. Department of Corrections, Minnesota (Nov.).

Middleton (1984). *Sentencing: The Alternatives.* NATIONAL LAW JOURNAL, April 23.

Man Sentenced in Assault Case. ASSOCIATED PRESS, July 22, 1995.

Man Who Spread AIDS is Punished. REUTERS, October 30, 1991.

McCarthy, P. (1992). *Fitting Penalty to Crime.* BOSTON GLOBE, May 24.

McPhee, M. (1996). *Graffiti Draws House Arrest.* BOSTON GLOBE, Jan. 28.

Michigan Killer Accepts Sentence of Celibate Living. NEW YORK TIMES, June 19,1981.

Muro (1987). *Stalking Justice in Oregon Town.* BOSTON GLOBE, January 16.

Murphy, S. (1990). *Collecting Fines Seen as Crucial.* BOSTON GLOBE, November 8.

Nealon, P. (1992). *Arlington Man is Sentenced for Sexual Assault of 2 Girls.* BOSTON GLOBE, Sept. 16.

Nolan, M. (1995). *Calif. Sees Prisons Filling as Colleges Decline.* BOSTON GLOBE, August 28.

Not Drunk? Tell it to the Car. NEW YORK TIMES, August 6, 1987.

Panel Says New York Courts Are Infested with Racism. CRIMINAL JUSTICE NEWSLETTER, 22:12 (June 17, 1991).

Penn (1983). *Risk to Society, Reliance on Probation is Increasing, and so is Opposition to its Use.* WALL ST. J., May 16.

Polluters Deserve Jail Time. PATRIOT LEDGER, Nov. 11, 1990.

Probation and Parole Populations Reach New Highs. Bureau of Justice Statistics Press Release, Washington D.C., Sept. 11, 1994.

Raab (1981). *New York Probation Aides Assert Office Fails To Watch Thousands.* NEW YORK TIMES, August 3.

Rakowsky, J. (1995). *Surgeon Sent to Prison in Child-Support Case.* BOSTON GLOBE, November 2.

Rangel (1985). *She's a Prisoner in Her Own House.* PATRIOT LEDGER, September 24.

Rapper Shakur Ordered Jailed. REUTERS, Jan. 23, 1996.

Richard (1983). *He Serves Sentence By Warning of Danger of Drinking, Driving.* BOSTON GLOBE, May 27.

Scarlet Bumper, Humiliating Drunk Drivers. TIME MAGAZINE, June 17, 1985.

Simon, P. (1993). *Molester Will Face Stiff Curbs After Jail.* BUFFALO NEWS, July 10.

Slumlord Seems to Like Sentence. BOSTON GLOBE, July 25, 1987.

Sniffen, M. (1995). *US Inmate Population Soars in '95.* ASSOCIATED PRESS.

"Stay Home" Sentence Given Child Molester. BOSTON GLOBE, June 8, 1980.

Stern, H. (1995). *State, Federal Prisons Reach Record 1 Million Inmate Level.* ASSOCIATED PRESS, August 10.

Tatz, D. (1995). *Quincy Court Pleased with Most Wanted Program.* PATRIOT LEDGER, August 4, 5.

Taylor (1983). *Instead of Jail, One City in New York Imposes Sentences of Work, Reparations, or House Arrest.* WALL ST. J., December 23.

Turner, *Unusual Sentence Stirs Legal Dispute.* NEW YORK TIMES, August 21, 1987.

Two Whites Ordered to Aid Black Church. BOSTON GLOBE, December 18, 1988.

Udevitz (1985). *More Would Go To Jail if Prisons Weren't So Full, Judges Say in Poll.* DENVER POST, March 16.

Whittman (1984). *Genessee County,* 3 VORP NETWORK NEWS.

Wilson, D. (1990). *A Sentence that Should Insult Every Volunteer.* BOSTON GLOBE, Dec. 12.

Wilson, D. (1988). *Drunken Drivers Visit the Morgue.* NEW YORK TIMES, September 21.

Zachary, G. (1995). *Economists Say Prison Boom Will Take Toll.* WALL STREET JOURNAL, September 29.

$20 Million Fraud Brings Tough Probation Terms. NEW YORK TIMES, June 4, 1989.

Speeches, Interviews and Unpublished Material

Armstrong, T. (1980). *Restitution: A Sanction For All Seasons* (speech before Fourth National Symposium on Restitution and Community Service Sentencing, Minnesota).

Cannon, M. (1984). *Developing A Rational Corrections Policy In An Environment of Hardening Public Attitudes Against Criminals* (speech before Ethics and Public Policy Conference, Washington, D.C.).

Domurand, F. (1995). "Supervising the Violent Offender in the Community: An Unmet Challenge," Paper presented to National Institute of Corrections Workshop, Maryland, March, 17.

Fallon, V. (1995). Georgia Director of Probation, Remarks to Office of the Commissioner of Probation, Boston, MA, April 24.

Gorczyk, J. (1996). Commissioner of Corrections, Vermont, Remarks to Restorative Justice Symposium, National Institute of Justice and Office of Victims of Crime, Washington, D.C. January 25.

Interview with D. Maloney, Director of Deschutes County Community Corrections, Jan. 9, 1995.

Interview with H. Sinkinson, Reparations Coordinator for Chittendon County, Vt., October 25, 1995.

Interview with J. Larivee, President of Crime and Justice Foundation, May, 1995

Interview with M. Carey, Dakota County Community Corrections Director, November, 1994.

Interview with R.B. Talpey, Supervisor, Intensive Supervision Program, Trenton, New Jersey, November 15, 1995.

Menton, A. (1995). Chief Justice, Connecticut, remarks to Massachusetts Probation Conference, Randolph, MA, May 11.

Schmidt (1987). *The Use of Electronic Monitoring by Criminal Justice Agencies,* (National Institute of Justice, Discussion Paper 2-87).

Wittman, D.J. (1996). Director, Genesee Justice Program, Genesee County Sheriff's Department, Batavia, N.Y. Remarks to Restorative Justice Symposium, National Institute of Justice and Office for Victims of Crime, Washington, D.C., Jan. 25.

Table of Statutes

Alabama Code
§ 15-18-66 (1982) **5.07**
§ 15-18-65 to -78 (1982 & Supp. 1985) **5.03**

Alaska Stat.
§ 12.55.100 (1985) **3.02**
§ 12.55.100(a)(2)(1980) **5.03**
§ 12.55.055 (1984) **6.03**

Arizona Rev. Stat. Ann.
§ 13-603(c) (Supp. 1985) **5.07**
§ 13-4201(4) (1978) **5.05**
§ 13-4201(4) (1989) **5.07**
§ 13-901(F) (Supp 1985) **5.03**
§ 43.2350-59 (Supp. 1985) **9.05**

Arizona R. Crim P.
26.7 **2.09**
27.1 **8.04**

Arkansas Stat. Ann.
§ 41-1203(2)(1) (1977) **7.03**
§ 41-1201(2)(f) (1977) **5.03**

Cal. Const.
Art. 1, § 28(B) **2.08, 5.03**

Cal. Penal Code
§ 1192.7 (West Supp. 1996) **2.01**
§ 1203(b) (Supp. 1986) **2.04, 2.09, 3.01**
§ 1203.1 (Supp. 1986) **3.03**
§ 1203.1b (Supp. 1987) **7.04, 8.03**
§ 1202.6 (West Supp. 1995) **3.03**

Cal. Vehicle Code
Art. 4, § 23235 *et. seq.* (West Supp. 1996) **8.03**

Colorado Rev. Stat.
§ 16.11-202 (1978) **1.02, 9.05**
§ 16-11-204(2)(c) (1978) **9.02**
§ 16-11-204.5 (Supp. 1985) **5.03**
§ 16-11-206(3) (Supp. 1985) **10.06**
§ 16-11-206(3) (1986) **10.06**
§ 16-13-101(2) (Supp. 1985) **4.16**

Connecticut Gen. Stat. Ann.
§ 53a-30(a) (West 1994) **3.05**
§ 53a-30(b) (1985) **3.05**
§ 53a-30(a)(2) (1985) **8.04**
§ 53a-30(a)(4) (1985) **5.03**
§ 53a-30(a)(6) (1985) **7.03**
§ 53a-30(a)(2) (West 1994) **8.04**

Delaware Code Ann.
Tit. 11, § 4105 (Supp. 1984) **6.02**
Tit. 11 § 5409c (1985) **2.09**

D.C. Code
§ 22-104a (1981) **4.16**

Table of Cases

Ott v. State, 690 S.W.2d 537 (Tex. Crim. App. 1985)   § 8.05

Owens v. Kelley, 681 F.2d 1362 (11th Cir. 1982)   §§ 3.04, 10.04

Patterson v. Commonwealth, 12 Va. App. 1046, 407 S.E.2d 43 (1991)   § 10.06

Patterson v. State, 572 So. 2d 508 (Ala. Crim. App. 1990)   § 10.05

Patton v. State, 458 N.E.2d 657 (Ind. Ct. App. 1984)   § 2.01

Patton v. State, 580 N.E.2d 693 (Ind. Ct. App. 1991)   § 10.04

Payne v. Robinson, 207 Conn. 565, 541 A.2d 504 (1988), *cert. denied,* 488 U.S. 898, 109 S. Ct. 242 (1988)   § 10.06

Payne v. Tennessee, 501 U.S. 808, 111 S. Ct. 2597, 115 L. Ed. 2d 720 (1991), *reh'g. denied,* 115 L. Ed. 2d 1110 (1991)   § 2.08

Peltier v. State, 119 Idaho 454, 808 P.2d 373 (1991)   § 10.05

Pennsylvania Department of Public Welfare v. Davenport, 495 U.S. 555, 110 S. Ct. 2126, 109 L. Ed. 2d 588 (1990)   § 5.07

People v. Allegri, 109 Ill. Dec. 781, 487 N.E.2d 606 (Ill. 1985)   § 10.06

———— *v. Anderson,* 189 Colo. 34, 536 P.2d 302 (1975)   § 10.04

———— *v. Arbuckle,* 22 Cal. 3d 749, 587 P.2d 220, 150 Cal. Rptr. 778 (1978)   § 2.09

———— *v. Arvanites,* 171 Cal. App. 3d 1052, 95 Cal. Rptr. 493 (1971)   § 3.04

———— *v. Aylesworth,* 532 N.Y.S.2d 322, 143 A.D.2d 353 (N.Y. Sup. App. 1988)   § 2.07

———— *v. Baker,* 158 Ill. App. 3d 756, 511 N.E.2d 219 (1987)   § 2.04

———— *v. Baum,* 251 Mich. 187, 231 N.W. 95 (1930)   § 3.04

———— *v. Becker,* 349 Mich. 476, 84 N.W.2d 833 (1957)   § 5.07

———— *v. Bell,* 579 N.E.2d 1154 (Ill. Ct. App. 1991)   § 10.07

———— *v. Belleci,* 24 Cal. 3d 879, 598 P.2d 473, 157 Cal. Rptr. 503 (1979)   § 2.04

———— *v. Blankenship,* 16 Cal. App. 2d 606, 61 P.2d 352 (1936)   § 8.04

———— *v. Bogan,* 540 N.E.2d 1135 (Ill. Ct. App. 1989)   § 10.07

———— *v. Bond,* 297 N.W.2d 620 (Mich. Ct. App. 1980)   § 5.07

———— *v. Boucher,* 179 Ill. App. 3d 823, 535 N.E.2d 56 (1989)   § 10.05

———— *v. Bravo,* 238 Cal. Rptr. 282 (Cal. 1987)   § 3.04

———— *v. Breau,* 101 Cal. App. 3d 468, 161 Cal. Rptr. 653 (1980)   § 10.06

———— *v. Brown,* 137 Ill. App. 3d 453, 484 N.E.2d 945 (1985)   § 3.05

———— *v. Bruce,* 102 Mich. App. 573, 302 N.W.2d 238 (1980)   § 3.05

———— *v. Burleigh,* 727 P.2d 873 (Colo. Ct. App. 1986)   §§ 3.04, 7.03

———— *v. Burnett,* 86 Cal. App. 3d 320, 150 Cal. Rptr. 126 (1978)   § 7.03

———— *v. Burton,* 117 Cal. App. 3d 382, 172 Cal. Rptr. 632 (1981)   § 3.04

———— *v. Butler,* 137 Ill. App. 3d 704, 484 N.E.2d 921 (1985)   §§ 3.05, 6.05

———— *v. Cagle,* 780 P.2d 12 (Colo. Ct. App. 1989)   § 10.05

———— *v. Calhoun,* 145 Cal. App. 3d 568, 193 Cal. Rptr. 394 (1983)   § 5.07

———— *v. Catron,* 678 P.2d 1 (Colo. Ct. App. 1983)   § 5.07

———— *v. Clark,* 130 Cal. App. 3d 371, 181 Cal. Rptr. 682 (1982)   §§ 4.02, 5.07

———— *v. Clark,* 157 Ill. App. 3d 371, 510 N.E.2d 1256 (1987)   § 10.05

———— *v. Coleman,* 13 Cal. 3d 867, 120 Cal. Rptr. 384, 533 P.2d 1024 (1975)   § 10.06

———— *v. Cookson,* 3 Cal. Rptr. 2d 176, 820 P.2d 278 (Cal. 1991)   § 3.06

———— *v. Cooper,* 497 N.E.2d 157 (Ill. App. 1986)   § 10.06

———— *v. Cottrell,* 141 Ill. App. 3d 364, 95 Ill. Dec. 858, 490 N.E.2d 950 (Ill. App. 1986)   § 5.07

———— *v. Crago,* 24 Misc. 2d 739, 204 N.Y. S.2d 774 (1960)   § 5.07

———— *v. Dailey,* 286 Cal. Rptr. 772 (Cal. 1991)   § 5.07

———— *v. Daugherty,* 104 Ill. App. 3d 89, 433 N.E.2d 391 (1982)   § 5.07

———— *v. Davis,* 123 Ill. App. 3d 349, 462 N.E.2d 824 (1984)   § 8.05

———— *v. Davis,* 127 Ill. App. 3d 49, 468 N.E. 2d 172 (1984)   § 8.05

———— *v. Diamond,* 245 N.W.2d 809 (Mich. Ct. App. 1976)   § 10.04

Index